KU-716-505

THE PRACTICAL HOME HANDYMAN

A COMPREHENSIVE GUIDE TO
CONSTRUCTIONAL AND REPAIR WORK
ABOUT THE HOUSE

Edited by
W. P. MATTHEW
Assisted by
EXPERT CONTRIBUTORS

ODHAMS PRESS LIMITED · LONG ACRE · LONDON

CONTENTS

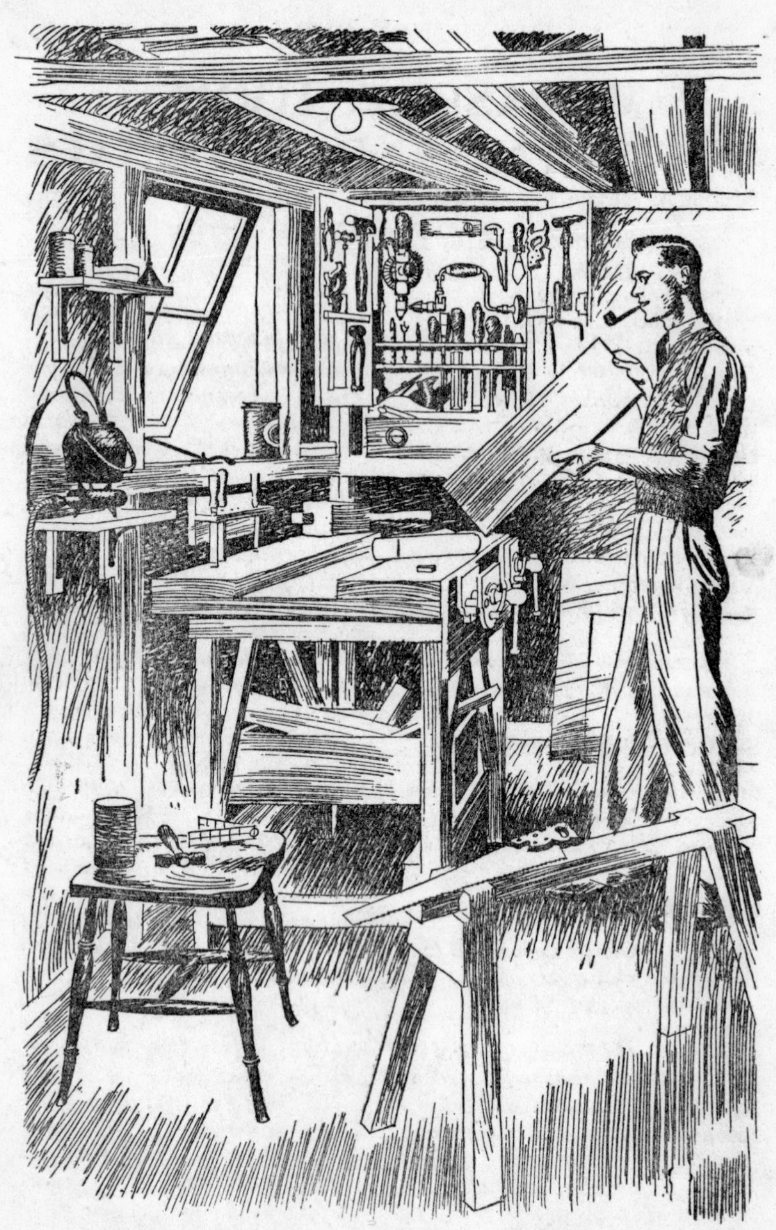

A WELL-PLANNED HANDYMAN'S WORKSHOP

SECTION ONE

WORKSHOP, TOOLS, EQUIPMENT AND MATERIALS

Selection and Care of Tools

THIS section contains advice in the selection of a useful tool kit, and quite a number of tools are described, but it would be wrong to give the impression that such a kit must necessarily be ambitious and therefore too expensive for the average householder. The tools need not be purchased all at once. It is, in fact, suggested that the particular tools needed for each job are bought when the occasion arises, and in this way a complete kit will be gradually built up. (See Fig. 1).

Hammers.—To begin with, buy a hammer (Fig. 1) or rather, two hammers; first, a claw hammer. Ask the assistant at the local toolshop to show you several; try them for weight and balance, and choose one that feels comfortable. Later on purchase a light tack-hammer with a wedge end. The two, together, cost only a few shillings.

It is advisable to see that they bear the brand or trade mark of a recognized tool maker, and to examine the wedging, where the head is secured to the handle, to make sure that the steel wedges are firmly driven home and show no signs of splitting the wood. Finally, when using a hammer keep the striking face clean and bright. Most bruised fingers and thumbs come from using dirty hammers.

Handsaws.—Next, purchase saws. As the prices vary and there is a wide range of qualities much depends on the amount paid. Pay just as much as can be afforded, and if it means waiting a week or two longer until it is possible to buy something really good, then wait. It may be just a matter of a shilling or two between a sweet cutting tool and strip of iron that gnaws its way painfully through its work. The hand saw comes first, and should be 24 or 26 in. long and with about 8 teeth to the inch. Look for the maker's name, and try the saw by hand for balance. Make sure that there are at least four rivets securing the blade to the handle, an infallible sign of a good saw. If possible, get one of the skew-backed pattern. Fig. 2 shows the correct method of holding the saw and Fig. 3 shows how to guide the saw when making the initial cut.

Tenon Saw.—The second need is a tenon saw, the most useful size being 12 to 14in. Apart from a good maker's name a brass back is the sign of quality for a tenon saw. Add to these two other useful and quite cheap types of saws, namely a keyhole saw, and a coping saw, which, generally speaking, can be utilized for everything for which a fret saw would be used.

Screwdrivers.—Now for a few of the smaller items. Two screwdrivers will be required, one about 10 in. long for general work with screws of size 10 and upwards, and

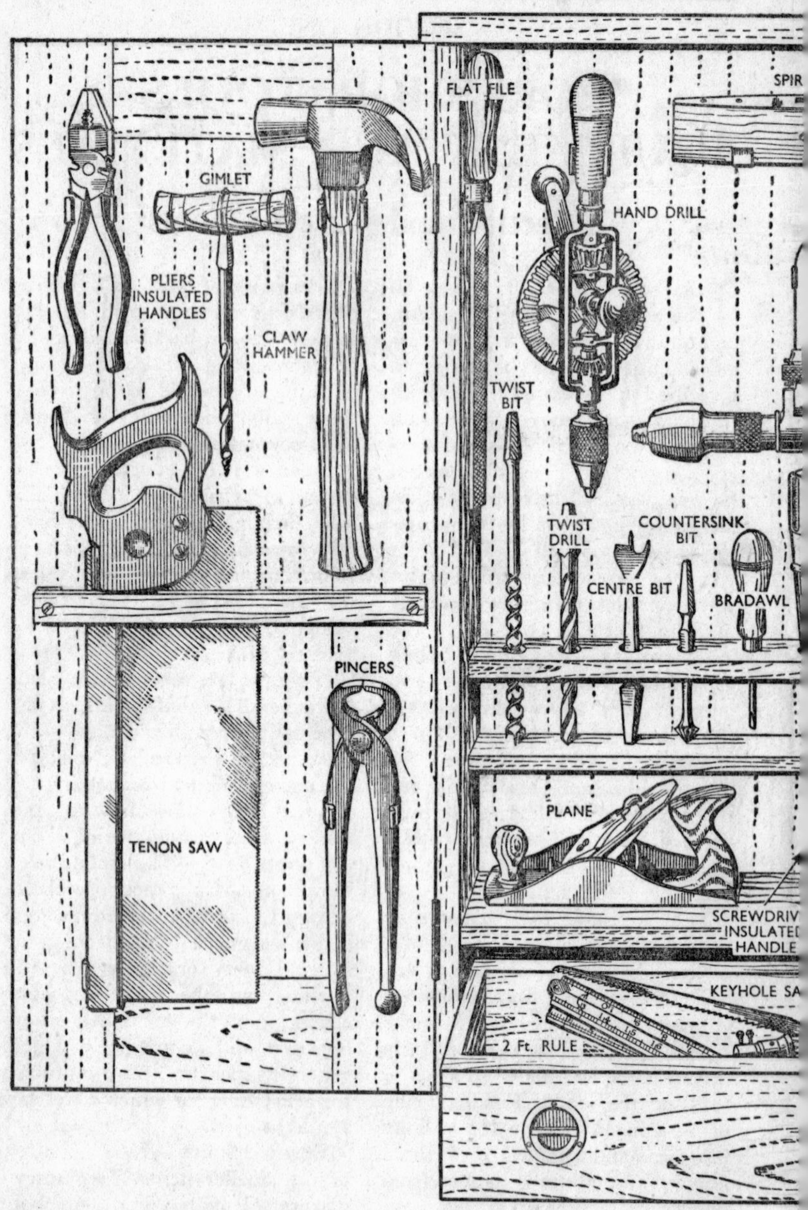

Fig. 1. A representative tool kit for the handyman, illustrating an efficient method of arranging and housing the tools in a cabinet. Such an arrangement ensures

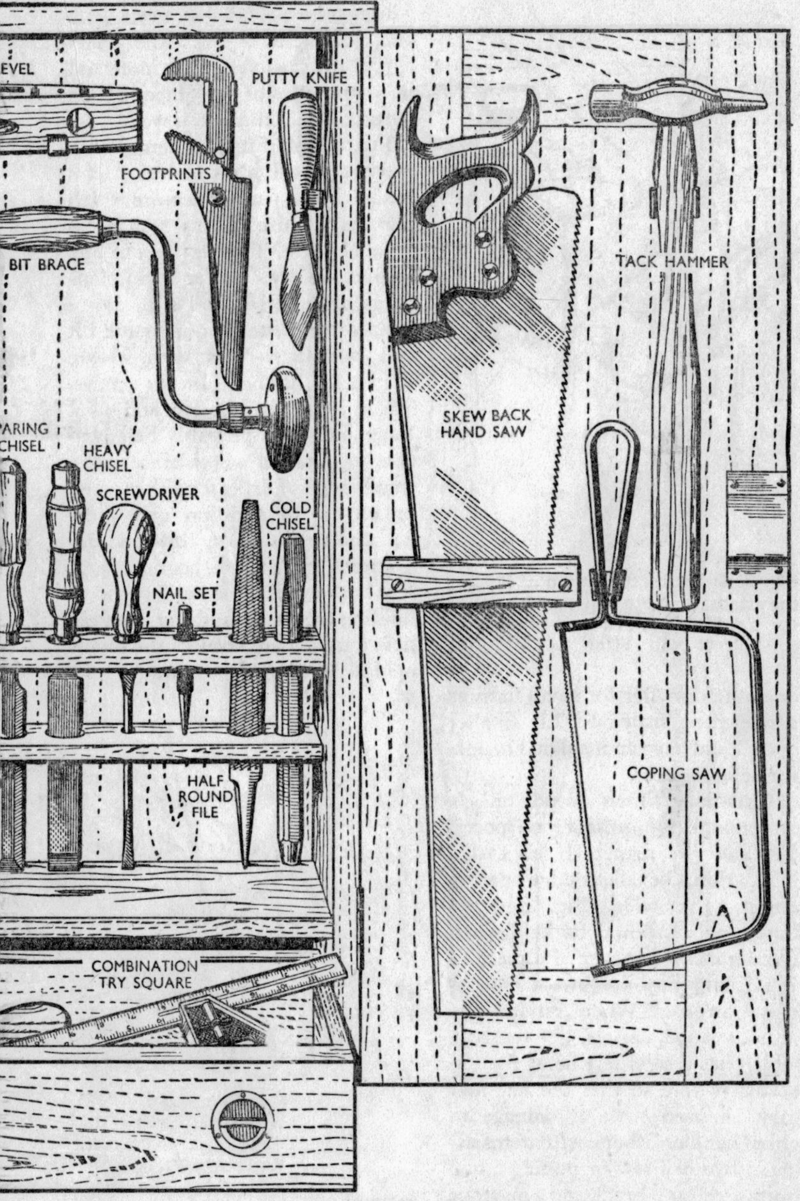

easy accessibility and, what is more important, permits quick selection of the required tool at a glance, without the delay often caused by lack of order.

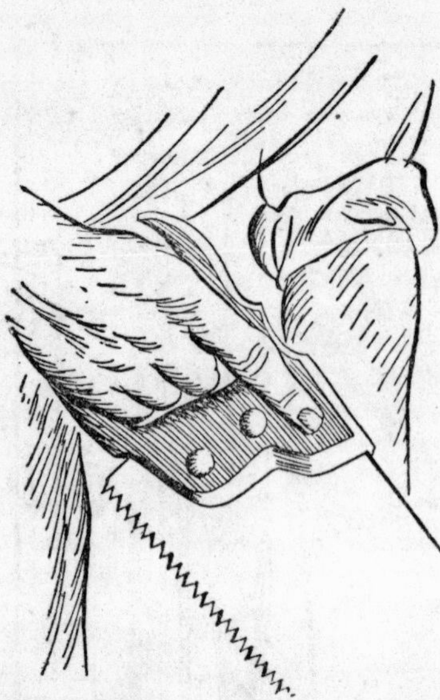

Fig. 2. The correct method of holding the handsaw. Note the position taken up by the index finger to control and direct the blade of the saw.

one much smaller for small fixtures and electric fittings. This smaller one should have an insulated handle for safety's sake.

Chisels.—Three wood chisels are enough for ordinary purposes, $\frac{1}{4}$in. and $\frac{3}{4}$in. firmer chisels and a long, thin, bevelled edge paring chisel $1\frac{1}{4}$in. wide. Fig. 4 shows how a chisel should be held when cutting away a corner of a piece of wood, and Fig. 5 shows a mortise chisel in use. When buying the heavier wood chisels, get the type which has a steel ferrule at the top of the handle so that the hammer may be used without damage to chisel handle. Other useful items include two nail sets or punches, one quite small for brads and one stout one for floor nails, etc.

Cold Chisel.—A steel cold chisel will also be useful, but get a long one, say 12in. × 1in. The extra length will cost very little more and is essential, for instance, when cutting a hole through a wall.

Brace and Bits.—A larger item is a brace with a set of bits. Get a ratchet brace, a useful feature which permits the use of this tool in restricted space. The best bits to buy at first are $\frac{1}{4}$in. $\frac{1}{2}$in. and $\frac{3}{4}$in. Jennings pattern, $\frac{3}{8}$in. and 1 in. centre bits, a rose-pattern countersink bit and two twist-drills with square shanks for boring holes for screws. These last should be $\frac{1}{8}$in. and $\frac{3}{16}$in. Later on it will probably be advisable to obtain a wheel brace and a small range of drills for either wood or metal. In addition one small and one medium-sized bradawl and a strong gimlet will be necessary. Fig. 6 shows the correct method of holding the brace, and Fig. 7 shows how a try square ensures the tool is held in an upright position.

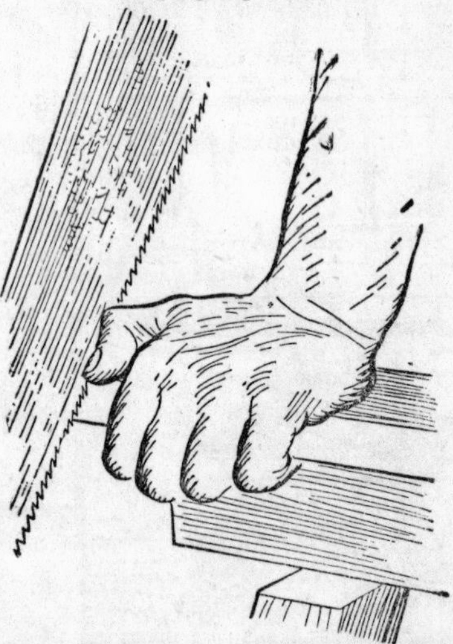

Fig. 3. Starting the saw cut. Note how the knuckle of the thumb is raised above the teeth and against the blade.

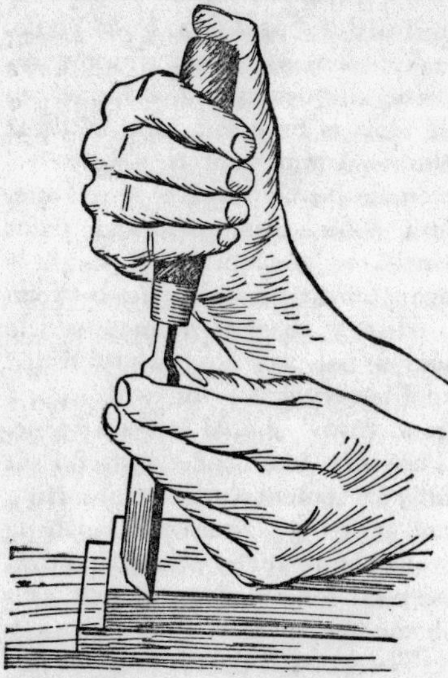

Fig. 4. Showing the method of holding a wood chisel when making a vertical cut. Pressure is applied by the right hand, the blade being guided by the left.

Eventually the need for a plane will arise, and it is worth while to save up until a metal one can be purchased (Fig. 8). The smoothing plane (Fig. 9) about 10in. long is most useful.

All tools must be carefully looked after, if the best results are to be obtained and this is especially true of cutting tools. A touch of oil saves a ton of rust, especially on saws, and tools should be kept in a rack or housed in a cabinet as shown in Fig. 1. Never leave them lying about on the bench. Instructions for making a tool rack will be found in the WORKSHOP EQUIPMENT paragraphs.

No cutting tool should ever be used for a minute after it has lost its edge, and though it is best to send saws to an expert to be sharpened as soon as they begin to need it, edge tools can, and should, be sharpened by their user on a good oil stone. First grade carborundum or india oil stones are to be recommended, also a bench oil can should be purchased for the lubrication of the oil stone.

Pincers.—No tool kit is complete without a pair of pincers (Fig. 10) and a pair of pliers. Any good tool shop will supply them.

Pliers.—These, like the small screwdriver, should have insulated handles, for though it is usual to switch off the power at the main when making electrical repairs and adjustments, the insulation on the pliers and screwdrivers is an additional safeguard against shocks. A pair of footprints is a useful accessory. These are a very handy type of grip which will firmly hold a pipe of any moderate diameter or any size of nut. They are invaluable, for

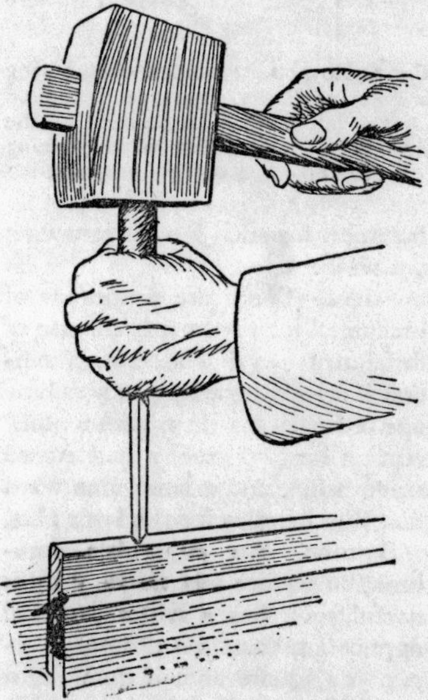

Fig. 5. The correct method of holding a mortise chisel. On narrow section wood, the chisel must be driven in carefully to avoid splitting the wood.

Fig. 6. How to use a brace when boring a hole, vertically. Pressure is applied by the left hand. The position of the head, as shown, assists in maintaining the brace in a vertical position.

instance, for such jobs as renewing tap washers.

Files.—There are a number of incidental jobs requiring the use of different types of files, but in general it is only necessary to purchase one ordinary flat rasp, with a quick cutting bastard face, a half round smooth file, and a small fine ward file. Buy handles for the large files.

Square.—An adjustable combination square and mitre, a most useful tool, has a wider practical application than the ordinary carpenter's square and, if possible, it should be included in the tool kit, particularly if the handyman has much to do with woodwork design. (Fig. 11).

Builders' and Glaziers' Tools.—For cement work, window repairs, and decorating, a special set of tools is necessary, and of these the most important are a trowel, a wooden float, a level, a putty knife, and some distemper and paint brushes. Get a 6in. trowel, and here again the difference in price between a clumsy, badly-tempered article and a balanced and well-finished tool is very small; for, with care, a good trowel should last a lifetime. The size recommended is useful not only for cement work but for mixing and applying plaster when repairing walls before redecorating, and may be used for a dozen different jobs in the garden.

The wooden float is used for finishing off large cement surfaces like garden paths; this tool may be pur-

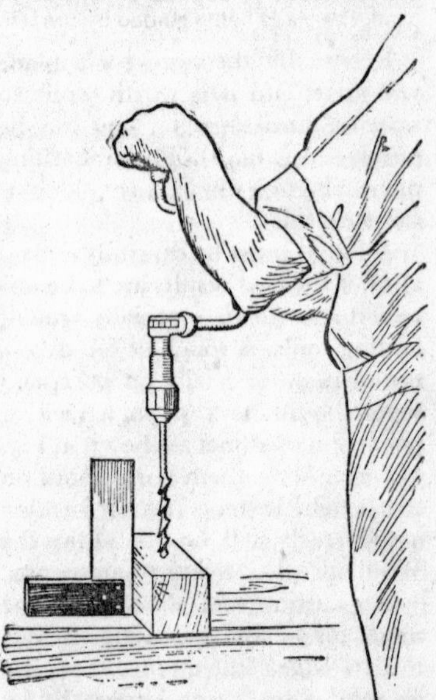

Fig. 7. Sighting the brace for vertical position, using a square. This method may be used when boring, as for Fig. 6.

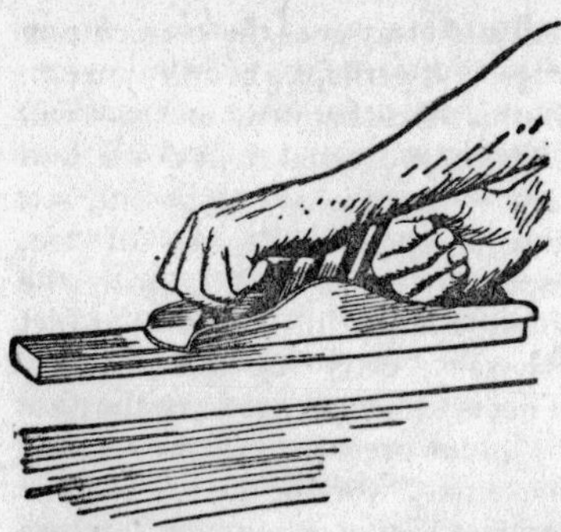

Fig. 8. Using a metal smoothing plane. Note the position of the hands for planing. The left hand guides the plane, the right hand supplies thrust.

chased, but it is simple in design and easy to make. A spirit level will be frequently needed. The one shown in Fig. 1 is a 12in. boat-shaped level and includes a plumb bubble. This last is invaluable when setting up fence posts or clothes line posts, or building yourself that long-promised workshop.

Brushes.—For decorating jobs two good rubber-set paint brushes should be obtained, one 1in. and one 2in. brush, and a distemper brush for walls and ceilings. The ideal distemper brush is the two-knot type similar to that shown in Fig. 12. However, these are really expensive and if the price is too high it will be found that a 4in. rubber-set paint brush, (Fig. 13), as an alternative will give very satisfactory results. It is certainly a better tool than a cheap distemper brush as this will probably shed bristles and disfigure the surface when used. When buying a putty knife, ensure that the blade is really springy and of finely-ground steel.

Paper-hanging Equipment.—For paper-hanging a pair of paper shears are more or less essential. A paper-hanging brush, and a small roller for pressing down the joins in the lengths of paper are also needed, but alternative implements are usually available in every household. For instance, if the wallpaper edges are trimmed at the shop any subsequent scissor work may be managed with the household scissors. A clean clothes brush makes an excellent smoothing brush, and an old chair castor makes a very efficient roller.

Special Tools.—The selection of extra tools chiefly depends on whether it is intended to specialize in a particular branch of work. It may be cabinet making, for instance, or metalwork and in either case special equipment will be required, but the items already mentioned will form a tool kit adequate for all the ordinary jobs about the house.

Care of Tools.—If it is important to acquire a set of good tools, it is no less important to ensure they remain a set of good tools. With this in view a few notes on their proper

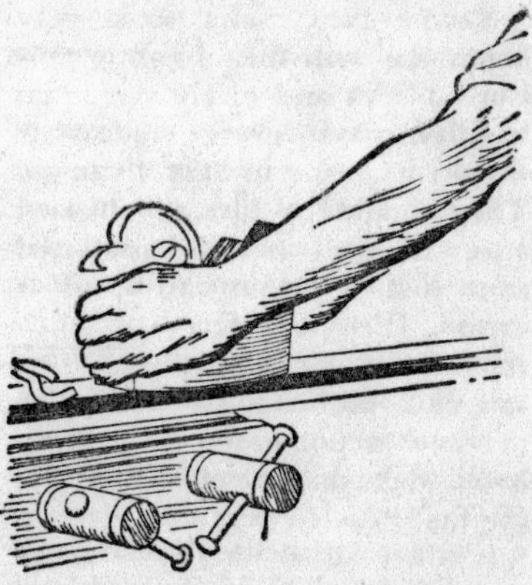

Fig. 9. Using a wooden smoothing plane. Note the position of the left hand which, as in Fig. 8, is used to guide the plane. When planing use a steady, but quick forward thrust.

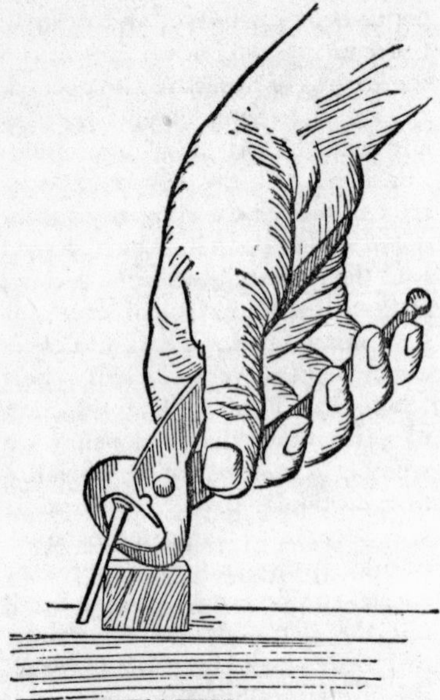

Fig. 10. Using a pair of pincers. A wooden block, placed under the pincers assists the final removal of nail.

care and maintenance are given in the following paragraphs.

Saws.—New saws look very handsome with their brightly polished blades and nicely varnished handles, and every endeavour should be made to keep them so. They should be carefully housed after use with the steel protected from rust by a thin film of oil or grease. Directions for the making of a useful saw rack will be found in a later section of the book. Make that one of the first jobs. Be careful when using any secondhand timber, to examine it carefully for hidden nails or screws. One touch of the saw teeth against a buried nail and away goes the keen cutting edge, and perhaps a couple of teeth. If this does happen, the saw will have to be dressed right down, and new teeth will have to be cut, set, and sharpened. Be careful too, especially when sawing with the grain (Fig. 14) of the timber to let the saw "carry its own weight". That is to say, do not force the pace by undue pressure. Not only does it make hard work of the job but one awkward movement and severe lateral pressure will be brought to bear on the fine ground blade with consequent danger of buckling it.

Examine the rivets in the handles of the saws occasionally, especially during the first few months. It may be found that they have slackened because of shrinkage in the wood of the handle. Tighten them until they grip firmly again (Fig. 15). When it is not in use stand the saw down by the side of the bench or sawing stool, by placing the handle on the ground. It will then be far less likely to get knocked down or to fall over than it would if the handle were uppermost (see Fig. 16).

Hammers.—About the only thing to be careful of, apart from keeping the hammer clean, is any tendency on the part of the head to become loose on the handle. This is easily corrected in the following

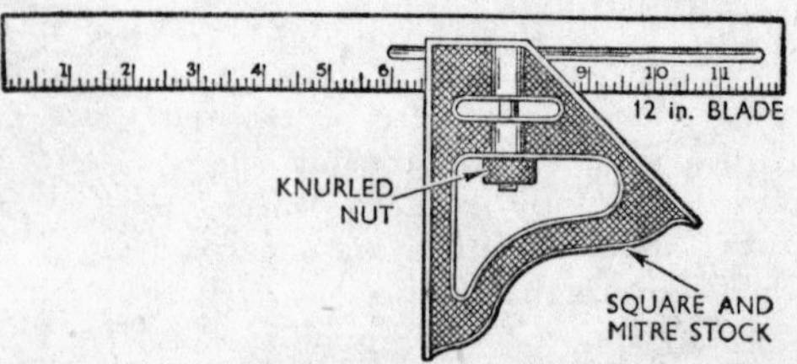

Fig. 11. An adjustable combination square and mitre with a graduated inch scale on a grooved, sliding blade, adjustment being made by nut.

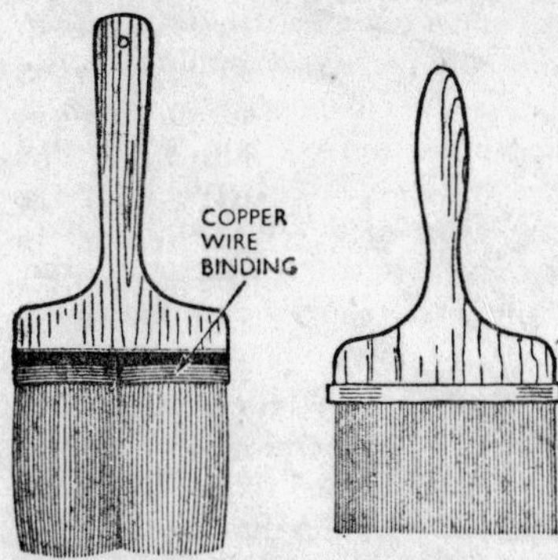

Fig. 12. Shows a two-knot wire-bound distemper brush. (Left).
Fig. 13. A rubber-set brush as a less expensive alternative. (Right).

manner. Give the butt of the handle a sharp blow to drive it up into the head. Then take a nail punch and give the steel wedge which secures the hammer head a couple of taps. This will send the head of the wedge below the surface of the wood which will now be protuding a little. The head will now be firm again and all that remains to be done is flush off the protruding eighth of an inch or so of the handle. This trouble is only likely to happen while the hammer is still fairly new and the wood of the handle liable to shrink. An alternative is to soak the hammer head in water for a few hours.

Screwdrivers.—There is not a lot to be said about the care of screwdrivers. Do not overstrain the screwdriver by using it on screws which are far too big for it. This is a common fault, particularly when dealing with a screw which has been in place for a long time and may be rusted in. The business end should be kept clean and in proper shape. Do not bang the wooden handle with a hammer or burr the bottom end of the blade. If, occasionally, a stubborn screw has to be dealt with, tap the handle with a mallet to jar away any rust from the screw head and apply a little oil to soak in the surrounding wood. Good quality drivers are made from hardened steel. A ratchet screwdriver is a boon because it avoids the necessity of removing the blade from the screw slot every half turn. Although this tool is not absolutely essential it may well be added as a useful extra when the main tool kit has been collected. On the question of length, use a long driver for large screws, and a much shorter one for small work. A screwdriver blade to

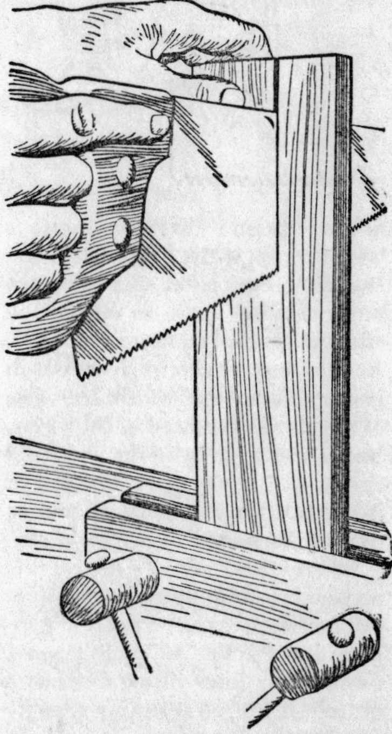

Fig. 14. Sawing with the grain. Allow the saw to cut, without applying any downward pressure on the blade.

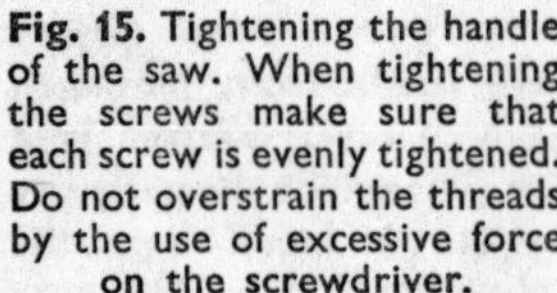

Fig. 15. Tightening the handle of the saw. When tightening the screws make sure that each screw is evenly tightened. Do not overstrain the threads by the use of excessive force on the screwdriver.

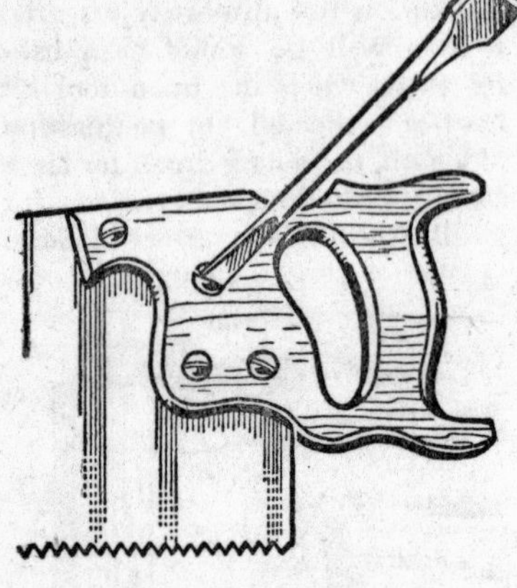

fit the carpenter's brace is useful for large screws; if the brace has a ratchet action the latter should be put into operation so as to enable the effort to be applied more gradually. Always use a screwdriver which is suitable to the width and size of the slot in the head of the screw. Never use a screwdriver as a cold chisel, and never make the end of it red hot for any purpose and so destroy its temper.

Brace and Bits.—Excepting occasional oiling the brace will not call for much in the way of maintenance, but the bits will amply repay careful handling. Store them in a bit roll. A bit roll is simply a length of green baize sewn into pockets, backed with stout canvas or other suitable material and finished with a strap or length of tape with which to tie it into a roll. The bits will lie quite snugly in these pockets with no danger of their cutting edges being spoiled by coming into contact with other tools. Use great care when boring into anything but new timber, to avoid meeting hidden nails, etc. and every now and then overhaul the whole collection, sharpening the cutting edges where necessary with the small ward file. Until accuracy is acquired in this sharpening process, be very careful to follow exactly the correct angle of these edges as they were left by the tool-maker.

Boring Tools.—The gimlet and the gimlet-pointed brace bits are the proper tools for making holes for screws. Bits of two different diameters for any given screw are required; one to make the hole for the

Fig. 16. A safe position for the handsaw when, temporarily, not in use.

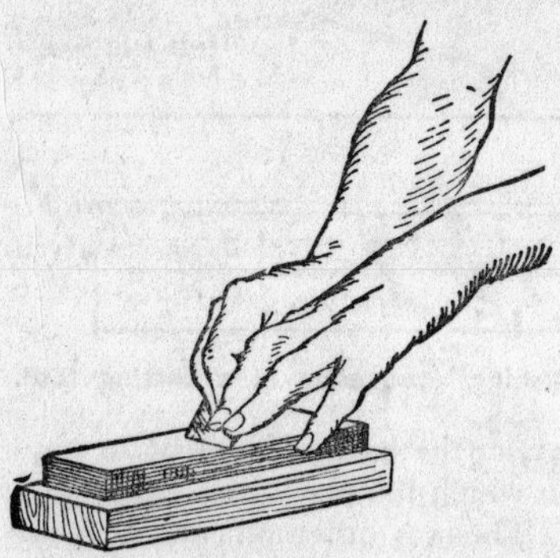

Fig. 17. Correct method of holding a broad cutting tool when sharpening on the oil stone. Apply even pressure on the forward stroke.

shank, and another (smaller) one to cut the hole for the threaded part. In hardwood, use a twist drill for the larger hole; such drills, with a square-taper shank, are made especially for wood, and have a point with a different angle from the metalworker's drill. A fretworker's Archimedean drill is very satisfactory for small work, enabling holes to be made quickly and accurately. Countersinking in wood is effected by a rose bit in a brace, but small

Fig. 18. Sharpening a narrow cutting tool. Be careful to retain the correct angle, relative to oil stone.

diameter holes can be countersunk with a twist drill of suitable diameter, giving it only a few turns. Sometimes a screw has to be let in below the surface, and the recess plugged with a piece of round wood afterwards. In this case the operation is called counterboring. Begin by making the larger hole (with, say, a $\frac{3}{8}$in. or $\frac{1}{2}$in. twist bit or centre bit); then continue with the hole for the shank to the proper depth, and finish with the smaller hole for the worm. If the order is reversed, it will be found difficult to centralize the $\frac{3}{8}$in. or $\frac{1}{2}$in. bit, and a ragged hole will result at the top.

Sharpening edge tools.—These consist of chisels, plane irons, and other such cutting tools, and when

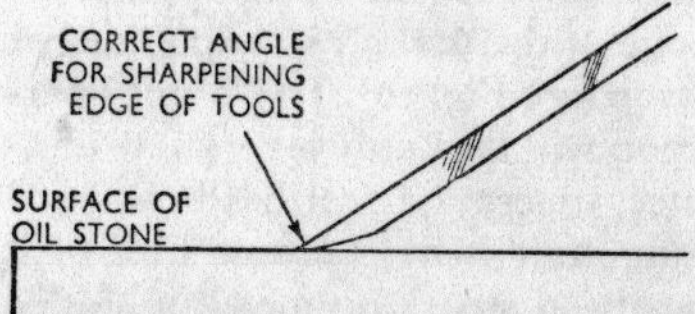

Fig. 19. Illustrating the angle taken by the tool, on the oil stone, to obtain a true cutting edge.

purchased from the shop they will be ground but not sharpened. The first thing to do is to sharpen them. Pour a few drops of oil on the oil stone. Now lay the chisel or plane iron (Fig. 17) with the bevel of the cutting edge flat on the stone (Fig. 18). Then lift it very slightly until it is at a reasonably correct angle (Fig. 19) for sharpening. Move the tool backwards and forwards on the stone, maintaining a steady pressure and keeping the angle of the cutting edge to the stone quite constant. Now turn the tool over and lay it flat on the stone, and in this

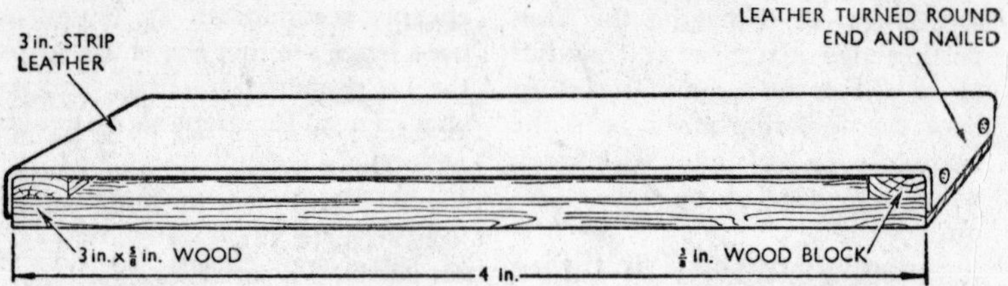

Fig. 20. A simple leather strop for "finishing" the edge of a cutting tool.

position rub it up and down a few times. The reason for this second part of the sharpening operation, is to remove the tiny burr of metal which is formed at the extremity of the cutting edge.

Most professionals finish the whole process by stropping the tool on the palm of the left hand. This is a dangerous business for the amateur but the same smooth keen finish may be obtained by stropping the edge of the tool on a simple leather strop (see Fig. 20). The whole operation will take only a very few minutes, unless the tool has been used long after it has become dull or it has been struck on metal (a hidden nail, for instance) and a notch has been made. In this case, continue the steady even rubbing until the edge is ground away beyond the extent of the damage. If it is deeply notched send it away to be ground. Most tool shops provide a two or three day service for grinding tools and sharpening saws.

Adjusting a Plane.—The adjustment of the plane presents no difficulty if it is a metal one. Lateral adjustment is by a touch of the thumb on a small lever which protrudes above the top of the plane iron, and the coarseness of the cut by a knurled wheel (see Fig. 21) at the back of the frog or base in which the plane iron rests.

The only other adjustment is the opening and closing of the mouth of the plane by means of two set screws in the metal casting which forms the bed of the plane. This will be secured by the manufacturer and should not be moved. One word of warning about the metal plane; its one drawback is the brittleness of the casting. It just will not stand being dropped. So never leave it where a careless movement of the elbow may knock it down. Also, when putting it aside for a moment, lay it on its side and avoid

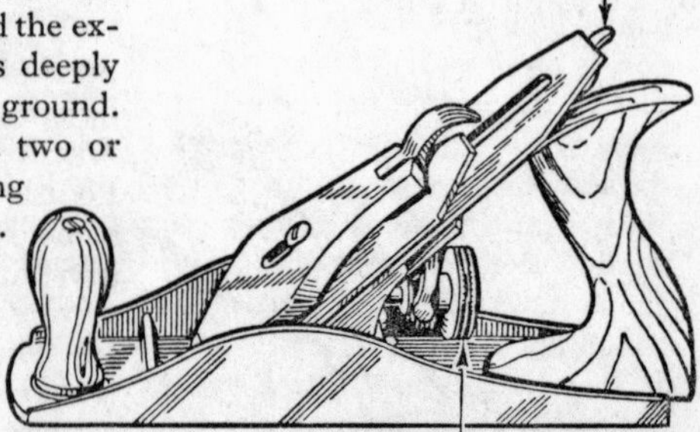

LEVER FOR
LATERAL ADJUSTMENT

KNURLED WHEEL FOR
ADJUSTMENT OF COARSENESS
OF CUT

Fig. 21. The points of adjustment for the plane. The lever is used to set the edge parallel with the base, the knurled wheel to advance or retard the blade to suit requirements.

the danger of damaging the keen cutting edge on a chisel or a handful of nails. For the same reason, turn back the adjusting screw until the cutting edge is quite withdrawn when the plane is no longer required.

Secondhand tools.—In buying secondhand tools the reader must be cautious. Badly worn wooden planes, for instance, will have been reduced in depth, so that the mouth has become widened, squares, for example, may be out of truth. But apart from this, a tool that has been well cared for may be bought with safety. Some of the more common moulding planes, rebate planes, spokeshaves and bull nose planes etc. may often be bought cheaply secondhand. In buying a used brace see that the chuck grips the bit properly, and that the ratchet (if any) functions as it should. In buying a secondhand saw, exceptional care is needed; in fact, it is not too much to say that such tools as saws and chisels should, if possible, be purchased on the advice of a craftsman.

Never buy secondhand files. They are occasionally offered for sale in markets, but a spent file is worthless. Sometimes files are revived by treatment with acid or by sand blast, but they are not to be recommended. New files are so cheap, and last so long in fair use, that it is a waste of money to purchase any others.

Arranging and Equipping the Workshop

LIGHT, warmth, and dryness are the main requirements of the amateur's workshop. Warmth it should be remembered does not necessarily ensure dryness, and indeed if the workshop is made too warm, it will probably become damp. The best way to secure dryness is by providing for ample ventilation; under the floorboards if it is a wooden building, or by opening the top of a window in other cases. With regard to light, if there is a window along one side of the workshop, the long side of the workbench should go against that wall. If there is a central fitting for the electric light, lead a long flex from the ceiling rose to a bracket over the bench, and suspend the lamp from that. Keep the light well up, out of the way when handling long pieces of timber on the bench.

A better way would be to run a length of vulcanised india rubber cable from the rose to a batten-lampholder screwed to a wooden block which is fixed to the wall. If this is done by an electrician, get him to fit a switch, combined with a plug point below so that an electric soldering iron or other appliance taking little current could be plugged in at need. A combined 5-amp. switch and plug outlet (the latter with a separate switch) is a standard fitting that can be purchased from most electrical dealers. It would be advisable for an earthed fitting (three-core flexible) to be specified, as most modern appliances are provided with an earthing terminal. As an example of the benefit of the plug point, a 500-watt bowl fire could be plugged in on cold days.

Warming the Shop.—This is not merely a question of warming the workman, but also of providing the warm atmosphere that will be needed if woodwork joints are to be glued together. Glue quickly chills and no satisfactory joint can be made on a cold day unless the timber is warm to the touch before applying the glue. So we must have some source of heat for such jobs, at any rate. An oil stove will do quite well for a small workshop, and it should stand on a square of sheet iron. It should also have a fender of the same material around it, standing on the bottom sheet and rising about 9 inches from the floor.

Fire Precautions.—Store the paraffin outside the shop, and do not forget that it is not safe to leave an oil lamp burning untended for long. Clean the stove periodically, and trim the wick when required. Sweep out the workshop regularly and bag up the shavings, etc. ready for burning under the garden refuse heap. The bowl fire can be used for odd-time warming, and should be given a stand on a slab of stone or brick, in some place out of harm's way.

Workbench.—A strong kitchen table can be used for light work, but it is not always firm enough for planing and other woodworking operations. This is mainly because the legs are open and are not connected near the bottom by braces. If the worker can obtain a strong table with square legs, it is an easy matter to screw four pieces of 4in. × 1in. batten about 3 inches up from the bottom, so as to connect the legs at front and back and the two sides. A flooring of ¾in. matchboard can be nailed to the top edges of the battens, stiffening the entire structure and furnishing a useful shelf for large tools, etc. Failing this, if the floor is not needed, nail on two widths of 6in. × 1in. floorboard from end to end, centred on the width of the short ends of the table; this forms a brace.

It is not difficult to construct a strong bench, and Fig. 1 gives the required information about the joints. The length may be anything from 4ft. 6in. to 6ft., according to the accommodation available, the width should not be less than 2ft. 3in., and a comfortable height for the average man is 2ft. 6in. First construct the two end frames. The legs are of 3in. × 3in. timber, and are connected at the top by a bearer cut from 4in. × 1¼in. deal; they are also connected near the bottom by a similar piece, the lower edge of which may come about 2in. from the bottom.

Any difficulty of jointing is avoided by screwing the bearer and the bottom rail to the legs, using No. 12 iron screws, 2½in. long. The holes bored in the rail and bearer should be large enough for the screws to pass easily. To assemble the end frames, lay the legs in their proper relative positions on the floor, with a bearer laid across them, and test the angles with a square. Now mark the position for a hole in one leg by passing the bradawl through the hole previously made in the bearer. Take away the bearer and start the hole where the awl has marked it. Put on the bearer again and screw it at the one hole, testing with the square before getting it too tight. Now get the bearer square with the opposite leg, bore one hole there, and turn in the screw tightly. It remains to bore for the remaining two screws, and insert them. Fig. 2 shows the correct method of holding a bradawl.

The screwing on of the rail near

the bottom is easy, because the legs are held in position by the top bearers; but test carefully for squareness, and measure from the bottom to ensure that the rail is the same distance up at each leg. A third screw can be put in at each joint for extra strength, if desired. Make up a second end frame in the same way. The two end frames are connected by top bearer rails cut from one-inch boards, not less in width than 4½in. These rails extend so as to cover the end of the 4in. × 1¼in. bearers of the end frames. Below, level with the lower rails of these frames, two narrower rails are fixed, cut from 4in. × 1in. deal. The same gauge of screw (No. 12), but only 2in. in length, should be used for the long rails. Lay the two end frames on the floor, in proper square position and at the right distance apart, and get an assistant to hold them while one top rail is screwed to one end. Get the rail square with the leg at that end, and tighten the screw so as to keep it from slipping. At the opposite end frame, get the rail square, and drive a nail in a little way (through one of the holes bored for screws), in order to fix the proper position.

Insert one screw in this second frame; then carefully pull out the temporary nail, without altering the location of the rail, and replace it with the proper screw. Go back to the first end now, and put in the second screw. Gently turn the partly assembled bench over to the reverse side; put on the top rail there, testing it and eventually screwing it in place as before. The lower rails are put on one by one, following the same precedure.

Cut the boards for the top, and nail them on, letting them come even with the edge of the top bearer rails at front, back and two ends. Tongued and grooved floorboard will make a good top. Saw down one board to bring the top to the required width if needed; plane off the tongue on one outside board and the groove on the opposite board in any case. Screw in No. 12 screws; countersink the holes in the boards so that the screwhead is sunk well below the surface. A diagonal brace can be fixed to the framework to stiffen it further (see Fig. 1A).

If it is decided to floor in the bot-

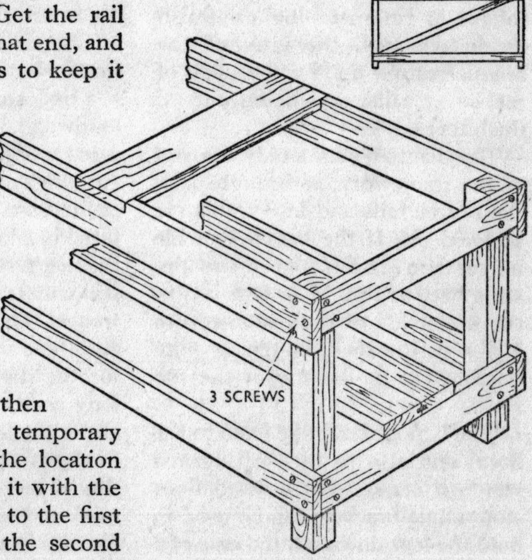

Figs. 1 and 1A. A part section general arrangement of workbench framework, joints and the diagonal side bracing; the latter being used to stiffen the frame.

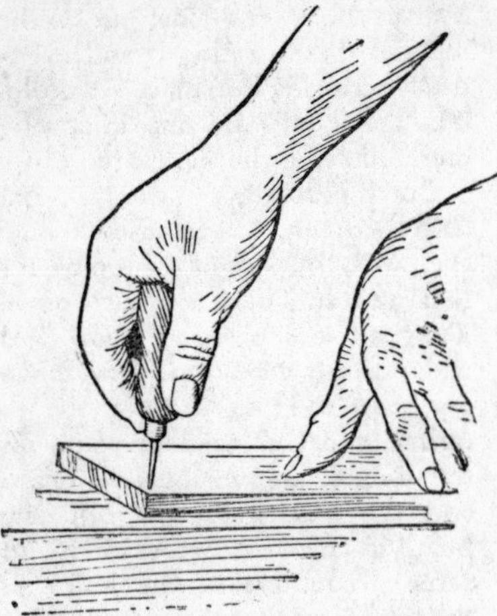

Fig. 2. When boring with a bradawl into wood, especially at the end of wood, apply the edge of the blade *across* the "run" of grain to avoid splitting.

tom, put the lower rails of the end frames on the *inside*, but the top bearers outside. Then the flooring (of ⅝in. or ¾in. matching) can finish inside the legs, the ends of the boards resting on the top edge of the lower rails, and being cut off flush there.

The diagram shows only one end of the framework, to indicate how the bearer rails and lower rails are screwed on. If the bench is made longer than 4ft. 6in., one or two 4in. wide battens should be screwed to the underside of the bench top to stiffen it. Let these battens go into notches cut in the top of the top rails.

The bench should be fixed to the floor, and also to the wall against which it stands. On a wood floor stout angle brackets can be used to hold the legs down. In the case of a concrete floor, drill holes for No. 12 Rawplugs and use No. 12 screws to fix the brackets down. For the wall, drive in wrought iron holdfasts at convenient brickwork joints, so that the eye of the holdfast comes against the side of a bench leg. Then, after getting the bench level and in proper position, put a stout screw through the eye and into the leg. Two holdfasts at each end should suffice; one at each end may do if a good fixing has been obtained to the floor. If the mortar of the brickwork joint is soft or crumbly, drive in a wood wedge against the holdfast to secure the latter; alternatively, rake out or chisel out a larger hole and cement in the holdfast, first bending over the extreme (pointed) end at right angles to form a grip in the cement.

Bench Stop.—The bench stop is an invaluable aid to the preparation of wood surfaces by planing and to provide a firm stop face for work of a similar nature. The stop is located at the top end of the working side of the bench.

The customary type of bench stop is shown in Fig. 3. It consists of a 1¾in. square section block of hardwood, 6in. long, and a hardwood wedge 5½in. long, 1¾in. wide, ¾in. thick at the top tapering to ⅜in. at the base. These components are fitted in a hole cut in the bench top, the rear face of the hole being cut to the same angle as the taper of the wedge. The location of the bench stop hole in the bench is a matter for the discretion of the user. So long as the top of the vice is not above the level of the bench no difficulty should be encountered in this respect. The hole should be marked off so as to be approximately 3in. in from the side face of the bench and at least 7in. from the top end of the bench. Having scribed the shape of the hole, which should be exactly $1\frac{3}{4}$in. wide by $2\frac{5}{8}$in. long, drill out a $\frac{3}{8}$in. hole at each corner and well inside the scribed lines. Using a keyhole saw, remove the surplus material and trim the sides of the hole with a paring chisel. All the sides should be vertical with the exception of the rear face which must be pared to the same angle as the taper of the wedge. Slide the stop in the hole, followed by the wedge which must be hammered in firmly but not excessively. Press the stop down until it protrudes about half an inch above the level of the bench. Lightly chamfer the top edges of wedge and stop. To alter the height of the stop tap its base to loosen wedge, re-position the stop to required level and secure it by driving the wedge home.

Pair of Saw bucks.—When sawing timber some form of stool or trestle is wanted on which to rest the board to be cut. A short piece of board to be cross-cut can be held with the knee on a single trestle, and the same applies to a board that is to be ripped (sawn down lengthwise). But a longer board will have to be supported at both ends, so that a pair of trestles will be needed. If, for example, there is occasion to take a room door off its hinges for planing, or for some other repair, nothing but a pair of stout trestles will do for supporting the door during the operation. These trestles are often called saw bucks, or sawing horses. While taking the measurements for one, and setting out the lengths and joints, it is very little more trouble to do this for a pair, and so provide two.

The saw buck as made by a carpenter is splayed in two directions; the legs slope back lengthwise, and also outwards. This is to provide a firm stand, while keeping the legs out of the way of the saw. Fig. 4

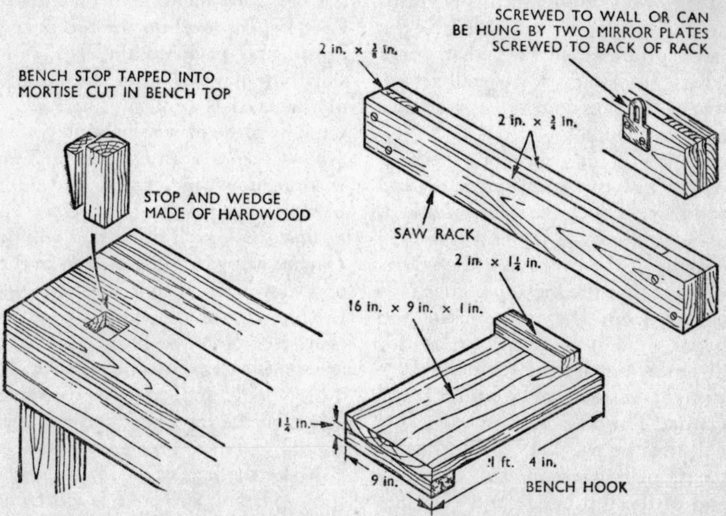

Fig. 3. General details of an adjustable bench stop for the workbench. Dimensions and assembly arrangements of saw rack and bench hook. These, for preference, and to give greater durability, should be made of hardwood.

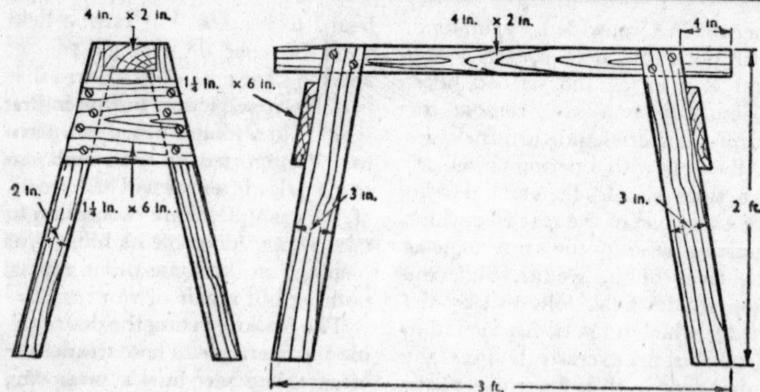

Fig. 4. Dimensions and general arrangement of a useful saw buck, showing front and end elevations. Side bracing for legs will not normally be necessary.

shows a saw buck in end elevation and in front elevation. The tops of the legs are notched out to receive the top beam, which is cut from 4in. to 2in. deal (wide face upwards). But the leg-tops, owing to the two-way slope, have to be cut with a slant or bevel, that is, a compound of the two slopes, and this is apt to be difficult for the novice. It is the same problem, in fact, that arises when making a wheelbarrow, where the legs join on in a similar two-way slope.

There is a simpler method, which will give ample strength and stability: slope the legs *outwards only*, as shown in the end view. On looking at the front view the reader will see that the leg-top comes four inches from the end of the top beam. Join it to the beam at this distance, but let the leg *come down straight* instead of sloping backwards. The two legs on one side will thus be parallel, as will the opposite pair. Measure 4in. from the end of the top beam, square a line down the side face of the beam, and fit on the leg-top square to this line. In other words, the distance from the end of the beam to the outside edge of the leg will be 4in. The legs are to be screwed to the beam at each side. The end braces should be screwed on after the legs have been fixed to the beam.

The lower ends of the legs will have to be squared off finally while the saw buck stands level on a floor. Rest a spirit level on the top of the beam, and pack up the legs with thin bits of wood until the bubble of the level is central. Then get a straight piece of wood about ¾in. × ¼in. to use as a straight-edge. Lay it alongside the legs of one end, narrow edge on the floor, close up against the legs. The worker will be viewing the saw buck as seen in the end elevation. Run a pencil along the top edge of the straight-edge, so that it marks a horizontal line across the legs of the saw buck. This should indicate the true line at which the lower ends of the legs should be cut to give a level stance.

Make the legs of 3in. × 2in. deal; the top beam, as stated, is cut from 4in. × 2in. deal. The end braces ought to be not less in thickness than 1¼in., and may be of any width

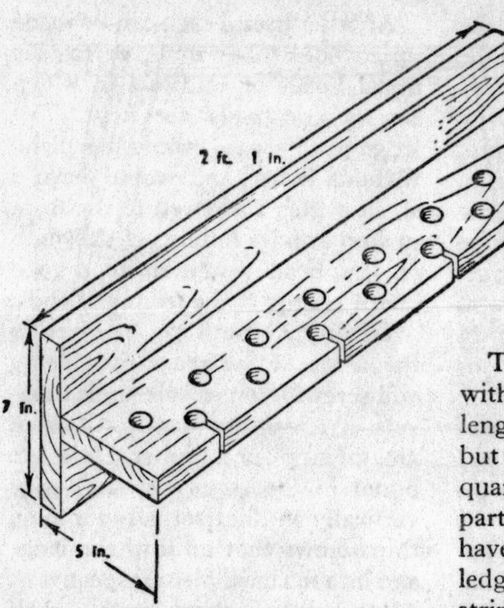

Fig. 5. Overall dimensions of a simple but efficient tool rack.

from 6in. to about 8in. They are screwed on with No.12 screws, the length being suitable to the thickness of the braces. A V-shaped notch may be cut in one end of the top beam, for use when ripping boards; it helps to prevent the saw damaging the end of the saw buck.

Tool Rack Over Bench.—A rack for chisels, screwdrivers, files and other handled tools is convenient, and is easily made, though it is not wise to leave edge tools continually in such a rack; they ought to be collected up and put away in a tool box when the job has been done. The rack shown in Fig. 5 is intended to be screwed to the wall of the workshop at the back of the bench. Rawlplugged holes should be made in the brickwork, if any, and the rack held by about four screws (for the length shown in the diagram). Some people fix the rack to the bench, but in this case the vertical back piece must be made higher to give clearance, and an objection to this is that hammering or planing on the bench jogs and jolts the tools, making an irritating noise even if it does not unship some of them.

The rack is shown 5in. wide, with a back piece 7in. high; the length illustrated is just over 2ft., but this is a matter of choice. Three-quarter inch deal will do for all parts; but, as many circular holes have to be bored in the horizontal ledge, it would be better to get a strip of hardwood or American whitewood for this part. Get the timber and plane it up to the chosen dimension. The ledge is shown merely screwed (from the back) through the back piece. It would make a stronger job to house it into the back piece to a depth of a quarter of an inch, but this involves cutting a shallow groove along the back piece. In either case, fit the ledge to the back, bore holes for the screws and put in about half of them, leaving out alternate ones for the time being. Then mark the position of the ledge carefully, apply hot glue, and quickly fit together again and screw up tightly. The screws previously inserted should be turned in first. Then insert the remaining screws and put the rack in a warm place for the glue to harden.

No. 8 iron screws will do for this job, and the holes in the back piece should be countersunk deeply to get the screwheads well in from the face of the wood.

The proper way to set out and bore the holes for the tools is as follows. Measure at each end of the ledge to get the centre line of the width, and connect these points by a scribed or pencilled line. The width shown in the diagram is 5in., so that the line comes 2½in. from the front edge. Measure in from the end a distance of 2in. lengthwise to give the point for the first hole; set a pair of compasses or dividers to span 3in., and step off the rest of the holes of the back row at 3in. intervals, starting from the two-inch point first marked. The front row of holes is started 3½in. from the end of the ledge, to bring these holes intermediate between those of the back row. Leave enough wood between the back row and front row, so that there is no risk of splitting out. The front row can be omitted, if desired.

Get a piece of waste board and lay it on the bench; lay the ledge over it and clamp both down to the bench firmly. Put a ¾in. centre bit in a brace and bore the first hole, going down through the ledge and into the waste piece far enough to leave a clean hole in the ledge itself. Proceed with the rest of the holes boring out slowly and carefully. If the brace has a ratchet action the latter should be brought into use, enabling slower and more gradual boring to be done. It will be seen, from the diagram, that some of the front row holes are slotted out to the front; this is to allow chisels with wide blades (which would not pass through the round holes in the ledge) to be inserted from the front and turned round with the blade broadside on. The slots are cut after the holes have been bored. The best bit to use is a screw-nose improved centre bit; these are cheap and efficient.

Another useful rack can be made up to hold other tools, or to take metal boxes or canisters in which screws and nails are kept. The ledge in this case would be plain, without holes, and would have a shallow guard screwed to the front to stop articles falling off. A length of 1in. bead would make a good guard or stop at the front and ends.

Greater strength can be given to the ledge of the racks by glueing and screwing on simple angle brackets of triangular shape, cut from 4in. × ¾in. planed timber. Holes are bored in the front (sloping) edge vertically and horizontally for long, thin screws that go into the ledge and into the back piece respectively. Alternatively, short steel shelf brackets can be screwed on at each end and at the middle of the length, under the ledge.

Saw Rack.—The saw rack shown in Fig.3 is made from two pieces of batten planed up true and separated by a thin piece of wood (⅜in. to ½in. thick). This latter forms a space through which the saw blade can be inserted, while the handle rests on the tops of the two battens. If a single batten were fixed to the wall, or to the side of the bench, and separated from the wall, etc. by two spacing pieces, the saw would not hang straight, so use two battens, and make up the fitment as illustrated.

The entire assembly, two battens and two spacers, may be fixed to a wall by two screws at each end, passing through the wood members and going into the wall or bench end. But a better method is to screw the front batten to the back one only, boring clearing holes through the spacers so that the screws do not bite into them. Thus the rack is fixed together independently. Procure two brass mirror plates and screw them to the back of the rear batten, so that the eye at the top of the plate is above the wood. Then hold the rack up against a wall where it is to hang, mark positions for Rawlplugs, and drill out two holes for the plugs in the brickwork. No. 8 screws will suit this job, and the handyman should procure screws having the worm formed right up to the head; otherwise the screw cannot be turned right in close to the mirror plate, and the rack will be loose.

Another method, for any situation where thin plates or other such fittings have to be Rawlplugged to a wall, is to make a hole with the drill or jumper of ample depth, and to use a shorter plug, so that the latter after insertion is about ⅛in. to ¼in. below the surface; this will allow an ordinary screw to be used. If a screw is forced into a Rawlplug after the wormed part has reached the top of the plug, the latter may be twisted round and loosened or drawn out.

Bench Hook.—This easily made gadget (see Fig. 3) enables such jobs as sawing the ends of battens square, or cutting off narrow wood to length, to be done comfortably at the bench. The hook is laid on the bench so that the thick stop at the under side rests against the bench front or end. A piece of wood is placed on the hook, resting against the top stop. By holding and pushing the wood against the hook with the left hand, it is easily kept sufficiently firm for sawing. The right hand is then free to use a tenon saw on that part of the job which projects to the right beyond the top stop of the hook.

To make a bench hook, procure a piece of 9in. × 1in. board, about 16 inches long. Plane up the top surface, and square off the front and back ends. The top and bottom stops are cut from batten 2in. wide and 1¼in. thick, or thereabouts. If a piece of oak or beech can be obtained for the stops it will greatly improve the hook, and add to its life. Also, the use of oak for the 9in. × 1in. board will help. Fix the stops on dead square; bore them for No. 12 screws, countersink the holes in the stops, and screw through from the bottom of the underside stop and the top of the top stop. Sink the screwheads well below the surface.

Vices.—Although wooden vices, with a wooden or steel screw, are still made for woodwork benches, the complete steel vice is usually preferred. The full-size joiner's vice is an expensive item, and generally the bench has to be cut away to fix this appliance. However, a simpler and lighter vice is made for amateur use, and can be fixed by its flanges to the top and front of the bench. A hole has to be bored through the top front bearer rail to let the screw of the vice pass. The makers give a printed leaflet with instructions for fitting, but any tool dealer will tell the purchaser what is necessary. The front of the bench is the usual site for the vice, and usually a point near the left-hand end is chosen, as this allows a board clamped for endwise planing to be worked from right to left.

We must consider the placing of the metalworking vice, if this is to be bolted or screwed permanently to the bench top. If the woodworking vice is fitted to the left-hand, the metal vice will have to go at the opposite end. It is true that a "portable" vice can be bought, and fastened for the time being by its cramp, but for this the top or end of the bench must project at least 1½in. to 2 in., and most woodworking benches have a flush front. A way out of the difficulty is to bolt down a piece of 9in. × 1in. board to one end of the bench, letting it overlap the bench end by about two inches. Then the overlap will afford a fixing for the portable vice. Cut a notch in the edge of the board, so that part of the cramp frame can be held against rotation. These screwclamp arrangements have a tendency to twist around when a strain is put on them, but the notch will do a lot to prevent such movement. If room can be found for a vice permanently, buy one that is bolted down by flanges to the top of the bench; this is much more satisfactory. If the pocket will allow it, purchase a vice with jaws not less than 2½in. wide.

Gas Ring for Gluepot.—Although an oil stove is a quite satisfactory means of heating the gluepot, a gas point is very convenient. If the bench is fixed against a wall, a gas pipe can be led near one end and terminated with an elbow and a tube nozzle with cock. A metal flexible tube can then be slipped over the nozzle (using a proper rubber connector), and joined to a small gas boiling ring. Do not get too big a ring; once the glue has been prepared, all that is needed is enough heat to keep it in the right condition for application. If the same ring is to be used to heat a soldering iron, buy one with a small central burner cone rather than one with the usual wider ring of holes at the outside. It will serve just as well for the glue, and will be much better for the soldering iron.

A slab of stone, a piece of slate, or a square of sheet iron should be put under the ring if it stands on the bench. One more point. Keep a shallow tin handy for the spent matches; this will be a reminder not to drop them on the floor among the shavings! This will reduce the risk of fire to a minimum: a precaution well worth adopting.

Materials for Constructional Work

TIMBER is stocked at the timber yards in two forms; *sawn* and *prepared*. Prepared timber is planed on some or all sides or edges, according to its intended uses. The planing of prepared timber naturally reduces it to something less than the nominal sizes by which it is sold. For example, a one-inch board in the rough, that is sawn, but not planed, will be approximately an inch in thickness. But "inch" board planed on both sides nd both edges will lose about an eighth of an inch in thickness and in width. If the worker requires planed boards that will measure an inch after planing, he should state this together with the type of timber required when ordering them, and thicker timber will be put through the planing machine so that the finished thickness is, in fact, one inch.

Quartering.—This is timber with such sectional measurements as 2in. × 2in., 3in. × 2in., 3in. × 3in., 4in. × 2in., and 4in. × 4in., and when sold *sawn* will measure approximately these dimensions. If bought to these nominal sizes as "prepared", each section will lose in breadth and thickness as explained above.

Plain-edge board, bought planed will be less than the nominal width and thickness, as previously mentioned. A tongued and grooved board, when fitted to another, will be less than its nominal width by the depth of the groove into which the tongue fits. Grooved boards are jointed by separate slips or tongues, sometimes called feathers, inserted into the groove of one board after glueing or painting, and then this board is pushed up to the adjoining board so that the tongue also fits into that groove. These slips must be free from defects.

Matchboard, or matching, loses in width by the same amount as tongued and grooved board, but is planed on one face only. For substantial work nothing less than $\frac{3}{4}$in. matching should be used, which in effect is $\frac{5}{8}$in. thick. But if it is required merely for covering in the back of a piece of kitchen equipment, then $\frac{1}{2}$in. matching will serve. Apart from its fragility, thin matchboard is often found to be defective at the tongues or grooves, there being so little thickness at these parts. Moreover, the parts in question are apt to break away when the boards are being fitted together unless great care is taken.

Weatherboard, in the cheaper grades is nothing more than featheredge board, two boards being cut obliquely from, say, a $\frac{3}{4}$in. board so that each tapers away at one edge. At the thicker edge the boards will be less than $\frac{3}{4}$in. by the material taken out by the saw blade. Here again, avoid the thinnest stuff, and take nothing thinner than $\frac{3}{4}$in. This type of board is used for fences, and thicker measurements will do for the outside covering of wooden sheds and similar outbuildings. But for any worth-while job where the boards are to be laid horizontally rebated weatherboards should be used. These are made with a rebate on the under side of the thick edge of each board, this rebated part fitting over the narrower edge of the next board below. Various grades are sold, cut from different qualities of timber. Generally, on outdoor work, it is almost a waste of money to use the cheaper or thinner kinds of board.

A still better material is moulded and rebated weatherboard which is shaped at the thin, or top, part as well as being rebated at the thick part. It looks nice and in fact has an altogether superior appearance, besides being far more durable and capable of more secure fixing. This type of board would be used for a good summer house, a sun-room, or for the timber sides of a veranda.

Battens, which are small boards measuring, say, 2in. × 1in., 2in. × $\frac{3}{4}$in., and so on, are useful for a variety of household jobs. Besides these, it is possible to get timber of 1in. × 1in. section, $1\frac{1}{2}$in. × $1\frac{1}{2}$in., 1in. × $\frac{1}{2}$in., and others. Quartering is also sold measuring 2in. × $1\frac{1}{2}$in. in section, but is too slight for most constructional jobs where such a material is normally used. Some of these slight sections are found mostly in the cheap portable buildings much advertised in gardening and other journals. They are worth what they cost, and the purchaser has only himself to blame if he expects to get a five-pound article for half

Fig. 1. Five types of weather boarding. B, the most commonly used and suitable for all general work, permits some adjustment of overlap. A, C and D, being rebated, and E, tongued and grooved, have a fixed overlap; but these possess a somewhat better appearance and superior weather-proof qualities.

that price. Incidentally this demonstrates the big saving possible when the handyman builds his own sheds, etc. Either he can spend the same amount on materials alone, giving his own labour and getting a first-class article, or he can actually save money by making the same shed as advertised and saving the labour cost.

Roofing Materials. — Corrugated steel sheets, galvanized, are made in various thicknesses, but nothing thinner than 24 gauge should be used for roofs; 22 gauge is much preferable for durability. The sheeting is made with 3in. and 5in. corrugations but the smaller one is generally used. Various stock lengths are kept, with a standard width of 2ft. 3in. This material cannot be painted satisfactorily until it has been weathered by exposure for six months or so.

Corrugated asbestos-cement sheets are an alternative material, better in appearance than steel but somewhat brittle. If put on carefully, and not subjected afterwards to blows or shocks, it is very lasting. Both these materials are fixed by nailing or screwing to roof timbers. Holes in the steel sheeting are made by punching with a sharp punch over a block of wood, but asbestos-cement must be drilled carefully with a twist drill (as used for metal) in a carpenter's brace or hand drill (see Fig.2). A curved washer is put between the top of the nail or screw and the sheeting. Holes are made in the "hills" of the sheeting, not in the "valleys". Both sorts of corrugated sheet can be used for the sides of sheds, etc.

Flat asbestos-cement sheets are used for lining the walls of outbuildings, and sometimes for the outside. The sheets are fixed edge to edge, with a small gap between. The joints are then covered by a strip of $1\frac{1}{2}$in. $\times$ $\frac{3}{4}$in. deal nailed through so that the nails enter the underneath studding in the gap between the asbestos-cement sheets. Holes in asbestos-cement sheets should always be drilled.

Wallboards, in many different materials, are sold for lining the insides of buildings, making partitions, etc., and some types also will do for use outside. Special types are made for keeping in warmth and keeping out noise. These are softer and more "open" in texture

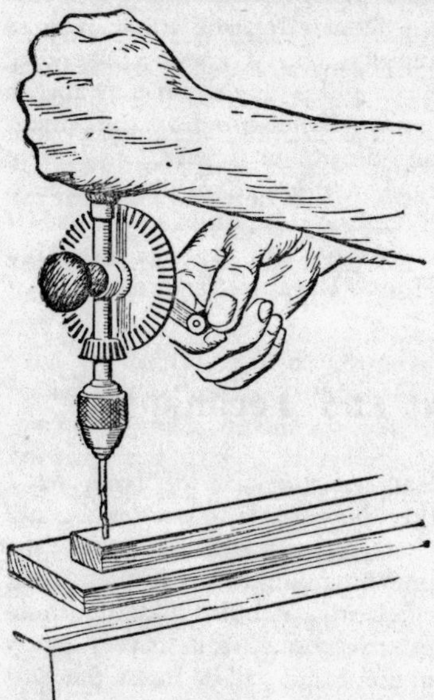

Fig. 2. When drilling vertically, through thin or soft material hold the brace, as shown, to keep the drill steady.

than the harder boards intended for other jobs.

Bricks, Cement, Lime and Sand.—The common pinkish-coloured bricks are used for all work where the surface is protected from the weather, as by roughcast or cement rendering. Harder and better quality bricks are needed for exposed positions. The best in appearance and durability are the facing bricks, used for outside walls. Another good quality is the stock brick, yellowish in colour. Bricks used for paving, or for doorsteps, etc. must be af a hard type (such as Blue Staffords or Dutch Clinkers), and the worker should ask for them specifically when purchasing. Engineering bricks, hardest of all, are blueish in colour, and somewhat more costly. Bull nose shapes (with rounded edge) can be used for the finishing course of steps, and many other "specials" are to be had for other positions where a shaped finish is wanted.

Roofing tiles including ridge and hip coverings are made in various shades and qualities. Slates are sold in many stock sizes. Except on porches or low roofs, the repair or replacement in both cses is hardly a job for the novice, who may do more damage to adjoining roofing than he originally set out to remedy.

Portland cement can be purchased in 7 lb. or 14 lb. bags, or larger quantities. Purchase no more than is necessary for immediate work, as it is troublesome to keep dry and may deteriorate if kept for some months. For extensive work cement should be bought in 1-cwt. bags. It is seldom sdvisable to use pure cement without sand, for this usually cracks after a short time. Mix the cement with sharp sand, that is, sand from which all earthy matter has been washed out. Washed sand sold by the builders' merchant is of this type; sea sand is not generally satisfactory. The proportion of sand to cement varies with different sorts of jobs but a good general mixture is 1 of cement to 3 of sand. Make a dry mixture of cement and sand and then mix it twice after wetting. Avoid adding too much water; the mortar, after mixing, should be plastic, but not fluid.

Lime mortar is a substitute for Portland cement mortar when great strength is not needed, but it is sometimes strengthened with a small amount of Portland cement. Lime, after slaking with water sprinkled on to it from the rose of a watering can, is mixed with sand to form the mortar. Lime can be bought in small lots or in hundredweight bags. It needs the same care as cement, so far as protection from moisture is concerned, and care should be taken to keep it from the eyes and away from clothing.

In all jobs which involve the use of cement, the parts to be dealt with must be well wetted before starting; for it is obvious that porous substances will suck up moisture rapidly, and if the brickwork of walls etc. is very dry it may absorb too much moisture from the cement and destroy or weaken its adhesive quality. Bricks, floor tiles, and such like, should be dipped in a pail of water before laying. See also House Repairs (External).

Soldering Equipment and Technique

The procedure and materials necessary to efficient soldering vary according to the type of work, but there are general principles which should be observed at all times. The surfaces to be united must be chemically clean, free from grease and dirt and sufficient heat must be applied not only to melt and flow the solder, but to warm the parts of the joint. The soldering bit must be clean and free from oxide. A flux is used to seal off the surfaces from the air and prevent oxidation, and to assist the flow of melted solder. On electrical work a non-acid flux should be used, to avoid corrosion and damage to the adjacent parts of the object; *but* (and this is an important consideration with the novice) in general it is easier to solder with an acid flux such as killed spirits. For ordinary work in which functional safety is not involved acid flux may be used providing the residue is removed when the work is finished.

One more point, solder, an alloy of tin and lead, can be used with resin flux applied *directly* on tin-plated objects, but for other materials the jointing surfaces must first be coated with a thin film of solder. The beginner should, for practice, test out the use of resin as a flux because it possesses certain characteristics which require some understanding before it can be used efficiently. Tubular solder, with an internal core of resin, is very handy in use, but it will be found that soldering will be improved by a touch of acid flux. Paste fluxes are much used and are excellent, but the liquid acid is preferable until the handyman is proficient. Acid flux incidentally, cleans the surfaces, besides preventing oxidation.

Joints can be "sweated" together in the following manner:—The method is to hold the surface of one joint over a flame, and meanwhile apply a little solder to make a thin film over the whole area of the joint face. Both surfaces are similarly treated. Next the surfaces are clamped tightly together and heat is applied, by holding the clamped joint over a flame, or by directing a blowpipe jet systematically over the whole joint. Two electric wires twisted together can be soldered by a tiny flame, properly applied and directed. Other minute jobs can be served in the same way.

Source of Heat.—An atmospheric gas burner, Bunsen type, is the best for heating the soldering bit, or for applying heat to work to be sweated. Unfortunately a certain amount of oxide is deposited on the bit, so that it requires frequent cleaning by wiping with a rag. Occasionally, after heating, it will need to be filed clean with an old coarse file (while still hot). A small block of sal ammoniac should be obtained, and the hot soldering bit rubbed on this occasionally to clean it (unpleasant fumes are given off).

The old-fashioned method of heating the bit in a clear fire has much to recommend it, but the worker must guard against too prolonged heating, which will burn away the working faces of the copper. When using a gas ring, choose one with a small ring of jets close together; cover the bit with a bent piece of sheet iron put on top, to conserve the heat.

Electric soldering bits are very satisfactory, but there is a time-lag in heating up, and the tool should be given ample time to attain the correct temperature. This may be determined by the simple expedient of applying a stick of solder to the working surface.

Patch on a Tinplate Kettle.—A typical job, which is described in detail hereunder. Scrape clean the surface around the hole; emery cloth may be used, but wipe off all emery dust afterwards. Cut a piece of tinplate to a polygonal shape (octagon, etc.) at least ½in. larger in cross dimension than the hole. Brighten the tin on top and under sides, with emery cloth. Sheet copper may be used with very good results but as sheet tin is more easily procurable this material is recommended here.

Procure a clean canister lid of tinplate for use as a solder tray; rest it on a piece of board or asbestos to prevent heat going through to the kitchen table, etc. Pour a little acid flux into the tray. Have a stick of solder (50/50 grade) handy, or a length of blowpipe solder. Get the parts of the job handy too, since the soldering bit must not be allowed to cool. Apply flux to the kettle around the hole, and also to the underside of the patch, using a spill of wood as a "brush".

Heating the soldering bit.—Light the gas ring, and put the bit across so that the middle of the copper as well as the pointed end gets the flame. Presently the flame will turn a vivid green, and when the colour is very pronounced remove the tool. Avoid overheating the bit, otherwise the solder may not adhere. Wipe the working faces of the bit on a thick, clean (non-greasy) cloth, and immediately put the bit in the tray, on the end of the stick of solder. The solder will run, and flow over the working faces of the copper bit, which is then ready for use.

A little pool of solder will form in the tray. The cleaning and tinning may take so much of the heat away that the bit has at once to be returned to the gas ring for a warm up; do not let it stay longer over the flame than necessary, and wipe it again on the rag when you take it off.

Hold the kettle firmly, bottom up, by some means. Put the soldering bit on the little heap of solder in the tray; it will pick up solder in a molten state. Now rub the bit around the fluxed margin of the joint area, and the solder should flow over the parts. All this is done in less time than it takes to tell; probably, after a little experience, the worker will be able at once to proceed to the next stage, which is that of tinning the patch. This consists of laying the patch on a wood block, holding it down with the tang of an old file and applying the soldering bit to the margins all round to give them a thin coat of solder. After heating the bit again, put the patch over the hole in the kettle, tinned side downwards, hold the patch firm with the file, and run the soldering bit around to melt the solder underneath and so attach the patch firmly to the kettle.

However, assuming that the slower method has to be followed, return the bit to the flame after tinning the part around the hole. Possibly the patch also can be tinned in the same heating, but be on the safe side, and never work with a cool bit, which makes for messy and slovenly results. In case of difficulty, merely stick the patch down at about two places at first, and complete the job after re-heating the bit. The edges of a tinplate patch must be well tinned in order to prevent eventual rusting.

Assuming that a copper patch is to be used, tin it rather more thoroughly on the underside, and in other respects proceed as before described. In dealing with a large area of copper it will be found that the heat will be drawn out of the soldering bit rather quickly, as copper is such a good conductor; this means heating the bit more often. Brass, tinplate and zinc can be soldered easily; zinc melts at a low temperature, so use a hot bit and get it on and off the work in the quickest possible time. On zinc, the flux should be neat spirits of salts, *not* the usual killed spirits.

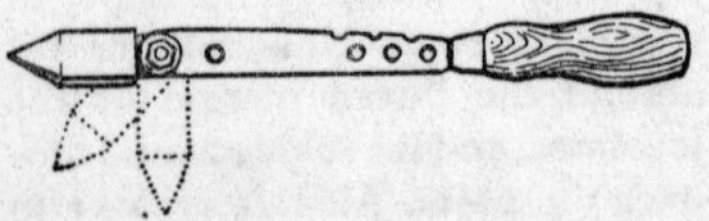

Fig. 1. Soldering iron with an adjustable bit secured by a nut on a steel shank.

General Hints.—Clean all surfaces thoroughly; throw away the tray when the solder in it begins to get dirty, and get a new tray. This solder, after frequent heating, loses some of its more volatile characteristics by evaporation. Keep the soldering bit clean and bright at the working surfaces. If it gets corroded, file it after heating up, as explained above. Keep the flux well corked up. Always test the bit on solder to ensure that the correct heat has been attained. Re-heat immediately the solder ceases to flow readily. Acid flux is corrosive to human skin and it will damage most material and should be used with caution.

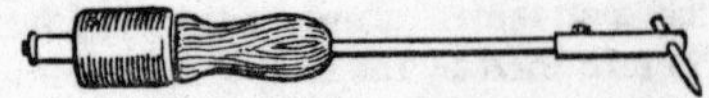

Fig. 2. Electric soldering iron with a special socket for interchangeable bits.

On a fairly large job, after the joint or seam has been stuck at intermediate points by applying solder picked up on the end of the bit, as explained earlier, the work has to be continued by slowly running the soldering bit along the seam, meanwhile holding a stick of solder close to and in front of the point. The joint or seam should be held firmly by thin iron wire twisted around the object, or by some other means. Often a joint is first secured by rivets or mechanically shaped seams, etc. and the solder used merely to seal the joint.

SECTION TWO

SIMPLE CARPENTRY

Airing Cupboard

Modern housekeeping has imposed new standards on the design and functional efficiency of household appliances and equipment. One amenity, however, has not been given sufficient attention by house designers. It is the provision of proper facilities not only for drying and airing, but storing the family washing in the most efficient manner.

In the large old-fashioned kitchens, the clothes horse, and airing rails suspended from the ceiling no doubt served their purpose very well, although in some instances the airing rails would be situated in inconvenient positions, and often above a smoky fireplace. In any event there is little or no room for airing rails in the limited space of the modern house or flat.

Builders do sometimes make provision for an airing cupboard located around the hot water storage tank. Frequently, the tank is installed in the bathroom where humidity is very much higher than in most other parts of the house. The temperature in such a cupboard is generally too high for the correct airing of clothes or linen because when the water is drawn from the tank the temperature drops and the tendency for the linen to absorb moisture from the air will be increased.

In consequence, the linen and laundered materials never become really dry and thoroughly aired. But in these conditions the tendency to high accumulation of moisture can be to some extent offset by increasing the ventilation of the bathroom by the simple expedient of opening a window and by leaving the cupboard door open when the room is not in use.

Nevertheless, owing to the fact that a high content of moisture prevails in the atmosphere, this disadvantage cannot be satisfactorily eliminated.

Under ideal conditions of course an airing cupboard would be located in a thoroughly ventilated room with separate means employed to generate a slow but even flow of filtered and heated air throughout the cupboard; the air temperature being controlled automatically.

But since these latter requirements are a little beyond the scope of the handyman, a simple but very efficient design of airing cupboard is outlined in the following paragraphs.

Position for Airing Cupboard.—Before proceeding further with the preparation of an airing cupboard it is advisable to give some consideration in the selection of the best, and at the same time, the most convenient position in the house. In general, apart from the foregoing factors one sound rule should be taken into consideration, never make use of walls directly exposed to the weather.

With regard to heating of the cupboard, carbon filament lamps are, as shown in Fig. 1, very satisfactory.

This cupboard will provide constantly dry warm air for the airing of freshly laundered linen, and racks for its storage when aired. An existing cupboard may be found suitable for the purpose, or a plywood cabinet can be made and fitted along the lines described. Dimensions are not given in the illustration (Figs. 1 and 2) since these must depend on individual requirements, but the general layout should be followed in principle.

The cabinet is heated by one or more carbon filament lamps. These are easily obtained and installed, have a long life, and are cheaply replaced. The current consumption is low, and there is no risk of overheating or fire. The size of the cupboard or cabinet determines the number of lamps required, and this requirement is best found by trial, starting with one lamp and adding additional lamps if necessary. It is obviously better to use a low power source of heat burning permanently day and night, than a higher power switched on intermittently. One 15 watt carbon filament lamp burning continuously will consume 2½ units of current in a week, and this should be adequate in a small cabinet.

The cabinet is made on a light framework of planed deal about 2in. × 1in. cross section. It is not necessary to make tongued or halved joints. The frame joints can be secured by screws or nails, but care must be exercised to ensure that all are square and true.

First make the two side frames as a matching pair, and carefully fix the back panel to these with panel pins. Battens of 2in. × 1in. are then fitted and screwed across the front, one at the top and one at the bottom. The assembly can then be stood upright and the slats forming the storage rack nailed to the side frame battens. The top and bottom and side panels are then fitted and fixed with panel pins, and the door hung on suitable hinges. If the cabinet is large and wide it is advisable

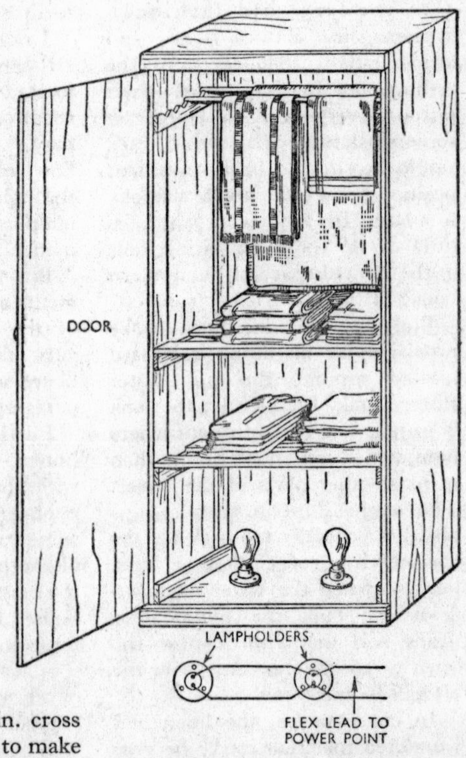

Fig. 1. Details of Airing Cupboard and wiring circuit for lamps.

to use double doors, as one large door, unless expertly made, is liable to warp.

A reasonably rigid door can be made quite simply by gluing and pinning plywood panels on *both* sides of a light wood frame. In this case the frame should be jointed with halved or mortise and tenon joints, so as to present flush surfaces for fixing the panels.

It will be seen in the sketch (Fig. 2) that the cross members at the top of the side frames are positioned a few inches down from the top. These members act as bearers for the removable airing rails and sufficient clearance must be left to allow handroom for handling and loading the rails.

The lamps are mounted in batten type lamp holders screwed to the floor of the cabinet and wired in twin flex to the nearest convenient supply point. There should be two or three inches clearance between the top of the lamps and the underside of the storage rack. It is important that the folded linen be stacked in piles on this rack in such a manner as to leave spaces up the centre and at each side, in order to allow free circulation of air. A sheet of cardboard or half a dozen thicknesses of newspaper should be laid on the rack under the linen to protect the bottom of the piles from excessive heat and to deflect the air currents. Warm air is carried upwards by convection, passing through the spaces between the slats, up round the piles of stored linen, to the airing space above.

The top part of the cabinet is provided with a number of removable rails over which is hung the newly laundered linen for airing. Broom handles may serve very well for this purpose, or for a shorter span, lengths of ½in. dowel rod may be preferred. The bearers supporting these rails are notched to prevent rolling and bunching.

Fig. 2. Distances between cross bearers and cross members should be arranged to suit requirements and overall height.

Very little ventilation is required. Indeed, too much ventilation is wasteful since cold air freely entering the cabinet not only reduces the ambient temperature but may, on occasion, carry considerable moisture. Some change of air there must be, in order to carry away the moisture taken out of the linen, but this requirement is likely to be met by opening the door in the course of normal use. Alternatively, the door could be left slightly ajar for half-an-hour during the day.

Bookshelves Built into a Recess

THE first design, as shown in Fig. 1 is a simple tier of shelves extending up to a height of about 6ft. 6in. The shelves can be of a suitable width to take ordinary novels, etc. 7in. clear or deeper; a width of 1ft. 1½in. is shown in Fig. 1. Here the recess is assumed to be 4ft. wide and 1ft. 1½in. deep. The height chosen will bring the top of the structure a few inches below the line of the picture rail, as usually fixed. This disposes of the awkward problem of lining up the cornice with the picture rail, which seldom looks well; further, the picture rail is usually painted, and so clashes with the treatment of the bookshelves.

Preliminary Work.—Take down the skirting board in the recess. It may have to be removed for some distance back, so as to get the entire board away; this would be cut to the required length and be replaced later. The shelving comes to the line of the chimney breast or other projecting part of the wall bounding the recess. The best treatment is to cut the skirting flush, and to form a "return" moulding on the edge to make a neat finish. After the shelving has been completed, a plinth board is fixed to line up with the skirting, and the ends of this plinth are chamfered off or moulded (see Fig. 1A) to match the pattern used for the front face. Thus, although the plinth and skirting line up, they are marked off by the slight moulding of the abutting ends. Attention to details such as this make a big difference to the appearance of the job.

Cut a piece of 1in. × ⅞in. batten, so that it will fit easily across the recess from wall to wall near the floor. Test the width of the recess with this rod at, say, 3ft. and 6ft. up from the floor. This will disclose whether the walls are reasonably free from bulges. The sides of the shelving will have to be vertical when fixed, but must also be brought close up against the wall (at the sides of the recess). Therefore, if the wall bulges a little at about the 3ft. height, some packing will have to be inserted at top and bottom in order to bring the woodwork vertical, and to give a firm backing. Correspondingly, if the wall is hollow or concave at a midway point, but is satisfactory at lower and higher levels, packing would be inserted between the woodwork and wall at the concave position. This packing should consist of pieces of thin plywood, or of layers split off plywood, pared down to give a satisfactory backing at the required place.

A gauge rod should be made: cut a length of batten, about 7ft. long, and square the two ends. Sweep out

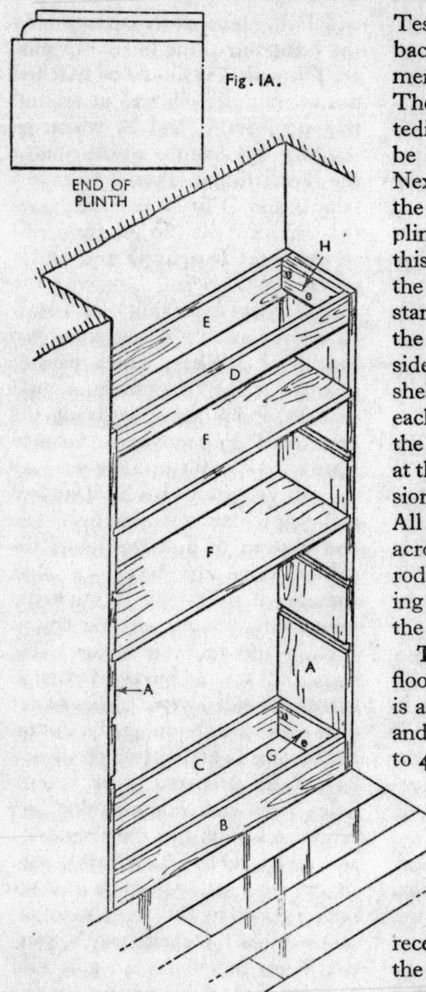

Fig. 1. General arrangement and assembly details of a bookshelf built into a recess. Fig. 1A illustrates the treatment of the return end of a plinth by suitably shaping a contour at the end of the moulding.

the floor of the recess; test the floor with a spirit level, and if necessary nail down a thin strip of wood at one side to bring the two sides level. Test for level also from front to back and make any similar adjustment which may be necessary. These preliminary details may seem tedious, but no satisfactory job can be carried out if we ignore them. Next, using the gauge rod, set out the distance of the top edge of the plinth from the floor line. Note that this line is the *levelled* line at which the foot of the bookshelf upright stands, so that it denotes, in fact, the lower edge of the bookshelf side. Set out the positions of the shelves, indicating the *top* side of each shelf. Mark off the position of the top edge of the bookshelf sides, at the 6ft. 6in. height, if that dimension be the one determined upon. All these lines should be squared across the selected face of the gauge rod, and carried round one adjoining face. The rod is used to mark the actual timber.

Timber for the Job.—One-inch floorboard, tongued and grooved, is as good material as any for sides and shelves (for a shelf length up to 4ft.). If the wood for the shelves is too slight, they will sag in course of time. The thickness specified is nominal; planed timber will come out $\frac{1}{8}$in. less in actual dimensions. Fig. 1 shows a recess 1ft. $1\frac{1}{2}$in. deep, so that the boards must be bought of a width that will make up this dimension when tongue is fitted into groove, and the tongue on the outermost board is sawn off. Remember that tongued and grooved board of nominal 6in. width will be only $5\frac{1}{2}$in. when fitted, as the tongue is cut out of the 6in. width; in other words, two such boards when fitted together will make up a total width of only 11in.

The worker may find it convenient to get the sawmill people to saw a board for each side, in order to get the desired total width. In assembling the bookshelf sides, put the grooved edge of one board at the back; then the tongues on all the boards will face the front. If a board has to be sawn to get the proper width, this will give a plain edge at the front; otherwise, if a board of ordinary width can be used, the tongue must be sawn off (or it can be taken off with a jack plane, perhaps the easiest method for a novice). The same considerations apply to making up the width of the shelves.

Assembling the Sides.—Saw the boards for the sides to length. Put one set together and stand it in the recess, close against the wall. Get a helper to hold it while testing for vertical position, and make notes where packing (if any) is required. This gives an opportunity to see if the front edge comes in line with the front of the recess. If the edges protrude slightly when the sides are fully home in the recess, remove the surplus material by plane. It may be advisable to make the width of the sides a fraction less than the depth of the recess from front to back. Take the side out and proceed to clean it up.

On referring to Fig.1 it will be seen that a batten (C) is fitted between the sides at the back, and that another similar board is fixed at the front. Note also the similar members (D) and (E) at the top. Between B and C and between D and E a short piece of wood (G and H) should be fixed to the sides by screws after the side boards are assembled and glued. Besides serving as a stop to fix the members B,C and D,E, these short battens hold the component side boards together. The sides (A) should be notched out at the back edge to fit around the members C and E, which *go right through* from one side wall of the recess to the other. The members B and D fit *between* the sides (A) and are nailed to the front end of the short battens G and H respectively.

The sides (A) having been cleaned up for assembly, get some hot Scotch glue ready, and a pair of cramps. Glue the tongues and grooves, and put the boards together with a sliding movement so as to squeeze out any surplus glue. Lay the side assembly on a level surface and apply bar cramps near top and bottom to pull the joints together. Give the boards a good squeeze; if they tend to open the joint midway, ease off one cramp slightly and move it along a few inches. Tack a piece of batten across the side at two places to secure the boards temporarily. Put on the battens G and H (which should have been prepared, with screw-holes bored and countersunk), then screw on firmly. Lay the assembled side on a level floor in a warm room to dry and set. Assemble the remaining side in the same manner.

Assemble the shelf boards, putting them together with glue and cramps; if short of cramps, use the latter to squeeze and hold the boards while short pieces of batten are attached temporarily, as suggested above. The net length of the shelves must be settled, of course. Whatever the distance between the inner faces of the sides when standing in place in the recess, add ½in. for the depth of two grooves (each ¼in. deep); this will give the extreme length for the shelves. It is safer to make the latter about 2in. longer in the first place, and to saw them across to the actual length later, when the sides of the structure have been fixed to the recess walls. This extra 2in. allows a clean final cut to be made at each end.

Grooves for Shelves.—When the sides are set hard, lay them down on edge, face to face, face-edge uppermost, and hold them together with a pair of G-cramps. If a bench is available, fix the two sides in the vice and support the opposite ends with a stool or a piece of quartering. Lay the gauge rod on top and transfer the markings for the top faces of the shelves. These marks will be made on the front edge of the side assemblies, both the latter being marked at the same time. Take off the cramps and square the marks across the inner faces of the sides. Remember that the marks indicate where the top face of the shelf comes. Measure the exact thickness of the shelf boards; if they vary, and they may, take the thickness for each shelf separately, and mark them 1,2,3, etc., to correspond with the grooves. Transfer the thickness to the side boards, *below* the shelf lines we have just established, and square a line on front edge and inner face as before.

Set a marking gauge to a bare quarter inch, and scribe this distance from the inner face of the side boards, on the edge of these, at back and front, at the places where the parallel lines have been pencilled on the board face. A hard and fine-pointed pencil should be used on the board face for marking; a fine scriber is even better. Use a fine-toothed tenon saw to outline the grooves; first saw down to the line at the front and back edges, then continue across the board. Take out the waste wood with a sharp paring chisel of a suitable width. Beware of making the groove too deep. At the back of the side boards, saw out the notches to fit, around the battens C and E.

Erecting the Shelves.—Lay the batten C in place at the back of the recess; stand the two sides in place, fitting over this batten. Get someone to hold the sides while the top back batten E is tried in place and its position marked on the back wall. Ease the notches if required. The position of batten E can be indicated by a pencil line on the wall at top and bottom edges. Bore two holes through batten E at about 6in. from each end, and mark through to the wall to give the point where a Rawlplug drill should enter the brickwork. If all this can be done while the helper is holding the sides in place, so much the better. Take down the sides; drill and plug the wall (use Gauge 12 screws, iron, countersunk, about $1\frac{3}{4}$in. long). Fix battens E and C.

Try the sides in place again; if correct, take out the right-hand one, say, and bore it for three screws: one each about 6in. from floor and top line, and another midway; see they come clear of the grooves. Mark the wall for plugs; drill and plug the brickwork, and fix the side. Proceed similarly with the remaining side. Fix the boards B and D; the former will come about an inch lower than the top of the plinth. The depth of the top batten D will depend on that of the piece of moulding to be used as a cornice. This cornice stands up above D far enough to allow a dust board made of plywood to fit on top of D, E, and A, and to fit behind the cornice and flush with the top of the latter.

Fit in the shelves one by one, the idea being to make them a tight fit but not so tight as to need more than a gentle tap with a mallet to get them home. Rely on the shelves to keep the sides in place, to some extent. Try a shelf in its groove; ease the back part of the ends of the shelf a little with a smoothing plane (or a block plane, if available), should this prove necessary. Hold a smooth piece of batten against the front edge of the shelf, and tap against this with the mallet. Be on the safe side, and ease any shelf that tends to stick.

Cut the bottom shelf to fit nicely in place, and screw it (Gauge 6 or 8 screws, countersunk, 1¾in.) to the top edges of battens B,C,G. This shelf should come flush with the front edges of the side boards. Screw on the plinth (see Fig. 1A); fix the cornice and dust board. Clean up the face of the work with two grades of glass paper used in succession, and the job is ready for staining and varnishing.

By facing the edges of the side boards, and those of the shelves, with oak, walnut, or mahogany strips about 1¼in. deep, and using a plinth and cornice of the same wood, a superior appearance is produced. The strips of hardwood ought to be grooved so that they would fit the tongue on the tongued-and-grooved board used for the rest of the structure.

Two-Tier Open Bookcase.—This is shown in Figs. 2 to 7. Each tier can be built in such a way that it may be dismantled and re-erected, and stands more or less free in the recess. Here again the depth of the recess has been taken as 1ft. 1½in. The lower shelf of the bookcase is 1ft. 1½in. deep; the top shelf is 8¼in. deep. Hardwood facing pieces (or pilasters) are used at the sides of the front, as in Figs. 3 and 7; the rest of the front framing also is in hardwood to match. The front part of the top board D (Figs. 2 and 3) should be hardwood. The facing pieces A are shown worked with a stop chamfer, but some other simple form or ornamentation can be substituted, if desired.

The preliminary work is much the same as for the shelving shown

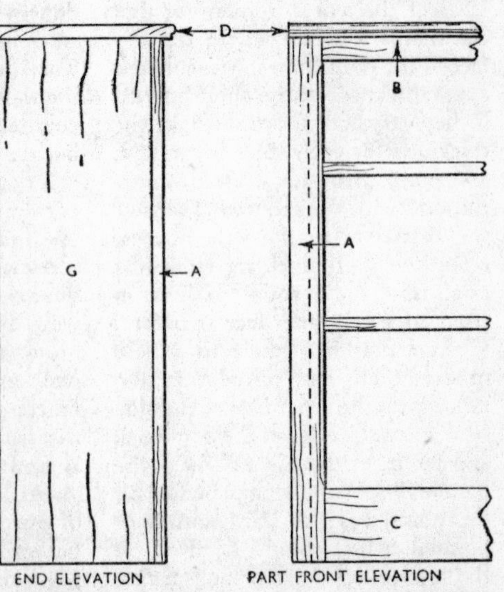

Figs. 2 and 3. An end and part front elevation of a simple bookcase for fitting into a recess, showing finished details of facing pieces and moulding.

in Fig. 1. But the sides of the structure are spaced in from the recess walls by the blocking pieces E; these pieces, plus the thickness of the side boards G, equal the width of the pilasters A. The blocking pieces E are screwed to the outside of G, but otherwise the assembly and setting out follow the lines of the simple shelving shown by Fig. 1. A bottom batten F (Fig. 4) is screwed to bottom of the uprights of the lower tier to support the bottom shelf (H). This shelf comes behind, and level with, the facing piece C shown in Fig. 3, which should be tenoned into A, or halved a little way to make a sound and neat joint. When the two lower sides have been glued and assembled and the blocking pieces E screwed on, the sides are stood in the recess, and the top board D screwed down to them. The bottom shelf H is then screwed down to the battens F. This lower tier must be an easy fit into the recess, as it stands by itself and is not normally fixed to the walls. Should it appear necessary to fix it, a back batten at top and floor line can be inserted as in Fig. 1, C and E, and these battens plugged to the back wall.

Prepare the top tier (Figs. 5 and 6). A back batten (not shown) may be needed at the bottom, and should be fitted in the same way as C and E of Fig. 1. Insert the shelves after the top tier has been placed in position on top of the top board (D) of the lower tier. The whole top assembly should stand firm by its own weight; but, if needed, two brass mirror plates may be screwed to both the top and bottom back battens, and screwed to plugs in the wall. If, however, the case fits tightly this will not be necessary.

Hardwood Facing Pieces.—The pilasters and the rails B and C (Fig. 3) should be jointed in some simple manner for neatness, either by short tenons or by a short halved joint, at the corners. Behind the cornice of the top tier there should be fixed a front rail like that of B in Fig. 3. The pilasters must be screwed to the sides G by fine screws (Gauge 6) let in by counterboring, and the top holes plugged with pieces of similar hardwood. Another method is to stop the holes

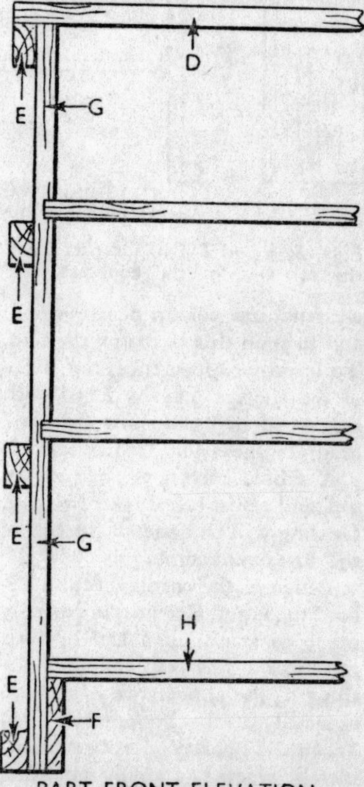

PART FRONT ELEVATION

Fig. 4. A part front elevation showing the constructional details and the use of blocking pieces, E, necessary to the fitting of the bookcase in the recess.

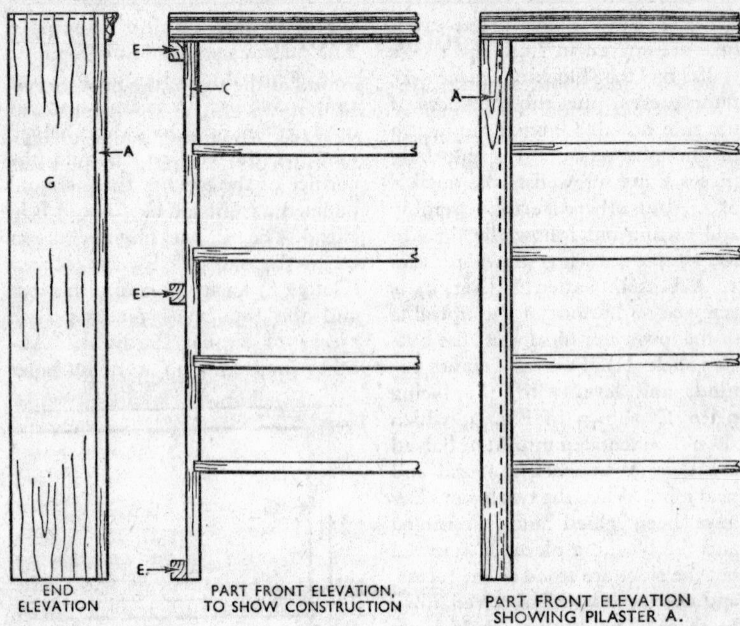

Figs. 5, 6 and 7. End and part front elevations illustrating the construction of the top tier for the bookcase, similar in design to that shown in Fig. 3.

with natural colour plastic wood, and to stain this to match the rest. To improve appearance, the edges of the shelves may be faced with hardwood strips to show the same grain as the front framework.

A simple cornice is fixed at the top, and a dust board is screwed on. Dusting will be easier if the top of the dust board comes flush with the top edge of the cornice, fitting behind the latter. Cornices are usually made to stand up a little, which produces a dust trap and adds nothing to the appearance of the job especially if the bookcase is low. When the bookcase has been completely erected, a small moulding may be mitred around the front and inside of the feet of the top tier, to provide a stop; "quarter-round," about ⅜in. across the flat face, is suitable for this; it is pinned down to the top board D with veneer pins.

The bookshelves, as illustrated in Figs. 2 to 7, are each of moderate height, but the number of shelves and height may be varied to suit the requirements of the handyman. In some instances it may be found more practicable, when the depth of the recess is excessive, not to carry the shelves back to the full depth. In order to eliminate the possibility of an unsightly gap at the back of the case a thin sheet of plywood should be secured to the back of the bookcase. The topmost shelf may be carried to the full depth of the recess. But if the top of the bookcase extends beyond the back it will be necessary to secure a light wooden batten to each side wall of the recess.

Clothes Horse

A SINGLE fold clothes horse, 4ft. high by 3ft. wide when closed, is a convenient size. The commercial article has rails mortised and tenoned to the posts, but with the comparatively slight timber such as that generally employed, this form of jointing should be avoided by the amateur, in the interests of easy manufacturing.

Fig. 1 shows part of a clothes horse constructed with round rails cut from birch dowel rod, ¾in. in diameter. This rod can be purchased at shops which supply cabinet materials, or from many timber merchants. The uprights (or posts) may be cut from beech or deal measuring 1½in. by 1¼in. in section. Since ¾in. holes have to be bored for the rods, we must use the timber so that the wider side is available for the boring of socket holes.

Preparing the Timber.—Buy wood, which, after planing to a good smooth surface, will not be less in section than 1½in. × 1¼in. Choose timber which is not bent or warped. When cutting the posts make them about 2in. longer than the finished length. Cramp all four posts together (after planing), and with the ends even. Square a line across all four, an inch from the end. Mark each of these ends of the posts "T" for top, before they are taken out of the cramp; also measure down from the top mark to the exact length (4ft.) and square a line across all four posts at this point so as to ensure posts of equal length.

Take them out of the cramp and (singly) square a line across the side faces of each post to connect the pencilled lines previously made. Thus we shall have a true line all around at the top of the post. Serve the bottom end in the same way. Next, set a marking gauge to half the width of the upright on the wide face (the setting will be approximately ¾in. depending on the *exact* width of the wood). Use the gauge to scribe a central mark down one side of one post; mark this side or face "I" for inside. Gauge and mark all the posts in this way.

Most people like to keep the lowest rail well above the floor level at say 1ft. 6in.; the other two rails are equally spaced over the remainder of the height. Proceed as follows: the top rail must come 2in. *down* from the top of the post; the bottom rail comes 1ft. 6in. *up* from the bottom. This leaves us with 2ft. 4in.; so if we set the middle rail at 1ft. 4in. *down* from the top of the horse everything will be all right. Here are the measurements down the post from the *top line "T"*: top rail, 2in.; middle rail, 1ft. 4in.; lower rail, 2ft. 6in.

Having decided on these dimensions it will now be possible to proceed with the final setting out of the different parts, as described in the following paragraphs.

Remember that these measurements are those for the *centres* of the holes. Set out one rail accurately with a rule and fine pencil; square lines across at the distances given. The crossing of the pencilled line with the gauged vertical line will show where the point of the twist bit must go in. Lay the four posts on the bench or on a table, with the top ends all close against a stop (such as a batten temporarily tacked across at right angles). As one post has now been marked, we can

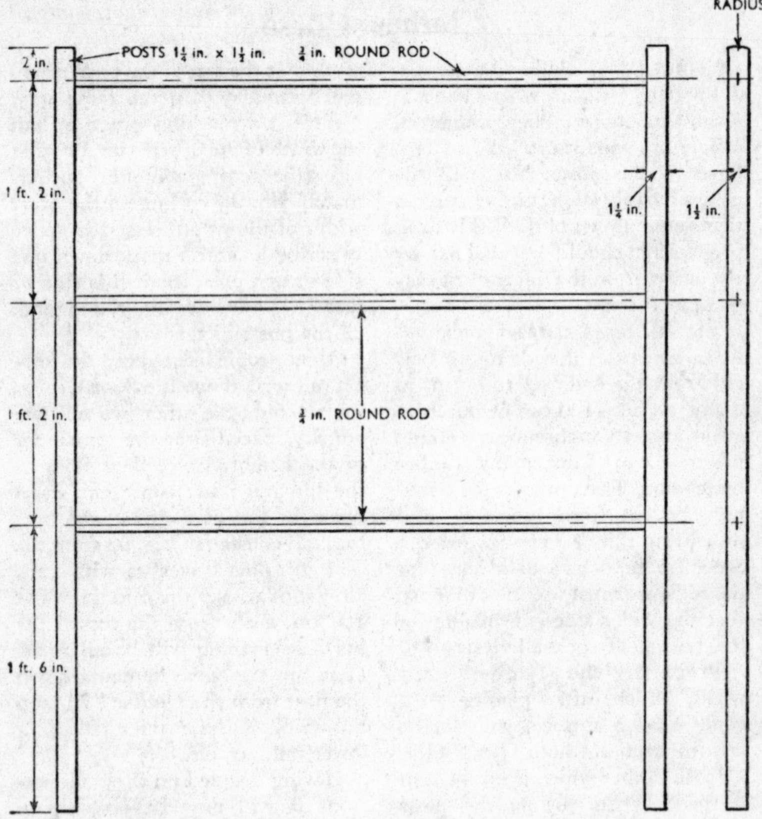

Fig. 1. Dimensions for one side of a clothes horse.

transfer the markings across the others with the square, while making sure that the pieces do not slip. So far, then, we have side faces of each post marked across, gauged vertically on the inner faces.

Next, mark the posts for pairs: that is, mark one "A-1", and the opposite post ,"A-2"; mark the remaining pair "B-1" and "B-2".

Boring for the Rails.—Bore a hole with a ¾in. twist bit in a waste piece of the same timber used for the posts; smooth off an end of a piece of birch rod and try it into the hole. It *must* be a tight fit, but not so tight as to cause a split. Dowel rod varies a little, and it would be a sound plan to bore a test hole in a scrap of wood and take the piece along when choosing the rod. If a test shows it as fitting slack, we can use a smaller twist bit ($\frac{11}{16}$in. instead of ¾in.); this will mean that the ends of the rod will have to be reduced a little in diameter. Coarse glass-paper will generally prove satisfactory in this respect. Twist bits in the intermediate sizes are obtainable only in better makes. But since

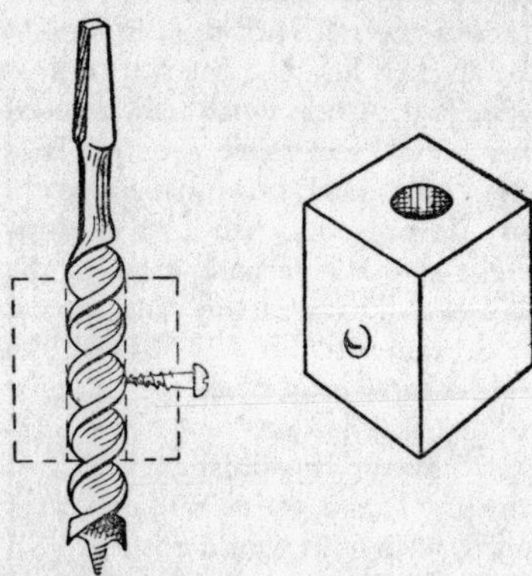

Fig. 2. Illustrating the use of a wood block and screw fitted to a twist bit so as to provide a useful depth gauge.

such a tool would be useful for many jobs, such as making or mending deck chairs, or ordinary Windsor chairs, it might be economical to buy one for the job.

The tapering on the ends must be taken well back, or else, in driving the rail in, we may split the post. Some sort of a depth gauge will be advisable: it may consist of a block of hardwood, about 1½in. high by about 1¼in. thick, bored out with the same bit. Put it on to the bit so that it allows a hole to be made about half-way through the posts; it is secured at this setting by an ordinary wood screw put through a tight hole in the side of the block to grip the flute of the twist bit, as shown in Fig. 2.

Lay one of the posts on the bench and clamp it down. Make an indentation with a metalworker's centre punch exactly at the crossing of pencil line and gauge line, tapping the punch lightly with a hammer. This will guide the nose or centre of the bit to the proper entry. Bore out the hole (Fig.3) until the depth gauge touches the surface; hold the brace square and upright, and press lightly if the wood is birch.

When a pair of posts are ready, lay them down with "inside" faces towards each other, and at the proper distance apart, so that the overall measurement across from outside edge to outside edge is 3ft. Cut a rod approximately to the proper length, 3ft. less twice ⅝in., the distance the rod goes into each post. Pare off the ends of the rod if necessary, to give a tight fit; otherwise, merely take off the rough edge with coarse glasspaper.

Insert the rod into the two topmost holes; tap it in with a mallet struck against the outside of one post. Measure with a rule across the assembly, having first verified that rail is square with post. Probably a fraction will have to be cut off one end of the rod to bring the overall width to 3ft. If so, ease off one post, take out the rail, and trim the end of the rail. With this rail as a guide for length, prepare the other two. Lay aside the pair of posts with the three rails for the time. Bore and fit

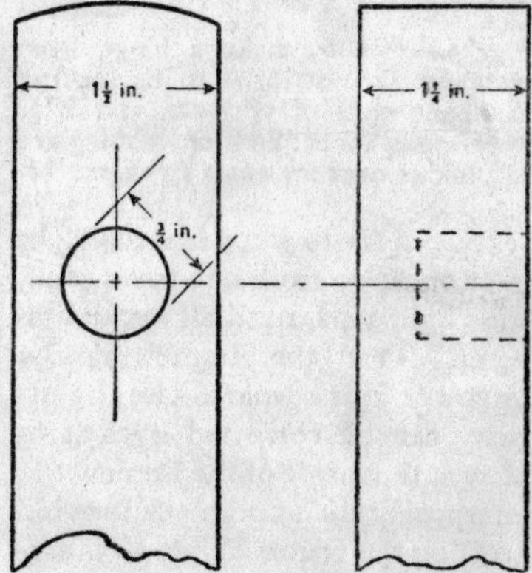

Fig. 3. When boring the sockets in the vertical rails to the depth shown, use the depth gauge as illustrated in Fig. 2.

the other pair, and make ready for gluing and assembling.

Assembling the Parts.—After heating the glue apply it thinly to the rail ends and put a little in the holes also. Lay one post on the bench, "inside" face uppermost; tap in the three rails; now bring the other post into position, and enter the free ends of the rails, easing them in gently. Have ready a block of clean wood, lay it on top of the topmost post, over a rail; tap the block with a mallet or a hammer. Next tap over the middle rail, and proceed to the bottom one.

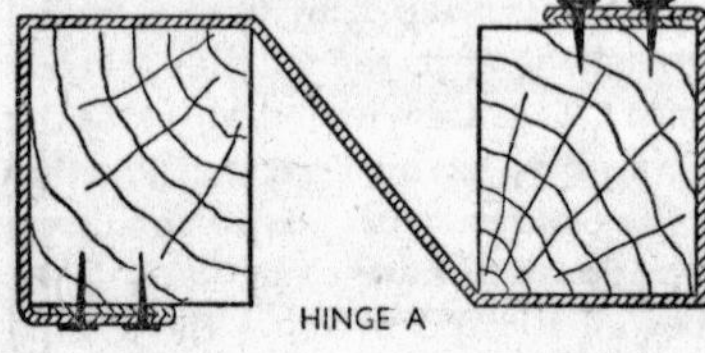

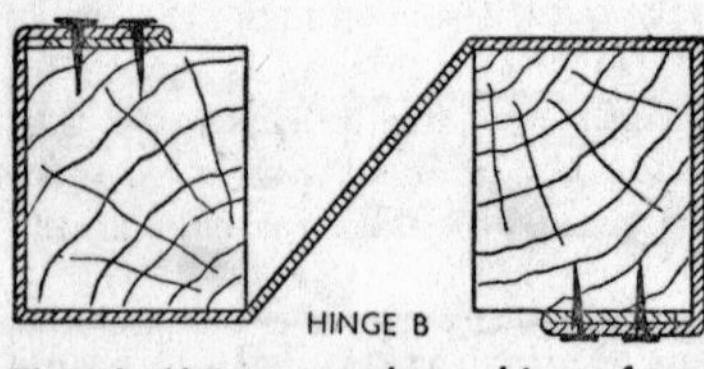

Fig. 4. How to make a hinge from webbing. One strip, A to be secured at upper ends of uprights, and B at lower ends. Note: Ends of webbing are folded over for extra strength.

Do not try to force one rail right in at once; go from one to another, with light taps, until all are driven home. Test the framework by square at four corners. Any irregularity can be corrected by a light blow at the inside of the framework, interposing the wood block to avoid bruising the frame. When all is satisfactory, lay the frame on a level floor; bore with a fine bradawl for a panel pin that will be driven in to secure the rail end; the pin should be an inch long for the size of post specified. A fine twist drill, as used for metal, will make a better hole than a bradawl, but must not go in too deeply—only through the upright at one side and just into the rail end. Drive in the pins, one at each end of the rail. Stand the frame in a warm place for the glue to dry and harden.

Whatever the finished width of the first frame, the second one must agree with it. It would not matter if the finished dimension were slightly under or over 3ft., provided both were alike. So assemble the second frame, gluing and pinning as before.

Points to Watch.—Clear out all chips from the bored holes; a gouge is the best tool for this job, but a ½in. chisel can be made to serve. Often a twist bit leaves part of a core at the bottom of the hole, and this must be cut out or smoothed off level with the gouge, etc. Test the holes for depth, by putting in a rule and noting the graduation on the rule at the surface edge. The improvised depth gauge mentioned earlier is not a guarantee of exact finished depth. Any doubts about depth of hole must be settled before gluing, since it is difficult to make corrections later. But if one rail proved long, it might be possible to increase the distance at the other two, and would not matter if they did not go right home, so long as they fitted tightly. But any adjustment to the first frame would have to be followed in the making of the second frame.

Holes might be taken right through the posts, the rails being driven right in and left flush. This makes a stronger job but is not so

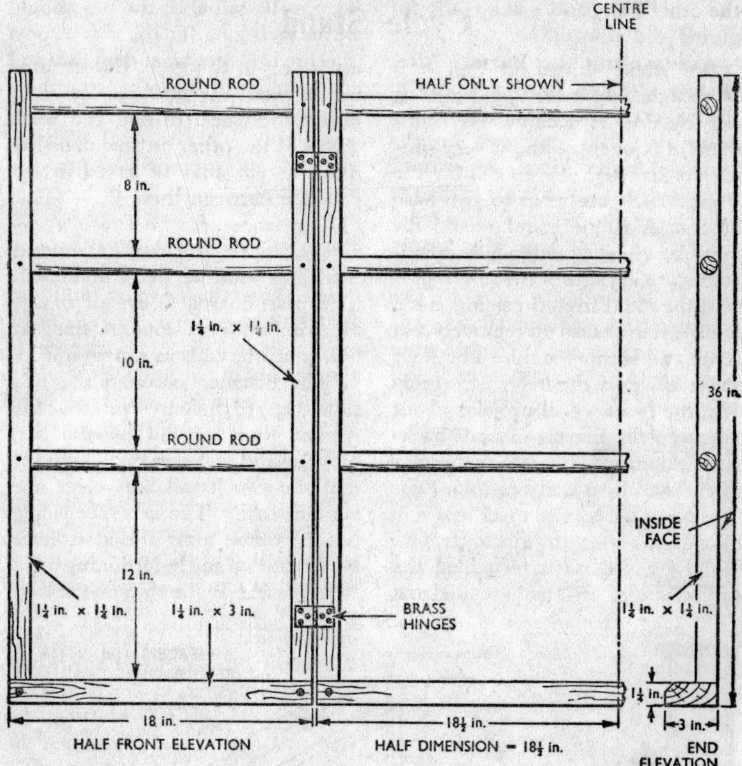

Fig. 5. End and part front elevation of an alternative arrangement of a clothes horse of sturdier construction showing use of metal hinges and base boards.

sightly. Put a piece of flat board under the post when boring, so that the wood on the under side of the hole does not break out. Take the twist bit right through, and go a little way into the waste wood, below, so that a clean hole results.

When the rail joints have set (24 hours after gluing) cut off the ends of the posts to the proper length, as marked earlier, The top ends should be rounded slightly, as viewed from the end. Clean up all surfaces with glasspaper; scrape off any glue that has exuded. Simple hinges of upholsterer's webbing should be secured by tacks or short, broad-headed wire nails. Fig.4 shows how the webbing is wound around the posts to form two opposed hinges. One of each A and B is to be fixed about nine inches from top of post, and one of each at nine inches from ground level.

Fig. 5 illustrates a clothes horse of somewhat more solid construction, having base boards on which the frames are mounted. Ordinary butt hinges are utilized and these, together with the base boards, make a steadier framework. One wide and two narrow frames are used.

Cycle Stand

THE stand shown in Fig. 1 is designed to take two bicycles, side by side. It occupies the minimum of floor space and is very simply constructed. Two slots for the front wheels are fixed to two base boards. A single stand would require base boards extended considerably at each side of the slot to prevent the stand from capsizing, but a double stand takes up relatively less space and is more stable. The floor space is approximately 3ft. 4in. × 2ft., the front wheel projects about 2in., and the bicycle extends backward about 3ft. 6in. from the rear of the stand, so that the total floor area occupied by two machines side by side is about 3ft. 4in. × 5ft. 6in. To the width must be added the projection of the two handlebars, according to the type. (By arranging to stand the machines head to tail, front wheel of one and back wheel of the other on the stand, as much as 9in. may be saved in the distance between them.)

First, measure the space available and make sure that the stand and machines can be accommodated. The base boards C are of 6in. × 1in. timber. The slots are fixed at 6in. from the ends as shown in Fig. 1. The distance between the two slots is approximately 22in., but the worker should stand up the two bicycles and measure them, and see that the two handlebars clear one another easily. The central spacing can be tested after the slots have been made up and before fixing them to the base. Lay the slots on the base

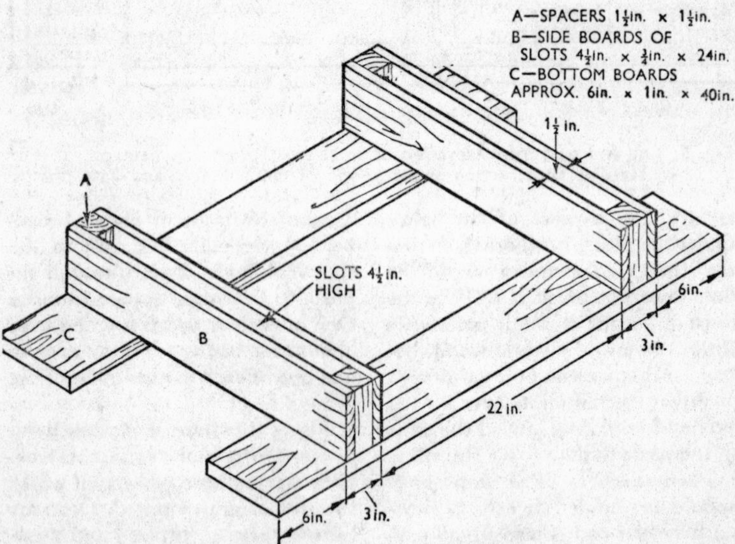

Fig. 1. A general arrangement of the cycle stand illustrating details of construction and location of component parts. The wheel slots are secured to the bottom boards as shown in Figs. 2 and 3.

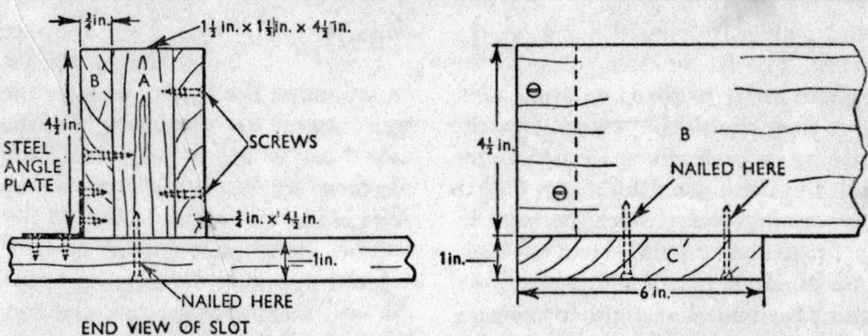

Figs. 2 and 3. Showing end and side elevations of wheel slot and method of securing the slots to the bottom boards, by screws, nails and angle plates.

boards at the selected distance, and try the bicycles in them with a helper supporting the machines. Mark the distance in from the ends of the base at which an easy clearance is given between the machines.

Figs. 2 and 3 show details of the slot assembly. The sides are of ¾in. × 4½in. board, 24in. long; the spacers are cut from planed quartering which is 1½in. on one side and may be the same or a little more on the other. The 1½in. face must be in the position shown by A in Fig.2; this determines the width of the slot for the wheels, and if it is too wide the bicycle will lean over instead of standing approximately upright. If, of course, the machine has 1¾in. tyres the slot must be made wider to suit. It should also be remembered that, since the construction of the slots is light, it must be well done. First screw the side boards (B) to the spacer blocks; this will be easier if the boards are first tacked on with two oval wire nails at each side and each end (1¼in. nails will do). Bore and countersink the screw holes, and use Gauge 8 iron screws, 1½in. long.

Take care that the lower end of the spacer does not project below the bottom edge of the side, or the slot will not stand level on the base.

Having completed both slots, and determined the proper spacing between them, square a line on the under side of each of the two base boards to indicate where the outside edge of the slots should go; in Fig.1 it is shown as 6in. from the end of the base. Lay the two assembled slots upside down on a bench or table (or on the floor), and rest one base board on them at the proper distance. The line marked on the under side (now visible) will afford a guide by sighting along it and the lower edge of the side board. Drive one 2½in. round wire nail through the base board and into the end of the spacer block (see Fig.2), thus lightly attaching the board to one side of the slot. Proceed to the other end and fix the second slot in the same way.

Now get the slot square with the base board, by using a try-square; hold the parts firmly and drive a nail up through the base board and *into one side board*, as shown in Fig. 3. The second nail, there indicated, can be driven in later. Turn the assembly right side up, and verify that the slot is square across the board. Then reverse the parts again, and put a nail into one side board of the other slot. This should ensure that the slots go on squarely, and stay so during the rest of the work. The fixing of the slots to the remaining base board will be easier, but they should be tested with the square before nailing. Complete the job by nailing each side board with two nails. Extra strength can be provided by screwing steel angles at the outsides of the slots—between the side board and the projecting end of the base board (see Fig. 2). The angles should be about 1½in. wide, and 2in. to 3in. high; they are put on with Gauge 8 iron screws, countersunk heads, ⅜in. long for the base boards and ½in. long for the side boards. Bore holes carefully for these screws, or the boards may split along the grain.

The stand may, if it is considered desirable, be secured to the floor so as to give greater stability but this should not be necessary in normal circumstances.

Draining Rack and Board

THE rack shown in Fig.1 accommodates twelve plates on the lower shelf, and the same number of smaller plates, or saucers, on the upper shelf. Both shelves swing upward, to a vertical position between the side pieces of the framework. The advantage of this arrangement is obvious where space is limited: when the plates or saucers have been drained in the rack they are removed from their spaces between the bars and put away, the shelves are swung upward out of the way, so that the sink above which the rack hangs is unhampered for its full extent.

The side pieces are 21½in. long, 2¼in. wide and ¾in. thick. They are connected at top and bottom by pieces 12in. long, to which the sides are screwed; but this attachment is not completed until the vertical rails are in position, and until the back rods of the top and the bottom shelves have been lodged in the side pieces. It is on the back rods that the shelves swivel upwards when the rack is not in use.

The top piece of the framework is 1¾in. wide and ⅜in. thick; the bottom piece is ¾in. wide by ⅝in. thick. These members, together with the sides of the shelves, are made of hardwood. The eleven vertical rails, and the corresponding eleven in each shelf, are ⅜in. in diameter, and ordinary curtain rods will serve admirably. The vertical rails have their ends lodged ¼in. deep in holes bored, at equal distances apart, in the inner edges of the top and bottom pieces of the framework.

The side pieces of the shelves are 9in. long, and the ends (front and back) are rounded. They are 1⅛in. wide and ⅝in. thick. They are joined (in pairs) by rods ¾in. diameter. The front rods (Fig.2) are positioned ¼in. in from the ends and fixed by screws passing through the sides. The back rods pass tightly through the sides of the shelves and project ½in. into the socket holes bored in the side members. The centre of the hole for these back rods is 1¼in. from the back end. Holes in the framework sides in which the back rods lodge are a shade more than ¾in. diameter, so that the movement is free when the shelves are raised or lowered (Fig.3). Distance between the outer edges for each shelf is 11⅝in. And front and back rods are 7⅛in. apart (inside measurement). The rails are sunk ¼in. deep in these rods, with a tight fit.

When the bottom shelf is lowered, further downward movement is prevented by the bottom piece of the framework, against the underside of which the inner ends of the shelf sides rest. In the case of the top shelf, this purpose is served by two stops set well back, one in each side member. These are pieces of ⅜in. diameter rail sunk ⅝in. deep in the side members and protruding horizontally a distance of ⅝in.

Holes are bored in the top member, for hanging. To keep the back edges of plates well away from the wall, a block 1in. thick is nailed or screwed to the wall. The screws or nails for hanging are inserted in this block. A similar block keeps the bottom member at the same distance. When the rack needs cleaning it is a simple matter to lift it from the two supporting nails or screws.

It may happen that a water pipe, or similar obstruction, passes down the wall where the rack would most conveniently hang. The pipe can be cleared by positioning a block, of the necessary thickness, on either side of the pipe.

A draining board (Fig. 3) is essential to easy washing-up, and it is most conveniently placed at the side of the sink opposite to the rack.

To be a permanent structure it should be of hardwood, preferably beech or sycamore, and the boards should be not less than ¾in. thick, if possible tongued and grooved to ensure tight and waterproof jointing. It should correspond with the width of the sink. Length may be dictated by circumstances of space; a useful length is 3ft. It may, of course, exceed that if greater length enables the end farther from the sink to be supported on a piece of board nailed to a right-angle wall.

The boards are held together by two pieces of timber 4in. wide and as long as the draining board is wide; they are secured to the top by screws from the underside. A raised ledge runs along the front and one end, as a barrier against items sliding off; this is ⅜in. wide beading ⅜in. thick, nailed to the top, thin

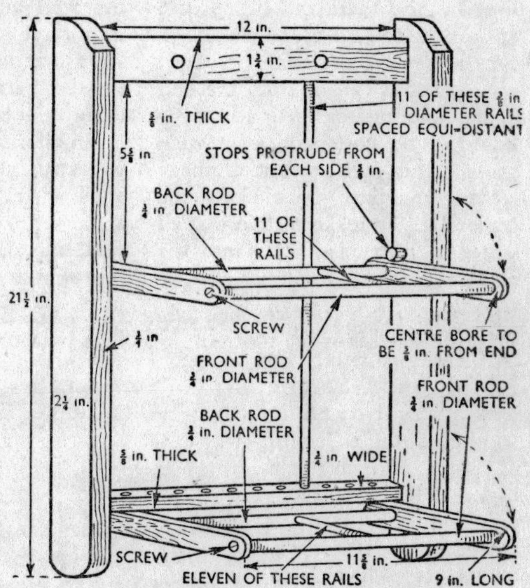

Fig. 1. General dimensions and assembly details of the two-shelf draining rack for attachment to the wall, adjacent to the kitchen sink.

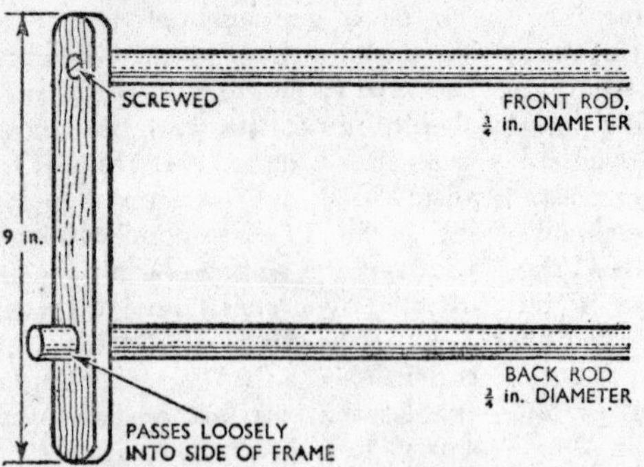

Fig. 2. A detail assembly view of one shelf in part construction.

nails passing vertically down through the beading. The corners, where the two pieces meet, should be neatly mitred.

If the surface is given a sufficient slope, about 1in. per foot of length, water will drain freely into the sink without the aid of the shallow channels which disfigure many draining boards. And there will be no drip at the outside edge of the sink if the board overlaps the edge by about 2in. At about 1in. in from the end of the draining board cut across the board, on the underside, a ⅜in. wide groove; this will prevent drainage water "creeping" back along the underside. To make certain that all water is diverted quickly into the sink, a piece of wood, shaped as shown in Fig. 3(A), may be screwed at the two lower corners.

The back of the draining board is supported on a length of timber, an inch thick, nailed to the wall. Then the board is fixed to it with brass screws, after recesses have been cut in the top edge of the support to take the ends of the strengthening pieces on the underside of the draining board. To protect the wall from moisture, a piece of wood the length of the draining board, 3in. wide, ½in. thick, is nailed to the wall, the lower edge being flush with the bottom surface of the draining board.

Unless the outer end of the board butts against a wall to which it can be fixed, a leg will be needed at the front corner. This may be a vertical piece of 4in. by 2in. timber, to the top of which a horizontal piece is fixed with its rear end going a few inches into the wall and cemented in. It is important to cut the leg the right length, or the draining board will be twisted. Secure the bottom of the leg to the floor by a small angle plate.

An alternative to the upright leg is a strut, its lower end cut at an angle so that it fits neatly into the angle formed by the floor and the wall, its top end also angled for screwing to the underside of the

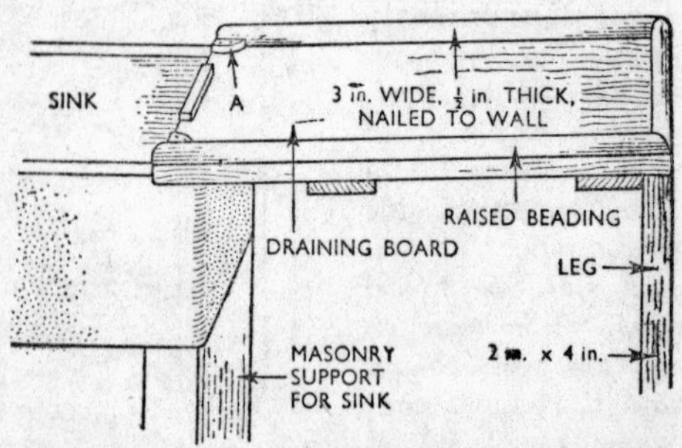

Fig. 3. Details of a draining board showing raised beading and, A, wood blocks to divert water drained from crockery into sink.

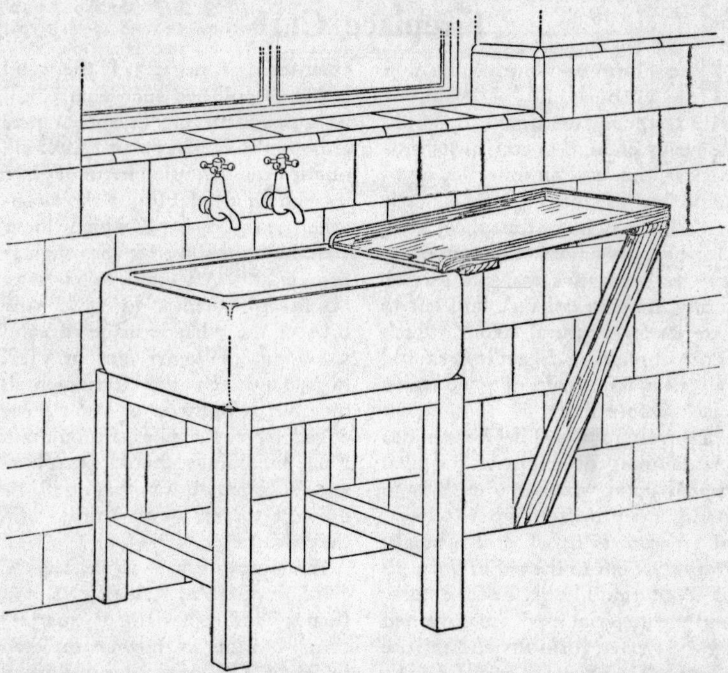

Fig. 4. A possible alternative arrangement of a simple draining board. The board should be secured to the wall by means of two large, strong angle brackets.

strengthening piece of the draining board. If this type of leg is adopted the strengthening piece should be screwed at the extreme end of the underside, the top of the strut then being fastened to this and not to the draining board itself (Fig. 4).

The leg may be painted to tone with the colour scheme of the scullery or kitchen, but the draining board should not be painted. It is cleaned by scrubbing; hot water is applied with a cloth, a little Vim shaken on to the damp surface and the scrubbing brush vigorously applied, after which it is wiped dry. The surface should never be left wet; always after use it should be wiped over.

Faulty construction may show later in cracks between the boards, where there should be a tight join. This must be remedied, by filling the crack or cracks neatly with a filler or with putty before water has a chance to soak into the timber and cause the wood to rot.

The space beneath the draining board can be put to good purpose, by fixing a shelf or shelves; or placing there a small cupboard on castors—so that it is easily movable when cleaning the floor. Shelves could be supported on battens one inch thick, nailed to the sink support, and to the leg; the inner end of the leg batten resting on block one inch thick, nailed to the wall.

Fireplace Curb

To conform with current fashion the curb should be plain, or with restrained ornament. It should be heavy enough to stay in its proper position and an inner facing of some fire-resisting material is needed. This may be of thin sheet iron, attached by screws. Sheet copper, a more decorative material for the lining, may be polished and left to take its own natural colour, which is not unpleasing. Sheet iron should be given two coats of good stove black before fixing.

Dimensions.—The length depends upon the width of the tiled hearth upon which the curb is to stand; a depth, from front to back, of 1ft. 3in. is usual, and a height from the floor to the top of the curb of about 3in. The style of the curb, and the material used, are governed by the type of furniture and the use to which the room is put. Oak is a good material for dining room, lounge or bedroom, but mahogany or walnut may be preferred. The decorative characteristics of grain and colouring in these hardwoods should be taken into consideration when selecting pieces of timber. Figured grain in oak possesses a fine decorative quality.

Ornamentation. — The inside and outside top edges may be moulded as in Fig.1. or merely chamfered as in Fig.3. If the wood is french polished such a curb will be quite satisfying in appearance, although somewhat plain. After all, undue ornamentation is out of place in such an article. Fig. 2 shows another simple shape which looks well; here the top edges are slightly rounded off. After this we come to "built-up" shapes, in which the base of the curb is made of solid wood 3in. wide by 2in. or 2¼in. high, and the top (ornamental) member is built up of a flat piece edged by two strips of moulding. Such mouldings should be robust and substantial, or they will be difficult to pin down firmly, and they will break off.

A compromise is to rebate the solid wood as at A in Fig. 4, and then to insert a strip of quarter-round beading as shown completed by Fig.5. The inner edge of the top is bevelled or chamfered slightly. Undoubtedly a solid curb is the best, and the workman can produce a pleasing shape by the use of planes and chisels. If some simple moulding is to be run in the solid, this part of the job should be done while the timber is in a single length, i.e. before separating it into the three component pieces. A good allowance for waste should be made; perhaps an extra foot in the total length. In working the moulding shown in Fig. 1 a shallow rebate should be planed first on the two outside faces; then with chisel and plane, the radius is gradually produced by the careful removal of the surplus wood. A heavier design,

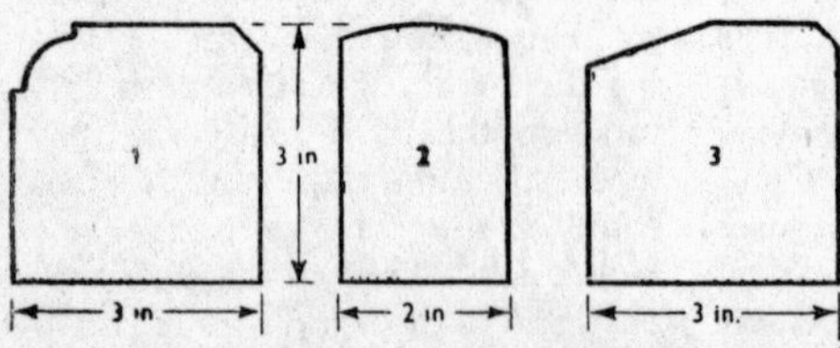

Figs. 1, 2 and 3. Three alternative cross sections of timber, shaped with simple ornament.

like that shown in Fig. 5 can be carried out in the same way, using a moulding.

When the curb is to be covered in sheet copper or brass, deal may be

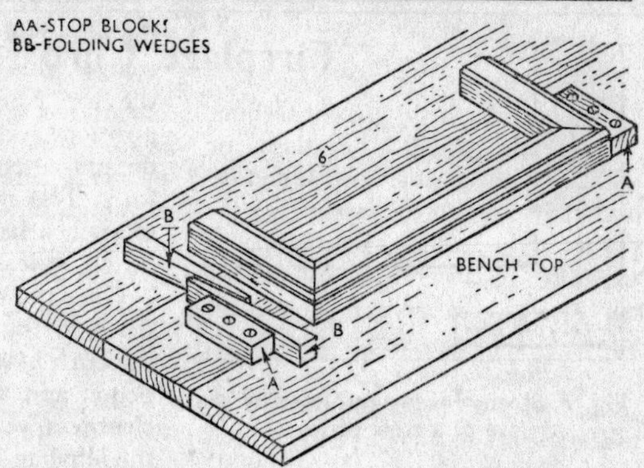

Fig. 6. How to assemble fireplace curb, when gluing, applying pressure by stop blocks.

used as a core. Good seasoned wood should be chosen. Ask the timber merchant to find a piece that has stood in stock for a good while, as in the ordinary way this timber gets very brief seasoning. It is safer, on the whole, to use oak as the core, though the cost is more and the labour greater than with deal.

Joints.—For the sake of good appearance the corners should be mitred. Three inches is rather deep, and the usual mitre boxes will not accommodate such stock. The only thing to do is to mark off the mitres with a mitre square, or a mitre template, and to saw down carefully with a fine-toothed tenon saw. It is essential to keep the saw blade upright with the work, while following the mark on the top. The corners

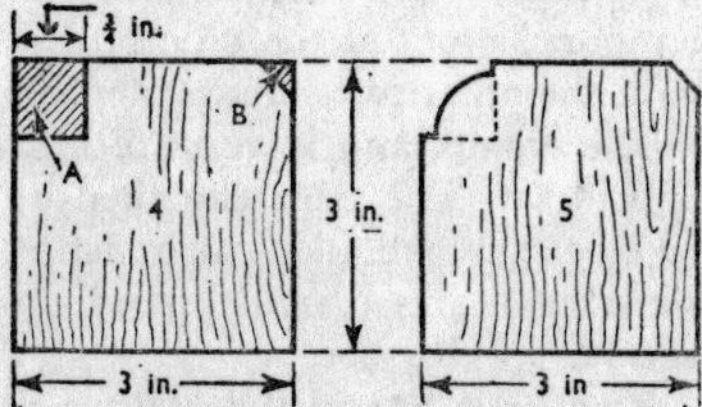

Figs. 4 and 5. How to utilize finished "quarter round beading," as an alternative to Fig. 1, for ornamentation.

are fixed by gluing and screwing; the screws go through into end grain in one member, which theoretically will not afford a good "bite" for the threads, but in hardwood it is practicable. The screws are sunk by counter-boring, and the hole left at the top is afterwards plugged with a round piece of the same wood to match the run of the grain. Thus, if the plug does match, the screw will also be hidden with reasonably unobtrusive effect.

A tip for any such job where a good grip is needed is to drill out a hole in the underneath member big enough to take a Rawlplug; the plug is then inserted, so that it is a trifle below the joint line, and when assembling the curb the point of the screw is carefully guided into the hole in the fibre plug. Two screws at each corner joint will be wanted, and they should be of No. 12 gauge, in "iron", and about 2½in. long. When the mitres have been cut and fitted, cramp the front piece of the curb and one end piece to the bench or to a table, in the correct position, with front and end fitting as tightly as possible to each other. Then bore guide holes with a fine gimlet, or a small bit in a brace, going through

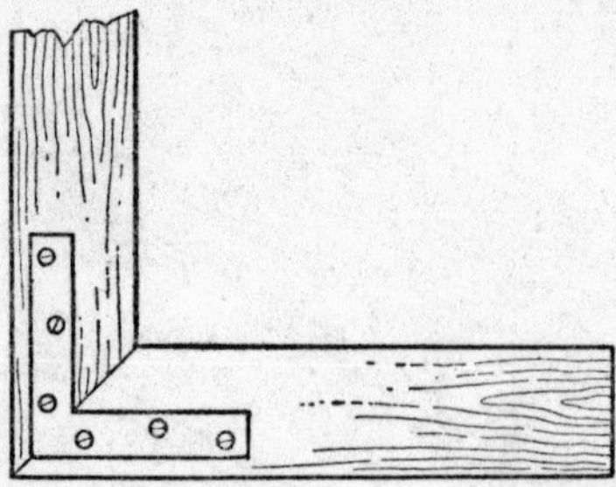

Fig. 7. Strengthening the joint by the use of a steel plate.

from the end piece into the front piece. Bore the *two* holes before taking the members apart.

This will give an accurate guide for enlarging the holes to the proper size. The next thing is to counterbore the *end piece*, and to enlarge the holes farther in, to take the shank of the selected screw. Finally enlarge the holes in the end grain of the front piece, to take the Rawlplug (if one is to be used), or to accommodate the worm of the screw. Secure the front piece again, with the remaining end piece in contact at the proper position, and repeat the operation of boring pilots, enlarging, counter boring, etc. for that joint.

Gluing and Assembly.—Try to rig up some simple form of cramp with stop blocks fixed temporarily to the bench about 2in. wider apart than the full width of the curb, and a pair of folding wedges that will be about 3in. wide when fully closed up, see Fig. 6. The idea is to glue the job, put it in this "cramp" between the stop blocks (close against one block), and then to tap in the pair of wedges at the open end, so that the whole assembly is driven up close. Have the appliances all at hand. When the glue pot is heated apply a thin coat of glue to the joint faces; lay the front piece and one end piece in position, and insert two screws but do not attempt to drive them in fully. The stop block should come to such a height that it clears one screw, at least.

Glue the other joint and assemble it in similar manner. Now put the curb between the blocks on the bench and tap in the wedges (for clearness we will assume they are at the left-hand side) until the ends of the curb are forced up against the mitred faces of the front piece. Next, drive in the screws at the end opposite to the one where the wedges are; turn them up quite tight. Take out the wedges, push the curb along so that now the left-hand end is hard against the stop block; insert the wedges now at the right-hand side and drive them up as tight as they will go. Turn in the screws now at the left-hand end. Owing to the counter boring, the screws will be sunk after the first few preliminary turns have been given, so that they will not foul the stop blocks or wedges. It may be found that only the top screw at each side can be got at, owing to the height of the stop block. In such case, drive home the accessible screw at each end, while the curb is cramped, and then, while it is temporarily out of the cramp, deal with the other two screws. Replace in the cramp, and leave until next day to set. The curb can then be taken out, but should remain flat on some level surface, undisturbed, for another twelve hours.

Further Strength.—Procure from the ironmonger two L-plates, about 4in. long on each leg. These are to be let in flush at each corner

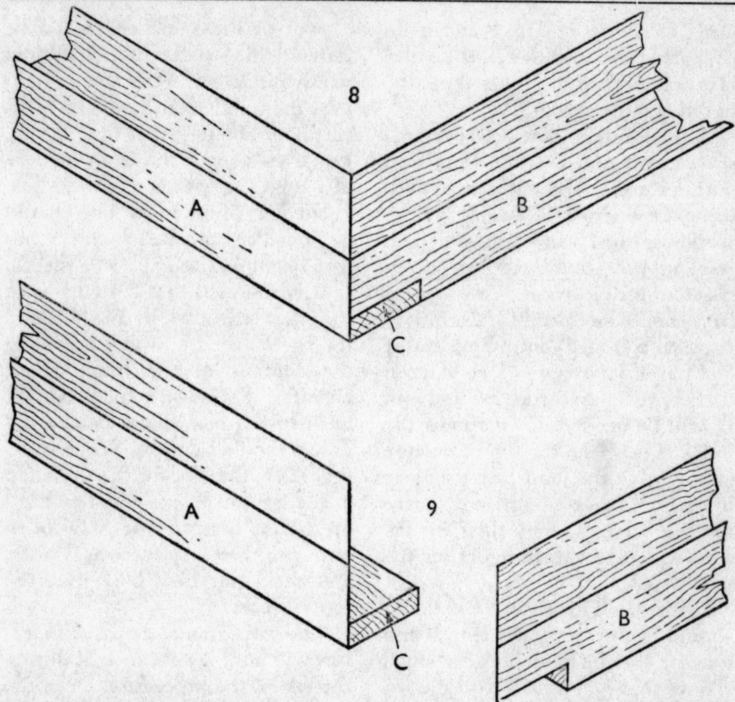

Figs. 8 and 9. Assembly details of mitre and half-lap joint for fireplace curb. The half-lap gives additional strength to the mitre and facilitates assembly.

joint, on the underside of the curb, and then screwed on (see Fig. 7). This job must not be attempted until the glue joints are indisputably firm and hard. Even then, be careful in chiselling out the shallow recess needed to take the plates below the surface, and do not strike heavy blows with the mallet. It should be pointed out that the L-plates will add much to the strength of a good glue-joint at the mitre, but will not compensate for badly fitting mitres, or for indifferent gluing and assembly.

Alternative Joint.—The mitre joint, glued and screwed, needs careful workmanship, but is the only one practicable for the amateur when the job must not show joint lines at the front or sides. An ordinary half-lap joint, as used in many jobs described in this book, is a substitute, but shows the joint.

The lap and mitre may be combined, as in Figs. 8 and 9, and then only a small portion of the joint will show at the end faces. The laps on the ends of the front piece are set out with a square and a steel point (a pencil is not accurate enough for this), then the mitre is sawn down to the exact depth required. A horizontal cut made from the end of the part A will separate the triangular piece of waste wood and leave the portion C, which fits into the notch cut in the short member B of the curb, as shown in Figs 8 and 9. In preparing the member B, the mitre is sawn first and fitted; then the notch is cut out.

Although this joint needs careful setting out and cutting, it is well within the capacity of the man with some experience of simple woodworking. Figs. 8 and 9 show a plain section (not moulded or ornamented) for clearness. This type of curb should be assembled *dry*, put in the cramp (Fig. 6) bottom upwards, and bored for screws. Two at each corner, going up through C and into B, will be needed. Countersink the holes. Then take the job out of the cramp; glue the joint faces; replace in the cramp bottom upwards, drive up the wedges, and turn in the screws. Leave twelve hours for the glue to set.

Lining.—The sheet iron lining should be cut to proper length and height, and be punched for small screws that will attach it to the inside face of the curb. If it is left all in one piece, and bent at right angles at the corner, take care it is accurately sized; if short in the long (front) section, the ends of the curb may be pulled in and the joint wrenched by the action of screwing the lining to the wood. This applies to the sheet iron lining; copper is more pliable and yielding, and may be attached with copper tacks instead of screws. Punch the holes along the flanges first.

Copper or Brass Covered Curb.—Construct the wooden curb as described earlier, except that the ordinary half-lap joint may be used at the corners. It is futile to use small mouldings for this type of curb, and the shape should be bold and simple, as in Figs. 2 and 3. Gauge 20 is suitable for the sheet copper or brass, which should be ordered in a piece of the desired width and length. It should go right over the wooden curb, and be turned under about $\frac{3}{4}$in. at the bottom. Lay a piece over the front section, of a length to overlap the mitre line about $\frac{3}{4}$in. (This mitre line should be pencilled across each corner before beginning to apply the metal).

It is assumed that the curb is in the position shown by Fig. 6. Bend the sheet over the wood, following the contour of the rounding or chamfering. Use only the hands for most of the bending; a pair of old gloves should be worn. When starting, allow the $\frac{3}{4}$in. for the underlap at the bottom inside edge; or bend up this lap first, so that the wooden curb can then be put to the copper, and the latter bent back over the top surface.

The curb, standing on the underlap, will hold the sheet tight during the rest of the procedure. Draw the curb close to the edge of the bench, and bend down the copper over the outer side. Finally, take the copper right down the front or outer face, and give it one or two gentle blows with a mallet to set it. Then, with the curb standing up, sides in the air, the underlap at the front can be taken over and driven down. Lay the curb face downwards for the final touches, using some soft material underneath to prevent bruising. When the underlaps have been formed, drill a series of holes, 2in. apart along the edges of the underlaps about $\frac{3}{16}$in. in from the edges. The holes to be drilled should be for No. 6 Gauge screws. Make a shallow countersink for each hole and drive in the screws, flush with the surface. If they do not come flush, file the heads.

Pelmets

THE use of the pelmet in window treatment should be confined to those windows which are greater in height than in width. The wide dwarf windows which one meets with in old-fashioned and reproduction cottages are much better treated simply with short curtains and without pelmets.

The designing, making and fitting of window pelmets form one of the most interesting and useful jobs the handyman can tackle to improve the appearance of a room.

Pelmets may be of either fabric or wood, the latter being most useful in effecting the more formal and simple designs.

The making of a wooden pelmet is very simple. It is a three-sided box with a cover board (Fig. 1). The ends are of ¾in. material with a facing of three ply, and the formal pattern is made on this facing piece. Hardwood, such as oak, walnut, or mahogany, should be used for the job and then stained and polished, or it may be constructed in white wood and painted to match the other woodwork in the room.

Fixing.—The pelmet should be deep enough to enclose the hanging device from which the curtains are suspended, say three or four inches, and it may be conveniently fixed to metal brackets fixed to the architrave, or frame of the window, or to wooden supports screwed to the edge of the architrave (Fig. 2). Very heavy pelmets may cause too much strain on the architrave mouldings, and an alternative method of fixing by means of holdfasts Fig. 4, to the cover board is shown at Fig. 5.

Strictly formal designs are most suitable for use with tall narrow windows and with French casement doors, as shown in Fig. 3.

An even more simple form of wooden pelmet may be manufactured by the use of deep section moulding, which may be purchased and cut to length with mitre joints to suit the angles and length required. This method of constructing a pelmet is particularly suited to a bay window, being both effective and unobtrusive in appearance. This type of pelmet is, of course, very suitable in many cases for use with the

Fig. 1. General dimensions of a simple pelmet design with a plywood facing and light, wood frame.

Fig. 2. Shows how to provide support for a wooden pelmet, by the use of a wood block screwed to architrave.

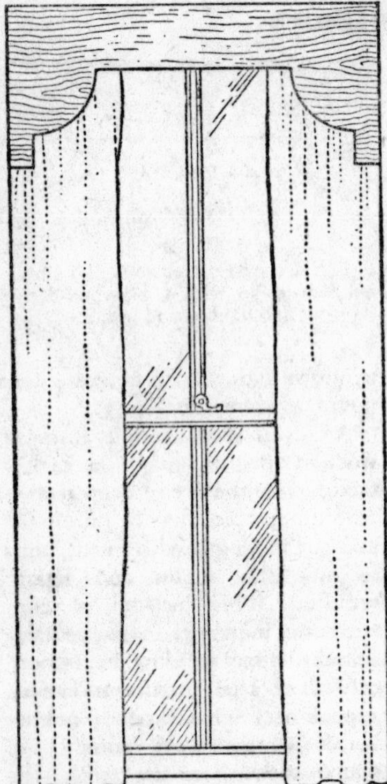

Fig. 3. A simple but effective design of pelmet fitted in place on a tall, narrow window frame.

ordinary sliding sash window.

Pelmets made of fabric to match the curtains may be used in a variety of ways and permit of less formality in design. Care should be taken, though, to avoid any suggestion of Victorian fussiness caused through over-elaboration. Whatever fabric is used, it will be

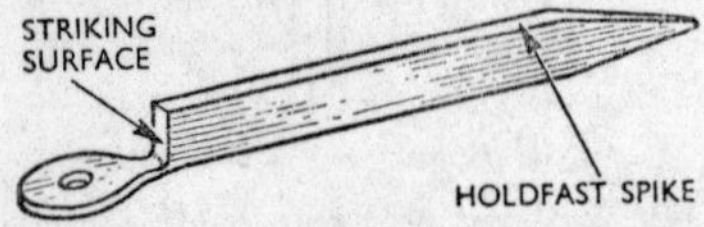

Fig. 4. Holdfast spike as an alternative means of attaching pelmet to wall.

necessary to provide a lining or backing. Buckram made especially for this purpose is the most suitable and may be bought in widths up to one yard. Buckram linings are essential for heavy fabrics such as velours and velvets. For lighter materials, such as cretonnes and silks or cottons, stout calico sheeting is quite good enough. The covering fabric is stitched to the lining after the shape has been cut out of both. In the case of buckram, hand stitching is to be preferred as it is beyond the capabilities of the ordinary sewing machine. The edges of the pelmet may be finished with a narrow gimp or braid.

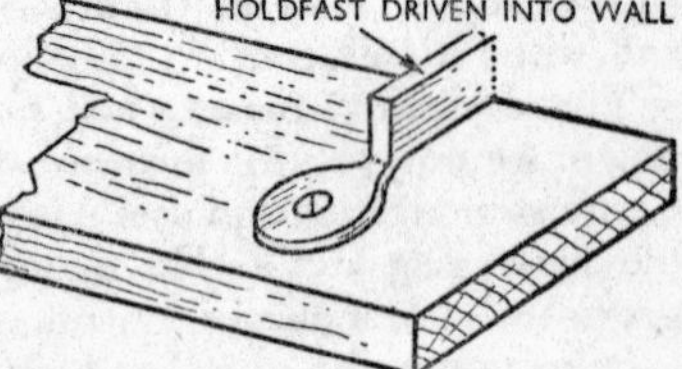

Fig. 5. The holdfast spike should be driven in about half its length into the wall to ensure security.

In order to ensure symmetry of design at both ends of the pelmet, it is advisable to cut a pattern out of stiff paper or cardboard and use the same pattern at both ends.

A point to remember is that, while a calico lining may be washed with the fabric cover complete, those pelmets mounted on buckram will have to be detached for washing as the buckram is stiffened with a glue solution. On the whole, it is better to manufacture pelmets from washable material, so that they may be renovated whenever it is necessary. When fixing such pelmets always be sure they can be removed without damage to the pelmet material.

Picture Frames

IN estimating the length of moulding required for making a wooden picture frame, the basis is the length and width of the picture plus the mount (if the picture is to be mounted). The length and width of the mount must agree with the distance between the limits of the rebate (the recess at the back of the moulding) as measured from side to side and from top to bottom. But there is an important addition to this; allowance has to be made for the width of the moulding, and also for a certain amount of wastage in cutting the eight mitres.

Each of these is cut, with a tenon saw, at an angle of 45 degrees. In marking for the cuts, a second thought should always be given. Each of the eight mitres must slope inwards to the rebate; the first attempt at making a frame can so easily be marred by going wrong, in this respect, with just one mitre.

For accurate cutting, a mitre block (Fig. 1) or a mitre box (Fig. 2) is desirable. One or other may be purchased, the box giving the greater accuracy because of its paired guide-lines. Construction of either presents no great difficulty. For the block, two pieces of wood each about a foot long and $\frac{3}{4}$in. thick, the bottom piece about 6in. wide and the top (that is, back) piece 3in., are screwed or glued together, the saw guides (mitre lines) then being marked out as shown, at 45 degrees, and sawn through to the depth of the bottom piece, the utmost care being taken to ensure the cuts are really vertical.

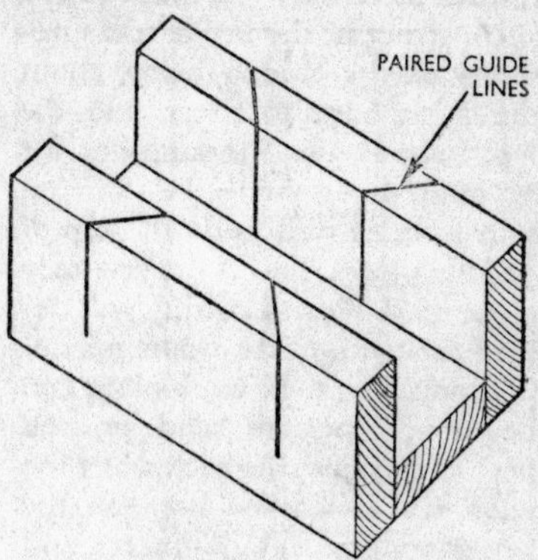

Fig. 2. The mitre box, constructed from three pieces of wood glued and screwed together, is a good alternative to the mitre block shown in Fig. 1. For deep section work, the mitre box is more efficient than the mitre block.

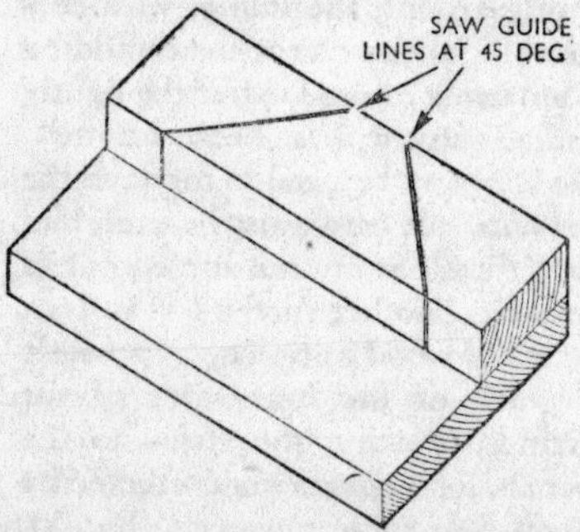

Fig. 1. This mitre block is constructed from two pieces of wood glued and screwed together. Guide lines cut in the upper block must be at exactly 45 degrees. These vertical guide lines must be sawn very carefully.

The length of moulding is held securely with one hand on the base of this block and pressed firmly against the top (back) piece and is positioned so that the saw-cut is made exactly where intended. Pressed to the bench, there is no likelihood of the block slipping.

With the paired guide-lines of the mitre box the tenon saw is held captive, and cannot deviate from the correct angle. As shown in Fig. 2, three pieces of wood are required to construct it, the inside measurements of the trough being about 4in. from back to front, and the depth about 3in. Marking-out for the guide-lines should be done on both faces as well as on the top of the side pieces, for on the accuracy of the marking and cutting will depend the truth of the frame mitres. The moulding to be cut is placed on the trough bottom, and pressed there and against the back while the tenon saw is worked between the corresponding guide-lines and through the moulding. Mark off the exact length for each side of the frame and carry the pencil marks vertically up the outer edge of the moulding. Having cut the first mitre, turn the moulding and ensure that the next mitre to be cut will agree with the joint angle to be made. The object of the pencil line on the outer edge of the moulding is to permit the moulded face to be turned uppermost and at the same time give visible location for the saw cut. Sawing from the face downwards avoids the chipping of the surface which is apt to result if the wood is cut through from the back to the face of the moulding.

An alternative method, dispensing with mitre block or box, is to mark the lines direct on to the moulding with a 45 degrees set-square or with a bevel gauge set at that angle, and do the cutting with the moulding in the bench vice, the jaws of the latter gripping the rebate and the outside edge. But this is practicable only when the moulding is plain-faced and flat; also it tends to be inaccurate.

When the four lengths have been cut they should be placed together, flat on the bench, to form the frame. Any inaccuracy in cutting will then be apparent, after testing with the large set-square, and can be remedied with a jack plane or smoothing plane used in conjunction with a shooting board. This, at its simplest, takes the form of a $\frac{3}{4}$in. thick base board to which is nailed or screwed an inch-wide strip of wood $\frac{1}{2}$in. thick, this forming an angle of 45 degrees with the perfectly straight edge of the base board (Fig. 3). The outer edge, against which the jack plane or smoothing plane, used on its side, will run, ensures each mitre being trued and smoothed at the same time. Pressure of the left hand, which holds the moulding against the inch-wide strip, keeps the shooting board steady on the bench.

After the eight mitres have been given this final attention, the frame is ready for gluing, newspaper being placed below the corners to prevent it sticking to the bench. There are several methods of clamping the frame while the glue is setting, one being to run a stout cord or string around the frame, with corner blocks to prevent the moulding from being injured. After the tightly pulled string has been knotted, wedges may be used to increase the tension, but care must be exercised that the sides are not forced out of square. Another method is to butt strips of wood as tightly as possible to each of the four sides of the frame, screwing the strips to the bench, looseness being corrected by the use of folding wedges (Fig. 4).

If the latter method is adopted, further securing of the mitres (when the glue has set) by nails or screws is simplified. Before the fine screws or thin nails are driven home, holes should be bored at the corners with gimlet or bradawl. If the string method of tension is adopted, and it is thought desirable to strengthen the joints after the glue has set, the nailing or screwing will require caution, to prevent both splitting and weakening of of the mitre joints.

The nails or screws should be sunk well into the wood, ample depressions being made for the head at the same time as the holes are bored. These depressions are later levelled up with wood-stopping, of a colour to match the wood. Alternatively, pieces of waste from the moulding can be cut to fit, and glued in.

Surplus glue should be cleaned from the jointed frame, and the wood should be rubbed with fine glasspaper, though use of this will be possible only on the back when the front face is heavily moulded. Then the glass, picture and backing can go into position, though oil paintings are generally left unglazed. If there is any difficulty with surplus glue on the face and sides of the frame this can be removed with a wad of cloth dipped in hot water.

The glass should be thoroughly cleaned, particularly on the inner surface. It should be cut to an easy fit for the rebate, though not too loose, and it should not be fingered on the inside while the picture is being placed on top of it. The picture having been put in place, a backing of thin plywood or very stiff cardboard is introduced and secured with glazing brads or other fine nails.

These are driven horizontally into the sides of the rebate, while the frame is flat on its face. It is advisable to make certain that the bench (or table) has no loose nails or other small items on its surface to scratch or indent the moulding, and a flat iron on edge, or a block of wood, should be pressed against the out-

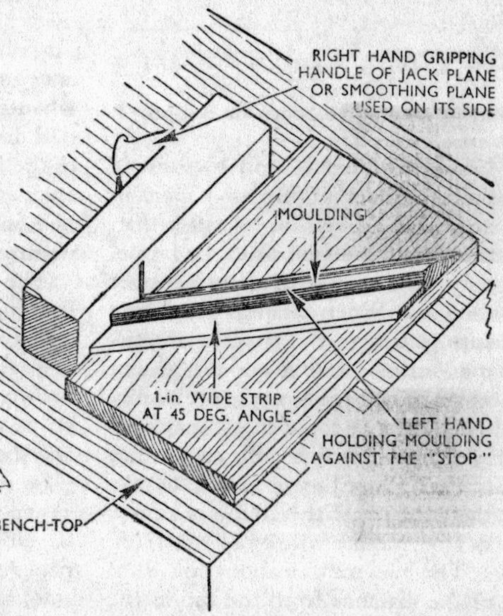

Fig. 3. Shows how to finish the joint face of a moulding on a shooting board, after cutting in a mitre box or block.

side edge of the frame (the edge that is being dealt with) as a support during the hammering. The backing must not be pressed down too tightly, or the glass may crack, but the brads must be sufficiently low in the rebate to hold the back securely in the frame.

Do not drive the brads in the rebate more than half their length.

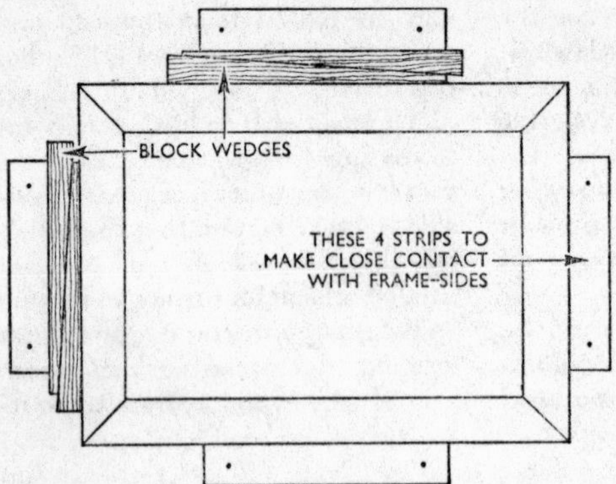

Fig. 4. How to assemble a picture frame after gluing, by use of wedges, and strips secured to bench or baseboard.

For a neat finish, and to exclude dust, a sheet of brown paper, in area a shade less on all sides than the overall dimensions of the frame, may then be pasted or glued over the back. When this has dried, any surplus due to the paper's stretching during pasting should be cut away. Small screw eyes (preferably the kind with loose rings) may now be inserted in line with each other in the back of the moulding, to take the cord or, if the frame is heavy, flexible picture wire or a light chain.

The eyes may be about one-third of the distance from the top of the frame, though this depends on the angle at which the picture is required to incline from the wall. If the inclination is to be slight, the rings will be inserted higher up. If the moulding is thin, the eyes should be screwed in cautiously, to avoid the screw points coming through to the front surface of the frame.

Generally speaking, the pictures on one wall should have the same inclination, and there should be some symmetry as to height. The most convenient method of hanging is from a picture rail, with hooks made for that purpose to take the cord, wire or chain, but ornamental wall hooks can be purchased if preferred, and fixed with long, thin nails. These hooks are specially suitable for hanging light pictures to lath-and-plaster walls. The simplest method of all is to drive a nail into the wall, though for appearance sake, this should be done only when the cord is so short that the nail does not appear above the top of the frame. It should be driven in at an angle, head pointing upwards, bedding it into a Rawlplug if the nature of the wall calls for plugging.

The passe-partout method of framing consists in using prepared strips of stout paper gummed on one side, the face being black, brown or any other colour. These strips are purchased in small rolls, and there is a variety of widths. The glass must be exactly the same size as the picture (and mount) and the backing of stiff cardboard. The paper is moistened on the gummed side, after being cut into four suitable lengths, and so attached to the backing and to the glass that the picture between is immovable.

Starting with the first cut strip, this is stuck to the glass and then bent down and under and attached to the backing, thumb and first finger being run along to compress it. This operation is most easily managed by having the assembled picture face upwards on the table, with the bottom edge extending a couple of inches or so beyond the table edge; a heavy book placed flat on the whole keeps it steady. The bottom edge is dealt with first; and when the paper strip is secure, the left and right ends are cut square and level with the glass.

The whole is then turned around so that the top edge can be dealt with similarly. Then the sides, the extremities of these being cut with the scissors at an angle of 45 degrees, to give each of the corners a mitred appearance. To hang the completed picture, two small rings are attached to the back, the attachment passing through the backing and then being bent flat; these should be secured in place before the sticking of the passe-partout is commenced.

A cardboard frame can be made by cutting four strips of stout cardboard to the desired width. The top and bottom strips should extend the full width of the glass, the two side strips ending square with the inner edges at top and bottom. These are then glued or pasted to the glass. When dry, picture and backing are placed in position; the procedure is then exactly as explained for passe-partout framing. If the cardboard framing is, say ¾in. wide, a very effective plan is to cover it with two contrasting colours, or shades, of passe-partout. It could be covered completely, first, with silver or gold, and then with black in such a way that a ¼in. margin of silver or gold is left to provide the required contrast.

Shelves

The essentials for strong shelving are (a) boards stiff enough not to sag noticeably over the span required; and (b) good supports at the ends and at intermediate points, according to the span. It is assumed for example, that several shelves are needed in the kitchen for pots and pans. The walls are of brick, coated with hard plaster or cement rendering. One end of the shelves can be fixed to the wall, but brackets must be provided for the other.

Saucepan Shelf.—Inch board is suitable, two pieces of 6in. tongued-and-grooved board being used to make up a width of a little under a foot. For the outer end of each shelf a steel bracket, 12in. × 10in. will be needed. A common length for shelves in such a position (flanking the sink, say) is about 3ft. 9in.; the bracket will be set-in about 6in. from the outer ends of the shelf, as illustrated in Fig. 1, page 66.

Begin by measuring on the wall the position of the *bottom face* of the shelf or shelves. It is a good plan to measure from the floor to the lowest shelf, and then to lay off the distances above, from the *first* line. Remember that the top of the shelf will come approximately 1in. higher than the line.

On the end wall we shall need a bearer for each shelf, cut from 1in. × 2in. batten, neatly planed, and cut back to a slope at the outer end. Prepare these bearers first, and bore holes for the screws. Use Rawlplugs to fix them to the wall, with No. 12 screws, 2in. long. Countersink the holes in the bearers, so that the screws go in flush. Square off pencil lines on the wall to show the line for the *top* of the bearer (*bottom* face of the shelf). Hold the lowest bearer in position, with a spirit level on

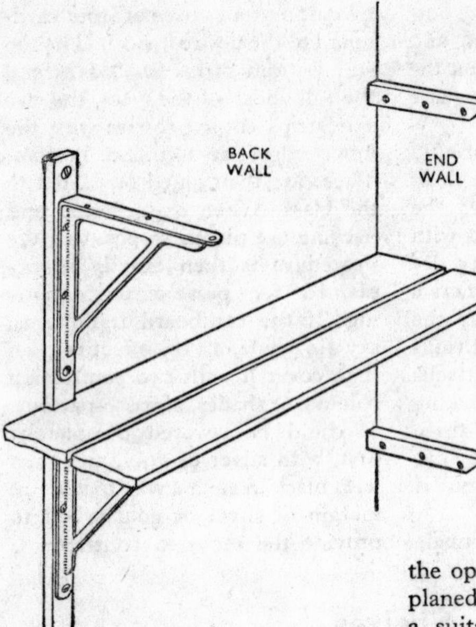

Fig. 1. How to utilize steel brackets and wood strips for mounting shelves.

Mark the back wall through the batten for plugs; drill the holes, and screw up the batten.

Cut the inch board to length; plane off the tongue, and let the grooved board on the other side go against the wall. The shelf can be stiffened by screwing a ledge (made from the 2in.×1in. batten) across the two boards underneath, midway in the length. Do this before fixing the shelf. The latter, at the open end, should be radiused, planed and sandpapered. To make a suitable radius a large dinner plate can be used to mark the curve, running a pencil around it.

The back edge of the shelf should be notched to fit around the vertical batten, close to the back wall. After fitting (but before fixing) the lowest shelf, the latter can be used as a guide for marking those above it, but screw on the ledge first. In any case, where several shelves are being fixed, do not fasten the lowest, or fix brackets, until the preparatory work above has been completed. If large saucepans are to be accommodated, remember that they often have a loop handle at the opposite side to the long handle; when turned upside down, the loop will stop the vessel lying flat, unless there is an open space at the far side of the shelf. In such cases, do not take the boards close to the wall. Otherwise, to make a neater job, a length of batten, planed, and chamfered along the lower front edge,

top, and verify the level. Use a fine awl to mark, through the screw holes, the place where the plugs are to go. Drill the wall for these latter, fit the approximate size of Rawlplugs and screw the bearer in place.

Fix the bearers for the remaining shelves. Now fix the vertical batten to which the steel brackets are screwed. The batten may be some of the same timber as used for the bearers; cut it to length, and chamfer the two front edges. Bore holes for the screws as before. Get someone to hold the batten in position while it is tested for vertical; a plumb bob and line will give the true upright, but it may be got approximately by measurement from the end wall, though the walls may not be dead true.

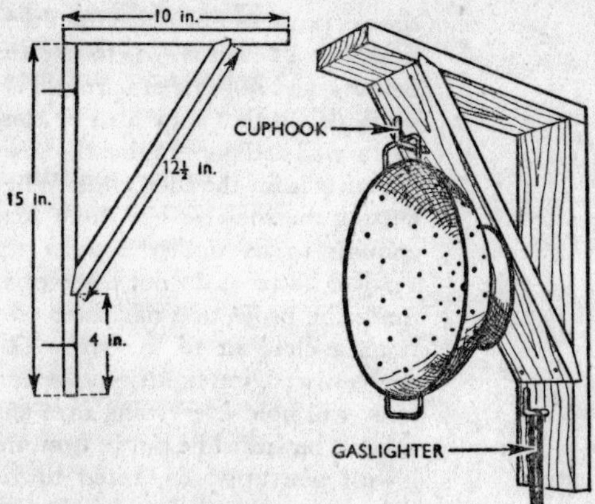

Fig. 2. Showing construction of a wooden shelf bracket and the incidental use to which it may be put for kitchen utensils and other equipment.

can be fixed to the wall under the back of the shelf. Oval brads can be nailed through the board obliquely into the top of the back batten.

When ready to fix the brackets, lay a shelf in place on the end-wall bearer, and adjust the height of the other end until a spirit level placed on top shows the shelf to be horizontal. Mark the position on the vertical batten (for the under side of shelf). Place the bracket so that its *top* arm is at the level line; and bore for a screw through one of the holes in the *vertical* arm of the bracket; screw this in, adjust the bracket for perpendicular, and put in the next screw. Lay the shelf in place and test with spirit level; if correct, proceed with further screws into the batten. Only short screws are needed to hold down the shelf to the bracket; No. 8 ⅜in. long, will do. Two oval brads will hold the other end of the shelf to the bearer on the wall. See also Figs. 2 and 3.

Fitting Shelves to a Recess.—Two types of recessed shelves are referred to. The case first dealt with is where the recess has a skirting and picture rail or frieze rail, and for some reason these are not to be cut, see Fig. 4.

Two vertical battens are fixed at each side of the recess, on the flanking walls; only one side wall is shown in the diagram, for clearness. The battens (of 2in. × 1in. or 3in. × 1in.) are cut at the bottom to fit close to the skirting, being bevelled for that purpose. At the top they are given a longer bevel to bring them over the picture rail; if this is a thick rail, the battens can be taken only part of the way up the mould-

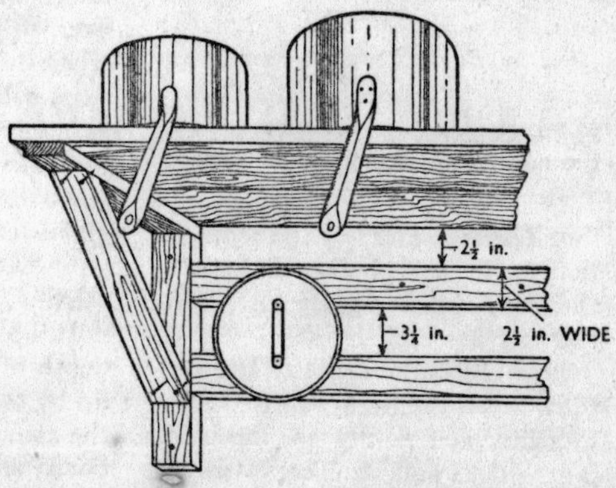

Fig. 3. Alternative method of arranging a single shelf by use of wooden brackets, shown in Fig. 2.

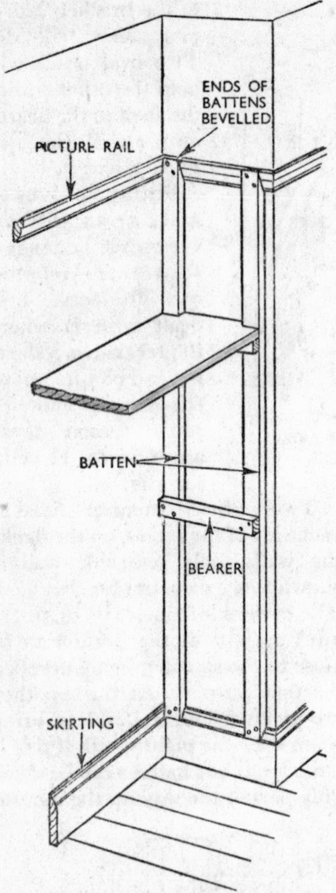

Fig. 4. Construction of shelves showing the method of attachment in a recess.

ing. The essential requirements are that the battens shall come close to the wall, and fit tightly to skirting and picture rail.

Nail the battens at top and bottom, after plugging them at two intermediate points to the wall. Next cut and fit cross-bearers where the shelves are to come; the sketch shows these screwed flush to the verticals and of the same thickness; but a better way is to use 2in. bearers, and notch them around the verticals, so that they also fit close to the wall and give double the bearing surface for the shelf ends. When cutting the shelves, get them long enough to fit tightly against the vertical battens; do not attempt to make the projecting narrower portions a close fit to the wall. The shelves, wedging tightly to the battens, will hold everything firm and solid. They must be put in from the lowest one upwards, tilted to get them started, and then gently tapped down with a mallet (or a hammer knocking on a block of wood). Undue force will loosen instead of tightening the job.

The second case is where the skirting and top rail can be taken down. Remove them, and fit the vertical battens straight through to the floor, and up to the height required. (If desired, a hanging wardrobe can be made by fixing a piece of matched picture rail, or architrave moulding, across the opening at the topmost point, level with two top cross-bearers, and fitting a dustboard of plywood on top). However, to proceed with the shelving, when the upright battens have been fixed solidly, screw on cross pieces as before, to take the shelves. Where the skirting and picture rail were taken down, short end pieces can be glued and nailed on to make a mitre joint with the meeting lengths of skirting, etc.

It has been assumed that the full depth of the recess has been taken up by the fitment; but if this is not the case, suitable pieces of skirting board and top rail will have to be fitted in, to make a neat finish. If metal rails are to be fitted, to take

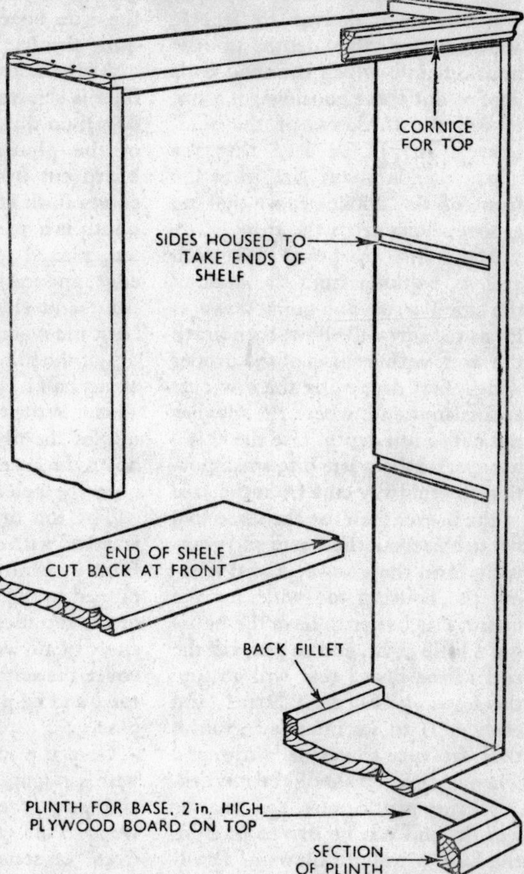

Fig. 5. Details of dwarf bookshelf showing framework joints and the general construction. The joints for the cornice and the plinth should be plain mitred, glued and nailed. Plinth fits outside front and sides.

wardrobe hooks, two special bearers should be fixed up, suitable holes having previously been bored in them for the rod ends. Then the rods will be inserted before screwing up the bearers. Do not forget also to put the hooks on the rods.

Dwarf Bookshelves.—Fig. 5 shows a set of shelves 3ft. high, 1ft. 11in. wide, and 6½in. deep. The principles here used can be applied to larger constructions, but the span should not exceed 3ft. between the sides, and the wood in such cases should not be less than an inch thick for the actual shelves. In the fitment illustrated the outer members are from inch board, while the shelves are ¾in. thick. Cut out the sides, an inch less in height than the total overall height; but the top and bottom boards the full width.

Use a marking gauge to scribe the line for the rebate at each end of both top and bottom boards, a little less than ½in. deep, and extending back from the end to the width of the side boards. Saw across with a tenon saw to the proper depth, and then remove the waste wood by chisel or saw it out with a *fine* saw, cutting entirely in the waste wood. Smooth off the rebate with a rebate plane, if one is at hand; failing this, use a broad chisel, and finish with coarse sandpaper wrapped round a square-edged wood block.

Cut and fit all rebate joints, and carefully square off the ends of the side boards. Do not fix together yet.

Cut the two shelves to length, allowing for the depth of the housings into which the shelf ends fit. Set out these housings, of a size to suit the thickness of the shelf boards. It will be seen that the housing ends about $\frac{3}{4}$in. from the front of the bookcase, so that no groove shows from the front.

Make two saw-cuts for each groove, working from the back of the side boards, and going down as far as the saw will allow; then finish the work with a chisel of the proper width, first deepening the saw cuts at the front end, where the saw has not cut to full depth. Use the chisel to separate the waste into small portions by midway cuts from the face of the board; then use the same tool flat to chisel out the waste and gradually form the groove. Avoid making the housing too wide for the board; it is better to have the housing a little tight, and to pare off the end of the board that will go into the housing. Fit each board (and each end) to its intended groove; they are sure to vary slightly, and when once fitted should be marked.

Having made sure the shelves *will* fit, and can be driven in from the back with light blows of a mallet, we can assemble the outside four members, and nail them through the top and bottom into the ends of the vertical pieces. Bore holes with a fine bradawl a little smaller than the nails. Lost head wire nails, 2in. long, are suitable, the heads being almost invisible after a slight punch down. Next tap in the shelves, inserting them from the back. Any defect in fit will force out the sides, so work carefully, and ease the shelf if necessary. A little hot glue can be used on the ends if desired, though nails put in from the side boards will hold the job quite firmly.

At the bottom of the bookcase a fillet is screwed down (Fig. 5, back edge); on this, and on the top edge of the plinth, is nailed down a board cut from stout plywood. It comes flush at front and back. The plinth is a piece of 2in. × 1in. batten, planed to a bevel at the top edge, and mitred. It is nailed to the front and sides. The fillet at the back must agree in height with the top of the plinth, and the latter, for about half of its thickness, must be square at the top, to provide a seating for the plywood. When nailing down the latter, use panel pins, and bore the holes first.

The top of the bookcase is finished off with a piece of moulding to form a cornice; this is mitred and pinned to the sides and to the edge of the top member of the frame. A sheet of plywood should be cut to cover the entire back of the bookcase, and be pinned on with veneer pins.

Give the job a good rub down with sandpaper, punch in the nails, and stop the holes with plastic wood. Stain with a solution of vandyke crystals in water, and a pleasing oak shade will result, depending on the strength of the solution. First test the colouring intensity of the stain on waste wood, letting the stain dry thoroughly to find out what the finished colour will be like. Be sure to lay on the stain evenly so as to obtain a quite smooth colouring effect. After staining, the grain may be observed to have risen, but a rub with medium sandpaper will remedy this. Finally, give two coats of oil varnish, allowing the first coat to dry before applying the second coat.

Step Ladder

STRENGTH is an essential factor in the design of a pair of steps, but lightness and dimensions which permit easy movement from one part of the house to another are important considerations. The steps to be described meet these requirements, but the dimensions may be varied according to the particular use to which the steps are intended to be put.

The timber used throughout is $\frac{7}{8}$in. thick (finished size) and of good quality deal. If the timber can be purchased ready planed both sides a lot of planing can be avoided. A couple of lengths of 9in. boarding, for instance, would provide the various components with a minimum of cutting. The quantities required are as follows :—

			ft.	in.	in.
Legs ..	2	lengths	4	3×2½
Top strap	1	,,		13×2½
Bottom strap	1	,,		18×2½
Treads ..	1	,,	7	0×5
Top piece	1	,,		15×8
Back piece	1	,,		13×6
Strings ..	2	,,	5	3×4

First mark off the bottom of one string at an angle of 30 degrees on the width and some 5 degrees on the thickness and cut off the waste. At intervals of 10in. draw guide lines parallel with, and measured from, the bottom. These guide lines indicate the centre line of the treads, the marking off for the saw cuts should therefore be $\frac{7}{16}$in. on either side of these lines. Now mark off a total length of 5ft. and saw off the waste, making the cut parallel with the bottom. Note that no saw cuts for the tread grooves have yet been made. Cut and mark off the second string similarly, remembering that

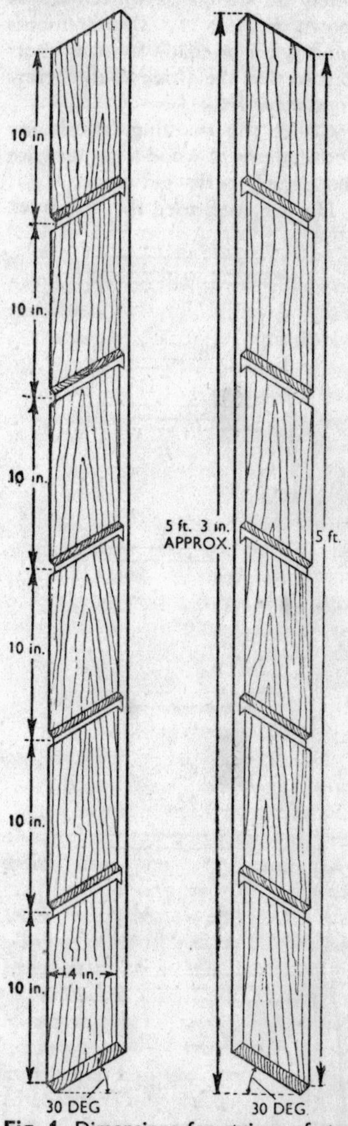

Fig. 1. Dimensions for strings of step ladder showing inside faces, each cut to house five treads. The angles at tops and bottoms of strings must match the angles of the tread housings.

the guide lines will face each other when the strings have been cut as shown in Fig. 1. Measurements must again be made from the bottom so that the strings will correspond exactly.

Check the marking by placing both lengths of wood together with the pencil marks outwards.

Having confirmed that the tread

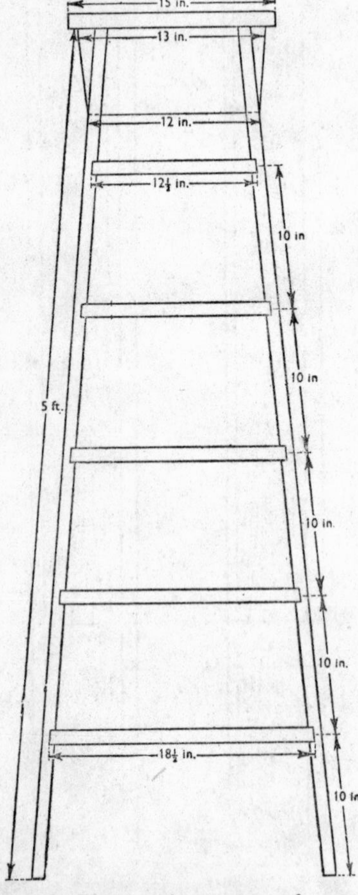

Fig. 2. Showing front view of step ladder and overall dimensions of the assembled treads strings, top and strengthening back pieces.

positions agree, lay the strings on edge, guide lines inwards, and position them 12in. apart at tread five and 18in. apart at tread one. Secure the strings in this position by tacking a couple of laths to hold them. By this arrangement the angle of the groove cuts can be marked. Mark off the depth of the grooves using a marking gauge set to ¼in.

The tread grooves can now be cut to the required depth with a tenon saw. Chisel out the waste. It is better to chisel out slightly less than the required depth, the final chiselling being done when the treads are fitted.

With all grooves cut, position and temporarily secure the strings as before and mark off the length of tread No. 1 from the strings. Remember that the ends of each tread must be cut to match the tapering angle of the strings, i.e. about 5 degrees. If the tread fails to fit the groove snugly, adjust the grooves to fit the length of the tread. In fitting the tread, see that all the projection is towards the front of the steps and none whatsoever at the back to interfere with the closing of the legs.

Mark off, cut and fit tread No. 5 in a similar way. Three 2in. nails should be used to secure the ends of each tread in the grooves of the strings. Drive in the nails and use a nail punch to drive the heads below the surface. Treads Nos. 2, 3 and 4 may now be marked off, cut and fitted. (See Fig. 3A.)

Take particular care to mark the exact length of each tread. Chamfer the forward corners of the treads. With these fitted, the most difficult part of the work is completed.

Before the front section of the

steps is complete, a back piece and a top piece must be fitted. (See Fig. 2). Cut the top piece first. It is to be 15in. × 8in. Lay it centrally over the head of the strings with a projection of 1in. to the front. Nail on with 2½in. nails.

The cutting of the back piece is a little more difficult. First cut a piece 13in. × 6½in. and plane one edge to an angle of 30 degrees. Try this under the top piece. It should fit snugly into the angle formed by the back projection of the top piece and the strings. Centre it and mark off the point of intersection of the bottom edge and the outside face of the strings. Mark off from this point to the top corner and cut. Nail into position. This completes the front section.

Next cut the legs in the following manner. Take the front section and lay it face downwards. Place one of the legs so that one end butts on the bottom edge of the back piece and the outside edge lies flush with the outside face of the string. Mark the top end of the leg and cut it so that it will butt flush against the bottom edge of the back piece. Mark off 4ft. 3in. and make a parallel cut. The other leg is dealt with similarly. It will be noted that the bottom ends of the legs are not at right angles to the edges of the legs.

Place the legs in position again on the front section. Mark off the bottom strap by placing a length 12in. from the foot of the legs. The top strap is marked off 3in. from the top of the legs. The straps can now be screwed on to the legs.

Back flap hinges (2½in.) are fitted to the legs as shown in Fig. 3 and then to the back piece. Care should be taken in fitting these

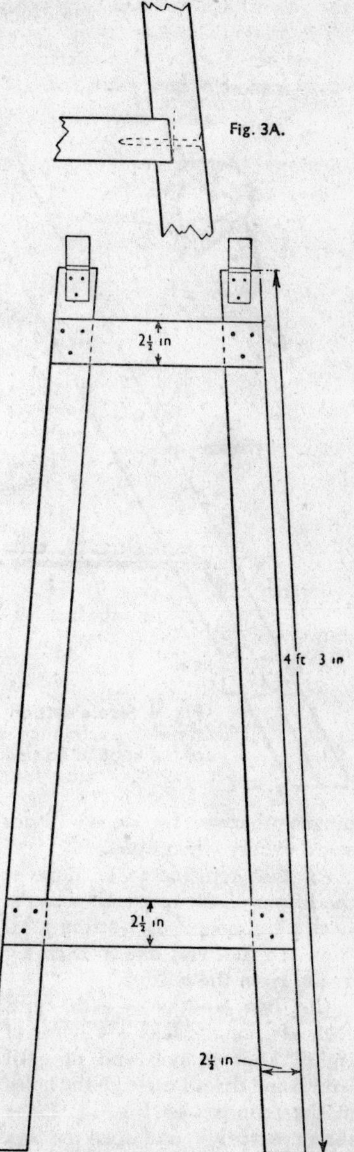

Fig. 3. Shows legs and straps assembled, back flap hinges in position. **Fig. 3A.** A part view of a tread housed and secured in a groove of a string by nail.

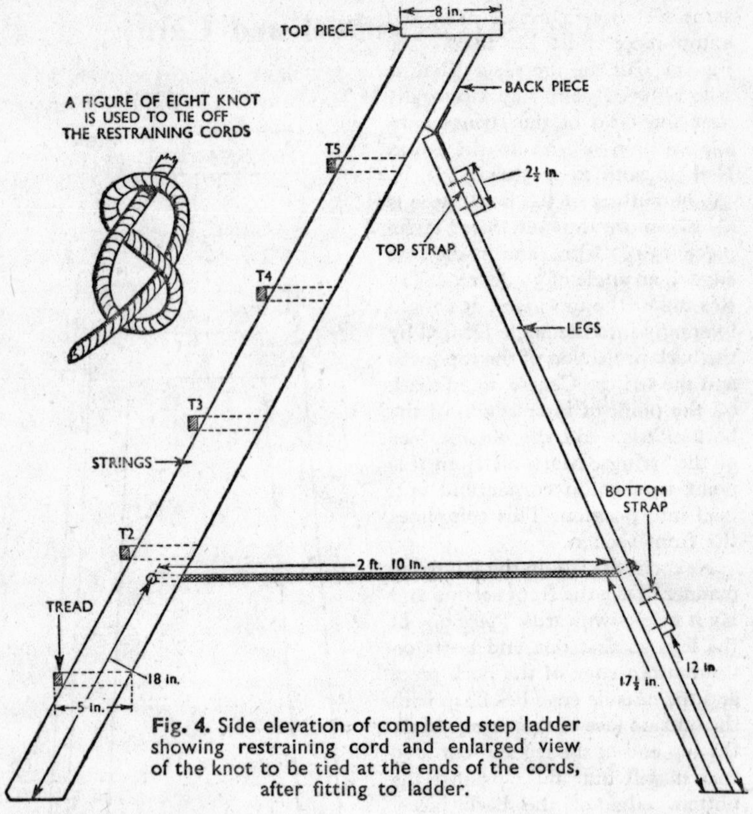

Fig. 4. Side elevation of completed step ladder showing restraining cord and enlarged view of the knot to be tied at the ends of the cords, after fitting to ladder.

hinges otherwise the steps will not stand evenly when open.

All that remains to be done is the fitting of the restraining cords. Drill a ⅜in. hole in each string 18in. from the foot and one in each leg 17½in. from the bottom.

Cut two lengths of sash cord, each 4ft. long. Make a "figure of eight" knot at one end of each length and thread through the holes in the strings (see Fig. 4). Place the steps upright and open the legs until the treads are horizontal. Make sure that this operation is effected on a level floor. Thread the restraining cord through the legs and tie off again with a "figure of eight" knot. Make the cord a little less than the actual measurement to allow for stretching. But be certain that each cord takes equal strain when the ladder is subjected to loading.

The steps are now complete and should stand firmly on a level floor although a little trimming of the bottom ends of the legs may be necessary to achieve this. Finally, sandpaper all corners and edges to prevent splinters entering the hands when using the steps. Finally, cut the bottom, forward corners of the strings as shown in Fig. 4.

Tables (Occasional and Card)

A FOLDING or collapsible table which can be used for card-playing, or an occasional side-table for tea in the garden, can be made with reasonably small expenditure in material and effort. The example shown at Fig. 1 may be constructed from oak or walnut if it is desired to obtain the best decorative results; but for a table of this kind, likely to experience casual handling, the use of deal is worth consideration, either stained or painted. If it is constructed from oak it may be left unpolished, although if used much in the garden a protective coat of good varnish may be applied.

The top, overall size of which is 21in. square (including the $\frac{3}{8}$in. beading) is of stout plywood and is covered with green baize, or with leather-cloth. Leather-cloth has one advantage in that it is easily cleaned with a damp cloth. A strip of plain beading fitted along the edges of the table top falls flush with the surface, holds the leather-cloth in position and gives a neat finished appearance to the table top.

The plywood top is on a frame (Fig. 2) $2\frac{1}{4}$in. wide and $\frac{1}{2}$in. thick; two of the pieces are $18\frac{3}{4}$in. long and are jointed to the two longer sides, each $20\frac{1}{4}$in. long, and glued. When the glue has set, the top is glued to this frame. Attachment of the covering, and fixing of the beading remains until last.

The four legs are each $30\frac{1}{4}$in. long, $1\frac{1}{4}$in. wide, $\frac{3}{4}$in. thick, and are rounded at top and bottom. At a point $16\frac{1}{4}$in. up from the bottom, where touching legs will cross and are attached, holes are bored, to take $2\frac{1}{4}$in. long bolts (Fig. 3). A bolt is passed through each pair of legs, from the outside of each of the two fixed legs, and the nut screwed home. One leg only, of each pair, is actually fixed to the underside of the table top frame, a single screw securing the leg to a metal bracket on the appropriate side. The brackets are fixed each by two screws to the inner edge of the frame and are located as shown in Fig. 4.

The two free legs are connected at the top by a rod, $\frac{1}{2}$in. in diameter; the rod-ends pass through holes of the same diameter bored $\frac{4}{5}$in. down from the top, this measurement being taken to the centre of the hole. There the rod is glued, the ends being flush with the outside edges of the legs (Fig. 5).

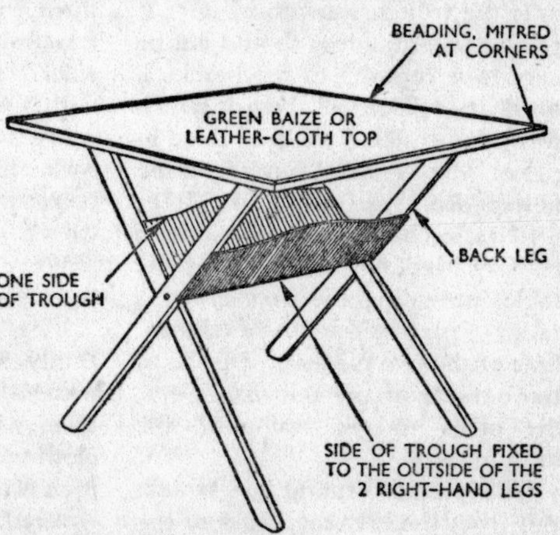

Fig. 1. Completed folding table suitable as a card or tea table for occasional use in the garden. Note trough attached to legs to hold books or papers.

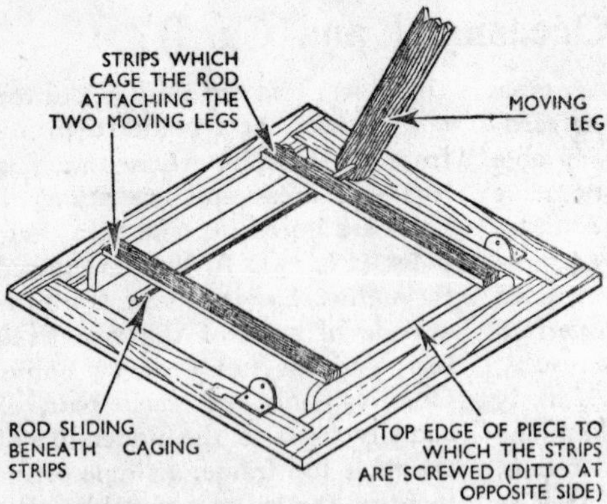

Fig. 2. An underside view of the folding table showing the general construction to obtain folding movement of the table top and legs.

secured when they are shaped with a spokeshave or fretsaw. Other wood lacking, a good quality piece of three-ply may be used.

When the table has been assembled, the "run" of the movable legs should be tried. If there is any stickiness here, too close contact between the leg-tops and the underside of the table-top, a shaving or two should be removed from these, until there is no hindrance to free movement. It will be noticed that as the free legs lodge securely in the angle of the framework there is no possibility of an accidental collapse; the only precaution to take is to see that the legs are open to the full extent.

To cover the top, cut the green baize or leather-cloth to an area which allows of the edges falling flush with the lower edges of the framework, and attach it to the surface and to the framework edges with the minimum of glue. If too much of the latter is used it may soak through the surface of the baize; when this is being smoothed down it must not be unduly stretched. A flat-iron will assist in banishing wrinkles.

The glue should be smeared thinly over the wood, and the material attached first to one edge, from which the baize or leather-cloth will be smoothed flat inch by inch until top and frame edges are covered. When the glue has dried, any surplus material is removed with scissors, then the ¾in.-wide beading is screwed to the frame

These legs move from one side of the table-top to the other when the table is collapsed, and are "caged" by two strips of wood each 15¾in. long, 1⅜in. wide, ¼in. thick. The strips are screwed to pieces 12in. long, 1½in. wide, ½in. thick, which in turn are screwed to the inner edges of the two longer sides of the frame (Fig. 2).

If the trough shown at Fig. 1 is to be added, the legs should not be caged, or screwed to the brackets, until the pieces of board which form the trough have been fixed in place. This is useful for containing newspapers, magazines or other articles, such as needlework, and in no way hinders the folding of the table, providing the precaution is taken of placing the sides as shown. One of the two pieces is screwed to the outside of the two fixed legs, the other to the inside of the movable legs.

The pieces forming the trough run from the extreme edges of the legs, and are 5½in. wide and ¼in. thick. Their top edges can be left straight, but a better effect is

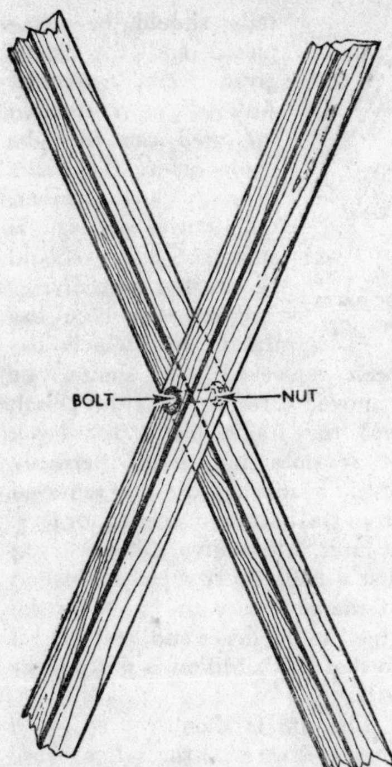

Fig. 3. Shows the midway pivot point for legs of the folding table.

edges, the ends of the beading being mitred to make a neat junction at the corners.

The heads of these, and other screws used in the construction, should be sunk below the surface of the wood, to allow of their concealment with wood-stopping; or sawdust from the wood itself can be made into a stiff paste with a little glue and worked in over each sunk screw-head. If the top should ever need re-covering, the beading can be removed for that purpose. If any object is to stand on the table semi-permanently, the baize (which is more likely to be marked, or worn, than leather-cloth) can be protected with a false top of wood to match, in kind and finish, the material used throughout.

A point to observe is that with each of the two bolts which join pairs of legs, a thin metal washer, about 1in. diameter, should be placed between the crossing legs so that these do not rub throughout their length when the table is collapsed or opened. Also it saves time and makes for accuracy when dealing with the trough-sides if both pieces of wood are worked together in the vice; the pattern to which the top edges are to be cut first being outlined on a strip of paper, which is then pasted to one of the pieces as pattern for the fretsaw or spokeshave.

A more formal occasional table, for the hall, or to take the wireless set, can be constructed in oak, walnut or mahogany (Fig. 6). The top, consisting of two or possibly three boards glued together, is 24in. long, 15½in. wide and ¾in. thick. The edges may be left square or, alternatively, may be "scalloped" with the spokeshave. The four legs are 27in. long and 1¾in. square. If these can be turned

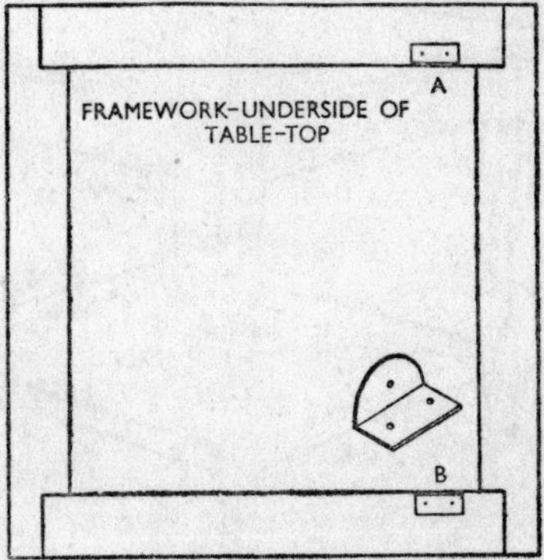

Fig. 4. Brackets A and B in position for securing legs. See also Fig. 2.

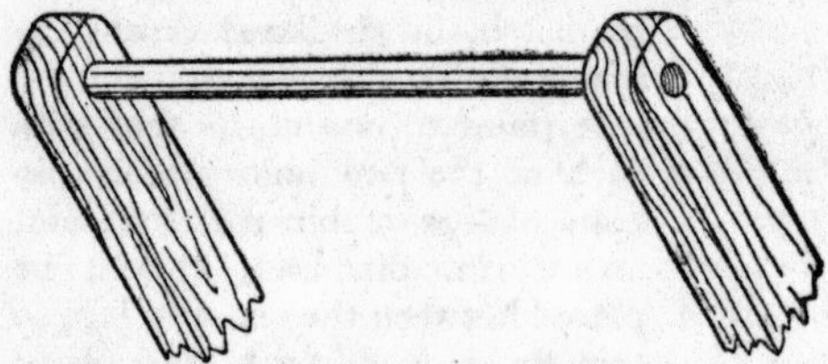

Fig. 5. A part view of top of sliding legs, illustrating the method of housing the rod in the legs. Use wooden rod with a good straight grain for extra strength. The rod must be a firm fit in the legs.

on the lathe, the appearance of the table is added to; or turned legs may be purchased.

The top rails are secured to the legs by stub mortise and tenon joints; the long sides measure 17½in. from leg to leg, the short sides, 10in.; the wood is 3in. wide and ¾in. thick. The tenons are ½in. long and ⅜in. thick.

The bottom rails are 1¾in. wide and ¾in. thick, and the jointing here is by dowels, ¼in. diameter and 1in. long. These rails are positioned 4in. up from the bottom of the legs; their lengths correspond, of course, with those of the top rails. Joints of top and bottom rails should be completed and the frame given a trial assembly. Any slight correction indicated can then be made before the frame is finally glued together. One dowel per rail is sufficient, and it should be situated centrally.

When the glue has dried, any which has been squeezed out should be removed carefully with the chisel, and the frame tested for level. If it does not stand perfectly level, a shaving can be removed from the bottom of the leg, or legs, at fault. Alternatively, if one leg is just a trifle short a piece of wood of the necessary thickness can be glued to the lower end, and shaped so that this addition is not noticeable.

The top is then secured, with glue and screws, the latter being inserted at an angle from the inner face of each of the two long pieces of rail so that they bite into the underside of the table top. Four screws are needed, each 2in. in from the ends of the long rails. This fixing is done by first gluing the top to the frame, taking care that the top is placed centrally. When the glue is dry, the positions of the four screws should be marked, ¾in. down from the top edges of the long rails, and a trial hole at each position bored with a bradawl or fine gimlet.

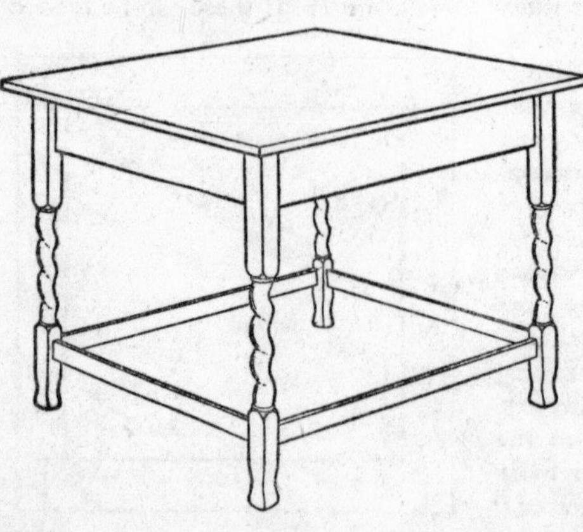

Fig. 6. A general view of a more formal occasional table for use in the garden.

The angle at which the holes are bored will

determine the length of the screw, from 1in. to possibly 1½in. It is sufficient if the screw passes about ¼in. into the underside of the table top. When the holes have been made, a larger gimlet completes the boring and the screws are driven home. The heads should be countersunk so that there is no projection on the inner face of the rail.

When the table is not in use do not leave it exposed to rain and damp. Store it in a dry sheltered position, preferably in some convenient place inside the house.

Towel Rails

The problem of fixing the fitted position of a towel rail can sometimes be solved by dismissing the wall altogether as a suitable site and attaching the rail instead to the inside of a door. That is certainly preferable to trying to plug a lath-and-plaster wall. If, however, the latter is of brick, no difficulty should be experienced in securing the backboard of the towel rail by long nails, direct into the mortar between bricks or into wooden plugs inserted between them.

Sufficient mortar must be removed, with a cold chisel, to allow of the plugs being driven in. These should be not less than 2ins. long and about ½in. diameter. More convenient are Rawplugs, purchased at an ironmongers; by their use with screws far less disturbance to the wall is caused, and their holding-power is great. But whether on door or wall, the roller towel fixture should be about 6ft. up from the floor.

In the example (Fig. 1), the backboard is 19in. long and ¾in. thick and 5in. wide, with the front edges slightly chamfered. Brackets to hold the roller are fixed ½in. in from each end, by two screws inserted from the back. These brackets (Fig. 2) are cut from a piece of wood to the length of 4¼in., width 2¼in. and thickness 1in. The shaping can be done with a spokeshave or by the combined use of saw, chisel and rasp.

On the inner face of the left-hand bracket is marked the position of a hole in which a spindle of the roller will revolve. The hole is ½in. diameter, ⅝in. deep, and its centre is 1⅜in. from the back edge of the bracket and 2⅛in. down. The hole should be bored with a brace and centre bit.

To allow of the removal of the roller when the towel has to be changed, the right-hand bracket

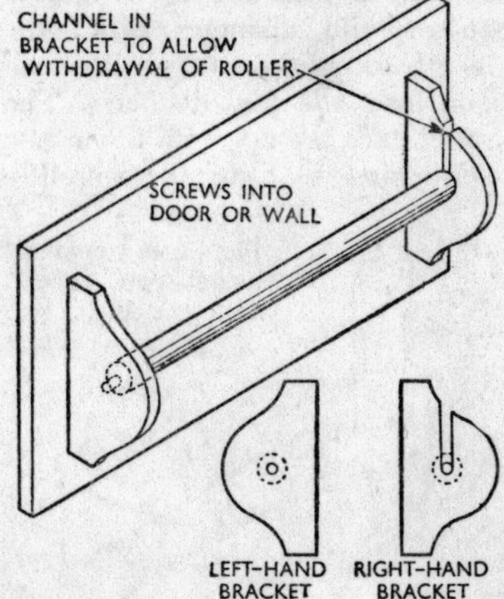

Figs. 1 and 2. General details of towel rail and end elevations of the two left-hand and right-hand brackets.

(Fig. 2) has, in addition to a similar hole on its inner face, a slot cut from the hole as far as the top edge of the bracket. This vertical piece to be cut away is removed by two cuts with a tenon saw after boring the central hole.

The positions of the two prepared brackets are marked on the face of the backboard, their inner faces 16in. apart. Their bases outlined in pencil on the baseboard, holes to take the securing screws are bored through the board, these holes then being extended into the corresponding brackets, about 1¼in. from the top and the bottom of each. When the screws have been driven home (from the back), the fitment can be attached to door or wall; a screw hole first being made a few inches in from either end and along the central line of the board, for fixing to the door, or nail holes bored for attaching to the wall.

If the roller cannot be bought ready turned, a piece, square in section, can be suitably planed to shape. The finished length is 16¾in., and diameter 1⅝in., the length including two spindles each ⅜in. long and ⅜in. diameter. The roller ends are cut with tenon saw and chisel to form the spindles.

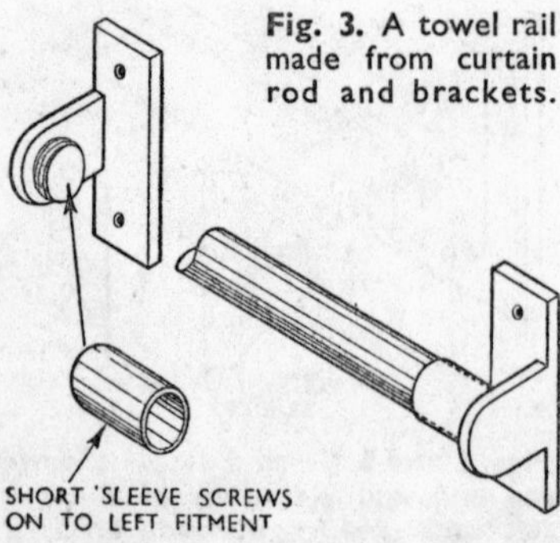

Fig. 3. A towel rail made from curtain rod and brackets.

Exercise great care when sawing the roller ends not to undercut the diameters of the spindles.

Having carefully cut the shoulders with the tenon saw, at both ends, the roller is held vertically in the vice and the end marked, with compasses, for cutting downwards with the chisel as far as the saw-cut. The chiselling should be done piecemeal, carefully working inwards from the circumference. The other end is dealt with similarly. The spindles should be perfectly round, and smoothed to run in the bracket holes without friction. The roller must revolve quite freely; if the fit is too tight, the shoulder can be suitably reduced in diameter.

This fixture may be painted, to match the wall or door; or it may be stained, or polished, or stained and polished. If there is likelihood of the brackets making contact with and damaging the wall when the door is opened right back, a door stop should be screwed to the floor to limit the angle of opening. A similar precaution saves the door from injury if the towel rail is fixed to the wall.

Lighter fitments for ordinary towels take a variety of forms, and these may be purchased at most ironmongers. Others, equally simple, can be contrived at home. For fixing a rail behind a door, perhaps the simplest arrangement of all consists of a length of brass stair rod, or a thin wooden curtain rod coated with white enamel paint, and gripped between two brackets of the type used for carrying small window curtain rods (Fig. 3). This does not provide much space between rail and door (or wall) but it serves its purpose.

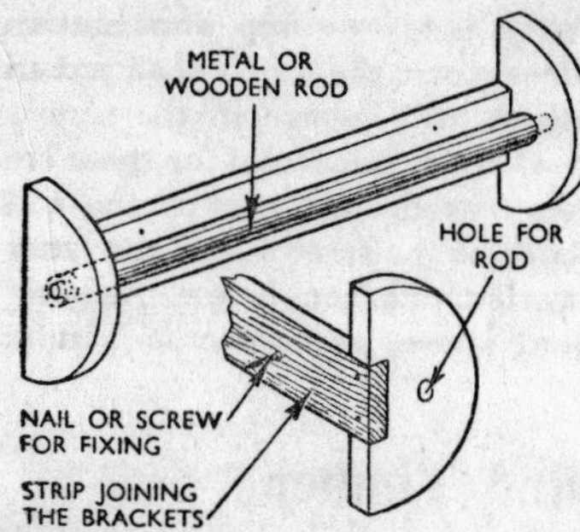

Fig. 4. A towel rail suitable for attachment to side of washstand or door.

Greater space is allowed in the fitment at Fig. 4, which is suitable for fixing to the side frame of a washstand, or to a door or wall. Two semi-circular pieces 1in. thick are cut 3in. long and 3in. wide, as brackets. These are joined by a strip 1in. wide and ⅜in. thick, its length being adapted to the frame of the washstand to which it will be screwed. If there is nothing to limit the distance between brackets (as on a wall) this should exceed by about 2in. the width of an ordinary towel. The strip is sunk to its own thickness centrally in the straight edge of each bracket and there glued and screwed. In the centre of each bracket, a hole is bored to take the metal or wooden rod. This fitment is made of hardwood, polished or stained or painted to match the surface to which it is attached by two screws or nails. Should any difficulty be experienced in cutting the brackets to the semi-circular form shown, these can equally well be oblong: 3in. wide by about 4in. long.

A swivelling towel rail is sometimes a great convenience, as in limited space; it is specially adapted for fixing to the side of a washstand (to the frame, not to a thin panel). As shown in Fig. 5, it consists of two pieces of wood only, the swivelling arm being attached to the back plate by means of two round-head screws which are lodged in fairly substantial brass screw-eyes in the face of the back plate. It is cut from a single piece of hardwood 3in. wide and ¾in. thick.

The back plate (supporting block) is 6in. long and rounded off at top and bottom. Two slender brass screws, 1in. up and 1in. down respectively, fix it to the washstand side as high up as may be convenient. The swivelling arm is of a length to fall short of the washstand front by about 1in. In the figure shown, its overall length is 16in. At 3in. from the inner end it is cut in 1in., and from that point it narrows to ¾in. at the outer end. The edges of the inner end are rounded, to allow of free move-

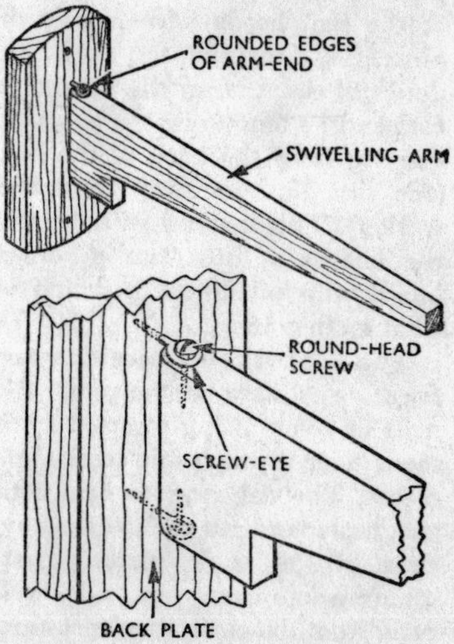

Fig. 5. A swivelling towel rail and a part view of the hinge on back piece.

ment against the back plate.

The two brass screw-eyes which form part of the hinge are screwed into the face of the back plate a shade in excess of 3in. apart, in line down the centre. When these are in place, the tapered arm is placed between them and pencil marks made on top and bottom edges where the round head screws (which will engage in the screw-eyes) are to go. Holes for these are then bored, but not to the full depth of the screws, and the latter inserted, one from below, the other from above, as shown in Fig. 5.

Using Secondhand Timber

Wood from packing cases, tea chests and similar sources can be turned into many useful articles. The first thing is to take the box or case to pieces carefully. Generally the boxes that come to hand for re-use are made of thin board, and any attempt to prize the boards from their fixings leads to splits and breakages. It is better to cut square across the box so as to clear the nailed portions of the ends. Perhaps by detaching them at one end it will be possible to prize up the other end so as to get at the nail heads with a pair of pincers and extract the nails. In doubtful cases, sever the boards at *both* ends; a tenon saw can be used, starting from the back of the box (the side farthest away from the worker). This method will shorten the boards a little, but a sound board will be obtained, which is what matters most.

Tea Chests.—The sides are fixed to square framework, the nails or rivets being inserted from the outside through thin steel angle pieces. The only way to deal with tea chests is to cut each side away, clear of the angle plates. First, square a line across one side, well away from the steel; then (presuming that the top of the chest is open, leaving one edge not protected by an angle plate) saw down two sides. Next, to get an entrance at the bottom of this side piece, bore a half-inch hole to admit the point of a keyhole saw, and saw along a line pencilled across. In plywood, it will not be easy to keep a straight cut with this saw, but the ply can be sawn square afterwards, when it has been detached by the three cuts mentioned. Thus one fair sized rectangle of plywood will have been removed from the box.

Proceed in the same way with the other three sides, which will leave only the bottom to be dealt with. Should the tea chest have all four sides on, then one must be cut away by using a keyhole saw in the first place. Another way is to cut through the corners with a hacksaw until the steel has been severed, and then to continue with an ordinary wood saw; we suggest a tenon saw because this, having fine teeth, will not mutilate or splinter the plywood; but a fine panel saw will serve almost as well, once the steel has been cut through. One side of the chest may have a small circular hole in it, closed with a tin lid. The best parts of the wood can be cut away, at either side, though for some jobs, the entire piece may be suitable. In making any finishing cuts on plywood, saw from the face or best side, since the tool will leave a burr on the under side.

Construction Methods.—Since box materials are slight and thin, there is little possibility of using them without a supporting framework. In other words, use them merely to clothe or line the articles which are to be made. But a very light framework will suffice for small work, and all that is needed is some quartering measuring at least 1¼in. × 1¼in. in section when finished. Thus, for a job to be finished off neatly, material sawn 1½in. square, may be used, and planed on all four sides, or two adjacent sides only, since at least two sides will be hidden from view by the lining which will be attached to them.

Another useful material for framework is batten, size 2in. × ¾in. or 1½in. × ¾in. Heavier jobs need 2in. × 1in. batten to stiffen them. No heavy nailing is permissible in this sort of work, but a much better job will result if screws are used freely, generally in Gauge No. 6. There is a very handy tool made which combines a boring appliance and a screwdriver. The screwdriver blade is secured in a simple chuck at the end of a spirally-cut spindle, something like the stock of an archimedean drill. When the handle is pressed down, the spindle revolves, so that a screw can be inserted or withdrawn, according to the direction in which the ratchet is set. Interchangeable with the screwdriver blades are three double-flute drills, excellent for making screw-holes in wood; they are fixed in the chuck by a simple "push" action, in place of the screwdriver blade. This appliance enables light work to be done quickly and accurately.

A dodge worth remembering for locating members that have to be screwed to a framework is to tack down the covering, e.g. plywood, with four panel pins. Then, with a bradawl or the tool mentioned above, holes can be bored through the ply and sufficiently far into the frame underneath. By now inserting about four screws, the covering can be fixed in proper position, for the remainder of the screws to follow. Also, if nails are to be used throughout, the fixing by panel pins will make this operation easier. But there is much to be said for the use of small countersunk screws in jobs where neatness and strength are desirable. Plywood can be attached with Gauge 4 screws, ¾in. long, and the heads will not be conspicuous after the work has been painted. It is seldom that salvaged timber is clean enough to be left "in the white", ready for staining and varnishing, but even then small screws, neatly inserted, are not a great blemish.

Rabbit Hutch.—This is intended to be protected by placing in an open-fronted lean-to shed, an airy position shielded from driving rain. It is suggested that it be made 1ft. 4in. high, and 1ft. 3in. from front to back, overall; the length may be 2ft. 6in. A partition divides the sleeping compartment from the run. The first is closed with a door, hinged to the partition frame by two pieces of pliable leather and held closed by a wooden button fixed to the frame of the left-hand side of the hutch. The leather hinges are screwed to the woodwork of the partition and to the

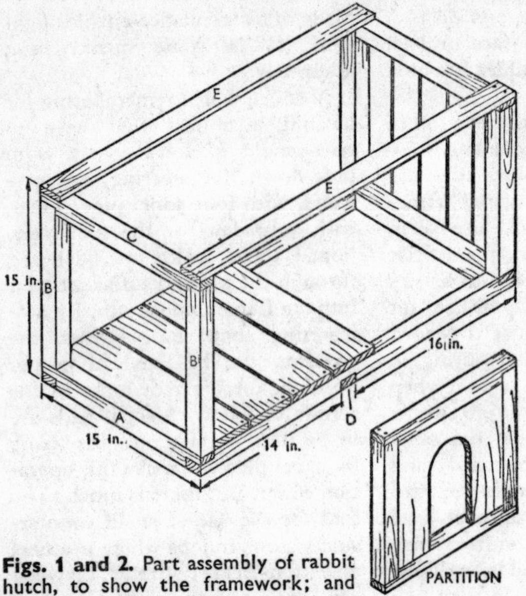

Figs. 1 and 2. Part assembly of rabbit hutch, to show the framework; and details of middle partition.

door frame. The run-front is hinged by its top edge, so that by lifting it upwards and outwards there is easy access to the floor of the hutch for cleaning. Steel hinges can be used here, though leather ones have proved quite serviceable.

Begin by making up the floor frame as shown in Fig. 1. The long pieces of 1¼in. wood are halved to the short pieces at the four corners, and the brace D that comes under the partition is notched in from underneath by a T-lap joint as shown. The diagram indicates short pieces of board from packing cases nailed across from back to front. If wood long enough to run lengthways is obtainable, the boards can of course be laid from side to side. Nail the halved joints with care, leaving room for a centre nail, 2½in. long, to be put in from underneath and to go into the upright member B later. The end frames are made up of three pieces. B is butted down on to the top surface of A and held with two 1in. oval nails put in obliquely. Then the entire bottom frame is turned upside down and the longer nail mentioned driven in to go right through A and about an inch into B. But the end frame ought to be assembled first by connecting the two uprights B with a cross-piece C, the latter being notched out slightly as shown, to rest on top of B. After the two end frames have been fixed, the floor boarding should be nailed on.

Make up the partition separately, as Fig. 2, allowing for the difference in height due to its standing on top of the floorboards. It is screwed down through these boards and into the cross-brace D. The top of the partition, of course, should be level with the top pieces C of the end frames. The partition strengthens and braces the whole job. Now make the roof (Fig. 3), first screwing on two lengths of batten at front and back (as shown by E, E in Fig. 1), securing them to the end frames and the top of the partition. Make sure the latter does not get out of upright. The final task here is to fill in the rest of the roof with short pieces of wood from salvaged boxes, as Fig. 3. Since these boards can meet on the top of the partition, we can use up quite short pieces. They will generally be thinner than the batten, but the thickness can be made up by tacking on three or four strips of odd plywood or similar stuff at each end, and over the place where the partition comes.

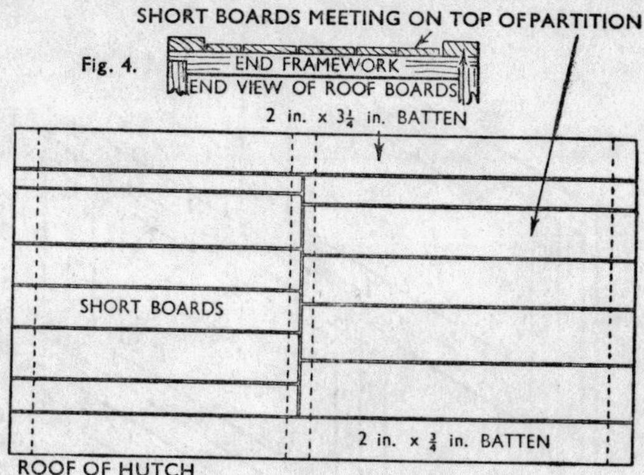

Figs. 3 and 4. Showing the method of using short boards to cover the roof of rabbit hutch, and cross-section of roof. Cover with layer of roof felt.

On top of all, nail some bituminous roofing felt, letting it project at back, front, and ends about an inch. This last operation, however, must be left until the back and ends of the hutch have been covered in with pieces of boarding, in the same manner as the roof. The ends and back should be covered with roofing felt, tacking it down with tin-tacks. A section through the roof is shown in Fig. 4.

The doors of the hutch are illustrated in Fig. 5. The dimensions suggested (see Fig. 1) are limited by the consideration that wood from old boxes is to be used, generally in short pieces. The hutch could be made six inches longer with advantage. Get some pieces of leather strap or belt for the hinges; make small holes for the screws with a bradawl, and fix the hinges with round-head brass screws, Gauge 4 or 6, about ⅝in. long. Soak the leather in lubricating oil before use. A simple staple will serve to fix the wire front against opening, and a small padlock can be added. A simpler fastening is a wood or brass button, as suggested for the door of the sleeping compartment. This door is represented as made up of short pieces of box wood (which are clamped together at the back by a cleat at top and bottom).

Instead of using the method shown in Fig. 1 for the end frames, they can be made up as independent units, and screwed down to the floor frame. This is a good method if, by using longer boards for the covering, the hutch can be

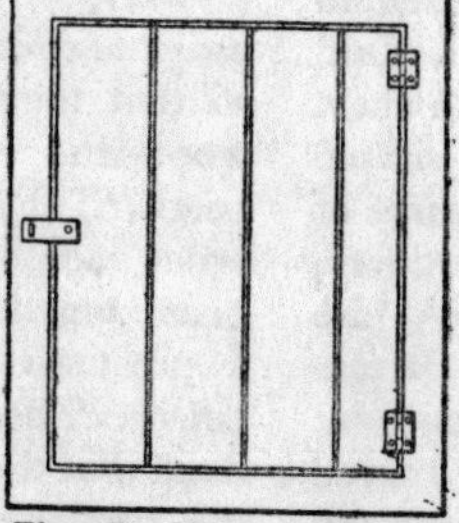

Fig. 5. Plain board and wire mesh doors for front of hutch. Hinge and staple doors as indicated.

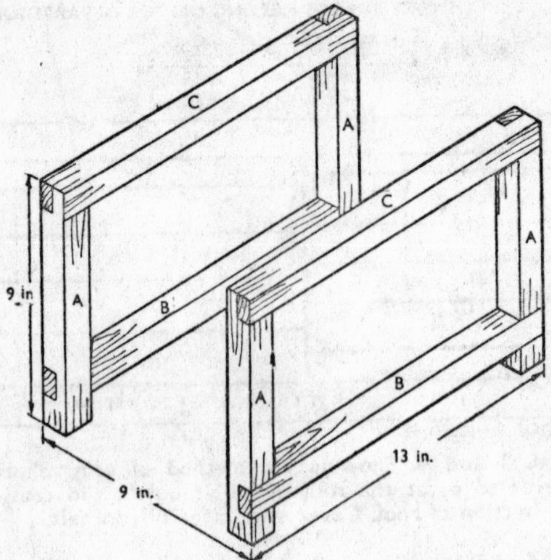

Fig. 6. Shows general details and overall dimensions of the framework for a slipper box. See also Fig. 7 for details of covering.

built longer, say to 3ft. or 3ft. 3in. The joints of the frames in this case should be halved as shown for the floor frame. When nailing boards to the framework, rest the structure on a solid floor, and get a helper to hold an old flat-iron, or a heavy hammer, under the part on which you are hammering. Bore all holes where there is any danger of splitting the timber. A hand drill, with a twist drill in the chuck, will do the trick.

Slipper Box.—This is 13in. long, 9in. high, and 9in. from back to front (see Figs. 6 and 7). Odd pieces of plywood from a tea chest will make the covering; the simple frame is built up of planed strips of square-section deal, 1in. square, see Fig. 6. The uprights (A) are 9in. high; the cross pieces (B) are notched in at 1in. from the bottom; the top cross-pieces (C) are halved to the uprights level with the top end of the latter. There are no cross-pieces to the narrow ends, as the plywood will be screwed on here to unite the back and front units.

For simplicity, the lid (Fig. 7) merely fits into the top of the box; having four mitred cleats of half-inch wood about 1½in. wide nailed on with fine panel pins from the top face of the plywood. The cleats should be thinly coated with a liquid glue before being attached. Four or five "spots" of glue will suffice, and the mitre joints also should be glued. As the cleats are nailed down, the glue will spread out over a wider surface; avoid putting on too much glue, as only a thin film is needed. The wood must be clean where the glue is to be applied.

In order to locate the cleats in their proper position, lay down the lid flat, *under* side uppermost; square lines across with a pencil where the cleats are to go; glue the cleats, lay them down on the lid, and drive in a few pins to fix them for the time being. Then turn the lid over, top side now being uppermost, and drive in ⅝in. panel pins so that they go through the plywood and into the cleats underneath. If the pins protrude on the other side, after the heads have been punched down slightly with a pin-punch, file off the points below. The cleats should be so fixed that the lid fits easily between the framework of the box at the top opening. If desired, the pinheads can be concealed by nailing around on top a strip of shallow bead or moulding, mitred at the corners.

It will be seen from the perspective sketch (Fig. 7) that the bottom edge of all four sides of the box, is cut away to a sweep for the sake of appearance. Grip the plywood in a vice, and saw the curve with a fretsaw or coping saw; finish with glasspaper rolled around a piece of broom-handle, etc. Always saw downwards, away from the face surface, to avoid burring the face side of the work.

The front and back frames, made up of pieces A, B and C, should be cut and jointed, and the plywood attached. Note that the ply projects at each side just enough to cover the plywood ends of the box; it is flush at the top, of course. Thus, looked at from the long side, no end grain will be visible. The piece B is better let into notches made in the outer sides of the uprights, where the joints will be hidden by the plywood facing. Also, the halved joints at the top should be similarly cut, to let the continuous piece be at the back. In order to get a finished flush surface, the plywood should be about $\frac{1}{16}$in. longer than the finished dimension at each side, to be rubbed down with glasspaper to the exact level last thing, after assembly of the complete box.

After covering the front and back frames, cut a piece of plywood to fit the bottom of the box and glue it in place. It should go in fairly tightly, but not so tight as to force out the plywood covering. Next nail on the end pieces of plywood. A spot of glue here and there between the ply and the surface of the uprights will make a stronger job. Lastly, lay the box on a table, end uppermost, and cut a piece of 1in. quartering to fit tightly between one pair of end uprights at the top, where the halved joint comes. Apply glue, and force the cross-piece into place. Hold it with a pair of cramps to the plywood facing until the glue sets. Later, fix a similar piece between the opposite pair of uprights, thus giving a neat and flush finish to the box opening.

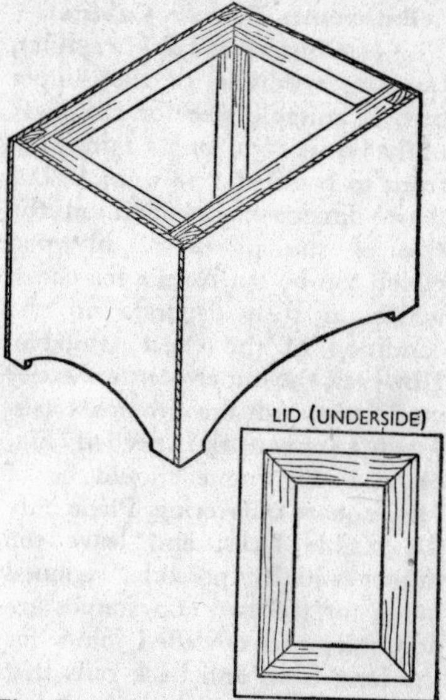

Fig. 7. Shows the completed slipper box and the construction of lid as viewed from the underside. Four mitred cleats, glued and pinned to lid.

Two coats of hard-gloss paint will give an attractive appearance to the slipper box. An alternative, after glasspapering to a smooth surface, and slightly punching down the heads of the nails or panel pins, is to stain with bichromate solution, or vandyke crystals, and to varnish the box.

Bathroom Box or Cabinet.—This (see Figs. 8 and 9) is a similar, but larger edition of the slipper box. A suitable size for the body of the box is 20in. long × 15in. from front to back, and 18in. high, but these dimensions depend on the size of the pieces of plywood which can be cut from a tea chest, which in turn depends on the condition of the chest available. However, the dimensions are easily modified to suit the circumstances. Again a framework is needed (Fig. 9), and this frame should be of 1½in. square quartering. Plane only the visible faces, and leave the timber as stout as possible. Tenoned joints for the two end frames are desirable, and dowelled joints for the long front and back rails that connect the end frames. Again, as in the slipper box, there is a top rail and another lower down, on which latter the floor of the box rests.

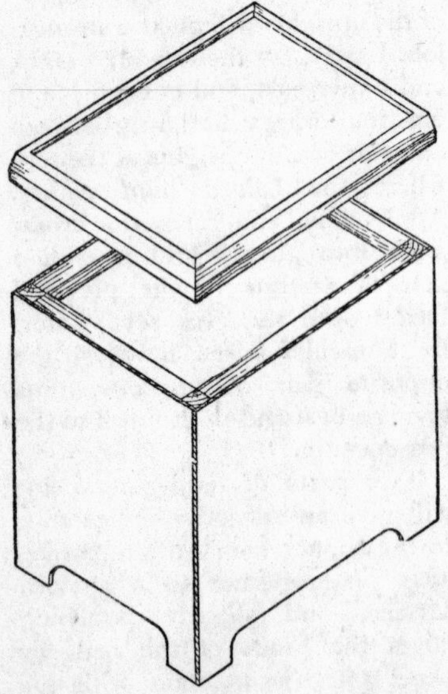

Fig. 8. A bathroom box or cabinet covered with thin sheets of plywood.

In this case we make up the two end frames as independent units. Cut and fit the joints; glue up, and leave in cramps to set. Next, cut the two long rails for each long side. Square the ends of the wood and bore for two ⅜in. dowels. A cardboard template can be marked out and applied to the places where the dowels are to enter, to mark the points for boring the posts. The same template will be used to mark the ends of the rails. Notch in a cross-bar to the bottom pair of rails, cutting the notches in the top or uppermost face of the rails. This bar is to support the plywood bottom; if pieces of board from boxes are to be used instead for the floor of the cabinet, the cross-bar may be omitted.

When the dowelled joints are set hard, and not until this is certain, the plywood sides can be attached to the carcase; small screws with countersunk heads are best in this case. Slightly countersink the holes with a brace and the proper bit; tack the plywood temporarily at two opposite corners, and then proceed to bore for, and enter, the screws. Put in about two to each post or rail, and then insert the rest in between. Watch for any tendency of the plywood to cockle; since it is twice-used material, this may occur, but can be corrected by working from the middle of the edges outward towards the margins, and not tightening the screws finally until all seems correct. If the ply be first fixed at the outside of the piece, it may cockle at the centre portion, and will be difficult to put right without making fresh holes. If we were using thicker plywood this trouble would not crop up.

The lid is "thicknessed" at the edges by gluing and screwing on some pieces of planed deal about ½in. thick and 2in. wide (Figs. 8 and 10). As with the slipper box, these are mitred, but in the present case they come flush with the edges, on the under side of the lid. Further inside the lid, some fillets of ¾in. × 1in. deal should be screwed on from below, to form a sort of rebate and guide the lid into its proper position. Glue and mitre these, leaving plenty of freedom for an easy fit. Also, at midway in the length, cut and fit a stiffening piece of the same material as used for the thickening pieces. This fits tightly across the lid underneath, and is glued in.

When all the glue joints are hard, glasspaper the top surface of the lid, and clean off the edges nicely. We now have to consider what is to be done with the top surface. A cork slab is the best material to use, if it can be obtained in a suitable size; in fact, the entire box could be proportioned to fit the slab, allowing for the lid to project about ¾in. at each side beyond the body of the box. The slab should be kept in position by a strip of moulding fixed to the edge of and standing up about ¼in. above the lid.

Assuming that cork is out of the question, the next best thing is a piece of good linoleum in some neutral shade and having no pronounced pattern. This is glued lown to the top of the lid, and finished off by a strip of bead mitred around the edge, as in the case of the cork slab, but not standing up nearly so high (see Fig. 10). The beading should be fixed first, before gluing in the lino, though the latter may be cut and fitted beforehand. When cutting pieces of material, wood, lino, glass, etc., always mark the top edge and one side edge by chalk marks. It is seldom that a piece of woodwork is dead square; therefore, having fitted a panel, always replace it in the same position as that for which it was fitted and marked; top, right-hand side, etc.

Good paint or enamel will make a nice finish for the bathroom box; this is preferable to varnish or polish in a situation exposed to dampness. If odd pieces of wood from boxes are used for the floor of the box, they can be covered over by a piece of lino, or even

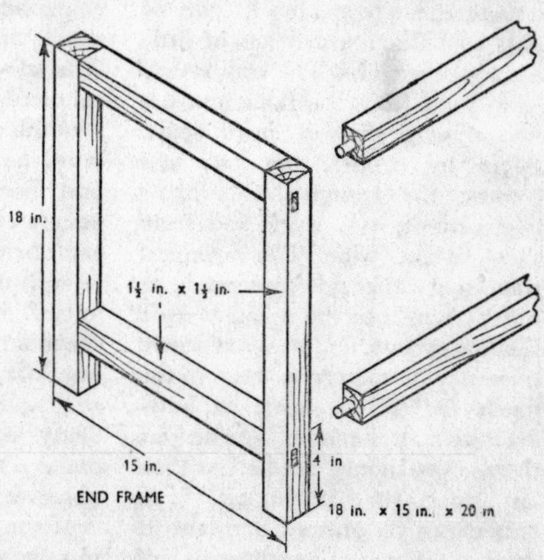

Fig. 9. Part frame and joint construction of cabinet.

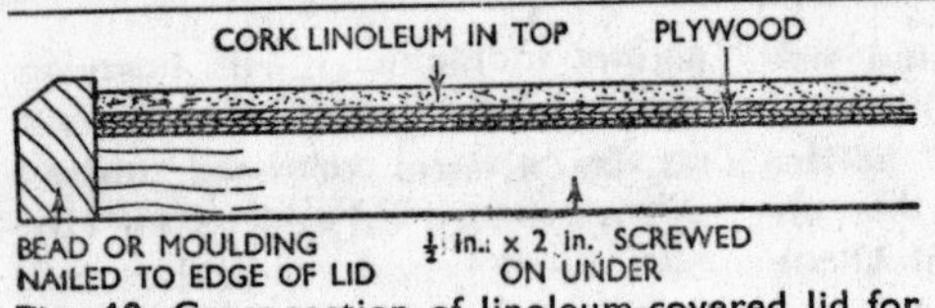

Fig. 10. Cross-section of linoleum-covered lid for the bathroom cabinet or box. Cut linoleum to exact size and secure in position with glue.

stiff packing paper. Two stout brass hinges, or a continuous strip of hinge as used for cabinets, can be fixed at the back edge. The amateur may find the continuous hinge easier to deal with, as the alignment is not so difficult.

The same style of box can be used for a lady's workbox, altering the dimensions, making the shape more of a square, and lining the inside with some simple padding. The bathroom cabinet as here described, will stand reasonable treatment, though obviously, with such thin plywood for the covering, it should not be subjected to rough handling.

Vegetable Rack.—This (see Figs. 11 and 12) being an open structure, can be made with narrow slats or boards which are of little use for other jobs. The rack stands 22in. high from the floor and has two sloping shelves, 10in. apart. Begin by making the two end frames; the uprights should be two battens, 1in. thick and from 1½in. to 2in. wide. The strongest way to fix the side bearers is to notch them into the uprights by a shallow groove, and to screw them; they may be merely screwed to the inside face of the uprights, however, without notching. The bearers themselves should not be less than 1in. thick, so that the 2in. × 1in. batten can be utilized here also if desired. Connect each pair of uprights by cross-bars of 2in. × 1in. batten at top and bottom, so that the outside measurement across the end unit is 11in. These cross-bars can be screwed on without notching, on the outside of the ends; they will serve as handles for lifting the rack. Now for the shelf bearers. Do not make the slope too acute. If the worker has a fairly large set-square handy, 60 and 30 degrees, this will serve admirably for marking the angle of slope, which is approximately 30 degrees. Take the upright which is to be the *front* right-hand side one; measure down from the top end 2in. and mark a squared line across the *front* edge. At a point 10in. lower down, square another line across. These indicate the top edges of the bearers for the shelves (see Fig. 11).

If the batten is 2in. wide, a second line this distance below each of the existing marks is to be scored with a pencil on the front edge; adjust the marking to the exact width of the bearer wood. The left-hand unit is to be marked to agree with the right-hand one. Lay the set-square flat on the unit, with the slope pointing downward and backward, the foot of the square even with the front edge of the upright and level with the top pencil mark. Draw the line of angle. Shift the square to the second *top* mark, 12in. below the one just dealt with, and mark the sloping line there also. Lay a rule along each line, continuing the angle across the back upright, and pencil it there.

If the bearers are to be notched in a little, mark the width and saw out the notch. If to be merely screwed across, lay the cut pieces of batten even with the top line, after having bored two screw-holes in each end, and mark the uprights with a bradawl through these holes. Bore the uprights and insert the screws.

So far the two end units only have been assembled. The next thing is to connect them at the back by a pair of cross-bars cut from 2in. × 1in. batten and screwed on at the back, outside, at the top edge and near the bottom one. A useful width for the vegetable rack is 14in. overall, but this could be increased or diminished slightly to suit the place where the appliance is to stand. Fig. 12 is a front view of the rack. Procure a number of thin pieces of sound wood from packing cases, all the same thickness. Fix about four slats across the bearers from side to side to form the vegetable shelves. Bore holes and nail them on. A stouter slat ought to be screwed on at the front or open side of each shelf for strength.

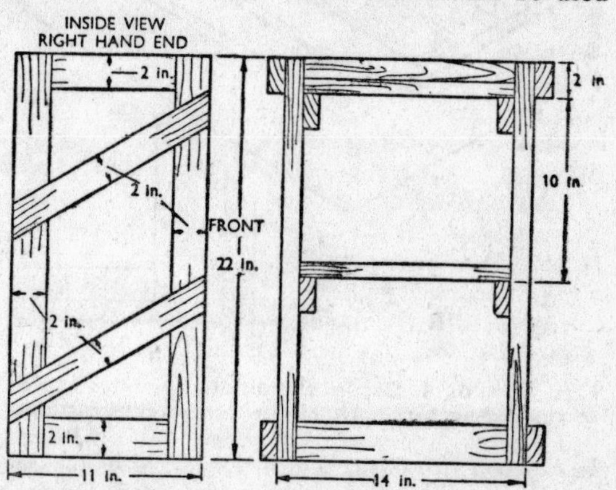

Figs. 11 and 12. End and front elevations of the framework and shelf supports for a vegetable rack.

All that remains now is to apply other slats to the sides and back of the rack, running vertically. If the framing has been done well, these slats will merely be used to prevent the contents of the rack from falling through, and need only be of quite thin wood. A rack of this description has done good service for six years, and is likely to last indefinitely. The main requirement is good sound joints in the rails and posts and bearers. The spaces between the slats should not be more than $\frac{3}{4}$in.

Seed Boxes and Trays.—Shallow boxes for starting seedlings are easily constructed from thin box material. If possible, the end pieces should be stout enough for the long side pieces to be nailed to the edges; failing this, and when only very thin wood is obtainable, angle pieces of square wood, about 1in. × 1in. in section can be used to unite the corners. A useful size is 8in. to 9in. × 12in. to 14in. for the sides, and a depth of 2in. to 3in. When only thin wood is used, a fillet of 1in. deal should be used to cleat the bottom boards together at the short sides, so that this thicker stuff can rest inside the box and the end pieces be nailed to it. If, however, the short sides can be formed of wood at least a full $\frac{1}{2}$in. thick, the sides and bottom boards can be nailed directly to the edges.

Trays for Fruit Storage.—Trays (see Figs. 13 and 14) about 20in. to 24in. long and 15in. to 18in. wide serve admirably for storing apples, etc. The bottoms are slatted with good openings between the slats to promote a free circulation of air. The slats can run the narrower way of the tray, so enabling short lengths of wood to be worked up. The sides should be 3in. high. The short ends ought to be of wood ¾in. thick, and the long sides of at least ½in. if the trays are to be made up without a framework.

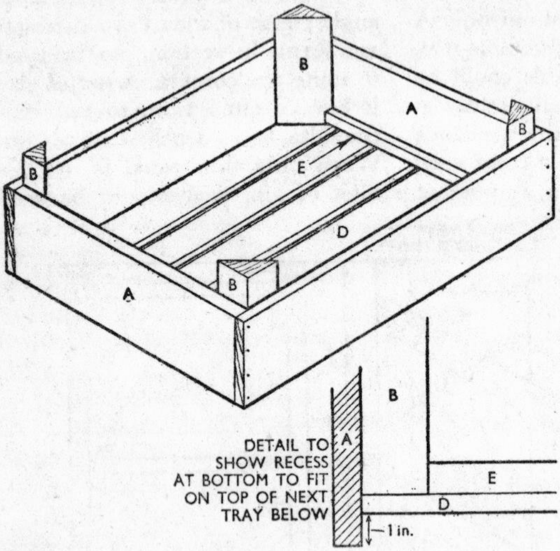

If the sides are made a little deeper, the trays can be arranged to stand on top of each other in a stack without the contents touching. The bottom of the tray in this case is fixed an inch up from the lower edge of the tray sides, forming a recess which fits on the top of pieces of square or triangular timber projecting up from the next tray lower down. All the trays must be made pretty closely to the same dimensions if this system is used. Instead of squared timber for the corners, triangular pieces cut from 2in. × 2in. square are best substituted. This makes a neater job inside the tray and leaves more room for the fruit. The triangular pieces can be cut by the worker himself from the ordinary quartering by sawing clean through from corner to corner diagonally down the piece.

Figs. 13 and 14. Details of fruit storage trays and a corresponding part view of the corner construction.

Fig. 13 shows one of the trays with the corner blocks projecting. A piece of ½in. × ¾in. deal should be nailed to the inside of the box to support the slats at each end, at such a height that the bottom of the tray is at least an inch from the bottom edge of the tray sides. The triangular corner blocks come down to this same level, with the slats below them and nailed at the corners to them. This is shown in the enlarged detail drawing (Fig. 14).

Converting Boxes into Useful Articles.—So far we have been considering boxes as material for re-making into various articles. Let us see what can be done with light boxes which are sound and can be used almost intact. Nail down loose boards; plane off rough edges and level up the top edge all round. The driving of a few more nails may help to strengthen the box, while the judicious use of a cross-brace or a diagonal brace will prevent "racking". A good way to stiffen up a box is to nail or screw braces across the bottom. When the box is to be made into a cupboard, this bottom becomes the back; the side which is placed downwards upon the floor should in that case also be stiffened with one or more cross-bars. Much depends on the size of the box; a fairly small one will be strong enough in itself if the boards are firmly fixed; a larger box will need additional support.

Useful Barrow for Garden.—This is made from a box about 18in. long by 11in. wide and 6in. deep (see Figs. 15 and 16). Strengthen it as suggested above. Steel corner pieces, as used for travelling boxes, can be affixed outside with short screws; use two angle plates for each corner, one at the top and another at the bottom. Stiffen up the bottom, and fix an axle tree cut from a piece of 2in. × 2in. deal; the two wheels are screwed into the ends. The axle tree is attached by two or three long screws which go through the bottom of the box from the inside, down into the 2in. × 2in. piece. Screws do not hold well in end grain, so the best thing to do here is to bore a larger hole to take a No. 9 Rawplug. Insert the plug into the end of the axle tree, and then proceed as for plugging a hole in the wall, that is, turn in the screw until the plug grips the sides of the hole. Put a steel washer under the wheel, between it and the end of the axle tree; another similar washer goes under the head of the screw, between it and the outer face of the wheel. The screws should be Gauge No. 9, round-head pattern, about 2½in. long.

The wheels are cut from wood at least an inch thick. Set a pair of compasses to a radius of 2½in. and describe a 5in. circle. If suitable wood is available a slightly bigger wheel will be an advantage. Cut the circle with a coping saw, and finish with a rasp. A keyhole saw can be

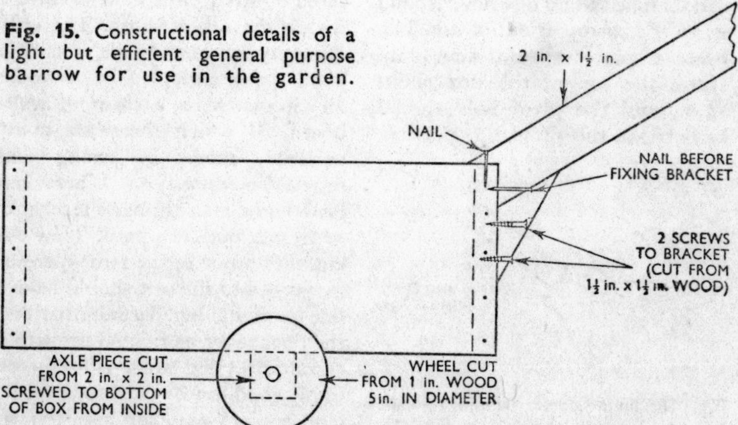

Fig. 15. Constructional details of a light but efficient general purpose barrow for use in the garden.

used, but will not cut so cleanly. The handle of the barrow is made from a piece of deal 2in. × 1½in. in section, cut to a "bird's-mouth" so that it fits tight to the top edge and front face of the box as shown in the diagram. Nails, or thin screws (Gauge No. 6), will secure the handle here. Underneath, a small shaped bracket (if made in oak it will last twice as long) is screwed to the box tight up under the handle; a short screw can be inserted last thing between the top of the bracket and the lower side of the handle.

The handle is shown fixed in the sloping position; if a swing-down handle is preferred it is easily arranged (see Fig. 16). Cut an oak bracket somewhat larger than the one shown, bird's-mouthed to the top edge and front face of the box, much as the former handle was fixed, but projecting outwards about 2in. This must be screwed very firmly to the box. The handle itself should be slotted to fit over the bracket, and a ¼in. bolt be put through a pivot hole made in the handle and the bracket. The handle can then be swung down horizontal when the barrow is out of use. The bracket piece should stand up above the top of the box about 1½in., and the pivot hole should be bored in this projecting portion.

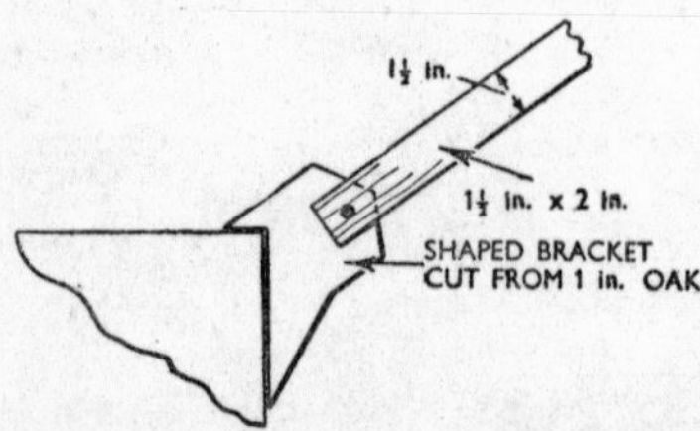

Fig. 16. Swing-down handle for the garden barrow shown in Fig. 15.

Child's Toy Truck.—Various toy trucks and wagons can be made out of small boxes, on the lines of the garden barrow described, altering the dimensions to suit the job. Metal wheels can be bought for these toys, or wood wheels can be cut from half-inch deal. Failing this, three thicknesses of thin plywood could be glued together and cut to shape with a fretsaw afterwards. Brightly coloured paint will transform a box into a toy that is sure to appeal to a child. The corners of the axle tree should be chamfered off, and the chamfer painted in a contrasting colour. The handle also should be chamfered.

Cupboards.—Fig. 17 shows a box 22in. high, 18in. wide, and 15in. deep. The idea is to fit two good shelves, and to close in the front with a simple door made from a piece of plywood to which a facing of 2in. × ½in. planed wood is screwed and glued for stiffening. The facing is shown fixed to the outer face of the door, but could just as well go inside. In the latter case a diagonal piece should be fitted tightly from corner to corner, within the other facing. The only difficulty here may be the procuring of a large enough piece of plywood; an alternative is a sheet of wallboard, of which there are many varieties, made in strong and durable compositions. These can be bought at a timber merchants or from a builder's yard. They are cut with a saw in the same manner as wood, but the saw should have a fine tooth. Failing these alternatives, the door must be framed up with a crossbar, so that two smaller pieces of plywood can be used to cover it, with a mock-panelled appearance.

The box as obtained will have a narrow edge; a thickening piece, of ¾in. deal must be cut and fitted to each long side, so that the door can be hinged to it. This thickening strip may be about 1½in. wide; it is screwed on, preferably by inserting the screws through the outer face of the box. Two shelves are shown, the top one less deep than the lower one, to give access easily. Cut and fix bearers for the shelves, again screwing them from the outside of the box.

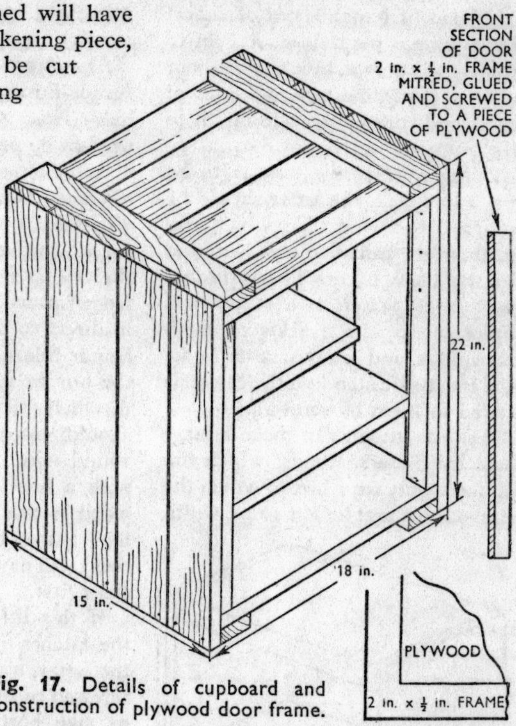

The door fits flat against the front of the box, and comes flush with the box sides. Fix a pair of hinges. As for a fastening, the simplest is a screw-eye inserted into the edge of the thickening piece so that the ring comes through a vertical slot cut in the door facing; a wood peg, or a split-pin attached to the door by a short piece of chain, can be put through the projecting eye to keep the door closed. The top of the cupboard can be made neat by tacking a piece of plywood or wallboard down between the two cleats. Alternatively, a "table-top" can be made by framing up a piece of either material (with a facing or thickening piece all round); the complete "top" is then screwed down to the cupboard. Details of the door are illustrated in part plan and end view in Fig. 17.

FRONT SECTION OF DOOR 2 in. x ½ in. FRAME MITRED, GLUED AND SCREWED TO A PIECE OF PLYWOOD

22 in.

18 in.

15 in.

PLYWOOD

2 in. x ½ in. FRAME

Fig. 17. Details of cupboard and construction of plywood door frame.

By the use of a similar box a meat-safe can be constructed. A large opening should be contrived at one side, so that a panel of perforated zinc can be affixed with a flat facing mitred around. The door should have a strong framework, preferably mortised and tenoned at the corners, though a well-made halved joint would pass muster. The perforated zinc with which the entire door front is covered can be tacked down at the back of the opening. A neat job will result if, over the edge of the zinc, a facing strip of ¼in. × 1in. deal (or plywood) is screwed to cover the joint. The meat-safe should be protected overhead (if it stands out of doors) by a simple penthouse or lean-to roof supported on brackets to shoot off the rain. The top and sides of the woodwork of the safe ought to be covered with good-quality roofiing felt. If the safe is to be fixed to a wall, the latter should be plugged to take screws which will go through "mirror-plates" screwed to the back of the box. Another way is to attach two stout steel brackets to the brickwork with Rawplugs and screws, and to let the meat-safe stand on the brackets (fixed to them by screws).

Do not attempt to make a large safe by these methods, which are suitable only for a box of which the dimensions are: height 18in., width 13in. and depth 12in. (approximately).

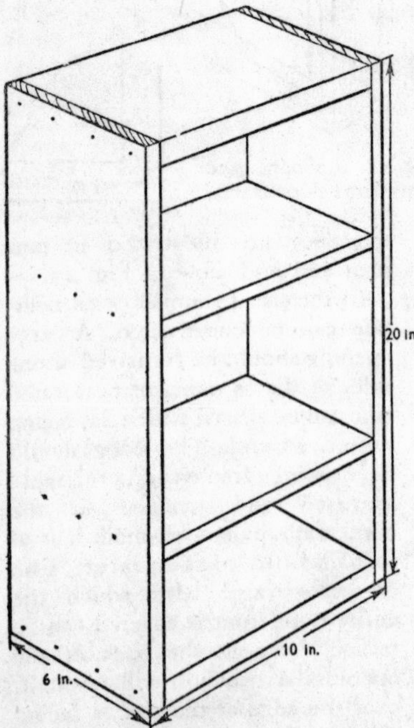

Fig. 18. General arrangement and dimensions for set of wall shelves over a sink, for kitchen utensils.

Shelves over Sink.—The simple fitment shown in Fig. 18 is made from a box in which starch used to be packed for the shops; it is 20in. long, by 10in. wide, and 6in. deep. There is little to do to it, after making sure all joints are sound, but to cut and fix the two shelves. If the shelves can be got from $\frac{3}{4}$in. wood they may be nailed in direct to the box sides, without bearer fillets. Square a line across the box to show the centre line of the shelf thickness, where the nails should enter. Nail in with $1\frac{1}{2}$in. round wire nails, boring all holes with a fine bradawl. If only thin wood is available for the shelves, four ledges or bearers to support them will have to be screwed to the sides first.

If this little fitment is fixed in the kitchen near the sink, or over the latter, a few cup-hooks can be screwed to the edges of the shelves to take bottle-brushes and other like implements for cleaning.

Blacking Box.—A small box can be made into a convenient blacking box, to contain boot brushes and polish tins, by fixing a central partition in which a handle has been cut. The box ought to be about 12in. long × 9in. wide and 4in. deep. The partition, which runs the long way of the box, can be cut from a piece of wood 7in. wide; bore two 1in. holes, on centres 3in. apart, and connect them by two horizontal saw-cuts to make the hand-hold. The partition is nailed to the two short sides of the box and also to the bottom. If a box, about 2in. wider can be obtained, it will be possible to fit two lids to cover the two compartments; hinge these to the partition at each side.

Knife Box.—A similar box can be made into a knife box, leaving the compartments open. It can be lined with green baize. Of course, the wood for this job must be sound and clean, and must be capable of a good finish. It may be left "white", for kitchen use, or it can be stained and varnished to "oak" shade. It is not worth while going to this trouble unless the raw material is sound, with a close grain, and able to be papered down nice and smooth.

General Hints for Second-hand Timber.—At builders' yards and similar places it is often possible to buy used fitments and joinery which are quite good for re-use where utility is the primary consideration. Doors and frames, window sashes and such-like, are examples. Look out for serious defects such as warped or twisted frames, which often render the fitment practically useless. As for second-hand timber, much material may be obtained which will do for fences, outhouses and similar work. When it comes to materials for indoor joinery and better-class jobs, there is less chance of picking up bargains. Generally, look out for nails (which may have broken off and left a part almost invisible in the timber). Before sawing or planing once-used timber, especially if it has been painted, examine it minutely for possible nails or screws in the line of the tool.

Nails which unite two pieces of wood can sometimes be severed by a hacksaw cut between the two pieces, thus freeing the joint. A nail which refuses to be drawn out can often be punched right through the wood, or pinched out when it protrudes far enough. Obdurate screws can be eased by pouring a little paraffin on the screw-head and leaving it for some hours. It may be easier to get the screw to turn if it is first attempted to drive it in farther by a clockwise turn or part-turn of the screwdriver; this will often break down the adhesion caused by corrosion, so that the screw can then be moved a little in the unscrewing direction. If the slot is choked up, try to true it by using a thin flat file on it, or scrape it clean with some pointed tool. A smart blow with a hammer on a cold chisel rested in the slot will often start a screw that refuses to budge. The paraffin soaking ought to be tried first before other methods, as if it succeeds, the screw will come out without damaging the timber.

When metal fittings are to be removed and the screws have rusted in, try to prize off the fitting if it is not in such good order that it is worth preserving. The heads of round-head screws which fix latches, etc. to gates can be chipped off by using a small and sharp cold chisel. Sometimes a hacksaw blade, taken out of its frame, can be got in between two metal parts to give the few cuts needed to sever a screw. When the head of a screw has broken off and the shank stands up enough to be gripped, file a flat on two opposite sides, and grip the shank with a hand-vice, by which usually it can be turned. If the shank is level with or below the surface of the wood, cut away the wood carefully with a gouge until enough of the shank is accessible to get a vice or pliers on the job.

SECTION THREE

FURNITURE CARE AND REPAIR

Upholstery

RENOVATING the upholstery of chairs, sofas, and settees is one of the jobs which may be tackled very satisfactorily by the home craftsman.

It should be noted, however, that this article does not deal with the extensive repairs to framework and upholstery which, properly speaking, are the province of the skilled upholsterer, but with the repair of minor defects.

Equipment.—A hammer, screwdriver or old chisel, pincers, an upholsterer's needle, and an appliance for stretching the new webbing tightly are all the tools required. The necessary materials are hessian and springs (where replacement of either is required), webbing, and a ball of good quality twine. A packet of ½in. tacks completes the list, except for such covered studs, brass head nails and ornamental binding as may be necessary to match the design or ornamentation of the article being repaired. If an upholsterer's needle is unobtainable, a packing needle such as that shown in Fig. 1 will do perfectly well. Buy the very best quality webbing you can get, as the success of the work will largely depend upon the strength and durability of this item. The twine should be real upholsterer's twine, and any extra effort expended in procuring the genuine article will be well repaid in both the strength of the finished job and the ease with which it is accomplished.

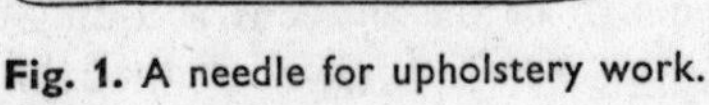

PACKING NEEDLE

Fig. 1. A needle for upholstery work.

The life of the twine will be considerably lengthened if it is drawn firmly across a lump of beeswax before use. The beeswax not only protects the twine from deterioration but discourages rust where the knots secure the springs.

For the purpose of these instructions it is assumed that the article for repair is an ordinary settee, but the method of working applies equally in the case of easy chairs or any of the more usual items of upholstered furniture.

Repairs.—The first operation is the removal of the canvas cover on the under side. Turn the settee upside down, supporting the centre of the seat on a chair (see Fig. 2). Release the tacks holding the canvas in place and remove it completely. If it is still strong and undamaged, lay it aside to be used again, but if it is faulty, measure it carefully for replacement.

To remove tacks from canvas and webbing, hold an old screwdriver or old chisel against the edge of the head of the tack and give it one or two sharp blows with the hammer. Be careful to sweep up all the tacks later as they are dangerous to the worker when kneeling at the settee during later stages of the work.

The webbing with the springs attached will now be exposed. Unless the repair consists of the

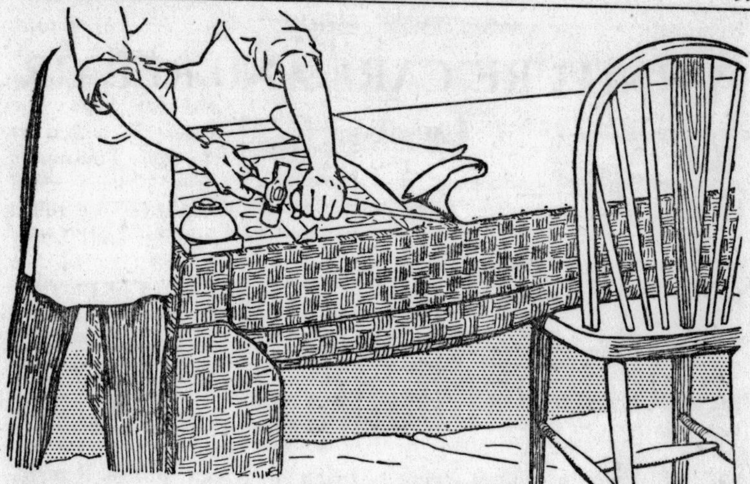

Fig. 2. Shows method of removing the canvas undercover from the bottom of a settee. Use an old screwdriver or similar tool to loosen the tacks.

replacement or re-fixing of just one or two faulty springs, it is advisable to replace the whole of the webbing. Release the tacks securing the webbing to the frame of the settee and cut loose the twine securing the springs. Make a careful note at this stage of the method used by the upholsterer to tie the springs in place. A typical method is illustrated in Fig. 3.

Next turn the settee back to its normal position and release the top cover all along the front of the settee and turn it back, complete with the stuffing. It will be necessary, of course, to remove first the covered studs, brass head nails, or other ornamental fixing, together with any gimp or binding employed. Lay aside specimens of all these for use when selecting replacement patterns.

The released springs should now be examined for wear and distortion. Take an old spring to the upholsterer's shop when ordering new ones, which are quite cheap. It may be necessary to buy a different size of spring from the original to allow for the results of long compression of the remaining springs.

Now for the front edge of the settee. It is assumed that this is boxed with suitably padded wood. Repairing a sprung edge is rather beyond the capabilities of the amateur, but it may be fairly simply modified by a wood frame and then treated as a boxed edge.

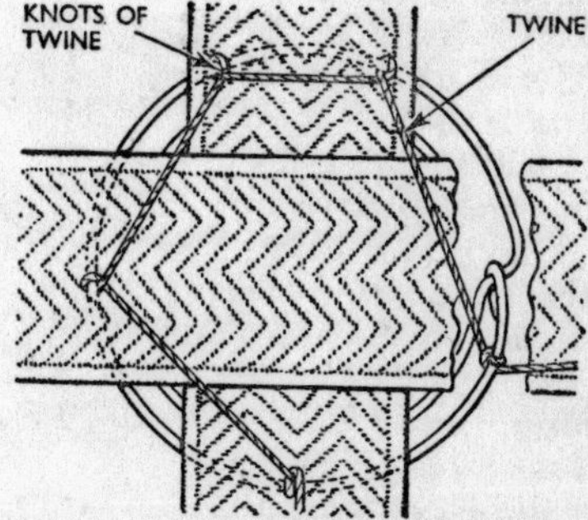

Fig. 3. A typical method of tying the springs to the webbing. Note knots.

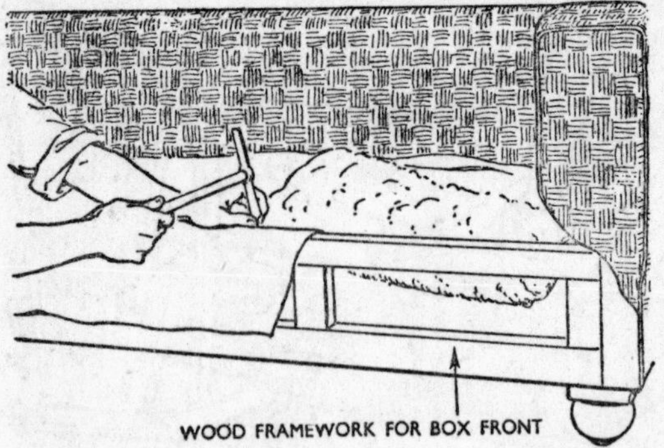

Fig. 4. A settee with box front, showing canvas being tacked in position in preparation for a rolled edge.

Fig. 4 shows a typical frame.

At this stage in the work it is convenient to examine the joints of the frame for any looseness or weakness. Ordinarily, these may be made good by gluing and screwing. A point to remember here is that when re-gluing any joint the old glue must first be completely removed, or failure will result.

When it is seen that the frame is satisfactory, cut a strip of new canvas or hessian about 5 or 6in. wide and the length of the front. Double back about 1in. of this, and firmly secure it to the top member of the front frame with tacks. A length of twine is now loosely tacked close to the tacked edge of the strip of canvas to act both as a guide, and a support to the stuffing for the rolled edge it is desired to form (see Fig. 5). Take the old stuffing, if you are re-using it, and beat it with a stick to loosen it and give an even texture, then form it into a roll by tucking it in and around the twine which is tacked at the edge. The canvas strip is then turned back over the rolled stuffing and firmly fixed to the top member of the front frame. The first operations are illustrated in Fig. 4.

Turn the settee bottom upwards so as to facilitate the fixing of any new springs. Remember, also, to strengthen the fixing of the old springs where necessary. The new springs should be secured exactly on the site of the old ones which they are to replace, and securely stitched. Note that in all good class work the springs are not only strongly secured to the canvas underside of the top cover, but are also tied to each other to prevent any chance of slipping. Examine the fixing of all springs which are to remain, and re-stitch firmly wherever it is necessary.

Fig. 5. View of box front settee, illustrating the making of a rolled edge with canvas and stuffing.

The new webbing may now be fixed in place. Since this bears the whole weight of the person using the settee, it is obvious that it must be firmly secured. Double back 1in. to 2in. of the webbing and secure it by three or four tacks to the site of the first cross strip. The outside end of the webbing is first fixed by

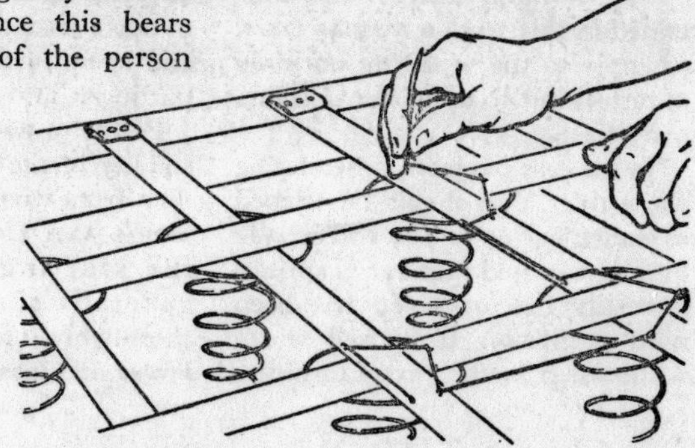

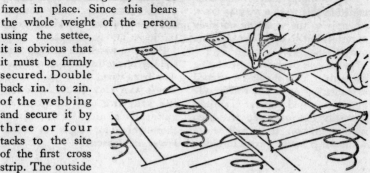

Fig. 6. Stitching the springs to the webbing of the settee.

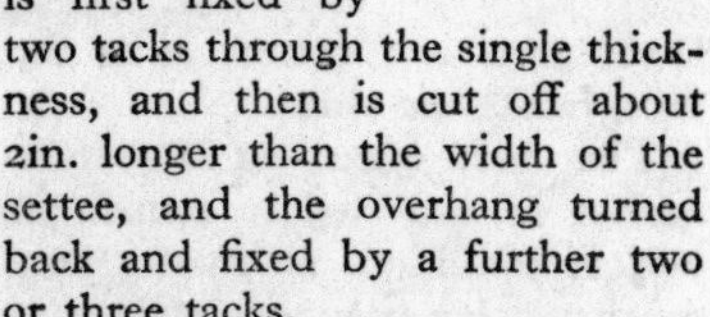

two tacks through the single thickness, and then is cut off about 2in. longer than the width of the settee, and the overhang turned back and fixed by a further two or three tacks.

Continue this process from end to end of the settee until all the cross strips are in place. Those from end to end of the settee are then fixed. Note that they are threaded alternately, over and under the cross strips.

The springs are now stitched into position at the intersections of the webbing (see Fig. 6). During this stitching, the string is joined in one continuous length from spring to spring throughout the whole job.

Now stand the settee back on its legs for the next stage, the replacement of the cover over the boxed front. The canvas lining is first stretched down and secured to the frame. Then the stuffing is carefully arranged and spread evenly over the rolled edge, the top cover drawn down and fixed (see Fig. 7). The edge of the cover is hidden by leather binding in the case of a leather or rexine settee, or by gimp in the case of a plush, velour, or similar-covered fabric settee. Suitable ornamental nails are used. With the fixing of the canvas over the springs and webbing on the underside, the work is complete.

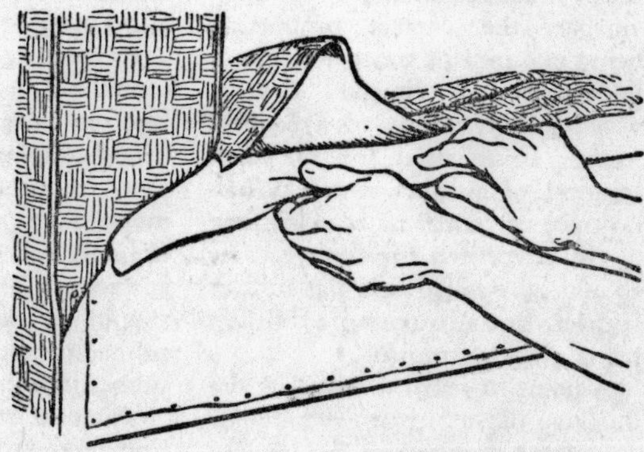

Fig. 7. Arranging the stuffing and canvas for the rolled edge preparatory to re-fitting of the settee cover.

The working instructions contained in this section may be taken to apply to the repairing not only of settees but to upholstered chairs and sofas.

In the case of chairs, when fixing the springs, they should be stitched as shown in Fig. 6. You will usually find that an odd number of springs normally five or seven has been used originally. It is well worth while when needing extra furniture of this kind to take the opportunity to buy a secondhand article cheaply and spend a few leisure hours in putting it into good repair.

Points to watch are strength and solidity of the framework and fredom from wood decay (see WOODWORM AND DRY ROT). Similarly, the stuffing and upholstery generally should be examined thoroughly, for signs of moth larvae and insects.

Furniture Upkeep

THE preservation of furniture depends chiefly on regular dusting and polishing and a good furniture polish applied by vigorous rubbing with a clean, napless cloth: for a high gloss not only looks good but preserves the wood. Apply the polish sparingly and thoroughly rub the surfaces with the cloth.

Cleaning Furniture.—A table or other piece of furniture which has become grimed cannot be expected to respond to any ordinary polishing. Grease and dirt must first be removed, by washing with warm water containing a very little vinegar, the correct proportion being one pint of warm water to a tablespoon of vinegar. Several washings may be needed, a chamois leather being used for the final removal of surplus water. When no trace of dampness remains, one of the advertised furniture creams should be applied and the surface lished, subsequent polishing being a weekly routine.

A point to remember is that the dusting of a room should be completed throughout before any polishing commences. Equal attention should be paid to the legs and lower parts of furniture as to the tops, fronts and sides.

The best piece of furniture cannot be expected to remain in perfect condition, no matter how much regular attention is given to it, if exposed to conditions which were never visualized by its makers. These include heat and damp. Too close proximity to a fire or radiator will induce warping or splitting of even the soundest wood. A consistently damp room can prove equally ruinous. The consequences of damp conditions are described under the heading of WOODWORM AND DRY ROT.

Removing Water Stains.—It sometimes happens that a tabletop, too close to an open window, becomes splashed by rain. In this case, moisture should first be mopped up with a clean cloth or chamois leather, and as soon as the surface is thoroughly dry the cream should be liberally applied and rubbed in, the surplus being finally rubbed off.

There is danger of water-stains from porous pottery vases or jugs or bowls used for flower display. Unless a vessel is of china, glass, or

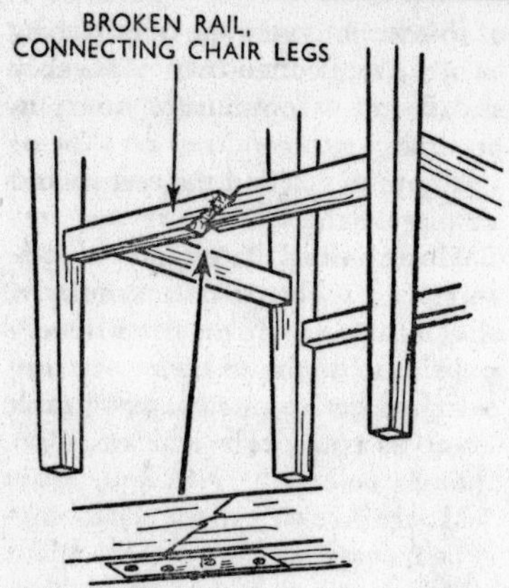

Fig. 1. Mending a broken chair rail by the use of a flat metal plate.

metal it should always be regarded with a doubtful eye as to its water-tightness. It is safer to put such vessels on a stand, such as a china saucer or a glass dish. If water-stains occur they can be erased when dry by extra vigorous rubbing with the polishing cloth. Stains of any kind which are not removed by treatment will generally respond to petrol, lighter fuel, or benzine, applied with a wad of clean cloth. When all signs of the marks have vanished, polishing in the ordinary way should leave the area spotless. If the stains (not ink-stains) are deep-seated the following alternative method, used with careful discretion, may be employed. Wrap a small wad of cotton-wool in a square of clean napless cloth, 2in. square. Apply a little methylated spirits to the pad and lightly rub the pad over the stain, using a regular circular motion. Do *not* apply an excessive quantity of methylated spirits and if the pad shows any signs of sticking add one drop of linseed oil to the face of the pad. See also the article dealing with Polishes and Polishing for details of polishing technique.

Table mats should always be used on polished dining tables to prevent heat from plates and dishes penetrating to the wood, and causing unsightly marks. Vigorous rubbing with a soft cloth, after the application of cream, is needed to remove them. Scratches cannot be removed, other than with a plane, but they can be made less obvious, in the case of dark wood, by rubbing into the affected surface a little dark brown boot polish and then briskly rubbing the spot with a soft cloth.

Removing Marks.—Dents in polished surfaces call for painstaking attention. They should be carefully filled with methylated spirit, and then a hot flat-iron should be held just above, as close as can be contrived without scorch-

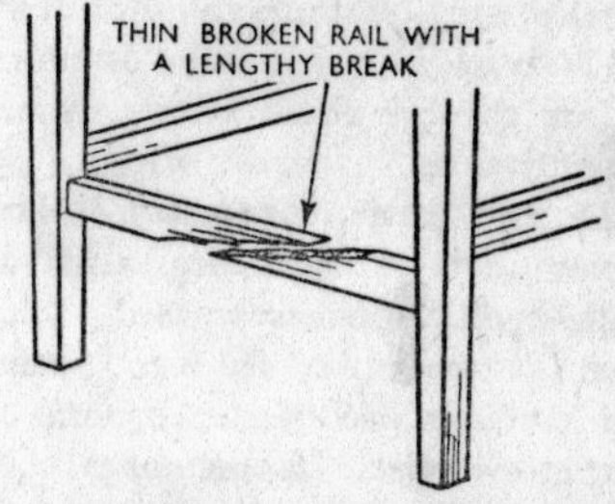

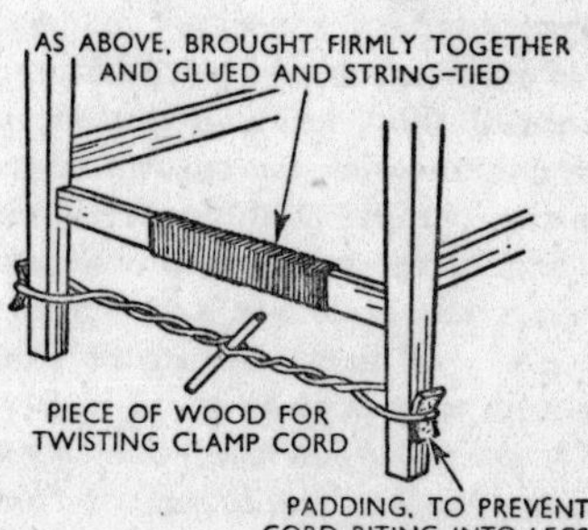

Fig. 2. Another method of mending a chair rail. Remove tourniquet after glue has thoroughly dried.

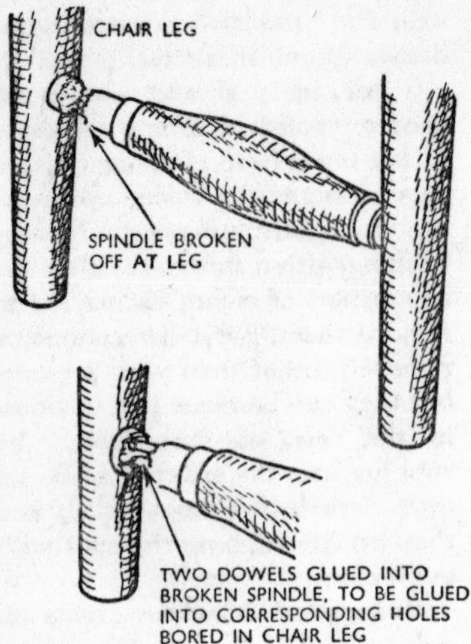

Fig. 3. Repairing a leg spindle by the use of two dowels inserted at break.

ing the wood. The heat thus applied should "draw up" the base of the dent. This treatment may need to be repeated once or twice before the blemish entirely disappears.

Dents and Scratches.—The lower parts of furniture, such as table-legs, bookcases and sideboards, are often damaged from the careless use of the broom or carpet-sweeper. If the corners of these appliances are not padded, this omission should be rectified. A piece of thick but soft leather, or similar material, nailed or screwed to the corners and edges of the broom or carpet-sweeper will prevent many a knock and scratch. A piece of heavy furniture close enough to a door to stand in peril of impact damage when the door is flung open can be safeguarded from injury by a door-stop screwed to the floor a couple of inches from the possible point of contact. The stop can be contrived with the aid of a disused cotton-reel if the shop article is not obtainable, the protruding rims of the reel being neatly removed and the reel stained or painted.

Unpolished Furniture.—The foregoing applies to a shiny surface, that is, one which has been french-polished by the makers. An unpolished deal-topped kitchen table deserves equal care and attention, though polishing cloth and cream will here give way to the scrubbing-brush, soap, and hot water. Stains which prove obstinate on a plain deal top can be shifted by dry-scrubbing, using a dry scrubbing-brush and very fine sand.

Cane Seats.—Chairs with cane seats need to have their pleasing appearance maintained by keeping the cane free from dust. An occasional scrubbing of the cane may be necessary, with hot water in which has been dissolved a little salt, a tablespoonful of the latter to each quart of water used. The scrubbed cane should then be dried off with a clean cloth and the chair placed out in the open (weather permitting, of course) for the drying to be completed naturally.

Leather Upholstery.—This furniture soon becomes dusty in corners, and the tucked-in areas. The dust should be got at with a stiff brush, and the leather occasionally washed with a mixture consisting of a tablespoonful of vinegar to a pint of hot water. The leather must not be made too wet, and it needs to be dried off promptly with a clean cloth. All-over washing may not be necessary, and attention may be restricted to the soiled areas. When the leather has dried, the job is completed by polishing with a little furniture cream.

Loose Joints.—These need to be looked for during the weekly attention. Chair legs and rails cannot be expected to remain firm for ever, and if any suspicion of looseness in the joints is neglected, strain is likely to be thrown on the piece as a whole, and what was a simple repair becomes a major operation. A great deal can be done with a little glue, and with angle-pieces, or flat metal plates, in effecting repairs.

Broken Chairs.—A chair rail that has cracked or snapped can be secured by means of a flat metal plate (most ironmongers have a selection of both these and angle-pieces) screwed to grip securely along both sides or surfaces of the breakage. It may not be possible to sink the flat plate in the wood, but if the thickness of the latter does allow of it this should be done; see Fig. 1.

If the broken rail or spindle is too thin, or its shape unsuited, for this flat plate attachment, the broken surfaces should be glued, brought together as closely as possible and there secured with a thin screw, or with two screws if there is space for these. Where only gluing is practicable, pressure should be brought to bear by means of a piece of thick cord carried around the extremities and the ends secured tightly, see Fig. 2.

Where this clamping-cord passes round chair legs these should be saved from bruising or denting by padding the angles with thick card-board or pieces of rag. When the encircling cord has been stretched tightly and knotted, the pressure is increased by twisting with a piece of wood inserted between the doubled cord, as shown.

A spindle that has broken off may be refixed by means of simple dowels and glue, see Fig. 3. Or it may be possible to dispense with dowels and use instead a long screw, the screw head being countersunk in the seat or other part through which it passes. Where surfaces are flat, secure joins can be effected with angle pieces or brackets (see Fig. 4). If possible, these metal brackets should be placed where they are not visible; and neatness of repair is enhanced if the brackets are as thin as is consistent with strength, and if they are sunk flush with the wood, a job for a sharp chisel. Screw holes should be bored, to reduce strain while the screws are being worked home, and to lessen the possibility

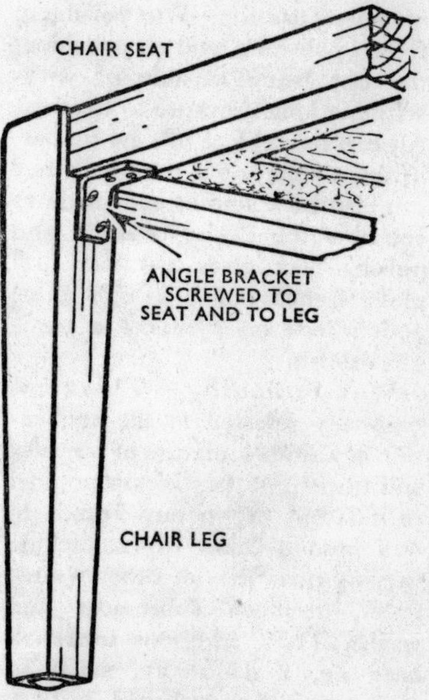

Fig. 4. Strengthening a seat rail.

of splitting wood at the joints.

A long break in a spindle or leg can be joined with glue, the parts then being bound round tightly with string until the glue has set, as previously described. The string is then removed, and fine screws inserted as reinforcement, the heads being well sunk and then concealed with a wood stopping or filling. The latter is sold plain, or ready stained, in tubes at the ironmonger's. This stopping is suitable also for filling in cracks generally, and for taking the place of chipped-out pieces which have become lost and so cannot be glued back into place.

Polishes and Polishing

POLISHING may be employed to produce varying degrees of gloss according to the type of medium used. All must rely to some extent upon friction for the final levelling and smoothing of surfaces treated, but perfect uniformity of gloss will also depend (as in painting) upon the checking of excessive porosity of the surface.

The three methods of polishing in general use are:—Wax polishing, french polishing, and oil polishing, the last being capable of withstanding long exposure to weather. All can be applied to new timber, or upon stain; or if required, they can also be coloured and made to combine the duties of stain and polish. Wax gives a rather dull gloss; french polish a high gloss; and linseed oil produces a semi-gloss finish.

Wax Polishing.—This term originally referred to the application of a simple mixture of beeswax and turpentine, but is now applied to different proprietary brands of wax base polishes which include varying quantities of other waxes, gums, resinous substances and spirits. These additions to a wax base do, undoubtedly, assist in obtaining a fine polished surface, but the simple beeswax base possesses a characteristic gloss which has its attractions. Although it is often more convenient to purchase a ready-made compound, the preparation of wax polish is simple; precautions must be taken to prevent the ingredients catching fire. A good method is to shred the beeswax into an earthenware jam jar, using just sufficient to half fill the vessel, place the jar in a pan half filled with water and heat over a low flame until the wax melts. Any tendency to boil over can be countered by the immediate removal of the pan away from the flame.

Take the jar of melted wax out of doors, or at least well away from any naked flame before adding the turpentine (or turpentine substitute). This should be added in the proportion of one part of turpentine to two of wax, the mixture being stirred well, and the jar should then be covered to prevent loss by evaporation.

Wax polish imparts a smooth, hard-wearing finish to new hardwood floors or furniture, but several coats rubbed well into the woodwork at daily intervals are required before the best results are obtained. When the more porous softwoods have to be treated, it is advisable to apply a preliminary coat of raw linseed oil (mixed with driers), or a coat of oil stain, in order to reduce excessive porosity. Such work is often carried a stage further and varnished prior to wax polishing; see VARNISHING, p. 179.

It is well to remember that surfaces finished with wax polish cannot be varnished or french polished unless one is prepared to tackle the difficult job of completely removing every trace of wax.

Oil Polishing.—Although the process is not widely known and has the disadvantage of being rather tedious and slow, it produces an extremely tough and durable finish particularly suitable for new hardwoods. Preparation consists of filling holes with plastic wood, sand-papering the whole surface and finally removing all dust.

The oil is prepared by mixing half a pint of refined linseed oil with one tablespoonful of liquid driers. This is applied sparingly with a piece of clean rag, giving about four applications at weekly

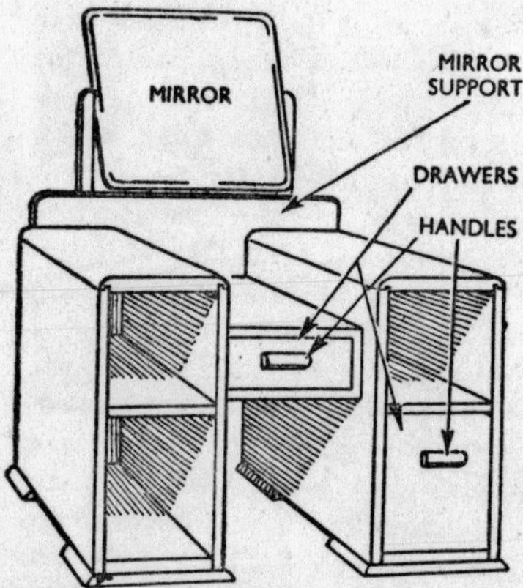

Fig. 1. Shows examples of parts to be removed in preparation for polishing.

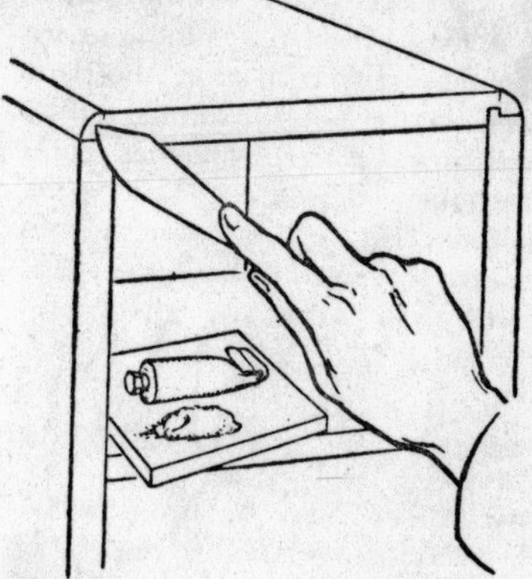

Fig. 2. Shows the method of applying stopping to holes and gaps in the wood.

intervals. The final coat is rubbed briskly to produce a gloss which, when hard, is capable of withstanding hot dinner plates.

French Polishing.—While absolute perfection in this craft demands considerable experience, there are many amateurs quite capable of producing a good finish upon straightforward work. Given the right working conditions and materials, any beginner should make good progress, in a few hours.

Conditions of dryness and warmth are of great importance. A cold draught, or damp atmosphere is almost sure to cause French polish to dry with a permanent whitish bloom, or with considerable loss of brilliance.

Brown french polish should be prepared from the very best quality orange shellac, or button lac. White french polish should be made from the best bleached shellac. Both can be bought prepared.

A stock mixture contains 4 to 5 oz. of shellac for brown french polish dissolved in one pint of methylated spirit or industrial

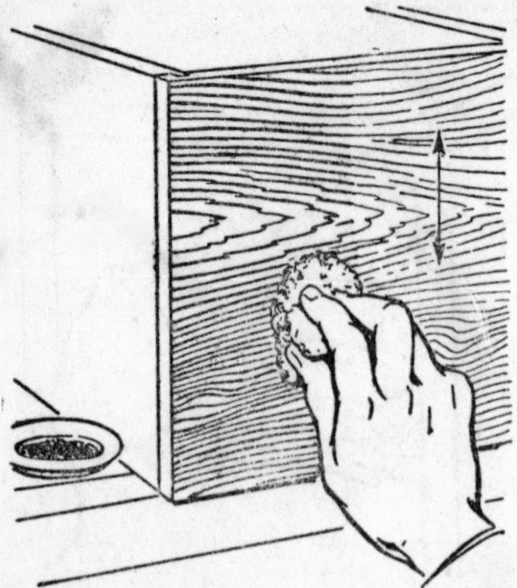

Fig. 3. Applying grain filling to the wood. Use the rubber across the grain.

alcohol. The standard mixture for white french polish contains approximately 6 oz. shellac dissolved in one pint of methylated spirit or industrial alcohol.

If the polish is to be brush-applied, the addition of one or two ounces of gum benzoin, or sandarac, will improve the gloss. The resin dissolves in about 24 hours, after which time the mixture is sieved through muslin, and bottled.

Other requisites will vary according to the demands of each class of work, but a fairly complete stock includes the following:—spirit stains, water stains, methylated spirit, plastic wood, grain filler, No. 00 sandpaper, refined linseed oil, camel hair mops, cotton wool, and clean calico, the last two being required to make rubbers for the application of the french polish.

New Woodwork.—Preparation of surfaces and polishing are generally carried out in clearly defined stages, in the following sequence:—(a) stopping and smoothing down, (b) staining, (c) grain filling (essential with open grained and soft woods), (d) oiling in, (e) bodying up, (f) spiriting off. Both new and old work should, as far as possible, be dismantled, handles and other obstructions being removed to allow free play for the rubber. See Fig. 1.

Stopping.—Cracks and nail holes may be stopped or filled up with plastic wood (see Fig. 2), which hardens so rapidly as to permit a general glasspapering of the surface within half an hour. Always rub in the direction of the grain, using a flat block of cork inside the glasspaper. If this fails to level the surface, a carpenter's scraper must be employed. Either method will clean as well as smooth the work, but any rust or ink-stains will have to be bleached out by several applications of oxalic acid solution.

Staining.—Chemical staining, of considerable value as a means of darkening the softer parts of wood grain, thereby increasing contrast,

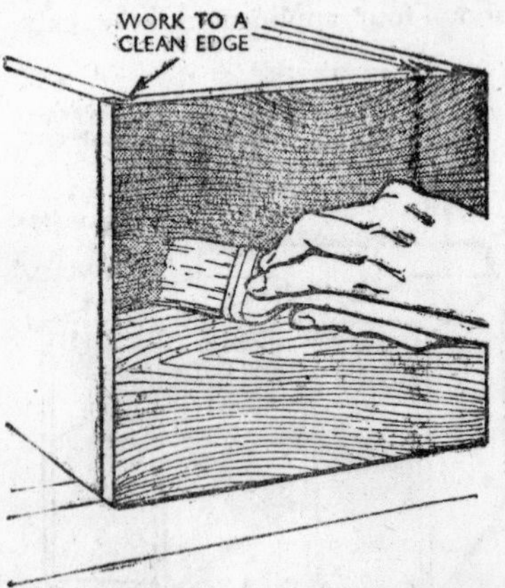

Fig. 4. When applying the first coats by brush, lay on with the run of the grain and work to a neat clean edge.

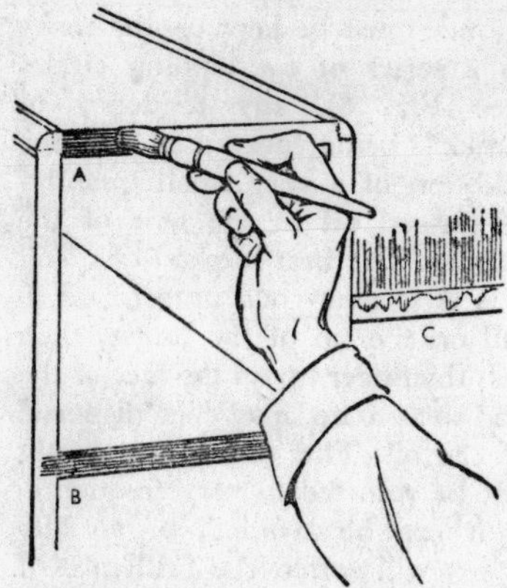

Fig. 5. Applying stain to narrow edges, at A and B. Do not overload the brush or the stain will dribble as at C.

may be used as an alternative to the ordinary water stain but it may also precede the application of a water stain. The usual materials dissolved in warm water, are (a) washing soda, (b) Epsom salts, (c) lime, (d) ammonia, or (e) bichromate of potash. The staining intensity of the solution of one or other of these materials should be determined by testing, and altering the proportion of water or stain material to suit.

Water stains are available in several forms, chief of which are the ready-prepared powder colours, alkaline dyes, concoctions of tea, coffee, saffron, turmeric, etc.; and the slightly opaque vandyke brown, mahogany lake, burnt sienna, etc. They may be applied with either a brush or a sponge.

Spirit stains, obtainable in powder form, are dissolved as required in methylated spirit. These have the advantages of being quick drying and deep penetrating and can also be used to colour french polish. A soft brush should be employed for the application of spirit stain, the work being covered a section at a time, and particular care being taken to finish off neatly and squarely at each joint, without overlapping upon the adjoining section. See Fig. 5.

Grain Filling.—Where the timber has open pores, it is quicker to fill these with grain filler, rather than with repeated coats of polish. A reliable composition is made from whiting, turpentine, and an appropriate colouring matter such as umber, raw sienna, mahogany lake, etc., which may be in either powder form or ground in linseed oil. Mix to a creamy consistency and rub well into and across the grain, using clean rag as a rubber (see Fig. 3). Surplus filler should be removed by fine sandpaper.

Oiling In.—This simply involves a sparing application of linseed oil to check excessive

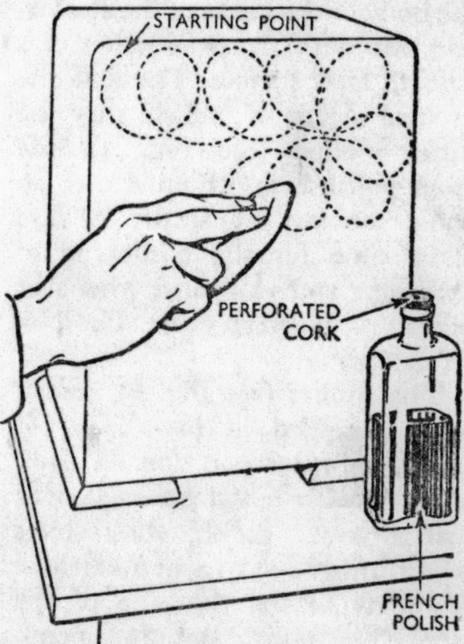

Fig. 6. Shows the direction and motion to be followed by the rubber when applying the final coats of french polish.

Fig. 7. Shows the direction in which the rubber is to be used when spiriting off.

porosity of the dry filler, a clean rubber being employed for the purpose.

Bodying Up.—This stage is mainly concerned with building up the body or thickness of the shellac, and also with the production of a smooth level surface. The first one or two coats of polish may be brush-applied (see Fig. 4), the stock polish being thinned with an equal amount of spirit. Always allow time for the hardening of each coat, and sandpaper whenever necessary, between coats. Use No. 00 sandpaper.

The rubber (see Fig. 6), cotton wool, wrapped in two layers of calico, is employed for all later coats. This is fed at intervals with half strength polish, the rubber being unwrapped to permit these additions to the top side of the wool. The polish can thus penetrate slowly and evenly to the face of the rubber, enabling it to be used in a semi-dry condition. The rubber must be kept on the move in a series of overlapping circles (see Fig. 6), any tendency to "stick" being prevented by the addition of a very small quantity of linseed oil to the face of the rubber. The best method of doing this is to allow one drop of oil to fall on the tip of the finger, then rub the finger tip on the face of the pad so as to make an even dispersal of the oil. This procedure should not be resorted to very frequently if it can be avoided, or an oily sheen will soften the brilliance of the finished surface.

Spiriting Off.—A separate rubber charged with quarter strength polish and applied in long strokes following the direction of the grain, should remove any rubber marks and produce a uniform gloss (see Fig. 7). The work is then finished with a clean rubber barely moistened with spirit only.

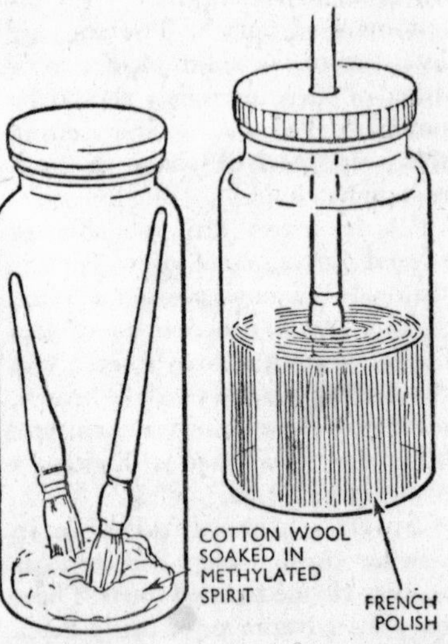

Fig. 8. Store brushes as shown. Single brushes in regular use may be suspended in the polish if the jar is sealed.

Old Surfaces.—These are prepared by washing with a warm solution of washing soda, followed by a rinse of clean water. Repair small defects with plastic wood and touch up with coloured polish. The work is then bodied up with the rubber, using slightly coloured polish to restore richness of hue. Store brushes as in Fig. 8.

Laying and Repairing Linoleum

NEW linoleum is usually fitted by professionals employed by the retailers of the material, but when one is changing room furniture, etc., and when moving house, the programme generally includes taking up and re-laying linoleum.

This is not a difficult business, but, on the other hand, it is not as simple as might be supposed from watching experts at the job.

A knife with a stiff blade is needed, and it must be sharp. A shoemaker's knife is excellent for the purpose, and it may be bought for a shilling or so; a broken table-knife, properly ground at the point, is a good substitute. Knives, specially designed for cutting linoleum are, of course, generally available, but the amount of this kind of work in the ordinary household hardly justifies the purchase of a special knife. A wood straight-edge is indispensable as a guide for long straight cuts. A tack hammer is required, and an ounce or two of those small headless brads used by shoemakers.

Begin by examining the floor boards for faults. First, the heads of protruding nails should be punched down, and all tacks extracted. Then see that the boards are flush, using the plane where necessary.

If the floor is of cement, fill in any holes or cracks with a mixture of one part cement to three or four parts of sand. Wet the holes thoroughly first, then fill them in flush and allow the cement to harden and dry before laying the linoleum. Linoleum should never be laid on a damp surface or it will be liable to rot. On wooden floors put down one or two layers of the specially made thick felt paper under the linoleum. Not only will this level out any unevenness, but it will soften the tread and reduce wear.

Fitting Linoleum.—Cutting and fitting the linoleum into awkward corners and round the hearth will present the greatest difficulty to the amateur, but there are one or two methods that will simplify the procedure. The first is exactly the same method as is used by dressmakers when cutting out a frock. Take a large sheet of paper and cut it out with scissors until it fits exactly into the awkward place. Then transfer this pattern to the linoleum and mark round the edge with pencil and cut accurately to the line. Another method, especially useful when fitting linoleum to a curved or crooked wall, is called "scribing", and this is made plain in Fig. 1.

Cut a short piece of wood about six inches in length and square on both ends and in one end cut a small "v" just large enough to hold steady the point of a pencil. Lay down the linoleum about five

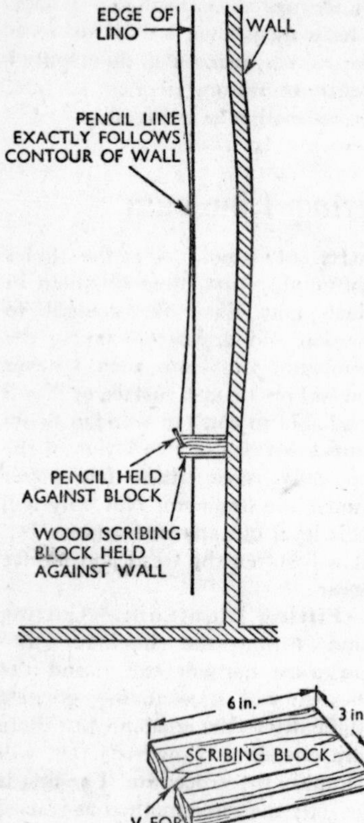

Fig. 1. Illustrates an efficient means of fitting linoleum to a wall contour.

inches from, and parallel to the wall, then, holding the wooden block against the wall, move it steadily along marking the linoleum at the same time. Be careful to keep the pencil steady and the block square to the wall. Having lined out the whole of the profile of the wall, cut accurately to the pencil mark and the linoleum must fit exactly to the wall, however crooked.

When laying patterned linoleum, match the pattern at the joints which occur in the middle of the room and make sure that it remains in the right place while marking and cutting it to fit the walls and corners.

At doorways, the edge of the linoleum should come just halfway under the door when shut. Difficulty may be encountered in fitting accurately round moulded architraves and door stops (see Fig. 2). The easiest way out for the house owner is to take a saw and carefully cut the thickness of the linoleum off the bottom of these mouldings and stops and so allow it to be slipped underneath.

After being laid, new linoleum will always spread to some degree, according to its thickness and quality, and provision must be made for this before finally fixing it down or it will buckle up into folds and wrinkles. A patterned linoleum must be matched and fixed at the centre joins and a gap of about a quarter-of-an-inch left round the edges of the room until spreading is finished, when these edges may be fixed. A plain or Jaspé linoleum should be fitted close to the walls and allowed to overlap at the joins so that it may be trimmed and fixed later. The mottled or Jaspé linoleums are a useful alternative to either plain or patterned types. They do not need matching, and their plainness gives an appearance of space.

Fixing Linoleum.—Linoleum cements may be obtained for fixing linoleum to cement or composition floors but their use is not recommended for wood floors as the consequent sealing of the floor may encourage dry rot or mildew in the floorboards and joists.

Linoleum squares patterned in

the same style as carpets and available in various sizes do not normally need fixing down. They are often much thinner than linoleum bought by the length, and benefit by having two or even three thicknesses of thick felt paper laid beneath them.

Since it is as difficult to fit and lay cheap linoleum as it is a good one, it pays in terms of labour as well as cash to buy the best you can afford. In living rooms and kitchens, where the traffic is heavy, it is important to purchase inlaid linoleums as the pattern is solid right through and there is no danger of the "bald spot" one so often sees in printed linoleums after a year or two of heavy wear by the kitchen sink or living room door.

Cleaning Linoleum.—Frequent washing is injurious to linoleum apart from the chances of water finding its way between the joins and setting up rot or mildew. A good wax polish is much to be preferred. Not only does a well-polished linoleum present a smart appearance but the wax protects and preserves the material.

Patching Linoleum.—After laying or re-laying linoleum, save carefully the larger cuttings as a useful reserve for patching later on, especially if the linoleum is patterned and difficult to match. It may be, of course, that a larger patch than can be covered by the trimmings may be needed, and in this case it is sometimes worth while to remove a piece of sufficient size from under, say, the piano or sideboard, and to replace this (where it does not show) with two or three small pieces, or even with one piece of the right size but a different pattern.

Consider the method to be adopted in this case. With the wood straight-edge and a sharp knife, cut out a rectangle round the damaged place. Cut right back into sound linoleum and cut right down to the floorboards. The worn piece may then be lifted up intact. Carry it over to the place from which it is decided to cut the replacement and lay it down so that the pattern exactly coincides. Fix it down temporarily with one or two brads. Now cut all round the edges right down to the floorboards. Then remove the brads and lift out the patch. If care has been taken to cut clearly and accurately, it will fit exactly into its new position and the pattern will match correctly. It may be found that as the patch has had very little wear in its old position,

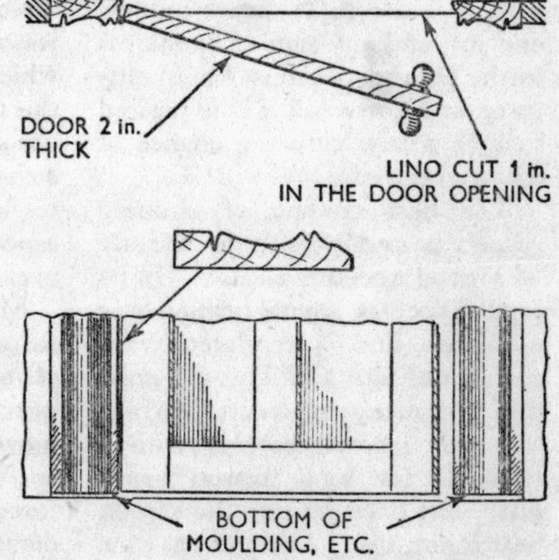

Fig. 2. Fitting linoleum at a door opening. Cut away the base of moulding, or stop to the thickness of the linoleum.

it will be thicker than the linoleum in its new place. If it is an inlaid linoleum set the plane to a really fine cut and carefully chamfer the edges of the patch until they are flush; if it is a printed linoleum, pack up the worn linoleum around it with a suitable thickness of folded newspaper before fixing.

Sometimes, the repair is a small one, necessitated, maybe, by wear from a chair castor. In this case cut out a new patch first of all, but instead of making it rectangular, cut it to an irregular shape. It will be much less conspicuous, especially in plain linoleum.

Having prepared the new patch, lay it down over the worn place in such a way that the pattern, if any, matches, and secure it with two or three brads. Cut all round the edges, lift out the old piece, and the patch will drop into place.

Care of Carpets

EVERY carpet should have a felt underlay, not only to give the carpet a softer tread, but to improve its wearing qualities and so prolong its life. Before laying the felt, examine the floorboards carefully for any protruding nails or tacks, and very uneven boards. The latter should be smoothed down with a plane or chisel after the nails have been punched well below the surface. The greatest enemy of carpets is damp. It causes mildew and rot, and any sign of dampness in the floorboards must be investigated and corrected if it is desired to give a new carpet a chance of a long and useful life.

The best method of cleaning carpets is undoubtedly by the use of a good vacuum cleaner. By its regular use, the annual beating over a clothes line is rendered completely unnecessary. This is a good thing, for many carpets are damaged by over-vigorous beating with a stick. If for some reason heavy gritty dirt does get into the carpet, beat it out, using a proper flat cane beater, and do not use too much force. Better to go over the whole carpet two or three times beating quite lightly than to make a determined attack on a small area and so damage the fibres. If a vacuum cleaner is not available, use a good stiff carpet brush regularly and always brush with the pile of the carpet, otherwise the dirt and grit will be brushed deeper into the pile.

To brighten the colours, a good carpet soap may be used occasionally according to the makers' directions but if possible avoid washing the carpet in the room in which it lies and in any case avoid the use of too much water. Never use salt or tea leaves; salt may have a chemical effect on the colours and tea leaves are liable to leave a stain especially on carpets with a light background.

Much damage is often done to carpets by the castors on the legs of furniture such as settees and heavy armchairs which are rarely moved. The comparatively small surface of the castor wheel is forced deep into the pile and soon damages the fibres, leaving a permanent mark, see Fig. 1.

The best way of avoiding the trouble is undoubtedly by removing the castor altogether and replacing it by one or more "domes" or "glides". These, as will be seen from Fig. 2, are small, plated circular studs and are simply fixed into the leg of the furniture by a tap or two of the hammer. In the case of the leg of a modern settee which is often five inches or more square, or in diameter, two or three of these may be used on each leg, see Fig. 2. They allow the heaviest piece of furniture to be slid about easily and silently on almost any surface and as they protrude only a fraction of an inch, leave no mark in the carpet or linoleum. Alternatively, where it is not proposed to move a particular item of furniture, such as a piano, it will be sufficient to house the castor in a bowl-shaped foot. These are commonly sold under the name of "insulators" and may be obtained in wood, vulcanite or glass, see Fig. 3.

It should be quite unnecessary to nail down the ordinary carpet, but occasionally one finds a little trouble with a corner that persists in curling up and forming a trap for unwary feet. Instead of nailing it down, try this: sew a small triangular pocket of hessian or canvas on the underside of the corner (see Fig. 4) and slip into

Fig. 1. Effect of castor on heavy pile.

Fig. 2. Fitting domes to table leg.

this pocket a small clipping of thin sheet lead. Any plumber will sell a piece for a few coppers. This should put an end to the trouble and probably, after a month or two it will be possible to dispense with the lead as the curly corner will have decided to behave itself.

Acid.—This is a case of real emergency and the utmost speed is essential. Take up the carpet and turn it upside down over a chair or bench. Then drench the area affected by the acid with a weak solution of ordinary washing soda or bicarbonate of soda and water, or with ammonia.

Moth.—If a carpet is attacked by moth, the best thing to do is to take it up and send it to a firm specializing in cleaning carpets, who will deal with the trouble so that the eggs or grubs deep in the carpet will be destroyed.

Inkstains.—These will usually yield to skim milk rubbed well into the pile with a cloth.

Soot.—Scatter coarse salt or

Fig. 3. Shows a castor in an insulator.

sawdust over the place and brush it vigorously into a dustpan. Repeat several times and finally wash carefully with carpet soap. It is fatal, however, to allow water near the place until all the loose soot has been removed.

Stains on Carpets.—Tea and coffee stains may be removed by a solution of borax and water in the proportion of two tablespoonsful of borax to a pint of water.

Tar.—This is best dealt with by applying a paste of fuller's earth and turpentine. Allow the paste to dry and then go over the place with a stiff carpet brush.

Stair Carpets.—The more sober the pattern chosen the broader the staircase will appear. Always purchase one yard more stair carpet than is strictly necessary to cover the stairs. It will then be possible to move the whole carpet up or down, say, twice a year. By so

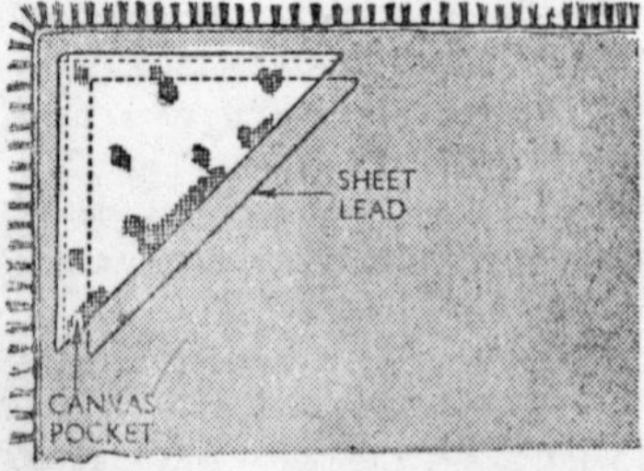

Fig. 4. How to prevent a curling edge.

doing, the portions that have been laid horizontally on a tread will now be vertical over a riser and so will enjoy a holiday for the next six months. This will obviously, practically double the life of the carpet.

Stair carpet should be laid with the pile towards the foot of the stairs so that the main tread presses it down instead of kicking it up. Finally, the provision of a small felt mat on each stair under the carpet is as good an investment as the felt underlay beneath the main carpets.

Non-skid Rugs.—Nothing is more disconcerting than to skid the length of a hall or room on a

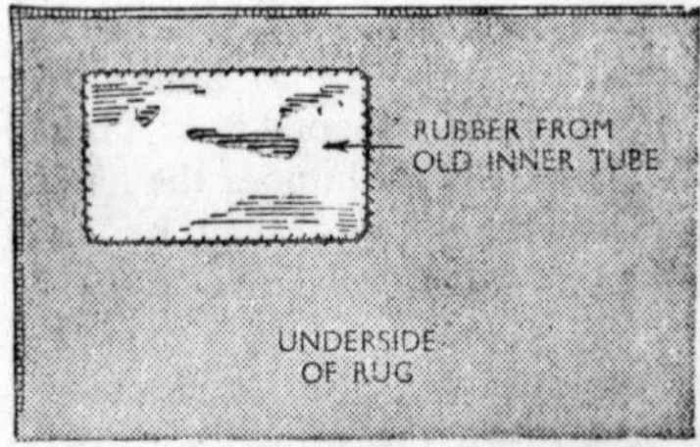

Fig. 5. How to prevent a rug skidding.

rug which is laid on polished boards or linoleum. It is possible to buy rugs which are backed with a rubberized non-skid fabric which hold to the floor quite firmly however highly it is polished. This kind of trouble, however, is easily cured.

Cut from an old cycle or motor inner tube four small squares of rubber for each rug. These may be stitched on the underside of each corner (Fig. 5) a little way in from the edge and the rug will never move under the tread. Be careful to put stitches at least half-an-inch in from the edge of the rubber patch otherwise they will tend to split the rubber and pull out.

SECTION FOUR

HOUSEHOLD APPLIANCES

Fuses

A FUSE is a short length of thin, fusible alloy wire mounted in a fuse box between the mains supply and house circuit. It is designed to melt if the wires of the circuit become overloaded, thus cutting off the current before overheating causes fire or damage elsewhere. The occurrence of a "blown" fuse therefore has to be taken at its true value: it is a safeguard against serious mishap.

Fuse Box.—The location in the house of the fuse box, or boxes (there may be two or more), should be known. In addition to the house circuit fuse boxes there is a mains fuse box, which the electricity supply company has sealed and which must never be interfered with by the consumer. This is on the street or inlet side of the meter, and is the concern only of the company's servants. The consumer's principal fuse box, to which the householder can attend as often as necessary, will generally be found close by the side of the meter, and there may be another, or others, elsewhere in the house.

Individual fuse boxes control their own particular circuits, so that a fault developing in one circuit will not necessarily affect the entire house. When a fuse blows, note should be made of the rooms affected. When once that is determined, searching for the fuse box concerned on any future occasion is eliminated.

Fuse wire, to replace that which has suddenly blown, should always be kept ready to hand. Supplies are obtainable from the electricity company or from a shop dealing in electrical appliances, and it is standardized for specific purposes. It is 5 amp. fuse wire for household lighting, 10 amp. for heating, 15 amp. for power. No other kind

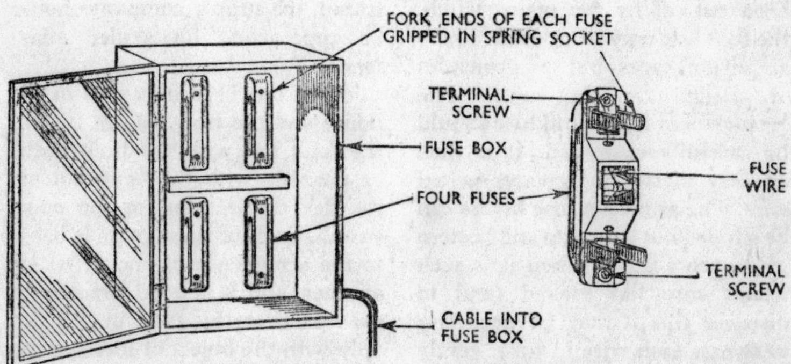

Figs. 1 and 2. Showing a typical fuse box and an enlarged view of a fuse.

of wire should be used as replacement for a blown fuse; neglect of this precaution may result, when a short circuit occurs, in the wires becoming overheated elsewhere, with dire consequences.

As a fuse box may be situated in a cellar, or in a dark cupboard below the stairs, a torch or lighted candle may be required to enable the trouble to be attended to. And as a fuse replacement in such circumstances is a two-handed job, the presence of someone to hold the light is a decided advantage. A small screwdriver, and a pair of scissors or pocket knife to cut a new length of fuse wire, complete the simple tools required. Before touching the fuse box, the main switch, which controls all points, should be turned off. All current, on the consumer's side of the meter, will then be cut off and the job can be proceeded with in perfect safety. After the melted fuse has been replaced with new wire, and the fuse box has been left as one found it, the main switch should be turned on again. This is an obvious procedure which is sometimes overlooked.

When the supply of current has been cut off by the main switch, the fuse box may be opened. There are several types, but the principles of design are the same. The arrangement of a sound fuse should be carefully examined. It is then an easy matter to replace melted wire. The porcelain fuse blocks can be slipped out from top and bottom grips, see Fig. 1. When it is seen which wire has melted (and to discover this it may be necessary to twitch each wire in turn, gently with the screwdriver) top and bottom terminals should be loosened, and wire adhering removed. A length of new fuse wire is then cut of sufficient length to allow of one turn around each of the two terminals after it has been passed through the fuse block, see Fig. 2. The terminals are then tightened with the screwdriver and the block replaced. Some fuses, such as those shown in Fig. 3, are separately enclosed, the cover being secured by a knurled nut. Fitting new fuse wire to this type of fuse is simple, and position taken up by the fuse wire after securing the terminals is shown in Fig. 4.

Every fragment of the "blown" wire should be removed before any attempt is made at replacement, and no surplus ends of the new wire should be allowed in the fuse box; they should be snipped or cut off close to the terminal. It also makes for neat and secure fixing if the wire-loop runs in the direction in which the terminal screw is tightened. The temptation to use a thicker wire than is appropriate may present itself in the case of frequent fusings, but the danger of this has already been stressed. If a fuse gives repeated trouble and the cause of the latter cannot be traced, the supply company should be approached for skilled assistance.

When one light only fails in the house and the fuse has not blown, the fault lies with the bulb itself, or possibly with the lamp-holder, the flex connections, or the point switch. Each of these parts is liable to the occurrence of one defect or another, and it is good practice to examine everything thoroughly not only with the object of locating the fault but of obviating the possibility of other defects.

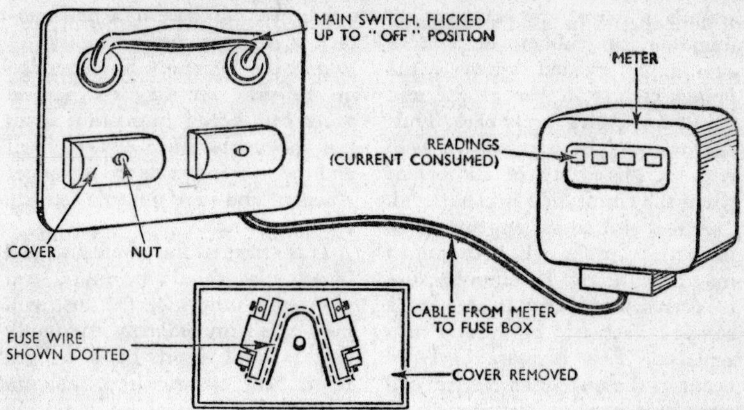

Figs. 3 and 4. An example of single fuses, separately enclosed, and view of fuse.

Test these possibilities in turn. Remove the bulb and try it in another holder which is known to be in good order. If it fails to light, the bulb is obviously defective and a new one is needed. If the replacement bulb gives no light, examination of the holder or connections or point switch is needed, but before this is done the main switch should be turned off.

Sometimes, the lamp socket spring plungers may not be bearing on the two lead contacts on the lamp's base, the springs actuating the plungers having become weakened. If this fault cannot be adjusted after the holder has been taken apart, a sound one must be substituted. Or it may happen that one of the two slots in the sides of the holder, wherein the projections near the base of the bulb should engage and be gripped, has partly broken away, this defect causing the bulb to be held other than squarely in the socket. In this case again, a new holder is indicated.

If nothing is wrong with the holder itself, the flex connections in the holder may be faulty. The connections need to be both clean and immovable, and it may be discovered that the flex wire has completely or partly broken at or close to a securing screw. If so, the short faulty portion should be cut away and the new end of the flex stripped of its covering. The bared wire should now be inserted in its correct terminal and the holding screw tightened up. It may be found advisable to treat both wires in the same way, so as to obtain equal length of ends.

A flex end is most easily bared of its covering by using a short sharp blade in such a way that only the covering is cut (at a point about ¾in. in from the end) the actual wire strands being untouched by the knife. A few extra seconds spent on this careful removal of the covering may save a further shortening of the wire due to the sharp blade partly severing the wire. Ragged threads of the material can be removed with scissors, and then the exposed strands of wire, now carrying no fragment of rubber or cotton, should be twisted between the fingers tightly, a ¼in. of the end then being bent sharply back. Thus compressed, the wire will be held without possibility of movement when the connection is completed.

A flex end which appears to be in perfect order when examined may be failing to function because of corrosion or dirt; it should be scraped clean and bright and then replaced. This is more likely to occur in the case of an electric bell push-button when its fitment is an exterior one, than in the case of an indoor lamp; but the possibility where indoor fitments are concerned is always worth bearing in mind. The point switch controlling the sound bulb which refuses to light up (and for which failure no other cause can be found) should be examined, the cover being removed for that purpose. The contact arm may have become corroded, and in this case gentle scraping so that the metal is left bright, on both sides, should prove effective. Or the contact arm may have lost its springiness, or become bent, and a little careful work with a pocket knife or small screwdriver will probably restore it to working condition. Purchase of a new contact arm may be necessary. A switch can generally be depended on to give service over several years, but there comes a time when the inevitable wear asserts itself and the working parts are no longer efficient, and here the sole remedy is a new switch.

It is essential that the cause of a blown fuse should be found and put right, otherwise the fuse will melt again immediately the faulty part is used again, be it a light bulb, bell, electric iron, vacuum cleaner, fire, cooker, or a sewing machine. The cause may be the frayed ends of different wires touching each other, or a break in the wire caused by a length of flex becoming kinked or knotted when put away instead of being loosely coiled. With the current off, such a break can be found by passing the flex slowly between the fingers and bending it inch by inch, when a break in the wire will become apparent by the readiness with which the flex suddenly bends at one point. It should be cut through at such a point, the exposed ends securely joined, and each join separately bound around with insulation tape. Use fairly wide tape and a good overlap.

Electric Points

MANY houses lack sufficient lighting plugs and power points to allow for increased use of electrical appliances, and existing plug points may often be in inconvenient places.

If it is proposed to add another electric point a little previous planning and consideration will save time and confusion. First, what is the new point required for, lighting or power? Lighting includes here small apparatus such as electric irons, vacuum cleaners, small electric fires, standard lamps; anything that does not exceed 5 amp. loading. Power (in the household) includes any apparatus with a loading in excess of 5 amp. but not exceeding 15 amp., such as electric motors, large electric fires, and so on. Such items as electric cookers may take considerably more current than that mentioned, but these are not considered here as they require an entirely separate installation.

There are varying sizes of plug points in houses, with both two or three-pin connections. The modern practice, however, is to standardize on 5 amp. three-pin types for lighting, and 15 amp. three-pin types for power, the third pin being used for earth connections. It is advisable to have all the plug points on the same circuit of the same type, so that all the appropriate household electrical appliances will readily fit into any socket (on the right circuit) in any room.

Second, at what point should the extension be commenced? The obvious answer seems to indicate the nearest "live" plug point. But this section of the wiring may already be fully loaded, and should that be the case, the new extension may have to be taken back to the fuse box at the supply intake. The arrangements of the supply intake in dwelling houses include the company's cable, sealing ends, cut-outs or main fuses, and the meters. From this point the wiring contractor fixes a main switch fuse and any additional sub-fuse boxes that may be required for the various wiring circuits, the power and lighting circuits being in separate boxes. A typical example is shown at Fig. 1.

The supply company does not forbid the running of extensions from the fuse box, providing it does not mean interfering with the mains supply connections. If the fuse boxes are erected as at Fig. 1, the extension may be made by connecting into the sub-fuse box without interfering with the mains supply. In a well-planned installation the sub-fuse box will have one or two spare fuse-ways, to allow for future extensions, and, by switching off the supply at the fuse switch, the connection of the new extension can be carried out with safety. Before commencing any extensions or repair of any kind the supply *must* be switched off.

The procedure to adopt when carrying out an extension to the wiring is to cut off the current and install the wiring first. The supply shop will furnish the correct size and type of vulcanized India rubber-covered wires or tough rubber twin, if the purpose is clearly explained. If possible, it is advisable to carry this wiring under the floorboards, as this usually gives a more direct run to the supply point and cuts down the length of cable required, at the same time ensuring a neater job.

The socket is then fixed to the skirting board and the connections made. It is necessary that these connections should be tight, and no bare wire should be showing after they have been made. The last part of the operation is the connection to the fuse boxes. Plenty of wire should be allowed at this end, as one wire has to go to a top connection and will probably enter the fuse box from the top entry.

Before connecting, check to see that the main supply is switched off, then insert the wire end in the

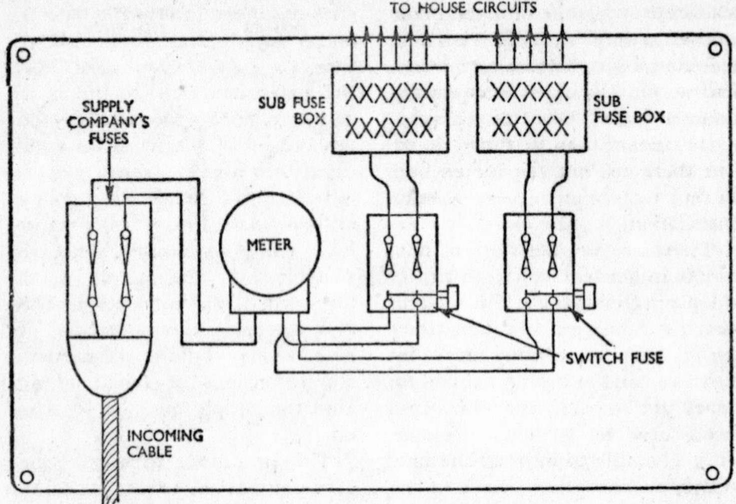

Fig. 1. A wiring circuit illustrating the arrangement of Supply Company's fuses and the disposition of the wiring for two sub fuse boxes. Note that each box is connected to a separate switch fuse on the house supply side of the meter.

brass connector and screw down firmly. The fuses should then be made up with suitable fuse wire; 5 amp. for lighting, 15 amp. for power purposes. The extension is then complete and the supply may be switched on. If spare fuses are not available in the sub-fuse box it will be necessary to install a new fuse box, in which case it should have additional spare fuse-ways to allow for future extensions. This new fuse box will require a supply, and when all connections are made

Fig. 2. Shows the general details of typical porcelain shrouded connectors.

to the new wiring the supply company must be approached to make the necessary connections to the main supply.

Quite simple alterations to the existing wiring may be carried out with flexible leads and multi-way adapters. Flex is available in two- and three-core types, and when purchasing, it should be stated clearly for what purpose it is required; the size of wire, and the current carrying capacity being specified. The multi-way adapters are very useful, especially in a house which is wired for two-pin plugs only, making it possible to take several pieces of electrical apparatus from one plug-point without incurring any work on the "live" side of the wiring.

There is, of course, a limit to the amount of flexible lead that can be taken from any one socket, and it should always be kept to a minimum. The trailing of long flex can prove dangerous when it is constantly walked on. It is as well to follow a strict procedure when dealing with an extension to, say, a standard lamp. Generally, a lamp of this description is movable to give additional light in any part of the room, hence a considerable length of flex may be necessary over and above that which is supplied with the standard lamp.

A piece of flex of the best quality should be obtained, with sufficient extra length allowed for making joints, plug connections and so on. Quality is important, as the flex will be used in a trailing position and may have to stand considerable wear; the better the quality the safer the job. In the case of a standard lamp it may not be possible to put a complete new flex from the switch to the plug point as the flex usually runs up the centre column of the lamp standard. If this is the case, a join will be necessary somewhere near the base, in a position where it will be subjected to as little wear as possible.

The join may be made by firmly twisting the ends together and covering with insulation tape, but a connector is better. Connectors usually take the form of a brass tube with screws at either end to clamp the wire in position, the whole connection being covered in a porcelain shroud. They can be obtained in single or double types for various sizes of wire (Fig. 2).

When the cleaned wire ends have been inserted in the connector and the screws tightened, the whole join should be covered with insulation tape as far back as the braiding. Connection of the flex to the plug completes the work. Right and wrong ways of connecting the flex ends to the plug connections are shown at Fig. 3. The wire should be placed under the washer and in the direction of the tightening of the screw, so that when the screw is tightened the wire will tend to close into a loop, the result being a very sound connection. If put in the reverse way, the wire may come out from under the washer, a bad connection resulting.

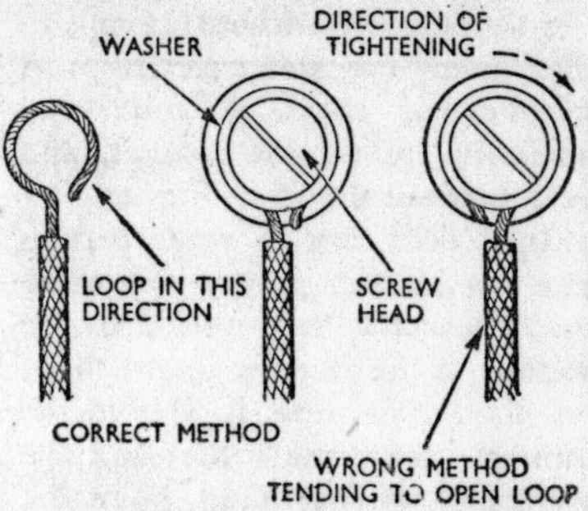

Fig. 3. How to secure wire to terminal.

Actual connection to the plug point can be made *via* a multi-way adapter, which will give facilities for supplying other apparatus from

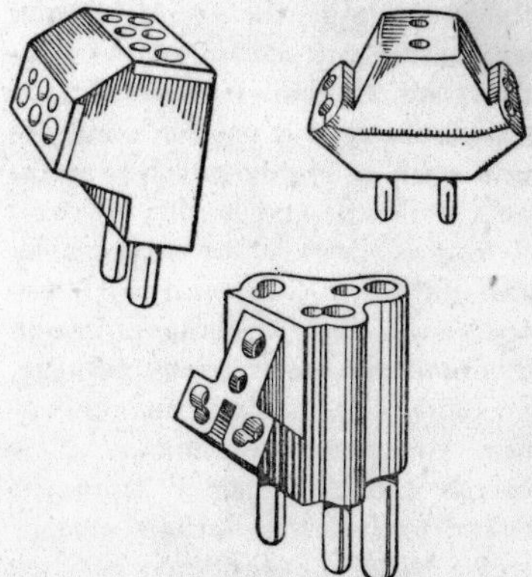
Fig. 4. Shows three types of multi-way adapters for two and three-pin points.

the same point without having to disconnect the standard lamp. A number of types of multi-way adaptors are on the market, and examples are shown in Fig. 4.

It is necessary to make certain that the adapter plug points make firm contact when inserted in the socket. If the plug is found to be on the slack side it should be removed from the socket and the split end of the plug point be gently splayed out by the insertion of a thin knife blade.

A wireless set should not be connected *via* a multi-way adapter, because it is almost impossible to get the necessary perfect connection with so many sliding contacts. Bad or indifferent contacts mean sparking, and this gives rise to crackling in the set. A wireless set should always be connected to one plug and socket to avoid that trouble. An electric clock is also better with a plug and socket to itself, for if an adapter is used there is a possibility that at some time the current to the clock may be interrupted by the connection of other apparatus to this point of supply.

It should be noted that, although there is no law or other regulation to prevent the house holder installing additional points, the supply company will not connect the wires to the main supply if the new wiring does not stand up to the insulation test standard required by that company. There must be nothing slipshod about it

Electric Fires

THE heating element of electric fires for domestic use are of two main types, (a) those in which the wire is in the form of an open spiral laid in the grooves of a fireclay former, as in Fig. 1, and (b) those having the wire tightly wound on a porcelain rod of relatively small diameter, see Fig. 2. The latter type is used in conjunction with a highly-polished parabolic reflector and is very efficient so long as the reflector is kept clean and polished. The fires with the open spiral type of element, though less modern, are still very popular, probably on account of their cheapness and easy maintenance. New spirals can be obtained from the electrical dealer in various wattage and voltage ranges and may be fitted at home with very little trouble.

Fitting a New Spiral.—In most cases it will be necessary to remove some kind of cover from the back of the fire so as to gain access to the screws and nuts that serve as terminals for the ends of the spiral and as connections for the mains leads. The screws and nuts will usually be found to be rusty and the application of a few drops of thin machine oil will make removal easier. To insure correct reassembly, note the positions of washers and wires. See Figs. 1 and 4.

The new spiral as purchased will be in the form of a closely-coiled spring some eight or ten inches long. This must be evenly stretched to the length required to fill the grooves of the fireclay element bar. Measure the exact length.

It is a good plan to lay a length of string in the grooves to find the exact length to which the spiral

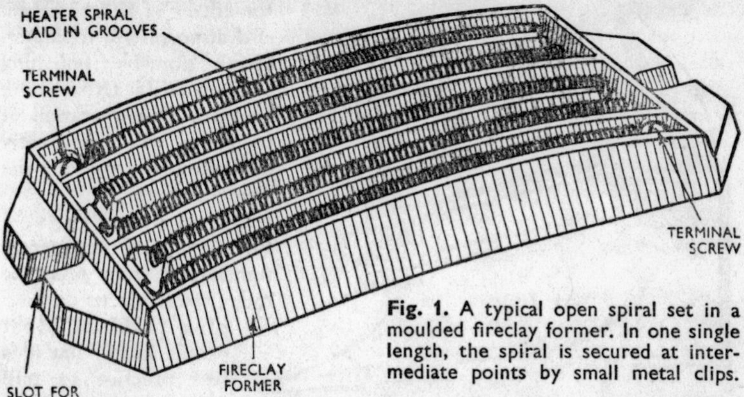

Fig. 1. A typical open spiral set in a moulded fireclay former. In one single length, the spiral is secured at intermediate points by small metal clips.

needs to be stretched. Having cut the string to the required length, get an assistant to hold one end of the string together with one end of the spiral, and, taking the free end of the spiral, pull it gently until it reaches the other end of the string. Do not overdo the stretching; it is better to have it too short than too long. Now secure one end with the screw and nut provided, and carefully work the spiral into the grooves and secure the other end in the same way. When replacing the mains connections see that the wires are clean and intact and that the insulation is in good condition. When a switch is embodied, check over all nuts and screws for tightness.

Temporary Repair.—It is not advisable to attempt to prolong the life of a broken spiral by joining together the broken ends, but an emergency may arise where some such expedient is desirable. If this should happen, do not fall into the common error of twisting the ends together, but proceed as follows. Cut a small rectangle of tin (unpainted or with the paint removed) about $\frac{3}{4}$in. long by $\frac{1}{4}$in. wide. Bend this into the form of a letter S as shown in Fig. 3. Insert the ends of the broken wire, one in each bend of the S, and flatten the tin between the jaws of a pair of pliers. It is important that the ends be made clean and bright with a piece of emery paper before making the join. This is because the high temperature to which the wire is raised produces a coating of oxide, a bad conductor of electricity. This oxide must be removed to ensure good electrical contact. A join made in this way is kept cool by the tin, thus preventing the formation of fresh oxide. Apart from electrical contact it also has greater mechanical strength and neater appearance than twisted wires.

Reflector Type Fires.—These fires have elements wound on a porcelain rod and are less subject to a burn-out than are the open spiral elements. Accidental damage may occur, resulting in a broken rod, in which case a complete new element may be obtained and fitted. The rod is held between two clips either by spring pressure or by a

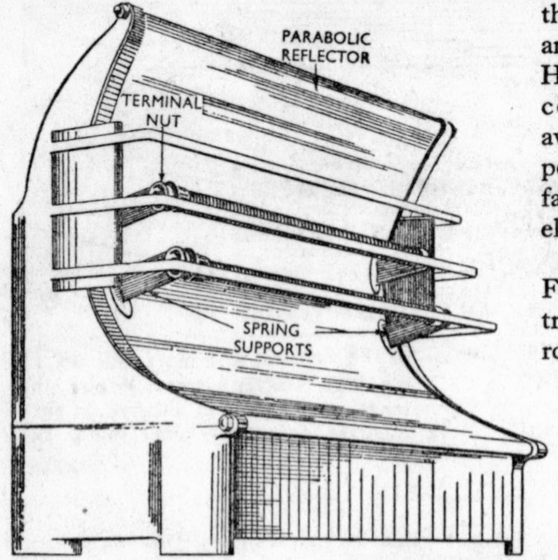

Fig. 2. An example of an electric fire fitted with porcelain rod element and a parabolic reflector. The rods are secured at each end by a terminal nut.

terminal nut at each end and the method of replacement is simple and obvious. So simple is it that the job is likely to be attempted without taking the precaution of first switching off the current. In all such jobs, however simple, it is always wise first to switch off the current and then to remove the plug, thus making sure that it is absolutely impossible either to get a shock or blow a fuse.

Care of the Reflector.—The efficiency of the reflector type of fire is derived chiefly from the reflector, see Fig. 2. This is scientifically designed by the makers and sent out with a highly-polished finish. If the high polish on the surface of the reflector is allowed to deteriorate, the reflector will not give a thorough radiation of heat. Frequent polishing is not necessary but an occasional rub over with methylated spirits and a chamois leather is sufficient to counteract the effects of alternate heat and atmospheric moisture. Harsh abrasive polishing compounds should be avoided. The operation of polishing will be greatly facilitated by removing the elements first.

Cords and Plugs.—Fires that are frequently transferred from room to room are liable to develop plug trouble. Most people know that it is bad practice to pull the plug out of its socket by tugging. This practice is often persisted in despite knowledge of the consequences; broken wires, damaged plugs and loosened sockets. The cap of the plug should be removed by unscrewing the countersunk screws from the underside. It may be found that one of the wires has come loose from its pin and needs to be re-secured. Another common fault is a broken wire within the insulation at the point where the flex enters the plug. This fault in its early stages may appear intermittently and give rise to burning of the rubber covering due to sparking. The

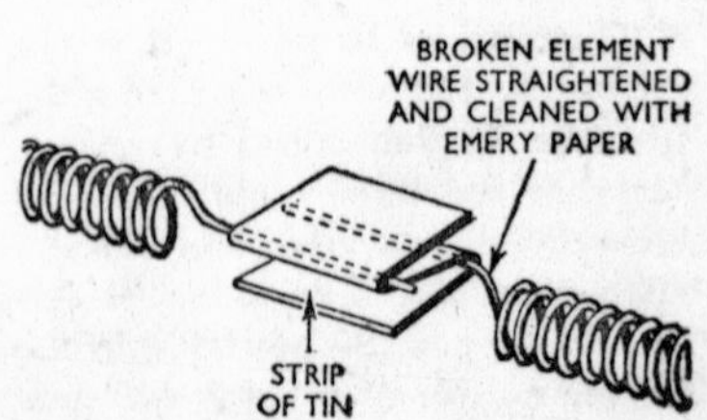

Fig. 3. A simple but effective method of repairing a fractured element.

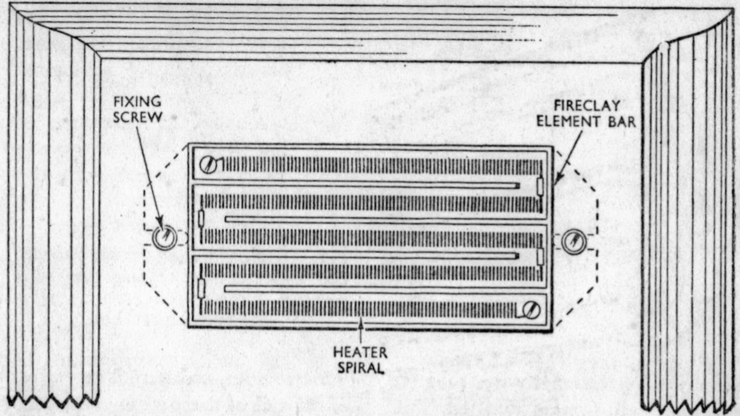

Fig. 4. A diagrammatic view of an open spiral fireclay former secured in position.

remedy is to make a clean cut right through the cord and strip back the braiding for about 2in. from the end. Then take each lead and strip off the rubber insulation, leaving about ½in. of the wires bare. Secure the wires to their appropriate pins. In the case of three-core flex and three-pin plugs it is important that the earth lead be connected to the earth pin. The earth pin is always the largest of the three, and the earth lead is always the one covered with brown insulation. The two other leads carry the current and are usually covered in red and white (or black) respectively. These can be connected to the two current carrying pins without reference to colour. Before replacing the cap, the loose ends of the outer braiding should be trimmed and the flex bound with twine to give a neat finish. Insulating tape may be used instead of twine but is apt to come loose when the adhesive dries out.

Electric Bells and Alarms

FIGURE 1 shows a simple bell circuit with push-button and dry batteries. When the circuit is "made" by pressing the push-button P the current flows from the batteries through the coils and the contact breaker B. This sets up a magnetic field about the magnet poles and attracts the armature A which breaks the circuit at B and at the same time causes the hammer to strike the gong. The break in the circuit cuts off the magnetic field and allows the armature to spring back and resume the position of contact at B. This cycle is repeated rapidly and continuously until pressure on the push-button ceases.

Adjustment.—The only adjustment to be made is by turning a screw at contact breaker B. If this screw is unscrewed far enough to leave a gap between the contact points, no current can flow and the bell will not ring. If, on the other hand, it is screwed in too far the contacts will not part when the

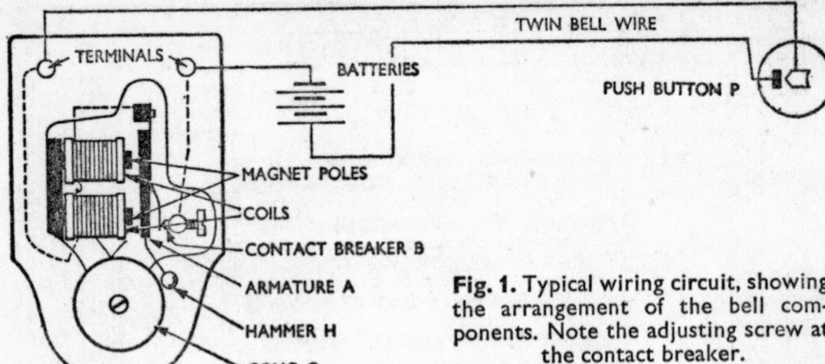

Fig. 1. Typical wiring circuit, showing the arrangement of the bell components. Note the adjusting screw at the contact breaker.

armature is drawn to the magnet poles and will remain jammed. The screw should be adjusted, while the push-button is being pressed, to a position between these two extremes to give the most satisfactory ringing. There is usually a locking screw to keep the contact screw in adjustment and this should be tightened when a satisfactory adjustment has been made.

Power Supply.—The power for ringing bells may be derived from wet or dry batteries or A.C. house mains. For general convenience, bell circuits are designed to operate at low voltage, and one or two dry batteries are sufficient for most house circuits. In cases where the wiring run is very long, more batteries may be needed to cope with the voltage drop in the line. The batteries are wired in series, i.e. the tail of the first is connected to the centre terminal of the second, tail of the second to centre terminal of the third, and so on. Fig. 2 shows three batteries connected in this way. The odd terminals at the end of the series, one tail and one centre terminal, connect up to the two wires from the bell. One of these two wires is cut at some convenient point, the two severed ends being attached to the terminals in the bell-push.

The batteries may be positioned at any convenient point in the circuit, generally on a shelf near the bell. Modern batteries have a long life but must necessarily be replaced from time to time, and it is cheaper in the long run to use the A.C. mains supply if available.

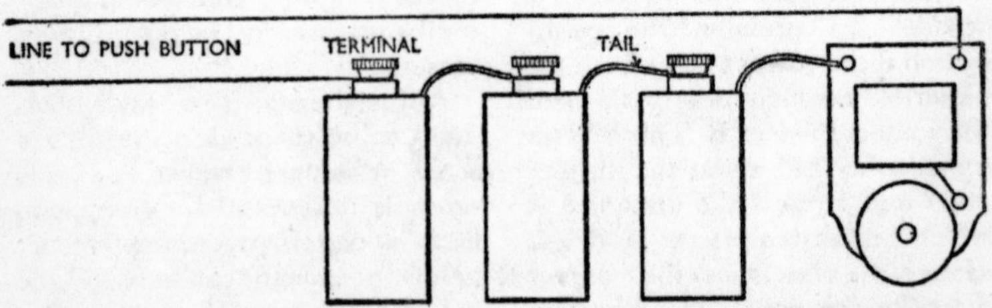

Fig. 2. Three batteries wired in series are a good remedy for conditions where the voltage drop may be occasioned by an excessive run of the wiring circuit.

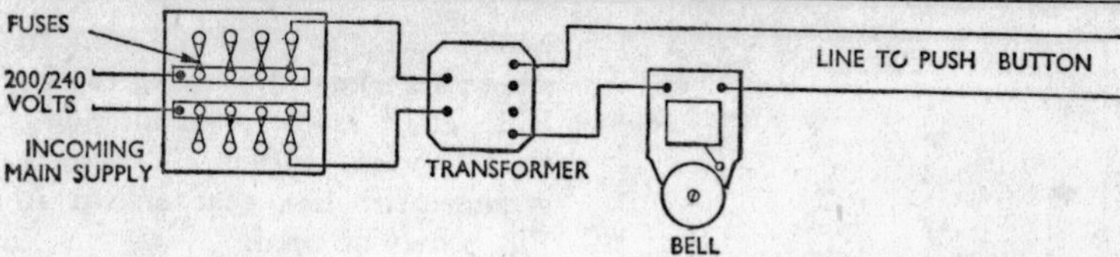

Fig. 3. Wiring diagram showing how to connect up a mains operated bell.

For this purpose a small transformer is utilized to step down the mains voltage of 200/240 A.C. to the low voltage required for the bell circuit. The transformer has a primary winding which is permanently connected to the mains through fuses, and a secondary winding with tappings to give, at option, 4, 6, or 8 volts, in some cases, 12 volts, to feed the bell circuit. No current is consumed except when the bell is ringing and even then the consumption is negligible. The wiring diagram for a mains operated bell is shown in Fig. 3.

Wiring.—The transformer should be fixed at the nearest convenient point to the fuse box carrying the house lighting circuits, and wired into the selected pair of fuses with vulcanized India rubber.

Twin bell wire is used for the low tension circuit to the push-button and it is usual to carry this on the top of skirting boards or picture rails, fixing it at suitable points with insulated staples.

The voltage required to operate the ringing circuit will depend partly on the bell windings and partly on the length and resistance of the circuit. The correct transformer tapping can be found by trial. The array of terminals on the transformer may be somewhat confusing at first sight. Figs. 4 and 5 show two typical arrangements of terminals and the voltage to be obtained between various pairs. The primary winding will be marked either "Mains", "Primary" or "200/240 volts A.C.", and the secondary winding will have three or more terminals giving various voltages from 2 to 12.

Multi-Point Circuits.—If it is desired to install a bell that can be rung from any number of push-buttons in different parts of the house, an indicator panel should be provided to show the point of origin of any particular call. A diagrammatic circuit of such an arrangement is shown in Fig. 6, but the layout of the wiring must be governed by the disposition of the points.

In the diagram the push-buttons, marked thus (P), are numbered to correspond with their respective indicator positions. Tracing the

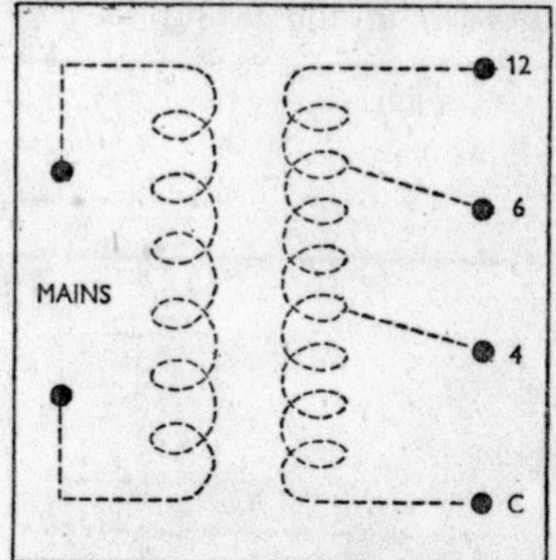

Fig. 4. Shows how the different voltages are obtainable on the transformer. See transformer in Fig. 3.

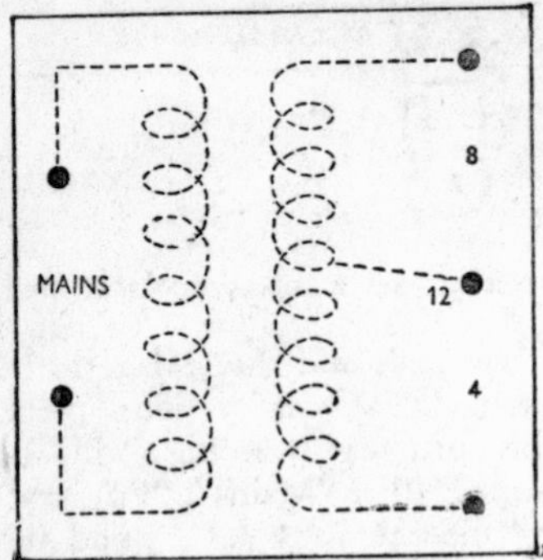

Fig. 5. Shows how to tap a transformer for different voltages. See also Fig. 4.

circuit from any selected push-button, it will be seen that current flows to the bell via its associated coil on the indicator panel. By this means, the coil is energized simultaneously with the bell and causes a white disk to flutter at the numbered indicator window below it. When the call is answered, the disk is restored to normal by hand, or drops to normal position automatically.

Burglar Alarms.—A simple bell circuit may be installed as a burglar alarm, and special concealed switches are obtainable for this purpose for fitting to door jambs, window sashes, etc. In situations where the wiring can be laid out of reach of an intending thief's wire cutters, a simple arrangement like that shown in Fig. 7 may be used.

The master switch shown adjacent to the battery is a single pole switch such as used for ordinary electric lighting. Its purpose is to render the system inoperative during the daytime. It is, however, subject to human fallibility, forgetfulness or even collusion. This objection can be overcome by using a time switch which can be set to cut in and out at predetermined times. In the case of shops or offices a time switch with a seven-day dial may be used and can be set to make due allowance for different closing times at week-ends and early closing days.

In locations where any part of the wiring is liable to be cut, the system shown in Fig. 8 should be adopted. In this case, the main circuit is normally energized and the alarm bell is on a secondary circuit which operates only when a break occurs in the main circuit. All the points to be protected are

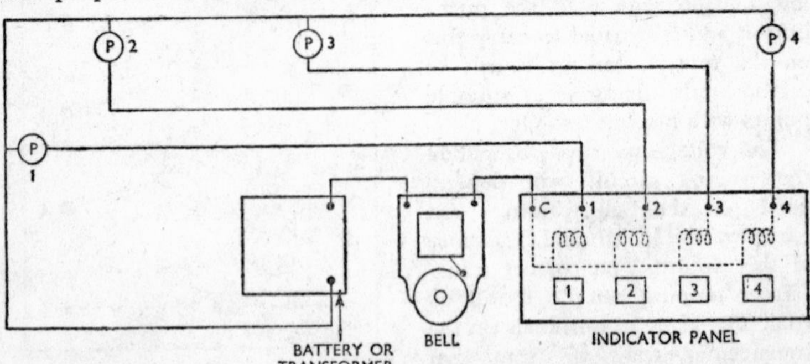

Fig. 6. A diagrammatic wiring circuit for a multi-point mains or battery bell system. Four push buttons, P, are wired in the circuit to the indicator panel.

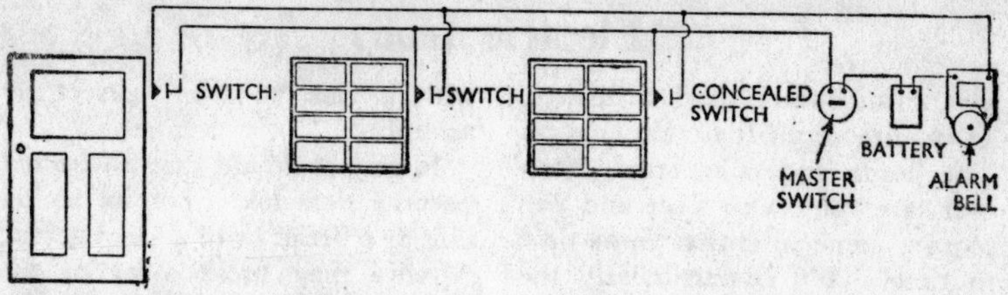

Fig. 7. A battery operated wiring circuit for a burglar alarm, with concealed switches located at windows and door. Switches close when door or window opens.

provided with switches of the normally closed type, in contrast to the normally open type shown in the previous system. These switches are all connected in series with a magnetic relay. In principle, the relay is a switch actuated by an electromagnet. The current flowing in the electromagnet maintains the switch contacts in the open position, and as soon as the current is cut off the contacts close under spring tension. These contacts are wired in the secondary circuit and operate the alarm bell.

The current consumption of the relay is very low, but since it must be continuously energized for long periods while protection is required, it is advisable to supply it from the mains through a transformer. The bell should be supplied from a battery and *not the mains*, otherwise the whole system could be defeated by deliberate interference with the mains on the part of an inside confederate. If such a contingency is possible, the bell, battery, and relay must be housed in a cupboard that is itself protected by the system. As it stands, the system is still not perfect, since a failure of the power supply would release the relay and give rise to a false alarm and cause unnecessary consternation. This defect can be overcome if desired by feeding the relay circuit from an accumulator instead of the mains transformer. The same accumulator would serve to supply the bell. It would be necessary to install a trickle charger to keep the accumulator charged from the mains. A trickle charger can be made with a suitable transformer and rectifier but it is beyond the scope of this article to give details of its design.

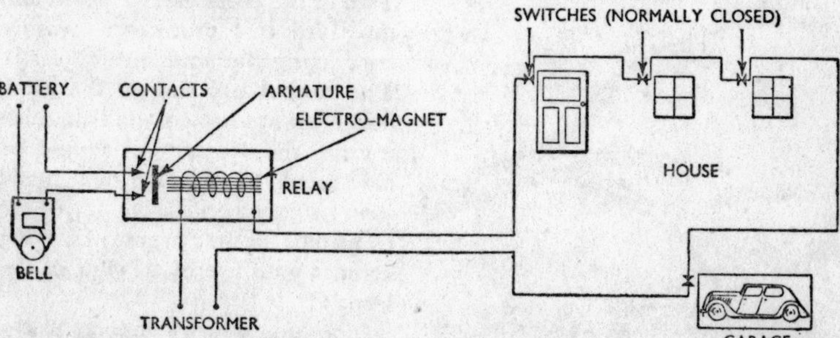

Fig. 8. Another wiring circuit for a burglar alarm. Note that the switches are closed. Opening of door or window also opens switch and sets off alarm bell.

Electric Irons

Electric irons, used with care, require very little maintenance. The cords and connectors, however, are subject to wear and will require some attention from time to time. This is particularly the case with the connection to the iron itself, due partly to the effects of transmitted heat, and partly to continual flexing of the cord at that point during ironing.

Whenever the iron fails to heat with the current switched on, first make sure that current is reaching the socket into which the iron is plugged. A blown fuse may be the cause, and this is easily checked by substituting some other appliance such as a table lamp. The next step is to examine the connector at the rear of the iron. The casing of this connector is made in two halves held together by two or more screws. Remove the screws with a small screwdriver and take the two halves of the casing apart. The internal brass sockets are apt to drop out at this stage, but this should be prevented until their disposition has been exactly noted with a view to their correct reassembly.

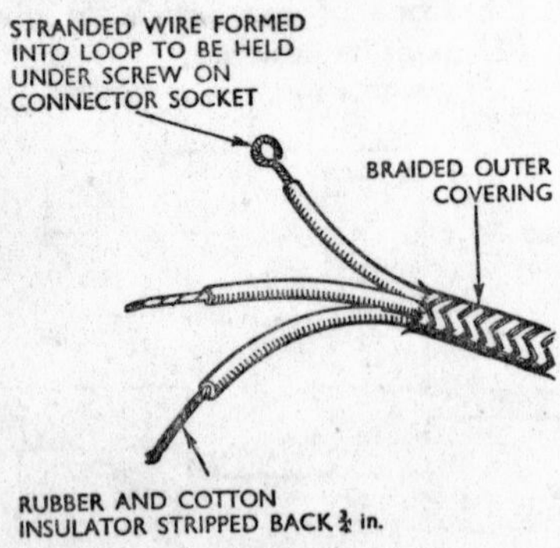

Fig. 1. Preparing the cable connections. Bind the end of the braided covering.

It may be found that a wire has become detached from its socket due to a break or to a loose screw. A wire may break away at the screw, in which case it will be visible, or the fracture may occur within the insulation at the point where the cord enters the casing, the symptom here being a limpness in the cord at that point. In either case it is best to make a clean cut and remake the joints to the brass sockets.

The braiding should be cut back with scissors leaving the leads free for a length of about 2in. Next, taking each lead in turn, strip back ¾in. of insulation, twist the strands of wire tightly, and form a loop for the screw to pass through, see Fig. 1. The tags thus formed are then assembled to the sockets with the screws and washers.

Early type irons (Fig. 2) are provided with twin-core leads, but all portable electrical appliances of recent manufacture should be supplied with three-core leads to conform with the Institute of Electrical Engineers regulations. Two of the cores carry current and the third is a protective measure connecting the appliance to earth. The rubber covering of the earth lead is always brown, to distinguish it from the others, and should be connected to the springy metal strip provided on the outside of the connector for the purpose of making contact with the metalwork of the iron.

The plug which connects to the wall socket should also be examined for faulty connections, and, if necessary, dealt with in the same way. Plugs of the three-pin type have a pair of pins (of equal size) which carry current and an odd (larger) pin to which should be connected the brown earth wire, see Fig. 3.

Heating Element.—It is uneconomical to attempt to repair a burnt-out heating element. New elements (see Fig. 4) are obtainable cheaply from any good electrical dealer, and can be fitted at home with very little trouble.

In most types of iron, the handle is anchored to the body by two nickled nuts. These can be removed with a spanner leaving two studs projecting. The handle can now be removed and the casing raised off the studs sufficiently to give access to the interior, where two more nuts will be found clamping down a cast-iron plate to the sole of the iron. These nuts and the plate are next removed, exposing the element. The element is wound on a flat mica former sandwiched between two pieces of similar material, and has two metal tapes which are attached to the pins at the back of the casing. Casing and element come away together and can then be separated by removing the nuts from the pins holding the tapes. The order of re-assembly with the new element is exactly the reverse of dismantling, and the only point needing particular attention is to see that all nuts are screwed up really tight.

Auto-control Irons.—The latest type of electric iron, with thermostat heat control (Fig. 5), are best dealt with by the maker's service department except for certain minor repairs which can be effected without special equipment.

If the tell-tale light in the handle (Fig. 6) is not lighting when the iron is working, it may be removed and checked with a torch battery. First remove the lamp housing, which is held by a single recessed

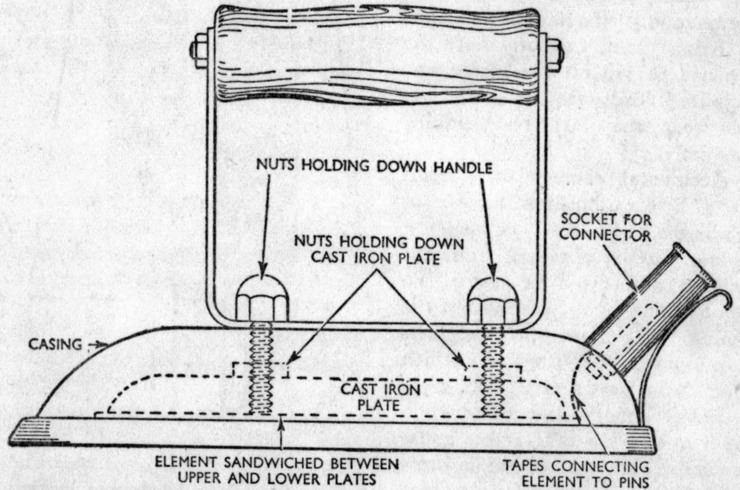

Fig. 2. A diagrammatic arrangement of early type iron having a twin core lead.

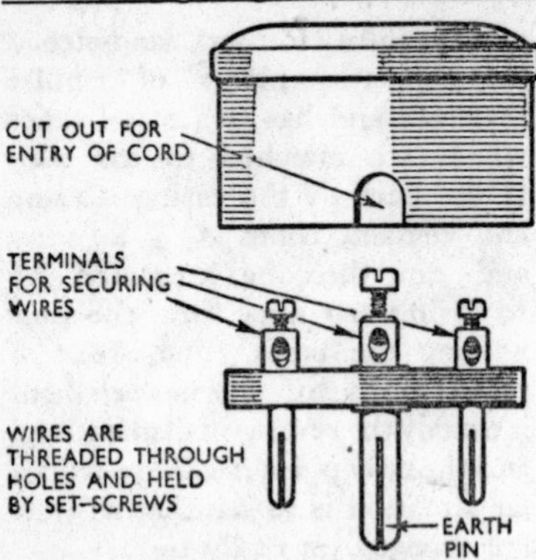

Fig. 3. Dismantled three-pin plug showing the points at which wires are secured to the terminals for the pins.

screw at the back of the handle. Inside the housing will be found a flash lamp held by two spring clips. This should be taken out and tested on a 2-volt battery, and a new replacement fitted if required.

The removal of the lamp housing gives access to the lead connections, which should be examined and if necessary, tightened. If any lead connection is broken and needs to be remade, or if a new flexible cord is being fitted, carefully note the points to which the different coloured leads are attached, and see that they are re-assembled correctly.

Accidental damage may result in a broken bakelite handle or porcelain body, in which case new spares can be obtained from the makers and fitted at home. To remove the body, disconnect the mains leads from their brackets and remove the centre screw which clamps the brown earth lead. Next remove the thermostat control knob by loosening the grub screw under its tail. This will reveal a brass nut which should be unscrewed with a suitable spanner. The body can now be lifted from the sole plate assembly and the handle removed from the body. Note the position of the asbestos washers between the handle and the body and locate them correctly in re-assembling the new parts.

The working temperature of the sole plate, with the thermostat set to "art silk", should be approximately 90 degrees Centigrade; the other settings follow automatically from that. Special apparatus is required for testing and adjusting the heat controlling mechanism and it is therefore necessary to return the iron to the makers or their service agents for fitting a new element, or any repair that calls for replacement or readjustment of the thermostat.

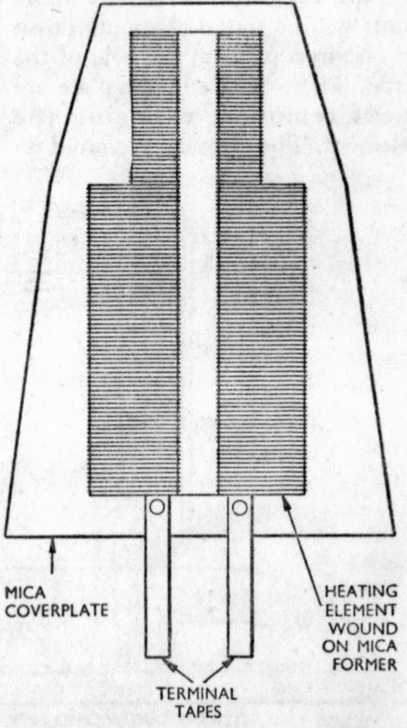

Fig. 4. A typical electric iron heater element, enclosed in mica coverplates.

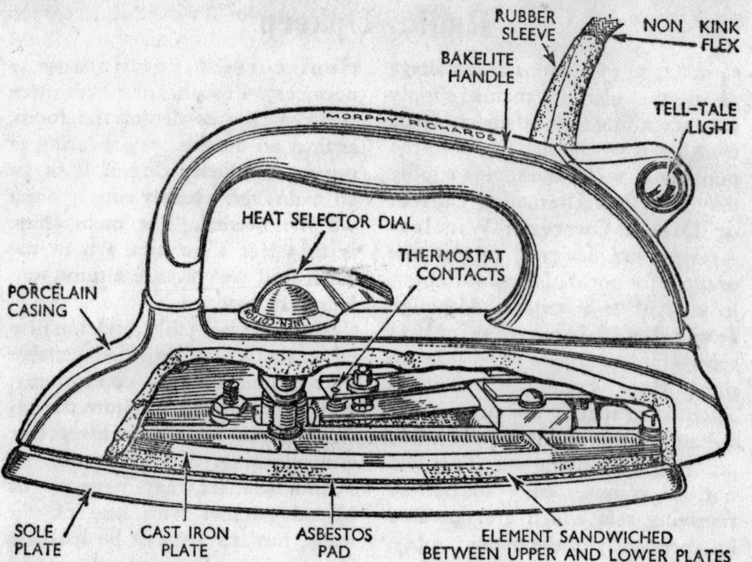

Fig. 5. A cut-away view of the interior of an auto-control electric iron, showing arrangement of thermostat control and internal components.

Caution.—Irons that are not provided with thermostatic control must be maintained at the proper working temperature by switching on and off as required. In this connection, a word of warning will not be out of place. The iron dissipates its heat in the process of ironing, and if it is left standing with the current switched on, the heat will gradually build up and cause damage to the iron and anything combustible that may be in contact with it. Therefore the iron should always be stood on a suitable heat-resisting stand and always switched off when left temporarily unattended.

The lead from power point to iron should be of adequate length and the ironing table ought to be situated in a position convenient to the wall plug so as to permit the unobstructed use of the iron.

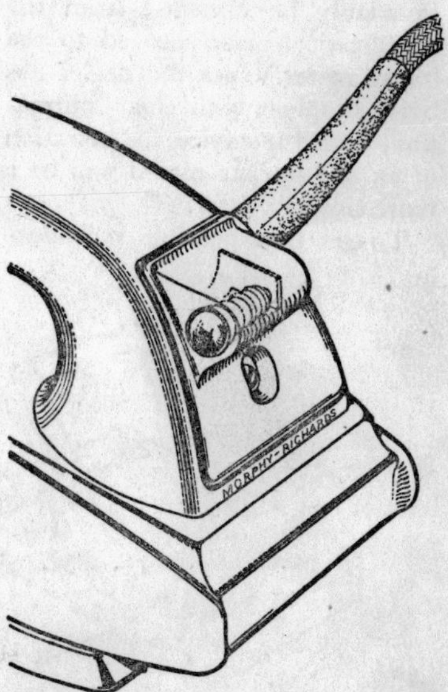

Fig. 6. Shows the position of tell-tale light to indicate when iron is working.

Radio Upkeep

THE type of current and voltage of the electric mains supply vary according to the district. Apart from certain variations in the number of volts, the mains supply may be either Alternating Current or Direct Current. Wireless receivers are designed to suit one or other (or both) of these variations in current and voltage. Although several versions of wireless receivers are made available to meet these contingencies it is essential to specify the current and voltage of the mains supply when ordering a receiving set. This will not, of course, apply to battery receiving sets which are operated independently of the mains supply. However, when it is proposed to purchase an all-mains set, the details of current and voltage may invariably be obtained from the specification plate secured to the house meter. Once the dealer has been supplied with this information, with his advice the selection of an appropriate model will be a more simple matter.

To get best possible reproduction, correct positioning is necessary. Probably the best place is across the corner of the room, against an outside wall, bearing in mind, of course, that if it is an all-mains set, a handy supply point will be needed. The main thing is to select a position where the earth lead will require a minimum length of wire.

If the set is a table model, a firm table should be provided capable of carrying the set comfortably, and large enough to allow the set to be turned around for inspection and cleaning. To allow for all factors the set may have to be placed parallel with one of the walls, but it must not be hard up against the wall, or resonance may occur and spoil reproduction. There should be about 8 to 12in. between the back of the set and the wall.

When the position has finally been decided upon, and the power plug made available, the connection of the earth and of the aerial completes the installation. It should be noted that when an outdoor aerial is used it is worth while to install a switch outside, to connect the aerial direct to earth in the event of a thunderstorm, and at the same time to isolate the set from the aerial. Such a switch can be obtained from a radio shop, and an example is shown in Fig. 1.

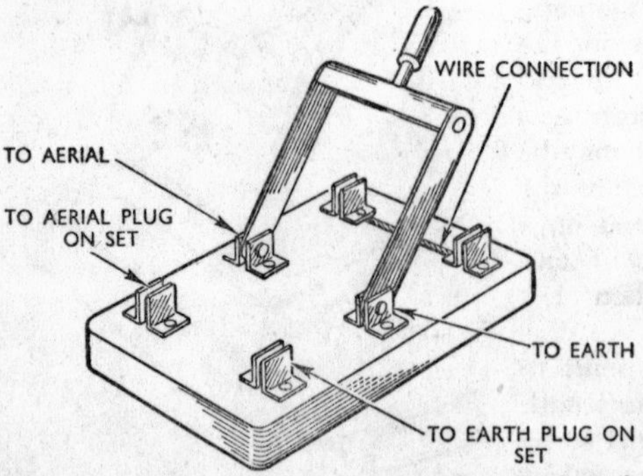

Fig. 1. Shows small hand-operated open switch used to earth the aerial and isolate the set when necessary, or as a precaution against lightning.

When the aerial and earth wires have been installed, all that remains is the actual connection to the set. Plugs are usually provided with the set, and the method of connecting these to the wire ends is shown at Fig. 2. The set is then ready for use.

If it is desired to have radio available in two rooms, this can be managed with the aid of an extension loudspeaker, as at Fig. 3. In every installation it is advisable to allow for this at the outset. Choice of the extension speaker will depend on the radio manufacturer's recommendation in the instruction book supplied with the set. All modern sets are provided with sockets to take an extension loudspeaker, which gives the most satisfactory reproduction if fixed in a corner of the room, fairly high up on the wall, say at the picture-rail level, with the speaker pointing down at a slight angle.

Lightly insulated wire of small section may be used for connecting the extension speaker, bell wire being quite suitable. If the speaker is likely to be wanted in a number of rooms, sockets can be permanently wired so that the speaker may be plugged-in wherever required. With these sockets, it is advisable to run the wires direct under the floorboards, to keep them as short as possible. Connections should be checked for tightness, for plug pins that fit loosely in their sockets give rise to crackling noises in the speaker.

The majority of modern sets are of the all-mains type, and with these the location of defects and the nature of running repairs are somewhat more complex than those relating to the battery set. But the latter, if an old model, will certainly need regular attention. If reception

Fig. 2. A two-piece single-pin plug with wire connected to loop end of the pin.

is poor, and results are generally unsatisfactory, fault-finding should commence with a careful checking of all external connections, and not until this is done should resort be had to dismantling the set.

Battery sets have a considerable number of plug-in connections, up to 4 H.T. leads and 3 or 4 grid bias leads and 2 accumulator leads. Each of these is a possible source of trouble, but much can be done by keeping all connections tight and clean, and by bearing in mind the golden rule, "Before disconnecting anything attach a label to it so that it will be refitted correctly".

Keep the inside of the set scrupulously clean, and occasionally check aerial and earth terminals, to ensure tightness. Make certain that the batteries are fully charged and replaced at regular intervals, and that the accumulator is also kept charged. The L.T. leads to the accumulator are usually of the spade type, and these must be kept free of acid corrosion, a smear of vaseline being applied after they are cleaned.

Should the battery receiver fail to give any signal, the following tests should be made with the aid of a voltmeter and battery, as shown in Fig. 4.

(1) Make certain the aerial and earth leads are connected up.

(2) Check loudspeaker leads for continuity and see they are securely

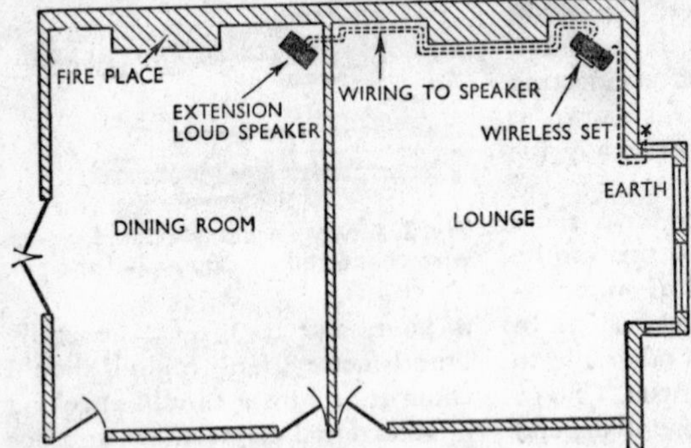

Fig. 3. Plan view of two adjoining rooms showing the wiring and suggested location of extension loud speaker in a suitable place, relative to set.

connected to the terminals.

(3) Test battery for voltage drop, and accumulator terminals for corrosion.

(4) Check all battery leads for a possible break inside the insulation.

(5) Test valves for continuity of filaments and see they are properly in their holders.

(6) Test for H.T. voltage on the anode of the valves.

(7) Test transformers and loud-speaker windings for continuity.

(8) Test any condensers across the H.T. supply for breakdown to earth.

(9) Inspect on/off switch to see if contact is good.

(10) Test all resistances for continuity.

The all-mains set requires considerably more skill to discover faults and rectify them. Indeed, it may be advisable to return the set to the dealer when the defect is persistent. The procedure to follow when the set ceases to function or is giving poor reproduction is to check all external connections before dealing with the set itself. Checks on similar lines to the battery set tests can be made under the following headings.

(1) Is the power supply "alive" at the plug-point?

(2) Are both aerial and earth connections in tightly and the connection intact?

(3) Are the loud-speaker plugs in firmly?

(4) Is the set switched on? (This may sound nonsensical, but it is a point to observe!)

(5) Test the mains leads for continuity.

(6) Is the wave change switch in the correct position? This should be tried in all positions for the test.

(7) If the set is for D.C. only, try the mains plug the reverse way in the socket.

(8) If it is an AC/DC set, check the resistance lead which is incorporated in the mains lead, to see if the connection at the plug end has been disconnected.

If all the foregoing points prove to be in order, the fault probably lies in the set. When working on an all-mains set, in no circumstances should the back be removed until the supply is switched off and mains plug removed from its socket. First free the interior of dust; an excellent way is to blow it out with a cycle pump or some form of light air spray.

Remove the valves, noting their positions carefully, and test the filaments in the manner indicated in the battery-set tests, remembering to pull the valve out by its base and not by the glass. If the fila-

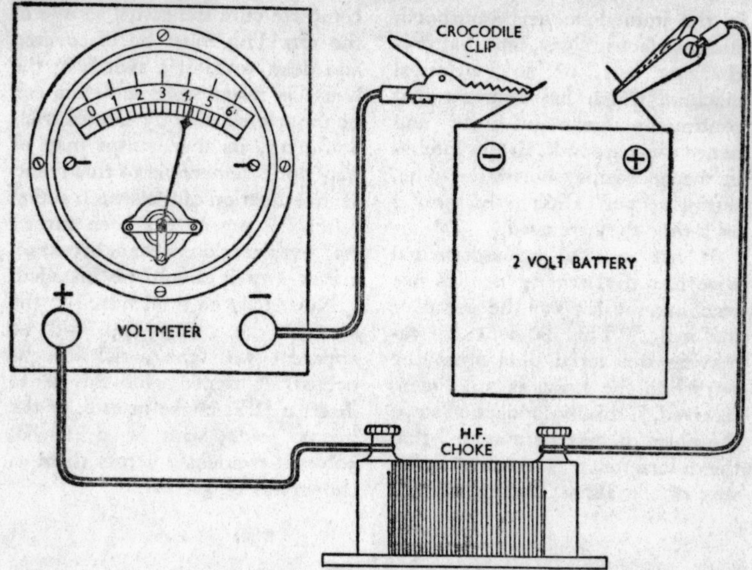

Fig. 4. How to use a voltmeter when making a continuity test with a two-volt battery connected across a high frequency choke.

ments are in order, a further check can be made by replacing the valves and switching on. With some valves it is easy to see if the filaments are alight, but with the metalized type it is not easy. To test these, switch off and place a hand on the valve; it will have become quite warm if the filament is in order.

If a filament is thought to be broken, the valve must be replaced with a new one. When putting a valve back into the set, make sure it fits firmly in position, and that valves with top connections are not touching any metal screens. (See also under VALVES).

If the set still fails to function, it may be necessary to take the chassis out of the cabinet to test all the components. Testing of components may have to be restricted to a continuity test if the only available equipment is a D.C. voltmeter and a 2-volt battery, as shown at Fig. 4. It should be noted that if condensers are being tested and continuity is indicated on the voltmeter this will show that the condenser plates are shorting, which will be one of the causes of failure.

Considerable annoyance may be caused by interference due to the operation of electrical machinery

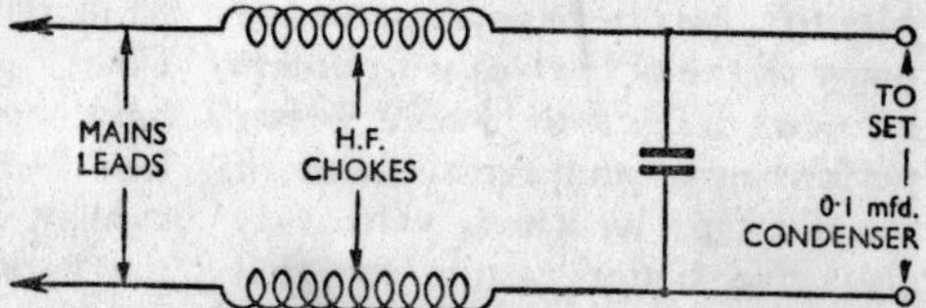

Fig. 5. Shows how to insert a high frequency choke in each of the mains leads with an 0.1 mfd. condenser across them.

in the immediate neighbourhood, such as electric signs, fans, battery-charging sets, or any electrical machine which has contacts that continually make-and-break and hence cause a spark. Even switches in the house may be troublesome, setting up a crackling in the speaker each time they are used.

It has first to be ascertained whether disturbing noises are reaching the set *via* the aerial or the mains. This is done by removing the aerial plug from the set while the noise is still being received. If this disconnection stops the noise, it may be assumed that the interference is coming in by way of the aerial, and to effect a complete cure the actual source of the crackling must be discovered and dealt with. If a switch in the house is responsible, and this can be discovered only by careful trial-and-error, its mechanism may or may not be amenable to treatment. If investigation of the switch action (after the supply has been turned off) reveals serious wear or breakage, a new switch should be installed.

Noise may be transmitted to the set *via* the mains and still be apparent with the aerial disconnected. A remedy for this is to insert a H.F. choke in each of the mains leads with a 0.1 mfd. 500-volt condenser across them as shown at Fig. 5.

Valves

VALVES, in common with other components in a receiving set, wear out with continuous use, and it is found that a marked improvement in the quality of reception is obtained if valves are renewed after, say, two years' continuous employment.

If a set is several years old, there may be some difficulty in obtaining a new valve of exactly the same type, number and manufacture as that already in the set. The original type may no longer be made. But that does not mean the end of the set's usefulness. Manufacturers have superseded many of the old valves with others of new design, to secure better performance, and replacement of the old type by a new valve may also give better results for that reason alone.

Before purchasing a new valve it is necessary to know the type of set: battery, alternating current or direct current, all-mains. The valve usually has the manufacturer's name, the type and number on the side or base. But, other details agreeing, it is not essential that the replacement be manufactured by the same firm.

Most valves have alternative equivalent made by one or other of the leading manufacturers; for example, should a power valve of the pentode type need replacing in an alternating current mains set, it could be obtained from at least four sources: Mazda AC/PEN; Mullard PEN4VA; Osram M.P.T.4; Cossor MP/PEN. These may not have characteristics exactly equivalent but they are approximately similar. By characteristics is meant the figures that indicate the performance of the valve used during ideal conditions, under the headings of the filament volts, filament current, amplification factor, impedance, mutual conductance, anode volts, screen volts, grid bias, anode current and optimum load resistance. The figures for these items are usually given on a valve data sheet sold with the valve, or they can be found in manufacturers' valve booklets.

One important feature of the valve is the type of base. It may be found that a valve needing replacement has an equivalent type in all the characteristics but has a different type of base, that is, more or less pins or a different fitting for the holder. At one time most valves had either four or five pins, and in the case of pentodes and screen grid valves an additional cap connection on the top or side. Today, the valve-base may have from four to nine pins, with top and side connections as well. The type of base, therefore, is of prime importance as the valve, although similar in all other characteristics, will be useless if it will not fit into the valve-holder in the set.

If it is not possible to obtain a valve with a similar base, the only alternative is to replace the valve holder with a new one capable of fitting the replacement valve: this means the purchase of a new holder at the same time as the valve. An example of a change of this kind is when a 5-pin screen grid valve with a top connection has to be replaced and the only available equivalent is a simple type having a 7-pin base. When a suitable valve holder is obtained it can be put in the place of the holder already in the set.

This change presents a difficult job, but with the aid of a soldering iron, and due care exercised with the connections, the alterations can be made. Make a note of all wires as these are removed from the old holder, fit the new holder into position and connect the wires to the solder tag with the same indicating letter as on the old holder; the top connection, if it be a grid connection, will then connect to the socket marked "grid". The sockets may not be marked on the new type of holder, but these can be identified from the valve maker's booklet.

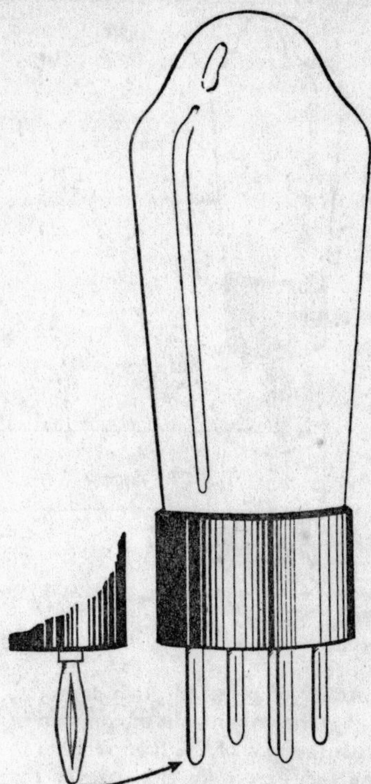

Fig. 1. If the pins of the valve do not grip they may be eased open as shown.

A valve may give considerable trouble although not being at fault itself. As it fits into a holder by a

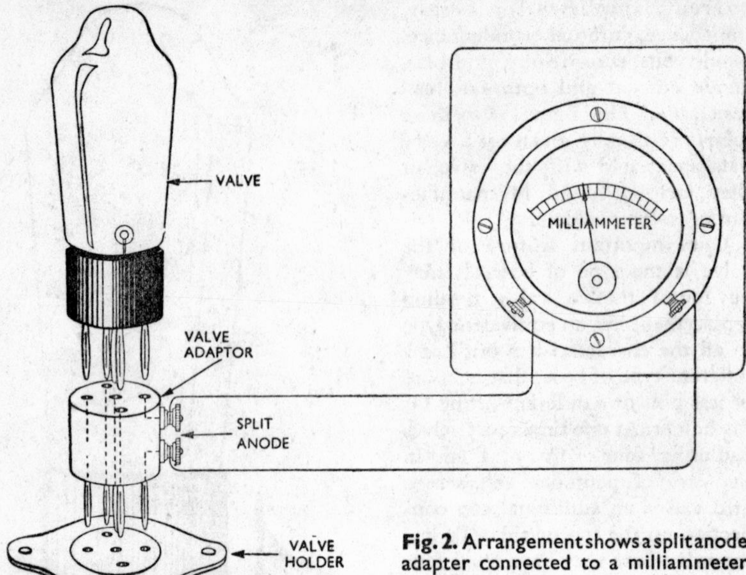

Fig. 2. Arrangement shows a split anode adapter connected to a milliammeter for reading current values.

number of pins, all push contacts, this is the only means of connection with the rest of the components in the set, except in the case of the cap connections, and often these also are push fits. It is possible for one of these contacts to be either dirty or loose, the valve in consequence failing to function.

If the pins are dirty they should be cleaned with fine emery paper. If the valve fits loosely in the holder, the set will proclaim the fact with crackling noises; the valve should be taken out and the split of the pin eased open with the tip of a knife (Fig. 1). The holder should also be inspected, and if necessary cleaned. If the sockets are very loose these can be improved by pinching-in each with small pliers. Removal and replacement of a valve should be done by gripping the base firmly and gently rocking it until the valve pulls out. It should not be pulled by the glass, or this may break away from its base.

It is possible to have a complete valve test at a radio dealer's. It is useful, however, to be in a position to be able to make various simple tests at home. They can be carried out with very little equipment, such as a voltmeter for reading direct current voltage, a milliammeter with three dial readings of 0 to 5, 0 to 50 and 0 to 150 milliamps for reading the current values, a split anode adapter as shown in Fig. 2, and a battery. This equipment allows for a continuity test, which is a test to ascertain if the circuit is continuous throughout, and the measurement of the anode current to be found.

A filament continuity test is a test to see if the filament wire of

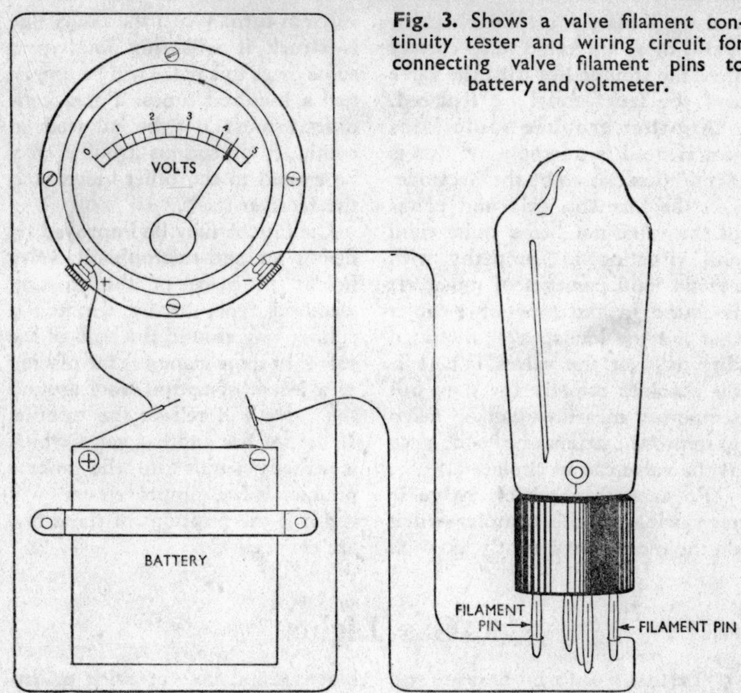

Fig. 3. Shows a valve filament continuity tester and wiring circuit for connecting valve filament pins to battery and voltmeter.

the valve is intact, and is quite simple to undertake with the aid of the direct current voltmeter and battery connected as shown at Fig. 3. If a battery valve is being tested, the battery in circuit should be 2 volts. If it is an A.C. valve, a 4-volt battery must be inserted. Should the filament of the valve be intact, the circuit will be closed and a reading shown on the voltmeter.

The anode current can be measured by using the split anode adapter and the milliammeter: both are shown connected up in Fig. 2. The split anode adapter is in the form of a removable plug and is an easy means of making a break in the anode wiring, all the pins being continuous except the anode pin, which is broken inside the adapter and the ends brought out to two terminals for connection to the milliammeter.

With the adapter fixed in the valve socket in the wireless set, the valve is placed in the top and the milliammeter connected to the terminals of the adapter, and the set then switched on. A reading will be indicated on the meter; if the valve is working in the correct manner the reading should compare favourably with that shown on the manufacturer's valve data for the particular valve under test. If the reading indicated is lower than the manufacturer's figures (obtained from the chart included in the valve carton) something is at fault; the voltages, both H.T.

and grid bias, must be checked, and if these are found to be correct then the trouble lies with the valve and the latter must be replaced.

Another trouble sometimes experienced is microphony; this is a condition caused by the electrode, i.e., the filament, grid and plates of the valve not being quite rigid and vibrating in sympathy with certain loud passages of music. It is found in the type of receiver that has the loudspeaker mounted directly over the valves. There is no absolute remedy for this, but temporary measures can be taken to improve matters until such time as the valve can be replaced.

To ascertain which valve is responsible for this trouble, switch on the receiver and gently tap each valve in turn. When the faulty one is struck it will ring loudly; in some cases this noise will be amplified a hundred times. These conditions must not be allowed to continue, or serious trouble may be caused to the other valves and the receiver itself.

Conditions may be improved by fitting an anti-microphonic valve holder in place of the existing standard type, or by winding a rubber ring around the bulb of the valve. In some instances the placing of a jacket of cotton wool around the valve will relieve the trouble. If the set has another valve which is exactly similar to the microphonic valve, improvement will result if the positions of these two are changed.

Gas Lights

VERTICAL mantle burners are still in use, though the inverted type has almost put them out of business. It is assumed that a new mantle is to be fitted to a vertical burner; take out the crutch which supports the mantle, and remove any fragments of the latter which may still be on the burner. Brush away any dust or flue with a camel-hair brush or similar brush with soft hair. The gas-fitter uses a little blower to send a current of air up through from the air "ports" below; failing something of the sort, get a piece of rubber tube about ⅛in. bore and fit to one end a piece of brass or copper tube about four inches long, which will enter the air ports. Put the metal end in place at an air hole, and blow briskly through the other end of the rubber. Pinch the tube after blowing and before taking an in-breath, or some of the dust may inadvertently be drawn into the mouth. Of course, a rubber bulb fitted to the metal tube would prevent this risk.

Leaving all adjustments as they are, turn on the gas and light it at the burner, without a mantle in place: the flame should be bluish at the inner cone and more of a purple colour at the outer part. It should be brisk and free, and not of a yellow or luminous type. The sliding collar which can be turned round partly to close the air holes should be manipulated slowly and gradually to stop any roaring; the collar in good burners can be fixed at the best setting by turning in a small screw. Another screw (see Fig. 1) controls the gas supply, and should be turned in a little if a yellow or luminous flame is seen.

Put on a new mantle and flare it off by setting a match to it; this burns off the protective dressing with which the mantle is coated. Any manipulation of the mantle must be done before burning off, since the fabric is too fragile to be touched afterwards. Next turn on the gas and apply a light. In correct adjustment the flame should just fill the mantle; if too much gas is getting to the bunsen the flame will be too high and will come through the top. Alter the air-collar adjustment again if needed. Turn out the light and let the burner cool before replacing the glass chimney and ornamental shade.

Inverted Burners.—The construction, though similar in principle to that of the upright burners, is different in some points. There is the sliding or rotating air-collar as before, but the gas control is usually a needle-valve operated by turning a milled metal or plain fibre disc at the end of the screw. Take off the globe; the mantle is held by lugs which fit on to recesses or brackets on the burner. Get a mantle of the proper size for that particular burner; take the old mantle ring to the shop to ensure correctness.

Brush out or blow the dust from the burner; owing to the inverted position this is easier than with the upright burner. Light the gas at the nozzle and adjust both gas and air supplies until the flame is the proper colour and not unduly noisy. Turn out the gas. Put on a new mantle and, after making sure it is in correct position, apply a match with the gas still turned off. Now turn on the gas and light at

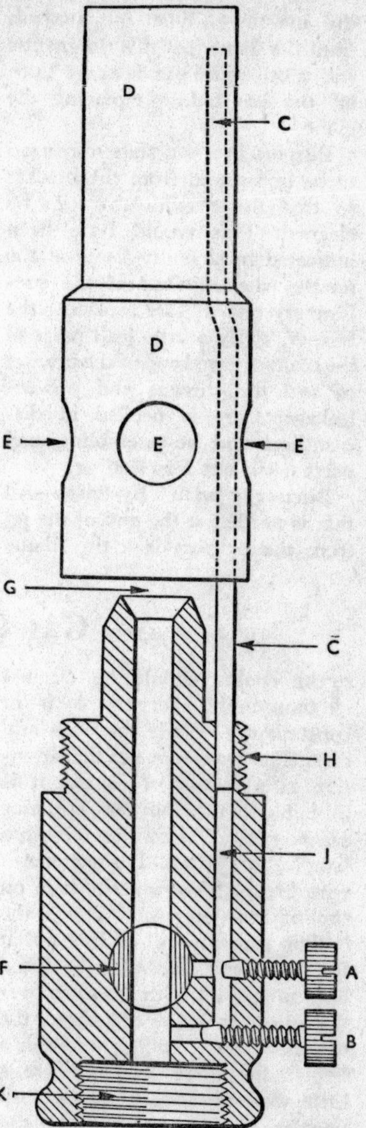

Fig. 1. Vertical mantle burner. A and B, by-pass jet adjustment screws; J and C, by-pass duct and tube; F, gas tap plug; G, main gas jet; K, threaded socket for bracket; H, thread to engage sleeve D; E air ports for gas jet.

the mantle. Adjust the controls until the flame just fills the mantle and is otherwise satisfactory. Turn off the gas before replacing the globe.

Burners in a bad state may need to be unscrewed from the bracket so that the needle-valve can be cleaned. This would have been indicated by a faulty flame at the nozzle when ignited at the preliminary test. Before replacing the burner, apply a little lead paint to the male-screwed end of the bracket to seal the threads and prevent leakage. Care is needed in dismantling and re-assembling any parts taken out for cleaning.

Burners with By-Pass.—All that is needed at the end of the jet from the by-pass is a tiny flame which will ignite the main gas supply to the burner when the tap is opened. If the by-pass control screw is not opened sufficiently however, the by-pass will not light (as it should) when the main tap is turned off. A few tests with the actual burner will disclose what is needed. Good burners have a steatite tip to the actual jet; the orifice may have become choked, and should in that case be cleared with a fine needle. Do not use a metal-worker's broach or other like tool for this job, or the hole may be enlarged. The burner may have to be dismantled, if very dirty or corroded. As mentioned earlier, a preliminary test for this purpose should be made before anything in the way of readjustment is done.

Gas Cookers

The cooker should be cleaned thoroughly every week if in constant use. While the oven and enamelled parts may get this attention as a matter of course, it is probable that the burners, etc. may escape notice. A stiff brush, with a handle, is needed. Do not use a wire brush. Take out the bars on top of the hot plate, above the boiling rings; it will be found that the "burners" can then be lifted out, as they fit with a socket over the injectors projecting from the taps. Get some boiling water in a largish flat bowl, and dissolve a little washing soda or some soap powder in the water. Dip the burners in, one at a time, and scrub vigorously with the brush, paying especial attention to the nipples or holes from which the gas issues and burns when it is connected up.

Next, sharpen up a wooden skewer, or some similar spill of wood, until it has a slowly tapering point which will fit into the holes in the boiling ring. The point need not be rounded; in fact, if it is left with squared facets, it will work better. Twist the skewer into the holes, so removing any incrustation which may have blocked them; resharpen the point from time to time as necessary. Never use a sharp metal instrument for this job. Before replacing the burners, scrub over the outside top of the oven with hot soda water to remove any congealed grease. Hardened grease can be cleaned off with one or other of the proprietary compounds available at most ironmongers, for this purpose.

The fretted plates above the grill need careful cleaning if an

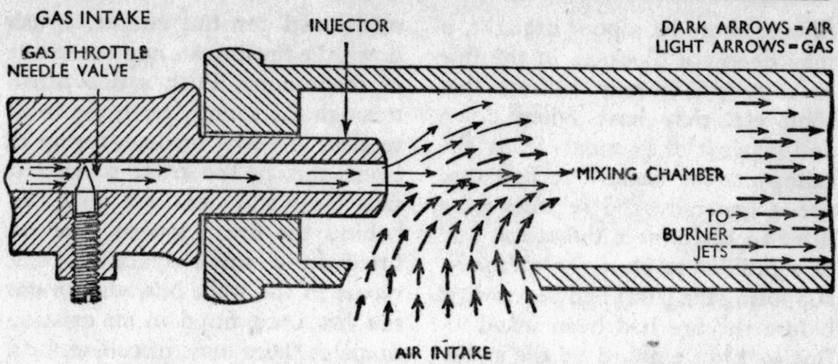

Fig. 1. Shows a cross-section of a typical gas cooker bunsen burner and how the delivery of gas is controlled before entry into mixing chamber via the injector jet.

offensive smell is to be prevented. After washing the bars, hot plate, etc., wipe them with a dry cloth before replacing; allow the burners to dry naturally, after shaking out any water within.

The adjustment of the bunsen part of the burners (see Fig. 1) should be left to a gas-fitter, and the adjusting screws should be left as they were set by the Company. The height of the flame, and its colour (the latter depending on the proper mixture of gas and air to the appliance) are matters which need skilled treatment. Tampering with any individual burner may do more harm than good; the gas-fitter can make a test when all the top burners are in use, to see that they *all* work properly under normal conditions. The oven burner (often nowadays a single long burner at the back) can be lifted out and washed in the same manner as the boiling rings; clean out the holes with a freshly sharpened skewer.

If the gas "lights back" and, after a bang, burns with a luminous flame the adjustment of the gas is faulty. But when the burners or the surrounding parts are hot, this lighting-back may be merely temporary; let the burner cool for a short time, after turning out the gas, and try again.

The flames from the boiling rings should not touch the bottom of any saucepan or other vessel in use; nor should they impinge against any bars, the appliance being so designed that the flames when in proper adjustment will be clear of the bars, supports, etc.

Gas Fires

A GOOD up-draught is essential for comfort and efficiency, and, of course, for healthy conditions in the room. Light a candle or a taper, and hold it just at the opening of the hood or canopy of the gas fire. The flame will be drawn up into the canopy if all is well, thus demonstrating that there is a draught upwards through the fire and into the flue. The extent of this up-current can be gauged by the vigour with which the flame is blown inwards and upwards.

Should there be a poor draught, it may denote a blockage in the flue or chimney, or may indicate that soot, etc. may have fallen down and against the outlet from the canopy at the back. The first case needs generally the services of a fitter to disconnect the stove, and of a builder to clear the chimney, supposing the latter had been swept before the fire had been installed. But soot not reached by the sweep may fall down later, so that sweeping the chimney anew may cure the trouble.

Supposing the second case to exist, it can be dealt with in the course of a general clean-up as below described. Take off the wire guard from the fire; take out the "radiants" carefully and lay them in a safe place: they will probably be brittle after use. Unscrew the metal fender or similar fittings at the foot of the fire. Now brush out all dust and fluff with a small paint-brush. Clean out the burner jets with a skewer, as described for the cooker burners; the suction nozzle of a vacuum cleaner will draw out dust and fluff from the burner nipples. Using the handled brush mentioned for the cooker, brush down the fire-bricks, and the inside of the canopy. Push a flue brush through the canopy from the front to clear any soot or dust, trying to bring this to the front so that it falls clear and does not go down behind the fire. Modern fires are fitted in a small specially built recess in the wall; but when a gas fire has been fitted in an existing fireplace there may, of course, be a good deal of space behind. Often, the only way of dealing with the matter is to have the gas fire disconnected and drawn out, so that the back space can be cleared thoroughly.

Put back the radiants, buying fresh ones to replace any that are broken. Defective radiants waste gas and impair the action of the fire to a very great extent. The flame should pass up through the radiants without being checked or diverted by misplaced or broken portions. Wrongly shaped ones, which do not properly fit that particular fire, are also a source of wasted heat. The adjustment of the burner control is a matter for a competent gas-fitter.

Oil Stoves

VAPORIZING stoves work on the principle of the paraffin blow-lamp. The heating tube has first to be made very hot before vaporization of the fuel will take place. This preparatory operation is done in the following manner. With the air outlet closed, a small quantity of methylated spirit is poured into the cup at the base of the burner and ignited with a match; this flame plays upon the burner, where the heating tube is doubled upon itself before going to the nipple. By the time the spirit in the cup is nearly burnt out, the tube should be hot enough to vaporize oil passing up to it. The heat of the spirit flame will have warmed up the reservoir somewhat, and so will have set up a pressure within. Normally, by this time some vapour, or some partly vaporized oil, will have emerged from the jet and will have become lighted by the spirit flame. After a few puffs and spurts, a steady roar should come from the burner, and the familiar bluish flame should appear.

In a few moments the flame should become stronger and more regular. Now is the time to give one or two strokes with the pump, but if the flame turns yellow, and spurts of liquid paraffin come out, it is a sign of premature pumping. Open the air outlet valve, to reduce pressure in the reservoir; the flame should then die down. Let the stove cool; fill the cup with methylated spirit and try again. A little experimenting will soon show when to start the pump.

Sometimes the flame, after starting properly, will light-back, and oil will take fire at the nipple; this is a defect due usually to a choked nipple, other things being correct. Avoid spilling methylated spirit over the reservoir; wipe off any surplus before igniting at the cup. Too early operation of the pump may force out liquid paraffin which drops down into the cup, mixes with the spirit, and burns noisily there. Open the air outlet valve momentarily, and the trouble at the nipple should cease; after closing the air valve, the flame should soon start up properly.

The following simple rules should be remembered:

1. *Priming.* Fill the cup with spirit to about ⅛in. from the top, the stove standing on a level surface. Stick to this quantity, and the action of the stove can then be judged.

2. *Pumping.* Start when the spirit is three-parts consumed; stop at once if liquid paraffin emerges.

3. *Air Outlet Valve.* Open the valve immediately any irregularity is seen; the flame will then die down.

4. *Nipple.* Clear this with the proper pricker every time the stove is to be used—before priming and lighting. Do not use any other implement on the nipple which might enlarge the aperture.

5. *Filling the Reservoir.* Do this only when the stove is "out", and after it has cooled. Do not overfill. About three-quarters full is enough.

General Hints. A full-size stove is better, even for "portable" use, than a miniature one. Procure a proper metal can for the priming spirit, one with a pouring spout. Use a small funnel for filling in paraffin. When buying a stove, get also the following spares: two or three extra nipples; a nipple key for removing the nipples; half a dozen prickers.

The pump can be unscrewed to fit a new leather washer. It may sometimes suffice to bend outwards the sides of the old washer.

Wick-type Oil Stoves.—These should not smoke or smell. Defects of this kind are the natural consequences of neglect, and are usually caused by failure to attend to the wick and those air vents which are intended to allow the passage of an uninterrupted current of air. It should go without saying that the outside of the oil reservoir should be wiped with a dry rag after every filling as a routine precaution against the collection of dirt and dust and the spread of an oily odour.

In cleaning and preparing for use a paraffin oil heater of a popular type (Fig. 1) the reservoir should be lifted right out, after the upper part of the stove has been tilted

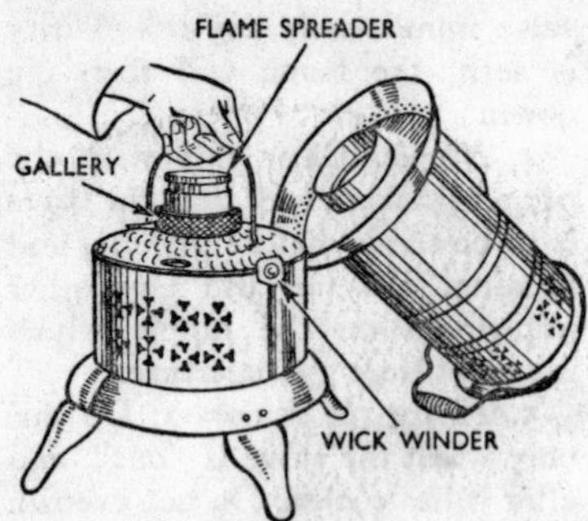

Fig. 1. Removing oil heater fount from the lower section of the heater casing.

back (a spring catch releases it). The reservoir should then be filled not more than three-quarters full. The opportunity should be taken, at the same time, to trim the wick and clean the burner parts. To get at the wick, the flame spreader must first be removed by twisting, and then lifting. The wick is then wound up to bring its top level with the top of the central tube. Burnt fragments can now be wiped away with a piece of cloth, loose threads snipped off with scissors, and a final gentle patting-down should leave the wick properly trimmed. Scissors should not be used other than for the removal ot fluffy bits, unless, through a period of absolute neglect, it becomes essential to restore the end of the wick by cutting it level. The regular removal of loose char should keep the wick in proper condition until it has burned down so short that a new one must be fitted. See arrangement, Fig. 2.

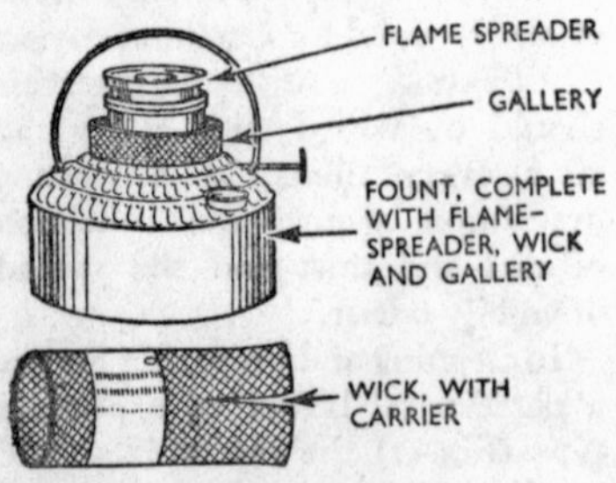

Fig. 2. The fount, flame spreader and gallery and view of wick with carrier.

Before the reservoir is replaced, the gallery of the heater should be unscrewed (anti-clockwise) and removed for cleaning. A small stiff brush rubbed once or twice over its perforation will dislodge any dirt that may have settled there. When the spreader has been similarly brushed, and any char on its underside scraped off, these parts are in a condition to go back.

In replacing an expended wick by a new one, the latter must be appropriate to the particular model of stove. After the flame spreader and gallery have been removed, the old wick should be turned up to its limit and then pulled right out along with its carrier. The old wick may then be extracted from the carrier and the new one slipped in, the straight edge of the new wick being inserted into the bottom of the carrier and coaxed upwards. It should finally be pressed against the spikes at top and bottom of the inside of the carrier so that it is gripped firmly.

The wick and carrier are then placed over the central tube and pushed down, the split ends being coaxed into the reservoir and the carrier forced farther down until the teeth on the winder spindle engage with the apertures in the carrier. The new wick having been turned down as far as the winder will carry it, the gallery is then screwed home and the spreader twisted into place. The wick should be given five minutes to soak up oil, when it will be ready for lighting. See also Fig. 3.

It is important to ensure that the carrier is replaced with its top uppermost (the top for a short distance down is unperforated) and that the cogwheel of the winder passes through one of the splits in the wick. Also, it is advisable to dry the new wick thoroughly first. One popular model simplifies wick replacement in that new wicks are purchased together with new carriers.

The wick should always be lighted in two or three places at once, after it has been turned up to the fullest extent (without straining the winder). The heater should then be closed down and the flame turned quite low for a minute or so. That gives the burner a chance to warm up, the flame afterwards being turned on full. Possibility of the heater smoking is then remote. When the flame is to be extinguished it should not be blown out, but the wick turned down as far as the winder will take it. It will be extinguished in a matter of seconds.

Wick economy is practised by ensuring that there is always sufficient oil in the reservoir to prevent the wick burning dry. If the latter should happen, the top ¼in. or more of the wick will have to be rubbed off, with fingers or cloth, and ragged pieces cut away by scissors. Heater models fitted with a damper (a revolving perforated plate at the top) should have this closed, for ordinary purposes. For boiling a kettle or saucepan, the damper should be open. Cleanliness of the exterior of the heater is ensured by rubbing over it occasionally a very little furniture polish, all trace of the latter being then removed with a clean cloth and vigorous rubbing.

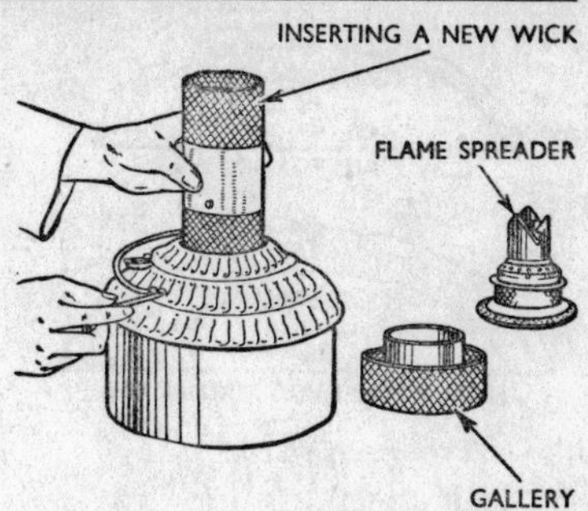

Fig. 3. Inserting new wick. Carrier is perforated to engage sprocket of winder at interior end of handle.

The bottom of the central draught tube, the function of which is to allow free circulation of air in the interior of the heater, should not be impeded by the surface on which the stove stands, such as a thick fluffy rug or mat. Ordinarily, the feet will raise it well above a surface, but if it is located on a rug or mat into which the short feet are likely to sink, a square of wood, or other firm and level base, should be provided.

The boiling stove, provided with

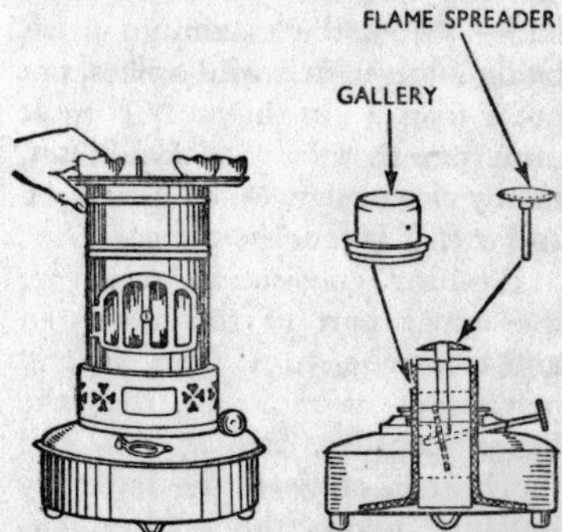

Fig. 4. A popular boiling stove. Right-hand view is a cross-section of fount.

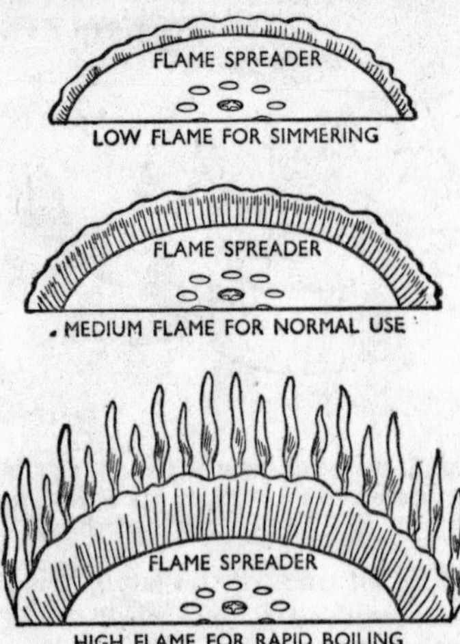

Fig. 5. Diagrams representing three types of flame. Low, medium and high.

a grid top plate, requires some care as to adjustment of the flame. Taking a small popular quick boiling model as an example (Fig. 4), when this has been lit, the door should be closed securely and the wick turned down very low. After a minute or so it can be turned up, for about the same length of time, to produce a small blue flame. The burner will then have warmed up and the wick can be turned for a larger flame, the maximum flame being blue with white spikes not more than a ¼in. high. It is most important that the wick should not, in any circumstances, be turned up so far that it touches the spreader.

Cleaning consists in removing the upper part of the stove (an anti-clockwise turn frees it and permits of its removal), then the flame spreader, freeing this and the burner of char, the latter by brushing across the perforations. With the wick level with the top of the tube, clean this as previously described. Replacement of the wick is effected in the same way as has been described for the heater.

Flame adjustment (Fig. 5) in the larger model boiling stove is in three stages, low for simmering, medium for ordinary boiling and cooking, high for rapid boiling. The low flame is a small blue one; the medium, blue with white points just showing; the high, for really fierce heat, a blue flame surmounted with ½in. high white points. The wick, when it requires trimming, should be raised level with the central tube, after collar and spreader have been removed, and wiped level with a soft rag.

It should be noted that this wick is chisel-shaped at the top, the slope being downwards to the inside, and this shape should be so maintained. Lack of frequent attention may result in the top of the wick burning unevenly, wiping with a cloth failing to restore the level. Instead of trying to restore the level with the scissors it is

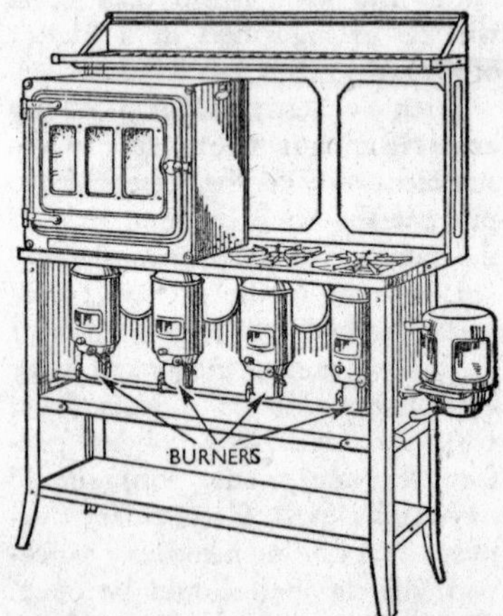

Fig. 6. Common type of oil cooker, having four burners supplied by a pipeline from a single reservoir.

better to empty the reservoir and with all parts replaced, light the wick and let it burn out. The ring of char left at the top can then be removed with the cloth and the top edge of the wick will be level once again.

The oil cooker (Fig. 6) calls for flame adjustment on the lines of the boiling stove, with the important difference that the high flame may be allowed white points up to 1in. high but no more. Here, the high flame, which gives intense heat, is only for rapid boiling, frying, and pastry baking. If the flame exceeds that limit, overheating of the burner will gradually produce a still larger flame, and apart from possible dire consequences to whatever is being cooked, smoking may result. A few minutes should always be allowed, with a medium flame, for the burner to warm up.

Daily cleaning of the wicks (to be kept chisel-edged with the aid of the cleaner supplied with the stove) increases the efficiency of the flame (Fig. 7). The slotted cleaner is placed on top of the burner tube (after removal of the spreader) and the wick turned up.

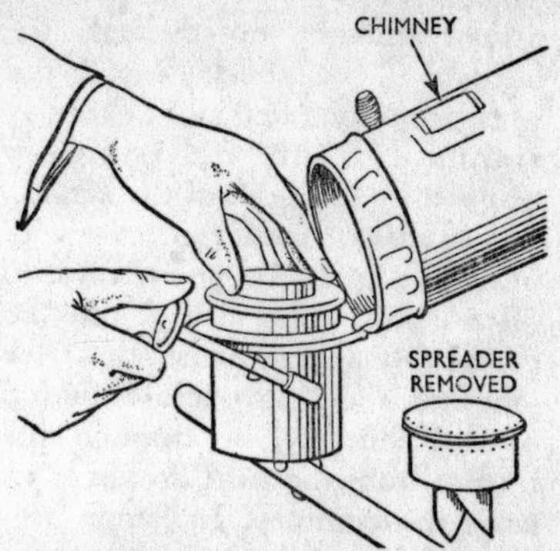

Fig. 7. Trimming and cleaning the wick.

As the cleaner is rotated the char is removed and the edge of the wick is left at the correct shape. Airholes in the base of the chimney are likely to become stopped up if a utensil boils over. If that occurs, the chimney should be tilted back and lifted so that the tongue of the cone is freed from the securing collar ring. The chimney being free, the cone (in the chimney's base) should now be removed and both parts carefully washed in soapy water. The external frame of the cooker should be cleaned with a little soapy water and a cloth, and then wiped quite dry. (See also Pressure Oil Stoves, page 148.)

Oil Lamps

The instructions for the maintenance and care of oil lamps are similar to those described in the previous article under the heading of Oil Stoves. The following details should, however, be given special note.

Fill with oil daily, and carefully wipe off any paraffin that may get on to the outside of the reservoir or on the burner. When first lighting a lamp for the evening, turn it down somewhat lower than the customary height; as the burner warms up the flame will rise a little. Do not buy a lamp with a *cheap* glass reservoir or one raised too high on a pedestal and therefore apt to be top-heavy.

Replace a broken chimney, even if it has only become shortened by the break. The chimney induces a proper draught up through the burner; if too short, it will not work properly. See that the chimney stands upright, and is firmly gripped by the sides of the carrier. If necessary, bend the brasswork inwards a trifle. Do not attempt to fill a lamp while still alight. To extinguish a lamp, turn the wick low first, then blow across the top of the chimney, or through the burner from the side; do not blow *down* the chimney. In lamps provided with an extinguisher, turn the wick low before operating the extinguisher.

Lamps with a tubular wick have an air passage through the centre of the burner, which permits a more plentiful supply of air than is possible with the flat-wick burners. The lamp should stand so that this opening at the foot is not blocked. Regularly clean the burners of all lamps by rinsing in warm soda water, using a stiff brush to remove any matter blocking the perforated parts. When inserting the wick, turn the wheel gently until it is certain that the wick has been gripped and is feeding correctly. Oil lamps using an incandescent mantle should be cared for and operated according to the maker's instructions. Apart from these special points, cleanliness and regular attention are called for, as with other types.

It is not safe to leave any oil lamp unattended for long; at the best the lamp may gather heat and the flame may rise too high, leading to a cracked chimney and a profusion of smoke. At the worst, the lamp may become overheated and cause it to become dangerous.

Mending China and Kitchen Utensils

THE repair of broken china depends, naturally, on the extent of the damage. A teapot or cup or saucer broken into small pieces is hardly worth mending unless it has some important or intrinsic value. Vases and antique pottery may well be repaired if the damage is not so great as to render the piecing together an almost impossible task.

Mending Pottery.—Simple breakages involving large fractures, without irrecoverable small chippings and fragments, may be mended by the use of liquid glues, several proprietary brands of which are available at most ironmongers' stores. A good cellulose base cement glue is a very efficient material. Apply the cement thinly to the broken faces, allow it to harden a little, then smear another thin layer on the faces and join quickly all the broken portions. If any additional temporary means of securing the portions together is practical this measure should be resorted to. Tall vases, and circular pots, having high walls may be judiciously bound with cord to retain the broken portions in position until the glue has set hard. After which, surplus cement may be trimmed off by a sharp knife or used razor blade. A piece of adhesive tape or muslin applied to the crack on the underside, or inside of the article will assist in strengthening the joint, see also Figs. 1 and 2.

Teapot handles or cup handles will not respond satisfactorily to this method of repair. These should be pinned or rivetted in the manner described later. Saucers, plates and small jugs, cups, etc. which are not too badly broken may be mended in the foregoing manner with cement, the broken part being held in position (for the plate or saucer only) as shown in Fig. 3. Cleanliness of the joint is important. Rubber bands may be employed on small jugs to keep the broken portions in place until the cement hardens.

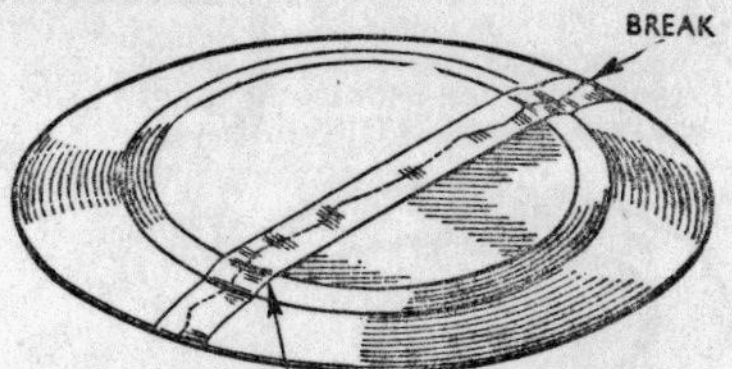

Fig. 1. A strip of adhesive tape applied to straight fracture after glue has set.

Riveting.—Riveting is a somewhat difficult method of mending pottery. The handyman, if he is interested in attempting this sort of repair, should practise the method of drilling the ware, on scrap pieces of pottery, so as to acquire a better sense of the more delicate treatment of the material than it is possible to describe.

First, purchase a small, but good wheel brace. The drill may be a very fine Morse gauge drill, the size of which will vary according to the thickness of the material to be drilled. Heavy pottery will require thick gauge wire to rivet the joints together. Ordinary metal drills will do the job fairly satisfactorily and hardened triangular section broaches of fine gauge may be used to enlarge the holes.

The position of the holes to be bored in the material should be gauged with the eye, the actual boring being made if possible with the article, for example the teapot, filled with water, the broken parts having been first secured if necessary by the process of cementing already mentioned. Do not apply heavy pressure on the drill when operating the hand drill, allow the speed of the drill to carry away the material. If the material is fairly thin it is advisable to drill the holes with the article completely immersed in water and as the drill penetrates the other side of the material the drilling motion should be even more controlled and slow so as to avoid chipping. Drill holes about $\frac{3}{16}$ in., or more, each side of the fracture and bind together by inserting soft brass wire of the same gauge as the hole. Turn in the edges of the wire as shown in Fig. 4. The total length of the wire used to make the joint should

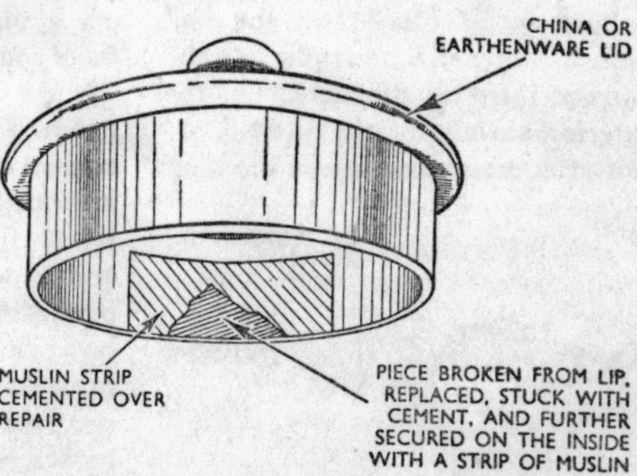

Fig. 2. Reinforcing small repair with strip of muslin.

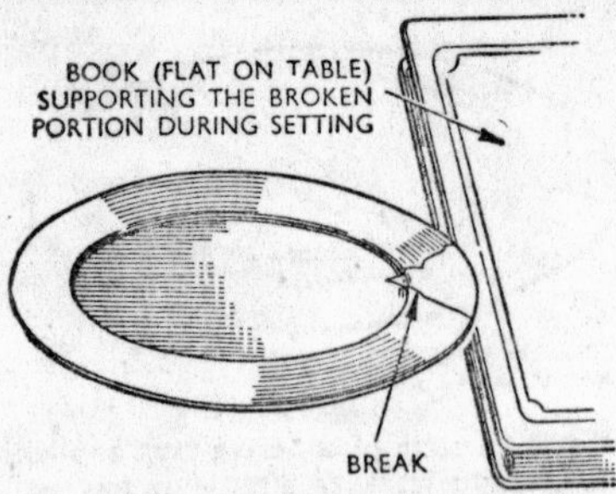

Fig. 3. Shows how to support a small fractured portion of a plate after it has been glued and fitted.

be the distance between the two holes, plus twice the thickness of the pottery, plus at least half the distance between the two holes.

Metal Utensils.—Pots and pans and metal utensils such as kettles, either enamelled or plain, may be mended if leaks occur in the base or wall, by fitting one of the sealing washers shown in Fig. 5. Leaking seams may be repaired by soldering, and dents may be removed by hard pressure with a blunt round metal tool or by a ball pein hammer. This latter method of removing dents holds good, if used correctly, with silverware, pewter, etc. but excessive force should not be applied. If the dent is placed over a hard wood block and the ball pein hammer can be applied to the convex form of the dent, i.e. the interior surface of the utensil, do not attempt to knock out the dent

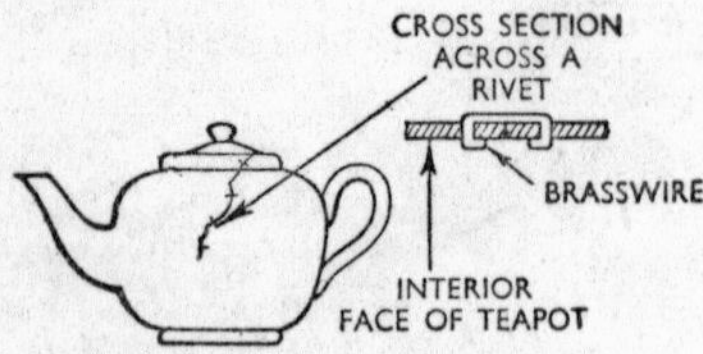

Fig. 4. Shows type of riveting for china.

in a few blows. Tap evenly and lightly all over the dent (the thinner the gauge of metal the lighter the tap), and continue until the dent has disappeared.

Where handle rivets fall out or are loose these may be replaced by those of similar diameter and material. If there are small cracks running from the holes where the handle is attached to the utensil, remove the rivets and cut a piece of thin gauge tin plate of sufficient dimensions amply to cover the positions of the rivet holes in the utensil. Mark off the positions of the rivet holes on to the steel

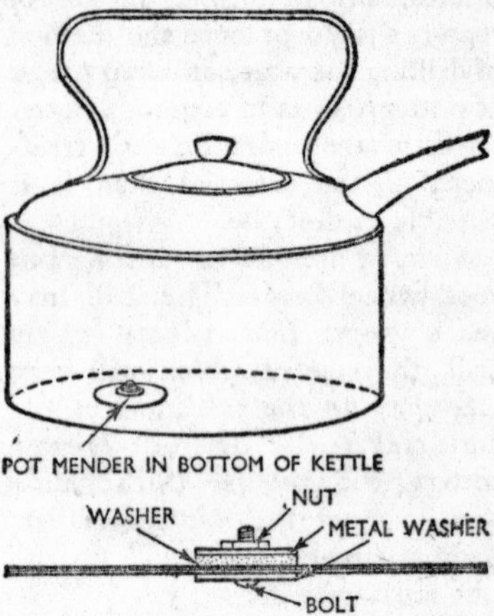

Fig. 5. View of kettle with pot mender fitted and cross-section of pot mender.

patch. Drill out the holes to the correct diameter and place it on the interior side of the material. Pass rivets through the patch utensil and handle, rivet holes. Then burr over the ends of the rivets by a ball pein hammer. Fractured hand-grips on kettles may be repaired by securing two shaped strips of wood by screws as shown in Fig. 6. Lids having broken finger grip knobs

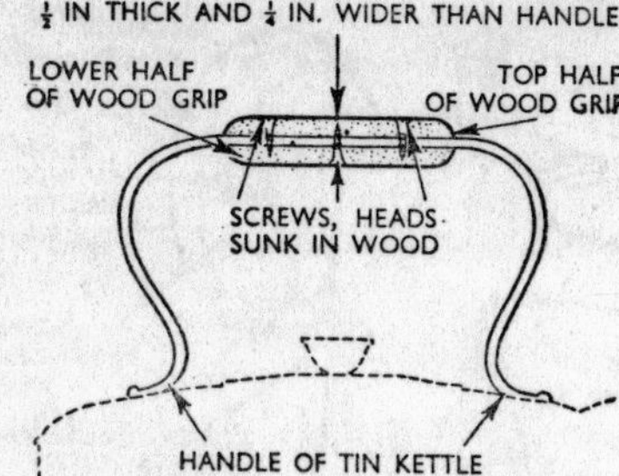

Fig. 6. How to mend a kettle handle that has broken at the hand-grip. Use straight grain hardwood and bore screw holes with suitable drill to avoid splitting of the wood along the grain.

may be renovated by the use of a cork, screw and washer as shown in Fig. 7.

Cleaning Metal Utensils.—Kettles particularly, and all kitchen utensils should be regularly cleaned and washed on the inside and outer walls and bases.

Kettles are very often subject to the formation of a white deposit containing lime. This furring-up of the kettle may be cured by the introduction of a tablespoonful of vinegar in a kettleful of water. The mixture should be left to soak into the deposit for a few hours, after which the kettle should be rinsed out. The harder particles may be prized away by a knife, and if this is not satisfactory, a further soaking in vinegar and water at a convenient opportunity is indicated.

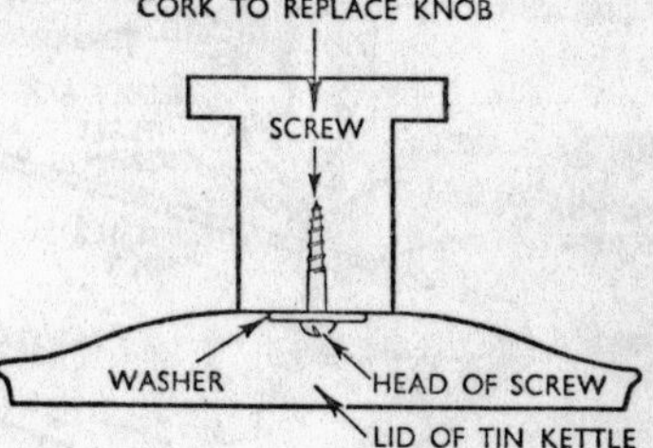

Fig. 7. How to fit a new handle to a lid.

When the kettle is once more thoroughly clean inside, make a practice of swilling and cleaning the interior every day so that the white deposit does not get a chance to form. A small pebble or marble placed in the kettle will discourage the formation of the deposit on the walls and bottom of the kettle.

Sewing Machines

HOWEVER careful the user may be to cover the sewing machine whenever it is not in use, dust and fluff will inevitably accumulate, and although these may be removed daily from the external parts, there is a great temptation to allow those parts which are out of sight to remain dirty until trouble occurs.

Oil, of the kind recommended by the makers of the particular model, is essential to the proper lubrication of working surfaces, spindles and bearings, but before any oiling is done, the dusting of all parts is essential and should be particularly thorough. The oil holes, which must be kept clear, are indicated in the maker's instruction handbook; each one should be located and given its single drop of lubricant.

The owner of a new machine may wonder how frequently cleaning and oiling will call for attention. The average user, running the machine for an odd hour or so, on perhaps two or three days of the week, should dust it both before and after use, and

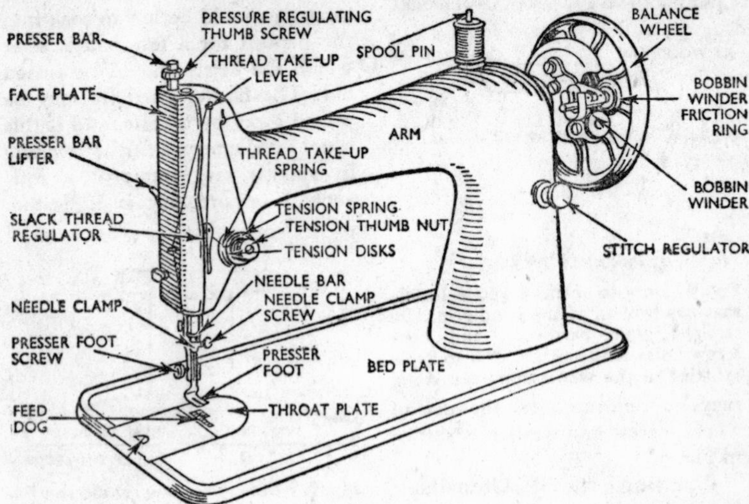

Fig. 1. Shows the main components and arrangement of typical design of sewing machine. For details of stand and treadle type connections, see also Fig. 3.

oil it not more often than about once a month. If used three or four hours a day regularly, oiling and cleaning once a week will be sufficient. If the machine is in regular use for most of the day, these attentions should be given daily before work commences.

The presence of too much oil, or oil of the wrong kind, must be avoided. A machine which is not used very often is, as a rule, the first to make known the fact that it has been unwisely lubricated. Hard running after a period of idleness indicates that oil has gummed in the bearings. This effect will be emphasized if the machine stands in too cold a room or in a cold draught. If the machine must be used during winter in a room without a fire, it should be given some chance to work efficiently by being warmed up a little for an hour or so before working. An oil stove or electric radiator should be placed near it to render the oil less cloggy.

If the machine still runs sluggishly, go over each oiling-point and apply a very small quantity of paraffin, first taking the precaution of spreading a sheet or two of newspaper on the floor to catch odd drips. The machine should then be run briskly for, say, three minutes. This should have the effect of thinning the oil and reducing bearing surface friction, and the gumming or clogging should disappear. Traces of oil will probably be observed here and there on the exterior when the rapid running ceases, and a scrap of non-fluffy rag should be used to remove the last traces.

Sewing machine oil, of the kind specified by the maker, should then be applied to each hole, after which the running should be easy and smooth. If the machine still runs unsatisfactorily a general overhaul is indicated. Only in this way can it be thoroughly cleaned of dust, grit and bits of fibre which are liable to cause stiff working no less than thick oil. Overhaul inspection must be done methodically, and if the maker's handbook is not available for a guide, a rough sketch should first be made of each part which it is intended to remove, so as to facilitate replacement.

Careful use of the screwdriver will prevent burring of the slots in the screw heads, and for safety the screws should be placed aside on a piece of clean cloth or newspaper or in a tin lid, while the work is proceeded with. If any parts are rusty they should be immersed for a few hours in paraffin, then polished with a clean rag. No harsh abrasive should be used. A little metal polish and plenty of rubbing may supplement the cleansing influence of the oil. It is not at all probable, of course, that rusting will occur in a machine unless it has been disused and neglected for a long time, but it *is* possible in the case of a machine purchased secondhand, and is a condition which should be looked for before purchase.

For purposes of thorough inspection, and for occasional overhaul, the thread should first be removed, then the slide plate, the bobbin, the needle and the presser foot (see Fig. 1). Removal of the throat plate will reveal the shuttle race, which can then be cleaned and oiled. Extraction of screws from the face plate will reveal oil-holes and joints for lubrication on the needle bar, presser bar, and the thread take-up.

To get at the underside of the machine head, in the case of a

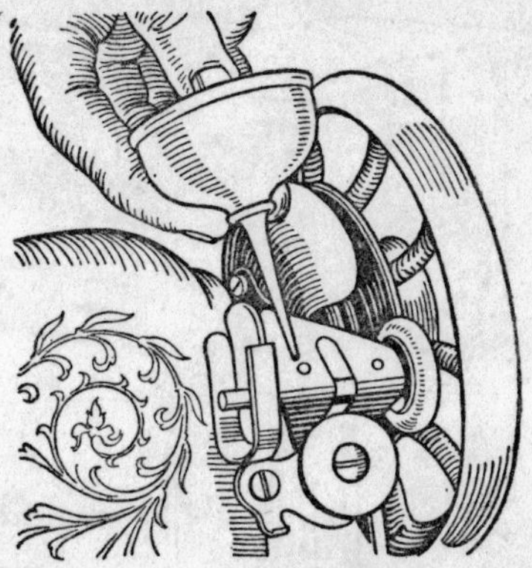

Fig. 2. Oiling the spindle of the bobbin winder friction ring. See also Fig. 1.

treadle machine, the belt is removed from the band wheel, by means of the belt shifter whose lever has to be moved to the left, whilst the machine is gently running; this displaces the belt to the right. It is then possible to hinge the head back, and if the balance wheel is then slowly turned the points where single drops of oil should be applied become obvious. Surplus oil should be removed with a piece of rag; the head may then be restored to the working position, and the belt replaced, while the treadle is gently operated so that the band wheel revolves towards the operator.

The hand machine needing these attentions will be lifted from its base after the removal of the securing screws, the latter being screwed tightly home again when the underside cleaning and oiling have been completed. It is customary to attend to the underside of the head first, the oiling points at the top of the machine being dealt with next. A clean and non-fluffy duster should then be

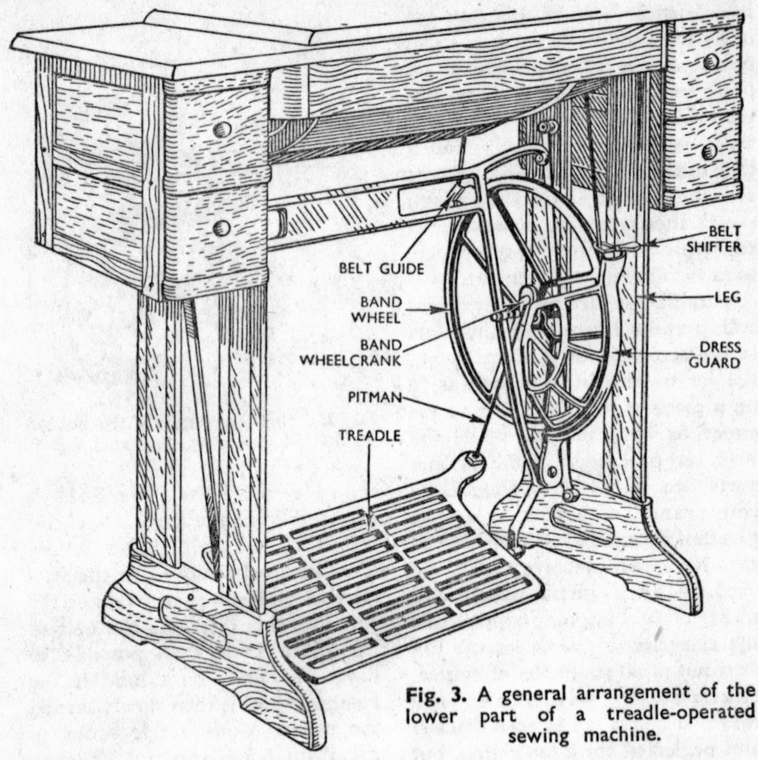

Fig. 3. A general arrangement of the lower part of a treadle-operated sewing machine.

used to remove all traces of oil on the exterior. A piece of odd material passed through the threaded machine will rid the working surfaces of oil, before the next piece of sewing is to be done.

In the matter of oiling the bobbin winder (see Fig. 2), very careful use of the oil-can is necessary. One drop only, at each of the two holes, is needed. If oil gets on to the rubber ring it will cause slipping, and the rubber itself will soften and deteriorate. Should oil contaminate the rubber, it must be wiped off instantly and thoroughly. If the rubber ring on the bobbin winder deteriorates from the effects of oil, the only remedy is replacement by a new ring.

Trouble with the treadle, the pivoted platform operated by the feet, can be avoided by regular oiling at the side-points, thus ensuring easy action. Other moving parts of the stand should likewise be kept dusted and lubricated (see Fig. 3). A noisy treadle may be quietened by tightening one or both the screws which form its pivots. Before the screw can be tightened up, the nut around its head must be loosened with a spanner, the nut being tightened again when the screw has been attended to. If, on working the treadle, the noise still persists, the opposite screw should be tightened. No more than the reduction of "play" should be aimed at, for if the screws are tightened unduly the treadle will be difficult to work.

It is essential that the machine, treadle or hand, should stand perfectly level, on floor or table respectively. When not in use the head of a treadle machine should always be lowered into its cabinet stand, and that of a hand machine kept covered up, to avoid accumulation of dust and the possibility of interference by inquisitive children.

A number of common troubles are traceable to the needles. The latter must conform to the type specified by the makers of the particular machine, and should be of the correct size for the thread and the material. The needle that is satisfactory for all classes of work has yet to be invented. A table setting out the relative sizes of needles and threads, and the class of sewing (the material), should be obtained from the makers of the machine, or their agents, and carefully followed. Needle breakage and many other troubles will thus be avoided.

Tugging at the material while the needle is still engaged may result in the needle becoming broken or bent. In the latter case it will strike the throat plate on the next downward movement and this will burr the hole in the plate and the slot in the presser foot. A bent or blunted needle may also be responsible for the breaking of the upper thread. Breakage of both upper and lower threads is sometimes due to over-tensioning.

Tension (pull) on the upper

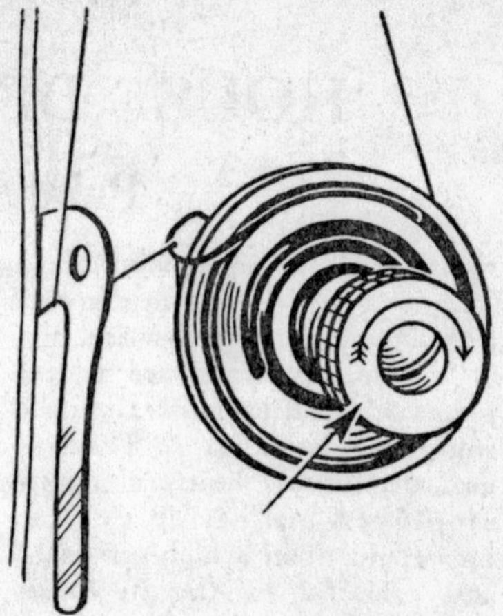

Fig. 4. Detail view of thread tension adjustment. Thread is gripped between disks and pressure applied by thumb nut.

thread (from the needle), for adaptation to different materials, is adjusted by means of a thumb nut (see Fig. 4). This is turned to the right when the tension is to be lessened. It is necessary that the presser foot should be down when upper thread tension is adjusted. Upper and lower tension should be approximately equal, the lower tension controlling the thread from the shuttle or bobbin case. Adjustment of the lower tension is effected by means of a small spring screw, which is tightened slightly to increase the tension, and loosened a trifle to lessen it. Any adjustment of the thread tensions should be accompanied by a test of the effect on the stitches.

If any difficulty is experienced with one of the older types of sewing machine, which cannot be rectified from the foregoing instructions, advice will be readily forthcoming from the maker's local representative for repair service.

SECTION FIVE

HOUSE DECORATION

Paint Brushes

THE final test of a paint brush is to be made only in use over a reasonable period of service, but, at the outset, there are several points which distinguish the good from the inferior brush. The type and quality of hair or bristle employed are of far greater importance than a highly finished and colourful handle. In consequence, it is the hair and its method of attachment which must claim the attention in the selection of a brush. Another consideration is the purpose for which the brush will be used.

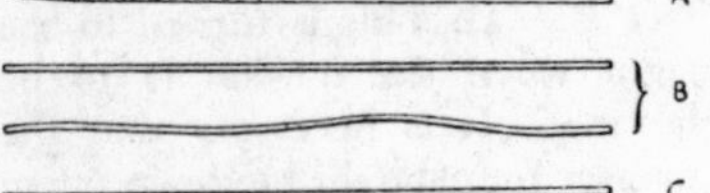

Fig. 1. Bristle characteristics. A, hogs' hair with fine taper, often with split end. B, horse hair, little or no taper, often wavy. C, vegetable fibre.

Oil paints and varnishes are too viscid to be applied and evenly spread with anything softer than hogs' hair bristle; there are, however, a number of finishes, chief of which are lacquers, french polish and cellulose lacquers, which require a very soft brush of squirrel, fox, or camel hair. Whatever the type of bristle (Fig. 1) employed, it is always desirable to select a quality of sufficient springiness to keep its shape during use.

The best paint brushes are made from full length hogs' hair bristles (previously sorted into equal lengths) which, by reason of their tapering shape, impart a combination of strength together with the fine, soft tips so necessary for good brushwork. Any trimming or cutting of the tips of bristles may form a more shapely brush, but if carried to excess will produce a brush too stiff for anything except the roughest of painting.

Qualities of Hogs' Hair.—These are not very easily distinguished. The creamy-white "lily bristles" are regarded as the best, followed by grey and black, in order of merit. There are, of course, various grades of each type, and while price is usually a good criterion of the quality of any reputable maker's goods, it is important to discriminate between limp, inferior bristles and those which exhibit the essential charac-

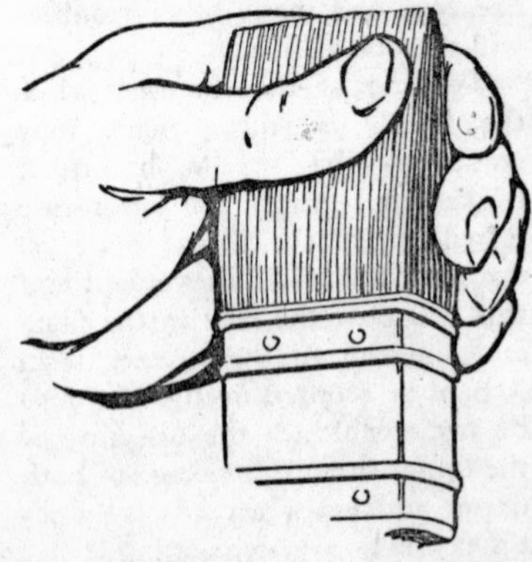

Fig. 2. Testing bristles for shape.

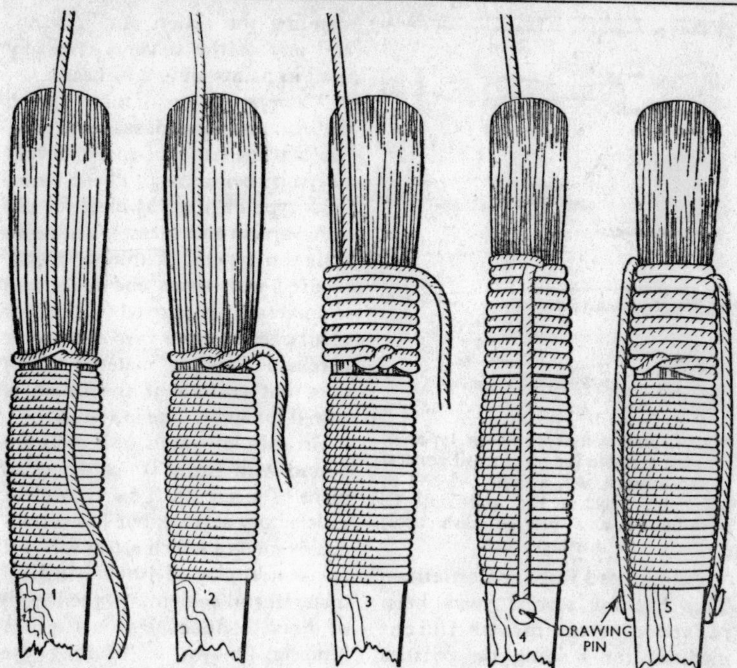

Fig. 3. Shows five stages of binding or bridling a sash tool. Use good quality thin cord and bind tightly. Secure the loose ends to the brush handle.

teristics of springiness and good shape. See also Figs. 4 and 5.

The long bristles employed in the larger types of both paint and distemper brushes are split at the tips into two or three strands. This is a desirable feature as it proves that a genuine full length material has been used. In smaller brushes this characteristic is not usually evident, but one can easily compare the degree of tapering (or lack of it) by firmly pressing (a) the base, then (b) the tip of a brush, between the finger and thumb: (b) should not be more than half the thickness of (a); see Fig. 2.

Hogs Hair Substitutes.—Both horse hair and vegetable fibre have at times been found intermixed with genuine hogs hair in the cheaper type of imported paint brush. These substitutes are noticeable by (a) their lack of spring; if bent at a sharp angle they usually remain crippled; (b) bristle and horse hair will, when burnt, give off the characteristic smell of burnt hair; vegetable fibre does not; (c) horse hair lacks the tapering shape of bristle and is smoother to the touch.

Vegetable fibre is quite unsuitable for use in paint brushes, and is more usefully employed in brushes intended for the application of caustic solutions such as those used for the removal of varnished wallpaper and the cleaning of stonework, etc.

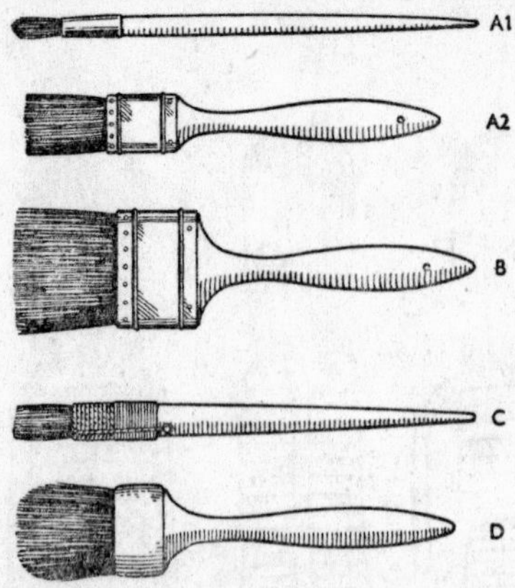

Fig. 4. Shows four common types of brushes suitable for most small general purpose work. A1, a fitch; A2 and B, flat paint brushes 1in. and 2in.; C, wire-bound and bridled sash tool; D, dusting brush.

Vulcanized Rubber Cement.—This has for several years been regarded as the most efficient medium for holding the bristles firmly in place. The words "Rubber Set" stamped upon a brush, indicate that not only has this type of adhesive been employed, but that the brush is capable of withstanding the action of oil, water, and any of the solvents normally used in paints and varnishes.

Metal ferrules are of three classes: the machine pressed, seamless type, has a plain band of metal devoid of rivets, being easy to keep clean. This type of brush is ideal for use with varnish and enamel. The more common type is of thinner metal, secured with rivets and nails, and is universally employed for brushes of all sizes. Copper wire also makes a reliable binding material which does not corrode if the brush is stored for some time in water.

Brushes known as sash tools are bound with string which serves in place of a ferrule. This type gives satisfactory service, but has certain disadvantages which are as follows: (a) weakness of both binding material and cement; (b) the length of bristle necessitates further binding (known as bridling the brush) so that it may be more easily controlled. See Fig. 3.

Distemper brushes are assembled in a different manner from paint brushes, the former being con-

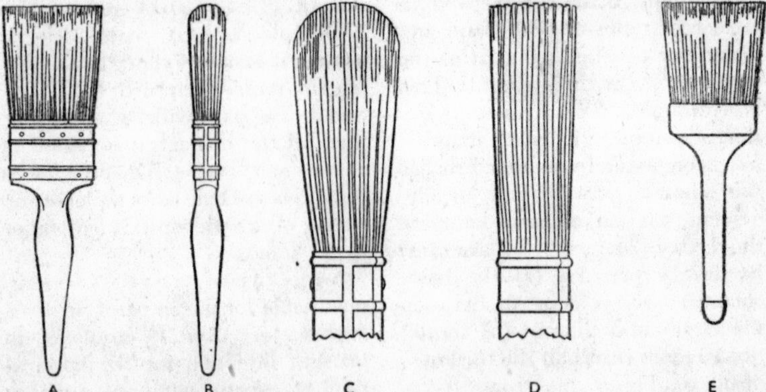

Fig. 5. A, rubber-set paint brush. B, end view of brush A. C, section of B, showing contour of bristles. D, end view of inferior brush showing flat, coarse contour of bristles. E, seamless ferrule varnish brush.

structed with a centre core of wood, to facilitate cleaning. When purchasing it is wise to reject any brush with a core of excessive thickness, i.e. more than one-third the total thickness; such brushes are inclined to open at the tip during use.

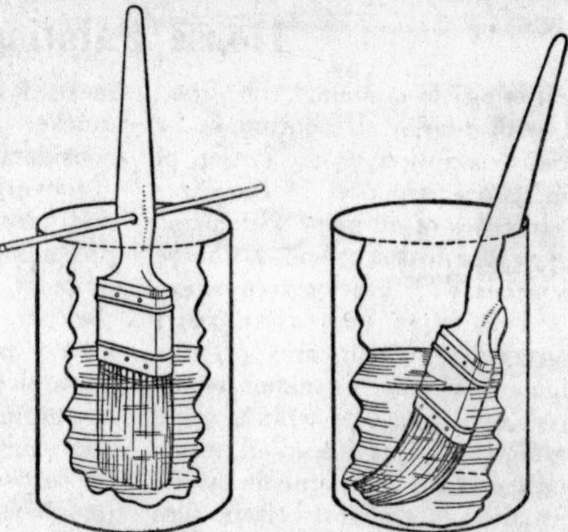

Fig. 6. Shows, left, a simple method of suspending a brush in solvent. Right-hand view illustrates the wrong method which distorts bristles, a defect which is often very difficult to rectify.

Before using a new distemper brush or one that has not been used for some weeks it is advisable to soak it in cold water for about twenty minutes. This causes the wood core to swell, tightens the binding, and thus helps to prevent any loosening of the bristles.

Storage of Brushes.—Paint brushes in daily use may be kept in good condition by simply standing them upright in a vessel containing sufficient water to reach the metal ferrule. The average brush should not develop a twist unless it is placed at a slanting angle; a better method, however, is to suspend the brush in water or (in the case of a varnish brush) in a solvent oil, utilizing the method shown in Fig. 6.

Brushes not required for several weeks or more should be rinsed in paraffin or white spirit, to remove as much paint as possible, then washed with hot water and common soap (not soda) until no trace of paint remains in the roots (base) of the bristles; rinse well in clean water and allow to dry in a cool airy place. This treatment will also be advisable when a brush is to be used for pale tints following its use in a dark colour.

When clean and dry, brushes are stored in the same manner as for new ones, i.e. placed in boxes containing a little flake napthalene to prevent damage by moth larvae. Store in a cool, dry atmosphere, because heat causes undue shrinkage and possibly warping of the wood, and dampness induces mildew which may have a detrimental effect upon the cement.

Note: Varnish brushes, particularly, should be washed immediately after use, with soap and hot water, if they are not to be used again for some time. It is difficult enough to clean brushes in which paint has dried, but varnish incorporates a high content of gums, and when the varnish has once hardened it will not readily respond to the application of a solvent. Brushes used for cellulose paints should also be cleaned immediately by rinsing them in the correct solvent. They should then be thoroughly dried by rubbing them on a soft absorbent cloth.

House Painting

THIS article is mainly concerned with interior oil painting, and a brief description, at the outset, of the nature and uses of the three main types of oil paint will enable the reader to select and use these materials with greater confidence.

Each type contains four ingredients, which are: (1) the pigment or colouring matter (which may, of course, be white), (2) a drying oil such as linseed oil, which binds or fixes the pigment by the formation of a slightly elastic film which makes it glossy, tough, washable, and resistant to variations in weather conditions, (3) a drier, which accelerates evaporation and enables the paint to dry in eight hours instead of as many days, (4) a thinner, such as turpentine or a reliable brand of white spirit, which, by thinning the paint makes it easily brushable, and dry quicker and harder, but which considerably reduces its gloss.

Fig. 1. Using blow-lamp and shave hook for removing paint from irregular surfaces, mouldings, recesses, etc.

By varying the proportions of oil and turpentine, it is possible to produce any of three main types of paint, or, if necessary, change the character of ready-mixed paint. Glossy paint contains five or six parts of oil (or varnish), to one of turpentine. Flat oil paints contain approximately one part of oil to six of turpentine. Semi-gloss paints (employed as undercoats) contain equal parts of oil and turpentine. For house painting it is safe to assume that glossy paints (particularly those containing white lead) will give reliable service upon outdoor work, and upon those positions indoors where frequent washing down is necessary. Flat oil paints are used for interior work only, and are employed mainly upon ceilings and walls, where their matt surface is often mistaken for oil-bound distemper. The similarity is limited to appearance only, however, for in practice a flat paint will be found to withstand considerably more washing down and is so much more stable than distemper that after thirty or forty years of accumulated coatings there is rarely any sign of chipping or peeling off.

When purchasing paint it is advisable to purchase "decorator's quality" from your local builders' merchant. Not only does he carry a wide range of paints but he will be able to give sound advice as to their suitability for any particular purpose. As some paints, particularly those containing a large proportion of zinc oxide (white), are unsuitable for outdoor use, while others are equally good for both exterior and interior work, it is wise to state your requirements clearly. Titanium oxide paints for both interior and exterior use are to be recommended, as they possess remarkable covering power and, unlike lead oxide paints, are non-toxic (i.e. safer to handle).

Surface Preparation.—This involves (1) the production of a smooth, dry surface, quite free from dust, grease, dirt, old wall-paper, or distemper, (2) special treatment for certain types of surface which are normally unsuitable for the reception of oil paint, (3) the application of a first or priming coat of paint (never glue size) when points (1) and (2) have received attention. This priming should contain enough linseed oil to correct porosity in the surface, and should be sufficiently thin to penetrate well into the material being painted, thus ensuring perfect adhesion.

Previously Decorated Surfaces.—These embrace six main classes, and their treatment should also indicate a line of procedure for others not included.

(A) The most easily prepared work is that previously finished in flat or semi-gloss paint. Here, a scrub down with hot water and sugar soap (or washing soda), followed by rinsing with clean water, is the only treatment necessary. Any roughness of surface can be rectified by rubbing with pumice-stone while the surface is still wet. (B) Glossy paint or varnish needs the same treatment, but will require more rubbing with pumice to produce a dull or matt surface, which will improve the adhesion of the new paint. (C) Blistered, cracked, or other work which is overloaded with paint would take many hours to rub down, but it should certainly be removed. The complete removal of the paint is a much easier and quicker job. Burning off with either a blowlamp or large bunsen burner is generally more satisfactory than the use of fluid, paint remover. (D) Distempered surfaces must be washed with hot water to remove as much as possible of the material. Soap will not be necessary except where grease is present, as for example, in kitchens. (E) Wall-papers require to be stripped off in accordance with instructions detailed in the section referring to PAPER AND PAPERHANGING. (F) Materials requiring special treatment include creosote, tar, tar or bitumen paint, asbestos sheets, and Portland cement. These are rendered safe for painting by first coating with a special sealing solu-

Fig. 2. Use a broad scraper on large flat areas and scrape with the grain.

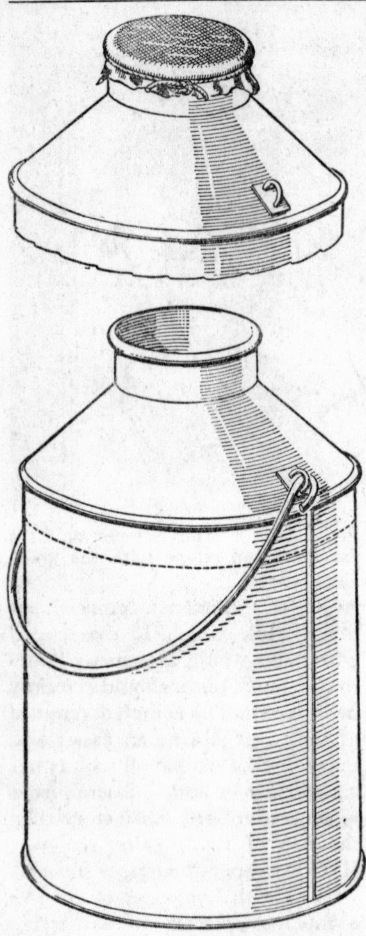

Fig. 3. How to make a sieve from a large paint tin. Cut along the dotted line and tie gauze on opening, as shown.

tion obtainable from any builders' merchants, or if the area is not too large, by coating with aluminium paint or a good shellac varnish.

Burning off a Door.—The removal of paint from mouldings requires time and care, so it is better to tackle them before dealing with the larger flat areas. Avoid undue charring of the wood and damage to the numerous sharp edges. It may be necessary to go over the work several times in order to leave a smooth surface free from patches of charred paint. The term "burning off" should not be taken too literally; actually the flame is used to soften the paint film in order that it may be scraped off with the shave hook (Fig. 1) (a special scraper for the removal of paint) and a chisel knife. Nothing will be gained by the application of too much heat. Not more than about 8in. of paintwork should be softened at a time, and the flame should then be removed while this is cleaned off. The broad flat areas demand a slightly different method. Here, a broad scraper will easily follow the flame in a slow continuous sweep of two feet or more. It will, of course, be found that continual cleaning of the scraper becomes very necessary, and that the best result is obtained when working in the same direction as the grain of the wood; see Fig. 2. The work is finally smoothed with No. 1½ glass paper and is then ready for knotting (i.e. treatment of knots in the wood by a special sealing liquid) and priming (painting) of the main surface.

Paint Removers.—There are certain materials such as glass, the thin sheet metal work of motor car bodies, and stained and varnished woodwork, which are easily damaged by a flame and must therefore be stripped by a solvent. Among the numerous types will be found a few which are non-inflammable; the remainder must be kept strictly away from any naked flame. Caustic soda solution, an efficient if somewhat drastic paint remover, is injurious to the skin and should be used with discretion, having regard to the surface to be repainted. All traces of the brush-applied solution should be scraped away from the surface and the whole area should be scrubbed clean and left to dry. Use a fibre brush to apply the solution.

Fig. 4. Illustration shows which parts of the casing rebate should be painted the same colour as the door. Do not paint end plate of door lock.

Solvents vary considerably; some are capable of penetrating three or four coats of paint in as many minutes while others require a longer period but usually penetrate more deeply. Whatever the type used, repeated coatings may be necessary (applied with an old paint-brush), as the various layers of paint are scraped off. Finally, wash off all traces of the solvent, using turpentine substitute (white spirit) and clean rags. The surface is then ready for painting.

Preparing the Paint.—Decorators' paint of the standard semi-gloss type, in common with many other undercoat paints, will usually require a little further thinning with linseed oil or turpentine, or both. Oil is added only when the porosity of new wood, plaster, etc. calls for this treatment. Equal parts of oil and turpentine are employed to thin undercoats intended for outdoor work, but for interior use a mixture of 2 parts turpentine to 1 of oil is generally preferable. A home-made sieve for straining off foreign matter from the paint is illustrated in Fig. 3.

The question of how much thinners to add can only be settled by trial. There is, however, some comfort to be gained from the knowledge that while over-thinning may necessitate an extra coat of paint, it is far quicker and easier than trying to smooth out (by glasspapering) the coarse brush-

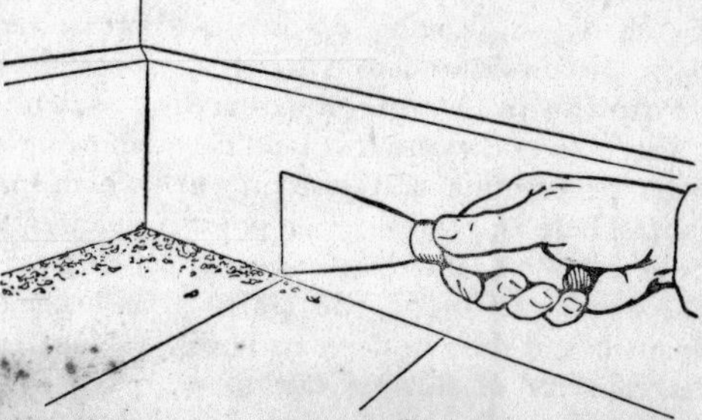

Fig. 5. Before painting skirting, all dirt and loose material must be scraped away from corners and angles of skirtings and floorboards, etc.

Fig. 6. When painting the outside of the window frame, paint the upper portion of the top frame A and the lower frame B in the position shown. Next lift the frame A to expose the unpainted portion of B and complete the painting on the outside of the window frame and sashes.

work produced by applying the paint too thickly. Thin coats, and more of them constitute good, sound, practice, and it is therefore advisable to thin out the paint and make repeated tests until it can be applied with the lightest pressure of the brush, leaving no brush-mark. Obtain clean edges as in Fig. 7.

Painting a Door.—Reference is made (see ENAMELLING) to the order of painting and stopping a door. There is, however, one point to be stressed, and that concerns the application of the paint. Enamels and their undercoats have the capacity of flowing out to a level surface after application, but ordinary paint cannot do this, and must be applied more sparingly until (with the brush almost dry) each section of the work can be crossed and laid off with the lightest possible strokes.

Attention is directed to Fig. 4, showing which door edge and which part of the casing rebate belongs to the side of the door being painted. A piece of clean rag is needed for the removal of paint which gets out of bounds. Before painting the door casing and skirting, scrape away any accumulated fluff which is often present in the angle formed by woodwork

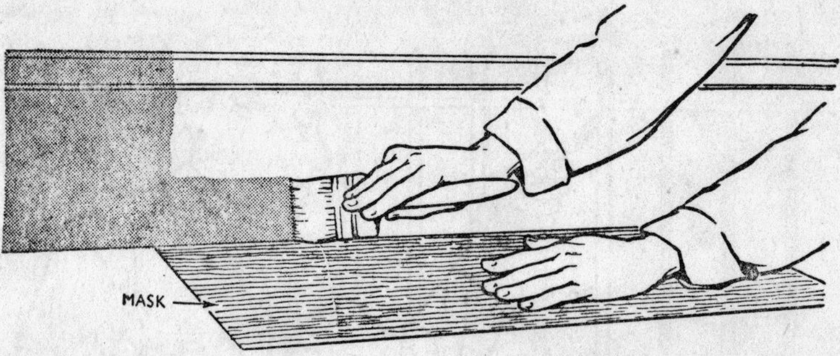

Fig. 7. Shows an efficient method of obtaining a clean finished edge on skirting by the use of a mask, made from a sheet of stiff card or similar material.

and floor; see Fig. 5. Furthermore, if the walls of a room are to be papered, it is wise to paint about ½in. of the wall adjoining any woodwork, otherwise it means working to a clean edge at the point where the two meet.

Cupboards may prove awkward unless tackled in the right way, i.e. by painting the inside parts first, then the shelves (working from the top downwards but leaving the top sides unpainted), then the door casing and door edges, thus leaving the doors until the last.

Walls and ceilings offer no special difficulties if painted in a series of strips as recommended for the application of oil-bound distemper.

Window Frames.—Both the outside and inside are subjected to rigorous climatic changes, therefore good white lead undercoats are recommended. The brushes required are a 1½in. flat, and a part-worn 1in. or ¾in. flat brush. The latter is particularly handy when painting to a straight line against the glass.

The procedure followed is to coat all rebates and edges of hinged or swivel type frames which open outwards, with the colour used for the outside, leaving edges which open inwards to be done with the inside colour. The window is then closed (not fastened) and the whole painted, working from the top downwards. This order of working will, of course, have to be varied in the case of sash windows (see Fig. 6) but on completion, the

Fig. 8. A good method of preventing damage to windows when using ladder for painting upper floor windows.

Fig. 9. When painting railings place sackcloth over brick work. Paint the edges, tops and undersides of the horizontal pieces and the vertical members.

window is left slightly open until the paint is dry.

Edges and rebate must be thinly coated to prevent subsequent sticking, while rust spots on metal casements should be well scraped before the first coat of paint is applied. If this is not done thoroughly, rusting will continue and cause the paint to lift. Some difficulty may at first be experienced when painting upon the putty or other parts in intermediate contact with the glass. It will be found that several long strokes (with the brush only lightly charged with paint) will be necessary to produce a nice straight edge, and if this extends for $\frac{1}{16}$in. upon the glass, so much the better. The paint will then fill in any fine cracks between putty and window pane. Any cracks between window frame and adjoining brick or stonework should be filled in with paint, putty, or if very wide, with cement mortar. It is good practice to lash a stout board to the top of the ladder (see Fig. 8) when painting upper windows is to be undertaken.

Fig. 10. When painting at any height, both hands should be free.

Iron Railings.—As the object is to prevent corrosion, the surface must be absolutely dry at the time of painting. It is of equal importance to remove by means of a wire brush and scraper all scale and rust prior to repainting with lead, graphite, bituminous, aluminium or other anti-corrosive paint. Use paper or an old sack to protect garden walls from paint spots, see Fig. 9.

Gutters and Rainwater Pipes.—Obviously, it is equally desirable to paint inside as well as outside the gutters. This necessitates cleaning out any accumulated leaves, dust, etc. and sweeping with an old brush in order to get the inside properly dry. A hook made from stout wire enables a small bucket to be suspended from either the pipe or from a rung of the ladder, leaving both hands free for the work involved, see Fig. 10.

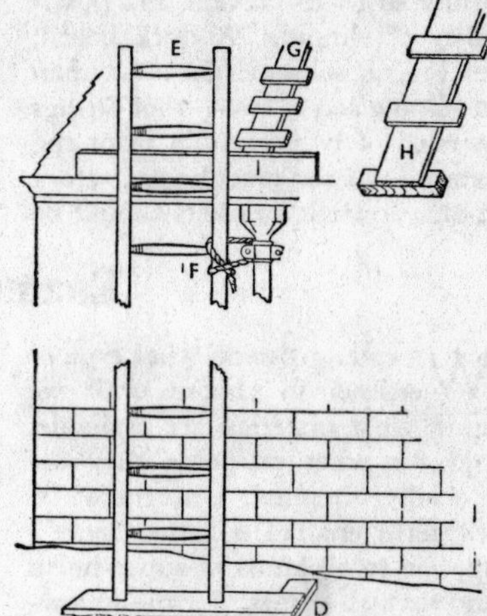

Fig. 12. Shows ladder E standing on boards arranged at D, on soft, uneven ground, and lashed at F for safety. The duckboard G, held in position by plain board I, interposed between ladder and lower end of G, the top end of G is shown inverted at H.

Fig. 11. Shows A, side view of ladder and safe angle; B, ladder wedged at C on uneven ground surface. Wedges may be pegged on forward side, by peg driven into ground.

The finest asset is an extension ladder which brings the work within easy reach, and enables one to see clearly and to paint with a small brush those awkward places behind gutters and fall pipes. Other articles of equipment include wedges, for packing the ladder foot where the ground is uneven (see Fig. 11), two stout boards or short planks for placing under the ladder, when working over soft uneven ground, and a length of thin rope to secure the ladder head to a wall pipe (or other fixture when roof work is involved), see Fig. 12. In addition, it is a great help to have someone at the foot of the ladder who will hold the ladder firmly so as to prevent any possibility of slipping. A duck board, see Fig. 12, will assist the handyman in gaining access to any roof fittings in need of painting. To paint the exterior of a greenhouse, stout L-shaped angle brackets should be secured at regular intervals at each end of the sloping roof so as to permit the laying on of strong boards to protect the glass and give access to the higher parts of the roof. It will then be possible to carry out the painting safely.

Enamelling

We cannot decide what type of enamel to choose until we know what materials are available, and for what purposes they are specially intended. Unfortunately, the term enamel is rather loosely applied to all kinds of super-finish and varnish paints, but the following are most likely to be of use to the handyman.

Super high-gloss enamel is still the best available finish where durability and a brilliant, lasting gloss is required. It is equally serviceable for interior or exterior work, and withstands plenty of washing without injury.

Bath enamel, as its name implies, withstands the action of soap and hot water.

Gloss enamel paints and hard gloss paints are frequently used for general house painting. They have several attractive features, the chief of which are: (1) a wide range of colours; (2) economy (they are only half the price of the super high-gloss type); (3) they have better obliterating power, and are calculated to save an undercoat; (4) the surface to be painted is more easily prepared when repainting becomes necessary; (5) like enamel, they are usually suitable for either inside or outside work.

As a rule, the two characteristics, gloss and obliterating power, are skilfully balanced by the manufacturer. It must be realized that high gloss is only obtainable by limiting the amount of coloured pigment, and as gloss is of greater importance in a finishing coat we must not demand perfect obliterating capacity. The undercoats should perform the duty of hiding all imperfections of surface. Gloss is imparted to the enamel by gums and residues of oils, while obliterating power is afforded by the inclusion of a suitable pigment, usually of an oxide specially suited to the purpose of the enamel.

Synthetic enamel paints or lacquers are similar to the above type except for the synthetic resin which forms an ingredient. Hardness, gloss, durability against weather, and quick-drying qualities are claimed for this class of paint, which is equally useful for a front door or a bicycle. An important point is to ascertain at the time of purchasing whether the material can be applied over ordinary paint, or whether a special undercoat is necessary.

Floor enamels are useful for giving new life to old linoleum, or for brightening and dustproofing cement floors. Some varieties are also capable of resisting heat, petrol, and oil. No undercoating is required for this product.

Cellulose enamels dry so quickly

Fig. 1. Rubbing down old paint with pumice. Use water liberally and wash surface frequently with water. Use circular motion with pumice pad or stone.

that only small areas can be satisfactorily dealt with unless a spraying plant is employed. They are too inflammable to be used near an open fire and usually require a special undercoat. The room temperature should be approximately 70 degrees F. when applying cellulose enamels. On no account must they be used upon recently applied oil paint. Cellulose finishes present that hard, smooth, surface found on motor cars, etc. If extensive work is to be undertaken with this enamel, try to arrange suitable ventilation so that fresh air is blowing the odour away from the face.

Bituminous enamels are water-resisting compounds, ideal for the proofing of concrete or Portland cement, or as protective coatings for gutters, rainwater pipes, garden railings, and ironwork exposed to weather or in contact with earth. The insides of cold water tanks and cisterns are often painted (when dry) with these compounds. A possible snag connected with their use is their liability to discolour a top coat of ordinary paint if this is applied at some future

Fig. 2. On new wood work all knots should be coated with knotting fluid or shellac before applying undercoat.

time without a special undercoat.

Flat enamels (non-glossy) are available for interior walls and woodwork. They present the smoothness, hardness, and freedom from brushmarks so characteristic of gloss finishes.

Preparation of Enamels.—The only safe rules to follow are those laid down by the manufacturer, but in the absence of other instructions, these materials should not be thinned or interfered with in any way, otherwise loss of gloss will invariably follow.

With undercoats it is different. A very dull gloss forms the ideal surface upon which to apply the finishing enamel. Thin coats build up the hard, smooth surface required, and it is usually necessary to add genuine turpentine or a really good substitute, as a thinning medium. On no account should paraffin or inferior grades of white spirit be used; their greasiness prevents proper adhesion and drying.

The amount to purchase can be calculated by roughly measuring the area to be coated and working on the basis that one pint of enamel (or undercoating) covers ten square yards. In terms of weight, this means that one pound of material covers approximately six square yards.

Surface Preparation.—Before the application of any form of paint it is better to know what conditions are most likely to ensure success. A well prepared surface will be perfectly clean, smooth, hard, and dry, and these conditions are usually present only on new work.

Previously painted work has first to be rubbed down (wet), see Fig. 1, with either a flat piece of pumice stone, or waterproof glass-paper. Then the work is well rinsed with clean water and dried with a washleather. Should the old paint be cracked or blistered, it is more quickly and easily removed by blowlamp or gas burner jet as described in House Painting.

Paint will neither dry nor adhere properly when applied to a dirty or greasy surface. Furthermore, it

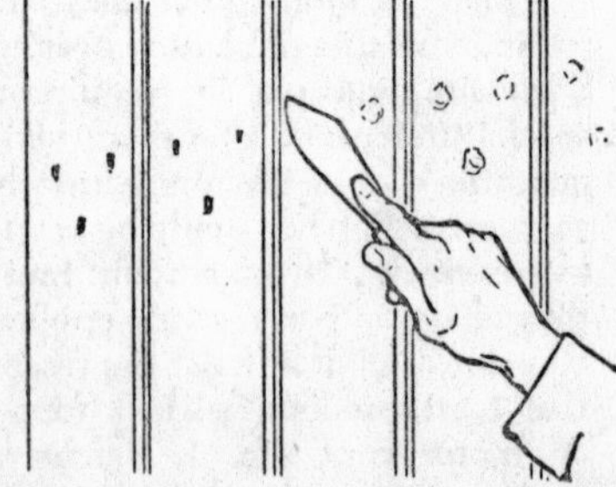

Fig. 3. Fill all nail holes and small crevices with putty or stopping as shown, and trim flush with surface.

causes flaking off and cracking of subsequent coats of new paint. Any roughness of surface becomes exaggerated by a gloss finish and also accumulates dust and dirt. Dryness is of paramount importance; to paint upon damp surfaces invariably causes blistering.

Walls coated with distemper or hung with wallpaper must be soaked, scraped, and washed down with clean water, and defective plaster must be made good (see GENERAL WALL REPAIRS). When dry, the surface is treated as new plaster, i.e. glasspapered and given a thin coat of paint containing plenty of linseed oil to check excessive porosity.

Preparation of New Woodwork.—After glasspapering woodwork, but before painting, all knots must be painted over with either patent knotting or shellac varnish to prevent them showing through and discolouring the finished paintwork, see Fig. 2.

Fig. 4. Wide depressions may be filled with stopping by use of a broad scraper.

Fig. 5. Numbers indicate door parts, to be painted in that order.

Undercoating fulfils the important duties of completely checking all porosity, levelling and generally improving the surface painted, obliterating old paint, and giving the right colour for the reception of the enamel. The number of undercoats required varies according to the finishing colour. White enamel often necessitates four coats, while dark shades (upon old work) only need one undercoat.

Filling Nailholes and Cracks.—On old work, this job is best done before undercoating, but on new work, after the first coat is dry. Linseed oil putty is commonly used, but a mixture of four parts putty to one of white lead forms a better stopping which leaves a smooth surface when

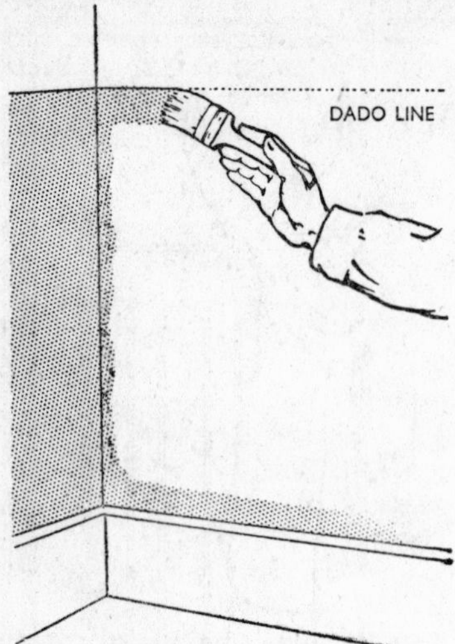

Fig. 6. Finishing the dado line. Note way in which brush is held in the hand.

pressed firmly into place with the putty knife (see Fig. 3). Larger cavities may be filled with stopping in the manner shown in Fig. 4.

Applying the Enamel.—Either a bathroom or kitchenette provides a variety of subjects suitable for enamelling. The ceiling and upper parts of the walls could be finished in cream coloured flat paint, and the dado (lower part of wall), door, window, and cupboards, in enamel (salmon colour). The skirting and door casing would then look well in black enamel. The bath may exhibit several rust spots and need renovating with the proper bath enamel.

The important essential in all this work is cleanliness, and all dirty work, including the scouring of the bath interior by pumice and washing of the floor, should have been completed, and the final undercoating applied, before any finishing colour is put on. Clean, dry brushes are also essential. These should not be so soft and springy as those required for undercoating, but stiff enough to spread the less easily manipulated enamel. Part-worn brushes, thoroughly washed in hot water and soap, are ideal for the purpose.

The enamel must be stirred well and then tested out upon the cupboard shelves, window frame, or other small area, in order to get acquainted with the different brush technique required. Enamel (as one might expect from its syrup-like consistency) is never easy to apply. It must be more slowly and forcefully brushed, and at the same

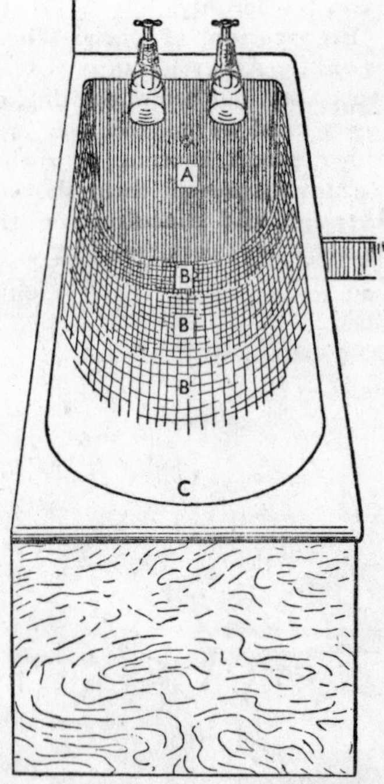

Fig. 7. Enamelling the bath. Note the two jars under taps to prevent water dripping. Start at A and finish at end C.

time more generously applied, than paint.

To obtain a perfectly even gloss and colour, the coating must be spread evenly; this can only be accomplished by varying the direction of the brush strokes, working firstly in the direction of the grain, until about two square feet is evenly covered, then brushing across the grain, and finally finishing off with the grain of the wood.

The adjacent section is immediately joined up to the first and the work continued in the same manner until completed. All brushmarks should disappear within fifteen minutes, and any runs which may have formed should then be levelled out with the brush. Apply less material to mouldings; especially at the mitres, where it is liable to accumulate.

A door is coated in sections, see Fig. 5. Finish the dado, see Fig. 6. Leave the door casing and skirting (because of the wide difference in colour) until the following day, when the paler enamel should have dried out sufficiently.

Enamelling the Bath.—The proper enamel and its undercoat are obtainable in quantities sufficient for one large bath, but where undercoating is not available, mix 1½ lb. of white lead with equal parts of carriage varnish and turpentine, until an easy-brushing consistency is reached; finally, sieve through fine muslin. Touch up those parts of the bath which are in any way discoloured; repeating the process (one coat each day) until the bath is of fairly equal colour. The whole surface will then require two or three coats to produce the perfectly even whiteness upon which to enamel. No glasspapering is to be done after the final undercoating lest the surface be soiled. Hang jars or tins over the taps to prevent drip and enamel the bath in progressive sections as shown in Fig. 7.

Four or five days should elapse before using a freshly enamelled bath, and then, for the first few occasions of its use, run in cold water before running in the hot, thus avoiding the effects of excessive heat during the hardening and drying period.

Varnishing

VARNISHES are quite as numerous and as varied in character as paints. Each is designed for a definite purpose and should not be expected to prove equally efficient when used otherwise. Spirit varnishes are hard drying, almost to the point of brittleness. Oil varnishes are sometimes sufficiently elastic to permit application over oil paint, while other types are designed especially for use upon floors, wallpapers, baths, boats, and almost every conceivable kind of material.

Oil varnishes constitute the most important class, and may, for convenience, be divided into two groups, the hard-drying varnishes (for interior work only), and the elastic varnishes, which contain a higher oil content and tougher resins, to enable them to withstand exposure to varying weather conditions. A general purpose varnish, which is claimed to fulfil both sets

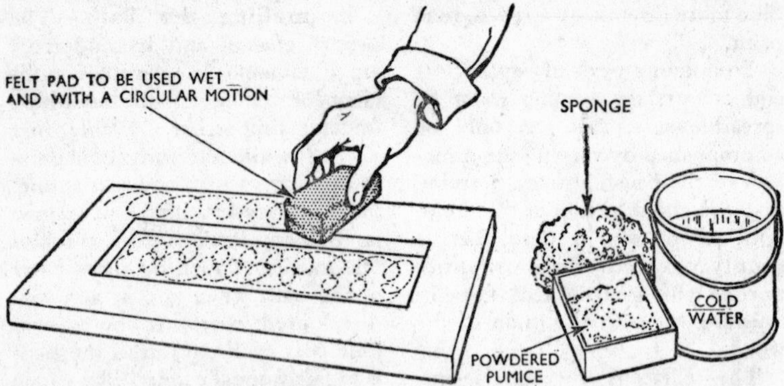

Fig. 1. Shows the use of a wet felt pad which has been dipped in pumice powder. When using the pad apply circular motion, sponge the surface often, with clean water and regularly charge the base of the felt pad with powdered pumice.

of conditions, can hardly succeed in meeting such widely different demands.

Synthetic varnishes are becoming increasingly popular for outdoor use, their quick-setting characteristics causing the surface to harden and become dust-proof, and often weather-proof, in two or three hours. In these, the linseed oil is combined with an artificial resin, frequently of the bakelite type, and the resulting product when applied to a surface will withstand a considerable amount of washing down without injury.

Flat, i.e. non-glossy, and egg-shell flat, i.e. semi-glossy, varnishes are intended for use upon an undercoat of gloss varnish, while others can be applied directly upon flat oil paint to improve and protect the surface. Such varnishes are quite unsuitable for outdoor work.

Spirit varnishes are simple solutions of shellac, wood resin, or other easily dissolved resins, in a suitable solvent such as industrial alcohol, naphtha, white spirit, etc. French polish is probably the best known type of spirit varnish, and the same conditions of warmth and dryness are equally essential during the application of all such spirit preparations.

Their suitability is strictly limited to indoor use upon new or stained woodwork, but not upon floors or painted surfaces. Articles of furniture, and shop or office fittings, offer a wide scope for these hard quick-drying, brush-applied varnishes.

Japanner's gold-size in an oil varnish combining a drying agent, but it possesses neither resistance to weather nor outstanding gloss. Its value lies in its capacity of drying within an hour, thus enabling it to be employed as a mixing varnish, or as a sealing coat prior to the application of a more expensive oil varnish upon anti-drying surfaces, such as new teak and Columbian pine.

Varnishes, specially manufactured for application on paper, meet the demand for an extra pale and durable oil varnish suitable for use upon sanitary or other wallpapers which are capable of withstanding the preliminary coats

Fig. 2. Stopping gaps and crevices between mouldings and wall with an improvised tool. This may be made, as shown, from an old table or kitchen knife.

of glue size. Its resistance to water and steam makes it ideal as a protective coating in kitchens, bathrooms, and humid situations generally.

Surfaces for Varnishing.—It may appear from the list of varnishes mentioned, that anything and everything can be successfully coated with the appropriate lustrous finish. But it is not only important to choose the right material for a job; there are other factors to be considered of equal or greater consequence.

Surfaces must be hard and firm, quite free from dirt and grease, they must present a smooth, non-porous surface, must above all, be absolutely dry, and, if possible, of a non-glossy character. Few surfaces comply with these exacting conditions, but good preparation must always aim at their production by such methods as the one shown in Fig. 1. A durable and satisfactory finish can never be obtained otherwise. Cracks, crevices and holes should be filled with plaster of Paris, putty or quick-setting proprietary cement, as shown in Fig. 2, the stopping being stained later to match, if necessary.

Other Essentials.—Absolute cleanliness is of major importance. The floor of the room should have been swept or washed, and the dust allowed to settle before attempting any varnishing in it. Varnish brushes must be clean and dry, and the vessels used for the varnish must be equally clean.

Fig. 3. How to hold the brush so as to work close up into corner recesses.

Painted surfaces should be of an egg-shell gloss (semi-flat) type, and be wiped down with a clean, damp wash-leather to remove dust. Outdoor work will obviously have to be postponed if rain, mist, frost, or dusty conditions prevail.

A warm temperature of between 60 degrees and 70 degrees Fahrenheit is a decided asset during the application of oil varnishes but this is not so important as the avoidance of a sudden fall in temperature during the early stages of drying. For this reason it is preferable to complete all varnishing during the morning, so as to have the work almost dry before nightfall. Newly applied varnish may also be chilled by undue exposure to draughts, the result of chilling being similar to that produced by varnishing upon damp surfaces, and manifesting itself by loss of gloss or by a whitish surface bloom.

Varnishing Painted Work.—Choose an oil varnish of a hard drying or elastic type according to the location of the work (i.e. whether inside or outside) and secondly, use the palest varnish available if the paint is of a delicate tint. No varnish is absolutely colourless, but some, particularly the dark oak varnishes, are suitable for use only upon dark or medium coloured backgrounds.

Varnishing requires a different technique from painting. The latter is applied sparingly and is finished with the lightest possible brush strokes, but varnish must be applied liberally and with enough force to spread the coating evenly. The work is then crossed and laid off as in painting but the toughness of the material demands slow, firm, brushwork throughout. Work up well into the corners of panels, mouldings, etc., using the brush as shown in Fig. 3.

The colour will be a good indicator of the evenness of the coating; if this is patchy, it will again be necessary to cross and

Fig. 4. When applying spirit varnish to a small panelled surface, brush with the grain on each part of construction.

lay off with the brush, taking care to complete each section of the work before the varnish begins to set. Two or three minutes is ample time for the varnishing of a door panel, and five minutes is about the maximum; otherwise, there is the possibility of brush marks failing to level out.

Each door or wall should be completed one section at a time, always joining up before the previous section has commenced to set; see Figs. 4 and 5. Pay particular attention to mouldings, for it is here that excessive coating may occur, which, if not removed with the brush, may crinkle or run.

After completing a door, it is wise to examine the job several times at ten minute intervals, to make sure that any runs are immediately noticed and levelled out with the semi-dry brush. See Figs. 6 to 8. It may be found

Fig. 5. Applying varnish to wall, in a vertical direction and in narrow strips.

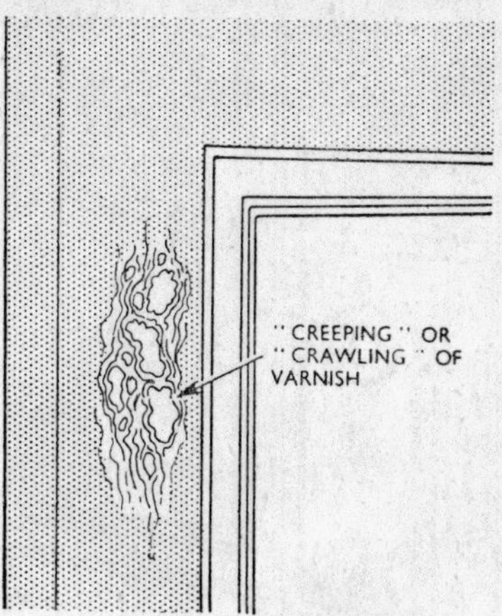

Fig. 6. If varnish is laid on too thickly it will tend to form wrinkled patches

(especially where turpentine substitute has been used in undercoats) that bare patches have made their appearance. These must be treated in the same way as runs, repeating several times if necessary.

Bare patches are a common trouble during the application of both varnishes and gloss paints. Such cases indicate a slight greasiness of surface which is easily cured by rubbing the unvarnished paintwork with a damp sponge (or wash leather) sprinkled with fullers earth.

Varnishing New Woodwork.—Hardwoods should first be stopped, sandpapered, stained (if required), and the grain filled (see POLISHING). The first coat of varnish or gold-size should then be applied rather sparingly and allowed to harden for forty-eight hours. The surface is then rubbed down lightly with fine waterproof sandpaper, using water as a lubricant, and the work dried off with the leather. Apply a finishing coat of varnish when the surface is sufficiently dry.

Fig. 7. Do not varnish the handle at A or the lock, B. Remove any runs at C.

Teak, Columbian, and Oregon pine are stopped, sandpapered, and then given a sealing coat composed of two parts japanner's gold-size to one part turpentine. The surface is then safe for either staining or varnishing.

Softwoods usually present surfaces of such uneven porosity that the application of stain or varnish immediately accentuates the fact by a marked difference in tone and colour. This patchiness can be greatly minimized if the work is given a preliminary coat of french polish or white knotting prior to staining or varnishing. For work of secondary importance, a coat of jellied glue-size will answer the purpose.

Staining and Varnishing Floors.—A stained and varnished floor margin makes an ideal surround for carpets and at the same time is more hygienic and economical than linoleum. If an oil stain and floor varnish are employed, the job will last for five to ten years without deterioration, providing that the surface receives an occasional dressing of floor polish. Varnish stains dry quickly and do not penetrate deeply, with the result that they are more easily marked.

Floorboards should be scrubbed clean and allowed to dry before stopping the nailholes with plastic wood. The oil stain consists of equal parts linseed oil and turpentine tinted with burnt umber and raw sienna; to this must be added about ten per cent liquid driers. One pint will cover approximately fifteen square yards when applied with a brush.

The stain and varnish must each be allowed twenty-four hours for drying and hardening off after

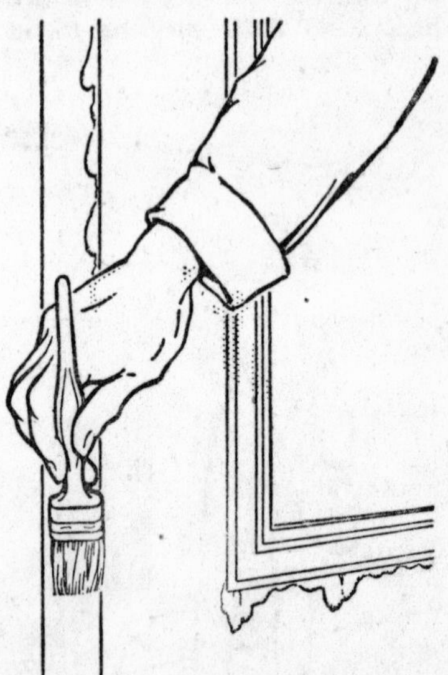

Fig. 8. Clean off any surplus varnish at edges of doors, corners of mouldings, etc., particularly at horizontal edges.

application. Two coats of varnish will be necessary, the amount required being calculated on the basis that one pint covers eight square yards of surface.

Varnishing Wallpaper.—There are two important essentials connected with papering and varnishing which, if neglected, will spoil the job. In the first place, it is obviously necessary to see that all joints and edges of the wallpaper are firmly attached to the wall; a point demanding special care during both the preparation for and hanging of the paper. All cracks between walls and skirtings or architraves must have been properly filled with plaster, otherwise varnish may creep behind the paper and cause discoloration. The second essential is the application of two coats of weak glue-size (brush applied), which serve as an efficient protection against the staining action of oil varnish.

Paper and Paperhanging

THE goods normally offered for domestic repairs include ceiling papers, white and tinted; lining paper, a plain white or coloured paper used for improving wall surfaces prior to distempering, or prior to the hanging of high class paper; ordinary wallpaper, plain and embossed; sanitary wallpaper, a smooth, washable paper suitable for bathrooms or kitchens; varnished paper, a sanitary paper with a high gloss finish; imitations of woods and marbles, usually finished with a glossy and washable surface.

Selecting a Wallpaper.—While the choice of colour and pattern depends very largely on the fancy of the individual, there are other factors to be considered which may help to avoid final disappointment.

Colour.—With regard to colour, many people choose a wallpaper in the lightest part of the room, e.g. near a window, and afterwards wonder why the papered walls appear so much darker than expected. Even in a well-lighted room, dark colours will appear darker, and light colours paler than the sample chosen. More thought might be given to the sensible use of both warm and cool colours. Warm yellows, pinks, and yellow-greens, for example, give an impression of warmth and brightness to sunless northern rooms, while the cooler tints of mauve, blue, and blue-green may be used with advantage to tone down the glare in sunny situations.

Pattern.—The effect of a large pattern (except in very large rooms), is to make a room appear smaller

Fig. 1. When stripping old wallpaper, thoroughly soak the surface with water.

Fig. 2. How to trim a roll of wallpaper.

ground for the display of furniture, choice pictures, etc. and when moderately light in colour give a pleasing effect of cleanliness and spaciousness to bedrooms and sitting rooms. A touch of bright colour can always be introduced by a suitable border or panel arrangement.

The value of semi-plain or mottled papers, especially when several nicely blended colours are used, should not be overlooked. It is often possible to find in them several of the colours present in the furnishings, thus helping to bring about a harmonious relationship.

and more amply furnished; small patterns have the opposite effect. Vertical lines, whether in the form of striped pattern or by the use of upright panel borders, impart an impression of increased height; horizontal lines seem to reduce height and accentuate space. Thus, defects in the proportion of a room may be rendered less obvious.

It is a great advantage, wherever possible, to see a roll instead of a small pattern-book sample. This will often bring to light any unsuspected spottiness or other undesirable features of colour or pattern. Lastly, do not be unduly influenced by the amount of gold in a pattern. Choose a wallpaper with sufficient colour interest to retain its decorative quality when, after two or three years the material has become discoloured.

Plain and Semi-plain Papers.—Both form an ideal back-

Removing Old Wallpaper.—Apply water, using a clean distemper brush; allow the water to penetrate and scrape off the paper as shown in Fig. 1.

Surface Preparation.—This is almost identical with the preparation recommended for distemper-

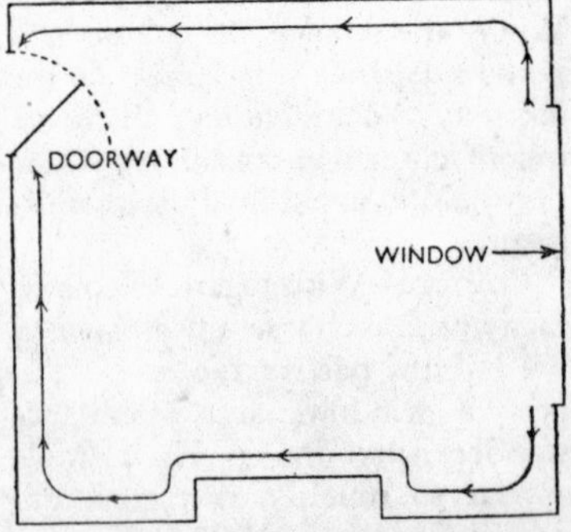

Fig. 3. Shows the directions in which paper hanging should progress.

ing, the modification necessary when paperhanging being the use of jellied size, as a preliminary to the application of the paper. Treatment suitable for the more difficult surfaces is listed as follows:

Painted or Varnished Work.—To prevent condensation, a cheap

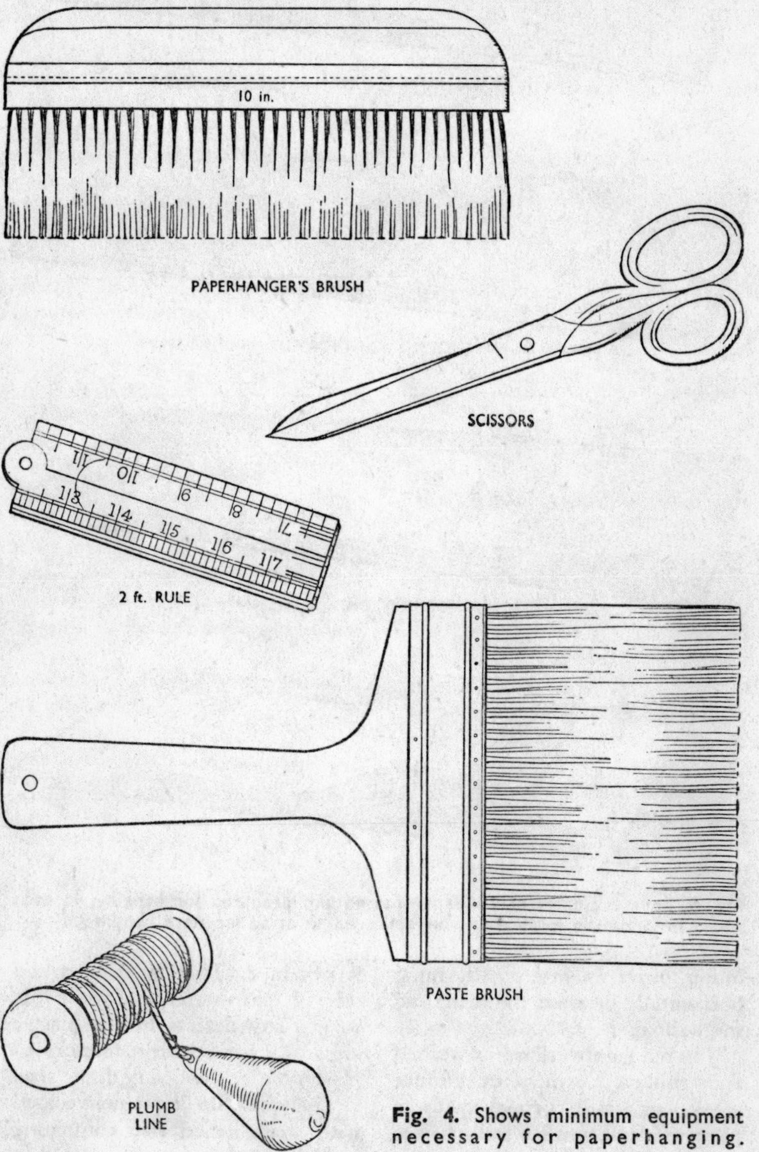

Fig. 4. Shows minimum equipment necessary for paperhanging.

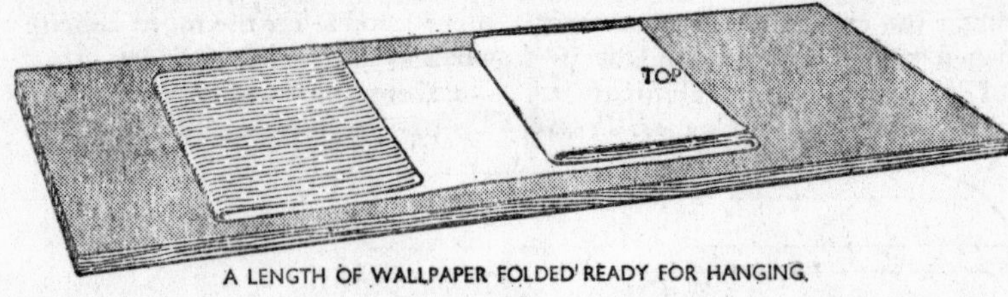

A LENGTH OF WALLPAPER FOLDED READY FOR HANGING.

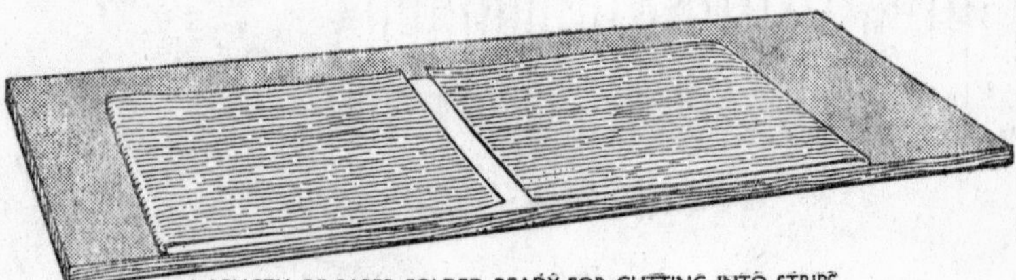

A LENGTH OF PAPER FOLDED READY FOR CUTTING INTO STRIPS

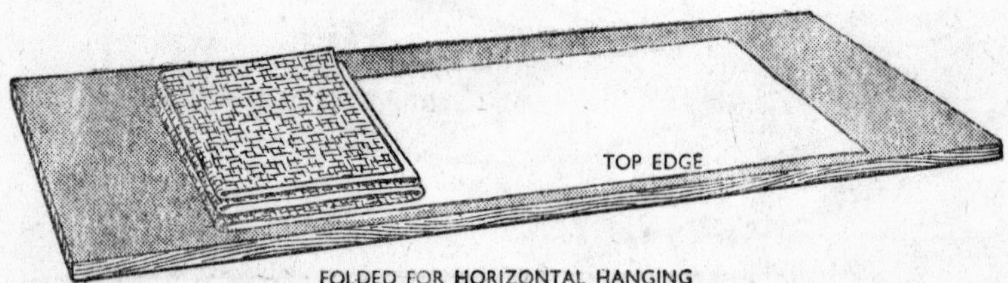

FOLDED FOR HORIZONTAL HANGING

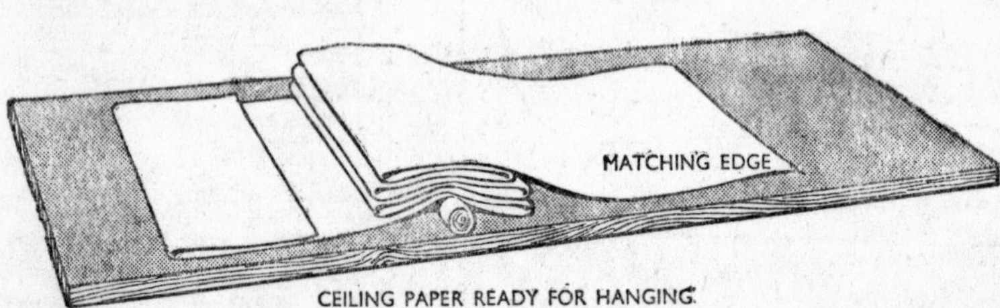

CEILING PAPER READY FOR HANGING

Fig. 5. Four examples of wallpaper pasted and prepared for hanging. In each instance the folds are to be arranged so as to facilitate handling.

lining paper is interposed, hung horizontally between the paint and the wallpaper.

The old paintwork is first washed and rubbed down with pumice stone, or (still better) with a pumice block, until a dull surface is obtained. This is then rinsed off with clean water, and while it is drying any defects in the plaster are made good with a mixture of plaster of Paris and very dilute size.

The whole surface is next coated with weak jellied size containing

Fig. 6. Using the plumb line to check the window frame. Note that in this case the window is not vertical and the adjacent strip of wallpaper must be cut accordingly, along the edge which will fit close to the side of the window frame.

1 lb. of whiting to half a bucket of size.

The surface may be lined immediately the size is dry.

Portland and Keene's Cement.—There is also the danger of atmospheric moisture penetrating through wallpaper to condense upon the hard, smooth surface beneath. The procedure recommended to prevent this is to roughen the cement face slightly with coarse glasspaper, and then coat it with size. Finally, cross-line it as for painted surfaces.

Asbestos Sheets.—There is some risk of the wet paste producing a chemical action likely to cause serious discoloration of the wallpaper. One coat of oil-bound distemper, applied after nail holes and joints have been made good

Fig. 7. Hanging first strip of wallpaper. Allow surplus at top and bottom and trim as required. Hold left edge away from wall until wallpaper is vertical.

with plaster, will not only serve as an effective insulator, but will act in place of a coat of size and render the work ready for papering.

Compressed Wallboards.—While the majority of wallboards can be sized and papered in the same manner as plaster walls, there are others which, owing to their tendency to warp, are best finished with distemper. Guidance on this matter will have to be obtained from the supplier or the manufacturer of the material in question.

The procedure adopted in the preparation of wallboard is: (a) coat all nail heads and joints with oil paint; (b) make good with

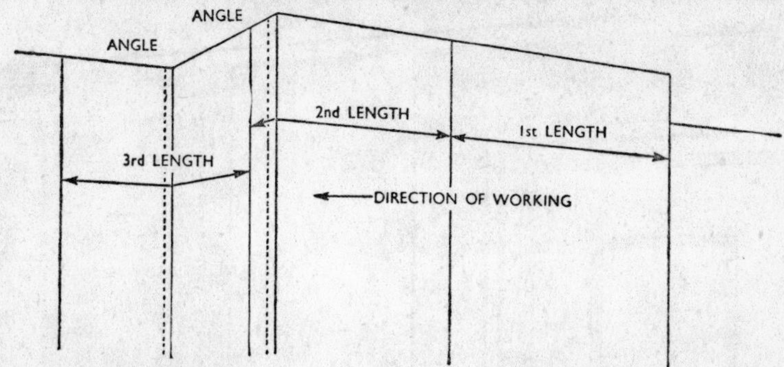

Fig. 8. Shows the direction of working and how to negotiate a series of wall angles.

plaster; (c) size the whole surface, and (d) paste a strip of muslin about 2in. in width over each joint. This treatment discourages rust and prevents the splitting of wall-paper over the joint.

Match-Board.—This is the most troublesome of all surfaces mainly because expansion and contraction of the timber speedily cracks or ridges any paper which is not reinforced in some way. The method usually followed is to stretch scrim, or muslin, over the whole surface, securing one length at a time with tacks, and finally coating the whole with glue size.

Measuring for Wallpaper.—A roll of English wallpaper is 21in. wide, and 11½ yd. long; there are, however, many instances where the odd ½ yd. is slightly soiled and has to be scrapped; it is therefore safer to assume that each roll contains 33 ft. of usable material.

It is bad practice to use two short pieces where a full length of paper is called for. With these points in mind it will be clear that a roll of paper can only produce 3 lengths of 11 ft.; 4 of 8 ft. 3 in.; 5 of 6 ft. 7 in.; and so on. This does not take into account any waste incurred in matching the pattern, nor the extra 2 in. allowed at the top and bottom of each length.

In measuring up the paper, first ascertain the height of the walls, adding 6 or 8in. for waste and matching. Then calculate how many lengths can be obtained from a roll, and the amount left over.

The next step is to measure the number of 21in. widths required to go round the room, noting at the same time the possibility of using up any short ends in positions over doors, fireplaces, etc. Divide the number of full lengths required by the number obtainable from one full roll. This gives the total number of rolls necessary for the main walls, and to this will be added any short lengths inside cupboards, over the fireplace, etc. Reference should also be made to the article on Plaster Walls and Ceilings for papering of ceilings.

Trimming.—This term refers to the cutting or trimming of the selvedges of wallpaper, and may be executed either with scissors or with one of the patent gadgets sold by decorators' merchants. Paper is usually trimmed before being cut into lengths. When some profi-

Fig. 9. Shows the method of negotiating the approach to, and head of door. Dark portions indicate wallpaper already hung. Cut and hang A and B in that order.

ciency has been gained, the operation can be carried out while sitting on a chair (see Fig. 2), but in the early stages it will be easier to use a table or pasting bench as a support for the paper.

Those papers which are thin enough to permit a lap joint when hanging, should have one edge trimmed clean, the other edge being left with about $\frac{1}{4}$in. of the selvedge untouched. Very thick papers have to be hung with a butt joint which necessitates the clean and accurate removal of both edges. Where the first method is adopted, the left-hand edge can be trimmed clean and the paper hung from left to right until the room is completed. A better method (see Fig. 3) is to commence at, and work away from the window, thus working from left to right on some walls and in the reverse direction upon others. Trim the paper accordingly, having determined the method.

Making the Paste.—Good surface preparation and good paste will do more than anything else to ease the work of paperhanging. A good paste will not only hold the paper instantly, but will allow the small amount of sliding which is of great assistance when matching a pattern. The best and cheapest adhesive is made from common (not "self-raising") flour, and is prepared as follows:

Mix 2lb. of flour with enough cold water to form a stiff batter; stir briskly until the mixture is quite smooth; add one large pinch of borax and then pour in about a gallon of boiling water, again stirring briskly until the paste thickens. When cool, dilute to a brushing consistency with cold water.

Hanging the Paper.—Professional paper-hangers employ more than the essential tools shown in Fig. 4, but the amateur will find that these, plus an apron with a pocket 12in. in width, will meet all ordinary requirements. An improvised paste-bench such as a large kitchen table should be wider than the paper and preferably about 6ft. in length. It is important that the bench be kept clean and dry, otherwise the paste will certainly soil the face side of the paper.

Make certain that the measurement is correct and cut about a dozen lengths, allowing the extra few inches for waste. These are turned pattern-side downwards, ready for pasting and folding as shown in Fig. 5.

As paperhanging is commenced at one side of the window, it is wise, before pasting the first length,

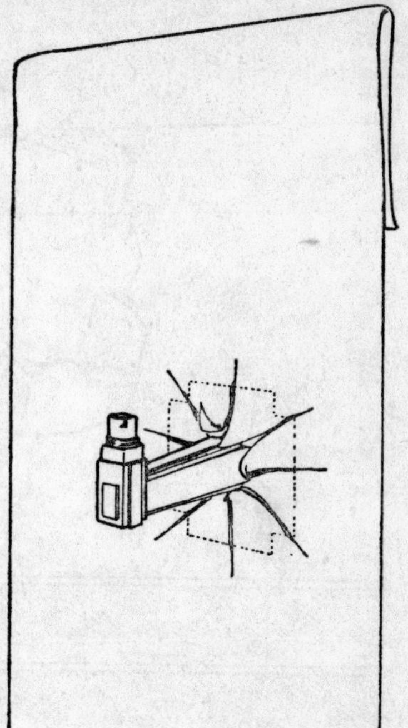

Fig. 10. Fitting wallpaper over a wall fitting, e.g. a lamp bracket.

to ascertain whether the window is plumb upright as shown in Fig. 6. If found correct, it makes the best guide in establishing a vertical edge for the paper; if incorrect, the paper can be plumbed while lightly attached to the wall, and any surplus along the window edge can be trimmed off afterwards. An alternative is to rule a vertical line 21in. from the window and make this the starting point.

To handle the first length, place the right edge of the paper against the ruled line, meanwhile holding the left edge a few inches away from the wall as shown in Fig. 7. By raising or lowering the left-hand the whole length is brought under control until some 3ft. of the right

Fig. 11. Paperhanging along a horizontal course. Line up each stretch before unfolding progressively. A and B show alternative joins at paper edges.

edge is properly placed and attached. The papering brush, which should, incidentally, be close at hand, can then be used to fix the remainder and brush out any wrinkles.

It is advisable, before trimming off the surplus paper at top and bottom, to check up once again with the plumb line. It may be found that the paper has been slightly twisted (probably by not using the brush in a vertical direction) out of straight and in that case the paper must be taken off and re-applied. It will soon be realized that while vertical and horizontal brush strokes do not affect the accuracy of a length of paper, any diagonal strokes will speedily twist the paper in the direction followed. Fig. 8 shows the progress of papering and the negotiation of wall angles. Fig. 9 illustrates the method used in arranging the wallpaper when passing the door frame.

Other points to note are: (a) always plumb the first length on each wall; (b) sponge off any paste from painted skirtings, etc.; (c) remove paste or fingermarks from the surface of a paper; this is not difficult if tackled immediately with a clean, damp rag; (d) where special fixtures are strongly secured to the wall, such as lamp brackets, switches, etc., which it may be inadvisable to remove, accurately measure the location of the fixture and mark off the position on the appropriate strip of wallpaper, then cut out the form of the fixture or, alternatively, cut the paper as shown in Fig. 10.

Paperhanging for Friezes.—When laying on wallpaper, following a horizontal course as shown in Fig. 11, the strip of wallpaper should be closely gathered in a suitable number of folds as illustrated and the first stretch should be carefully lined up before progressively extending each fold.

Distempering

THERE are three distinct types of distemper, each possessing its own peculiar merits, and a brief knowledge of their differences and characteristics will be of material assistance in selecting the best material for any particular job.

Types of Distemper.—Broadly speaking, all distempers consist of dry colours, like whiting (chalk), and various tinting or staining colours, well mixed with glue-size or other fixative and diluted with water. An oil-bound distemper contains, in addition to the foregoing, a fair amount of oil emulsion to give a washable and waterproof finish.

In addition to the glue- or size-bound distemper, and the oil-bound variety just mentioned, there is another popular type known as washable distemper, which (although not as resistant to water as the oil-bound class) is yet capable of withstanding a light sponge down. Any attempt to clean size distemper in this manner would be disastrous, for the whole coating is very easily removed by moisture.

When and when not to use. This problem must be faced sooner or later, and with several products at our disposal it frequently happens that one type of distemper may be a complete success where others would fail. On the other hand, there are materials such as iron, glazed tiles, glass, oil-painted or varnished surfaces, and woodwork, which are quite unsuitable for the reception of distemper of any kind.

Good surfaces are those of an absorbent nature, providing also that they are permanently dry and free from undue movement. A slight roughness of the surface assists adhesion, enables a thicker coating to be applied, and gives a better finish. Such surfaces as plaster, cement stucco, wall board, plaster board, asbestos, brickwork, stone, and paper, offer the right degree of porosity for all types of distemper and rarely give trouble, but woodwork, owing to its seasonal expansion and contraction, is liable to cause flaking.

Special attention must be given to Portland cement and hard wall plasters of the Keene's cement type when highly finished by the plasterer. Although fairly porous, these materials present smooth, hard and cold surfaces which encourage condensation. In these circumstances the best distemper is the one which does not permit moisture to penetrate, i.e. the impervious oil-bound type.

Unsuitable Surfaces.—Obviously, iron surfaces would rust and discolour any form of water

Fig. 1. Mixing the distemper and thinning out with liquid size.

paint, but non-ferrous metals being free from this objection often prove satisfactory when coated with oil-bound distemper. The action of heat or of excessive humidity in the atmosphere are the destructive elements which destroy the fixative and cause premature flaking of any distemper.

Painted or varnished surfaces have two serious drawbacks, first on account of condensation which occurs sooner or later when such materials are coated with either size-bound or washable distemper, and second because old paint or varnish is always sufficiently elastic (especially in hot weather) to expand and crack any harder coating applied over it.

Newly Plastered Work.—Time and material will be wasted by any attempt to decorate these surfaces before excessive moisture has had time to dry out. The period necessary will vary according to conditions, making it difficult to lay down hard and fast rules; but it is suggested that the following will serve as a guide:

Repair work, approximately 1in. in thickness and extending down to the old brick or stonework, a fortnight.

New work (hollow backed), such as lath and plaster ceilings and walls, or partition walls or breeze blocks, a fortnight.

New brickwork or concrete, if plastered in spring or summer, two to three months; if in late autumn, six months.

Old wallpaper will prove unsuitable when printed in dark, contrasting colours, when damaged by dampness, or when the paste has become perished and lost its

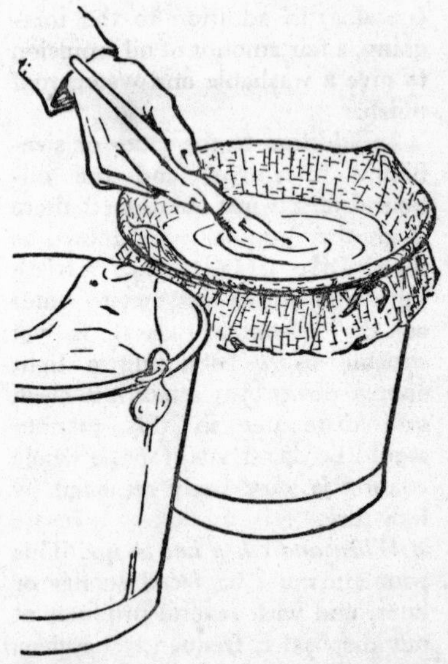

Fig. 2. Straining the distemper. Brush through sieve in small quantities.

Fig. 3. When removing old distemper apply water liberally by brush. Wash with sugar soap, if necessary, and rinse off with a clean sponge. Wash small areas at a time and change the water at regular intervals.

adhesive properties. (This latter failing does not apply to odd, loose edges which are easily pasted back.)

Purchasing Distemper.—What type to purchase, and in what quantity, are the next problems. Choice of colour is a personal matter, but it is wise to select warm tints (yellow, pinks, and colours containing these hues) for sunless rooms facing north and east, keeping the colder blues and greens for rooms of a southern aspect.

Oil-bound distemper is particularly suitable for walls of kitchens and bathrooms, and in situations where slight dampness exists, for here it is less likely to show that marked patchiness exhibited by other distempers. Washable types are useful for living rooms and passages, while ceilings, bedrooms, and spare rooms may be finished in ordinary size distemper.

The amount required is calculated on the basis that each pound of distemper purchased will cover (when thinned with water) six square yards of surface, one coat only. The average ceiling of 5 by 4½ yards will therefore require 4lb., but it is always wise to mix a little too much in case the surface is exceptionally absorbent. Whether bought in paste or powder form, containers of 4, 7, 14, 28, and 56lb. are usually available, the larger amounts being more economical.

Mixing Distemper.—*Powder distemper* is added slowly and well stirred into its own weight of water to render it ready for use.

Fig. 4. Distempering a wall. Apply distemper in strips and overlap previous strips before they dry. Note assistant erasing brush marks with stipple brush.

Paste distemper mixes more easily if warmed for a few minutes over a gas ring; cold water is then added a little at a time, any lumps being stirred and ground out against the side of the pail. When quite smooth, dilute to a brushing consistency.

Home-made distemper is cheaply and easily prepared, and although not so finely ground as the ready made types, is perfectly reliable. Any decorators' merchant sells the materials, which are mixed as follows:

(1) Place 3lb. of ordinary whiting in a clean pail, pour on ½-gallon of cold water and leave to soak.

(2) In another pail mix ¼lb. concentrated size with ½-gallon of boiling water. Now pour off all water not absorbed by the whiting and stir until a smooth paste results, adding liquid size as necessary. See Fig. 1.

(3) Any desired colouring must next be prepared by mixing separately (and thoroughly) in a little water. Lime green, lime red, lime blue, yellow ochre, umber, or a vegetable black, may be used

Fig. 5. "Cutting in," i.e. distempering at picture rail and skirting, then joining up.

(single or intermixed) to tint the whiting to the desired colour. This must be ascertained by trial on a slip of paper which may be dried near a fire in a few seconds.

(4) Sieve, in small quantities, through muslin to ensure a smoother mixture. See Fig. 2.

(5) Add liquid size until of brushing consistency.

Applying Distemper.—Correct preparation is important, especially when work is to be finished in oil-bound or washable distemper. Old distemper must be completely removed by washing, scraping and sponging with water until no trace remains. Obviously, an oil-bound distemper cannot be removed, but washing with sugar soap is advisable to remove dirt, grease and any parts on the point of flaking. See Fig. 3.

Defective plaster (see PLASTER WALLS AND CEILINGS). Minor cracks and holes should be filled with a mixture of plaster of Paris and distemper.

Bad stains on ceilings must be prevented from discolouring the new work. A preliminary coating of the part with either flat paint or

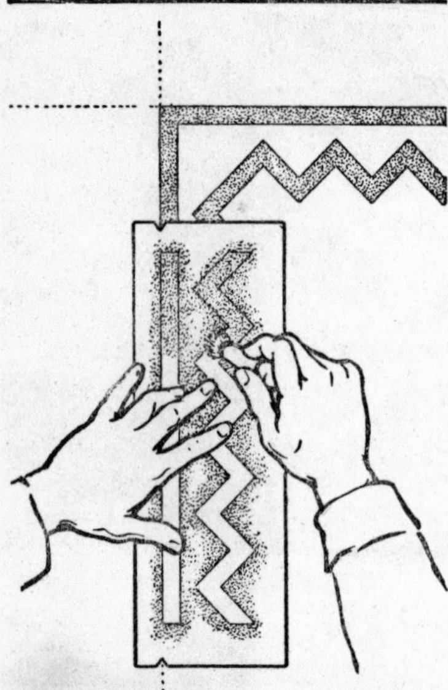

Fig. 6. How to apply simple stencil border. Note guide lines on wall, and notches at the ends of the stencil plate.

oil-bound distemper is usually effective.

Painted or varnished surfaces. The best preparation is to hang with lining paper (see PAPERHANGING) to minimize condensation.

Asbestos sheets. All nail heads should be painted to prevent rusting; then fill and level all joints and hollows with stopping.

First Coating.—Definite rules are laid down as to the proper undercoat for each type of finish employed, the object being to eliminate uneven porosity of the surface. Oil-bound distemper is usually mixed with an equal quantity of petrifying liquid (obtainable from decorators' merchants) and water, or with water only if the surface was previously finished in this type of distemper. Washable, or size distemper should be applied over a first coat of weak jellied size mixed with a quarter of its bulk of the finishing colour.

Final Coats.—Distemper dries quickly, and therefore must be applied rapidly and with a wide brush. Close doors and windows until the job is finished, and distemper the walls.

When applying distemper always coat each strip of surface before the edge of the previous one is dry. Apply a liberal coat with brush strokes worked vertically, but do not miss even the smallest part, for touching up afterwards will show prominently. See also Figs. 4 and 5.

The completion of each wall provides an ideal opportunity for

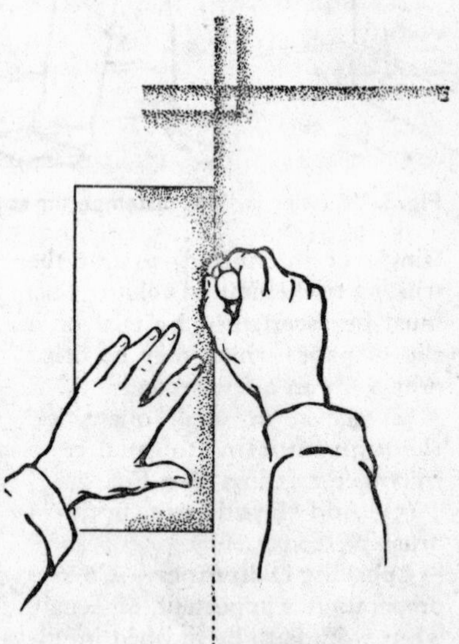

Fig. 7. Stippling a plain border design, using a mask with a straight edge. Do not overload stipple brush with paint.

the removal of any splashes from paintwork or floor. If tackled immediately with a clean damp cloth, much hard work will be avoided and the job left in a workmanlike manner.

Neat stencil and stipple line borders may be applied to the wall in contrasting colour, by a stencil plate cut as shown in Fig. 6. Use a good stencil brush and do not overload with colour. Mark off the base lines in pencil as a guide before applying stencil pattern to wall. Fig. 7 illustrates a simple method of stippling a border to a wall or similar surface by the use of a plain mask and stencil brush.

Whitewashing

The term whitewash, now somewhat loosely used, originally applied to a simple mixture of whiting (chalk) and water, without any fixing agent. This mixture has long been employed in ordinary dwelling houses, but for ceilings only, and its chief attractions are cheapness, fineness of texture, whiteness, and the ease with which it may be removed when necessary.

Limewash, which rivals whitewash in popularity, is a simple mixture of either slaked or hydrated lime and water, but this type of wash is not nearly as smooth working, nor as white, as that made from whiting. On the other hand, it is easier to apply, is more hygienic, and can be used for both interior and exterior work. Limewash possesses the property of permanently fixing itself to the surface coated. Although this may be an advantage out of doors, it is liable to produce a rough and overloaded surface after repeated applications to indoor work.

The two materials, whitewash and limewash, do not take to each other very well. If limewash is applied over whiting, the colour will dry patchy and the work will probably flake off. If, on the other hand, whiting is applied over limewash, the surface seldom dries out free from yellowish stains. The need for testing old surfaces is apparent, and fortunately this may be quickly done by rubbing with a wet cloth. If the coating washes off it is whiting or distemper; if not, and if its surface is of a dead flat, roughish nature, it is limewash.

Whitewashing a Ceiling.—This operation is more easily accomplished when the floor space is cleared of furniture. Heavy pieces can be left in the room if protected by dust-sheets, and wallpaper can also be protected by pinning up large sheets of paper. Carpets should be rolled up and removed as shown in Fig. 1.

It will not be necessary completely to wash off the old material, as in distempering; a light wash over with clean water (applied by brush) is quite sufficient to remove the surface dust, and if cracks are stopped at the same time with a mixture of plaster of Paris and whiting, the surface can be whitewashed immediately afterwards. It is, in fact, much easier to apply whitewash while the ceiling is still damp from the washing off.

Always commence at the lightest end of a room, applying the white-

Fig. 1. When whitewashing a ceiling protect walls and furniture from splashed whitewash. Use two ladders and a stout plank to facilitate the brush work.

wash as quickly as possible and working from left to right in a series of narrow (about eighteen inches wide) strips. Keep the whitewash rather thin, and stir every few minutes to prevent settling.

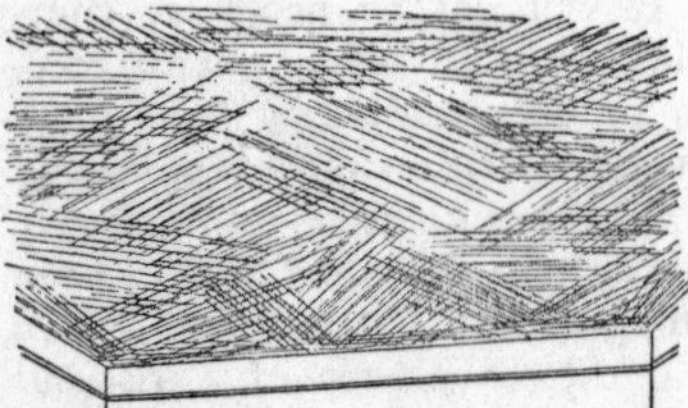

Fig. 2. Brush on and overlap the whitewash in a variety of directions, as shown.

The best results will be obtained by applying a very liberal coating and laying off in a variety of directions, as indicated in Fig. 2.

A ceiling cannot be completed without some splashes, but it should be possible to avoid the unsightly mess so often seen. Here are a few hints which cannot fail to produce cleaner results: (1) commence the work with a "dry" brush; (2) do not dip too deeply into the whitewash, two inches is sufficient, followed by lightly tapping the wet bristles against the side of the pail to remove surplus colour, see also Fig. 3; (3) never stand the brush in the whitewash; (4) scrape the bristles on the edge of the bucket whenever the whitewash begins to work its way towards the base of the brush; (5) avoid slapping the ceiling with the side of the brush; and (6) a large brush, with bristles at least four inches in length, is less likely to cause splashes than one with short bristles.

Removal of Whitewash.—This job is rarely necessary except when a surface is overloaded or flaking, or has to be papered. In the latter instance the job must be done thoroughly, but if the work is a preliminary to re-whitewashing, it can be carried out entirely by the aid of a distemper brush and frequent changes of water. It will be found that several applications of clean water will speedily remove the old material, and this can be supplemented, in parts, by a broad scraper.

Awkward details such as plaster mouldings, enriched corbels, etc. need careful treatment if the original shape is to be preserved. Such work is more easily and efficiently executed by the aid of a small brush and one or two pieces of wood shaped to fit into quirks and other hollow places (see Fig. 4). The excessive application of water may soften the plaster and add to the difficulties. It is most unwise to treat enriched plaster mouldings with any form of water paint; a flat oil paint is by far the best material for the job.

Fig. 3. When charging the brush do not dip in deeply, draw brush over lip of pail.

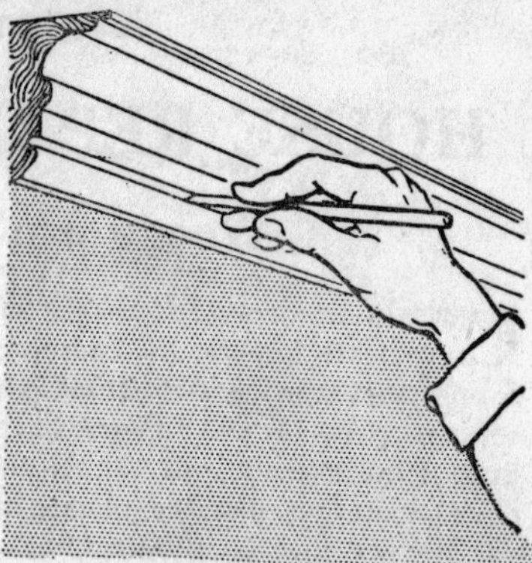

Fig. 4. Cleaning out the contour of a moulding, using a wooden pointer shaped to suit the work.

Limewashing.—Limewash is used in factories, workshops, bakeries, cellars, chicken houses, and other places requiring an antiseptic and cleansing wash. It can be tinted in the same manner as other whitewashes by adding a lime-resisting pigment such as yellow ochre, lime green, Venetian red, lime blue, umber, or black, the dry colour being well mixed in water before combining with the limewash.

When required for outdoor use, its weather resisting properties are greatly improved by the addition of boiled linseed oil, melted tallow or soft soap; one pint of oil or fat is stirred, a little at a time, into a pail full of rather stiff limewash; the mixture is then thinned for use in the usual manner.

SECTION SIX

HOUSE REPAIRS: INTERNAL

Woodworm and Dry Rot

CERTAIN timbers such as teak or cedar are practically immune from insect attack and possess high resistance to decay. Others have little natural resistance to insects or deterioration, due to exposure to varying weather conditions. Some have a high degree of durability if constantly submerged in water; this is true, for example, of elm, which will withstand prolonged immersion without deterioration, but it is apt to decay if left overlong in the ground.

The circumstances in which timber diseases and insect attack occur largely depend on the quality and type of timber, the uses, correct or incorrect, to which it is put, the degree of dampness, and the natural characteristics of durability for a specific type of timber. These factors cannot be described in greater detail in this entry; but, for the handyman, the following general information may be regarded as a good general guide in the prevention and cure of timber diseases and insect attack.

Wood is subject to two main forms of deterioration, attack by the larvae of certain small beetles and rotting by the parasitic activities of fungoid growths which, stimulated by damp conditions, attack and consume substances in the wood tissues, notably starch.

Woodworm.—There are several species of beetles whose sole purpose in life appears to be the selection of timber on which to lay their eggs. These eggs later develop into larvae or grubs which burrow into the wood and obtain, simultaneously, natural protection and a source of food. The extensive tunnelling of the grubs progressively undermines the structural strength of the timber, which, if subjected to a constant load, will eventually collapse. The grubs of wood-attacking insects may be found in living or dead trees, seasoned and unseasoned timber, fences, furniture, structural timber, and even in timber submerged in water.

Although each species possesses special characteristics and preferences (the pin-hole borer beetle and not the larvae, for example, being responsible for the excavation of the tunnels), the method of attack and nature of damage are very much the same for all the species. There are, also, variations in the lapse of time necessary to the completion of the life cycle for one species or another. The three species in most common distribution throughout the British Isles are the death-watch beetle, the powder-post beetle and the furniture beetle. There are others such as the longhorn beetle and the pin-hole borer, but it is proposed to deal only with the effects and treatment of insect attack in general.

Although the powder-post beetle is responsible for an immense amount of damage, principally in timber yards, the furniture beetle is no doubt most often encountered by man since the field of its existence is closely associated with domestic wood fittings and furniture. It is the grub of this beetle therefore which has earned the term woodworm, generally applied when wood is found to have been attacked by burrowing insects. The furniture beetle, approximately $\frac{3}{16}$in. long, will select, by the peculiar mechanisms of its instinct for survival, crevices in joints and obscure corners of rough unpolished or untreated wood surfaces, i.e. the undersides of tables, the unexposed surfaces of cupboards, etc. in which to deposit its eggs.

The presence of the grubs may be detected (if not by the very small entrances to the tunnels) by the fine dust, called frass, which may be discovered on the carpet or floor, particularly if the furniture has remained undisturbed for a reasonably long period.

The tunnels excavated by the grubs of the furniture beetle are about $\frac{1}{16}$in. in diameter and follow random directions, as shown in an exaggerated form in Fig. 1, frequently intersecting until the whole body of the wood is affected. As previously mentioned, some timbers are more liable to attack than others. Honduras mahogany is more prone to insect attack than cedar, which contains an oil that discourages the presence of wood beetles. Birch does not possess a high resistance to insect attack. Sapwood is more often attacked than sound mature timber. In general, wood with large grain pores and sapwood suffer most. The furniture beetle, however, will attack most softwoods and hardwoods, sapwood and heartwood. The death-watch beetle, notorious for its destruction of heavy timber in ancient buildings, shows a decided preference for wood containing sections of sapwood and an attack, as has been proved by recent research, is often preceded by the onset of dry rot fungus indicating the partiality of the death-watch beetle for damp, unhealthy wood in the early stages of decay. The powder-post beetle infests wood with its larvae, which will consume and reduce the interior of a piece of timber to a friable mass while leaving the outer surfaces more or less intact.

There is only one sound remedy for timber which is severely affected by insect attack, particularly if the component is designed to support a constant load, as with rafters, beams, joists, floorboards, etc.; remove it and replace with new sound timber, preferably treated with a preservative. The quick conversion and discarding of affected wood is a general practice,

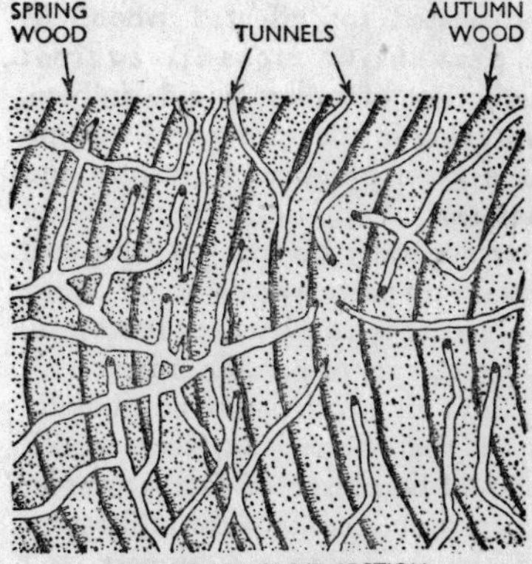

Fig. 1. A cross-section of wood showing, in exaggerated form, intersecting tunnels made by woodworm.

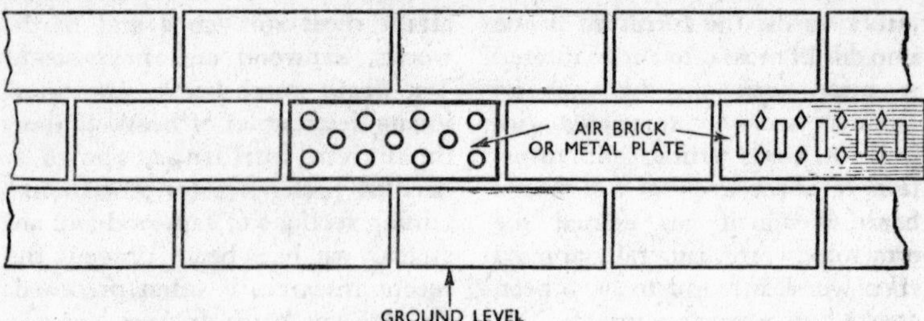

Fig. 2. Ventilation air brick or metal plate in wall surface. These are shown closely adjacent for convenience, but in practice are much more widely spaced apart along the outside walls of the house.

among other precautions and preventive measures, in timber yards. This is not always possible with pieces of furniture, but certain practical methods for halting damage and exterminating larvae may be adopted by the handyman, although it is emphasized that there is, as yet, no ideal remedy.

Preservatives in the coal tar group (creosote, solignum, etc.), useful for spraying external woodwork or roof timbers, joists, floorboards, etc. are good deterrents and, if impregnation of the wood is successful, will often kill off the grubs. Repeated spraying is advocated for affected wood. As a preventive measure against infection of other sound timbers, spraying in the spring and autumn is a good practice. Furniture and internal domestic fittings should not generally be sprayed with coal tar group preservatives as the odour is somewhat objectionable. Turpentine, or paraffin mixed with a fluid antiseptic, sprayed liberally over the affected surfaces, which should be presented face upwards, if possible, so as to allow infiltration of the fluid into the tunnels, will give good results. This work should be effected in conditions ensuring good ventilation. Rub wax polish liberally over the affected surfaces to seal the tunnel entrances. Similarly, fill the crevices and gaps between joints with wax. If it is an antiseptic wax polish so much the better. Small wooden boxes or ornamental objects may be completely immersed in turps so as to ensure efficient saturation and flooding of the tunnels. It should be remembered that paraffin and turpentine are solvents of paint and should not be used when it is imperative to preserve a painted surface intact. There are also many effective insecticides on the market and it is generally possible to select one that is suitable for the job. The use of water-soluble salts, in trade use, for the elimination of grubs is not recommended to the handyman as they are mostly of a poisonous nature and require a special technique in application. Fumigation, likewise, is a specialized process employing noxious chemicals, giving off poisonous vapours. Very low oven heat may, of course, be employed on wood, unlikely to be damaged in the process, to kill off the grubs. Recent research in insecticides suggests that more effective methods may be made available for the elimination of wood-attacking beetles, but it is not improbable that impregnation of seasoned timber with such preservatives, by the open tank immersion or pressure impregnation methods, before distribution from the timber yards to the manufacturer, will be the most effective means of preventing the onset of these pests.

Dry Rot.—More common than attack by insect is the rotting of wood tissues caused by the activities of organisms in the parasitic growth of fungus. The fungoid growths commonly seen on living and dead trees and on seasoned and unseasoned timbers are actually the fruits or flowers of the parasitic organism which attacks the wood. These organisms, called hyphae, microscopic in size and fibrous in shape, will only be found in damp humid conditions or where the timber is heavily saturated with moisture. The hyphae penetrate into the wood, from which they extract food and assist the generation of spores in the fungoid growth, finally reducing the wood to a soft friable mass. Most timbers are subject to dry rot if the surrounding atmosphere is humid or where moisture in the wood becomes stagnant by long standing in unventilated conditions. The hyphae will also explore every surface of wood in the vicinity and will traverse brickwork, metal and other surfaces in search for more material to attack. Hyphae actually penetrate mortar and brick in their persistent efforts to extend the field of damage. The best preventive measure against the infection of wood is to ensure good ventilation, freedom from saturation by moisture and the liberal use of a deterrent in the form of an approved preservative, many of which are available from builders' merchants and ironmongers, etc.

In the house, the handyman is advised to inspect all the sources of ventilation and to look for any evidence of dampness in timber and wall surfaces. It should be noted that perforated bricks or metal plates shown in Fig. 2 are installed in the outer walls of the house to give free ventilation to such timber as floorboards, joists,

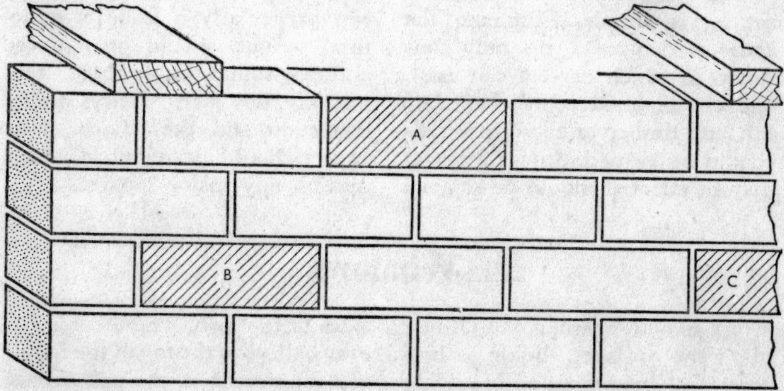

Fig. 3. A limited number of bricks may sometimes be removed at points A, B and C and replaced by air bricks or gratings to increase wall ventilation.

and other internal structural timbers. These bricks or ventilation points must always be free and uncovered and any evidence of dampness should be investigated. Where these air bricks do not exist it is permissible to make a limited removal of solid bricks at the position where damp occurs, as shown in Fig. 3; but this measure is not generally advised unless there is evidence to prove inadequate ventilation. Metal gratings should be fitted in place of the bricks. Walls which have ceased to be entirely weatherproof can be responsible for the onset of dry rot in timber by creating damp or humid conditions, the moisture tending to filter downwards and into timber. Damp timbers in leaky roofs and patches of flooring such as those beneath sinks, baths, and basins are specially subject to this defect, and suitable commonsense measures should be adopted to prevent the saturation of the wood. In regard to repair of walls, roofs, and floorboards reference should be made to the appropriate sections in this book.

The treatment of contaminated timber is simple. Eliminate the cause of dampness, the only condition in which dry rot can exist, and ensure good ventilation. Any infected timber or loose materials should be burned. Such timber as may be affected should be scraped and cleaned thoroughly. The use of a blow lamp on the defective surface is advised wherever this method can be utilized without injurious results; a slight charring or roasting of the surface, no more than would be necessary, say, for the removal of paint, being sufficient. Afterwards, spraying or painting with an approved preservative will give additional immunity. A good solution is 2 parts of zinc chloride to 100 parts water. Another solution, also brush applied, is a mixture of 2 oz. of corrosive sublimate to every pint of water. Be thorough in examination of all timber adjacent to the visible area of infection. External timbers may be treated with creosote, or other coal tar group paints. Even timber that looks sound may be in the early stages of infection so it is a wise precaution to apply a preservative to this timber by spraying or brushing. Apart from the ordinary use of oil paints, a hot solution of five parts boiled linseed oil to one of coal tar, brushed on, is a good sealing agent against damage to external timbers. Any timber badly damaged by dry rot, particularly if it bears structural weight, should be removed and new sound timber fitted. This measure, however, requires careful discretion and the advice of an expert should be obtained before making any major repairs.

Windows

The smooth opening and closing of the ordinary sliding sash is controlled by concealed balancing weights which are attached by cords to the left and the right top sides of the sash. These cords run over pulleys in the top of the frame, and the weight on the end of each cord rises and falls in the space provided in the interior of the frame. The balancing weights secured to the cords for the top sash are slightly heavier than the total weight of the sash. This ensures that the top sash will not tend to slide open from the closed position. The balancing weights of the bottom sash for a similar reason should be about equal to the total weight of the bottom sash. When a sash cord breaks, after long use, its metal weight temporarily ceases to be of use in the operation of raising or lowering the sash, until the broken cord has been replaced by a sound one. The broken cord can generally be detected because part of it hangs loosely outwards on its pulley, or the cord may cause the sash to jam in the frame. Access to the weight is provided by a pocket in the side of the framework, sealed by a strip of wood which is removable, see Fig. 1.

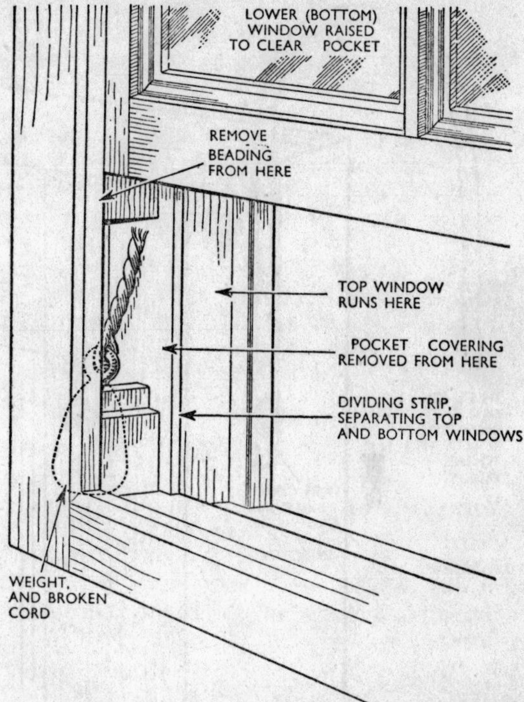

Fig. 1. Shows a part of a window sash, with pocket covering to the lower sash balancing weight removed.

Renewing a Sash Cord.—To replace a broken cord with a new one (sash cord is generally available at ironmongery or builders' stores), remove the length of beading, which runs from top to bottom of the frame, on the side where the break has occurred. To avoid damage to paint and wood, carefully lever out the beading, using a screwdriver or wood chisel inserted close up to each of the securing nails; it will then come away without trouble if bulged out at the centre. With the beading removed, the lower sash (if that is the affected one) is raised just far enough to clear the horizontal beading at the bottom and swung to one side; its only attachment to the window frame then being the sound cord. Support the sash on a box or chair.

The pocket in the frame may be located by looking for the horizontal cracks marking the top and the bottom of the strip. If it is not apparent, because of a covering of

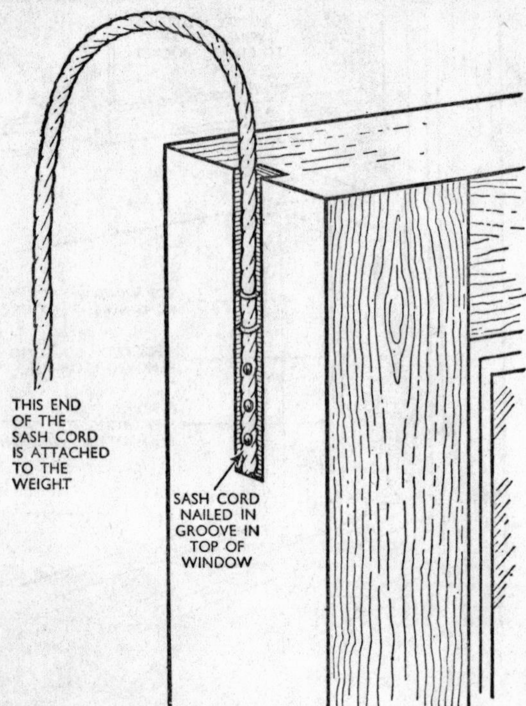
THIS END
OF THE
SASH CORD
IS ATTACHED
TO THE
WEIGHT
SASH CORD
NAILED IN
GROOVE IN
TOP OF
WINDOW

Fig. 2. The end of the sash cord must be firmly secured in the slot by staples and clout nails.

paint, a light tap or two with the hammer will cause the joint to show. The strip is then levered out with the screwdriver inserted at the bottom, and the weight lifted out of the pocket.

The two broken pieces of cord have now to be removed: one from the weight, the other from the top of the window which has been swung clear. The latter piece is attached by clout nails and also, in some instances, by staples, see Fig. 2; these should be extracted by pliers or pincers. The piece of new sash-cord must match the combined length of these two pieces exactly, and when the new piece has been cut to that length, one end is to be passed over the pulley for attachment to the weight. Tie a piece of string to the cord-end, and to the free end of the string attach a thin piece of lead about 3in. long by ¼in. diameter. Pass this over the pulley and allow the weight to carry the string down and inside the channel to the pocket opening. Draw down the cord, detach the string and be careful not to draw the top end out through the pulley.

The cord is then pulled gently through the pocket opening, just far enough to enable it to be tied to the metal balancing weight in the same way as the old one was fastened. Do not waste any of the cord in so doing. The top or free end can then be nailed in the window sash groove which the old piece had occupied. It will be necessary to lift the sash close to the frame while the nails and staples, see Fig. 3, are driven through the new cord. The repair thus completed, the cover is replaced over the pocket opening, the window goes back to its original place, and the beading, which was removed at the beginning of the operation, is nailed back in position.

Dealing with a top sash, the cord

of which has broken, it will be necessary to extract the lower sash, first by removing the beading on the same side of the frame as the broken top cord, then by raising the lower window an inch or so (to clear the bottom beading) and pulling it right out of the frame; it is then released so that it hangs, inside the room, by its two cords. Separating top and bottom sashes, at each side, is a long parting bead running from top to bottom, and this has next to be pulled or levered out of the groove that holds it. The strip is usually not nailed or otherwise fastened, but if paint prevents it being shifted it will need to be prised out.

That allows the top window sash to be swung down into the room, exposing the groove at the top of the sash to which the new cord is to be attached. The replacement is carried out in the same manner as when dealing with a bottom window. When this is completed, the top sash is replaced in position, the long upright parting-bead next, then the "lid" of the pocket goes back, and finally the lower window. The whole is made secure by nailing the side beading on the frame.

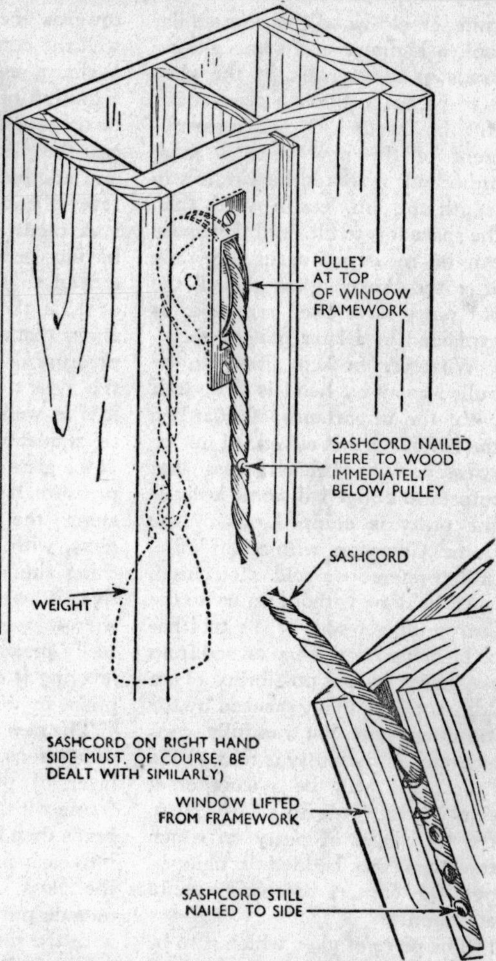

Fig. 3. When attaching sash cord in the slot of sash secure it temporarily, to the side of the window frame by one nail, to eliminate pull of balancing weight.

When the occasion arises to change one cord, examine the other three for signs of wear and renew these at the same time if necessary.

Glazing.—To replace a broken pane of glass the simple requirements are a new pane, some putty, a putty-knife or an old stiff-bladed knife, an old wood chisel or similar tool, a hammer and some glazing brads or short nails. If the glass is to be cut at home a glass-cutter will be needed. Exact measurement of the new pane is most important; it should be ⅛in. less in length and ⅛in. less in width than the space it is to fill. And that space can be measured accurately only after the broken glass and all the old putty have been removed, as explained in a later paragraph.

Whatever broken glass can be pulled away by hand is first dealt with; the importance of guarding the hands against cuts need not be stressed. The broken glass that refuses to budge will come away as the putty is chipped out of the frame. Chipping, with a stiff knife, or for preference an old wood chisel, must be done without injury to the surrounding wood. If the tool has to be helped with a tap or two from the hammer the possibility of an adjacent pane being cracked by the vibration must be carefully considered. As the putty is removed, a few brads will be encountered; draw these out with pliers. Next, the thin layer of putty on which the glass was bedded is chipped out, the corners receiving careful attention.

The piece of glass which is to be cut (minus the ⅛in. on length and width previously mentioned) is placed on a flat and speckless table or bench, overlaid with an old blanket to protect the glass, and the first measurement is marked off with a ruler against the edge of a tee-square lodged against one straight edge. The cutter, gliding against the side of the tee-square leg, is drawn firmly but lightly from the farther edge of the glass towards the operator. If all goes well the cutting is accompanied by a sharp, even sound; if there is a grating noise the glass is simply being roughly scratched, in which case the glass should be turned over and another attempt made on the reverse side.

A clean and continuous cut having been made, the glass is moved to the edge of the bench or table, the cut being immediately above that edge. Downward, quick pressure of the hand should cause the glass to part cleanly; and here it is as well to wrap the hand in a thick duster, in case of an accident. If the glass does not respond to the pressure, tapping on the underside, along the parting line of the glass, with a knife-blade or something similar, should prove effective. Where the surplus is of only narrow width it may be more easily persuaded to come away by levering it carefully with a pair of pliers or pincers.

The new glass reduced to correct dimensions, it is bedded on a thin layer of putty pressed into the frame with the thumb, a couple of brads then being lightly hammered into each side of the frame to hold the glass down to its bed. The outside putty is then applied, first with the thumb, then smoothed to an even slope with the blade, the latter being drawn from one end to the other. A certain amount of the bedding-putty will be squeezed out, on the room side of the glass, and this is cleaned off with the knife. A coat of paint applied to the putty completes the job.

This reglazing has to be done from the outside, and may involve the use of a pair of steps, or a ladder. There is, of course, the simple expedient of sitting on the window sill. However it is safer to take the window completely out of the frame and shift it to a table or bench where the work can be done in comfort. To do this, the beading is removed from one side of the framework, the sash cord then being pulled until the weight at its end has been hoisted as far as the pulley, and there the cord is pinned, with a large-headed nail driven through it into the woodwork immediately below the pulley so that it cannot slip back, see Fig. 3. The sash-cord on the other side is dealt with in the same way. The ends of the cords that are nailed to the top of the left and right sides of the window have then to be freed, thus enabling the window to be lifted right out. Reversal of this procedure, after completion of the reglazing, sees the window in action again. In dealing with a top sash it will be necessary to take out the vertical dividing-strip, as already detailed.

Plaster Walls and Ceilings

LIME plaster, as used by the builder, consists of slaked lime and sand impregnated with hair; the lime must be thoroughly slaked before use. Too-hasty use of the lime results in the presence of many unslaked particles which later may bubble and spoil the work. For this reason the handyman can, if desired, use one of the many alternative proprietary brands as they may be found easier to handle than the slaked lime plaster which requires much preparation and some delay. For all plastering, the surface must be well wetted, and all loose material, or old crumbled plaster, must first be removed.

Plaster.—Internal walls are plastered in three stages, the first coat being ½in. in thickness of hair mortar, employed to roughly level the surface beneath. The second or floating coat of mortar, ¼in. to ⅜in. thick, is intended as a true levelling coat, and the final or setting coat is a $\frac{1}{10}$in. to ⅛in. layer of fine white plaster, designed to produce a smooth, hard surface. This finishing coat is also occasionally known as a skimming coat.

A good mortar contains three parts sand to one of lime, mixed to a stiff paste with the necessary water. Strength and tenacity are improved by adding one handful of soft, chopped hair or fibre to one bucketful of mortar. To accelerate setting, place the amount required on the mixing board, make a hollow in the centre and add plaster of Paris (one part to eight of mortar); mix with water, then combine the whole mass: this latter method should be adopted mainly for small areas of repair. The final coat may consist of one part slaked lime, one part plaster of Paris to two parts fine sieved sand. The less plaster of Paris mixed in, the slower will be the setting characteristics.

Lath and Plaster Partitions.—In the case of partition walls covered with plaster on wooden lathing, make a close examination to discover the cause of any evident defect. The laths may be loose, decayed or broken, or the woodwork supporting them may have

Fig. 1. Removing lengths of defective laths. Replacement lengths may be butt-jointed or gapped.

warped or twisted. In bad cases a suitable area of plaster must be cut away to expose the laths where these are nailed to the nearest studs, so that faulty laths may be replaced. Laths can be bought at a builder's merchant, and should be matched for thickness with those of the partition. If laths are broken, cut them by a hammer and 1in. chisel as shown in Fig. 1, midway on a stud of the partition, so that room is left to nail the end of the new piece there, and also the existing end of the old lath that has been left. In some instances it may be possible to do this without altering the position of the nail in the existing part of the old laths. See, for example, the open joints and the method of removing defective laths in Fig. 1.

In dealing with old partitions it may be found that an attempt at extensive repairs may bring down adjoining areas of plaster. If this happens it will be fairly evident that the main area of plaster has badly deteriorated.

When, for example, the existing plasterwork crumbles away at a touch it is futile to attempt localized patching; the entire area should be stripped and re-plastered, a task that may require the services of a builder. The lathing having been made satisfactory, brush all dust and fragments of plaster from the bad portion. The plaster may be applied in two layers if the patch is fairly small, a coarse one which should adhere to and protrude behind the laths, and a fine coat which is to go on top and make a smooth surface.

Before plastering, cut back the lower layer at the edges of the patch (see Fig. 2), so that the new plaster gets behind the old top coat and forms a kind of dovetail "key" to the surrounding plasterwork; this can be done with an old, pointed kitchen knife. See that the spaces between the laths are freed from old plaster, leaving an interstice through which the new material may be forced so that it exudes at the back and spreads out, forming a key to the lathing and holding the plasterwork securely.

Material for the Patch.—To repair a small hole, and for defects in plaster at corners or by door or window openings, use a quick-setting cement which may be obtained from a builder's merchant. Several brands of quick-setting cements suitable for this type of repair are available under trade names. Keene's cement, a preparation of plaster of Paris and alum, calcined and powdered, is an admirable example. Manufactured in two grades for rough and fine coats it sets to great hardness and strength in a few days. Of the two grades, coarse and fine, the latter is white and the former pink in colour. For small jobs it can be applied as a single layer to fill completely the hole or crack, the holes or cracks being cut back at the edge as described above. Parian cement, prepared from a combination of gypsum and borax, is another quick-setting cement which sets in about five hours. Another material that can be used for small jobs is pure plaster of Paris; it sets very quickly indeed and does not permit long for smoothing off after application. Proprietary quick-setting plasters can, of course, be used in extensive repairs for both under layer and top coats.

Quick-setting plasters should be mixed and used strictly according to the maker's instructions. In one brand, for example, the plaster has to be mixed with an equal quantity of sand for use on lath work; for solid walls (no laths), *two* parts of sand to one of plaster are advised. Usually such plasters are recommended only when the space between the laths is not less than a ¼in.; however, the spacing is generally ⅜in. The proprietary plasters are sold in coarse and fine grades, and some also in haired plaster. Hair, it should be noted, is introduced into plaster not only to strengthen, but to bind the material together and is recommended for ceilings on that account. Enquiry of a builder's merchant will aid the reader in selecting the best preparation for the nature of the work or repairs to be undertaken.

Method of Procedure.—Spread a dust sheet or newspaper below the portion of wall to be treated. Damp the surface of lathing and the edges of the hole with a brush and water; a wide distemper brush is most suitable for large patches. Mix the plaster on a board, being sparing with water until it is seen, by experience, how the material works up. A brick trowel will do for small jobs,

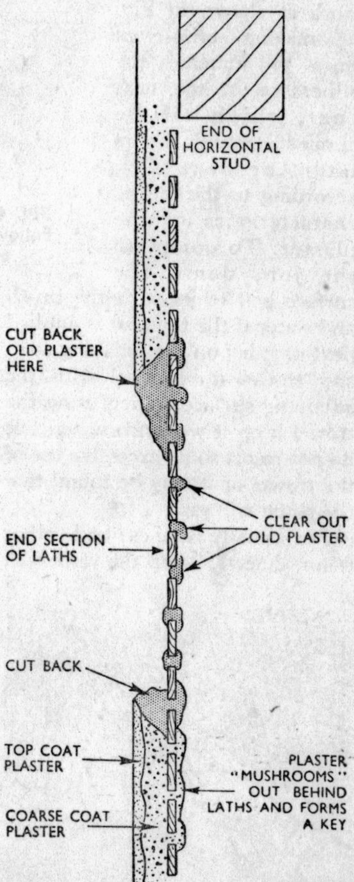

Fig. 2. An end view, cross-section of a lath and plaster wall, showing old plaster removed and areas to be cut back to form a key for new plaster.

though a flat (plasterer's) trowel would be more convenient for larger areas. Lay on the plaster, and press it well into the lathing, until a fairly level surface is produced up to the thickness of the surrounding underlayer. Score the finished work as shown in Fig. 3, making criss-cross lines to increase the adherence of the next coat, which will be applied several hours later, or next day, according to the setting characteristics of the plaster. To complete the job, damp the surface and edges with the brush and water if the top coat is applied next day; lay on the finishing coat, and trowel it off level with the adjoining surface. When using the trowel keep it wet with water, but do not resort to an excessive use of the trowel or it may be found that the patch will sag.

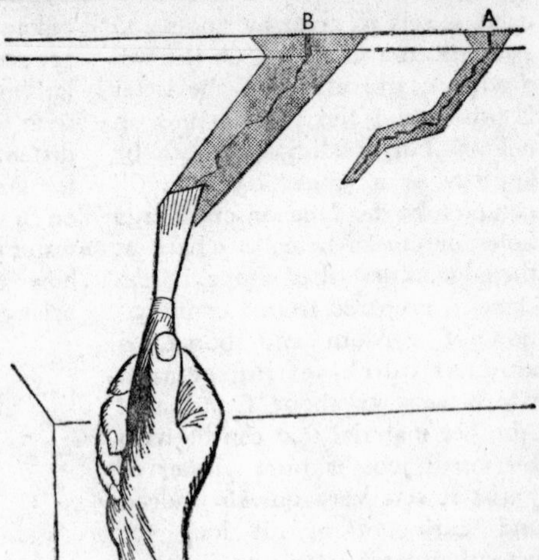

Fig. 4. Cutting out plaster to repair a crack. Follow main line of crack as at A or B, and cut at angle, dovetail fashion, as shown.

For small patches and other minor defects, damp the work well and fill in with the plaster selected. On solid walls the procedure is generally the same, except that a good bond should have been secured by roughening or pock-marking the surface to form a key, and by raking out the mortar joints. In patching the work, damp it well having first cut back the edges and brushed away all dust. In some cases it will be found upon removing the defective plaster that a metal mesh is secured to the wall. This mesh, which is another form of key surface, must be thoroughly cleaned and brushed, before applying new plaster.

Fig. 3. Scoring the underlayer surface to increase adherence of next coat of plaster. using a simple wooden tool.

Walls and Ceiling Stains.—These are usually met with in bedrooms and attics, and are commonly due to dampness arising from defects either to roof or gutter. See also WOODWORM AND DRY ROT. Smoke and soot may also cause discoloration as, for example, in old houses where the accumulated deposit may impregnate a plaster ceiling and this cannot be removed by washing.

The treatment of all stains consists of curing any dampness (at the source) and then sealing up the affected part by coating with flat oil paint, oil-bound distemper, or white shellac varnish. If this precaution is not taken, the stain will continue to strike through any number of coats of distemper. Where a ceiling is to be papered, it is better to use one of the many excellent damp preventive paints as a sealing agent.

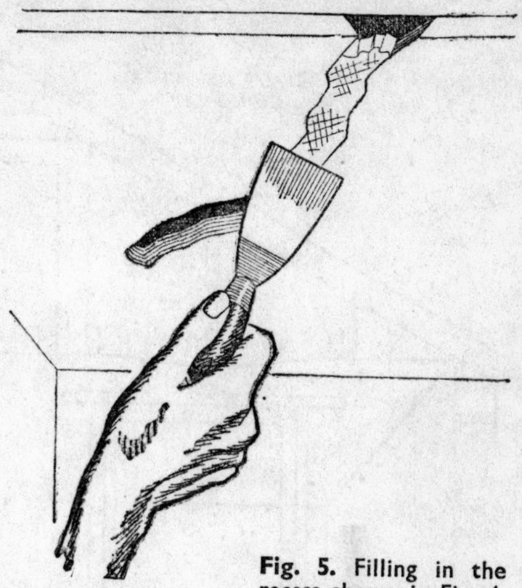

Fig. 5. Filling in the recess shown in Fig. 4.

Cracked Ceilings.—Cracks may develop as a result of vibration caused by heavy road traffic, or by the natural settlement of a building. The treatment will depend upon (1) whether the crack is of a simple character, i.e. with both edges level, or (2) is of the more awkward type with one edge higher than the other. In either case it is necessary to wash off the old distemper or strip off any paper so as to produce a clean surface, before commencing repairs. Cut away the plaster at the sides of the crack, making a slight undercut, following the line of the crack as shown at (A) or (B) in Fig. 4. The area should be made wet with clean water brushed into the gap, then stopped or filled with, for instance, Keene's cement, or plaster of Paris mixed with weak glue-size. The more thoroughly the plaster is worked in the recess, the less likelihood is there of further cracking. Finish it off flush, as shown in Fig. 5.

Where the edges of a crack are out of plane, i.e. not on the same level, the best and only permanent job is to cut out or widen the crack in order to disguise the fault on the surface.

It requires some courage, but the wider the channel cut out the more gradual will be the unavoidable slope, connecting the two edges.

The alternative would be the rather risky expedient of bevelling with plaster to build up a slope from the lower to the higher edge; perhaps with disastrous consequence when the door slams.

Sagging Ceilings.—It is not difficult to ascertain the cause of this trouble, but the remedy is sometimes very simple. Occasionally, however, it involves the temporary shoring up of the affected part. It is a job within the capacity of the handyman, but a matter for careful discretion.

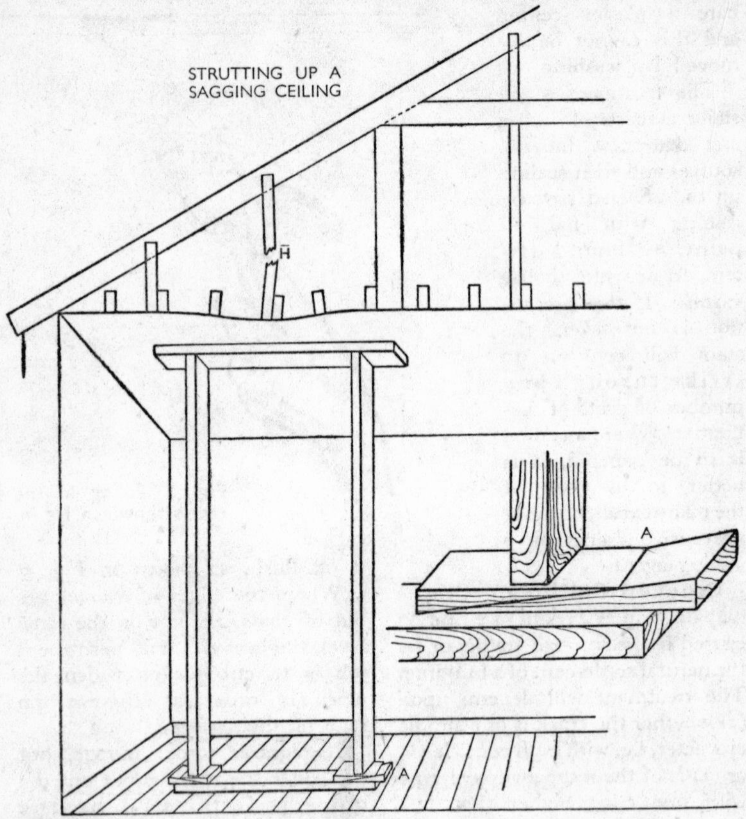

Fig. 6. How to strut up a ceiling which has sagged as a result of the broken hanger H. New hanger must be fitted while supports are in position. Note block wedges A.

First of all, find out whether the ceiling is of lath and plaster, plaster-board, or of the plastered, re-inforced concrete type.

If of the last-named class, the structure will, usually, be sound, and making good consists of hacking down the defective plaster and replastering with one or two coats according to the thickness. If lath and plaster ceilings sag and there is evidence of floor sag in the room above, strut with wedges as shown in Fig. 6. Remove the floorboards in the room above, where the sagging occurs in the ceiling of the room below, and investigate the cause. If light hand pressure, however, will restore the plaster to its original position it is probable that only the plaster keying or laths, not the floor joists, have broken, and the former method of inspection should not be resorted to. Small areas of plaster may be nailed up to the joists with clout nails driven below the level of the plaster, and covered

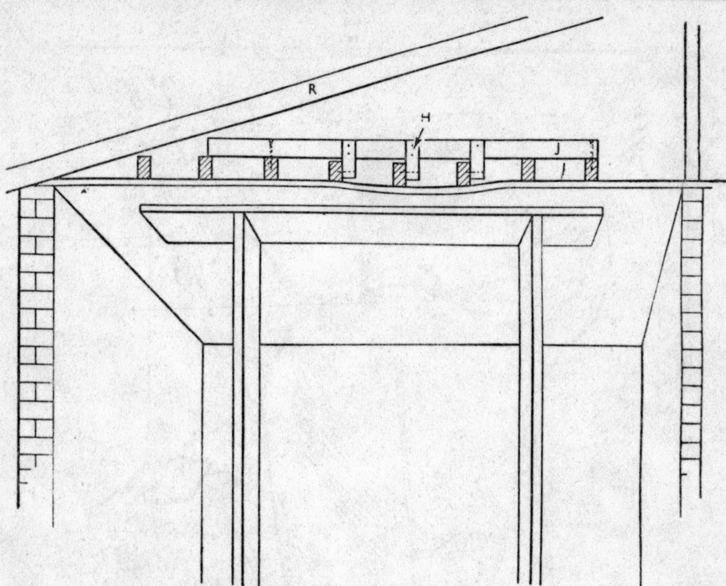

Fig. 7. Another form of repair to be used where rafters R, will not bear added strain. A joist (J), is used with short hangers (H), to distribute weight evenly.

with plaster afterwards to conceal their presence. If serious sagging of the plaster or breakage of laths has occurred, the whole area of plaster must be removed, the laths replaced by new ones and plastering carried out as described previously.

Plasterboard which may have come away from the ceiling joists may be made good by large-headed galvanized nails, along the line of the joists. While considerable pressure may be necessary to push back the bulging part, it must be remembered that this material is very brittle and easily damaged, therefore be particularly careful not to break the plasterboard when

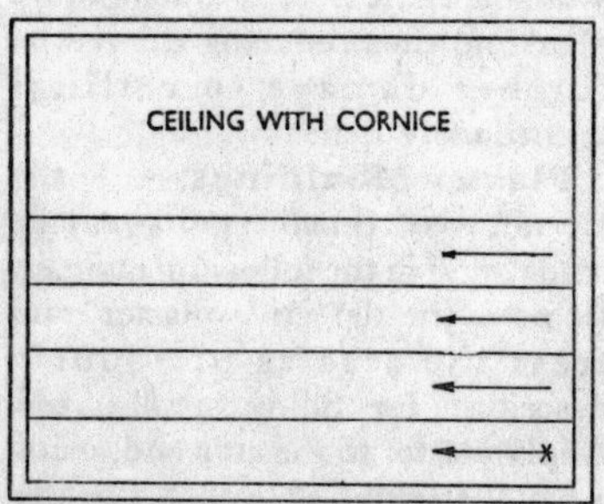

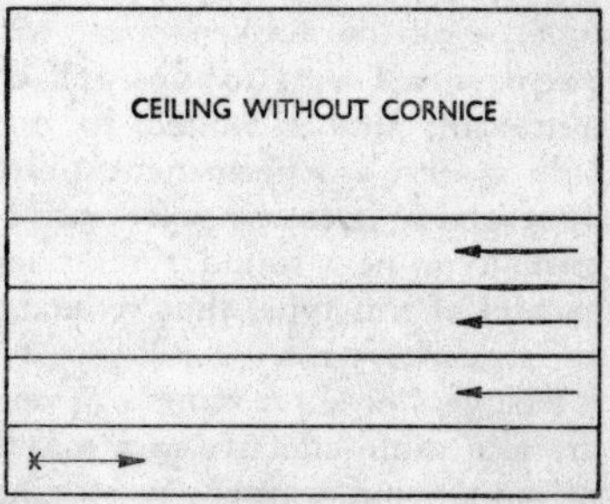

Fig. 8. When papering a ceiling surrounded by a cornice, apply all strips in the same direction. If there is no cornice, apply first strip in direction indicated.

Fig. 9. Applying ceiling paper. Note folds held in left hand together with a stiff roll to support paper. After first stretch, open and apply one fold at a time.

countersinking the nails or screws.

Where, as previously mentioned, severe sagging of the plaster exists, due to structural defects, the ceilings *must* first be shored or propped up from below and then secured or strengthened from above, as shown in Fig. 7.

A weak or broken joist will require a five foot length of 4in. × 2in. timber bolted to one side to serve as a permanent splint. It is advisable to use preservative-treated or new sound timber for repairs of this type, thus reducing the risk of dry rot.

Hangers or short struts of wood are also quite effective as a means of supporting warped or sagging joists (see Fig. 6). Where the rafters are too old and weak to take the strain, an 8ft. length of 4in. × 2in timber may also be fixed as shown in Fig. 7 across the top of the joists and will provide means whereby shorter struts can be secured. It will help considerably, when working in a loft, to use any available spare boards as temporary planking, thus reducing the risk of further damage to ceilings immediately beneath.

Plaster Mouldings.—Repairs are not easy. Small repairs may be made good in the following manner. Remove the defective plaster and treat the area as previously described for filling small areas. Apply plaster to the area and, using a metal straight edge that overlaps the extreme length of the patch, draw it lightly over the contour.

Another method is to draw a template, cut to match the contour of the moulding, over the plastered area; but the moulding must be simple.

The extensive repair of a heavily ornamented moulding is a highly skilled job, involving the manufacture of plaster moulds to match the form of the moulding, and a specialized understanding of the principles and materials involved. If the moulding is badly affected, it is advisable to obtain the services of a competent plasterer.

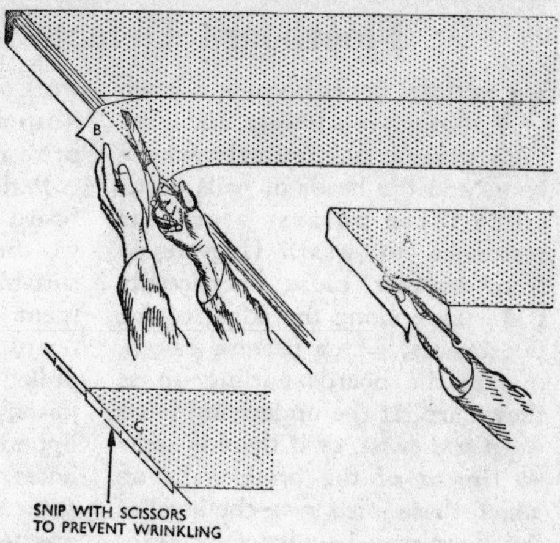

Fig. 10. Mark the end of paper, as at A, and trim with a pair of scissors, as indicated at B and C.

Papering a Ceiling.—The important essentials for a beginner are: (1) good preparation of the surface; (2) good paste; and (3) a ceiling of less than 9ft. across. Both (1) and (2) together with the use of tools and equipment are explained in the article on PAPER AND PAPERHANGING, page 185.

White lining paper needs no preparation, but patterned paper requires trimming, i.e. the complete removal of one, and the partial removal of the other, selvedge. The pattern can then be matched and the lengths cut, allowing a few inches at the ends for waste. Two step ladders and a plank form the scaffolding, and it is best to work from right to left when hanging the paper. A straight cornice mould is the best guide line for the first length, but where no cornice exists it will be necessary to rule a pencil line 20½in. away from the wall, and hang the first length in the reverse direction, taking care to keep the selvedge edge along the pencil line; other lengths are hung from right to left. (See also Figs. 8 and 9).

Pasting and folding must also be worked from right to left, to achieve the result indicated; it will then be easy to support the paper upon an odd roll held in the left hand, with the thumb gripping the folds. By employing this method it will be possible to release one fold at a time as required, see Fig. 9. The right hand remains free to unfold and attach the first few feet of paper to the ceiling and then to apply the remainder by brushing. See also PAPER AND PAPERHANGING. Waste ends should be systematically trimmed as shown in Fig. 10 so as to ensure a clean and accurate finish.

The main points to watch when papering a ceiling are: (a) to prepare each length of paper carefully if wall projections have to be negotiated; (b) do not overload the paper with paste; (c) do not use a stiff narrow smoothing brush.

Floorboard Defects and Repair

WOODEN floors become uneven through much wear, and leave high places, particularly where knots and the heads of nails occur since these possess a greater resistance to wear. Unevenness from another cause occasionally takes place along the edges of the floorboards, which become raised, due to the boards curling up as they warp. If the underlying joists warp and twist, or if there is some settlement of the brick walls on which these joists rest, the level of the floor may be disturbed. This type of defect is encountered more often in older buildings, and is outside the scope of repair for the handyman. Another defect to which wood floors are subject is caused by a fungus, and full details of this type of defect together with insect attack is described under the heading of WOODWORM and DRY ROT, page 204.

Replacing Worn Floorboards.—First study the diagram of a wooden floor given in Fig. 2. The joists, as will be seen, are usually 2in. wide or a little more. The boards, which cross the joists at right angles, are nailed at the centre line of the joist. If the ends of two boards meet in the form of a heading joint on one joist, both boards must be nailed to the joist. To remove the boards without damage is not easy, but on the assumption that one board is due to be scrapped, in any case, we can bore a round hole as near as convenient to the side of the joist, and enter a keyhole saw to sever one board close up to the joist. If the other end of the cut board runs to a heading joint. on another joist, work back along the board, levering it up at the intervening joists, and prize it off the joist where it ends.

Perhaps only part of the lifted board is defective, in which event we can cut it across to end on a suitable joist, ready for replacement later. In levering up the board, the nails will most likely be pulled up out of the underlying joists; rest the board, bottom side uppermost, on a stool or sawing horse, and tap the nails back sufficiently for the heads to be gripped by pincers, or by the claw of a claw hammer. Obstinate boards may have to have the nails punched right down into the joist to free the board. If a heading joint is not conveniently near, the board may have to be cut through at two places to remove the bad part. Electricians and gas-fitters often use a special floorboard saw, with a curved cutting edge; it is possible to saw straight across one board without damaging the boards at either side. The handyman, however, will generally bore a half-inch hole and cut across the board, using a keyhole saw, as previously mentioned.

Find the run of the joists. The positions of the nails will indicate this, and on the assumption that they mark approximately the middle line of the joist, measure an inch to either side of the nail, and square a line across, with a try-square. Mark a pencilled line. Put a fine bradawl through the board about a quarter-of-an-inch away from the pencil line, on the free side, then bore a hole with a brace and a half-inch centre bit or twist bit. If these dimensions have

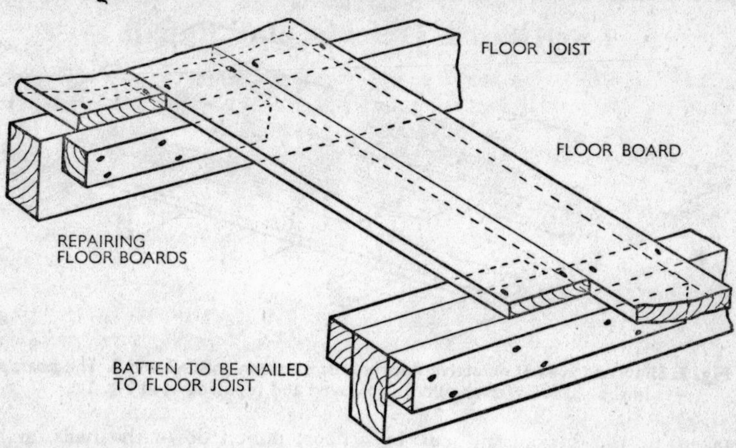

Fig. 1. Shows how short lengths of battens secured to the sides ot floor joists may be used to repair an area of defective floorboards, as indicated in Fig. 2.

been correctly established the joist will be visible, and the saw can be put through to cut alongside the joist, across the board.

As soon as the cut is long enough, take out the keyhole saw and enter a compass saw, or a small panel saw, and complete the cut.

Beware of gas pipes, or the casings of electric cables, when cutting the boards; they run usually in the space between joists. In some cases the electric wires may be merely protected by lead sheathing. When there is a room below the floor where work is in progress, some guide to cables, etc., can be got from the position of the lighting fittings on the ceiling below.

Having severed the board, the ends of the fixed parts can be trimmed up with a sharp chisel to a square edge. If several boards have to be cut away, take them back to joists one or two away to right or left from the one originally selected for the patch. In other words, break the joints, so that a board spanning over a given joist is next to one at which a board ends, and so on. Thus we shall not get a weak line of joints running along the same joist. A typical job is shown in Fig. 2; the joists are numbered, and the floorboards lettered. A heading joint is shown at X, X, on board B. It is not always practicable to make heading joints when replacing the boards, and the best thing to do is to support the ends of the replacement boards by nailing or screwing a stout batten to the side of the joist where the end of the new board will rest. The batten ought to be at least 1¼in. thick and about 3in. wide; take it half-way along and under the boards adjoining the one that it will support. This arrangement is illustrated in Fig. 1.

Two boards can be scarfed, that is, cut through obliquely, when they have to be jointed over a single joist. In this instance it is assumed that both boards can be

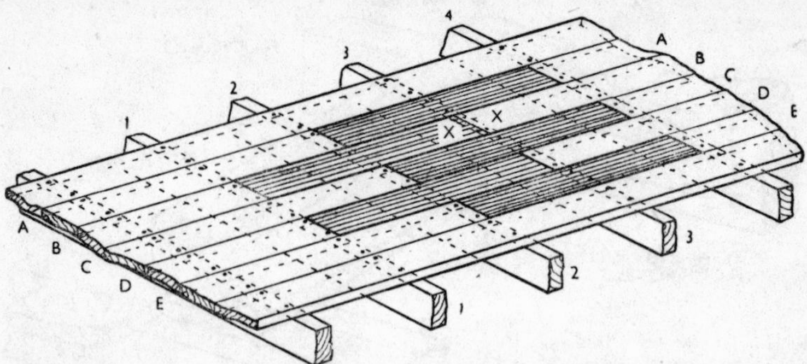

Fig. 2. Shows an area of defective floorboards between joists 2 and 3. The boards in the shaded area should be removed and repaired as in Fig. 1.

taken to the bench and cut by a tenon saw to a suitable angle. This makes a neat and sound job, the nails being driven through the scarfed portion. The angle can be marked across the edges of the board with an adjustable bevel.

Levelling a Worn Floor.—Sweep the floor, and brush out the cracks with a stiff brush (a wire brush is excellent for the purpose). Scrub down the floor and let it dry well before beginning operations. Then go along the boards with a hammer and nail punch, driving down the nails well below the surface, so that they will not damage the sharp cutting edge of the plane iron. Set the smoothing plane to make a medium cut and work over the high places. Follow the grain, attacking the place from a different direction if the wood tears or plucks. In bad cases a broad chisel may be convenient for removing the worst part. Next, reset the plane to make a finer cut; trim the edges of the boards and take off any irregularity here.

After new boarding has been laid, it may be found that the ends stand up higher than the old floor; punch down the nails, and taper off the end part of the new board so as to make a gradual change. Of course, in order to make a really good job, the replacement boards ought to be reduced in thickness to match the older flooring, though this may not often be practicable.

Repairs to Parquet and Wood-block Floors.—Loose blocks in a floor, if there are not many, should be removed. It will then be possible to scrape out the old mastic (a bituminous preparation) underneath. Put in fresh mastic, which must be warmed before use, and bed in the block. If the defect is extensive, the repairs may be more than an amateur can successfully undertake.

Parquet floors are glued and, invariably, pinned; dampness may cause the parts of the design to come loose, and in such cases the cause of the dampness should be found before attempting a remedy. Hot Scotch glue can be used to stick the different parts of a pattern together if a whole unit is defective. These diamonds, etc., are bedded on to a piece of low quality linen or other material with an open weave, which helps to hold them together. It will probably be best to unite the various parts of an element first, and let the glue harden, before re-laying, so as to ensure that all the joints are firmly set and safe to handle.

Door Defects

DEFECTS to doors, in so far as they are due to faulty hinges, can be corrected by alterations described in the section referring to HINGES. Most other defects are caused by the frame dropping at one side, or by warping of the door. When the frame drops, there will be points diagonally opposed, at top and bottom, where the door sticks or jams (Fig. 1, A); at the opposite side to this point the door will show a gap between it and the frame or the threshold (B), so that draughts may get through and cause annoyance (see also DRAUGHTS). Normally nothing can be done to the door frame, so that it is a case of making the best of a bad job, which means that we must adapt the door itself to overcome the altered conditions.

The first thing to do is to prevent the door from sticking; probably it will stick at both top and bottom, at diagonal corners. Plane off the high place at the top (A in Fig. 1) until the door is free here; it will be easy to locate the point at which the material should be planed from the edge of the door, by looking for the place where rubbing between door and jamb has taken place. With care, standing on a pair of steps or on a chair, a smoothing plane can be brought to bear on the door when open, but the end grain at the door stiles, may be difficult to plane in this position. In such a case the door must be taken down by unscrewing the hinge plates attaching it *to the door frame.* Instructions for doing this are given in the article on HINGES. First note also where the door must be eased at the bottom.

Remove the door and place it edgewise on the floor, with the faulty top edge to the left, and take off the high corner by smoothing plane. Then rectify the bottom corner if defective, and rehang the door. The next thing is to fill any gap caused by the dropped frame. Plane down the surface of a thin piece of deal, of the same width and thickness as the door, so that a long feather-edged piece results. It should not be a tight fit between top of door and top of frame; all that is wanted is to exclude draught and make a tidy finish. When the wedge slip fits, open the door, and nail it on top with veneer pins. Drive in two only at first, just enough to keep the slip in place for a test. Open and close the door, and see if it works easily; if not, take off the slip and plane off its top edge slightly; another way is to cut an inch or less off the thick end of the slip and then replace it so that it is now farther back than before. Tack it on again and try the door. When satisfactory, glue and nail the slip securely.

If an outer door shows daylight at the bottom (B in Fig. 1), a similar feather-edged slip can be nailed there to the threshold, but should be of hardwood. A better job is to nail the bottom slip to the edge of the door itself, after cutting and fitting while the door is hung. Of course, if it is tight, the job of taking the door down must be repeated to ease the slip, but this cannot be avoided.

Much of what has just been said applies to outer doors. Room doors can generally be adjusted by manipulating the hinges (see HINGES). The bottom of a room door is seldom a close fit to the floor, in order to allow for passing

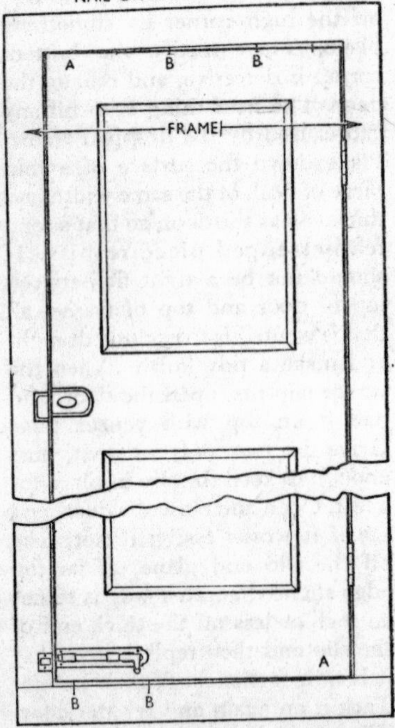
PLANE OFF HIGH CORNER AT A
NAIL ON TAPER SLIP AT B.
A
B
B
FRAME
A
B
B

Fig. 1. Shows how door lock and bolt are thrown out of register, and where excessive gaps may occur as at B, causing the door to stick or bear heavily at A. These defects may be due to warping of the door or the frame.

over floor coverings, so that it is the top and sides that have to be eased. Side tightness can often be remedied by adjusting the hinges.

Warped Doors.—Sometimes, as a result of warping, a door will not come close to the stops at sides and top; it may be close at one side and not at the other. The thing to do here is to move the stops to suit the door, provided the hinges are correct and nothing can be done with them. Refer to the instructions given under the heading FLUSH DOORS. In the case of an outer door it may have a stop moulded or formed on the door frame, which latter is cut out of the solid. A wedge of hardwood should then be cut to fit against the existing stop to close the gap. Test it as described above for the slip at top or bottom of door, and when it is correct, nail it on strongly.

Weather Changes.—In the case of outer doors especially, an adjustment made during warm, dry weather may prove too tight when the door later expands under damp conditions. This should be borne in mind and allowed for, and too drastic remedies avoided if the job is tackled in summer time. A sticking door, like a sticking drawer, may right itself later, so it is as well to bear this point in mind.

General Hints.—When a door rattles it may be due to the stops permitting too much clearance or play. In bad cases, move the stops in nearer, or tack a piece of thin felt along inside the stops. Always watch for any hindrance to the door latch or lock bolt when making readjustments at the stops. Readjustment of the latter may involve an alteration to the striking plate or box staple. For loose hinge screws, see also FIXINGS AND FITTINGS.

When a door frame drops, the bolt usually requires removal and refitting; usually the bolt staple is easier to move than the bolt itself.

Similarly, if the door warps, the bolt may be out of line with the socket or staple; the latter should be packed out a little to bring it again into register with the bolt. If the striking plate or box staple is out of register, an attempt may be made to rectify it. A striking plate is fitted when the lock is of the mortise type. Remove the plate, after noting where it must be altered; file downwards or outwards the slots for latch and lock bolt respectively, until they will again admit these parts. Put the plate in position, and mark where the wood must now be chiselled away to let the bolts enter. Take off the plate again, carefully cut away the wood, and refix the plate.

In the case of a box staple, the recess in the wood will need to be cut lower down, or deeper, according to the defect. Plug the old screw holes and bore fresh ones in the correct positions; after this, refix the staple. This is a ticklish job, which needs accurate observation and marking. Much harm may be done by inaccurate work. After completing the task, cut slips of wood to fill any gap left by moving the box staple. Some staples have a flange which is let into the edge of the door frame and screwed there; this complicates the job, as it is necessary to make an accurate fit in two directions. Plug the old screw holes, and proceed as described above. When deepening or altering a recess, take off only a little wood at a time, and try the fit before going further. If the staple has to be packed out, instead of being let in deeper, cut a thin slip of wood, or a piece of strawboard, and do not screw up too tightly; the latter material is quite easily compressed if it is forced up too hard.

Flush Door

IT is presumed that a room door fitted with a mortise lock is to be the subject of the operations. First of all, examine the door to make sure it hangs correctly and is unwarped. It is impossible to make a success of a door that has bent or warped out of the flat.

In order to avoid complications, endeavour to work so that the hinges need not be shifted. This means, if both faces of the door are to be covered flush, that the plywood cover on the *inside* face (the side where the knuckles of the hinges are) will have to be bevelled back and cut around the knuckles. The plywood, of course, adds to the thickness of the door, but if the edge mentioned is bevelled, the fact that the door projects inward here will hardly be noticed. At the locking side, the door stop can be adjusted so that the face of the door, after covering, comes flush with the door casing. The door stops will have to be taken down and replaced to suit the added thickness of the door on the outer side (opposite to the knuckle face).

The lock will not be altered, and the striking plate also should stay as before. Refer to the articles on Door Defects and Hinges. Obviously, any defects should be noted and remedied before fitting the flush covering or in the process of that work.

Furthermore, the door furniture will have to be taken off, and it is possible that a longer square spindle will have to be bought to allow for the extra thickness of the altered door.

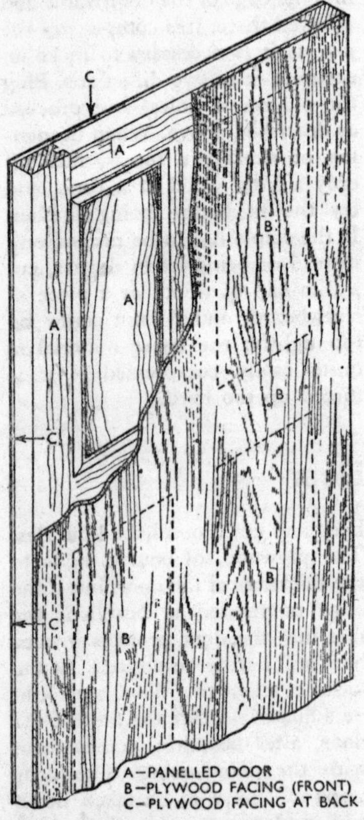

Fig. 1. A flush door. Location of door furniture omitted. If the door is fitted with a mortise lock it should be removed to facilitate the planing of the plywood edges if necessary.

Take off the door furniture first, unscrewing the handles, drawing out the spindle and removing any escutcheon or finger plates; mark these plates for the face of the door from which they were taken. Next unscrew the hinges from the door frame or casing, *not* from the door itself. The way to take off the door is explained under the heading Hinges. If any moulding around the panels stands out from the general level of the door face, this must be taken off or planed away and sandpapered down level. If the door is painted, polished or varnished, take a cabinet scraper and scrape off the paint, etc. all around the door framing, that is, the stiles and rails or upright members. The object is to leave a clean surface to which glue can properly adhere. If the door is merely stained, a rub with coarse glasspaper at the places mentioned will suffice. Remember that furniture polish, grease or oil will repel glue, and must be removed before gluing is commenced.

Plywood.—Choose two sheets of oak-faced plywood with a pleasant grain figuring (see also Fig. 1), which reasonably match on both faces of the door. Cut it to size, one piece for each face of the door. Mark the pieces for the respective side, and for top and bottom. See that they are used for the corresponding positions as indicated. The plywood may be left a little wide and long, and planed down after fixing. It should be cut with a fine-toothed panel saw, while resting solidly on two trestles or similar supports. This is a job where a helper is required. The saw will leave a burr on the underside, so cut from the top or best side, to leave the burr on the side that will not show.

Fixing the Flush Facing.—The method recommended is to get the main fixing by means of fine screws (Gauge 4, ⅝in. long), and to use 1in. veneer pins where the board shows any tendency to belly out. Hot Scotch glue will be applied to the under side of the board where it will come against the cleaned parts of the frame, and these parts also are to be spread with glue. The worker will need as many small cramps or hand-screws as he can provide up to about eight or a dozen. Go around the edges of the plywood, about an inch in from the outer edge, and bore holes with a drill to take the shank of the screws. These holes should be placed about a foot apart. Countersink the holes somewhat deeply, but leave enough wood for the screw head to bite on. After the screws have been inserted, the holes are filled with plastic wood, which on drying, is sandpapered level, and stained to match the oak. Plastic wood will not adhere in very shallow holes, so countersink as deeply as is safe. Screws are to be inserted wherever there are crossbars or intermediate rails or uprights in the old door. There is not time to do all this once we have laid the plywood in place on the glued surface, for the glue will chill quickly. The work should be done in a really warm room, if the temperature outside is very low.

Get the glue ready, and make arrangements to keep the pot warm so that the glue will retain the right consistency for applying. Use sandpaper to smooth off any burr left by the drilling process on the underside of the plywood; try the latter in place, while the door is resting ready for the job. Then apply glue to the door frame, fairly liberally; lay the plywood in place and test it at the edges for correct position. Tap four 1in. veneer pins partly through at the corners, to prevent movement of the sheet; these pins will have to be pulled out later. Now, working from the middle part of the door, bore holes one by one into the door frame for the screws, going in through the holes already made in the plywood. Insert the screws and turn them until they are securely home (avoid overtightening). Work from the centre out towards the edges of the door, to sides, top and bottom. If these operations proceed without a hitch, insert the screws in the holes bored along the edges.

Now is the time to use the cramps, interposing slips of waste plywood between the jaws of the cramp and the faces of the door. Take out the temporary pins first inserted. Watch carefully to see that the sheet does not bulge or belly out between the screwed fixings; by taking out a screw here and there such a defect can be at once remedied. Speed is as important as cautious and accurate assembly if disappointment is to be avoided. Perhaps here and there a veneer pin can be driven in so as to take down any swelling, but if the door face is level there should not be much trouble. Go over the screws to ensure they are fully home, after which the door, with cramps on, should be placed more or less upright against the wall in a warm room, with the faced side showing. It will thus rest on the uncovered edge, and there will be no end pressure on the plywood edge at the bottom.

The second side of the door can be tackled after the glue has set hard. But before the second side is put on mark and bore the holes for the door furniture, i.e. handle, spindle and keyhole. These are marked with a fine bradawl from the uncovered side of the door, where the existing holes will guide us. The spindle hole is merely a round one of ample diameter; after marking its centre with a fine bradawl from the uncovered side, bore through the exposed or outer face of the plywood sheet with a brace and bit; this will avoid splitting out the plywood.

Similarly, mark *two* holes to show where the bit has to go in at top and bottom of the keyhole; bore these holes through the exposed face of the plywood panel, as before. See the article on LOCKS for directions about boring for door furniture. A keyhole saw can be used to connect the two holes and form a slot to allow the door-key to enter. Do not drill and saw out the second piece of plywood until it is finally fixed.

The final job is to glue on and fix the second sheet of plywood. Lay the door on some clean paper to protect the face already covered. Proceed with the attachment of the second sheet of plywood as for the first. Allow this side to rest until the glue has set hard, and then clean off the edges of the plywood sheets all round, using a block-plane and a chisel, and finishing with sandpaper. Mark and bore the holes for spindle and key. If the door was painted, the edges will have to be cleaned and stained to match the oak face. The edges of the plywood will need to be stained also, and Vandyke crystals dissolved in a little water make a good stain for the purpose. Do not make it too dark, although the stain when wet always appears somewhat deeper in colour than after it has dried in.

No polishing or varnishing should be attempted until it is certain that the stain has thoroughly dried in. French polish is the best, if the worker has had some practice, but do not make the door the first job. An alternative is to brush on glaze of similar composition, and to rely afterwards on good applications of good quality wax furniture polish, which in time and with plenty of elbow-grease, will give a satisfying gloss. Another alternative is to oil the door faces with one of the furniture oils. Several applications should be made over a period of two or three weeks to get the best results.

When all the rest of the work has been done, the door furniture can be replaced; as mentioned earlier, the spindle, if short in the first place, may need replacement by a longer one, which can be bought at most ironmonger's shops. Usually, however, there is ample length as fitted.

Door Stops.—Take off the stops carefully if they have to be used again. Prize them away with a thin chisel; the nails may come out easily, or the stop may pull away over the heads of the nails, leaving the nails to be pulled out with pincers. In some cases the edge of the stops may need to be planed down to reduce the width, though usually there is plenty of room in the casing to allow the stop to come farther back, and it is merely a question of refixing in a suitable position to accommodate the extra thickness of the door. Knock out the nails, and use new oval brads to fix the stops again.

But before putting the stops back we must rehang the door, so as to see where they should go. The door being hung again, cut some slips of cardboard, about as thick as a penny, and, the door being fastened by its latch, place one of the long stops against the door face, with two pieces of cardboard interposed, one about 6in. from the floor and the other at the same distance from the top. The idea is to allow a little clearance between the door and the inner face of the door stop. After the latter has been fixed, there will be the thickness of the cardboard between it and the door face. Tack the stop in place temporarily with two nails driven only part of the way home. Put up the top stop similarly, and the opposite long side. If all is correct, and the door shuts satisfactorily, without too much play, proceed to nail the stops home. The nails are driven in, punched home, and the holes stopped with plastic wood or putty; the latter should only be used when the main surfaces are to be painted.

Since so much trouble has been taken to furbish up the door itself, it is worth while, when the other decorative finish is in keeping, to fix new door stops made of oak. About $2\frac{1}{4}$in. $\times$ $\frac{5}{8}$in. is the usual section for this, and it may be moulded on the outer edge or be left quite plain. A chamfer looks well on oak. Fix the stops in this case with $1\frac{1}{2}$in. lost head nails, which can be punched in and the holes filled with plastic wood for staining or polishing. Plastic wood can be had in natural shade to match the wood, or in a darker colour suitable for dark oak finish. Try out the selected kind, before use on an actual job; this is necessary because the colour will be slightly different after drying.

Drawer Repairs

THE repairs referred to hereunder will apply, mainly, to such fixtures as built-in cupboards, dressers, etc. Drawers in other furniture are not subject to so much wear, and in any event the repair of defects in this superior class of furniture is usually a job for the skilled craftsman. However, minor repairs may be undertaken on the lines recommended here.

It is not much use attempting to remedy defects in drawers unless one understands the basic construction of this piece of equipment, so the principal parts are shown in Figs. 1 to 5. The drawer, a small box, is unlike ordinary boxes in that its two sides and front are extended below the bottom of the drawer. They run on horizontal slips built into the dresser, and are guided by other slips rising vertically a little way from these runners (Fig. 4); or by the inner face of the dresser sides, Fig. 1. In course of time, the bottom edges of the drawer sides get worn away by the constant opening and shutting; if the sides

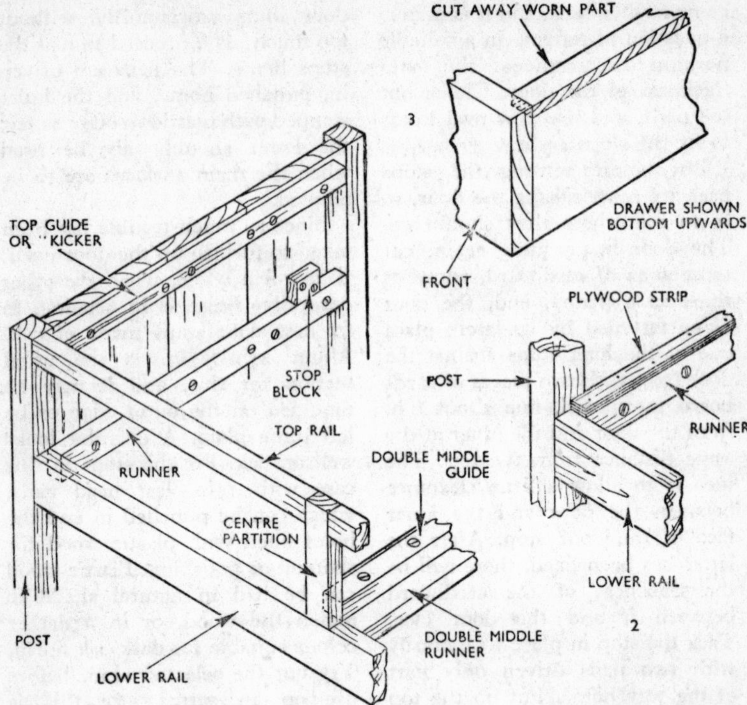

Figs. 1, 2 and 3. Show the general arrangement of framework for containing drawer, repairing a runner, and repairing a worn drawer edge with plywood strips.

are comparatively hard, the runners wear. This wearing away is greater at the back, so that the drawer becomes tilted, the front no longer fitting squarely into the opening.

Another defect of wear is that the drawer kicks up at the back as it is pulled out. This is prevented in good work by guides known as kickers (see Fig. 1), which are screwed to the framework at such a height that although they allow the top edges of the drawer sides to pass freely, they prevent any rising of the back portion. Of course, the top guides may wear, or the top edges of the drawer sides. When there are two drawers side by side, a central upright partition (see Fig. 1) is fitted to the framework, with a wider runner which carries the inner edges of *both* drawers. Often this central runner is poorly fitted, particularly at the back, and may have dropped a little. Most of the fixing in such work is by glue, with glued angle blocks added at suitable points to afford extra strength.

Dampness will cause the glued surfaces to part away at a joint, and any sudden jar during removal may break the joint. The remedy is usually to refix with screws or fine nails, also coating the joint with hot glue after scraping away any old glue. This re-gluing is possible only when the old joint is good, clean and unsplintered.

Yet another common defect is the absence of a stop block to prevent the drawer being pushed in too far. Very often such a block is fixed to the sides of the drawer opening (see Fig. 1), at or near the termination of the guides that rest on the runners. Here again, glue is often the only fixing, and the block may be driven off by rough use of the drawer. It should be fixed again, with glue and screws. In cabinets, and in some kitchen furniture, a different kind of stop is used, consisting of a thin fillet of wood (see Fig. 4) glued and nailed to the bottom rail of the drawer opening, as far back from the front as will allow the drawer front to go in flush. The fillet must be thin enough to clear the drawer bottom, which is fixed about half-an-inch up from the bottom edge of the sides; and the drawer front, held by the fillet, cannot go in any further.

Stops of this kind frequently get pushed off; they become loosened, and then an unlucky push will

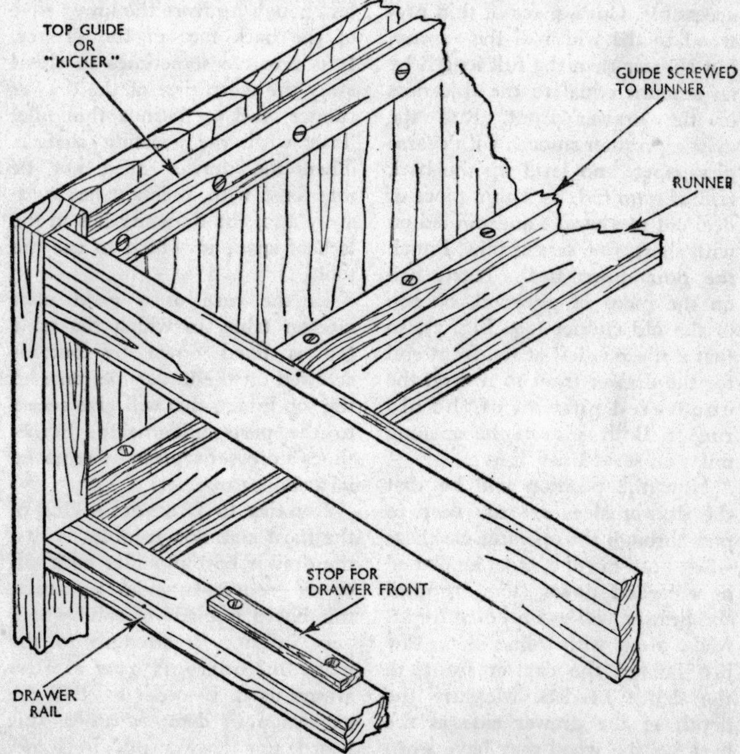

Fig. 4. Details of a typical arrangement of framework for containing drawer, showing kicker, runner, runner guide, drawer rail and stop for drawer front.

wrench them off the nails, or pull out the nails. At any sign of defective working here, the fillet should be replaced by one of hardwood, glued and fixed further by fine screws taken well below the surface. Neglect of this prompt remedy may mean that the heads of the nails will score the bottom edge of the drawer front, or do other damage. In a cabinet drawer the stop, if loose, may break away some of the wood of the drawer front.

Repairs to runners and Guides.—A badly scored runner is difficult to repair, as it is not very accessible. Cut a piece of thin plywood to the width of the runner, but shorter than the full length by an amount equal to the thickness of the drawer front. Rub the existing runner smooth with coarse glasspaper, and level up the back end, if required, by a thin piece of deal cut to a wedge and pinned on with short, fine veneer pins. Punch the pins down flush. Next, nail on the piece of plywood, on top of the old runner (see Fig. 2), so that a space is left at the front end for the drawer front to rest on the uncovered portion of the old runner. Both sides of the opening must be served like this.

Now the position will be that the drawer sides are too deep to pass through the opening. So these sides, bottom edge, must be planed or chiselled down (Fig. 3) until the drawer will again enter freely. Make a cut with a fine tenon saw just behind the drawer front, to the depth needed. Measure the depth of the drawer side at the back, as the wood may have worn away to some extent. Use a marking gauge to get a line along the drawer side to indicate the amount of wood to be cut away. Then carefully pare away with a sharp chisel. More cuts with the saw may be made at intermediate points along the side, to prevent the chisel going down too deeply. Finish off with a bull-nose rebate plane, if one is available, and finally with glasspaper. Gauge the remaining side of the drawer and cut this away to the same depth. Try the drawer in place, and if it needs easing, take a little more off the bottom edges.

This method can be used only when the drawer bottom is fitted far enough up from the lower edge of the back face of the drawer. It is possible sometimes to chisel away the worn part of the drawer runner, and to fit in a thin fillet flush with the existing surface. Then the drawer need not be interfered with, unless it has worn away also; the difficulty lies in the lack of space in which to use the tool.

In the case of a good class kitchen table, in which the table top is fixed down by buttons screwed on the underside, take off the top intact; this will give access to the parts underneath. Sometimes a dresser top can be removed in a similar manner.

Repairs to Drawers.—One of the most common troubles is that the drawer bottom slides back out of its groove. In older furniture, this board is made of solid wood, very inferior in strength to the plywood bottoms now almost always used. In order to allow for expansion in damp weather, this board was always put in loose, without glue. Further, although a nail, or in better work, a screw,

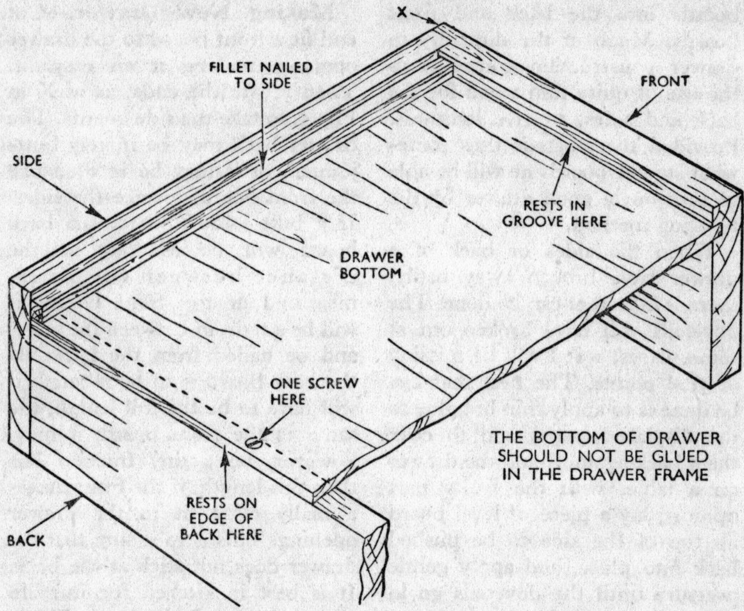

Fig. 5. Part section details of a drawer, bottom side up, showing location of fillet at the lower edge of drawer and the method of securing drawer bottom.

is generally inserted through the rear edge, where it projects beyond the back of the drawer, no other nails or fixings are used. The idea was that this single screw or nail could be easily withdrawn, and the bottom board pushed forward, if necessary.

Owing to the constant movement of the drawer in and out, the bottom board sometimes cuts a slot outwards from the fixing screw or nail, or breaks off a piece of stuff behind the screw. Where possible insert a screw through at some other point over the rear edge. If the board is badly broken, fit a new one from the thinnest plywood. Usually the bottom rests in a groove in the front of the drawer, and on top of hardwood fillets nailed to the drawer sides. These are shown in Fig. 5. Sometimes a grooved fillet is nailed on; the bottom board then slides in from the back, is pushed into the groove in the front, and is fixed with one screw at the back, as described. A moulded fillet, or a bead, is usually nailed on from the inside of the drawer, to hold the board down and make a neat finish. But of course, if a grooved fillet is used, it will show a moulded edge on top.

Good drawers are dovetailed, because this form of joint is the best for jobs where the front of the box has to stand a pull. The making of dovetails is a difficult task that needs accuracy and skill. For ordinary kitchen furniture a suitable and strong drawer can be made up by rebating the side boards into the back and front boards. Much of the difficulty in drawer construction comes from the use of quite thin wood for the back and sides, to give lightness. Provided the amateur uses somewhat stouter boards he will be able to turn out a good drawer by the rebating method.

When the sides or back of a drawer have broken away badly, there is little that can be done. The dovetails will have broken out at some places; wood will be missing at vital points. The best that can be done is to apply thin hot glue to the displaced parts, and to coax them back again. Stand the drawer on a table, with the faulty part upmost; lay a piece of level board on top of the side to be pushed back into place, and apply gentle pressure until the dovetails go in again. If the side has warped outwards, place a heavy weight on top until the glue hardens; span the front and back with a piece of board, and put the weight on that, thus equalizing the pressure. A few veneer pins may be driven in after the side has gone back, and before the glue gets cold. But do not hammer or knock the joint after this, or the jarring will break the glued joint.

Always drill a hole for the pins, through the side and just entering into the under part; a fretwork drill will do quite well for this job.

Making New Drawer.—Cut and fit a front board to the drawer opening, making it an easy fit. Then rebate the ends, as at X in Fig. 5, to take the side boards. The drawer back may be merely butt-jointed, or it may be rebated like the front board, to take the sides. If a butt joint is used, the back board will be as long as the distance between the sides, measured at the front board; it will be a tight fit between the sides, and be nailed from the latter. If the back board is to be rebated, it will have to be the full length, the same as the front board; it may, however, be a tiny fraction less than this length, if the front makes a really close fit to the drawer opening. This is to ensure that the drawer does not stick at the back. It is best in kitchen furniture to allow plenty of clearance. There are so many changes of air, owing to cooking and laundering, that a closely fitted drawer would be sure to stick in damp air.

Nail fillets on three sides to support the drawer bottom, as in Fig. 5. When this has been done, turn the drawer right side up, slide in the bottom from the back, and tack in pieces of quarter-round moulding on top of the bottom, closing the latter down to the fillet underneath. These pieces of moulding should be mitred, and be nailed to the drawer sides.

Draughts

When the point of entry of that elusive and annoying current of air known as a draught has been located, an end can be put to it in a variety of ways. The trouble may be due to loose hinges and screws or the door itself. If this hangs incorrectly as a result of bad workmanship or the use of unseasoned timber (which, in dry-

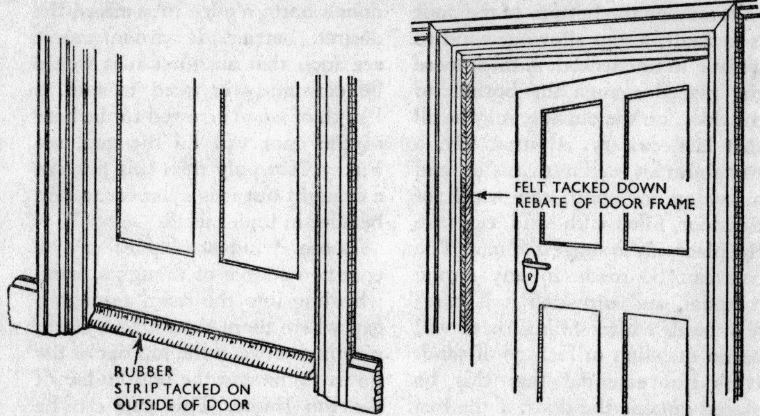

Figs. 1 and 2. Show how to reduce draughts originating from excessive gaps between floor or frame and door. Fit the draught excluders on outer side of door.

ing, has shrunk and left a gap between the edge of the door and the jamb post), a strip of felt tacked down the rebate (see Fig. 2) will almost certainly stop any draught at that point. But some study of the possibilities of practical repairs to the door should be made. Sometimes, however, warping and distortion, without rendering the door unserviceable, are not sufficient to justify the extensive repairs involved, in the elimination of a draught.

If the gap is unusually wide, a double thickness of felt may be required, or a strip of linoleum covered by a strip of felt. If that proves ineffective, the door should be increased in width by the addition of a strip of wood nailed or screwed to its inner edge, that is, the edge bearing the hinges. (See DOOR DEFECTS and HINGES for general door repairs). In some instances it will be found that the use of screws of the same diameter as the original ones, but ½in. longer, will secure the hinges without plugging the holes. The door should then shut correctly.

If it needs force to close it, a shaving or two removed from the side on which the lock is fixed may be all that is necessary. This may not have to be done from top to bottom of the door; removal of a shaving of wood at the point where the binding occurs will probably give satisfactory results. Complications with the setting of the lock make it impracticable to take off more than a little from this portion of the edge, but it may be possible to put the matter right by sinking the hinges a trifle deeper into the door post, thus pulling the door closer to the frame. If the door cannot be shifted in that direction and it does not appear likely that removal of a shaving from the point where binding occurs will do the trick, the door must be taken down and the hinged side of the door planed, after removal of the hinges, of course. These will then need to be sunk a little deeper than they were originally.

It may be the bottom of the door is at fault, a gap allowing wind to whistle in unchecked. A thick loose rug placed against the bottom of the door, on the outside, may be all that is necessary. Alternatively, a bag about an inch in diameter, and matching in length the width of the door, filled with sand, can take the place of the suggested mat. The bag can be made in any strong material, and provided it is carefully sealed after filling there will be no question of leakage of sand. It is not essential that this be placed outside the door; if the bag is made with a ¾in. flap it can be tacked to the inside of the door at the bottom. Alternatively of course, a strip of rubber may be secured to the bottom of the door as shown in Fig. 1.

An outside door may fail to make close contact with the doorstep, thus being partner to a draught. If the doorway is effectively shielded by a porch, an outer mat of sufficient thickness lodged at the door's bottom edge may afford the desired barrier. If circumstances are such that an outer mat would be constantly exposed to rain, a length of wood screwed to the base of the door will fill the gap, see Fig. 3. Not only does this prevent a draught but it is a barrier to rain beating in underneath.

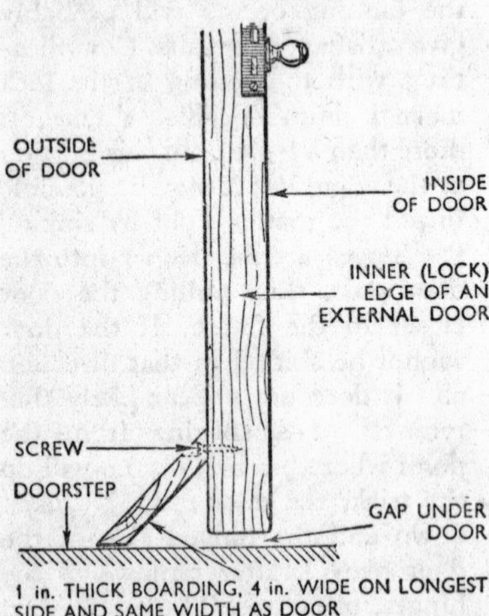

Fig. 3. Shows how to reduce draught to a minimum, on an outside door.

Loose window frames are a common source of draughts, wind whistling into the room through a gap where there should be a closer meeting between the top bar of the lower frame and the bottom bar of the top frame. This gap can be sealed by using a sandbag as described for blocking the bottom of a door, but of lesser diameter. Placed over the crack where the two sashes meet no draught will get past it. Or a length of stout brown paper can be rolled, and stitched, to form a plug for insertion in the crack, see Figs. 4 and 5.

Yet another remedy for a draught is a lath, or other thin strip of wood, tacked to the top bar of the lower frame and extending over the gap. With the necessary clearances cut in the lath there is no difficulty in opening the window. A coat of paint to match the colour of the sash will render this inconspicuous.

That area of a floor not generally covered with linoleum or carpet may be an unsuspected source of draughts, which can come up through gaps between boards. The obvious remedy is to cover the bare surround with linoleum. If this is not desired, the cracks between the boards may be filled with strips of thin wood, or laths, which have been treated by plane to give a tapered edge. The thin ends of these lengths are then inserted in

Figs. 4 and 5. Show two simple methods of preventing draught at gap between two sliding sashes. Sandbags as shown, are very efficient but should be used mainly for outbuildings or in rooms where appearance is not important.

the gaps and driven firmly in with mallet or hammer. Using a nail set, drive any protruding nail heads into the floorboards. Then plane away the surplus edges of the strips until they are flush with the floor. The finished edges should then be stained to match the flooring.

For lesser gaps an easily worked filling is indicated. For this purpose, putty at once comes to mind, but it does not readily take a stain. Another filler for floor cracks consists of pulped paper and glue. To make this, newspapers are shredded and then soaked in boiling water. The soaking should continue for several hours. Then the liquid is poured away and the sodden paper scraps are kneaded between the hands until a smooth pulp is obtained. Place the pulp in a can. Thin, hot glue is then poured over the pulp and the whole stirred with a stick. A table-knife or small flat trowel is a handy tool to press this filler home into gaps or cracks that need filling. When the pulp has been inserted it should be made very firm by pressing well in and adding more pulp to fill the space made. When it has dried, stain should be applied to match the boards. Several other fillers available at ironmongers will serve the purpose admirably if used according to the directions accompanying them.

A gap between floorboards and skirting, and many a chilling draught gains entry this way to a room, may be plugged with the same mixture, or with one of the fillers previously mentioned. Or

¾in. quarter-round beading may be nailed or screwed either to the skirting or to the floor, so that the gap is completely covered. Where pieces of this beading meet at a corner of the wall a neat mitre joint is easily made with a saw, and when finally in position a coat of paint to match the skirting completes a neat job.

Needless to say, the beading should be carried right round the room, or at least wherever the eye rests at floor level, for the sake of appearance. With a very old and uneven floor it may be found that even after the beading is in place there are still gaps here and there between the base of the beading and a sunken board. These must be filled in with one of the fillers already mentioned, or draught exclusion will not be really satisfactory.

Perhaps the most trying instance of a draught is presented by a bay window recess. These recesses appear to breed draughts, which are, upon occasion, sometimes difficult to trace. A curtain of heavy material hung from a rod to enclose the space completely is the quickest and most certain remedy here. It can be made to pull right across, or the curtains may be in halves, meeting with a generous overlap at the centre. This does not, of course, eliminate draughts, but during the hours of darkness the curtain is certainly efficient.

There are occasions when air must be let into a room on a generous scale, and at the same time even the least suspicion of a draught avoided, as in a case of sickness, when the patient will profit by all the ventilation possible. This can be managed, where sash windows are concerned, by pushing up the lower frame a distance of six or nine inches, the gap exposed at the bottom being completely blocked with a piece of board cut to fit. This can be secured in place with a couple of ordinary sliding bolts, making the removal of the board when the window is to be closed down a simple matter. When this scheme is adopted, fresh air enters the room gently by way of the gap between upper and lower frames and there is no suspicion of a draught.

There are people whose habit of never closing the door when entering or leaving a room appears to be incurable, and in whose trail a windy draught is inevitable. This annoyance is best met by the purchasing of a fixture which will automatically close the door, obtainable from most ironmongers. There are several satisfactory types from which to choose; attachment to both door and doorpost being equally simple in each instance.

Waste Pipes and Traps

UNDER every sink and wash-basin, and also under the bath-waste outlet, there is a trap consisting of a pipe bent to form a U-bend suitably adapted to the run of the pipe into the drain. The function of the trap is to hold a certain amount of water in the U-bend, with the object of sealing off the inside of the room from foul air that might otherwise enter from the drain. When the sink or basin is emptied, water runs through the waste pipe and the trap, displacing the water already in the U-bend, but leaving the latter filled up to the requisite level, at the finish of the flush.

At the bottom of the bend there will be found a clearing cap or plug, screwed into a bush incorporated in the lead pipe. Upon unscrewing this cap the contents of the U-bend will run out, so that a pail or bowl should always be put beneath it at such times. With the cap removed, a bent wire, or a piece of flexible metallic tubing, or thin cane, can be worked into and around the bends to clear any obstruction. This is one way of clearing the trap and the waste pipe, for it is frequently in the trap itself that a blockage occurs.

Use of the Force Cup.—Every householder should possess a medium size rubber force cup for emergencies. They cost only a few shillings, and are obtainable at most general stores supplying household equipment. These appliances work on a pressure-and-suction principle. Assuming that the kitchen sink waste runs sluggishly, or not at all, the following procedure should be adopted. Run water into the sink, about two inches deep, then take out the waste plug. Place the force cup over the plug hole. Fill up the overflow hole or holes temporarily with cotton waste or old rags, so that these holes are airtight. *Press down* firmly with the handle of the cup, so that pressure is communicated to the column of water in the waste pipe and trap. Do this three or four times; as you release the pressure on the handle, try the effect of *pulling up* the force cup, which will suck up water, and loose pieces of refuse blocking the pipe. By a combination of these actions most blockages can quickly be cleared, either forcing the obstructing matter down the pipe and through the trap, or drawing it up into the sink.

Should this procedure fail to clear the pipe, unscrew the clearing plug from the trap, as previously explained, and try to hook out any blockage with a bent wire. Do not omit to put a big pail below the trap, if much water is in the sink. If the pail fills up, clap the waste plug into the sink outlet for the time, and empty the pail. If the bent wire does not reach far enough, use a flexible metallic tube device (curtain spring wire), working first from the clearing opening in the trap, and then from the grating in the sink. Blockages which do not respond to ordinary treatment may be loosened by emptying the sink and trap, and then filling the sink outlet through the grating with washing soda; pour boiling water down to dissolve the soda, and wait awhile before again endeavouring to clear the obstruction by force cup. A good precaution against the occurrence of obstinate obstructions in the waste pipe is to use the force cup whenever the waste water tends to drain away sluggishly.

Baths and Lavatory Wastes.—The procedure here is the same as for sinks; try the force cup first. Bath traps are sometimes hidden behind the panel enclosing the side of the bath, more particularly in modern type baths, and are less accessible to the use of a flexible tube. Regular use of the force cup is therefore recommended, to make sure the flush through is complete and effective. However, use the flexible tube as required, and probably it will not be necessary to open the clearing cap at the trap. In the case of wash-basins, regularly inspect and remove any hair and odd scraps of soap, which often collect on the grating of the waste outlet. This simple precaution will prevent the occurrence of obstinate obstructions in the drain pipe. Really hot water poured down occasionally, with or without broken soda filled into the opening, will dissolve congealed soap which has collected below, a frequent nucleus of obstructions. This remedy is inadvisable during exceptionally cold weather, as the basin may be cracked by the sudden change of temperature.

Traps to Gulleys.—Every drain gulley outside the house, into which a waste pipe or rainwater pipe empties, has or should have a trap incorporated, to seal it off. However, in the summer months a neglected gulley may give off an offensive odour and regular cleansing is required. The iron grating should be lifted and the trap cleansed of sludge. A bucket of clean water to which has been added enough crystals of permanganate of potash to colour the water a deep pink should be thrown down the gulley at least once a week in hot weather.

Tiles (Internal)

THE tiling of a hearth or fireplace front is made up in the factory into complete slabs. When tiles become loose they should be carefully prized out. Chip the backing to a level surface and, similarly, clean the backs of the tiles. When cementing the tiles back in place remember that the tiles must be flush with those surrounding the area of repair. Use the jointing cement sparingly. Several brands of proprietary cements are obtainable at ironmongers' for this purpose; follow the maker's directions. Generally the joint surfaces of tiles and backing should be well primed with water so as to prevent excessive absorption of moisture from the cement which would lower its powers of adhesion when setting. The cement when prepared for use must be thin but not too fluid in consistency. Apply a thin buttering of the cement, and firmly press the tile into place, when it should soon adhere in position.

Where one tile only has come away, and can be returned exactly into its former position, so that the recesses of the tile will register again with the protuberances of the backing material that formerly filled them, we may omit the cutting away and levelling of the background. Try applying Seccotine rather liberally, and immediately press the tile back into place. In this instance do not wet the surfaces first. A *thin* mix of Keene's cement (sold at most oilshops as a powder resembling plaster) can, of course, be used for similar jobs where it is anticipated that no cutting away will be needed. But with all such repairs there is a probability that the tile will be a little high at the finish, as the new cement must take up *some* of the depth in the recess.

Wall Tiling.—Here again, odd tiles may be put back as explained above, but when larger areas are affected the backing surface and joint faces of the tiles should be cleaned and levelled. The glazed tiles used in kitchens and bathrooms are fragile, and damage to adjoining ones may be done by unskilful manipulation. Broken tiles can often be matched, more or less, at the builder's yard or by a builder's merchant.

Fixing Shelves.—Glass shelves to support tooth-brush holder, glasses, etc. are usually laid on special brackets plugged to the tiled surface. The first thing to do is to mark accurately the position of the brackets so that they will bring the shelf to the desired height. The points at which the screws are to enter must be indicated by a dot exactly central with the holes in the brackets. Obtain a tile drill, which must be of the same gauge as the wall plug and the screw to be used. Make sure the screw chosen will pass through the bracket and that it is not so long as to permit the plain shank to enter the wall plug. In attaching fittings that are thin (as metal brackets, mirror plates) use screws having the worm or threaded part taken quite close up to the head. If the unthreaded shank of a screw reaches the plug before the fixture has been drawn home, the plug itself may be turned round and loosened by any further driving of the screw; this is the reason for using the special screws previously mentioned. These are obtainable at most ironmonger shops.

Usually screws of No. 6 gauge and ¾in. long will suit these jobs, so that we need a No. 6 drill and No. 6 wall plugs. The drill is put into a carpenter's brace and turned fairly slowly while the tool is kept pressed close against the tile. (A percussion drill, as used for ordinary plugging in brick, etc. is not suitable for tiles). A light tap just sufficient to mark the glazed surface of the tile may be made with a metalworker's centre punch, struck with a *light* hammer, to start the drill and ensure that it begins at the right spot.

When the holes have been made, insert short plugs, cut off close to or a trifle below the face of the tile. The brackets, etc. may now be screwed on. If the worker has an odd tile, similar to those to be drilled, he would do well to practise on this first. Do not overdo the final screwing up, or the plug may be pulled forward and loosened.

Floor Tiles.—These are usually laid on cement mortar. Loose ones should be taken up and the backs and edges cleaned. Chip or scrape off any old mortar that would prevent a close fit of the tile against the surface beneath. Brush out any dust and dirt, and clean out the surface. Any lumps must be chipped off and the whole area to be re-tiled must be made level. If only one or two tiles are affected, an attempt may be made to replace them by using a grouting (semi-liquid solution) of Portland cement and fine (sieved) sand, equal parts. Mix this up to a thin consistency, so that it will pour easily. Damp the cement surface with water and a brush, and soak the tiles in water. Now pour the grout on the cement surface, and re-lay the tiles. Make sure they go down flat and level.

Take up any that are not satisfactory, and remove any lumps that impede them.

Next, mix up a little mortar (half-and-half, as before, but using less water), and work it down between the sides of the tiles with a small trowel as used for pointing brickwork. Do not attempt to clean off the tiled surface until later, when the mortar has begun to get firm; then rub the floor with a ball of newspaper, which will clean it better than anything else. A few hours later the floor can be wiped over with a damp cloth; to remove the worst of the cement, and a day later it can be washed in the ordinary way to remove the smears that will be left.

If the above method is not practicable, owing to the state of the cement beneath the tiles, or because many of the latter are affected, we must roughen the cement floor to improve the adhesive qualities of the surface for the new mortar; a cold chisel and a hammer will be needed for this job. Brush out any dust and fragments of mortar; damp the surface, and also soak the tiles. Lay mortar, not too watery, to the required level, and press in the tiles. Use a straightedge to get the level from adjacent tiles, and tap down any that need it by a light blow from the end of the trowel handle. Fill in the joints and clean off as directed above. As cement is prone to deteriorate from atmospheric causes, always purchase fresh cement for any small jobs such as this, and disappointing results will be avoided. Three parts sand to one cement is a satisfactory mixture for this kind of work; use only that quantity of water which will make the cement plastic enough for the purpose. Do not mix more than is required for the immediate task in hand.

Minor Repairs to Tiles etc.—In general, small holes and cracks, or similar defects in tiles should be made good with plaster of Paris mixed with water; it sets very quickly, and becomes unmanageable even more rapidly, so mix only a small quantity at a time. Press it into the hole or crack, using an old table-knife with a thin blade. Trim off surplus stopping and, later, stain the stopping to match the colour of the tiles. Patches of plaster at tile borders may be repaired with Keene's cement, which is less troublesome to the beginner than ordinary plaster as used by the builder. It is essential to brush out all dirt and dust, and to damp the area inside the patch. The edges of the old material should be undercut at the back, so as to form a key to hold in the new stuff. Reference should also be made to the article PLASTER WALLS AND CEILINGS, see page 213.

If the bad patch goes through to the undercoat of plaster, or even to the lathing, the repair should be done in two stages: first make good to the under layer, and then, an hour or two later, or next day, finish off flush with the wall surface. If the work is done in two stages, the undercoat should be scratched to roughen it and provide a good adhesive surface for the top coat. Small jobs can be done quite well by the use of a bricklayer's trowel; the plasterer uses a flat trowel with a handle at the back. A flat wooden trowel is generally used for rough work and a steel one for finishing the surface.

Washbasins

A FAIRLY heavy jar or metal article dropped or dislodged from the shelf above a lavatory basin is quite capable of cracking it, and if the fracture is not promptly repaired it will not only result in leakage, but the fracture will probably extend, causing parts to become dislodged, and the basin will have qualified for the rubbish heap.

What at first sight may appear to be a temporary repair, made with the aid of soap, whiting and a piece of linen or muslin, will endure for years, providing the job is carried out with some care and nothing further falls into the basin. These reinforcements are applied to the outside; the inside of the basin may need only trifling attention, to be attended to when the major repair has been effected.

The soap (any kitchen brand, uncoloured for choice) is reduced to a thick paste with a knife blade after softening with water, until it is easily workable with the fingers. An equal quantity of powdered whiting is added to the soap paste and thoroughly mixed. Any lumps in the mixture may be picked out and if it is too stiff a few drops of water should be added to give it the right consistency. It must not be fluid but rather like putty; if it tends to be sticky, work into the mixture a little more of the whiting.

This is then to be plastered thinly over the cracked area (on the outside of the basin) after the surface has been thoroughly cleaned with one or other of the proprietary scouring powders sprinkled on a damp cloth, and then dried. The mixture is most easily applied with the flat of a flexible knife, and the layer should extend about an inch on either side of the crack. When this has been evenly smoothed, a second layer is to be added, though the total thickness need not exceed about $\frac{1}{8}$in., the outer edges being smoothed down flush with the surface.

If the crack runs in more than one direction, or if there are two or more cracks, each branch of the fracture, of course, must be covered. The final step consists in placing on top of the mixture a strip of some white thin material such as linen or muslin, to the full length of the covered area and a little more in width. This is smoothed down with the same knife-blade until it is attached to the adhesive mixture (Fig. 1), and, until the whole is quite dry, no water should be allowed in the basin. When it is obvious that the patch is dry and hard it can be given a thin coating of white paint, and when this is

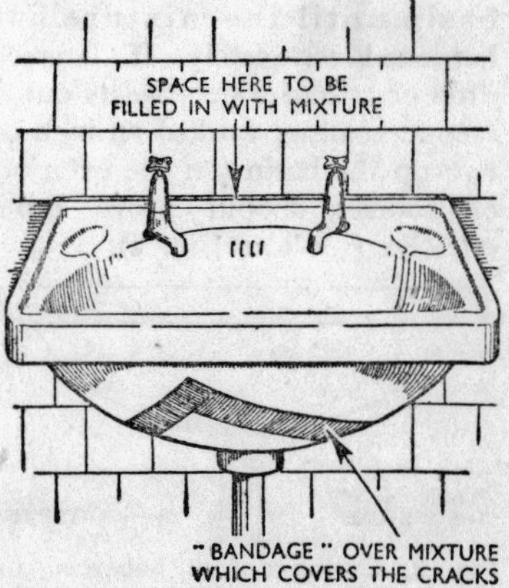

Fig. 1. Repairing a cracked washbasin.

no longer tacky the basin can be used again.

If, in cracking, small pieces were chipped from the inside, these can be stuck back with a waterproof glue, the smaller surrounding crevices, if any, being made good with a suitable filler, or any similar preparation having a plaster of Paris base, several brands of which are sold under proprietary names. The places whence the chips came may alternatively be neatly filled with the same substance, mixed according to the directions issued with it at the shop.

A leak where the outlet pipe joins the bottom of the basin may be repaired with red lead putty (red lead mixed with linseed oil) or a brand of plaster of Paris filler, a sufficient quantity of the powder being tilted into a saucer and cold water stirred in until it is of the proper consistency for application. This mixture should be put on with a pliable knife and worked into corners with the finger-tips. The junction should be wiped dry first and no water allowed in the basin until the mixture has hardened completely. If, later, a drop or two of water sweats out, a second coating, worked an inch or two up the basin (on the exterior, of course) should prove quite effective (see also Fig. 2).

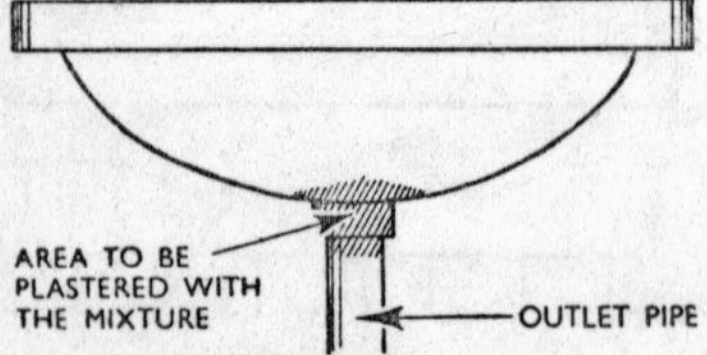

Fig. 2. Curing a leak between the bottom of the washbasin and the waste outlet pipe joint.

The same mixture may be used to fill a space at the back of the basin where it joins tiles or the wall, this space first being cleaned of soap or grease by means of a piece of stick and a rag dipped in hot water. If the wall is papered, this should be eased up a trifle in the neighbourhood of the repair, and pasted down again after the mixture has dried.

Again, a hard, quick-setting plaster compound will prove useful in refixing a plug-chain in its socket, if it has been attached to the basin in that way. The sides of the small socket are first cleaned and then smeared with the stiff mixture, and the fixed end of the chain pressed firmly in. If necessary, sufficient of the mixture should then be added to fill the small hole completely. Jobs such as these are perhaps most safely done last thing at night, when the basin will not be used again until morning; otherwise a cautionary notice should be displayed, to prevent the repair being ruined by some hasty hand.

Too vigorous rubbing must not be indulged in when cleaning a repaired basin. Though this will stand up to all ordinary usage, sudden pressure on a weakened area may prove too much. Routine cleaning consists of the daily use of one of the specially recommended scouring powders (not so harsh as to jeopardize the glaze) applied with a damp cloth. When the entire surface has been wiped with this, another cloth completes the operation, and flushing will leave the basin spotless.

Obstinate stains, failing to respond to routine cleaning, may respond to the following. Apply a hot strong solution of oxalic acid to the stained parts, allow it to penetrate the stained surface, then rinse the surface. When the water drains off, the stains should go with it. Do not attempt to remove stains with a harsh powder; this will do no more than roughen the surface, thus providing a foot-hold for soap and grease. Oxalic acid is poisonous and should be used with discretion. A stain of long standing, such as is sometimes caused by a dripping tap (particularly where there is a trace of iron in the water), may call for a repeat of the foregoing method, and, of course, a new washer for the faulty tap. Another, safer, and very effective method for greasy and dirty basins is to make a thin solution of soft scouring powder and paraffin. Rub vigorously with a cloth saturated in the solution, flush out the basin and wipe the surfaces with a clean damp cloth.

If the taps are of brass, there should be no splashing, or prodigal use, of the metal polish, and the polishing cloth should be kept from contact with the glaze of the basin. The labour and frequency of cleaning the basin are increased by sluggish action of the outlet pipe. If used water runs away reluctantly it will almost certainly leave a smear. For the clearing of clogged waste pipes, see instructions under WASTE PIPES AND TRAPS.

A raised beading fixed along the edge and ends of the shelf, having a rise above the level of the shelf top of ½in., is useful in reducing the possibility of articles falling into and cracking the basin.

Smoky Chimneys

SMOKE consists of particles of carbon which are carried away by the updraught of hot air. In terms of combustion, smoke represents wasted fuel. But it is not possible, in ordinary open grates (or in many closed furnaces) to prevent some unburnt fuel escaping in this way. The amount of smoke should not, however, be excessive in proportion to the fire. It is not the function of a chimney to provide a convenient exit for smoke and gases from the fire. That is a domestic necessity which coincides with the more important purpose of creating a draught with the object of improving combustion. Since we hear so much about fuel economy it should be explained that the warmth emitted from a fire is in proportion to the amount of fuel that can be efficiently consumed in a given time. Thus, in grates which work well and are furnished with a damper in the fret that closes in the space under the grate, we can open the damper after lighting the fire, and close it somewhat when the fire is well established. The use of the poker, within reason, opens more spaces for the air to penetrate, besides letting down ash or cinders that hinder the combustion of fuel. True economy lies in having a good fire when warmth is needed, and in keeping the fire low, or not lighting it, at other times. It is *not* economical to have a poor fire which gives off little else than smoke because it is kept too low to burn properly.

The chimney works on the

principle of simple air convection. The column of air within the chimney, heated by the combustion of fuel in the hearth, possesses a natural tendency to rise, causing more air to be drawn over the fire. The fiercer the fire the greater the draught. On damp, humid days, i.e. when the air is heavy with moisture, a fire will tend to burn sluggishly until it is well alight. Therefore, on a damp, cold day, burn some newspaper in the grate before laying and lighting the fire. This will do away with the smoke trouble otherwise experienced on such occasions. For a similar reason, be more generous with the wood and paper, and get them well alight before putting on much coal. Many fires are stifled by too-hasty shovelling on of fuel. Aim at keeping a small, bright fire until it is well established, then add more fuel gradually, in small lumps at first. By this means the correct draught will be maintained to ensure good combustion. Never overload the fire with fuel. A mere piling on of coal will give room heat only in the latter stages of combustion after much smoke, i.e. wasted fuel.

To prevent the generation of excessive quantities of smoke, good modern grates have the fire-back so shaped that smoke, etc. from the front of the fire must pass through the region immediately above the glowing area of the fire, near the back, and much of it is consumed in the process. Smokeless fuels, such as anthracite (which are less gassy and not so volatile as ordinary coal) do, nevertheless, give off a certain amount of smoke, and also unconsumed gases. In a domestic boiler fire, for example, a small area towards the back should be poked open so that red heat of the fire is exposed to the passage of smoke, thus burning the gases that would otherwise escape up the flue. This is a wise precaution after stoking up for the night. Sometimes the gas accumulates until it ignites with a sudden bang, accompanied by a cloud of dust from the fire into the kitchen and, perhaps, the blowing down of the front door of the furnace. If a glowing area is left uncovered, the gas will burn away (or most of it) as it is liberated from the fuel.

A smoking chimney is generally an indication that it requires sweeping. Some people are inclined to have the chimney swept at regular intervals regardless of the circumstances; but though this is an excellent rule, it should not exclude the summoning of the sweep at an earlier period if the chimney seems to call for it. The nature of the fuel may have changed, or weather conditions may have demanded more frequent fires. Be wary of devices sold as chimney cleaners. Only the sweep's brush will properly remove accumulated soot; moreover, his operations will disclose if the chimney has become blocked by fallen bricks or mortar, and give a warning if attention is wanted in this respect.

Boiler Flues.—A smoky flue is often due to an accumulation of soot in the space below the point at which the cast iron stove pipe enters the brick flue. Soot gathers here in a sloping heap and will eventually partially or entirely choke the end of the iron pipe. Open the access plate bolted to the bend of the pipe and scoop out the soot. At the same time, thrust a flue-brush down the pipe below and clear away any soot clinging to the pipe bore. Make sure, by shaking the damper vigorously, that this soot gets down into the furnace. Do not attempt to do this work with the fire burning. Inspect the cement pointing around the stove pipe where it goes into the brickwork; if it is cracked, chip it away and make a new joint with one of the fireproof cements sold for the purpose. If air enters the flue at this point, it may stop the fire from drawing properly, and is almost certain to cause a smoky flue. In order to function properly, air should be drawn in at the base of the furnace, to pass through the fuel bed and supply oxygen to the fire. Most domestic boiler flues are efficient, and leaks into the flue higher up may not have any noticeable effect, but in a few instances such leakage may prevent efficient working and cause much annoyance.

To avoid draught troubles it is inadvisable to take a boiler flue pipe into a disused flue of old construction, and it is bad practice to take the stove pipe into a flue already serving another fireplace. The domestic boiler should have an independent flue. If a boiler is installed in place of a cooking range, the flue opening that formerly served the range, ought to be diminished in area. If the flue pipe from the domestic boiler is merely taken up through the plate above, even though it be carried up some distance, the result will be less satisfactory. Owing to the enlarged space, a low pressure region will be produced here and will reduce the draught. Too large a chimney may cause downdraught and excessive smoke.

Structural Defects.—Some chimneys smoke only when the wind is in certain quarters, and little can be done as a cure. A cowl will sometimes cure this trouble, and the local builder should be able to advise. Chimneys should be taken up some feet above the highest point of a building, or of adjoining buildings. The presence of tall trees near the house will sometimes affect the chimneys. Wind eddies set up by the shape of the roof and the position of adjoining or near-by buildings are often the cause of downdraught, generally noticeable only when the wind blows from certain quarters. Cowls or similar appliances designed to reduce downdraught will improve matters, but expert advice is necessary. Tallboys, as they are called, mainly act by increasing the effective height of the chimney. Some cowls are mechanical in action, one member revolving in the wind. In time the moving parts get corroded and fail to work properly. Some specially shaped down-draught preventers act by utilizing wind action so as to induce an upward current of air in the chimney without the assistance of heat.

When an old-fashioned fireplace opening is converted to a modern grate, generally of smaller size, the larger opening should be properly reduced by brickwork. Skilled men should be employed to do such work, as there are many technical pitfalls which only experienced workmen can foresee.

Similarly, serious defects in the structure of the chimney flue should be left to the builder.

Fixings and Fittings

NINE-TENTHS of the trouble caused in the average house by faulty and worn locks, hinges, electric lamp fittings, etc. is due to lack of regular inspection and, with regard to fittings having moving parts, lack of lubrication. It is a good plan to go right through the house every six months with a screwdriver and an oil can, and to inspect and attend to every fitting from the padlock on the garage door to hinges on the skylight.

In general, screws should be inspected to ensure that they are secure. All moving parts such as hinges, window catches, etc., should be lightly oiled or greased and any metal parts, in places where corrosion is likely to occur, should be regularly examined for rust. This is particularly important with chromium fittings and an occasional touch of oil rubbed into angle corners of the form of the fitting wiil prevent deterioration of the chromium plating. Regular, systematic care means that not only will the house be free from irritating noises, but the bill for replacements will be small. In this article, imagine a tour of inspection and maintenance is being carried out, and the most likely places in which to look for signs of trouble are suggested.

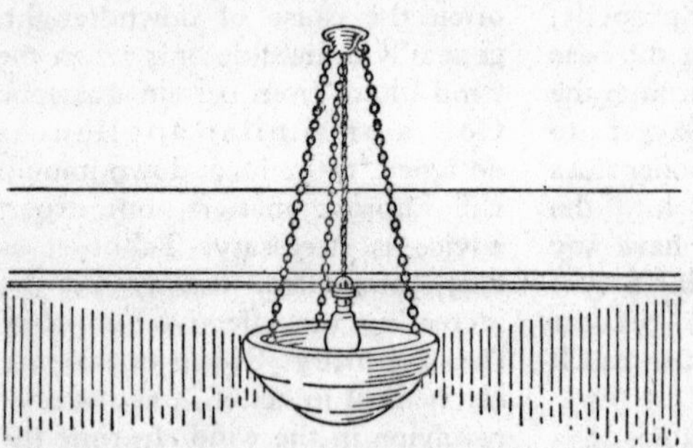

Fig. 1. Ceiling bowl suspended from special bracket. Ceiling bowl and bulb should, as a rule, be roughly level with the picture rail.

Door Fittings.—Begin at the front door of the house, and examine first the hinges. These will usually be three-inch or four-inch cast iron butt hinges, and will have four screws in each wing of each hinge. Take the screwdriver and test each screw for tightness. It may be found that one or two of them, particularly in the upper hinge, will not tighten at all; they may just turn round and round without gripping the wood. The hinge may even be quite slack, allowing the door to sag forward.

Remove one of the screws, take it to the ironmonger's, and purchase new screws of the same thickness but $\frac{1}{4}$in. or $\frac{1}{2}$in. longer. These will bite into new wood and tighten satisfactorily. If for some reason it is impracticable to use a screw of extra length, such as would occur if there is insufficient thickness in the door frame, it will be possible to get over the trouble either by using the old screws again after first slipping a wallplug into the screwhole, or by cutting wood plugs for the holes. See also article on HINGES, page 260.

If you choose the latter method, use a piece of dry timber for your plugs so that they will not shrink and become loose. Dip the end of each plug in lead paint before driving it home. The paint will act both as an adhesive and a preservative. To effect this repair it will be necessary to remove all the screws from one wing of the hinge and fold it back clear of the recess in the door or door frame, so be careful to support the door by wedging it up from the floor before releasing the screws. When you are quite sure that all the screws are holding tightly, oil each hinge. There are several brands of oil sold for domestic use and most of them are sold in tins complete with a spout for easy application.

The next thing to inspect is the bolt. It may be difficult to shoot the bolt home because settlement of the house structure or sagging of the door has thrown it out of alignment. If the door is hanging satisfactorily, take off the socket, plug the screwholes and refix it in its proper place. Lastly, smear the barrel of the bolt lightly with petroleum jelly.

The spring flap of the letter box will work all the easier for its ration of oil; also examine the bolts and nuts which secure it to the door for signs of slackening.

Fittings on Sash Windows.—These consist of the sash cords, pulleys and the catch which is fitted to the centre or meeting rails. The pulleys will normally only need a little oil but it will be advisable to check the tightness of the screws. A little tallow rubbed into the sash cords, especially when they are new, pays dividends in preserving the cords and easing their operation. If the cords show signs of wearing or fraying, they should be renewed; the directions for effecting this repair will be found in the entry referring to WINDOWS. The catch needs lubricating and may also need adjustment. This adjustment will usually take the form of a little packing of stiff card introduced under one half of the catch to compensate for shrinkage in the wood.

Casement Windows.—Deal with the hinges exactly as with those on the doors. This is especially necessary in the case of the upper hinges as any slackening here will allow the sash to sag forward and so give rise to endless trouble. Check the adjustable casement stays and the catch for adjustment and again use the oil can.

Watch for Rot and Rust.—These are the two most common defects, and the metal of windows and frames is usually the first point of attack. Therefore, while checking the fittings and fastenings, examine the lower parts of wood sashes for rot. Pay particular attention to the end of the stiles or side members of the sash frame and make a note of any part which is bare of paint. Examine carefully the edges of steel casements for signs of rust, and as a first precaution, smear any such places with oil. Later at a convenient opportunity, clean off the rust with emery cloth until the metal is bright and clean, then apply two coats of paint.

Electrical Fittings.—Only too often these are completely ignored until something goes wrong. Regular checks would not only prevent trouble, but would enable such adjustments, replacements or repairs to be undertaken at a convenient time, instead of causing an emergency that has to be dealt

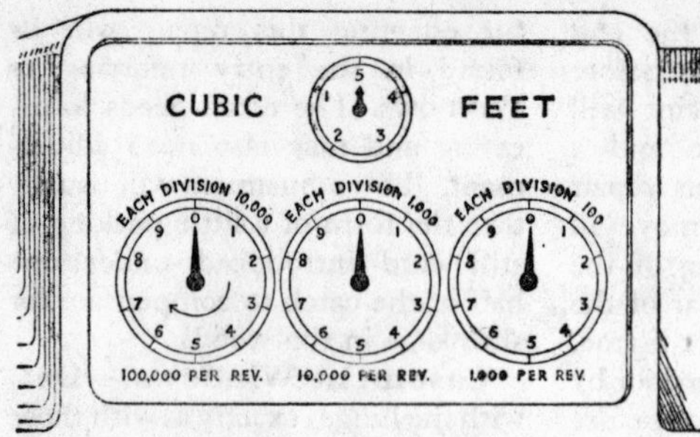

Fig. 2. Gas meter. The smallest dial records the flow of gas from **1** to **5** cubic feet.

with by candle-light at midnight. Take a small screwdriver, a pair of pliers and a roll of insulating tape, and carefully check the electric fittings in one room at a time. Do the job in the daylight and *do not* forget to turn off the electric supply at the main switch before beginning the inspection. Examine the flex at its point of entry at all fittings especially at ceiling roses and lamp holders. See also Fig. 1. These are the points where fraying is apt to take place. If there are any signs of fraying, detach the flex, cut back to sound wire and re-connect. Be careful never to suspend heavy shades from the flex. Diffusion bowls in particular should be independently hung, and special plates may be bought to fit over or in place of the ceiling rose and furnished with three stout hooks for this purpose. A point worth mentioning in this connection is the advantage of so adjusting the height of lamp bulbs and diffusion bowl that the line of light thrown by the edge of the bowl coincides with the line of the picture rail or paper border. The maximum reflection from the ceiling is thereby obtained. Fig. 1 makes this point clear. Test the screws in all fittings for tightness and keep a sharp lookout for places where the covering of wires is faulty and the bare wire liable to be exposed. Cover this with insulating tape. Check all portable equipment such as fires, irons, vacuum cleaners, etc. Make provision for possible emergencies by laying in a supply of fuse wire, together with an electric torch or a box of matches and a candle. Store this equipment in some accessible and convenient place. A small shelf near the fuse box is ideal. Then, when a fuse blows (and they seem always to blow at night) it will be possible to find the things needed for repair, without fuss or annoying delay in the dark.

Gas Fittings.—Carry out an occasional check of the gas installation, particularly for leaks; see also HOUSEHOLD APPLIANCES. We have all heard the old joke about looking for escapes of gas with a match, but make sure you know how to look for one, or even how to find out if there is a leak. Fig. 2 illustrates the arrangement of the dials on the gas meter. The small one set above the other three is intended to register a very small consumption of gas, as little as five cubic feet per revolution. Turn off hard *every* gas jet in the house and note the exact position of the pointer on the small dial. At the end of an hour or so examine it for any change in the reading.

The slightest passage of gas through the meter will be registered, and movement of the pointer will indicate leakage of gas. To locate the leak, the best guide is still by sense of smell. The usual places where leaks occur are at the joints of pipes, the junction of pipes with fittings, and in the fittings themselves. To locate the exact spot, make a thin solution of soap and water, smear it on the suspected length of pipe and the escape will bubble up through the soap film just as it would from a punctured cycle tube. A temporary repair may be affected by covering the place with very thick grease or soap, the pipe being bandaged with rag firmly secured with string. The gas company should then be informed so that they can send the fitters to make a permanent repair. One other thing to watch is the adjustment of the tightness of the control taps on gas fires, etc. It is very dangerous to allow these to become or remain slack so that a careless movement may easily knock them round.

This article on the checking and overhaul of the fixtures and fittings of the house may impress the average householder as a rather formidable addition to his responsibilities, but many of the jobs take only a minute or two to do and none of them is difficult, especially after regular attention. A house is, in actual fact, a machine designed to meet the material needs for human comfort, but like all machines, its efficiency is dependent upon the care and attention it receives. In the interests of comfort and functional efficiency, no detail should be overlooked.

Curtain Fittings

EXAMINE all curtain rod or pole brackets when the house is being spring cleaned and the curtains are down. The fixing screws to brackets may loosen through rust, and the brackets will sag; often the weight of the poles and curtain will be found to have pulled the top part of a bracket forward away from the woodwork. Remedies are (1) to relieve the bracket of weight by taking down the pole temporarily; (2) to unscrew the bracket and to plug the hole with plastic wood or a wood plug; and (3) to re-fix with screws of the same gauge (thickness) but greater in length. If the hole in the bracket will admit a thicker screw, use one of a stouter gauge as well as longer than the old one. When the woodwork at the old hole is split or spintered, stop this hole as before, but move the bracket up or down a little, or sideways, so as to let the screws go into new wood.

Long or heavy poles should have one, or sometimes two, intermediate supports as well as the end ones. If the old-fashioned wood rings are used, put on one midway, and attach it by a brass or thin steel strap to the window frame or ceiling above. This will suspend the rod or pole midway in its span. The same dodge can be used with metal rings on a thinner pole. A piece of strip brass, about $\frac{1}{8}$in. thick by $\frac{5}{8}$in. wide, can be bent to a hook to embrace the pole at the lower end, and bent to a right angle to screw to the window frame at the top end. Two holes for wood

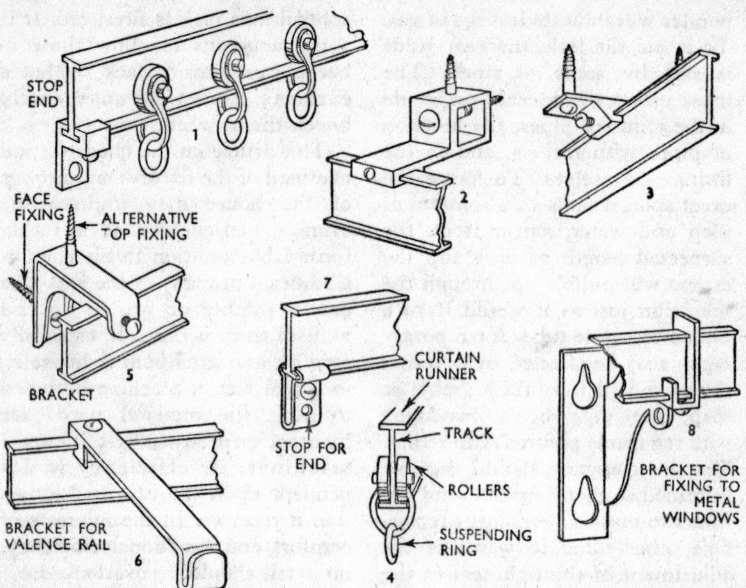

Fig. 1. A representative selection of curtain rail fittings for a variety of purposes.

screws should be drilled at the top end. In some cases the angle bend at the top is unnecessary, if the strap can be fixed flat to the face of a bay frame or the woodwork of a window.

Long spans over window bays, across halls, etc. need especial care for the sake of safety. Where a pole is to run clear from wall to wall, a builder should be asked to cut in and fix sockets in the actual brickwork; the rod then can be a length of "gas barrel" (nominal ½in. gauge). The rod would then be fixed permanently, but the rings required would have to be put on first. The piping can be painted first.

Curtain Rail.—By far the best means of supporting ordinary curtains is to fix up rails around a bay or across a window; runners are inserted on the rail, end stops put on, and then the curtains are attached by means of hooks inserted in the well known pocketed tape sewn to the top edge of the curtains. Once fixed, these rails and fittings last for many years, so that it is economical to install a good make, stout and well finished. Do not skimp the brackets, but put up the full quantity per unit of length recommended by the makers. Fix them firmly, boring the holes in the window frame carefully. The outer portion of the hole, for about a quarter-of-an-inch deep, should be made a little larger in diameter than the deeper part, which receives the worm of the screw. Get a helper to support one end of the rail while the brackets are spaced out and the screw holes marked.

Wherever the direction changes, bend the rail gently with two hands across the knee, avoiding sharp bends and taking the curve around easily. At each point of change from the straight, fix up a bracket on each side, right and left. Do not finally tighten the set-screws that hold the rail in the brackets until all the brackets have been screwed to the woodwork. Then make any little adjustments needed, and screw up the set-screws tightly. Add the end stops, and put a trace of oil on each pair of rollers or runners.

If curtain rails are already in position, give them a periodical inspection, and tighten up any brackets on the woodwork. Also correct the alignment of the brackets if needed (first loosening the set-screws holding the rail in place). Where joins in the rail cannot be avoided, the pieces are connected with bridges. In good class systems these bridges are screwed to the window woodwork, either at top or face. It is better to fix the rail in a single piece which will go the full length. The rail can be cut with a hacksaw; if the worker does not possess a full-size saw, he can manage with a miniature one which costs about one shilling and sixpence, and is handy for many jobs. Support the rail on a bench or table when cutting it. Take off rough edge at the cut end with a file, or the stops and bridges may stick when being put on.

Metal Windows.—Standard metal windows are provided, near the top, with two tapped holes into which short screws can be inserted to attach special fittings for blinds or curtains. Among the fittings illustrated (Fig. 1) is a bracket for use in such situations. It will be seen that there are two keyhole-shaped holes, to be put over the screw-heads and slid down until the narrower part engages behind the head of the screw. As supplied and fixed, metal windows have the necessary metal-thread screws inserted; all that is needed is to loosen them, put on the brackets, and re-tighten.

Fittings.—Those illustrated are: (1) portion of rail with stop-end and runners; (2) bracket, showing two alternative positions for the fixing screw—either into woodwork at back, or into the window frame at top; (3) bracket for attaching the rail to woodwork or ceiling overhead; (4) curtain runner, end view; (5) another rail system with bracket: this is made in rust-proofed finish for use in coastal regions where sea-air might corrode brasswork; (6) bracket to hold a valance rail, which fits into the hook-shaped carrier at the front end; (7) stop-end for the system shown in (5); (8) left-hand bracket for metal window frame.

Spring Expanding Curtain Rod.—This is excellent for lightweight work and shorter spans. The "rod" is cut to the proper length, and a screw eye is screwed in at each end. Two hooks are screwed into the woodwork, one at each side; the eye at one end is hooked on, and the rod is stretched until the opposite end can be hooked up. The proper allowance for stretch is 1in. to the foot, or 3in. per yard. Fix up the hooks, measure the distance between, and cut the rod to the proper distance short of this total measurement. Cutting can be done with a "three-square" file or with a wire-cutter or pair of cutting pliers. The screw eyes, once inserted, are difficult to withdraw from the ends of the rod, so make sure all measurements are correct before inserting the eyes. Instead of fixing eyes to the rod, hooks may be substituted, and a pair of screw eyes fixed to the woodwork. Bore a hole with a fine awl when fixing either; start the threaded end gently, and twist up tightly with a pair of pliers.

Many people merely thread the spring rod through a hem in the curtain, but this is not the best or the proper method. Special runners or "glides" can be bought to slide on to the rod before the eyes are inserted. These runners have loops or rings into which the hooks threaded in the curtain can be fixed, as with curtain-rail fittings described above, and the curtains will then slide easily without risk of tearing or other damage.

Sometimes it is required to fix curtains on spring rod so that they stand a few inches away from the face of the window. An easy method of doing this is to fix up a pair of steel japanned shelf brackets, about 5in. × 4in., attaching the longer side to the woodwork; the eyes of the rod are then attached to the end screw-hole of the bracket by an S-hook at each end.

Locks

There are many variations in lock design and innumerable specialized uses which determine their size and shape, but for the purpose of this entry only the more orthodox types, for use on doors, are described. These consist of the spring latch, the locking latch, the dead locking latch, the dead lock, the mortise lock, the rim latch and pin-tumbler lock.

A latch is a fastening device which can be operated without a key; the commonest sort is the thumb latch used on gates and outhouse doors. Spring latches are often used on cupboard and room doors. This latch may be operated from one side, or from either side, by turning a handle. When the door closes, the bolt (which has a bevelled end) is pushed in by the striking plate fixed to the door frame, and springs out again into the slot in this plate, so fastening the door until the handle is turned.

A spring latch is incorporated in many door locks, properly so called, and usefully applied as a night latch when fixed to exterior doors. On leaving the house, or entering it after having used the key, the latch fastens itself automatically when the door is pushed to the closed position. Inside the house the latch bolt can be opened by turning the handle; from the outside it can be operated only by the key. This is more properly known as a locking latch, and is the principle upon which the pin-tumbler latch (Yale pattern) works.

Most room doors have a locking latch. That is, the lock has two bolts, the spring bolt, acting as described above, and the locking bolt, which must be shot or drawn back by using the key. So the door can be opened (provided it has not been left in the locked state)

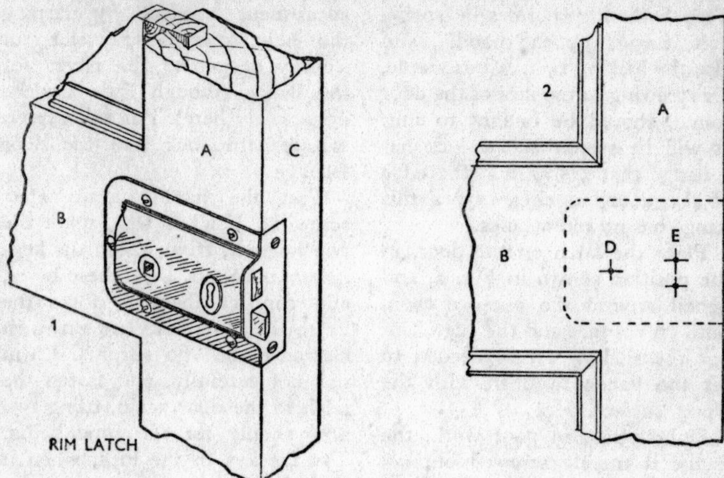

Fig. 1. Shows a rim latch secured to door and Fig. 2 illustrates the points at D and E which must be bored out to provide access for handle spindle and key.

by merely turning the handle. Locking latches, even of good quality, unless fitted very securely, may be opened by force.

For extra security a dead locking latch, or a plain dead lock can be substituted. This must be locked or unlocked by a key. Thus, if the householder takes the trouble to lock the door behind him, it is secure against unauthorized entry, even if a pane in the door should be removed. An alternative is to fit a dead lock in addition to the ordinary night latch, using the dead lock on occasions when the house is to be left unattended. People are apt to be careless of security in the matter of locks on outer doors. An extra ten or fiteen shillings spent on having better or more secure locks will perhaps save many pounds.

Fitting a Lock to a Door.—Good practice is to use a mortise lock, which is let into the edge of the door; as a result no one can tamper with the lock mechanism. But on less important doors the rim latch is more often fitted; this is merely screwed to the face and the edge of the door, as shown in Fig. 1. The fitting of a mortise lock to a door is a difficult task which (as a rule) should be undertaken only by a skilled craftsman. When a lock is to be fitted to a new door (for instance, that of a shed or outhouse), it is better to use a rim latch. Also, if the mortise lock of a door goes wrong owing to the wood of the mortise breaking out, a rim latch can be substituted, if the old lock is taken out and the mortise and other holes are carefully plugged. So here are given instructions for fitting the rim lock or rim latch only.

Purchase a rim latch, or rim lock, according to the situation and the requirements of the door. A rim lock is shown in Fig. 1.

This lock incorporates a spring bolt, turned by the handle, and also the locking bolt. A box staple, for screwing to the face of the door frame, should be bought to suit. It will be seen that the lock has a flange that fits against the edge of the door; in cheap types this flange has no screw holes.

Place the latch on the door, in the position shown in Fig. 2, and pencil around the outer margin, both on the face and the edge. Cut out the shallow recess needed to set the flange in flush with the wood surface.

Quite often, in poor work, the flange is merely screwed on, *not* recessed into the wood. Put the lock in position again, and while it is held tightly against the door edge, mark with a fine bradawl the centre which will locate the position of the hole to be bored for the handle spindle.

This hole is bored at D in Fig. 2, and should be large enough to avoid any possibility of the spindle sticking or binding in the hole. The door should be shut, or wedged in the open position, while boring.

When this operation has been completed, put the latch in place, and push the handle spindle through. Verify that it works easily, and that when the latch flange is hard up against the door edge there is no hindrance to its rotation. Make any adjustment needed, by rasping the hole towards one side, or slightly deepening the recess for the flange (though little can be done safely here). Put two screws through the lock into the door face.

Test the handle again after screwing. If all is well, mark the two holes E, from which the keyhole will be cut. Bore these holes, and connect them to form the keyhole slot; leaving enough clearance, but no surplus. Clean the slot carefully, and fasten the latch to the door again, using two screws only for the time being. Try the key in the lock, when it should function easily.

It remains to fix the box staple to the face of the door frame with the two long screws that should have been obtained for it. If the door has an architrave moulding, this may need cutting back a little to allow the staple to be fitted flat, in direct line with the latch. Shoot the lock bolt, and try the staple over it to find the proper position. Then screw the staple in place; try the lock again, and if satis-

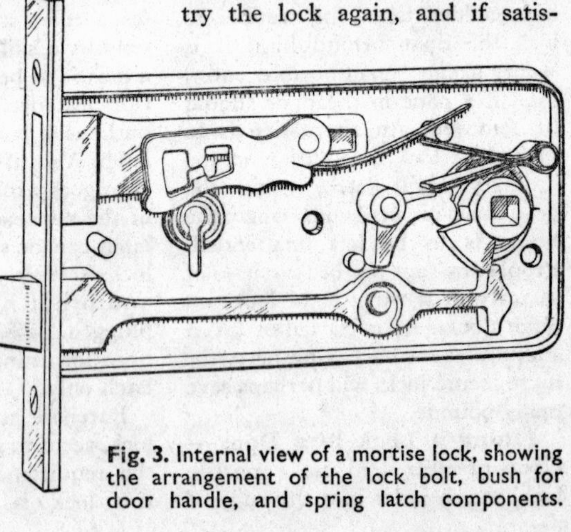

Fig. 3. Internal view of a mortise lock, showing the arrangement of the lock bolt, bush for door handle, and spring latch components.

factory, insert the remaining screws in the face of the lock, and also those through the flange on the edge. Enough clearance must be allowed between edge of lock and the striking part of the staple, but not too much.

Care of Locks.—Put a little oil on the spring bolt occasionally. At the same time observe if the hinges are in proper order, and oil them. When the action of a lock seems weak it is probably the spring that is faulty; more often the latching bolt will show this trouble. Sometimes the handle itself is fitted with a return spring inside the casing. Assuming that the handle is in order, take off the lock and open its casing. From a study of what has been said above, the rim lock will be easily removed. Take off one knob or handle, by undoing the locking screw or stud that attaches it to the squared spindle; sometimes the hole in the knob is threaded, while that in the spindle is plain, but this order may be reversed. Withdraw the spindle and proceed in the following manner:

Unscrew the lock from the door and brush off any dust from the back of the casing. One or two screws will be seen, which secure the back plate to the case; remove these screws and put in a safe place. Gently prize off the back plate; take care that the contents of the lock do not spring out and become mixed, as identification of the parts, for the purpose of reassembly, may be difficult. This will not matter so much when we have noted and memorized the fitted positions of the parts. A double flat spring will be seen which operates the bush in which

Fig. 4. The spring latch return spring.

is the squared hole for the spindle, see Fig. 3. This is the one most likely to have become weak, and the one that most frequently breaks. If the spring seems weak (it can be tested by turning the follower, without dismantling the parts), take it out and buy a similar one at the locksmith's or ironmonger's. They are quite inexpensive. If too long in one or both arms it can be cut off short with a pair of side-cutting pliers. If the end is jagged, hold it against a grindstone or bench grinder.

Before replacing the spring (shown in Fig. 4), brush out all dust, and give the working parts a touch of oil; another opportunity may not come for a long time. Bad rusting can be treated with paraffin and the parts rubbed bright with emery cloth.

The removal of a mortise lock is a little more difficult. Take out the spindle as before; unscrew the face plate on the edge of the door. When fitted on good locks, this plate is secured to the end plate of the lock by two metal screws; after removing these the two wood screws that fix the end plate of the lock in the door will be accessible. Having removed the two wood screws, withdraw the lock from the mortise as shown in Fig. 5; a screwdriver can be put through the spindle hole to assist, but take care not to damage the door or lock. The lock casing may

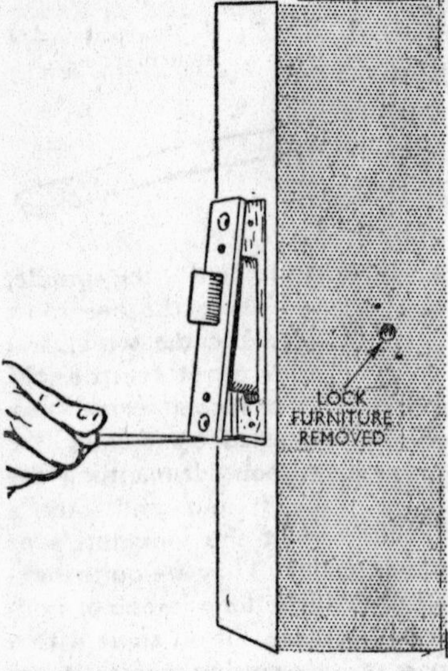

Fig. 5. Removing a mortise lock. Ease out the lock, applying screwdriver alternately at the sides and top of the plate until it may be withdrawn by hand.

be opened by unscrewing the securing screws of the casing cover plate. As the working parts in a mortise lock are closer together, more care must be taken to note the fitted positions of the components. In other respects the procedure for replacement of springs, etc. is as for the rim lock.

Striking Plates and Staples.—If a door drops or warps, the position of the striking plate (or, in a rim lock, the box staple) may be wrong, and the holes will not register with the bolts of the lock. After any necessary adjustment has been made to the door itself, the plate or staple should be moved so that it registers correctly with the end face of the lock.

Pin-Tumbler Lock.—These, of the Yale pattern or other type, are in almost universal use for entrance doors. When fitted by the builder they seldom give trouble, though the staple may have to be adjusted for an alteration in the position of the door in course of time. As with mortise locks, the fitting of a pin-tumbler lock is a job for the skilled craftsman, who will also possess tools and gauges to facilitate lock fitting. Sometimes when all keys are lost the lock itself has to be taken to the ironmonger for a new key to be made by reference to the lock. Take out the long screws securing the body of the lock to the back of the door, then those that hold the cylinder will be accessible and can be withdrawn. It is better not to tamper with the cylinder; deliver it, intact, to the locksmith.

When keys are to be cut from a pattern key, give the locksmith the original key, *not* one made from that key, which may vary slightly from the original sold with the lock. This applies particularly to pin-tumbler locks, but generally to *all* types. If possible, get the keys cut by a competent locksmith. It is better to obtain a hand-cut key from a good locksmith, rather than an indifferently duplicated key, cut by an unskilled operator.

Hinges

Of all the general types of hinges, the *butt hinge*, used for room doors, cabinets, cupboards and similar furniture, is perhaps the most commonly known. Steel butt hinges employed for room doors, have to support a good deal of weight, plus the leverage exerted when the door is opened or closed. This type of hinge comprises two plates and the knuckle, through which latter the pin goes. The plates are sunk into the edge of the door and into the frame of the door so as to be flush with the surfaces, or slightly below, with the knuckle centralized on the crevice between door and frame. Examine a door that has been correctly hung and verify these points. It will be seen that the door does not fit closely to the frame, but that there is a regular clearance of about $\frac{1}{16}$in. on the top and vertical sides. In good quality joinery the wide edges of the door are bevelled back a little from the inside to the outside for further clearance. Hinges of room doors are commonly fitted with a space of about 6in. above the top one and twice this amount below the bottom hinge, but this depends on clearing any joints in the door system.

Fitting Butt Hinges.—Two hinges are customary for light doors, with three for heavier ones such as entrance doors. In fitting up a new door the worker will need two marking gauges, and two thin wedges. Prop the door against a bench or table, with the hinge edge uppermost. Open one hinge and lay it in position on the door edge while the place is marked with pencil to give the *length.* The top edge of the hinge should be 6in. down from the top of the door.

Close the hinge, and applying a rule to the top end of the hinge, measure the width from the centre of the hinge pin to the outer edge of the wing or flange. Deduct $\frac{1}{8}$in. from this distance, whatever it is; the result will be the *width* of the recess to be chiselled in the edge of the door. Set the marking gauge to this, and scribe along the door edge, resting the stock of the gauge against what will be the inside face of the door. Gauge for both hinges in this way and carefully adjust the gauge (or, better, set a *second gauge*) to the thickness of one wing or flange. This gives the *depth* of the recess to be cut, and this depth should be scribed by gauge along the inside face of the door for both hinges. Square off the lines to denote the exact length of the recess, from the marks pencilled earlier.

Fixing Hinges to Door.—Using a fine tenon saw, cut down along the squared lines, until the depth line is reached. The point of the saw must be used, and it will not be possible to go down full depth at the back. Two other similar cuts can be made, in between, so as to facilitate removal of surplus wood by chisel. Use a sharp firmer chisel or a paring chisel, and outline the back margin by accurate cuts, taking care not to go down too deep; also complete the cuts at the side where the tenon saw could not go down full depth. Next, the chisel is used at the inside face of the door to incise the line here and eventually to cut out the waste wood and so form the recess. The reader, unless he takes great pains, is likely to take out too much wood. When the recess is correctly cut, fit the hinge, and using a bradawl, bore the holes for the screws. Insert the screws and turn them until they butt firmly in the hinge.

Door Frame.—Take the *first* marking gauge and outline the width of the hinge on the inside edge of the door frame, at the approximate position (top of hinge

6in. from top of frame, plus top clearance, $\frac{1}{16}$in.). Get an assistant to hold up the door in position against the frame, with the hinges opened out and the plates close against the door jamb. Use wedges (under the bottom of the door) to raise the door so as to obtain accurate top clearance. Alternatively, the method shown in Fig. 1 may be usefully adopted when removing or fitting hinges. The butts must come back to the scribed lines made by the *first* marking gauge. Use a fine awl or a steel scriber to mark the position for the top and bottom of each wing or flange, and to confirm the marks scribed by the first gauge.

Remove the door, and with the *second* marking gauge, scribe the line for the depth of the recess. Cut out the latter, replace the door with wedges beneath, an assistant standing by to hold all steady; bore for one screw first, in one hinge, and insert the screw; do the same with the second hinge, one screw only for the present. Slip out the wedges, and test the door gently. It will probably be quite satisfactory, and the wedges can be replaced while the remainder of the screws are inserted and turned home. Should a mistake have been made (perhaps in positioning the screw hole) it can be corrected. A wrong hole can be plugged with a small piece of hardwood, driven in tight and cut off level with a chisel.

It is assumed that the dimensions of the new door have been checked so as to ensure correct clearance on the top and vertical sides. After the door has been hung, stops will have to be fixed on the frame, not right up to the face of the door, but approximately $\frac{1}{16}$in. from it.

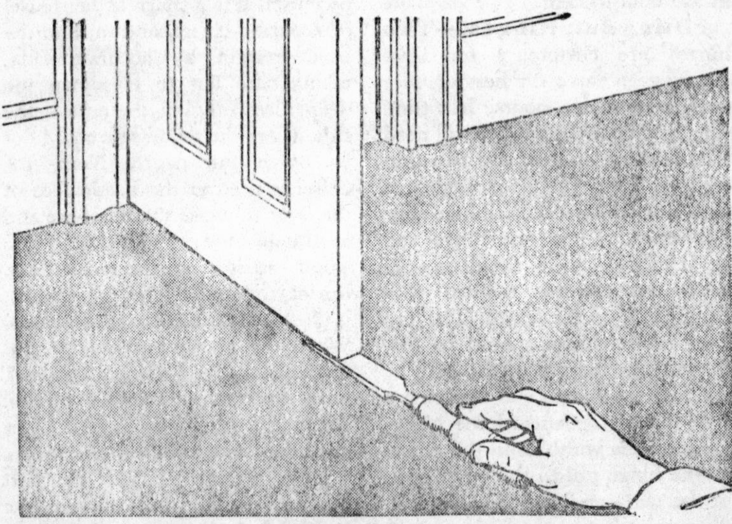

Fig. 1. When removing or fitting a hinge the door should be wedged at its outer edge to maintain the correct position. When both hinges are to be fitted or removed, wedge up full width of door and obtain assistance to hold door steady.

Rising Butt Hinges.—These are like ordinary butt hinges, but the plates are separable; one has a pointed pin fixed in the knuckle, while the other has an open eye which fits over the pin. The pin plate is fixed to the door frame, and the eye plate to the door. These hinges (Fig. 1) are *not* reversible, and the purchaser must specify right-hand or left-hand when ordering. The mating edges of the knuckle are formed in a spiral, so that the door rises on the fixed wings or flanges of the hinges in the door frame.

The procedure for fitting and fixing is as for ordinary butt hinges, but the door frame cannot be marked direct from the door in this case. Fix the eye plates to the door, then measure the distance from the top of the door down to the top of the hinge. Add for clearance, which in this case the amateur might increase a trifle. As the door in the open position is somewhat higher than in the closed position, it is customary for the joiner to bevel back the door slightly at the top and towards the hinge stile, to give clearance towards the end of the closing movement. However, since the object of fitting rising butt hinges is to enable the door to clear a thickish carpet and yet shut down draught-proof at the finish, the craftsman's method ought to be followed rather than allow too great a clearance.

Cross Garnets and Tee-Hinges.—These differ little, as shown in the illustration (Fig. 2). As both hinges are employed extensively for outbuildings, gates, etc. they are usually japanned or galvanized to prevent corrosion. In ledged doors the hinges should be fixed *over* the ledges, so that there is an adequate depth of wood below the screw; secure the hinges by screws to the door or gate first, letting the centre line of the knuckle coincide with the dividing line between door and frame. Support the door from below with blocks or wedges, and mark where the wings or flanges of the hinges come on the frame or fence post. While an assistant holds the door, bore one or two holes through those in the small flange of each hinge. Insert the screws and test

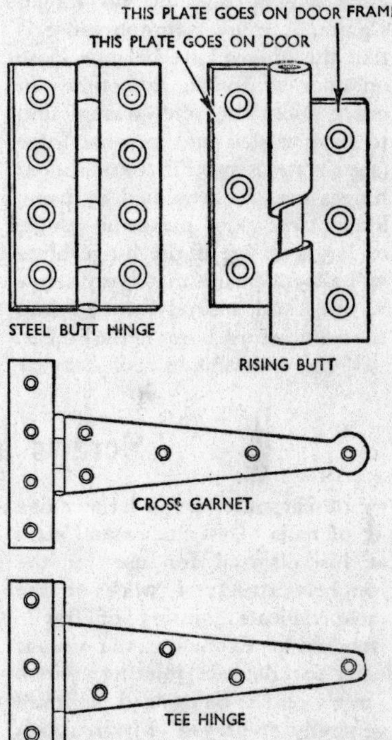

Fig. 2. Four common types of hinges. The rising butt hinge is designed to raise the door when the latter is opened so as to clear any slight obstruction, such as a carpet.

the door. If the test is satisfactory, insert the remainder of the screws.

Outside doors generally have an inch or more of clearance at the foot, so that thick wedges or blocks must be used to raise the door for hanging. When fitting hinges to an old door, there is the latch and possibly other fastening to be considered, so in some cases these must be taken off and refitted.

Defective Hanging of Room Doors.—When a door jams or sticks, the first task is to diagnose the cause. The frame may have gone askew, and be no longer square. A more common cause is that the hinges have become loose on door or frame. Sometimes in outer doors the screws are found to have rusted and become loose (see FITTINGS AND FIXTURES). Loose hinges may be remedied by using longer screws of the same gauge, or larger gauge if the hinge holes will allow. Ensure that every screw is tight and securely turned into the countersunk bores of the hinges.

If the door should stick because the frame of the door has warped, stand back from the door and examine it closely in the shut position. Perhaps the crack on the hinge side is not parallel, and the door is hanging *outwards* towards the lock stile; in such cases the top corner at the lock side will bind on the frame, and the bottom corner on that side will bind on the floor or threshold. Try tightening up the *top* hinges in the door and frame; if this does not cure the trouble, slightly deepen the recess in the frame for the top hinge, and also use a slip of cardboard as packing behind the corresponding plate of the lower hinge. A very trifling alteration may do the trick.

Should an examination show that the door is high at the top on the lock side, and that the bottom corner on the hinge side is binding on the floor, exactly the reverse of the method above outlined must be used; slightly deepening the recess for the bottom hinge, and packing out the top one, see also paragraphs on DOOR DEFECTS, page 225.

Screws and Nails

THE carpenter has a large range of nails of all shapes and sizes at his disposal for use on the roughest structural work or the most delicate jointing of fragile woodwork. Excluding the use of nails for delicate jointing, where screws cannot be utilized, nails are generally employed only in rough joinery, but no hard and fast rule can be applied to their incidental use for special work. Screws are, for instance, more or less essential for parts that may have to be dismantled without damage at a later date, but their use is not confined to this function only. In fixing parts by nailing, a good deal of force has to be applied by hammer blows; not all jobs will stand this. Another rough division may be made; nails are suitable for fixing one member to another at right angles, where the nail has to go into end grain. There is plenty of depth to allow a sufficiently long nail to be driven in, whereas a screw might not grip at all. If we wish to fix two fairly thin members together flat face to flat face, the only feasible way of doing this with nails is to drive right through both members, letting the nail be long enough to protrude on the under side, and then to clench the nail with a hammer blow. This is a very rough method, but is much used for certain work, for example, in nailing the boards of a ledged door to the ledges or cross members. For good class work screws are usually employed, provided the thickness of the ledge is sufficient to give adequate depth for the screws.

Screws are used extensively for attaching locks, latches, bolts and all sorts of fittings and apparatus to woodwork. If the fitting has a countersunk hole for the screws, then the screws with countersunk heads, as shown in Fig. 1 should be used. These are designed to be screwed in flush with the surface. Cuts and scratches may be sustained when using a latch or handle from which the heads of screws protrude, either as a result of careless fixing, or the use of a countersunk head when the plate of the fitting is not intended to take this type of head. When the plate has merely a plain hole, use the screws with a round head, shown in Fig. 1. On good class brasswork provided with countersunk holes there is an alternative to the simple countersunk head: this is a countersunk screw with a raised head shown in Fig. 1. A neat and pleasing finish may be obtained by the use of this type of screw.

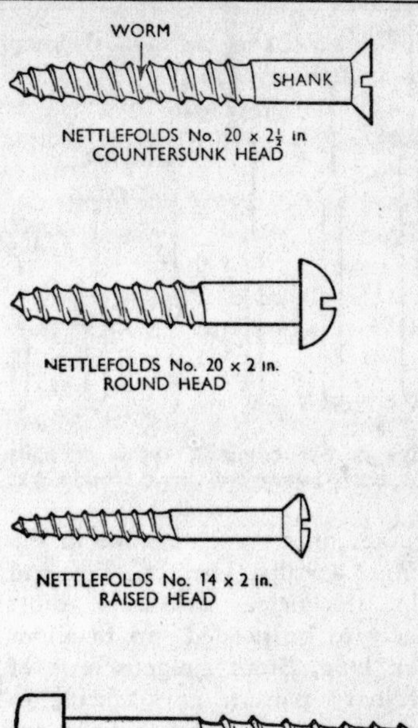

Fig. 1. Typical screws. These types are available in a wide variety of sizes.

Screws for Heavy Work.—Fig. 1 shows some typical examples of fairly heavy screws, the countersunk and round head screws are Gauge 20. They are made in lengths of 1in. to 7in., though the lengths above 3in. would have to be ordered, and would seldom be called for. Coach screws, used for heavy work, have a variety of uses; a typical one is shown in Fig. 1, this being 2½in. long, by $\frac{7}{16}$in. diameter at the shank. The head is square, to take a spanner; hexagonal headed screws are made, and are easier to turn in cramped quarters, since the spanner can be applied at six positions instead of four. The full range of diameters is from $\frac{3}{16}$in. to ½in.; lengths range from ¾in. to 8in., though only the

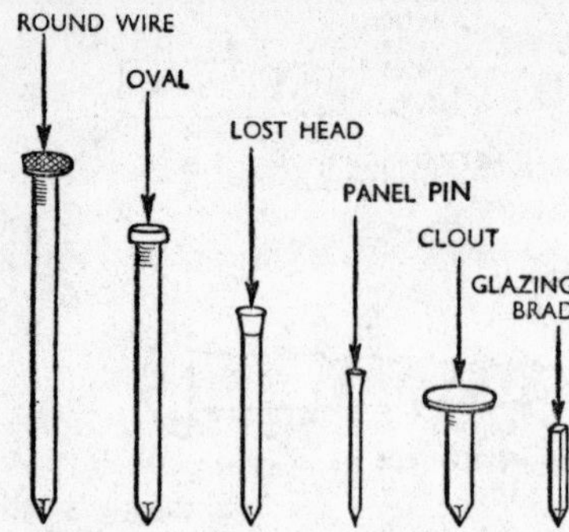

Fig. 2. Six common types of nails for both heavy and light woodwork.

stouter ones are obtainable in the longer lengths. The ¼in., ⅜in., and ½in. thicknesses are those most likely to be needed, up to about 4in. long. Stout gauge screws of ordinary pattern are difficult to drive, so that coach screws are better wherever they can conveniently be employed.

Choice of Screws.—The type of metal used in the manufacture of screws influences their use. Brass screws are much less strong than steel screws. When turning a brass screw into oak it is quite easy to break the screw, or to break off one side of its head, unless the hole has been bored carefully to give an easy clearance to the shank (see Fig. 1), and also to leave enough material for the worm to bite into without making the hole *too* small. In driving a screw we are, in effect, driving in a long, tapering wedge. The spiral arrangement of the worm enables the force to be applied very gradually. If a suitable hole is made for the worm, this hole, of course, being smaller in diameter than the top part, bored to clear the shank, the screw cuts a counterpart thread in the wood. Only a combined twisting and pulling motion will pull out the screw, unless very great force is used in proportion to the size of the parts and the nature of the timber.

Early wood screws lacked the gimlet point, and had to be forced into the timber with subsequent danger of splitting the surrounding wood. The gimlet point, however, assists the entry of the screw into the wood, by providing a lead for the worm thread, once it is given a good start. Where brass screws would naturally be preferred on account of appearance, and there is a doubt of their being strong enough, we can use brass plated mild steel screws. These will rust, of course, if used for exposed work or in places where conditions are conducive to dampness, but for all ordinary purposes they are satisfactory.

Always use steel screws where a strong job is desired. For outdoor work, galvanized screws should be used. Brass screws would naturally be used for indoor work where brass fittings are to be used; also for all sorts of small fancy articles and for furniture. Nickelled, chromed and coppered finishes are available for many sorts and sizes; aluminium screws should be used for aluminium fittings.

It is common knowledge that most screws have a plain shank between the head and top end of the worm thread, that is, the worm does not start until some little distance down from the head. This is satisfactory for fastening wood to wood, or for attaching fairly thick plates or fittings, but where thin fittings, or mirror plates are concerned, we need screws which are wormed right up to the head, or nearly so. Such screws can be obtained from most ironmongers, in lengths and gauges suitable for the purpose mentioned. This is an important point to observe when using wall plugs: the shank of the screw should not enter the plug, or it may cause the latter to twist round and become loose. When screws of the proper type are not available, cut the plug a little short, and push it in so that room is left for the shank before reaching the plug.

For most household purposes, screws in Gauges 6 and 8 are suitable. Gauge 12 is the one for workshop jobs such as making up a bench or a sawing horse. It is seldom that anything stouter will be needed. For the innumerable small or delicate jobs it is possible to get the inexpensive small screws in Gauges 00, 0, 1, 2 and 3, both round head and countersunk. Purchase them in the original box or carton, and they are less likely to be mislaid. Larger screws can be purchased two or three dozen at a time, and should be kept in small boxes or tins. If they have to be mixed, put a long size and a short in the same container; they will be easier to pick out than if several very near sizes are stocked together.

Nails for Household Jobs.—The wire nails illustrated in Fig. 2 will meet all general needs. Round nails, in lengths of 1in. to 3in., can be bought in half-pound lots and put into some simple box or tray ready for use. Oval nails are better for some purposes, but the head has less holding power than the bigger round head of the ordinary wire nail. Where a very inconspicuous nail is desired, use the lost head type; this has a round shank and a small head, like that of the panel pin. Panel pins, nominally intended for securing panels in joinery work, are useful for a variety of home jobs. Amateurs often confuse them with veneer pins, which are much finer and, if anything, more useful. When fine pins or nails are required, ask the ironmonger to display the various types.

Clout nails have large round heads and are short in the shank; they are used for fixing felt to wood, and similar jobs. There are special nails (galvanized) for fixing corrugated iron to woodwork, and curved washers are sold for use with them. Galvanized screws can be used as an alternative for corrugated sheeting; and there is also a drive-screw, or screw-nail which is driven in like a nail and twists during this operation.

Gimp pins are made in various short lengths; besides the nominal use for tacking gimp edging over upholstery, they are handy for many household purposes. Cut tacks are usually of poor quality and vary much in shape and finish; a better quality is made and should be used for preference. For fastening down carpets and other floor coverings use carpet nails with large heads. When nails with small heads are used the carpet is likely to be torn in the process of lifting for spring cleaning.

Always bore starting holes on woodwork of importance. If nails are used to attach one part to another, a clearing hole is needed in the top member, and should continue a little way into the underneath part to give guidance.

SECTION SEVEN

WATER SUPPLY

Hot Water Supply and Heating

For the average small house an independent boiler is the most convenient. It should be the correct size for the duty it has to perform. Heating system boilers need to be selected by a heating engineer, as there are so many variable factors to be considered. As to fuel, coke of proper size, as supplied for boilers, is very convenient, but more difficult than anthracite to keep alight continuously. By careful stoking last thing at night, and a knowledgeable manipulation of the dampers, however, this trouble can be avoided. Much fuel is wasted by haphazard stoking. During periods when little hot water is needed, keep a low fire. The bed of ashes on the bars will itself slow down the functioning at "off" times. Half-an-hour before hot water in more quantity is required, clear the fire bars with the rake, let the fire draw up for a few minutes, and feed in more fuel. Every chimney and flue has its own characteristics, which must be learnt so that the best use can be made of the dampers.

General Hints.—When about to burn up kitchen refuse, wait until a good red fire exists in the boiler, and then put in the refuse, as dry as possible. Remember that bones and similar matter will calcine to an inconsumable body like a clinker, and clog the bars. Have the boiler chimney swept at least every summer; at regular intervals examine the point where the smoke pipe enters the brickwork, to make sure the exit of the pipe is not choked by soot which has fallen down and become heaped up there. Clinker left uncleared on the firebars will tend to burn away the latter, so always clear the bars every night or morning. Where a boiler fire is to be kept alight for days together, it should be let out at least once a week to permit a thorough cleaning out of the furnace.

If water does not get hot enough, there are several things to suspect. First, make sure that no tap on the hot-water pipe line is dripping continuously; even a slight drip will entail a constant waste of hot and an intake of cold water. Make sure, too, that the fire burns briskly and that the flue and chimney give a good draught. There may be a permanent defect in construction or fixing which prevents sufficient pull on the smoke pipe. In the case of an old house to which a boiler has been fitted in place of some other appliance, the flue may not be sealed, or may even communicate with the flue for a fireplace in another room. Much depends on the duty demanded of the boiler, which may be more than such a boiler can normally fulfil. A heating engineer can deal with this matter. Even such a defect as a smoke pipe badly fitted to the brick flue may cause continued inefficient working. But independent domestic boilers have a wide margin of power over and above that normally needed, and it is exceptional for them to fail to give satisfaction.

Lagging the Pipes.—If the hot water is unsatisfactory in cold weather months a good deal can be done by lagging the pipes and the hot storage cistern. Special felt or other insulating material in coils can be bought to wrap spirally around the piping in exposed positions (such as in the roof space) to conserve the heat. The hot cistern may waste a lot of heat, and unless this is compensated for by the use in an airing cupboard, it is a dead loss. Even in an airing cupboard the gain is questionable, since few people need this service twenty-four hours a day and seven days a week. To lag the cistern, box in the front with thin wood; usually there is only a small space at the sides, between the cistern and the walls of the cupboard. Fill in dry sawdust all round; take it over the top of the cistern, and cover over the latter with boards, leaving openings where the piping emerges. Probably the pipes themselves will supply enough warmth for airing clothes.

Heating Systems.—Much of what has been said above applies to these also. In a combined system, the tendency may be on some days to rob the boiler for hot water and so get less warmth from the radiators. Lagging of piping which may give off heat where it is *not* needed, e.g. in the roof space, is an obvious precaution to take. But even in the roof space, if the house has a cold aspect, it may be well to use discretion in lagging, as the piping above may serve a good purpose by preventing a freeze-up.

When radiators are first brought into use after a stand-by period, the air release valve on each should be opened to allow accumulated air to escape. This may be necessary also at other times if air accumulates in a radiator, though this question is too complex for discussion here. If a heating system has been emptied by draining radiators, pipes and boiler, the air valves have to be opened temporarily when refilling the system, since the incoming water drives air before it, and vents must be provided. Generally, in times of frost, all radiators on a circuit should be kept in use to guard against freezing; isolation of any one or more at such times may cause them to freeze. The heat output from a radiator may be improved for all practical purposes by fixing a flat shelf above it on simple brackets. Metallic paint on radiators blocks a good deal of radiant heat emission, and should not be used.

Use only good fuel for a heating boiler. Kitchen refuse is best disposed of elsewhere. Heat is obtainable only from combustible substances, and it is futile to stuff the boiler furnace with wet vegetable matter which, so far from contributing heat, needs other fuel to enable it to burn at all. Further, the flues get choked and the dampers also. Boilers of all types, whether for hot water or for heating systems, need periodical cleaning. In some districts the pipes and waterways get furred-up with scale much sooner than in other districts. Formerly, the only practical treatment was to take down the boiler and clean it by mechanical means; piping, too, had to be treated in this drastic manner. But today, there are descaling liquids and compositions which, put into the boiler, etc., will remove the scale. A heating engineer will advise on such matters.

Boilers should be emptied in the "off" season, and sediment or other loose foreign matter drained out. There is a residuum which does not normally get into active circulation by the pipes; by coupling a hose to the drain-cock at the bottom of the boiler, this can be flushed out. The local hot-water fitter should be asked to do this job once a year. It is not generally advisable for the householder to interfere with taps or valves on the system or to shut off the hot water circulation.

Flushing Cisterns

THE water closet flushing apparatus is known in the trade as a water waste preventer, because it delivers a measured quantity of water at each operation. The cistern fills to a predetermined level, and when the handle or chain is pulled down, all the water is discharged. Water company regulations forbid any device which would allow a continual flow of water to run down the w.c. pan until a stopcock was turned off. In recent years attempts have been made to popularize a flushing valve that delivered a measured amount of water when the cock was turned, but such devices are only permitted when there is no danger of water being wasted.

Prevention of waste is more present in the mind of the companies than in that of householders. An example is the overflow pipe that projects through the wall from a cistern, and gives exit to water if the cistern level gets so high that it might overflow. People say, "Why don't builders fix these pipes so that they just discharge into a head or trough on the down pipe outside the house?" The answer is that the pipe is, properly speaking, a warning pipe, intended to warn the householder when water is being wasted by the failure of the regulating apparatus of the cistern, whether it be a flushing cistern or a storage tank in the loft. It must therefore discharge conspicuously to give prompt notice that something is amiss.

The overflow outlet is some little way below the top of the cistern or tank. Some modern low-down w.c. suites (Fig. 3) have a vertical pipe for the overflow, with the top of this pipe open, and at the proper height for the purpose. This enables the lead pipe joining the overflow to the exit outside the wall to be connected at the bottom of the flushing cistern, instead of through one side.

In no circumstances of household economics is the old adage "Prevention is better than cure" more applicable than in the maintenance of cistern ball valves. If entering a new house, ask the builder to supply half-a-dozen spare valve washers for the flushing

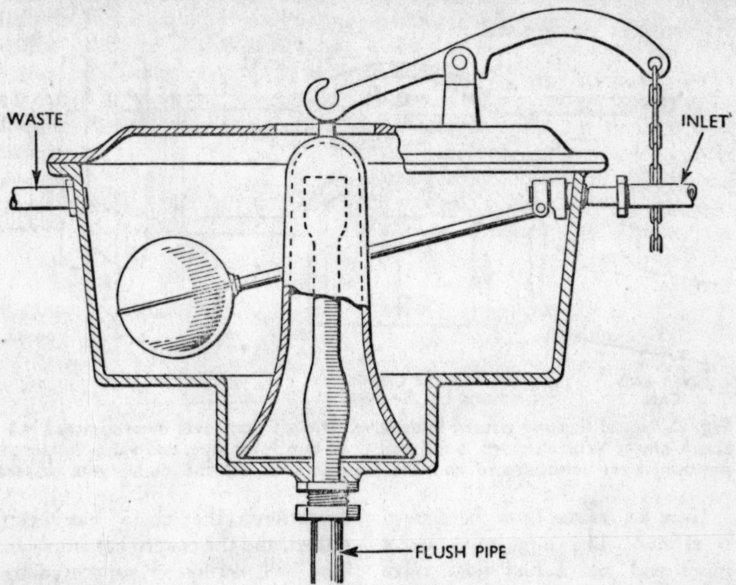

Fig. 1. Siphonic type of cistern. When in operation chain lever raises bell which, as it returns to original position, creates a siphonic action at top of flush pipe causing water to be drawn inside the bell until cistern is practically emptied.

cistern; also some for the storage tank in the roof. Replacement is easy when the spare washers are at hand; it is a very different matter when the householder has to fit a washer at short notice and without foresight. He then has to immobilize the cistern, which includes putting the w.c. out of commission for the time, while he picks out the old washer and takes it down to the ironmonger's to get another one of the same pattern.

How the Cistern Works.—The ordinary cistern with a cast-iron body or shell is usually one of the valveless, siphonic type; see Fig. 1. Open your own cistern and examine it; it is done by lifting off the lid, since though provision is made for fixing the lid by two bolts they are hardly ever fitted. The lever to which the pull-chain is fixed is connected at the opposite end to the bell, which fits loosely over a stand-pipe that is practically an upward extension of the large pipe that carries water from the cistern to the w.c. pan below.

When the chain is pulled, the lever raises the bell; when the chain is released, the bell falls down by its own weight and splashes water up inside it, and so forces some over the top of the stand-pipe. This water carries down with it any air in the pipe, and sets up a siphonic action. Atmospheric pressure on the surface of the water in the cistern body forces this water also up over the top of the stand-pipe, and the flush continues until the well in the cistern is practically emptied.

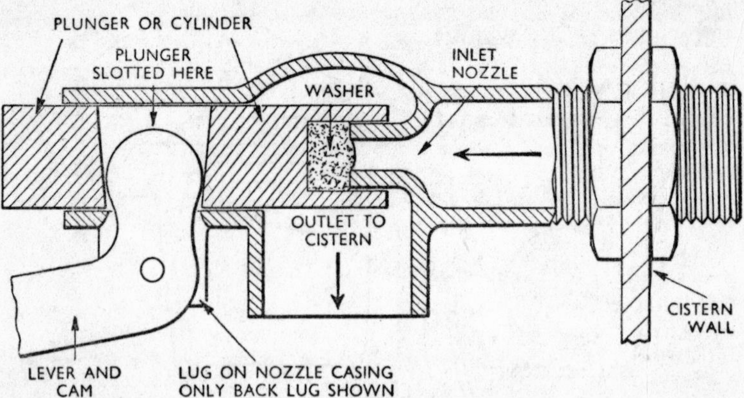

Fig. 2. Typical flushing cistern inlet valve. The ball float lever incorporates a cam above hinge. When cistern is full ball float cam lever operates valve to closed position, over inlet nozzle and the washer seals off the delivery of water.

Now let us see how the cistern is refilled. The inlet pipe at its inner end has a ball float valve fitted (see Fig. 2); when the valve lever is raised to a certain height it forces in a plunger or piston that seals the inlet nozzle. There is a little recess in the inner end of the plunger, in which a washer of hard rubber is inserted, so making a water-tight seal to the small hole in the end of the nozzle. Owing to the comparatively long lever arm on the ball side, this hollow float can exercise great pressure as the ball is lifted up by the rising water. But if the washer is faulty, or has perished, even this pressure will not suffice to seal the nozzle, and so we get water continuing to flow when it should have ceased. Another cause of faulty action is a ball that leaks and becomes partly filled with water, so that it does not float properly, or ceases to float. Copper ball floats develop minute holes in time, through which water enters.

Going back to the sequence of operations, the chain has been pulled, and the cistern has emptied. The ball, no longer supported by the water, falls to the bottom, and water gushes in as the valve is opened fully; gradually, as the cistern fills, the water level rises, and the ball is slowly lifted until the leverage exerted closes the nozzle once again. There is little to go wrong with this type of cistern, and faulty action is almost aways due to the need for a new washer.

Fitting a New Washer.—Turn off the water at the main, if the cistern is filled direct from the rising main. If it is supplied from a tank in the loft, find the outlet in the bottom (usually) which serves the flushing cistern; cut a broomstick to a taper at one end so that it can be pushed into the hole in the storage tank from which the supply comes, thus cutting off the water to that appliance. In some houses there is a stopcock on the pipe that serves the flushing cistern, and it has merely to be screwed down.

The water being turned off, pull the chain to empty the cistern. It will be seen that the valve arm is connected to the valve proper by a split pin that goes through two holes in a bridle or a fork on the nozzle. Close the twin parts of the pin with a pair of stout pliers, when it can be pulled out by a bradawl or some such tool put through the loop at the opposite end. Take care of the pin, which should be of brass or some other non-rusting metal. The lever will now come away, and the plunger can be pulled out; note which way it fits, so that the slot is right side up on replacement. With a stout needle pull up the edge of the old washer until it can be grasped and extracted. The recess is larger below than on top, and the washer may have spread out somewhat. Put in a new washer, which will need easing past the narrower top entrance just mentioned. Replace the plunger, insert the lever, and push in the split pin; open out the prongs of the pin with a knife blade slightly, so that it will not pull out in working.

Turn on the water again, ordinary working pressure, and watch the cistern as it fills. When the valve shuts off, the water ought to be up to, or not far below, the line moulded on the inside of the cistern body. But one cannot tell for sure how a cistern will behave until some hours have elapsed; after apparently sealing, a valve may go on allowing a trickle of water to enter until the warning pipe again drips. Further, as the washer gets compressed by the working of the lever, the cistern may fill higher a few hours, or a couple of days, after the job has been done. If the cistern is frequently used such a defect will only become noticeable during the night, or some other time when it is not in use.

If the cistern does not fill high enough, so that the siphon action

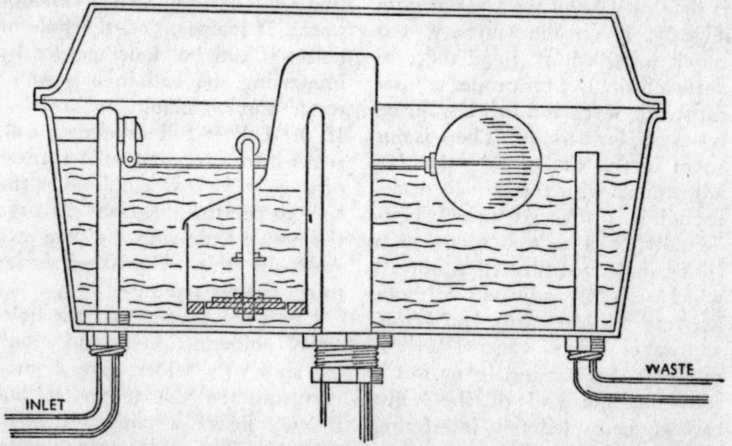

Fig. 3. Modern type siphonic cistern. This cistern employs a modified form of siphonic action, the bell being replaced by a plunger, plunger disk and a fixed siphonic head which is directly connected to the flushing pipe.

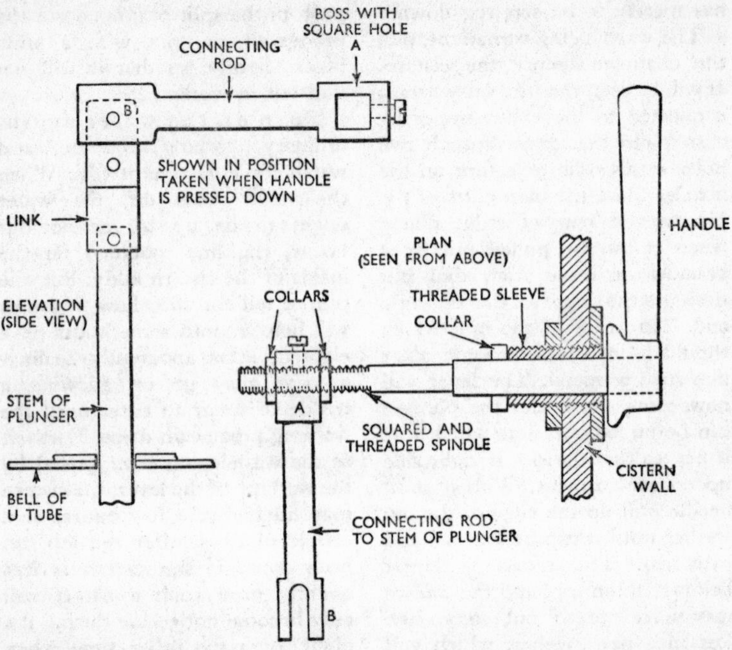

Figs. 4 and 5. Side elevation and plan view of connections between cistern flushing handle and plunger disk in U tube or siphon head in the cistern.

is defective, bend the lever arm *up* slightly; if on the contrary, too much water enters, bend the arm *down* a little. But for proper adjustment, the lever and ball should be taken off, for bending. There is not room in the cistern to make this adjustment with the arm in place, though it is often attempted. Incidentally, it is as well to mention (1) an improved float (flat-topped) which can be adjusted without bending the lever arm; and (2) an adjustable valve which can be regulated by turning in or out a screw at the end of the valve casing, again without interfering with the lever.

Leaky Float.—If this is suspected, take out the lever and shake the ball to see if it contains water. If it does, find the hole or holes; it can be done usually by immersing the ball in a bowl of water and watching for bubbles. If the ball is full or almost full, shake it to detect the hole; a smear of soap will show a bubble at the spot to confirm diagnosis. Enlarge the hole a little with the tang of a small file; this will make it easier to get the water out.

Clean the area around the hole, apply soldering flux, and "tin" the spot with solder; enough may flow into the hole to seal it, but if not, insert a copper nail or rivet, and flow solder over to make an air-tight joint. Scrub the patch afterwards with a nail brush and some soda water, to remove the flux, if an acid one has been used, and rinse well with clean water. A new ball float can be bought at an ironmonger's or a builders' merchant's and is merely screwed on to the end of the lever after the old float has been unscrewed.

Low-down Cisterns.—These (Figs. 3 to 5) work on another plan, as a rule, and the mechanism now described may be found also in ordinary flushing cisterns as well, see Figs. 3 and 4. Open up a flushing cistern and look at the mechanism. The principle is the same as in the bell type of apparatus shown in Fig. 1, but the method of operation is different. The cistern handle is connected by a lever to the stem of a plunger or disk, this stem working through a hole in the top of an inverted cup which forms the lower portion of a U-tube; the long straight arm of the inverted U is a prolongation upwards of the flush pipe, and corresponds to the stand-pipe of the cistern shown in Fig. 1, p. 271.

The handle and connecting parts are shown in Figs. 4 and 5. On pulling down the handle outside the cistern the plunger is raised; in rising, it lifts water up into the U-tube and thus starts the siphonic action, which continues until the cistern is emptied. The lever, links, split pins, etc., are of non-corrodible metal, and this type of appliance should not need attention, except occasional new washers to valves. But the lock nuts, or collars, on the handle spindle *may* shift, so that the lever connecting the handle with the link on the plunger stem may get out of alignment. This might cause the handle to stick down, but the adjustment is an easy matter, which entails loosening of the set screw to the collars and resetting the connecting rod at the proper distance.

Children should be warned not to treat this type of cistern roughly; no force is needed, and the handle merely requires to be gently pulled down to its full extent.

Cold Water Storage Tanks

THE cold water tank usually situated in the roof space should be protected against dust and dirt by a wooden cover on top. This cover should not come close down on to the top of the tank, but be spaced from it by battens nailed on underneath, so that an air space of about an inch is left between the under side of the cover and the flange of the tank. Fig. 1 shows how a simple cover can be made. Plywood is recommended as a material which requires little preparation. The cover should have a framing all round the edge, and this frame should be halved together at the corner joints. See Fig. 2 for the joint at the corners. Cut some lengths of batten, about 1¾in. wide by 1in. thick, and cut two pieces exactly the length of one side of the cover; the remaining two are to be the length of the width of the frame cover. Two screws are put through at each joint, and the plywood is nailed to the frame by ⅝in. round wire nails, or small screws may be used.

The cover is to go on so that

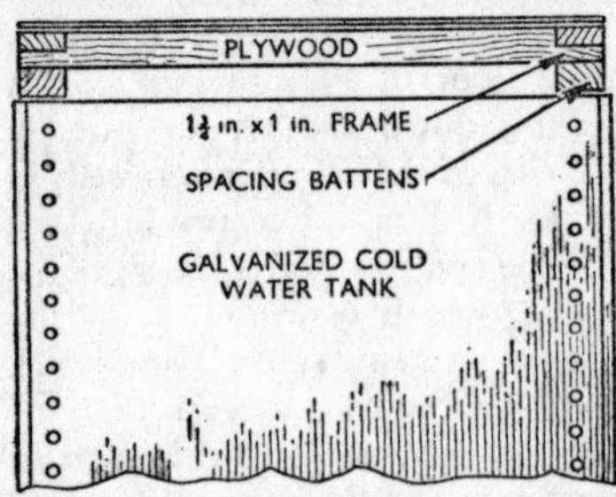

Fig. 1. End elevation of raised, wooden cover for cold water storage tank.

the flush side is uppermost. Now for the battens to raise the cover and leave an air space; screw two pieces of the 1¾in. batten to the under side, flush with the flange of the tank. These directions assume that the inlet cock goes through the *side* of the tank, which is a good arrangement; sometimes, however, the rising main is brought up so that the inlet pipe goes *over the top* of the tank, and in such a case the wooden cover would have to be cut around the pipe.

Access to the Tank.—Floorboards should be nailed to the joists in order to provide a safe track from the trapdoor over to the tank, which often is placed some distance away, near one of the outside house walls. Other boards should be fixed around the tank on the side where any maintenance work will be done. The use of loose boarding is inadvisable and invites accident.

It is a good investment to have a proper electric light point run to the tank loft, with a switch near the trapdoor. But this is not a job for the amateur. It is dangerous to use a trailing flexible connection to a lamp holder on the landing below. Few trailing flexible cables, after a period of service, are absolutely safe against leakage; if the worker inadvertently grasps part of the tank, or the water pipe, with one hand, and perhaps touches the flexible cable or the lamp holder with some other bare part of the body, a dangerous or fatal shock may result. A proper inspection lamp, with heavy insulation, can, of course, be used with reasonable safety, but a permanent lighting point is to be preferred. In frosty weather the properly fixed lamp may be left alight at night, and its continuous gentle warmth may prevent freezing.

Ball Float Valve.—New washers are fitted in the same manner as for a flushing cistern. Since access is more difficult, make sure that a proper job is made of the washer replacement, and that spare washers are at hand. General precautions against frost are described elsewhere in this book, but one good method of protecting the incoming main pipe may well be mentioned here. Usually this pipe runs up vertically from the room below (generally the kitchen), and is left bare for the distance between the lower ceiling and the tank. Make a wooden casing with three sides, to encase the pipe against the wall. The diameter of the pipe will determine the dimensions of the case, and the wood need not be thicker than ⅝in. If the diameter of the pipe is 1in. allow an extra 1½in. on the depth and width of the case. The casing encloses the pipe, being fitted on from the front, and is fastened to the wall by about two holdfasts at each side.

Drive wooden plugs, at suitable places, into the brickwork joints, and then knock in the holdfasts so that the flat top comes against the side of the casing. There is a hole in the holdfast for inserting a screw into woodwork. The casing should go down close to the laths of the ceiling below, but should not impose any weight on them. After fixing the contrivance, fill it from the top with dry sawdust, which can be shovelled in around the pipe with a garden trowel. The hooks, etc. which hold the pipe to the wall should be loosened, and pieces of ¾in. batten put behind the pipe. The idea is to surround the pipe with the insulating material, so that some gets behind as well as on the other sides.

A better but more elaborate way of constructing this insulating tube is to make a board to fit behind the full length of the pipe, and to fasten the pipe to the board with proper clips secured by screws. Make the casing so that it will fit *over* the board, which means that the width of the board must be the same as the inside width of the case, a loose fit. The casing can then be fastened on by about two screws at either side, these screws going through the sides of the casing and into the edges of the board. Fill in with dry sawdust as explained above. Any short horizontal portion of pipe may be lagged with strips of felt wound around it and secured by string.

Do not put an oil lamp in the tank loft to warm this space in frosty weather. No oil lamp or stove is trustworthy enough to be left for hours unattended. Instead, open the trapdoor, and let the warmth from the rest of the house circulate above. When attempting to thaw frozen pipes in the roof space, do not use a blowlamp; usually it is the ball valve that gets frozen, and this can be thawed in many cases by pouring boiling water over it. Sometimes the ball gets trapped by ice formed on top of the water in the tank Break the ice around the ball and lever, and use boiling water for the rest. In any case, the blowlamp method should be left to a plumber. Apart from the danger of fire, the amateur may melt or weaken the lead pipes.

Hot Water Vent Pipe.—In many houses which are provided with a domestic boiler, a pipe will be found at the side of the cold water storage tank, the pipe standing up some distance and having its end turned down over the tank. This pipe is to vent the hot water system in the event of pressure developing. On occasion, some water may be forced up this pipe, which is why its end is turned down and brought over the open cold water tank. Obviously, if we close in the top of the tank, any water that comes out of the vent will splash over and prove a nuisance. Nothing must be done to alter the height of the vent pipe, which provides a safety valve, or

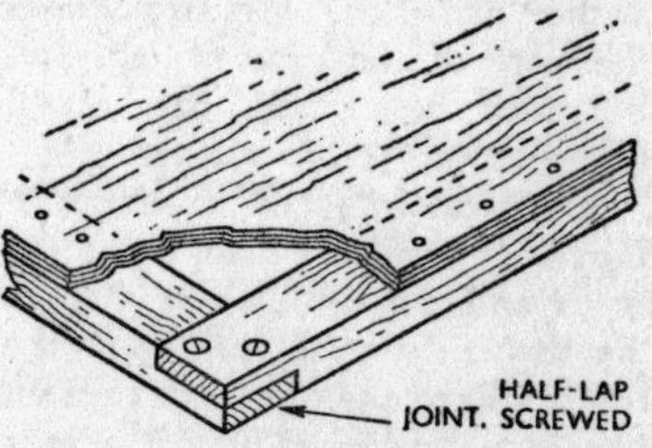

Fig. 2. Details of half lap corner joint for frame of storage tank plywood cover.

to obstruct its open end. The best thing to do is to cut a fairly large round hole in the wooden cover, immediately below the outlet of the vent pipe. If the level of the water in the tank rises above the safe level due to a faulty inlet valve or ball float, deal with the defect along the lines described in FLUSHING CISTERNS, pages 272 and 274.

Washers and Taps

THE ordinary tap, whether for hot water or cold, is one of the screw down type, but for low pressure lines a plug tap may be fitted. The screw down tap requires a certain minimum head of water to lift the jumper that closes the outlet. For this reason it is pointless to fit a screw down tap to a water butt, for example; a plug tap will be better suited to the purpose. Since in house systems the storage cistern is invariably placed at an upper level, there is a sufficient head of water (the distance above the point at which the highest tap is fitted) to operate the screw down tap.

At the kitchen sink a bib-cock (one with a turned-down nozzle) is fitted; a stop cock is also usually fitted for cutting off the water from a branch or from similar internal arrangement and needs occasional replacement of a worn or deformed washer. The usual size for house taps at sinks and basins is known as the "half-inch"; this size defines the bore of the pipe or tap, and is much less than the actual diameter of the tap washer.

A typical bib-cock is shown in Fig. 1. It consists of the body, the cover and the spindle; see Fig. 2. To the end of the spindle at the top is affixed the crutch or capstan handle, according to pattern. Fig. 1 shows a crutch or tee handle. The cover of the tap screws into the body with a flanged joint, there being a leather washer or gasket between the two mating surfaces to seal them. Just above the flange on the cover a hexagon is formed, to afford a hold for a spanner of the proper size. There is a coarse thread on the inside of the hole through the cover, in which the lower end of the spindle works. In this end of the spindle is a recess to accommodate the stem of the jumper, Fig. 2. When the spindle is screwed down by its handle, the jumper is brought close to the seating of the tap, closing the hole leading down through the inlet. A fibre washer (for cold or hot water) or a leather one (for cold water) is bedded on to the lower side of the jumper disc, and held there with a small nut, as shown in Fig. 3 (left-hand diagram).

This washer must be changed for a new one when the tap continues to run or to drip although properly shut down. The top part of the cover incorporates a hollow metal plug or gland with a milled head flange. The plug, which is threaded on its outside diameter, will be screwed partly into the cover, forming a guide for the spindle encased in the hollow bore of the plug. This plug is also a gland that seals the chamber below (known as a stuffing box). A small amount of packing made from tow is wound round the stem of the spindle, and compressed by screwing the plug partly into the stuffing box. This seals off the spindle against leakage. It is seldom necessary to re-adjust the position of the plug, but if it tends to leak it may be screwed down a little more but not so much as to render the tap difficult to operate.

Sometimes, especially in the plated taps used in bathrooms, the tap cover is enclosed by a skirt with an internal thread, which screws on to an external thread at the head of the cover. In such a case it is necessary to remove the tap handle from the spindle; the handle is usually secured by a set-screw at the side, but in some patterns a set-screw may be found under the little disc marked "H" or "C". This disc can be unscrewed, to give access to the set-screw. After removing the handle, the skirt can be drawn up over the spindle and removed.

Cold Water Tap.—Shut off the water at the nearest stop cock. Put a spanner on the hexagon of the tap cover, and gently try it in the normal unscrewing direction, i.e. anti-clockwise. Some taps have to be unscrewed *in the opposite* or *clockwise* direction, so try this if the cover does *not* move on reasonable pressure towards the left. Always grip the tap body with the free hand to minimize the strain. Probably the cover will unscrew at a slight effort; take it right off. The jumper, which is a loose fit in the end of the spindle, may stick inside the tap body; if so pull it out with fingers or a pair of pliers.

There are two main types of jumper: (a) the one already described, where the washer is

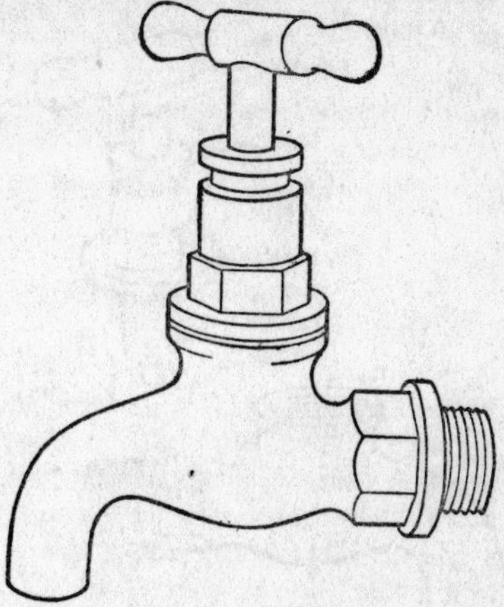

Fig. 1. A common type of general purpose brass bibcock tap. See also Fig. 2.

held on its disc by a nut, as shown in A, Fig. 3, and (b) the type where the washer is fixed permanently on the under side of the jumper B, Fig. 3, and a complete new jumper must be used to replace it. This will not be ascertained until the tap has been dismantled for the first time, so the handyman must then obtain a suitable replacement from the ironmonger; either a loose washer for type (a), or a complete jumper with integral washer for type (b). Spares should in any case be bought for future needs.

All that is necessary for the self-contained type is to insert the new jumper and screw on the cover again. First, however, unscrew the spindle until the tap is in the open position. When a loose washer has to be put on to a jumper of type (a), grip the stem in the vice, wrapping rag around so as not to bruise it; undo the nut with a spanner or a pair of pliers; prize off the remains of the old

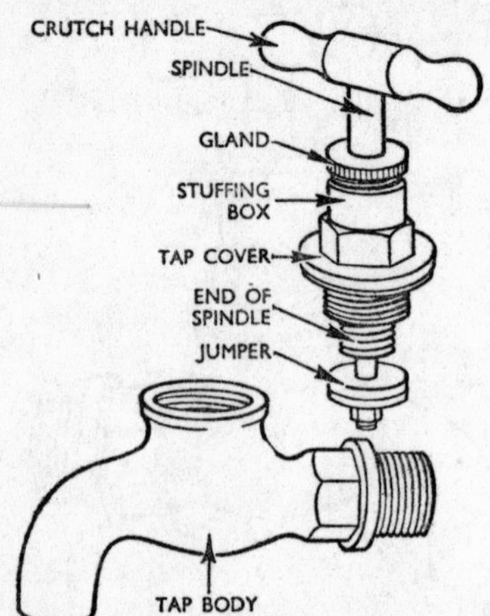

Fig. 2. Shows the partly dismantled components of a typical bibcock tap.

washer and clean the seating. Put on new washer, and screw the nut back.

When a stop cock on the cold water main has to be re-washered, it is essential that the water shall be cut off at a point farther back—perhaps at an outside stop cock in the forecourt. Even then it is probable that a considerable amount of water will still flow, since cocks which are seldom operated, and which receive no attention for years at a time, may not shut down tightly.

Hot Water Tap.—Here the problem is that we are seldom able to cut off the water entirely from the tap, since there is the full hot water cistern supplying the tap, and above that the cold storage tank. The next best thing is to reduce the flow by opening other hot water taps on the same system so that water may flow harmlessly into a bath, or into some other basin or sink than the one being dealt with. Arm yourself with a swab or a housecloth, and have all tools at hand, including washers or jumpers of the presumed size. All being ready, open the other taps just mentioned; open also the tap being operated upon. Next unscrew the tap cover, take it off and immediately clap the swab over the opening, to stop the water gushing upwards. Pull out the jumper, if it has not come up with the tap cover; insert the pliers or fingers under the swab to do this.

Quickly put on a new washer if the jumper is of type (a); or insert a new jumper into the tap body if of type (b); screw on the cover again.

Taps at Basins.—Much damage may be done to an earthenware or vitrified china basin by undue force being used in trying to unscrew the tap cover. The stress is communicated to the ledge at the back, where the tap is fixed through, and it is quite easy to crack this part. Unless the cover comes off easily it may be wise to let the plumber undertake the job here. Taps at the bath are dealt with in the same way as at sinks, but more care must be used, or the enamel of the bath may be damaged.

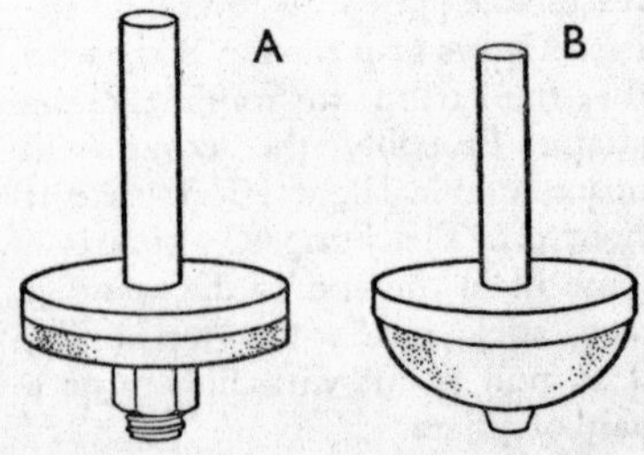

Fig. 3. Shows the two types of jumper washers. A, is detachable from the stem. B, is fixed to the stem and flange.

Water Pipes

A LEAK in a water pipe cannot be repaired until the area of the crack (or the burst) has been dried, and before this can be done the supply of water to the pipe must be cut off, and the pipe drained by turning on the tap. If there is an indoor stop cock the water can be shut off at that point. If the pipe is fed direct from a cistern the latter must be emptied (by leaving the tap running), and prevented from filling again by raising the ball cock as high as it will go, retaining it in that position (see Fig. 1) until the leak in the pipe has been attended to.

If neither of those preliminary measures is possible, the water should be turned off at the main. At an intermediate point between the street-mains and the house-supply a stop cock is provided. This can be turned so that the entire house-supply is disconnected. A long T-handled key is necessary to operate the stop cock, and this item is generally available only from a plumber or an ironmonger, apart from the water company officials. In all probability the long metal key will have to be borrowed from one or other of those sources, or purchased for a few shillings.

This main, outdoor stop cock may be below the pavement, or below the pathway leading to the house, with a metal trap above it, set flush with the surface; in some instances it is just inside the front door, beneath the floor. The householder should, however, familiarize himself with the positions of the main stop cock and any stop cocks on the distribution pipes in the house.

When the leaking pipe has been drained of water, the crack should be dried with a cloth. Meantime the plumber should be called in, since the nature of the repair requires the skilled attention of an experienced man. The defective area of the distribution pipe can then be sealed by soldering, after the area has been cleaned in the usual way; or the bulbous, swelling joint, typical of professional repairs, can be adopted. If the leak is of a serious nature, a burst, for instance, immediate and more drastic action may be necessary. The quickest way to deal with a burst is to flatten the pipe for about three inches or so on the supply side of the crack, with a hammer, so that a complete stoppage is caused, a cloth being held firmly over the hole whilst the hammering is in progress, to prevent the operator being deluged. Call in the plumber.

This method, however, entails substantial repairs, but damage by an uncontrolled flow of water is prevented or at least curtailed.

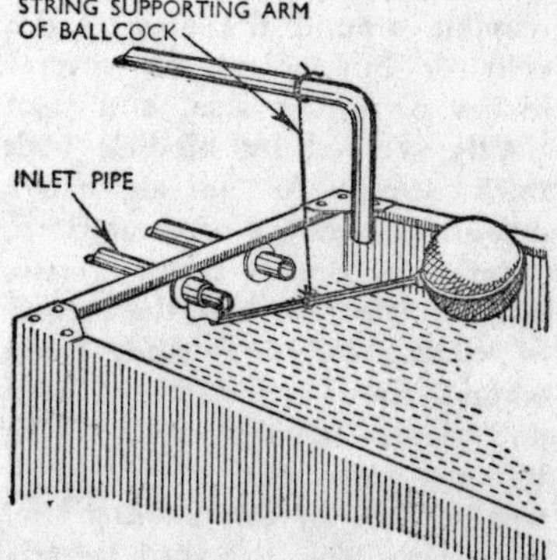

Fig. 1. Raise the ball cock until water ceases to flow, and tie as shown.

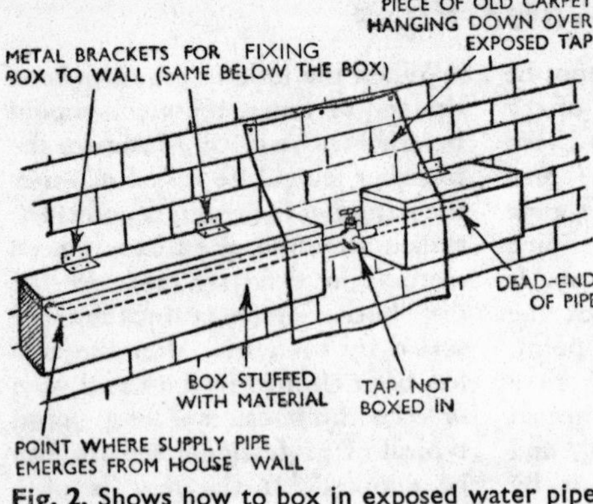

Fig. 2. Shows how to box in exposed water pipes and tap. Allow certain amount of space between tap and boxes for easy accessibility.

The short length thus dealt will later be sawn out and replaced with a corresponding piece of new piping; a job which the plumber is more capable of undertaking than the average amateur. So much for the lead or composition piping. If the pipe is of steel, hammering will be impracticable. Here an emergency repair can be attempted by using an old inner tube from a bicycle tyre, or strips cut from a discarded inner tube of a car tyre, as a tight bandage.

This must be wound tightly as possible around the area of the split or burst, and for several inches on either side, and then tightly secured by binding with thick string. As an alternative measure a bandage of stout cloth, covered well with motor grease, can be tried; several thicknesses of cloth, thickly greased, being wound round the affected area and tightly secured with string binding. A new section of steel pipe will be fitted by the plumber later to replace the damaged length.

Precautions against bursts caused by frost take several forms. The simplest, when a house will be unoccupied for a period during winter, is to turn off the main stop cock and then turn on all the taps; when water has ceased running the taps should be turned off, and the house may be left with the comforting knowledge that however low the temperature may fall the pipes will be unaffected by frost, because there is nothing in them to freeze.

That safeguard, however, covers only the period of non-use. The water supply may be needed again before the winter has passed, and more efficient preventive methods are necessary. Exposed pipes naturally, are mainly affected, and those leading from a cistern or tank in a loft or attic. These can be protected by wrapping them around closely with sacking or felt. These must be put on as thickly as possible and bound in place with string. Felt strips for this purpose can be obtained at stores and ironmongers.

But where outdoor pipes are concerned these materials, being exposed to rain, even when heavily insulated by paint or tar, tend to become sodden; and, as a result, will encourage freezing of the water in the pipes. Where severe frosts are likely, the safest plan is to box the pipe in. A three-sided box can be constructed from any odd timber, of sufficient length to cover the run of pipe and about 4in. wide and similar depth; this should be stuffed with sawdust, straw, hay or even newspaper before being secured to the wall (Fig. 2) with metal brackets, screws and rawlplugs.

There should be no cracks between box and wall to admit frost, and the pipes should be insulated from the wall by ¼in. strips of wood. The outdoor pipe particularly in need of this safeguard is one with a dead end, such as that which extends through the wall to a tap for feeding the garden hose. The outside tap itself may, of course, be covered in, but if it is needed during the winter it can be protected by means of a suitable piece of old carpet nailed to the wall a few inches above the tap and extending downwards some inches below the run of the pipe. The piece of carpet is left loose at the bottom, to enable it to be turned back for access to the tap.

Pipes in bathroom and scullery are likely to suffer in a hard night frost, and where it is not possible, or not desired, for appearance sake, to adopt the wrapping precautions, the next best thing is to leave a gas or electric light burning all night in a position where the water in the pipes is most likely to feel the benefit. An astonishing degree of protection is secured in this way.

Outlet pipes, which carry away waste water from bathroom and scullery, present only a foot or less of length, as a rule, outside the wall; but this is a very vulnerable portion. A half-shut or leaky tap will provide sufficient moisture to result in a freeze-up in this free end. It commences with icicles forming at the open end of the pipe, and these may increase in diameter, with the accumulation of drips, until the end is completely stopped and a plug of ice forms within the pipe.

In that condition it is not possible for water to escape from the sink or bathroom, and it is possible for the sink, or the bathroom basin, to become full as the leaky tap continues to drip, and eventually overflow, with consequent damage to the ceiling below the bathroom or to the scullery floor. A gas or electric light, as suggested in a previous para-

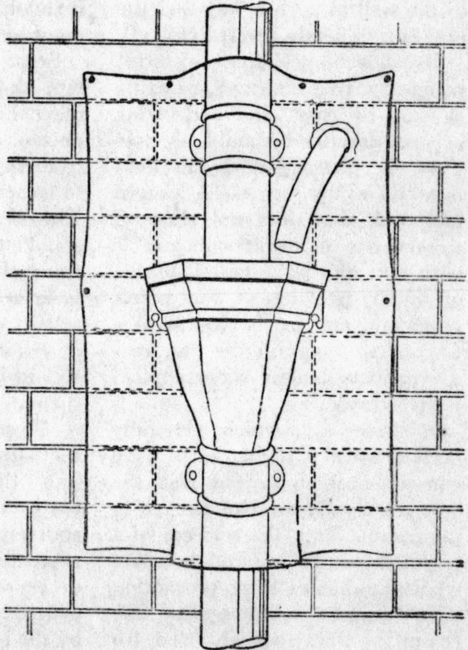

Fig. 3. A simple method of preventing freezing up at the lower end of an exposed outlet pipe.

graph, in the room will probably prevent this stoppage, unless the frost is very severe. But, of course, the taps should not be allowed to drip. See page 278.

Should the outdoor portion of outlet pipe freeze-up, boiling water should be poured over it, out of the window, or from a ladder if that gives easier access. Two kettles of boiling water will generally suffice to start the ice-plug melting, when it should fall away and no damage will be done. Unfortunately this stoppage is seldom discovered until the basin or sink refuses to empty itself. Apart from ensuring that all taps show no tendency to drip, an extra safeguard is several thicknesses of sacking, or a piece of carpet, fixed to the wall in such a way that the pipe is completely covered (Fig. 3).

Overflow pipes from cisterns, being as a rule high up, are easily affected by frost, and a covering as just described should, if possible, be fitted before the first frost of winter comes. A cistern ball cock that does not shut off tightly has a result comparable with that of a leaky tap, a dribble of water freezing at the pipe's outer end and in the course of a few hours necessitating the employment of boiling water applied from outside.

A freeze-up, which generally occurs in the night, may have consequences so serious that the water supply to the house is interrupted until the services of a plumber can be secured to effect wholesale repairs, so no precaution which can be taken against this form of mishap should be neglected. Until the thaw comes a burst does not, as a rule, make itself evident: unless, maybe, a stray icicle becomes noticeable on an indoor pipe where the crack has occurred. And even that clue may escape notice, especially if the pipe leads from an attic tank. The generous and timely wrapping of pipes in all exposed places therefore must not be overlooked.

Damage to an outdoor water pipe (such as one that leads out through an orifice in the house wall to provide water for car washing or to feed the garden hose), may occur through slight but frequent "play", due to looseness of the fixture which secures the short outdoor length to the wall. This fastening, usually a metal hook with a broad, curved grip, should be immovable in the brickwork and it should clasp the pipe firmly at a point as near as possible to the tap.

Some pressure on the pipe and tap, downwards or sideways, is inevitable when a hose is connected, or a bucket is being filled from this outdoor tap. This tends to loosen the fastening in the wall. The metal hook, in this event, should be removed, and the hole from which it is withdrawn should be enlarged and plugged with wood so that when the hook is reinserted it holds the pipe firmly. This should be given attention whether the pipe is of iron or lead.

When hammering the hook, the latter should be so directed into the brickwork joint that the broad grip will clasp the pipe squarely, and the last few blows need to be made cautiously in order that the pipe shall not be dented as a result of undue pressure by the grip. Instead of the hook, a metal strap may be firmly fixed to rawlplugs in the wall surface.

SECTION EIGHT

HOUSE REPAIRS: EXTERNAL

Wall Repairs

THE weatherproofing of house walls is an important factor in house building and one of the early essentials in the building up of the walls is the inclusion of a damp-proof course, a short distance above ground level as shown diagrammatically in Fig. 1. The conditions and manner in which the damp-proof course is laid will vary in accordance with the type of wall construction. The materials employed for the damp-proof course may be of lead or copper sheets or bituminous covered lead, slate or a bituminous composition. Apart from this essential, and the natural weatherproof qualities of good brickwork, perforated air bricks or gratings are situated about the same level of the damp-proof course to give free ventilation, particularly suitable in cavity walls, i.e. walls which have an air space running vertically through the height of the wall. Such walls often possess similar air bricks or gratings at the tops of the walls just below the eaves of the roof. The layers of mortar between the bricks are also treated in a special way so as to reduce saturation of brickwork by moisture.

The damp-proof course prevents the rising of ground moisture. The air bricks ensure a free passage of ventilating air, and the treatment of the mortar by pointing accelerates the clearance of surface moisture. Other factors enter into the effective weatherproofing of brick walls but for the purpose of this entry the foregoing description has been simplified to suit the type of repairs referred to in the following paragraphs.

Dampness in Brick Walls.—Dampness in brick walls may arise from one or more of several different conditions. These may be categorized as follows: (1) Deterioration of materials, mortar, brickwork, damp-proof course, and joints between wall and windows, doors, sills, etc. (2) Obstructed ventilation of wall cavities. (3) Inferior or badly laid damp-proof course, permitting moisture to rise from ground level, defects which may involve major repairs. (4) Inadequate ground drainage, i.e. waterlogged soil, penetration of moisture through walls due to cracks or high porosity of walls. (5) Roof leakages which pass the full volume of drained moisture on to the wall and cause the accumulation to drain downwards in the wall. (7) Walls which, for example, surround a courtyard, and from lack of the drying action of sun or wind, tend to retain a high content of moisture. (8) Frost, the effects of which tend to cause deterioration of wall surfaces. Some of the methods for countering these and allied defects are described hereunder.

Waterproofing Walls.—The best occasion to select for the

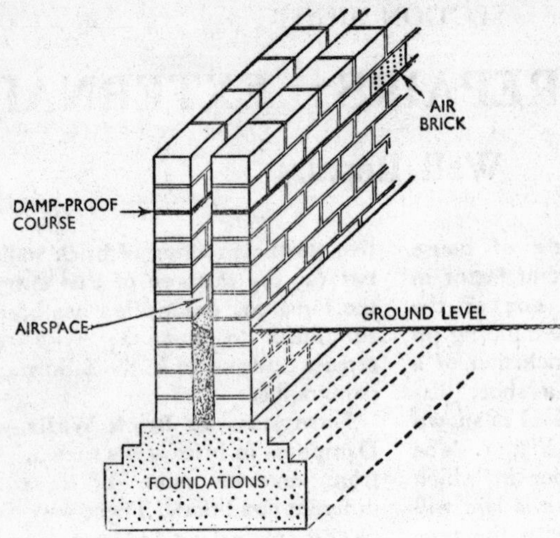

Fig. 1. Shows location of damp-proof course, air brick and air space in the brick wall of a house.

weatherproofing of walls, the surfaces of which have deteriorated, is, of course, during a spell of fine dry weather, because all walls retain a certain amount of rainwater or atmospheric moisture. Thoroughly air the rooms of the exterior walls to be treated. There are several very good proprietary brands of weatherproofing liquids, which may be brush-applied to external walls; some are transparent, while others incorporate a colouring agent natural to the material employed. Chief among the weatherproofing liquids are silicate of soda (transparent), paints with a silicate base, bituminous compounds, oil-bound distempers, whitewash, limewash, and gloss oil paints. The application of such weatherproofing agents is similar in method as for those described in the general instructions on INTERIOR DECORATION. They may be brush-applied or sprayed, but as the latter method involves expensive plant the handyman is confined to the former method. *Cement slurry* with a high sand content is often a useful weatherproofing agent in the treatment of cracked or eroded surfaces, but is not an entirely satisfactory covering and will flake away if the cement content is too high. If a waterproofing of the walls by one of the foregoing methods is considered necessary it will first be advisable to give some attention to the pointing of the brick mortar, before applying the waterproofing compound. Increase in porosity of mortar courses may be countered by the periodical painting of mortar as shown in Fig. 2. No. 6 "Flat Flitch" is a good brush for this purpose.

Re-pointing Brick Walls.—The cause of dampness may be due partly to inferior mortar or its deterioration from another cause. In any event, if the mortar between bricks shows definite signs of erosion and looseness rake out the affected section with a small pick, to a depth of about ¾in. in the manner illustrated in Fig. 4.

As an alternative to this, the mortar may be removed by hammer and a small cold chisel. Examine the layers of mortar to see which type of pointing method has been adopted. There are two varieties of mortar for pointing; one is *oil*

Fig. 2. Painting the mortar courses will increase weatherproofing qualities.

mastic, a stiff paste of fine sand, red lead and boiled linseed oil. The red lead is a strong colouring agent and therefore influences the selection of this mixture where appearance is also a consideration. Oil mastic is efficient.

Cement Mortar. A stiff mixture of one part by volume of Portland cement to four parts of fine sieved and washed sand in water. A small addition of lime will improve its smooth working qualities. Mix on a board, clean surface or bricklayer's hod or hawk.

Preparing Mortar Joints.—After raking or hacking out the mortar along the affected sections, as in Fig. 4, brush away all loose mortar dust and prepare the pointing material. Before applying cement mortar thoroughly wet the interstices of the wall. This is necessary otherwise absorption of moisture, by the wall, from the cement mortar will make repointing difficult. Use a brush similar to that shown in Fig. 3 to wet the mortar courses. This precaution is not to be adopted for repointing with oil mastic, linseed oil priming being used.

Applying the Mortar.—The mortar or mastic is applied to the interstices by a small pointing trowel. Finish the surfaces flush with the bricks; then use the jointing trowel shown in Fig. 5 or a small pointing trowel. Point the

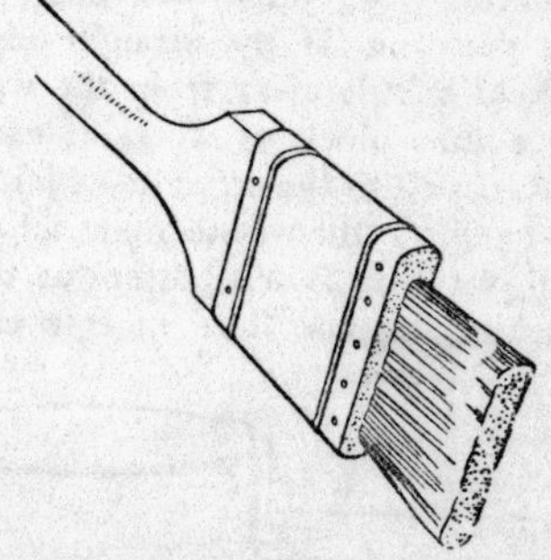

Fig. 3. An old paint-brush trimmed at hair roots, for brushing out mortar courses will be found very useful.

Fig. 4. Preparing defective mortar courses for repointing, by raking or hacking out defective mortar with a small pick. Apply water to courses before repointing.

mortar in the usual way, remembering that the slope of the pointing for horizontal courses should be outwards and downwards. Then, using a straight-edged board and the trowel, trim away surplus material from the lower edge of the pointing. If the straight-edge is held a little away from the wall by a thin block of wood at each end (nailed to the straight-edge) so as to allow the waste material to fall away—so much better for the working results. The mortar can of course, be pointed by making the surface a curved or V-shaped concave, but these are more difficult of execution. Irregular courses may perhaps be best pointed with an ordinary trowel as shown in Fig. 6, page 289.

Fig. 5. A small jointing trowel suitable for pointing mortar courses.

Defective Bricks.—Where cracks are evident in the brickwork, of such a nature as to cause dampness, these may be filled with the aforementioned mortar or mastic. If heavy erosion or deterioration of brickwork has taken place, new bricks may be replaced after removal of the old ones, but the utilization of this method is obviously somewhat limited in scope.

Leaks at Windows, etc.—Excluding the possibilities of

serious dry rot in the woodwork, as a result of dampness (see WOODWORM and DRY ROT) where leaks between joints of wall and frame occur, the use of oil mastic can be very satisfactory. If the gap is large, pack with painted wood strips or wedges and fill the gap to within 1in. of the wall outer surface, then point up with the cement mortar or oil mastic as required. In instances of bad decay of wood, removal of the defective woodwork is the only sound remedy to be considered.

Roof Leakages.—In general, gutters and gutter drain pipes, either of which may become defective (see also GUTTERS AND DRAINS), are the main causes of downward filtering moisture in a wall. These should receive careful attention. All roof leaks must be attended to at the earliest opportunity (see SLATES AND TILES).

Air Bricks.—If earth or refuse are piled up against air bricks, say, for example, during garden digging along a wall, air ventilation of the brickwork will be reduced and damp may rise over the damp-proof course. The air bricks should therefore be clear of any obstruction likely to encourage the accumulation of a high proportion of moisture or rainwater.

General Notes.—Rainwater butts should be mounted on grids and be at least 2in. away from the wall. They should not be permitted to leak. Where damp patches appear on external walls adjacent to the ground level look for the cause and, if practicable, dig in the earth a slanting trough, away from the wall, and fill with loose small rubble mixed with a little earth. Do this only if no logical cause other than ground dampness or waterlogging of a local nature can be found. Sweating or condensation of hard impervious bricks or other surfaces will respond to any efficient measure for increasing the

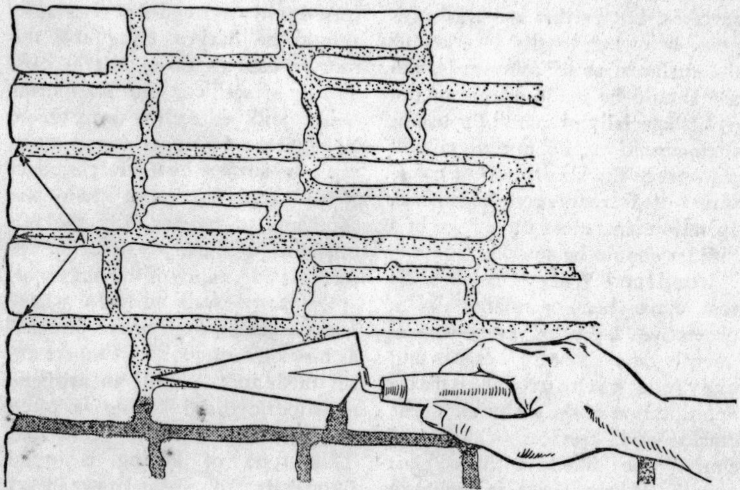

Fig. 6. Pointing irregular mortar courses. Note the pointing angle of mortar at A.

Fig. 7. Pointing regular brickwork mortar courses. Apply mortar flush with brickwork then point mortar to downward and outward sloping angle.

free flow of air over the affected surfaces, but as this is not always possible owing to the location of the surfaces, as in courtyards, the use should be made of one of the paints specially prepared for use in such conditions, i.e. one which will discourage the absorption of moisture or its formation on the surface. In serious instances the advice of a builder should be sought.

Rendered Walls.—Brick walls that have been rendered by a protective layer of cement frequently develop narrow cracks and crevices without any undue deterioration of the material. These cracks and crevices should, of course, be filled with cement mortar. Where there is evidence of deterioration of the material by loosening away, bulging, or powdering, the defective area should be hacked away and the mortar courses raked out as previously described, cement mortar being laid as shown in Fig. 8; large areas being trimmed flush with the surface by a straight edge. When applying more than one thickness of mortar, key the top or joint surface by scoring to increase adherence of the next coat.

On some wall surfaces where natural keying does not exist, such as may be found where timbers are set flush in the wall, an artificial or superimposed keying is often employed to facilitate rendering. This type of keying is quite frequently of special expanded sheet metal or heavy wire mesh.

Fig. 8. Rendering a brick wall. The mortar courses are raked out to provide a key. Apply water to the wall by brush and lay on the mortar in an upward direction.

This should be brushed clean and thoroughly damped before the application of new mortar. In some instances wood surfaces may be keyed by the liberal use of large head or clout nails. These are driven into the surface at close intervals, but the heads of the clout nails are not driven flush with the surface. They should be approximately $\frac{3}{8}$in. to $\frac{1}{2}$in. clear of the surface to provide a good key.

Gutters and Drains

It is not generally known, perhaps, that a gutter is fixed so as to provide a gradual slope towards the rainwater pipe into which the water discharges. This necessity is provided for when a house is built, but defects that arise later may cause the gutter to sag, thus forming a pocket into which water collects until it overflows over the top of the gutter itself. In the same way, blockage of a gutter by leaves, a bird's nest or other obstruction may cause an overflow. Gutters may leak at the joints between lengths, where the end of one piece fits into a shouldered recess formed in the end of the adjoining length. Putty is laid between the joint faces, and around the screws that secure the two ends, so as to render the joint watertight.

Rotting of the woodwork to which the gutters are fixed, or rusting of the screws that attach the gutter brackets, will cause the gutter to loosen or sag. The cast iron gutter may rust and develop holes or other defects. Regular care in the way of clearing out obstructions, and the painting of these parts when the outside of the house receives its periodical overhaul, will prevent most of the trouble likely to occur. At the time of overhaul, the gutters should be inspected for loose joints and any other defects. The brackets should be carefully inspected, and any that are loose should be made secure. At least once every year all gutters should be cleared with a garden trowel or similar tool. Do not rest a ladder against the gutter. This is often done with bad results to the gutter. Hang a bucket to the ladder by a simple hook, and put into it all debris removed from the gutter.

A balloon grating of thick wire mesh can be bought to slip into the gutter outlet, and so prevent blockage by birds' nests. If, however, this grating is not kept clear of leaves, etc. no useful purpose will be served. In any case, if a nest is observed, it will naturally be removed at the first opportunity. In a severe rainstorm almost any gutter will overflow for a short time, owing to the excessive delivery of water from the roofs, but the clearing of gutters every spring will prevent any possibility of the gutters being stopped up.

Lead Gutters.—So far we have dealt only with eaves gutters, attached to the feet of the rafters or to other woodwork at the face of the wall. The gutters to flat roofs, and other gutters formed in the roof itself, are usually of lead laid on suitably shaped woodwork. The same care in clearing away debris is necessary, and in ensuring that the outlets are unobstructed. There is one important precaution which the householder should take; never walk about on a lead gutter, or on any other roof leadwork, in nailed shoes. Put on a pair of rubber-soled shoes, or slippers, or the lead may be damaged. Better still if any work has to be done over lead, lay down some boards, and tread on these.

Rainwater Pipes.—These should be inspected and repainted periodically. If any defects are noticed (such as the appearance of damp walls adjacent to the pipes) in between these periods they should receive prompt attention. A new length of rainwater pipe of suitable size can be bought and fixed. The defective section should be freed by prising out the nails that go through lugs at the top end, and the pipe lifted out. If the length is an intermediate one, the pipe above or below will have to be loosened before the defective length can be removed. If a pipe of standard length will not do, it can be cut with a little care. Lay the pipe down on two wooden blocks, or on some bricks, so that it is properly supported; tie a piece of tape round the pipe so as to provide a guide for cutting.

Saw the pipe with a hacksaw. Do not try to cut right through at any one part of the circle, but aim at making a groove right around the pipe first. Saw a little way, and then rotate the pipe towards you, so that an uncut portion is presented to the cutting edges of the teeth of the saw. A practised hand, after cutting a groove all round, will give the pipe a smart tap at one or two points with a hammer, and the pipe will break neatly at the groove. But the beginner will do well to persevere with the sawing until the pipe separates. It must be well supported, and the weight must not be allowed to come on the half-severed part, or the pipe will, very probably, crack.

Bath and Lavatory Wastes.—These empty into a cast iron "head" outside the house. See that the outlet from the head is free; leaves and even birds' nests may choke it. It may be desirable to cut a flanged lid, to the shape of the head, from sheet lead or zinc.

Drains.—As far as traps and gullies are concerned, this matter is dealt with under WASTE PIPES. There is little that the amateur can do for drain blockages and other defects. He may, in fact, cause more damage in seeking to do work that needs much experience.

Occasionally a w.c. pan may become blocked. Procure a pliable cane, and gently try to poke the obstruction down. The pan is fragile, and may easily be damaged by rough treatment. If the blockage is stubborn, the amateur may take up the manhole serving the system, and observe if the blockage extends there also. Couple up the garden hose, and direct a strong stream of water at the exit from the inspection chamber. Try with a long stick to poke the obstructing substance through this exit, taking very great care to avoid damage to the earthenware pipes. A combination of this treatment with hosing may get the drain flowing again. If the pipe entering the chamber is blocked, turn the hose here and try to ease out the blockage with a stick.

A stubborn obstruction such as this would most likely have given warning some time earlier, by the sluggish action of the pan, but cases have been known where it was not suspected until a complete stoppage occurred. If the treatment just outlined does not cure the trouble, call in a builder. Although special rods for clearing drains, etc. are well advertised in the general press, and are also recommended as being useful for other jobs, the amateur will be well advised to refrain from interfering with drains other than by the simple methods previously described. It is true that the rods would serve to free an obstruction which showed at the inspection chamber, but the various hook and screw devices sold with drain-clearing appliances are likely to do much damage in inexpert hands.

Rainwater Gullies.—See that gratings are not blocked by leaves or other matter. Take up the gratings periodically and clear out any soil washed into the trap. Flush the gullies in very dry weather, especially if an offensive smell of sewer gas is noticed. The water seal in the bend of the trap may have become ineffective by evaporation, and a pail of water and carbolic fluid may be added if desired to restore the seal and block off any unpleasant odour.

A word about deodorant fluids and powders; if the drains smell, they should be inspected. Exclude the simple case just mentioned, where the defect is merely dried-up water seal. Little is gained by substituting a tolerable or even pleasant odour for an unpleasant one; the cause of the latter should be sought, and steps taken to remove the cause. The use of a deodorant is a health precaution, not a cure for defects in drainage when it ceases to be of much use.

Replacing Slates and Tiles

The first requisite is a ladder, which can be hired from a builder's merchant. An ordinary ladder is better than an extending ladder; if, however, purchase is contemplated and can be justified on general grounds an extending type is the most suitable for general use. Erect the ladder so that its top extends a few rungs above the eaves. As a safety measure, during the course of the work, arrange for a second person to stand by the foot of the ladder and ensure that it does not slip or move. See that the foot stands firm and level; if necessary put a wedge under one side to bring it level.

It is dangerous to put any pressure or weight on the gutter; do not attempt to deal with slates out of arm's reach when on the ladder, especially on a high roof. Builders use a duckboard, which is hooked over the ridge of the roof and lies upon the slated or tiled surface, but even in experienced hands this is none too safe a contrivance. Apart from safety considerations, an inexperienced person may do extensive damage to adjacent slates and tiles while making a small repair.

Slates are fixed to battens, or to a close-boarded roof, by two nails, as Fig. 1. Three rows of battens are involved, and the head of the slate lies upon the top batten. The slate is nailed to the *next lower* batten (upon which rests the head of the next lower course of slates); while the slate we are dealing with overlaps the *third* batten to a small extent. Any given portion of roof is thus covered by three thicknesses of slate, more or less. A cracked or broken slate must be removed, as a rule, by cutting the nails that hold it. For this job a slater's ripper must be used, if it is possible to purchase or, preferably, hire the tool. The tool invariably has a cranked handle and an arrow-shaped head with two V-shaped cutting notches. It is thrust between the slates and the notch on one side brought against the nail to be cut; the ripper is then brought vigorously against the nail in one or two strokes until the nail is severed or pulled out. The ripper is then moved along to deal with the second nail, after which the defective slate can be removed.

Unless several adjacent slates are taken off, which is neither desirable nor practicable as a rule, we cannot fix the replacement slate by nailing; the point of attachment is hidden by the slate of the next course above. The new slate must therefore be attached by a clip made of stout zinc or copper or thin lead sheet (Fig. 2) bent over

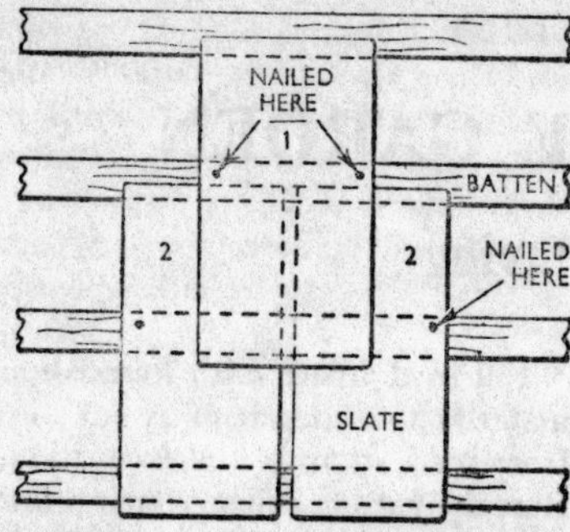

Fig. 1. Shows example of nailing overlapping tiles to battens. See also Fig. 2.

and behind the top of the slate beneath the one to be fixed. Another method is to nail the top part of the clip to the batten, through the narrow space left between two adjacent slates of the underlying row. In Fig. 1, this gap is somewhat exaggerated for clearness. The tail of the clip is left lying flat on the slates; the new slate is slid up into place, and the clip is now bent up and over the bottom edge of this slate in the form of a hook, and pressed down closely, see Fig. 2.

Replacing Defective Tiles.—We can deal here only with plain tiling, since the repair of the so-called single-lap tiles is more involved. Plain tiles are laid with a double lap, in a similar manner to slates, the tile in any one course overlapping part of those in the next two courses lower. But tiles, besides being holed for nails, are formed with "nibs" projecting downwards underneath the head, and these nibs hook over the battens. Not every course is nailed, but, generally every fourth or fifth course, thus facilitating repairs or replacements, since, in many cases, it is necessary only to unhook the adjacent tiles and take out the broken ones. Nailed tiles can be freed by the use of the ripper, as for slates.

Clay tiles are very fragile, and in consequence it is only those parts of the roof easily accessible that can be dealt with by the amateur. Do not disturb any tiles but those immediately concerned; take out the broken ones and put new ones in their place. Put back any others that may have been removed for the purpose. Tiles can be levered up with an old, flat knife or a putty knife, and may be propped up by thin wooden slips or wedges while the one to be removed is worked out. Sometimes it is possible to get at tiles on the high part of a roof from inside the roof space, and to put in a new one. But it is only in open roofs (tiles on battens) that they are accessible in this manner.

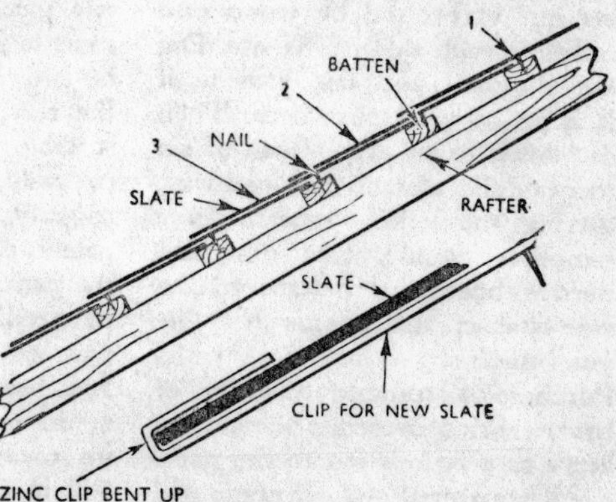

Fig. 2. Side elevation of slates and battens and a cross-section detail of zinc clip for new slate.

SECTION NINE

JOBS IN THE GARDEN

Crazy Paving

STONE slabs of irregular shape but all of even thickness are employed to lay a path of crazy paving. Such material can be bought from stone yards by the ton. The superficial area covered by a given weight of stone will depend on the thickness and nature of the stone, which varies in specific gravity according to its type. A thickness of 2in. is usual. Buy the stone near at hand if possible, as carriage from a distance adds a good deal to the cost.

The first job is to set out the paths, if they do not already exist. Cut a couple of boards, the exact width of the path to be prepared, for use as gauges. Drive in several stout stakes at each side of the proposed pathway, spacing them about six feet apart. The true line of the path is indicated by two strings stretched between end stakes at each side of the site. Dig out the turf and lay it aside if it is to be used elsewhere. Then dig down to an even depth of six inches all along the pathway, leaving the sides vertical. As a temporary guide, tack thin and narrow boards or battens to the side stakes; the boards may be ½in. thick by 4 to 6in. wide. Purchase a suitable quantity of broken brick or larger clinker, to serve as a foundation to the path. Similar material of finer grade will be needed for the top layer of foundation; see Fig. 1 opposite.

Fill in the path with foundation material to a depth of about 2in. from the bottom of the excavation. Run the garden roller over it a few times to make it firm, or tamp it solid with a rammer. Follow with a thinner layer of finer grade material, and roll that also. Drainage will be improved if the surface is given a slight camber, so that it is higher at the middle than at the sides. A board can be lined out with pencil to a suitable curve, and then sawn or spoke-shaved away until its lower surface gives the desired camber. When the fine stuff is laid, stroke it down lengthwise with a cambered board to shape the surface before rolling. See also GARDEN PATHS.

Paving Laid on Sand.—Spread a bed of sand for about a yard at one end of the site. Try one or two pieces of crazy paving on it, so as to judge the depth of sand to be laid down. Then carry on with the rest. Dump heaps of sand at suitable positions alongside the pathway. Also sort out the stone roughly, and dump loads at appropriate places along the edge of the path. Much time may be taken in needless journeys unless this part of the job is systematized. It is best to begin to lay the stone at the margins, and to work them up to the middle of the width. Fill in the path with large pieces of stone as far as possible, particularly when laying in sand. If a

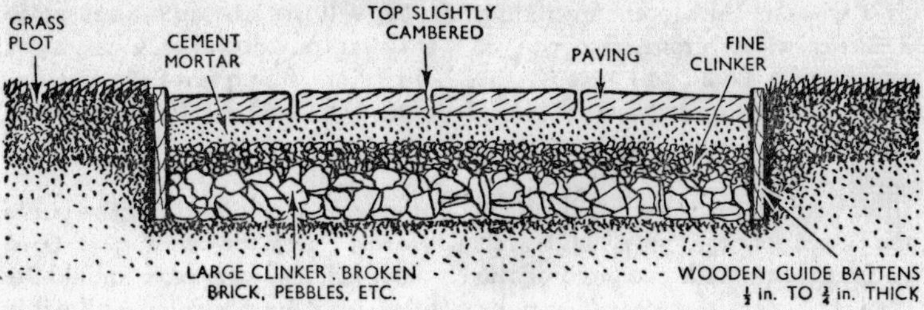

Fig. 1. A cross-section of garden path, showing the foundations, intermediate layers and top layer of crazy paving. Fill in the joints between paving with mortar.

large piece has to be cut or broken, use a heavy hammer (club hammer) and a bricklayer's bolster, or a large cold chisel. Strike with the chisel along the required line on top of the slab; then turn the stone over and work from that side also; this will weaken the stone along the desired line of breakage.

Laying in Cement Mortar.—A mixture of about four parts sand to one part Portland cement is suitable. After excavation of the pathway, proceed with the two layers of rubble or clinker as before described. Roll and ram the top layer after getting it to the proper camber. Mix up a quantity of cement and sand dry on a board, or on a cement floor near by. Mix the stuff twice in the dry state, using a shovel and rake. Then sprinkle it with a watering-can having a rose top and mix thoroughly by shovel. Avoid making the mixture too wet. Sprinkle the pathway with water at the place where work is to begin.

Lay a thin bed of mortar, and proceed with the setting of the stone; a distance of ½in. between the edges of the slabs is usual, but the joints may be left a little wider if they are to be pointed later.

When ceasing work for the day, leave the slabs irregular at the finishing point, in a zigzag line across the path. If the joints are to be filled in with cement, this can be done with a bricklayer's trowel as the stones are laid. Assuming the joints are to be pointed, perhaps in a coloured or a white cement, rake out the joints an hour or two after laying, but avoid using the path for the time being. Then a day later, the joints can be filled with the pointing material and levelled off flush.

General Hints.—A club hammer can be used to level the slabs, and bed them down into the sand or the cement immediately after laying. Often a light blow with the end of the handle will do what is needed. After laying, the stones must not rock; should there be any sign of this, lift the slab and remove a little of the bedding material where needed, or add a little more. When paving has been laid on sand, sweep over the section of work completed with a stiff broom, to fill the cracks with surplus sand; do not brush too heavily. Similarly, after laying paving in mortar, and filling the joints with ordinary mortar, brush over with an old broom, sprinkling a little water from the can if necessary. This will grout the slabs. (Grouting consists of filling a more or less fluid cement mixture into crevices).

Mortar should be filled in at the sides of the path, and well packed down with the edge of the trowel. Later, the boards can be removed if desired; in any event they will rot in time, but since they are put down only as guides during the filling in of the foundation, this will not matter. It *is* essential, however, that a good side edge should be formed with cement mortar, independently of the guide boards. After the latter have been taken up, ordinary soil should be filled into the hoes left by boards and stakes. Ram in the earth.

Clothes Line Post

THE post may be a fixture, set in the ground permanently, or it may be arranged to be lifted out of a socket and put aside after the weekly laundering operations are finished. We will deal first with the second case. A wooden socket is commonly used, but a concrete one is far better. Dig out a hole in the ground, 2ft. deep and about 15 to 18in. square. It is important to have enough space to wield the spade and shovel to dig and clear the hole, and matters may be made much easier by allowing a little more room. At the bottom of the hole lay a piece of paving stone about 2in. thick, see Fig. 1.

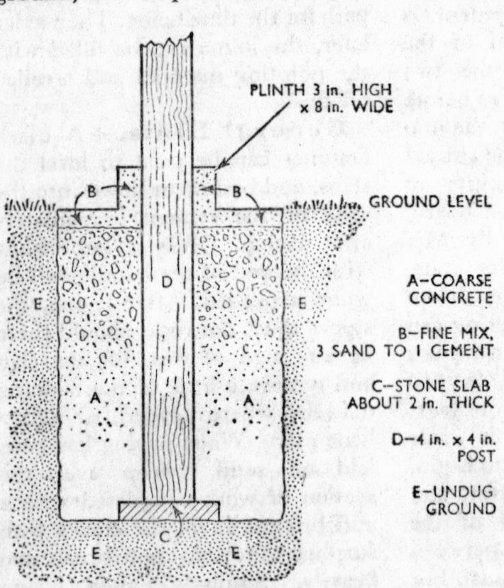

Fig. 1. Shows the lower part of the clothes line post set in the concrete base. Paint lower part of post.

Mix up some concrete near-by on a platform or on a firm path if one is handy. Use broken brick or stone, or washed shingle, not sea-beach shingle, for the aggregate, and mix in the proportion of 5 or 6 parts shingle, etc., to 1 part Portland cement. Mix well in the dry state, twice; then water with a rose, and mix twice wet. Do not use more water than is needed to make the concrete manageable. The shingle, or hardcore, should contain small pieces as well as bigger ones, so that the interstices are filled as the stuff is rammed into the hole.

For the post, use red

deal, 4in. × 4in. section; add 2ft. to the height desired above ground, which will give the total length of the timber. A short length of the same stuff can be used as a core to fix temporarily in the hole when filling in the concrete, but instead of this (as the 4in. × 4in. is rather expensive), we can make a mould out of four pieces of ¾in. or 1in. board, cut to proper width and nailed together so that the *outside* dimension is that of the post section, plus a little for easy clearance (see Fig. 2). The core mould is thus a square tube whose outside measures about 4⅛in. on each side, and it should be at least 2ft. 2in. long. Do not nail the mould together too tightly, as it may have to be broken out when removing it after the concrete has set quite hard.

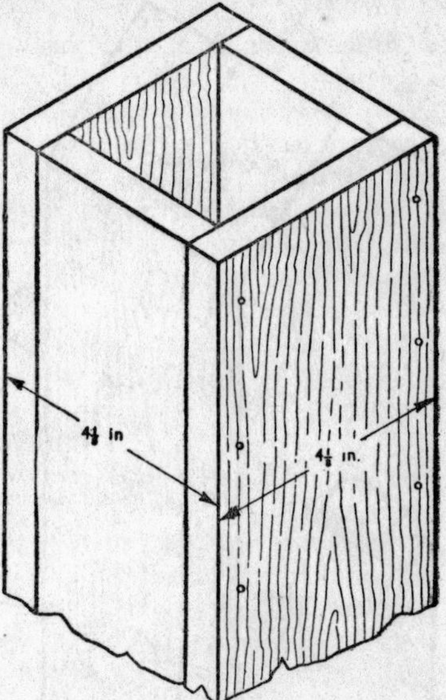

Fig. 2. Outside dimensions of box core for preparing concrete base.

Making a Concrete Socket.—When the hole has been dug and cleared of loose earth, lay in the piece of paving stone, as mentioned above, and set the mould on it, centrally in the hole and facing squarely the way in which the post is to face. See that the mould sits fairly on the stone slab, and fix it by four pieces of board tapped down edgewise between the side of the mould and the side of the hole, two near the bottom and two more right at the top. The bottom ones are left in, but the top two are taken out when the top part of the hole is being filled. Now proceed to shovel in the concrete around the mould; ram it down from time to time. Stop at about an inch from ground level, when the mould should stand up about two or three inches above this. Do not try to smooth off the top surface at present. The concrete will have to be left for about twelve hours. Push some sacking into the hole in the mould to prevent soil, etc., from falling in.

Shaping the Post.—Saw off the top of the post to a V-shape (Fig. 3), thus providing a surface that will shoot off water. But chisel away the sharp edge at the top. For a good job, cut a piece of sheet lead or zinc to make a cap for the post, as in Fig. 5. Nail on the lead or zinc with galvanized nails. About 8in. down from the top of the post, bore a hole right through one face, this hole being of a size to give a tight fit to a piece of broom handle or similar stuff that is available. At a point 2in. lower down, bore a similar hole through at right angles to the first one, and drive in a piece of round wood here also, as Fig. 3. Some housewives prefer a pulley arrangement, so

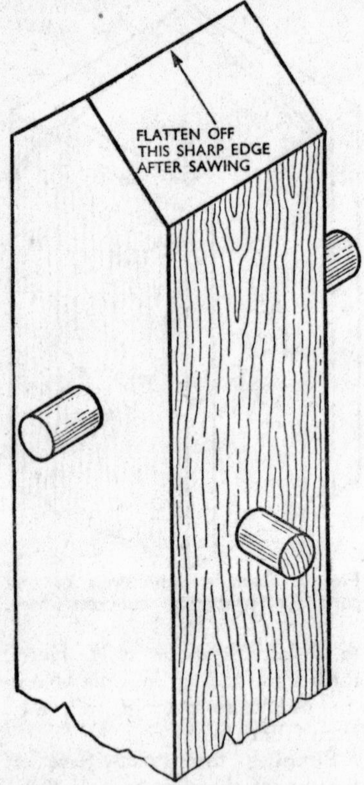

Fig. 3. How to shape the top of clothes line post. Bore holes and insert two pegs as shown, to support lines.

that the line can be raised or lowered; in this case the post merely needs a stout galvanized pulley screwed in at the front face, and a galvanized cleat screwed on lower down to fasten the loose end of the clothes line.

Finishing the Socket.—When the concrete is hard, pull out the core mould, if necessary driving in two of the side boards with a hammer and cold chisel so that it can be got out in pieces. Set the clothes post into the socket temporarily. Now we have to make a neat finish at ground level. Mix up some cement-and-sand mortar and lay on the top of the concrete, going right up to the sides of the post, which is left in place all through this operation. Have ready four pieces of smooth batten, 3in. × 1in., and long enough to make a little box measuring about 8in. on each side (Fig. 4). Nail three sides together, and leave the fourth piece loose, so that the mould can be got around the post. Lay these pieces of batten on top of the cement layer just applied, so that they form a mould around the post. See that they are square and level.

Fill in the cement-and-sand mortar until it is flush with the top of the box; leave it until it sets hard, taking precautions that the post is not interfered with meanwhile. Next day, remove the box, and a neat finish will have been provided, in the form of a square plinth standing up about two inches above ground, as seen in Fig. 1 at B. A simple stopper should be made to close the top of the socket and exclude dirt when the clothes post is not in place.

Permanently Fixed Post.—Dig out a hole as before, but taking

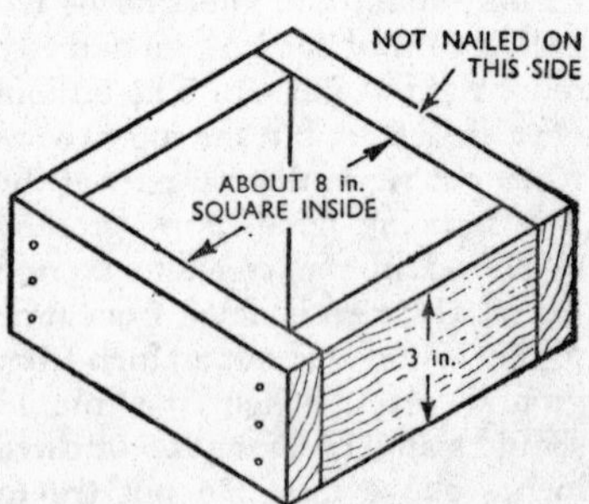

Fig. 4. Shows top box core for shallow cement plinth shown at B, in Fig. 1.

it to 2ft. 6in. deep. Prepare the post as required. A piece of stone should be put at the bottom for the post to stand on; further, if two rectangular pieces are available, one can be wedged into the hole at what will be the front and back of the post, close up to the latter. The hole can be filled in with broken brick, rubble, or other similar stuff, finishing off with soil. Before the post gets too firmly set, it should be tested for uprightness on two faces at right angles, and the filling corrected, if necessary. An earth rammer can probably be hired or borrowed for this job, and will prove invaluable; it is difficult to consolidate the soil properly without a rammer.

Instead of using stone slabs at back and front, two pieces of inch board may be nailed to the post near the bottom, to take the thrust exerted by the weight of the clothes on the line plus that caused by wind. In either case, once the post has been set fairly in the hole, and chocked by pieces of brick, etc. to stop it moving out of place, soil or hard core must be rammed in, between the board face and the side of the hole—or between stone slab and the hole—to ensure a solid support.

Some people prefer to set posts in concrete, but it is alleged against this practice that a wood post rots more quickly in concrete. There is a useful compromise which makes the best of both methods: fill in the hole with hard-core up to two inches or so from the ground level; then make a simple edging of 3in. × 1in. battens held tight with stakes driven in *outside*, and complete the job with about 2in. of concrete to just above ground level, trowelling it off fairly smooth at the time of laying.

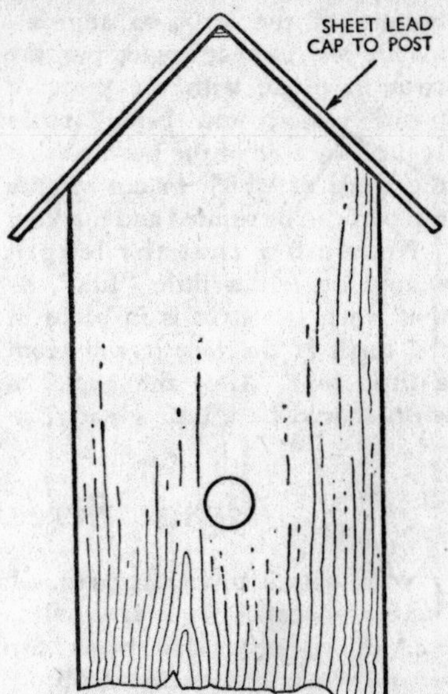

Fig. 5. Cap the post with zinc or lead sheet to prevent wet rot.

Repairs to Clothes Posts.—A post set in the ground may become loose, owing to the constant pull in one direction. Later this looseness becomes general all round. One remedy is to take out some of the top soil, to ram the remainder tightly, and to fill in about 6 or 8in. of concrete on top. The post should be strutted temporarily in two directions until the concrete has hardened.

Another remedy (which may be used to supplement the first one) is to fix a stout diagonal strut (4in. × 2in. in section) to the front of the post, where most of the pull comes. Dig out the ground where the foot of the strut is to go, taking it down about 12in. A piece of flat board under the foot of the strut will help matters. Cut off the bottom of the strut to approximately the correct angle; put the strut in place, with the piece of board under, and bring it up against the side of the post, so that the angle at which to cut off the top part can be sighted and marked.

Remember that the length should be left a little "full", so that when the strut is in place in the earth at the foot it will seem a little long. Also, the angle as sawn should be a little greater, so that the top of the strut will fit nicely against the post when driven down in the nailing. These points will be obvious during the course of the work. Set the strut in the ground and ram it tight. Then drive in two 6in. nails, through the outer face of the strut and into the post. Start the nail holes with a brace and bit, or a suitable bradawl. As the nails are driven home, the strut will come close up to the post and make a firm fixing.

Rustic Screens and Arches

GOOD sound timber is essential for success. Stack the poles, etc. in an airy, dry place for several weeks before use. Strip off the bark, cut off all branch ends close, and trim with a spokeshave or draw-knife. Timber rots much more quickly if the bark is left on.

Construction.—The main members should be stiff and stout; poles should go into the ground some 18-24in., and the butts should be the thickest ends. Well dope the butts with creosote before setting them in the ground. Short and slender posts can be driven with a mallet after pointing, but heavier posts need proper holes dug for them. In erecting a screen, first set out the line on the ground with stakes and twine. Dig the holes to one and the same side of the line, or central on it, throughout. Erect the two terminal posts of any main bay or portion of the screen or pergola; then, at a suitable height, stretch a line across horizontally. A simple plumb-bob suspended on a string from the top line will give the true vertical, and indicate where to place the intervening upright members. Similarly, a "line level", a short spirit level with holes or hooks for fixing horizontally to a line, will give any cross levels needed; owing to the irregular surface of rustic timber an ordinary spirit level is almost useless here.

After setting the main posts in the lengthwise run of the screen or pergola, insert any opposite posts to pair with them, using a simple home-made try-square which can be made in a few minutes from 2in. × 1in. batten. The next job is to tie the pairs of posts together by top bars (joint as shown in Figs. 2 and 3), and by cross bars lower down (as shown in Figs. 4 or 5). One or two diagonals (Fig. 1) should be worked in, since they stiffen the structure very considerably.

It is advised that holes should be bored for the nails in the outside members of all rustic work. A gimlet, or a similar bit held in a brace, should be used. Bore carefully, or the timber will split. Previous boring avoids heavy hammer blows, which weaken the

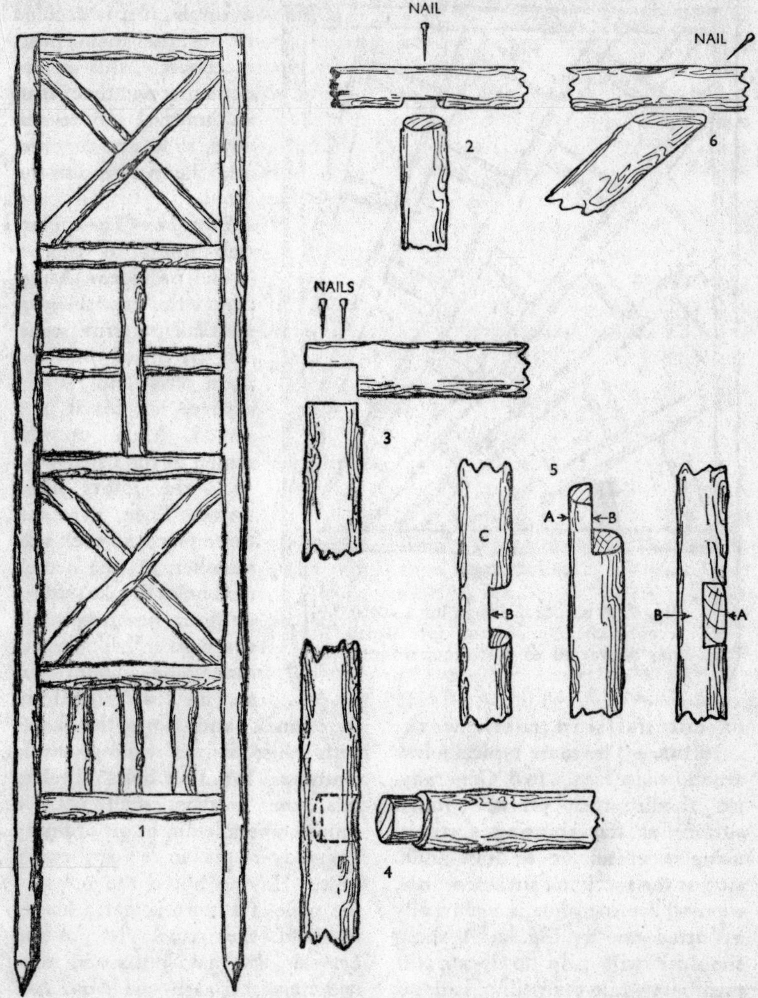

Fig. 1. Shows the side frame for a rustic arch and Figs. 2 to 6 illustrate typical joints that may be used in the construction of rustic arches, screens, panels and pergolas. Where diagonal bracing pieces cross, joint each piece as shown in C, Fig. 5.

whole structure. In top joints such as Fig. 2, we can use a coach-screw to pull the top bar down to the post if the latter is stout enough. Bore a clearing hole in the top bar, and a smaller hole (it must go deep enough) in the post. Much depends on the kind and condition of the timber as to whether it will take a screw and hold tight. Failing a screw, a 4in. to 6in. round wire nail must be used. Never make use

Fig. 7. A practical design for a rustic screen, the dimensions for which may be varied to suit requirements.

of cut nails in rustic work.

Joints.—The more typical joints are shown in Figs. 2 to 6. Generally, we should trim off the rough surface at the abutting surfaces, using a chisel or a draw-knife. Recess the receiving surface a little, even where the joint is technically a butted one as Fig. 2. A slight shoulder will help to locate the members while the nailing is done; if the latter is sound and accurate, the shoulder will give support in addition. While all main members must be fixed while in the erected position, we can use a more convenient process for the filling or panels of the screens, etc. This is to assemble the panels separately, and to attach the complete unit to the main framework afterwards. For example, if it is decided to set the main posts in concrete, this can be done first and then, after an interval of several days, to let the concrete set, the panels can be fitted.

Panels.—The spider-web motif in Fig. 7 (which provides a change from the usual geometrical patterns seen), can be fitted between main posts and rails in a space left for it in a screen. Make up the screen in the usual way, with the joints illustrated. Then, at about three places in each side member of the panel, drill holes to take (easily) a $\frac{3}{16}$in. coach-bolt. If the worker has a wheel brace, he should put a $\frac{1}{4}$in. twist drill in the chuck and bore the holes with this; it will allow ample clearance for the bolts. Failing this, use a twist drill with a square taper shank, or an ordinary $\frac{1}{4}$in. auger bit in a carpenter's brace. Having bored the holes in the panel framework, get a helper to hold the panel in position between the main posts and rails, and mark through one *panel hole* at one post to indicate where the *post hole* is to be drilled. Take out the panel, bore this one hole, and put a bolt through. Then deal with the hole in the other post and, after marking, bore this. If the first was put through near the top end of the post, bore the next one near the lower part of the second post. Put on nuts and tighten a little; mark the posts and rails for all the remaining holes. Take out the panel once more; complete the boring, and finish the job. Another method is, after fixing the panel with two bolts at each side, to bore *entirely through* posts or rails *and* panel-frame members *from the outside*; then the bolts can be knocked through and locked in position by nuts. A drill or auger bit of suitable length is indispensable for this quicker method.

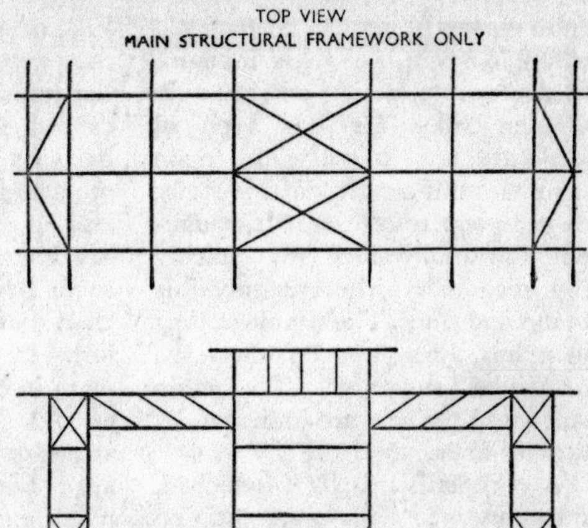

Figs. 8 and 9. Plan and side elevation of a strong pergola. Intervening areas between the main timbers may be filled in with designs in light rustic wood to suit individual requirements.

Screens.—Do not overdo the ornamental panels; let some of the intervening length of the structure be plainer, to set off the panels. Utilize this plainer portion to work in some stout and strong members that will resist wind pressure. A screen and one or more archways can be combined in a pleasing composite design to suit personal taste. Similarly, a screen can be made part of a pergola, or can flank the latter. Wherever the structure turns at an angle a much stronger post should be used at the turning point. It should be strutted at the foot in two or three directions to provide extra strength.

Arches.—Fig. 1 shows a straightforward design which is easy to assemble. It can have a square head, or if suitable timber can be picked out which has a natural arched form, this can be utilized instead. The fewer joints there are in the cross bars, the stronger the arch will be, so that a plain form of head is the best. Make up each side of the archway separately, leaving good long butts to go into the ground. Match the two sides; then insert the butts into holes dug for them. Brace the two sides together temporarily with two pieces of batten, and then nail on the top bars that will span between the sides. Here again we can use bolts to fix the head of the arch to the horizontal bars of the arch sides. In fact, this is the preferable method, avoiding any heavy hammering.

Pergolas.—We must not lose sight of the main function of a pergola, which is to afford support to climbing plants. This involves the use of many fairly slight cross members on top of the main framework; if the latter is made strong enough, the filling can be renewed when, in a couple of years, it begins to deteriorate, as it probably will. Golden rules for this type of structure are to make the main members sufficiently stiff and stout; to use good sound joints throughout; and to introduce cross-bracing (by diagonals) wherever possible in top and sides. The simple outline diagrams, Figs. 8 and 9, show the principles suggested. The main structural timbers are indicated by heavier lines.

A pergola is usually a detached, free-standing structure, and on that account must depend on its posts for the main support. So make the end posts, and some intermediate ones of stouter timber than the rest. Fix short struts (see Fig. 9) to these particular posts; they need not be unsightly. Often the middle part of the pergola is carried up higher than the end parts, as in Fig. 9; this will give an opportunity of using stouter stuff, and of working in some cross-bracing here. Since the pergola spans over a pathway, there is no chance of putting in low cross-bars between the two side screens; but work in bars up higher, just giving enough headroom below. Side struts to the main posts will help, also, but the main support, as mentioned earlier, must be got by using stout posts, and by taking them down deep enough for stability against broadside wind-pressure. This is most important in exposed positions.

Fences and Wire Netting

CLOSE-BOARDED garden fences offer great resistance to the wind and are apt in time to be made unstable as a result of wind pressure. Because the boarding impedes the prevailing wind, the uprights are subjected to buffeting and are liable to become loosened in the ground. This places a great strain on the cross pieces, which may eventually snap, causing a whole span of the fence to collapse.

At the first sign of this trouble the upright should be securely supported. This may be done with stout wire if the prevailing wind is away from one's own land, or with a timber crutch if the post inclines inwards. The anchoring wire may be lapped around the top of the post and its lower end secured to a stout stake driven into the ground at a sharp angle three or four feet to the front from the base of the post, see Fig. 1. If the use of a timber stay is indicated, the top of this should be wedged beneath a wooden block screwed to the post's top, the lower end being jammed against a brick or other substantial object buried a foot deep well out from the line of the fence, as shown in Fig. 2.

It is essential, of course, that this stay should extend to the post's top, or near to it. If its upper end is lodged too low down it will act not as a support but as a lever to help the wind lift the post clean out of the ground. The limb of a tree, fairly straight, two or three inches thick and sawn to the proper length will serve the purpose quite efficiently.

To prevent further trouble with the wind, the boarding may be

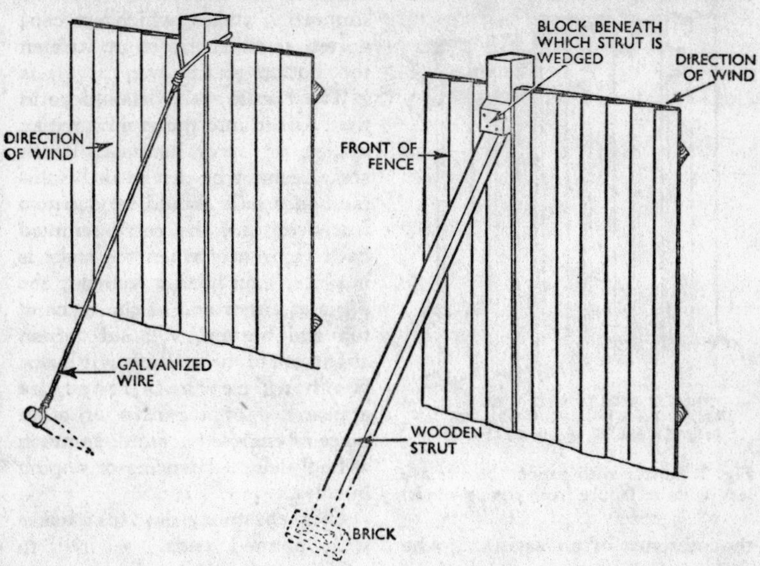

Figs. 1 and 2. Show alternative methods of bracing or strutting the main uprights of a fence. Note the indications of prevailing wind direction.

removed and then replaced spaced out with gaps of two to three inches between boards, see Fig. 3. Removal of the boarding needs care to prevent splitting. During the replacement the opportunity arises to discard those boards showing greatest wear. Supporting cross pieces which also are defective can be replaced at the same time with less heavy timber, say 2in. × ¾in. The object of spacing boards in this manner is to allow the wind to pass through the gaps and so reduce strain on the uprights; this procedure, however, may not be appropriate in all cases. If, for example, a thoroughly efficient wind-break is desired it would be useless. But even here it is generally possible to decrease the height of the boards without sacrificing that protection from the wind to any appreciable extent, thus lessening the total area exposed to the force of the wind and thereby lessening the strain imposed on the uprights.

If new posts are needed, a timber merchant should be asked for something superior, in the way of well seasoned timber, free from defects. Lower ends last longer if soaked in creosote (merely painting the surface with this preservative is insufficient), or if generously tarred before the post is lowered into the hole, which should be at least 2ft. deep. All fragments of broken wood from the old post should be removed, and the hole deepened and enlarged. If several new posts are being dealt with, a cord line is desirable to ensure perfect alignment.

The job is eased considerably by

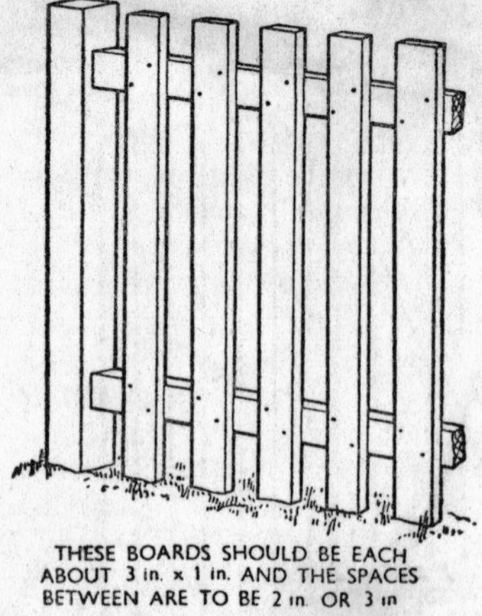
THESE BOARDS SHOULD BE EACH ABOUT 3 in. x 1 in. AND THE SPACES BETWEEN ARE TO BE 2 in. OR 3 in

Fig. 3. Fences with gapped boards are less liable to failure from strong winds.

the presence of an assistant, who will hold the post upright whilst the soil is returned and rammed hard all around. Even the hardest ramming will be ineffective if the hole is completely filled in before being rammed. The soil should be returned a little at a time and rammed down in layers. Consolidation throughout the full depth is then secured. If the soil is of a light, loose nature, bedding the bottom 12in. of the posts in concrete is worth considering, to give security and permanance to the bedding of the posts.

A length of boarded fencing, wrecked in a gale, might well be replaced temporarily with hurdles. These can be obtained in a variety of heights, and when in position are not displeasing. They do not give the complete protection against strong winds afforded by close boarding, but adequately serve every other purpose. It goes without saying that the taller the hurdle the stouter should be the supporting stakes, which are connected together by stout wire at top, bottom and midway.

The hurdle stakes should go in first, driven into the ground with a mallet, or heavy hammer. If the stakes cannot be driven in by this method a hole should be dug two feet deep and the earth rammed back vigorously when the stake is in place. Taut lines, attached to the posts at either end of the fence at top and bottom, will aid correct alignment of the intermediate posts. Nothing detracts from the appearance of a garden or other piece of enclosed ground, so much as badly aligned fencing or sloping hurdles.

Cleft chestnut pales (split stakes with pointed ends), secured to galvanized wire at intervals of about two inches, form an admirable fence where complete privacy is not a prime consideration and strong winds have not to be baffled. Lengths of this fencing are supplied in rolls, and erection is not difficult. Where cost is considered prohibitive, purchase might be restricted to galvanized iron wire and rough but substantial stakes, the latter to be stapled to the wire before erection.

Two rows of wire are needed, one to run nine inches down from the top line of the stakes, the other nine inches up from the bottom. The distance between the stakes (2 or more inches) must be the same at top and bottom or the result will be unsightly, and the stakes (or pales) must all be of the same length.

Stout posts at each end of the fence are very necessary because these will absorb much of the strain imposed when the fence has been erected, although intermediate posts or stakes, driven deeply into the ground, will be used. These will be positioned and aligned by a taut line at ground level. The posts at each end of the fence, as substantial as can be procured, should be sunk 2ft. deep and each should be provided with a strut secured in line with the run of the fence as shown in Fig. 4.

The outer ends of the horizontal wires will be twisted round the posts at each end and there firmly secured. Intermediate posts should be set up about 6ft. apart, and the horizontal wires stapled to them on the side most exposed to the wind. The paling can now be unrolled as far as the first intermediate post, and attached thereto with a couple of twists of wire, top and bottom. This procedure is repeated until erection is completed.

An alternative method can be resorted to in wiring stakes (split or otherwise) directly to two lines of strong galvanized wire. Posts at each end and the intermediate posts are first erected, two rows of stout wire are then stretched horizontally from end to end and twisted around each intermediate post. The stakes are then driven into the ground and fastened to the wires at 3in. intervals or according to requirements. This type of garden fencing is often useful for making a run for fowls, and wire netting may be substituted for the stakes or poles if preferred.

A wire netting fence is admirable as a garden division or boundary. Posts 3in. square and 2ft. longer than the intended height of the fence are first thoroughly creosoted, and after the liquid has been given time to soak in the posts are erected, with 2ft. of the length underground. The wire netting, unrolled as required, is attached to the end posts and intermediates with staples. If assistance can be had, the wire should be unrolled 8 or 10ft. at a time and strained, staples being driven home when it is seen that the top edge of the netting is running level. The assistant is useful for holding each support firm while the staples are being knocked in. Taut lines, stretched between the end posts at top and bottom should be used to secure a straight run and ensure that the intermediates are really upright.

Ramming at the base needs to be thorough, and struts should be provided at the extreme ends (as previously described). It is quite in order, however, to omit one strut, or both, if other firm anchorage exists, such as a wall to which the extreme posts can be secured.

A combination of boarded fence

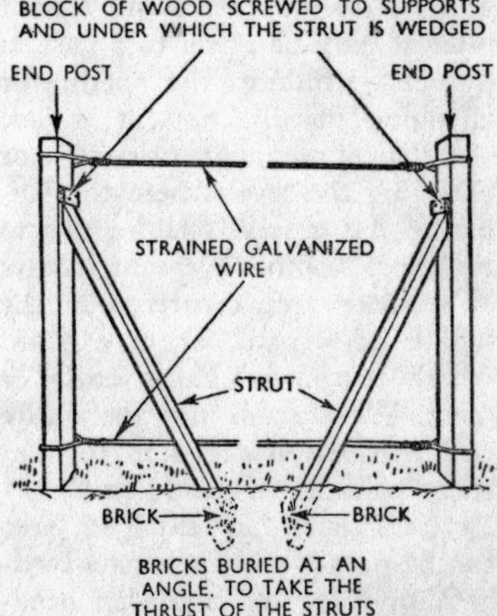

Fig. 4. An example of strutting and wiring of end posts for a fence.

surmounted by wire netting will secure increased height, where the garden fence is too low to support climbing roses or other plants. For this purpose netting has an advantage over a trellis extension in that it offers much less resistance to the wind, an important consideration in most districts. Uprights, about $1\frac{1}{2}$in. × 1in., should be nailed or screwed to the existing supports, the overlap extending for at least 2ft., and they should then be creosoted.

Galvanized iron wire should be run across these additional uprights, both at the top and at an inch above the top edge of the fence. The wire netting is stapled to the new uprights, and its top and bottom edges are then wired at intervals to the horizontal lines. These lines keep the netting taut and prevent sagging. Stapling the netting may present some difficulty if no assistant is available to brace the new uprights while the work is in progress, but in this case the netting, well stretched, may be secured to the posts with a turn or two of wire, at top, bottom and midway.

Maintenance of a boarded fence, apart from the details already given, consists chiefly in nailing up loose boards immediately they show signs of coming adrift, and in ramming at the base of supports when this is necessary. Ivy or Virginia creeper growing over the fence should not be allowed to push stems between close boarding, loosened. These plants should never be allowed to assume such dense growth that the fence is overweighted. Furthermore, dense growth will quickly cause wood rot in the timbering of the fence.

Garden Paths

FIRST determine the width and direction of the path. Added interest may be given to a garden by (1) winding the path, or changing its direction at angles; and (2) by stepping, terracing, or changing the level where the layout of the ground enables this to be done. Another pleasant feature is a wider area contrived in the length of a path, or at a point where two main paths cross or meet. Whether or not the entire path is paved in stones of irregular shape or uniform slabs (see CRAZY PAVING), such an enlarged area can be paved, and perhaps a bird-bath or some other garden ornament placed in the centre.

A square, or an octagon, is a pleasing shape for the paved space. A circular plot can be laid out by fixing the centre point, and then using a taut cord, or a length of lath, of the chosen radius (half the diameter of the circle). Tie a long nail to the outer end of the cord, or drive it through a hole at the corresponding end of the lath, and so scribe out the circle on the ground. The centre point may be a stake driven in. If a lath is used, put a nail through the inner end, and let it be driven into the top of the stake.

Laying Out the Paths.—We will assume that the garden plot slopes down from the house. Provide some stout stakes about 18 to 24in. long, pointed at one end and

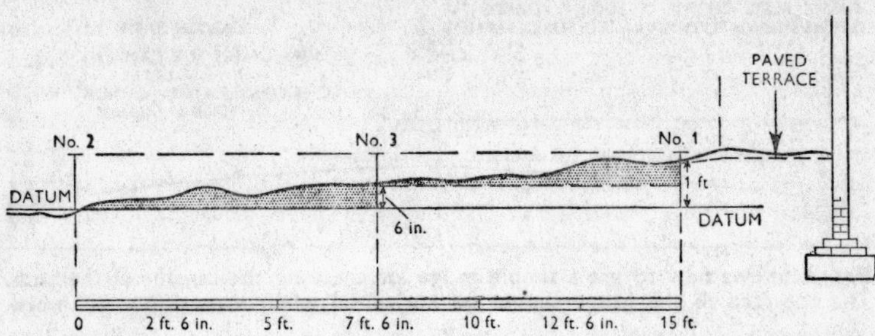

Fig. 1. Side elevation of sloping ground showing the dimensions for stepping a garden path for a 1ft. drop in 15ft. Remove earth as shown in shaded area.

square at the top; also a straight and level piece of batten, to be used with a spirit level. Two questions must be settled first: the direction of the path, and its level. With some simple stakes (not those mentioned above, which are for levelling) and some fine twine, outline the sides of the pathway, driving in stakes at the sides, about 12ft. apart, and connecting them lengthwise with the cord. Cut off a piece of batten to the exact width of the pathway, for use as a gauge. Ignore questions of level for the present, and merely outline the path and its direction. If a winding path is desired, the stakes must be more numerous, so as to indicate fairly closely where the path is to curve.

Levelling.—This does not mean making it flat, but denotes the determination of the slopes desired, the steps to be formed, and any drops in level that must be made. If the slope of the ground is an easy one, we may slope the path to correspond with the general line of the ground. But drive in two levelling stakes, one at the top end of the sloping piece and the other at the bottom, or at the point where the path is to take a fresh direction, or to change its level. Assuming that the drop is about 1ft. in 15ft. (see Fig. 1) drive in the top stake (No. 1) until its top is about 4in. above the ground (a short stake will do here, provided it is firmly set). Drive in a second stake (No. 2) at the bottom, letting it stand up a foot higher from ground level than the first one, i.e. 1ft. 4in. high.

At a point midway in the length of the slope, drive in a third stake (No. 3 in Fig. 1); rest the straightedge on the top of stake No. 1 and also on the top of No. 3. Tap down No. 3 until a spirit level laid on top of the straightedge shows the bubble central: stakes 3 and 1 will then be at the same height. Now proceed from No. 3 to No. 2; rest the straight edge on both, and adjust No. 2 until its top is level with No. 3 (and of course with No. 1). By measuring the height of the respective stakes above the ground it can be seen what is the drop in level between the highest point and the lowest.

A gradient of 1 in 15 (which we have assumed) is an easy one, but for the purposes of appearance and interest, we may decide to construct the path here in *two level*

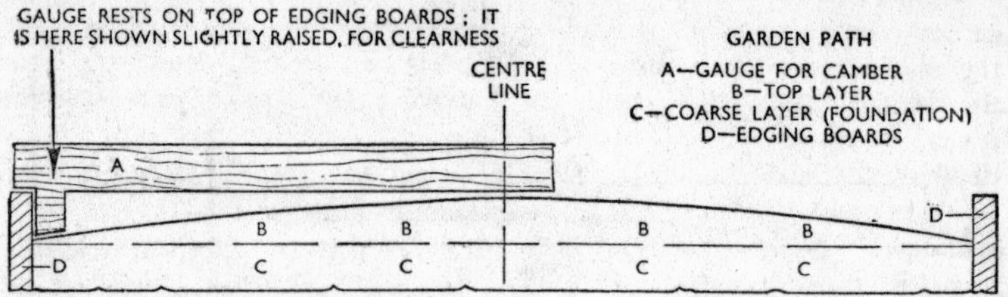

Fig. 2. Shows how to use a simple gauge for checking the camber of the path. The top face of the gauge should be horizontal when in position, as shown.

portions, each one dropping six inches. Clear the grass, etc. around the stakes with a mattock or a hoe if the turf is not to be saved. If it *is* to be preserved, use a spade or a turfing tool. Leave the levelling stakes undisturbed. Alongside stake No. 3 (at the midway point in the length of the 15ft. strip) drive in a peg approximately level with the surface after turfing. If the ground has sloped evenly, this will be six inches lower than the ground level at No. 1. Next outline the margins of the path with an edging tool or a sharpened spade. Dig out the soil, working upwards towards stake No. 1, where the depth should be 10in. below the top of the stake. Drive in a peg alongside No. 1, until a straightedge on this peg and on another peg by stake No. 3 gives a level indication.

Repeat the operation between stakes 3 and 2, driving a peg alongside No. 2 and taking out the soil back to No. 3 until a second 6in. step is formed. This is the basic method of dealing with a slope, or of first finding a level along or across a portion of a garden plot. When levelling an area for paving, work from a centre peg, and level out to the corners, if it is a rectangular space; by arranging the levelling pegs to stand up two inches or three inches (as the case may be) above the ground level, the tops of the pegs will mark the upper surface of the gravel or paving as finished. But the projection must be uniform with all the pegs.

Constructing the Paths.—On level sections, or portions where the slope is slight, we can proceed at once to take up turf and dig out the ground to a depth of 4 or 5in. for a foundation. The path will have been outlined by stakes and twine, as described earlier. The foundation may be made of any available solid material: coarse clinker, with a layer of finer clinker on top; clay heavily impregnated with gravel, with clean gravel on top; broken brick with fine clinker or gravel above. For CRAZY PAVING, see under this heading, where also are general directions for paving. The nature of the foundation necessarily depends on that of the soil; less thickness is needed on good firm ground. Shovel in the coarse material, roll it and ram it, using the rammer in places where the roller will not go. Spread the stuff with a length of straight batten (do not use the straightedge made for levelling, or it will be ruined for its own job).

The piece of batten cut to the width of the path (mentioned

earlier) can be used for spreading the material along the path, while the longer batten will serve to spread it from side to side. A depth of 2in. (in a total of 4in.) will be sufficient for the coarse or foundation layer. The next step is to fill in and spread the finer stuff. On a 4in. bed we have thus approximately 2in. for the top layer. Here we have to consider the drainage of the path, and it ought to be cambered so that the middle is about an inch higher than the sides. So the fine clinker or gravel must be heaped more freely at the middle line, and graduated off at the sides. Much can be done by rolling to produce an even camber.

Strictly speaking, a wooden gauge should be cut from a piece of batten, conforming on its under edge with the desired camber, but the striking of the necessary arc and the cutting of this gauge are difficult. As a compromise, make a half-width gauge like Fig. 2. A rise of 1 in 36 is usually enough, but for clearness, Fig. 2 shows a sharper rise of about 1 in 24.

If some thin edging board can be fixed at the sides of the pathway a neater and better job will result. Even if the edging rots and breaks away, the path will by that time have become stabilized. For a permanent wooden edging, use 4in. × 1in. board, fixed to stout stakes (1½in. × 1½in.) driven in the ground outside the path. Space the stakes not more than 6in. apart; where two lengths of edging board meet, use stakes of 2in. × 1½in. section, so that there is room for firm nailing. A less strong edging will not give satisfaction.

A fine clinker or gravel top layer can be bonded by a mixture of three sand to one Portland cement, mixed to a thick fluid and poured on the path after it has been finally rolled. This fluid mixture is known as slurry. Brush it over with an old stiff broom. This will by no means give a proper cement surface, but will add to the firmness and appearance of the top. At the sides some sort of gutter can even be formed by treatment with a garden trowel, in combination with a bricklayer's trowel, while the cement-impregnated layer is plastic. It may even be worth while to use a little more slurry here, to make a good job of the edges.

Drainage.—Although we have spoken of level portions of path, there ought always to be a slight slope or fall lengthwise, to cause water to run off, independently of any camber provided. Such a fall can be arranged when laying out and digging for the foundations.

Garden Frames

SIMPLEST form of garden frame is a wooden box without a lid, a sheet of glass covering the top. This is useful for raising seedlings, striking cuttings, and for covering a plant that needs winter protection. Owing to its small size its uses are limited. For ordinary purposes, involving the use of more ground space, the orthodox frame is to be recommended. This consists of a stout wooden construction with one or more movable lights (a light being the glass and

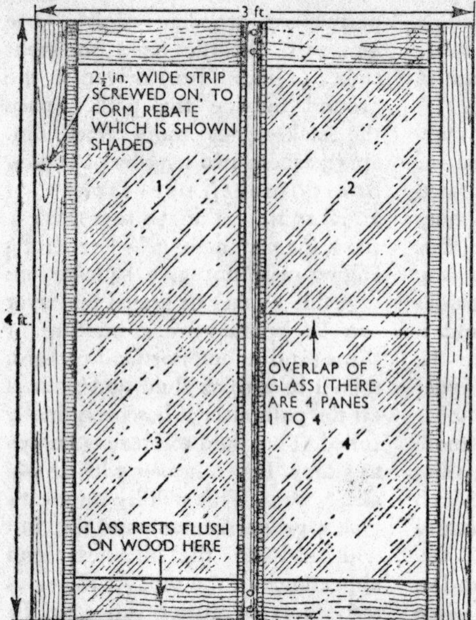

Fig. 1. Garden frame light. General dimensions. Note that panes 1 and 2 at top of light overlap above the lower panes 3 and 4.

difficulty may be overcome by joining the underside of the light to the back of the frame by a pair of stout butt hinges. To get at the interior of the frame the light is raised and hooked back to the wall or fence: the hook and chain being sufficiently strong to prevent any possibility of accident.

It is, of course, more convenient when the light slides back; and for general purposes two single-light frames are more valuable than a two-light frame. Seedlings and cuttings need to be hardened-off from the close atmosphere of the frame to open-air conditions, and the transition must be gradual. With two single-light frames the hardening-off process will be easy. The young plants are transferred from the frame in which they received very little ventilation to the second frame where air can be given in increasing amounts, while backward plants not yet ready for hardening-off remain for a further period in the first frame. The space made available in the first frame may then be used to raise more seedlings or to strike more cuttings.

A spare glazed window sash of the right kind makes a very useful light. It is not so useful if it consists of a number of small panes with wooden bars running across; these impede the escape of rain, as does the lower part of the window sash. Without transverse bars, a window sash comes nearer to requirements, its only drawback being the bottom part of the frame-

its framework, as shown in Fig. 4).

As the object of a frame is to afford protection against inclement weather and to trap the warmth of the sun, it should be of stout construction, completely waterproof and free from draughts. Also, the light (or lights) should slope down to the front so that rainwater readily runs from the glass.

The best site for a frame is one sheltered by wall or fence from the north wind, the frame being backed against the shelter, with the glass sloping to the south. If the available space is limited, the frame may have to be so close to the wall or fence that it is not possible for the light to be pushed right back when the contents of the frame need attention. That work. But this disadvantage may be overcome, to some extent, if the sash is placed on the frame so that its "weather" face points upwards.

It is waste of time trying to adapt to this purpose a window sash that has outlived its best days. There must be no looseness at the joints, or it will twist when handled and the glass will be broken; although something may be done to strengthen the sash by screwing metal angle-pieces at the corners. There must be no suspicion of decay in the woodwork, for the light must withstand rain from without and the action of moist atmosphere within.

As the sizes of window sashes vary, it is important when selecting the sashes that the garden frame should be constructed to match the dimensions of the sash. If a new light is to be constructed a useful size is 4ft. long by 3ft. wide, overall measurement, made of sound deal 3in. wide and 1¼in. thick, with the corners mortised and each secured with a dowel. See also Figs. 1 and 2.

Rebates to carry the glass (and putty) are contrived by screwing to the sides and top end of the new light, strips of wood 2½in. wide by ½in. thick. The bottom end has no rebate, the glass resting flush (or almost flush) upon it so that there is no obstacle to the escape of rain-water.

A length of ordinary sash bar divides the light down the centre, the ends being cut to fit the top and bottom rails, where they are secured by screws.

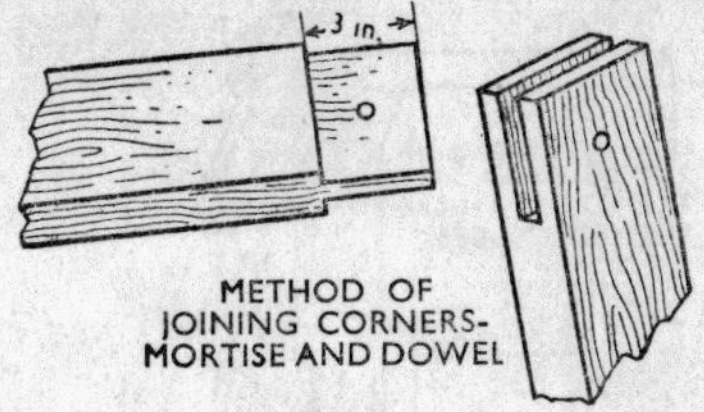

Fig. 2. An open mortise and tenon joint to be painted and secured by dowel.

Ordinary window or picture-frame glass may be used satisfactorily for the glazing of the sash, but as the light will be moved frequently any jarring movement must be avoided. The panes of glass should be puttied-in (see under WINDOWS), so that they overlap: about ¾in. of the bottom end of an upper pane projecting over the next lower pane. This is to prevent any possibility of rain dripping through, for plants hate drip. And though a moist atmosphere in the frame may be desirable in summer, to accelerate growth, the atmosphere must be dry in winter. Moist interior conditions in summer are induced by syringing.

To retain the panes of glass in position against the slope of the frame and to increase the holding

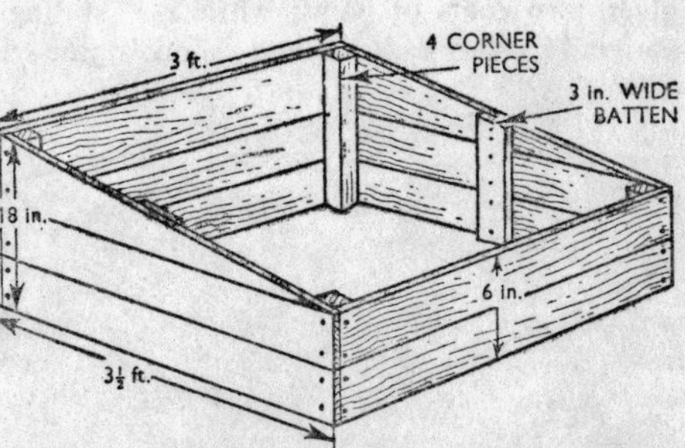

Fig. 3. Single light garden frame, showing main overall dimensions and general arrangement of the components when fully assembled.

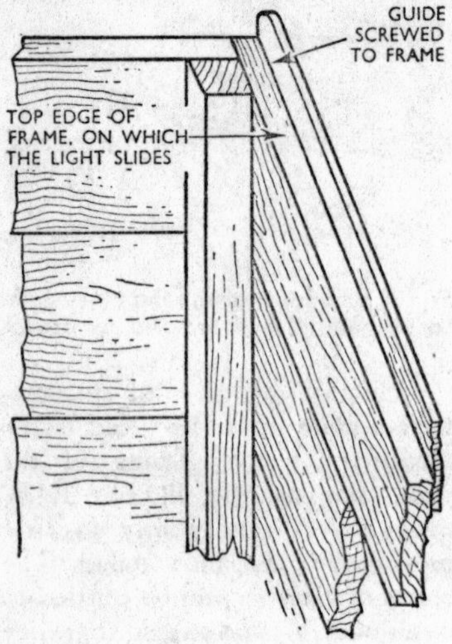

Fig. 4. Top corner view of frame showing the location of guide at side.

power of the putty, insert brads in the sides of the light at the bottom of each pane, so that these latter are supported before the top putty is pressed on. A light should consist of as few pieces of glass as possible, consistent with safety, because grime is apt to collect at the overlap, thus obscuring daylight.

When the frame light has been glazed, the woodwork should be given two coats of paint; white is generally used, well worked in on both sides. A light of the dimensions given will fit a frame $3\frac{1}{2}$ft. long by 3ft. wide; it can be 12in. deep at the front, and 18in. deep at the back, Fig. 3. The difference between length of frame and length of light allows of overhang of the latter at back and front, a further safeguard against entry of water. Some advocate the gouging out of a $\frac{1}{4}$in. deep channel or groove from side to side of the underside of the bottom end of the light, so that water shall not seep back into the frame. But if there is sufficient overhang, and a forward slope (of the angle indicated), the groove will not be essential.

Seasoned timber 6in. wide, not less than 1in. thick, and preferably tongued and grooved, is used in constructing the frame. Corner uprights, 2in. square, are cut to length as shown; and to each pair (a short and a long upright) the sides are screwed or nailed; then the front and the back are similarly attached. Across the centre of each side is then screwed a batten 3in. wide, 1in. thick, the tops of these, and the tops of the corner pieces, being sawn flush with the top edge of the framework.

To both sides, guides for the sliding light are screwed strips 3in. wide, 1in. thick. These are to project (see Fig. 4) so that their top edges fall level with the top faces of the light when this is in the closed position. Without these guides the light is apt to slide to left or right when being moved. Construction completed, the frame is given two coats of paint

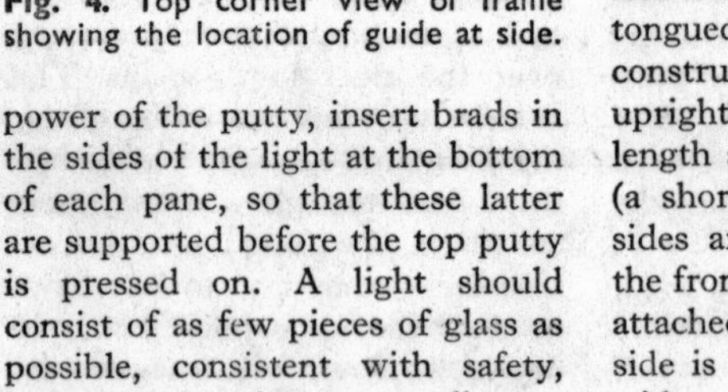

Fig. 5. A two-light garden frame, which may be divided temporarily by a light partition at the centre to support the inner sides of lights.

(green is the generally accepted colour) inside and out, working well into the corners. Fumes of the paint must be given time to dissipate before the frame is put to use.

To safeguard the lower part of the timber from decay through contact with the soil, the frame may be placed on a permanent border of bricks or flat tiles, lodged end-to-end. Either encroaches very little on the area of soil within the frame, and their provision should add years to the serviceability of the frame. There should be no spaces or cracks between the members of this slight foundation for wind to penetrate. Naturally, the site will be levelled before laying down the tiles or bricks, and the soil on which they are to rest will be made quite firm. With bricks, it is advisable to sink them half their depth, to prevent shifting.

Construction of a two-light frame (Fig. 5) is on similar lines, the width being increased to 6ft. with the addition of a centre-piece running from back to front. This centre-piece divides and supports the inner edges of the two lights. It is made of two pieces of ¾in. or 1in. timber, as shown in Fig. 6, screwed together. The lower piece is sunk in the frame at back and front, its top edge flush with the frame, and there screwed or nailed. A groove ¼in. wide and deep is made in the lower piece, on either side of the piece against which the lights will slide. The grooves run full length, their purpose being to carry away any rain-water that may trickle in between the lights. It will be noted that the two-light frame is further strengthened by two battens, screwed to the inside at front and back (Fig. 7); the tops of these should be cut to take the ends of the central dividing piece. A three-light frame will be 9ft. by 4ft., depth remaining as before; two dividing pieces, with corresponding battens, are provided.

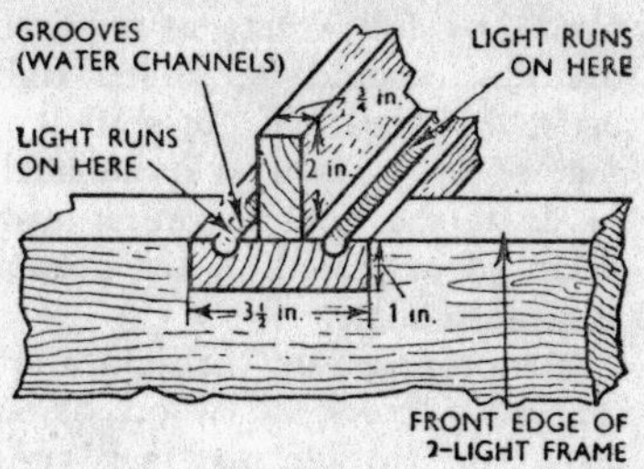

Fig. 6. A detail of the two-light central dividing piece showing water channels.

For easier handling of the lights when these have to be pulled back, metal handles may be screwed to the rear of each. When complete ventilation is to be given to the

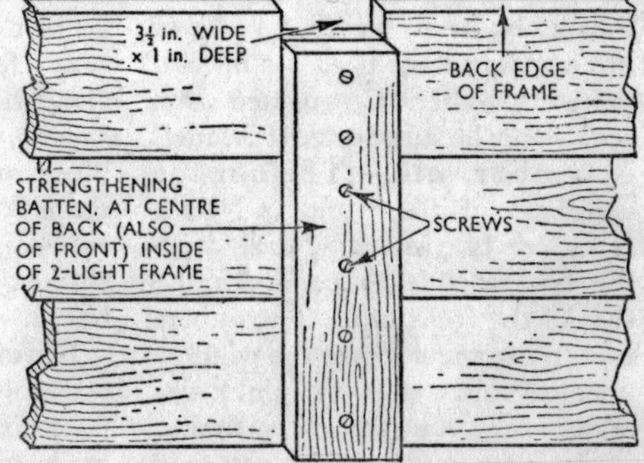

Fig. 7. Strengthening battens are fixed to the frame, front and back, immediately below central dividing piece which is screwed to the boards.

frame, or full access is required, the light should be pulled right back; the wind will not shift it in that position, as it is quite likely to do if the light is precariously balanced or rested on the ground at a sharp angle.

For propping up the light a few inches, a block of wood or an inverted flower pot is placed between the front edge of the light and the frame; or a stout stake will do. Whichever is used, the support should be given to both sides of the light; otherwise strain is thrown on the side without support and the frame of the light may become distorted.

Pieces of putty which may fall away or become loose should be renewed, and an annual repainting, particularly of the wood parts adjacent to the ground, will postpone the day when signs of decay become evident in the woodwork. Cracked panes of glass must be changed before the broken pieces drop on the seedlings, and to keep the frame weather-tight. Clean the glass panes at regular intervals.

Garden Shed

The shed described is a portable building, made in four main units, erected on a concrete or wooden base and bolted together. It can be dismantled in about half an hour. The principal members of the four frames should be mortised and tenoned together, but half-lap joints, carefully cut, and fitted, may be substituted. The roof is of corrugated asbestos-cement sheets, screwed to timbers resting on the tops of the end frames. The sheets are fixed separately, after the four units of the building have been set up and bolted together. Corrugated iron sheets may be substituted if desired.

Timber, etc.—The outside members of the front and back units are of 3in. × 2in. deal, with the narrow side to front. In the case of the front unit the members that frame and support the window opening also are of 3in. × 2in. material; all the rest of the timber is 2in. × 2in. section. It is assumed that the timber has been purchased to rough size, i.e., not planed. A ledged and braced door of simple construction can be made by the worker, and covered with matching or good weatherboard nailed on vertically. It is quite possible that a light door (half-glass would be an advantage) may be picked up by the reader at second-hand prices, or bought new. In that event the dimension of the door opening will, of course, be adapted to suit. A simple window frame and sash is easily made. The standard types, generally obtainable from a builder's merchant, will be too heavy for the job. The sides of the shed should be covered with good quality matching or weatherboard. The matching must be nailed vertically. Weatherboard must be nailed in horizontal lengths, each thick edge overlapping the previous board.

Floor.—A concrete floor is probably the best. But if a wood floor is preferred it should be made up of 1in. floorboards, with a plain edge, nailed to 3in. × 2in. joists, the latter spaced at 18in.

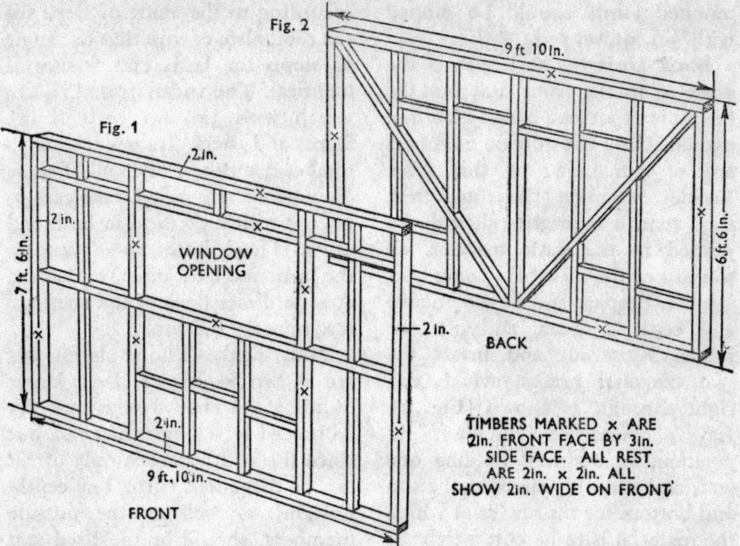

Figs. 1 and 2. Show general arrangement of front and back frames for garden shed.

intervals, measured from the centre lines.

Clear and level the site first. The joists, when laid, will run from front to back of the shed, and if it is considered advisable to lift the floor a little higher, three lengths of timber, 3in. × 2in. can be laid down first, running from side to side of the shed, one at the front, one at the back, and the third midway between. These are known as sleepers. Spike the joists to the sleepers at the proper spacing, then nail on the boards, which will run from side to side of the shed. Make the floor surface about 6in. longer and wider than the overall dimensions of the building, giving a 3in. projection on all sides.

Front Unit.—The overall dimensions of this unit are 7ft. 6in. high and 9ft. 10in. long. The outside members and the other stout ones marked with a cross in Fig. 1 must be cut to the full dimensions given, as they will be mortised and tenoned. Cut and joint the outside members; next deal with the 3in. × 2in. horizontal members. These posts are tenoned into the sill (bottom member) and the head (top member). Where they cross the horizontals they are halved to these latter, since the horizontals themselves are tenoned to the outside posts. The remaining studs (vertical and horizontal) are cut where they meet other members, and are tightly fitted and nailed (butt jointed). Note in Fig. 1 that the short cross members are shown staggered, so that the ends of adjacent pieces are accessible for nailing through the uprights. Be careful, in finally fitting the studs after the main members have been put together, not to drive these tenoned joints asunder by using too long studs elsewhere. The tenoned joints should be pinned with ½in. dowel rod.

Back Unit.—The length is the same as in the front unit but the height is a foot less, namely 6ft. 6in. overall. Only the outside members are of 3in. × 2in. in this case. Besides tenoning these together, the central upright should be jointed in the same manner, all the rest of the members being butt jointed. Prepare and fit the outside and central pieces, and pin the joints. Next cut and insert the two diagonal braces, which run right through as shown (Fig. 2). Lay a piece of 2in. × 2in. in position, an assistant holding one end, and carefully mark at the top and bottom for the angles at which the material is to be cut; a tight fit is necessary. This done, cut and fit the four uprights that remain, breaking joint at the intersection with the diagonal braces, and nailing obliquely to these diagonals at the intersection. Finally, fix the eight short horizontal pieces that stiffen the unit.

Door End.—In height, the two end units are two inches less than the front and back units, sloping off from 7ft. 4in. at the front to 6ft. 4in. at the back. This is to allow for the depth of the 2in. × 2in. purlins (mentioned above) on which the roof sheets rest. These purlins are spiked to the tops of the side frames, and the boarding on the outside of the sides is notched to let the purlin ends pass. Mortise and tenon the outside members and the post that forms one side of the door frame. The cross piece that acts as the head of the latter frame should be tenoned.

Care is needed in cutting the top of the posts to the proper bevel, according to the angle of slope for the roof; also, ensure that the angle of slope for both end frames is identical. The width overall is 6ft., which with 3in. for each of the front and back frames makes a total end width of 6ft. 6in. If these dimensions are varied, take care to get the width identical in both end units. These latter *stand between* the front and back units, so that the outside dimensions of the shed are 9ft. 10in. by 6ft. 6in.

Plain End.—The studs for this are shown in Fig. 4. In a larger building the ends would normally be braced by a single diagonal, but since the width here is only 6ft. it can be dispensed with. The centre upright, as well as the outside members, should be mortised and tenoned; the rest of the joints may be nailed.

Sheeting.—The boarding of the four frames is a simple matter, but in the case of the end units the position of the roof purlins must be settled, and the tops of the boards cut where they encounter the ends of the roof timbers. These boards will project 2in. above the top members of the unit and be cut off level to the proper slope, the notching for the purlins being done later. If horizontal boarding is adopted (i.e. weatherboarding), this projection will not be needed; the top board will be cut off level with the top member of the unit. After the purlins have been fixed and the corrugated sheets screwed down, a barge board consisting of a piece of 6in. × 1in. plain board is nailed to the ends of the purlins to cover the gap.

Roof.—The dimensions of the actual roof, measured over the front, back and end units, are something larger than the plan dimensions measured at floor level, for the slope of the roof adds to the length of the sides. But the shed has been designed to take 7ft. lengths of corrugated asbestos-cement, and this length will give a sufficient overlap at back and front. If, however, the pitch of the roof is to be altered, the length will be changed proportionately.

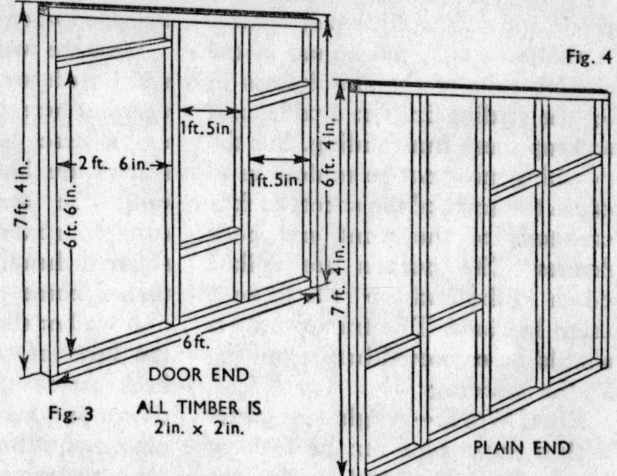

Figs. 3 and 4. The overall dimensions and general constructional arrangements of the framework at each end of the garden shed 2in. × 2in. timber used throughout.

The sheeting will run in a single piece from front to back; as the effective cover of a 2ft. 6in. sheet is 2ft. 1½in., we shall need five sheets in the length of the shed. The minimum satisfactory overlap at the sides of the sheets is one and a half corrugations, equal approximately to 4½in.

The asbestos-cement sheets should be *drilled* for the screws, using a twist drill with a square taper shank, in a carpenter's brace, or an ordinary round-shank drill in a wheel brace. Holes are made at the *tops* of the corrugations, not in the valleys, since water would run through in the latter position. Galvanized round head screws should be used, and one of the bent washers, specially supplied for this work, placed under the head of each screw. The hole must be an easy fit. These sheets are very satisfactory, but must not be subjected to jars or knocks.

The purlins on which the sheets are fixed will rest on the tops of the end frames, which are sloping, of course, whereas the tops of the front and back frames are square across. These latter timbers should be shaped by jack plane to make a bevel which will correspond to the slope of the sides. The bevel should be marked first at each end of the top rail; then a line should be carried along the inside face of the front rail, and along the outside face of the back rail, to mark where the slope should finish.

This should be done before the frames are boarded. With care the proper angle can be taken, to scale, from the dimensions in Fig. 3 and transferred by an adjustable bevel to the timber. Failing this operation, the operator may plane down the lowest edge of both front and back frame members so as to get an approximately correct seating for the corrugated sheets. These sheets, the operator must note, are screwed direct to the tops of the front and back frames. Two purlins will be sufficient, placed on the top of the shed so as to divide the span into three approximately equal spaces. A shallow notch can be cut in the sloping rails of the end frames to let the purlins drop in a trifle, and so keep them from sliding. But the notching must not be so deep as to cause the ends of the sheets to foul the tops of the front and back frames. The purlins are spiked down to the end top rails to keep them in place. The frame timbers should be creosoted before putting on the boarding.

Final Work.—A light zinc gutter with a down pipe can be fixed at the back of the shed, under the projecting eaves, the pipe discharging into a butt below. The gutter must slope a little down towards the outlet. After assembly, the boarding should have two good coats of creosote or some similar preservative.

Assembly.—It is advisable, after cutting and fitting the boarding, to leave the first three boards loose at each end of each frame. Tack them in position, not driving the nails right home; follow on with the rest of the boards, properly nailed on, until the three at the opposite end are reached, leaving these off after fitting. Stand the back frame in proper position on the shed floor, assuming that a wood floor has been laid, and hold it temporarily by two struts of quartering, one at the back and another at the front.

An assistant should be available during this operation. When the back frame is located in the correct position, bore two holes in the sill, near the ends, to take a $\frac{3}{8}$in. coach screw; bore a little way into the floor with a smaller bit, so that the worm of the screw can bite. The proper place for the screws is over a joist, but this cannot always be managed when assembling the parts.

Now the worker will see why the end boards were left off, since the opening here gives elbow-room to use a brace and bit. The coach screws are knocked down lightly until the screw bites, then a suitable spanner is put on the squared head, and the screw is turned home.

A washer should be placed under the head of the screw. With the back frame thus partly fastened down, put one of the end frames in place, abutting against the back properly; get an assistant to hold this steady while a hole is bored for one of the fixing bolts, at a point about 18in. up from the floor line. Mushroom-head bolts (often called coach bolts) are to be used, of suitable length to go through the 3in. thickness of the corresponding posts of the end unit, plus the thickness of the boarding of the shed sides.

Gently fix the end boards of the back frame, which were left off, tapping in the nails enough to hold the boards in place. Now bore through, from board to inside of shed, going through the post of the end unit; tap the bolt through with light blows, the head at the outer side. The square on the bolt, just under the head, will need to be driven in, and will hold the bolt tight against turning. Put on a nut and washer at the inside, and turn up finger-tight. Mount a step ladder (do not rest it against the job), and put in another bolt about 18in. from the top. Test the angle made by back frame and end frame, to see that they are square; insert two bolts in the sill as before. Proceed in the same way with the remaining end frame. Take down the two struts first put up, but nail a couple of pieces across the top of the side frames, to hold these steady.

Now offer up the front frame to the job, getting it in line with the posts of the end frames. If necessary, withdraw the screws holding the end frames to the floor, and adjust these frames for width. If all is satisfactory, bore for bolts, insert them, and then tighten all bolts. A third bolt at each corner can be put through now, for extra security. With an old brush, paint all the bolt ends with grease against rusting, slacking back one nut at a time and re-tightening it; this is a cleaner method than greasing the bolt end first, before insertion, and can be done when they are being finally tightened with the spanner.

All that remains is to nail on the loose boards firmly, and to put on the roof.

When erecting a shed on a concrete floor, the two frames first put up can be held together by a pair of large G-cramps over the adjacent posts. More strutting is advisable, since the frames cannot in this case be held down temporarily to the floor. The coach screws used with a wooden floor help to hold the shed against wind pressure, which might otherwise cause the shed to shift or slide on the floor.

With a concrete floor, the same result can be obtained by setting four bricks on the base at each angle, outside the shed and firmly cemented down to the base concrete or foundations.

Lawn Mowers

WHATEVER the type or make of lawn mower there are general directions which must be observed, in the interests of the operator, the lawn, and the machine. The most obvious precaution is, perhaps, most often neglected: the clearing of the lawn of stones and other small rubbish before mowing commences. The knives of a machine rotate at great speed, and it needs only the introduction of a small stone, or nail, between the knives and the bottom blade (which between them do the cutting) to damage the mower.

The counsel of perfection, therefore, is that the lawn should be swept each time before the mower gets to work. The alternative is for the operator to inspect the grass closely, walking methodically up and down the lawn, picking up any stones, nails, etc. which would otherwise damage the knives when the mower is in use. The bearings should be freshly oiled between operations. This makes a great difference to the results and to the operator of the machine by reducing labour. The holes through which oil is to be dripped are easily located. If any have become clogged with dirt, a piece of stiff wire will effect a clearance. Thick oil is a hindrance to free movement, and it is apt to collect dirt and pieces of grass. Ordinary cycle oil is a good substitute if the oil recommended by the makers cannot be obtained.

It is not possible for any machine to cut wet grass satisfactorily; even a motor mower will jib at that.

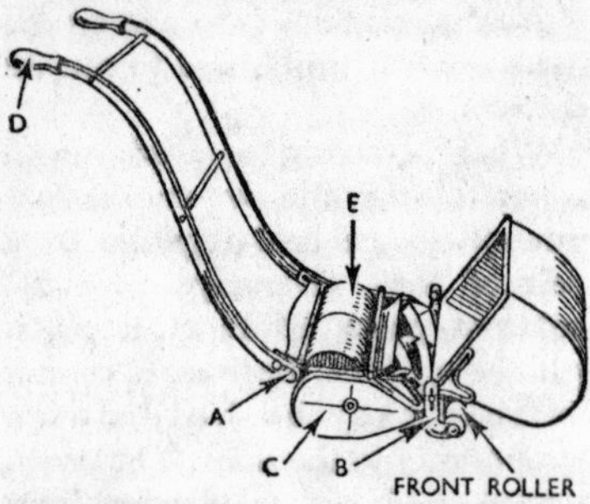

Fig. 1. View of typical lawn mower. A, bolts for adjusting handle height; B, front roller bracket; C, gear cover; D, handle; E, rear roller, geared to cutter.

Moderately dry grass is the best for mowing and, if there is any choice in the matter of time, the cool of the evening will cause less discomfort to the operator of the machine. Short strokes, then a pause, then another stroke, and so on, constitute a common and bad method of mowing. The machine should be run briskly and without pause to the end of the strip.

Bearing down on the handle, or handles, is another common error. The operator should stand up to the machine, so that the front rollers are always in contact with the ground. In some models it is possible to adapt the height of the handles to the user's requirements, the angle being altered by loosening bolts on either side of the base of the handles, and retightening the bolts when the angle has been adjusted, see A, Fig. 1.

Regulating Cut.—The closeness of cut can be regulated; in some types of machine by adjusting the bottom blade to the cutting cylinder (the knives); on other types the bottom blade is fixed and the cutting cylinder has to be adjusted to the blade. The method, in either case, is simple, tightening or slackening of screws being all that is required. These screws fix the positions of bearings located immediately above and at either end of the cutting cylinder. The makers issue printed instructions covering this and other points regarding operation and maintenance, and a leaflet or pamphlet can always be obtained on application, the number or name of the model being quoted.

Importance of this adjustment must not be disregarded. If the cutting cylinder and the bottom blade make too close contact the machine will be very hard to work. If the bottom blade rubs on the ground the mower will be difficult to push, the grass will be pressed down and imperfectly cut, turf will be sliced off, and the knives may be damaged. Always the bottom blade should clear the ground by not less than ¼in.; if the grass is long, the front roller should be lowered so that the blade is raised anything up to about ¾in., then when the long grass has been shortened the front roller is raised to the normal height to complete the close cutting.

On some types of machine the bracket on either side, carrying the spindles of the front roller (B, Fig. 1), is marked with indentations, these enabling the roller to be adjusted at perfect level, whatever the height. Cutting cannot be satisfactory unless the roller really is level. To see whether the bottom blade is clearing the ground, and by how much, the machine should be turned on its side, or turned right over, and a ruler or a straight stick placed across the wood roller and the side wheels (in the case of the side wheel type), or across the wood roller and the large land-roller (in the case of the roller type, Fig. 1). This will show the height of the blade: the latter should clear the ruler or stick by not less than ¼in.

When a grass box is used, the weight of this (loaded with cuttings) should be borne in mind. If the turf is damp, this added weight will tend to force the bottom blade down; the blade should therefore be somewhat higher than normal. When cutting without a box, the curved metal plate immediately behind the knives should be removed: the cuttings will not then be thrown forward to impede the forward movement of the machine.

To prevent damage to blade and knives when the machine is being moved along a path to or from the lawn, the handle should be depressed, to raise the front roller well clear of the ground; or in the case of the side wheel type the wooden handle should be thrust right over to the other side so that the knives are raised from the ground and taken out of gear.

At least once every season the knives will require sharpening. Like every other edge tool they become blunted with use; and here again the maker's instruction leaflet should be studied for the correct method of sharpening the knives. It is possible to have the knives sharpened by a firm specializing in the care of lawn mowers, but this is rather expensive, and it is worth doing at home. To sharpen the knives without removing from the machine, the edges of the knives are first liberally coated with oil, dripped on from the oil can; ordinary lubricating oil serves. Then fine emery powder is sprinkled on the oiled edges, also on to the oiled front edge of the bottom blade.

Knives and bottom plate are then adjusted so that these make light (not tight) contact throughout the full length, and the knives are briskly rotated in a backward direction, so that the abrasive puts on a clean cutting edge. In one model of the side-wheel type the procedure is as follows. After the knives and bottom plate have been adjusted so as to touch, the side

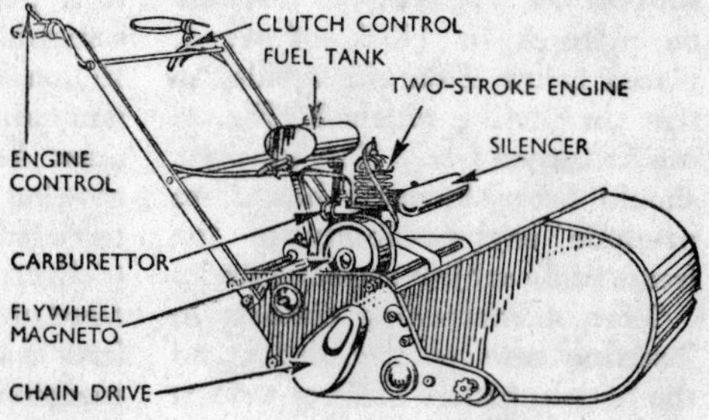

Fig. 2. A typical motor lawn mower, showing the main components and disposition of hand controls.

driving wheels are taken off, and the pinions (together with their pawls) are exchanged: that is the left and right pinions are changed over, the wheels then being replaced. Oil and fine emery powder are then applied, as previously described, the wood handle is pressed down with the left hand until the driving wheels can turn freely, the end of a spanner is inserted in a hole in the right-hand driving wheel (right-hand when standing at the handle), and this wheel is turned rapidly backward, reversing the motion of the knives. The grinding (sharpening) completed, the pinions are replaced in their original positions. With some models of the side-wheel type, a grinding pin is supplied for working the right-hand wheel in the above manner.

The roller type is sharpened similarly. With one of the most popular makes, the gear cover C, Fig. 1, is removed from the right-hand side. One of the wood handles, D, Fig. 1, is unscrewed and then screwed into the larger gear (revealed by removal of the gear cover), this wheel being turned rapidly backwards until sharpening is completed. Here it is essential to support the frame of the machine on a brick or block of wood, placed below it on either side, so that the driving rollers E, Fig. 1, can be turned freely. The supports should be of identical height, to preclude any possibility of the frame being subject to undue strain.

Test of sharpening consists in inserting between the blades and the bottom plate a piece of writing paper, or a leaf, then sharply rotating the knives. The paper or leaf should be cut neatly, as though with scissors. The test should be applied at intervals along the bottom blade, and adjustments made until the cut is perfect at all points. If the knives drag against the bottom blade, the grinding should be carried a stage further, more oil, emery powder and rotation applied until the desired result is obtained. The powder should not be allowed to penetrate into the machine; it must be shaken on carefully so that none finds its way to the gears or other moving parts. Clean away all traces of emery powder after the completion of the grinding operations.

There will come a time when the bottom blade will be chipped perhaps or blunted, or its extreme ends (not subjected to the general wear) will be higher than the remaining portion. These defects may be remedied by grinding the blade on a grindstone. The blade should be removed (on some types attachment is by countersunk screws on the underside) for renovation by grindstone.

Another counsel of perfection is that the machine should always be thoroughly cleaned, and edges of the knives and bottom blade be greased, after mowing and before it is put away. Mowing being a somewhat laborious task, this desirable attention is more often ignored. In that case, the cleaning must be done before the next mowing starts: knife edges being carefully scraped, the back (delivery) plate cleaned, rollers freed of dried grass, and oil dripped into every point provided. If the machine has been allowed to become very dirty, it can be cleaned by washing it with hot water and soap applied with a hard brush, this to be followed, after drying, by lubrication of the working components.

The efficiency of a motor mower (Fig. 2) engine depends on the same careful maintenance as the engine of a car, and here the maker's handbook should be carefully studied.

General Hints.—After using the mower wipe the cutting blades and working parts dry. Always store the machine in the toolshed, garage or under a shelter. Damp and moisture can quickly cause deterioration of both the appearance and working efficiency of the machine.

If the machine is to be stored away for the season thoroughly clean all components with a rag and stiff brush. Then dilute some petroleum jelly in a little cycle oil, which can be mixed to a smooth paste in a deep can. Using a small paint brush apply the jelly to all the unpainted metal working parts.

Examine the painted parts and if there are any spots which are blistered or show signs of flaking, scrape the paint from the affected area, rub briskly with emery paper until the metal is clean, and apply paint to match the original colour.

Garden Hose Reel

THE cheapest form of reel is a skeleton drum on which the hose is coiled. To rotate it, it is rolled along the ground. The first measure to be taken when such a reel has been purchased is to give it an extra coat of lead paint as a protection. Generally such articles as purchased from the shop have a pleasing, but not very durable, coat of colour. If the painting is deferred until after the reel has been in use for some weeks, spots of rust may appear, and no amount of painting afterwards will restore the surface to its original pristine condition. Rust may have penetrated under the edges of the corroded area, and will continue to eat away the metal.

Avoid any knocks or blows to the metalwork; use the reel gently always, and store it in a sheltered position when it is not in use. Empty the hose of water when coiling it up. In the case of a reel which has suffered damage or wear, go over the surface with a steel scraper and remove the paint around any rusted places. Next rub down the rusted spots with coarse emery cloth. Paint the bad places with red-lead mixed in linseed oil; when this is dry, apply ordinary lead paint over the same places. Finish with an overall coat of the same paint.

In the case of a reel with a frame, the treatment is also that outlined above; the bearing on which the reel rotates should be kept clean and well greased.

A wooden frame can be made for the simple reel first described if there is a central hole through which some sort of spindle can be inserted. Make up two A-shaped standards of stout wood, the cross-piece being on the outer side. Fix these standards to a stout wooden oblong frame to rest on the ground, so that when the reel is suspended it will clear the frame by a couple of inches.

Bore a hole through the side of each standard at the top, to take the spindle for the reel.

If possible, make the hole in the woodwork large enough to take a short piece of brass tube to act as a bearing for the spindle; the inside diameter of the tube must be suitable to the spindle thickness, to allow of easy rotation. If a piece of threaded steel rod is used for the spindle, it can be kept in place by nuts and washers on the ends, outside the wooden standards.

General Information.—Never leave the hose unreeled for any great length of time (i.e. exposed to the varying weather conditions) for, although imperceptible at first, deterioration of the material is accelerated by this form of neglect. Oil will also damage rubber.

Garden Gates

DEFECTS to gates are most usual in the posts and hinges. Posts rot or become loose after some years, and may deteriorate in a much shorter time if poor work or bad material has been used for the job. Let us take the case of posts which, though reasonably sound, have become loosened. First try to find the cause. The gate, if one of a pair (as at a car entrance), may not meet its fellow fairly; undue pressure will be applied to the post if an attempt is made to force it to close against the opposite gate. The meeting edges of the pair of gates must be eased so as to permit them to close together. Here it must be pointed out that such an adjustment, if made in the dry weather, should take account of the fact that the gate will be tighter, owing to swelling, in the wet season. However, assuming that the cause has been diagnosed, it can be dealt with later. Gate posts may loosen for other reasons, and will themselves cause the gate to jam, so we must not mistake the effect for the cause.

First Aid for a Loose Post.—Procure a piece of steel angle (see Fig. 2) about 1½in. × ¼in. × 2ft. 6in. Get the local blacksmith to cut or forge one end to a point for driving into the ground. At the opposite end, get three holes drilled to take ¼in. coach-screws. While a helper holds the loose post in an upright position, carefully drive the angle-stay into the ground, close up to the post, as in Fig. 1. It may be well to point the lower end of the stay very slightly inward, merely to prevent it going the other way and being too far away from the post. The stay may twist as you drive it, so guard against this by using hammer blows designed to correct any such defect. If a club-hammer can be borrowed, as used by the bricklayer or mason, this is the best tool for driving in the stay. When the latter has gone down about 18in. into the ground, fix it to the post by three coach-screws about 2in. long and ¼in. in diameter. Start the holes in the post with a gimlet, but do not go too far or make them too big. Insert a coach-screw, give it a gentle tap with a hammer, and proceed to turn it in by using a spanner of the proper size on the square head. In a single gate it is usually the post on the hanging side which fails first—that is, on the side to which the gate is hinged. But both posts may need support in this way.

Decayed Post.—If the top portion, from (say) an inch above the ground, is sound, the best repair is to use a concrete "repair post." This is placed close up to the existing post, in a hole carefully dug, and is bolted to the old post. The gate should be taken off first, and the post strutted or stayed so that it will not get out of place.

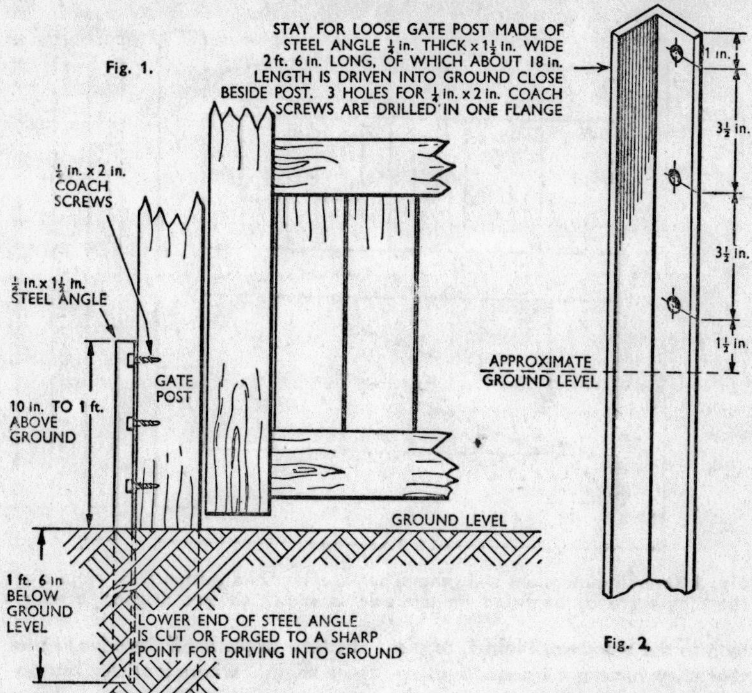

Figs. 1 and 2. Showing how to strengthen a gate post that has been weakened or has become loose in the ground. Drill the L-section stay as shown in Fig. 2 and drive into the ground as close as possible to the post. Gate should be removed to facilitate this work. Ensure post is vertical and tamp down earth all round.

The earth is replaced and rammed hard around the post and concrete butt. Makers of these repair-posts supply full instructions for their use. When the old post has gone beyond repair, a new wood or concrete one must be substituted. There are difficulties, however (such as getting a proper alignment), in this task which almost takes it outside the competence of the average handyman.

Sticking Gates.—When it is not the posts which are at fault, look to the hinges. Screws may have rusted, the hinges themselves may have become eroded by rust; in bad cases fit new hinges, choosing robust strap hinges in preference to cross garnets or the Tee pattern. If the clearance will not permit any other than the existing type to be used, bolt them *through* the gate with ¼in. coach-bolts instead of using screws. Try to avoid the old positions, on account of enlarged screw-holes in the posts; plug any old holes and trim off the plugs level with the surface. The gate should be packed up with blocks and wedges to the proper height before taking off or fixing hinges.

Besides attending to the hinges,

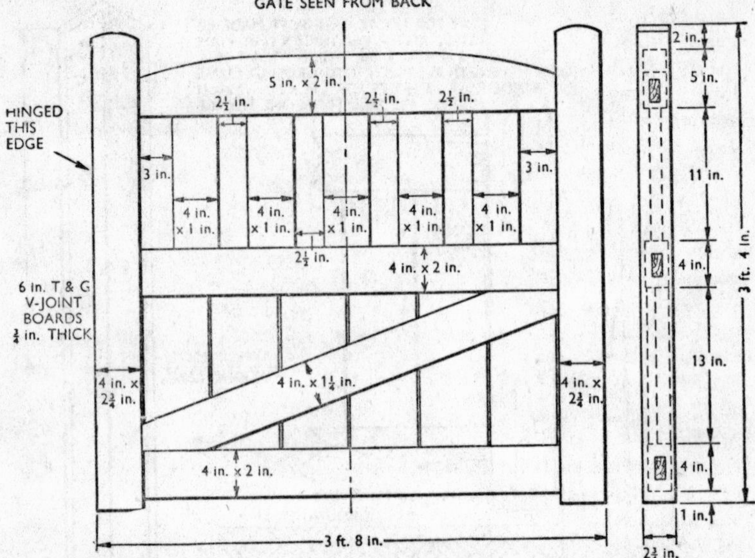

Fig. 3. Overall dimensions and general arrangement of a garden gate. Note that the hinges are to be fitted on left side as shown to suit diagonal bracing.

look to the woodwork joints, to see that they have not opened and so made the gate wider than at first. This would be corrected before rehanging the gate, as would any easing needed where the gate closes against the stop on the latch side. For loose joints, tap the side members of the gate frame close home against the shoulders; further, bore holes through the frame where the tenon passes, so that two pins cut from ⅜in. dowel can be driven through. The dowel should be a tight fit; if there is any doubt about this with the purchased rod, cut pins from oak or birch to a slight taper and drive in carefully. These pins need not be truly cylindrical; in fact, if they are octagonal they will be better, so long as they go in somewhat tightly. Trim off any projecting tenon ends with a chisel. Now is the time to plane off the edge of the gate slightly where it sticks, but do not overdo it, and be careful of the places where the tenons come through and show end-grain.

Fit a new latch if required. In the case of a pair of gates, give an eye to the stop-block in the centre. If it is doubtful, dig it out and put in a new one. With a little ingenuity a cast concrete one can be formed in place, the socket for the bolt being made of a piece of gas-barrel of suitable diameter. All that is needed is a mould or box formed of stout wood, into which the concrete is poured. This box should go down into the ground far enough to give strength; when the concrete has set hard, the box is knocked off, and the paving made good around.

Making a Garden Gate.—While there is almost endless

variety in the patterning of light gates, there are certain requirements which must be fulfilled if long life and satisfaction in service are to be ensured. In the mechanical sense a gate is a rather poor contrivance, since it hangs from a post which has to sustain not only the weight of the gate, but the stress due to leverage as the gate swings to and fro. So long as gates are not unduly wide, and are of light construction, they will answer even if the diagonal brace shown in Fig. 3 be omitted; but this brace, extending up from the lower part on the hanging side, helps to sustain the weight and transmit the load to the post at the best place. Further, such a cross-member, if tightly fitted and properly fixed, holds the gate together.

The gate illustrated in Fig. 3 is dimensioned at 3ft. 8in. wide, as for a single gate. A pair of such gates, but each 3ft. 6in. wide, would serve very well for the garage entrance to a forecourt. The sectional sizes given for the posts and rails are about the minimum for strong construction. Dealing in detail with the components, the stiles are cut from 4in. × $2\frac{3}{4}$in. timber. The three rails are all 2in. thick, tenoned into the stiles. The top rail is cut from timber 5in. wide, in order to allow the swept top to be got out. The middle rail is rebated on its *lower* edge at the front, so as to take the vee-joint match-boarding shown. The lower rail is similarly rebated on its *top* front edge. Behind this matchboard panel (our diagram shows the gate as seen from the back), a diagonal brace is fitted tightly and nailed to the stiles and rails. The thickness of the brace, and the depth of the rebate in the middle and lower rail, depend on the thickness of the matchboard used, which comes flush with the front of the gate. Our diagram, assuming that this panel is $\frac{3}{4}$in. thick, puts the thickness of the diagonal brace at $1\frac{1}{4}$in.

Between the middle and top rails, five slats cut from 4in. × 1in. timber are tenoned. The tenons need only be short ones. A simpler method is to plough a groove along the respective edges of the top and middle rails; to fit the slats (in this case of about $\frac{5}{8}$in. timber) into the groove, and to fill in the intervening spaces of the groove with blocks level with the rail. Yet another method is to use $\frac{5}{8}$in. slats and to make the mortises the full size of the slat ends. Another variation is to use round members instead of slats, sinking them into holes bored in the two rail edges. Sometimes it may be considered preferable to let the matchboard panel run through to the lower edge of the bottom rail, fixing it over this rail, which then must be of thinner timber—i.e. $1\frac{1}{4}$in. thick if we are to use $\frac{3}{4}$in. matchboard. Objections to this practice are made on the ground that the lower ends of the matchboard quickly rot despite the use of paint. It will be noticed that the bottom of the gate is kept well above the ground line.

Latches.—There are many types of latches designed for use on garden gates and the majority are quite simple to fit. The choice of any one of them is, of course, a matter of individual taste and requirement. The height and side at which the latch is secured are largely matters of convenience and requirement.

Garden Roller

THE roller here illustrated and described is made by filling an empty steel drum with concrete. The drum is not used merely as a mould, but is retained as the outer skin of the roller, and the concrete gives the necessary weight. Many of the types of drums available are formed with a number of corrugations at different parts of the height, and these would render the stripping of the mould difficult in any case.

Size and Weight.—Fig. 1 shows a drum which is 14in. in diameter and 18in. high. Such a drum when filled with concrete would weigh about 1¾ cwt. Wash out the drum with strong soda water or potash solution if it has contained anything of a greasy nature. Cut away a sector of the top (flat) portion (see Fig. 2), in order to allow the concrete to be filled in. Find the centre of the top and bottom, and make a hole that will allow a piece of gas-barrel to be passed through tightly (Fig. 1, B). The gas-barrel (or pipe) should be of the nominal size known as "half-inch", which will allow a rod of ⅝in. diameter to pass through to serve as the axle of the roller. The outside diameter of the gas-barrel is approximately ⅞in. (actually 27/32in.)

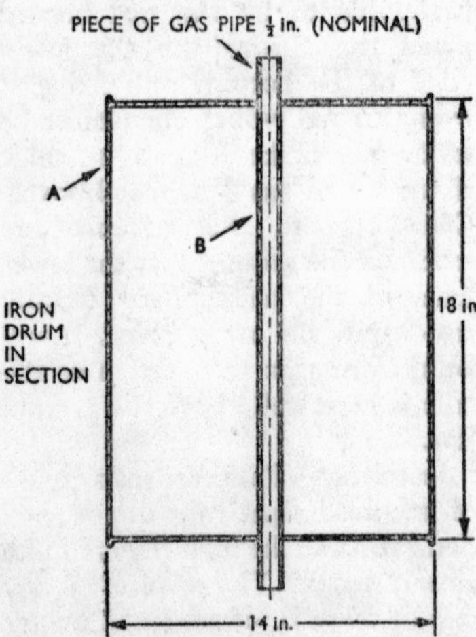

Fig. 1. Cross-section of an iron drum the ends of which have been drilled to accommodate a length of gas barrel or pipe approx. ⅞in. outside diameter.

Making the Roller.—Bore the central holes in top and bottom of the drum; push the piece of gas-barrel through so that it projects about three inches at the bottom and an inch or so at the top; stand the drum on the ground, level, so that the bottom part of the gas-barrel goes into the soil. Mix up enough concrete from gravel and Portland cement; three of gravel to one of cement will serve. Wet the inside of the drum, and fill in the concrete, tamping it down with the end of a piece of quartering. Don't put in large pieces of aggregate, and avoid empty "pockets" in the filling. Let the concrete stand a week to set and harden.

No more of the drum top should be cut away than is necessary to allow the concrete to be filled in easily; rely on the metal elsewhere to stiffen the roller and to hold the the spindle tube in correct upright position. The next job is to saw off the ends of the gas-barrel where they project; if there is an upstanding rim or flange to the drum, the gas-barrel must be left long enough to clear this, or else the side irons will not fit. No rim is shown in the diagrams, but many of these details depend on the kind of drum which is obtained; the dimensions of the yoke, etc. should be modified accordingly. When the ends of the gas-barrel have been sawn off, clean out any burr on the inside of the bore with a half-round coarse file.

Side Irons and Handle.—Two views of the side irons are given in Figs. 3 and 4; the latter shows how they are bent to reduce the span and fit them to the piece of oak which forms the shaft. They are let in flush to this shaft, in a shallow groove formed at each side. Four ⅜in. bolts secure the irons to the woodwork. Near the top end of the oak shaft a hole is bored to take a piece of ¾in. (nominal) gas-barrel, which forms the tee or cross-piece. It is driven tightly through, and secured further by a ¼in. bolt which passes clean through the oak and the tube, with a washer and nut underneath. (In making this hole for the bolt, drive the tube in place, and drill straight through the oak shaft and the tube at one go, so ensuring that the holes register.) The hole in the shaft to take the pipe itself should be approximately 1in. in diameter (actual outside diameter of the tube is $\frac{17}{16}$in., or $\frac{1}{16}$in. larger); make an "inch" hole with a bit, and enlarge it with a half-round rasp until the tube can be driven through.

The side irons should be made up from mild steel strip, 1½in. wide and ½in. thick. This is a job for the local blacksmith, who will bend and drill the pieces if given a drawing and the actual dimensions. These details will vary with the size of the drum to be used, and must be modified so that the same amount of clearance is given to the axle of

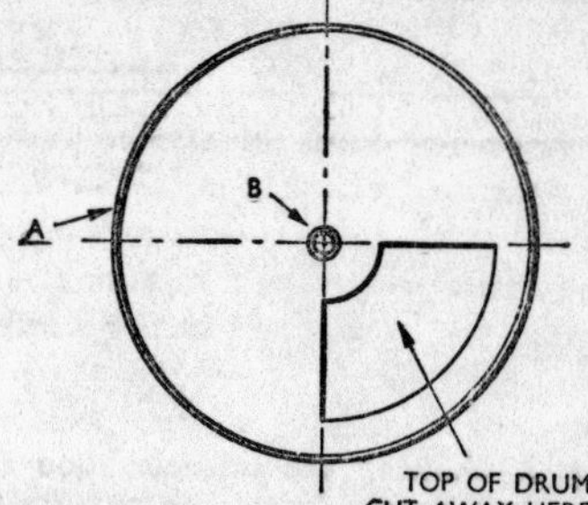

Fig. 2. Shows end view of iron drum cut away to facilitate filling in with concrete. A, outside of drum; B, gas barrel or pipe fitted in drum.

the roller. The bends need not follow our drawings closely; all that is needed is that the irons close in so as to fit against the oak shaft. It will be seen from Fig. 3 that a hole is to be drilled at 1in. from the wide end of the yoke; this hole, an easy ⅝in. in diameter, is for the axle. At 9in. from the same end (8in. distant from the centre of the first hole), another is drilled, but only ½in. in diameter; this is for a long half-inch bolt which acts as a stay to the yoke and keeps the side irons at the proper spacing. The head of the bolt comes close against one side iron at the outside. At the tail end, where the bolt is threaded, a nut should be put through *inside* the side iron, and then a washer and nut put on outside in the usual way. Alternatively, if we bolt in a short piece of 3in. × 2½in. wood temporarily to keep the spacing, we can ask the smith to rivet in a length of ⅝in. rod as a stay. But this means a little more trouble in fitting the side irons to the oak shaft, and in assembling the roller in the yoke.

Assembly.—Having got the side irons bent and drilled, fit them temporarily to the oak shaft and

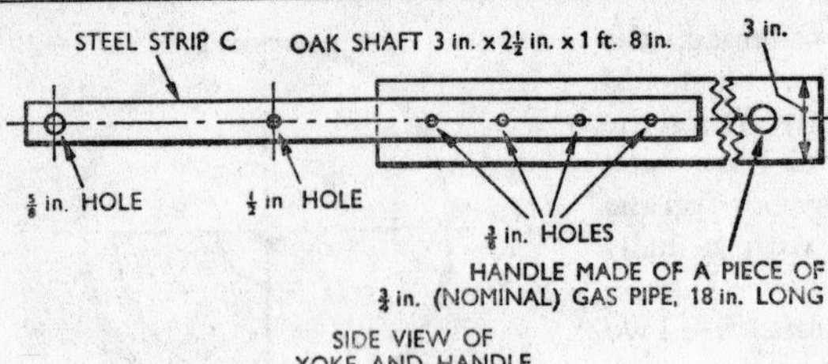

Fig. 3. Showing the side elevation arrangement of the yoke and handle for the garden roller. See also Fig. 4.

to the axle adjustment, however. Grease the axle and slip it through the gas-barrel, and put on a plain nut at each end, screwing it up so that about ⅛in. play is left between the inner face of the nut and the end of the gas-barrel. Next slip on a washer outside each nut and put on the two side irons. When the latter have been coupled together by the bolts, support the entire yolk and handle on a packing case so that it is level with the axle; now screw on an outer nut, leaving a little play between this and the side iron. When it has been made certain that the assembly is correct, a third nut should be screwed on outside of all, at each end, as a lock-nut to prevent the second one closing in on the irons. Two spanners are needed now; one is slipped over the second nut, while another is used to grip the outer nut and give it the slight extra grip to secure all firmly. Do not overtighten the lock nut.

The innermost nut (that on the inside of the side iron) may tend to slip; this can be prevented by one or two blows with a small cold chisel, which drive some of the metal of the axle into the nut itself, and so lock it against rotation. A better method for the handyman with some dexterity in metal-working, and the necessary tools at hand,

mark carefully for the four ⅜in. holes to take the bolts. Bore these holes, and then again try in the irons, inserting bolts and loosely screwing on the nuts. The next job is to put the axle through. This is a length of ⅝in. mild steel rod, threaded at each end far enough down—where it comes through the gas-barrel—to take nuts and washer. Going by the dimensions given in the diagrams, this means that the axle should be between 22in. and 23in. long; and the threaded part should extend at each end about 3in. inwards.

The axle is inserted and adjusted to the roller, and then the side irons are put on separately; next the oak shaft is bolted in place between the irons, and the staybolt put on and tightened up. First as

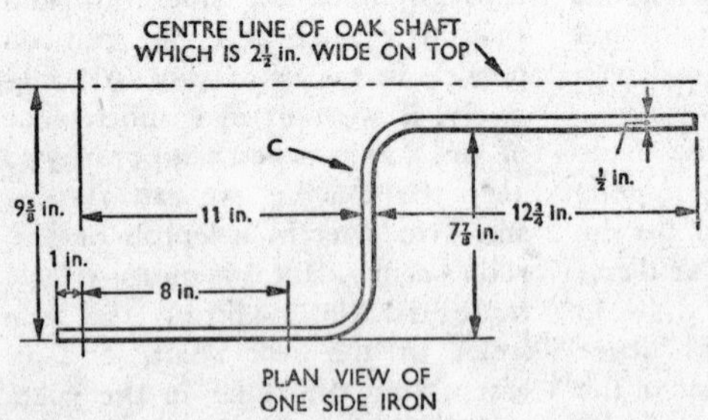

Fig. 4. Shows the plan view and dimensions of one side iron to form the yoke for garden roller. See also Fig. 3 for attachment of handle to side irons.

is to use a slotted hexagon nut for the innermost one. For this method, the nut is put on at the proper distance, and then is locked with a split pin which passes through two opposite slots and also through a hole which must be drilled through the axle. Also, by using a slotted hexagon nut and drilling the spindle again, we need only a single nut (the slotted one) outside the side iron. This is preferable where it can be adopted. Make a point of greasing the axle at these parts, otherwise rust will accumulate and jam the spindle.

Sun Parlour or Garden Shelter

A LEAN-TO type of roof has been chosen for this building because of the ease of construction, and also because this style allows of a more pleasant frontage. Again, the building is shown made up in four units or sections, plus a separate roof assembly. This involves the use of a little more quartering for the framework, but simplifies the work of construction. Moreover, the building is then portable and can be removed from one site to another.

Dimensions.—The frontage is 12ft. overall; the ends measure 8ft.; the height at front is 8ft. 3in., and at back it is 6ft. 9in. The roof, with its purlins and framework, adds a little to the total height, and the floor beneath the building raises the latter about 4in. from the ground level. Note that while the front and back units are the full width stated, the units for the two ends are narrower than the 8ft. overall width quoted above, since these units fit *between* the front and back frameworks, and therefore the thickness of the framework and its matchboard covering must be deducted in order to get the net width of the end-unit frameworks.

The reader should closely examine the skeleton view of the entire framework shown in Fig. 4; it gives all the timbers and indicates clearly where the end units fit into the structure. The appearance of the various sides when clothed with matchboarding is seen in Figs. 1 to 3. There are windows in both ends, and another at the back. Further, the two openings in the front of the

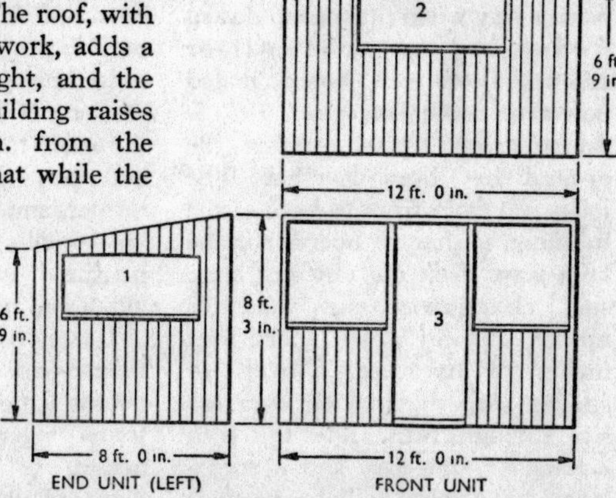

Figs. 1, 2 and 3. Show elevations of end, front and back units respectively of the garden parlour or sun shelter. Each unit is cladded with match boarding nailed to the framework, which is shown fully assembled in Fig. 4

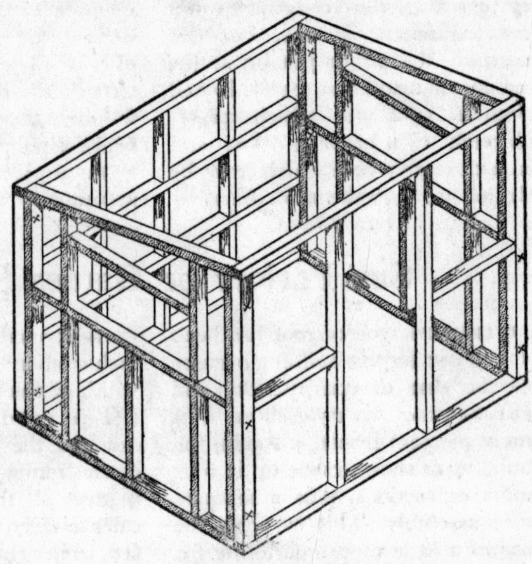

Fig. 4. The framework for the garden shelter or sun-parlour. The units should be firmly secured by bolts, nuts and washers at the points indicated by X.

building, to left and right of the doorway, may be closed in by removable glazed sashes in windy weather; or one opening may be closed and the other left empty. Such sashes would be held by stops nailed down to the top and bottom of the opening, and secured by iron buttons screwed to the face of the window frame. A half-glazed door is also optional. For convenience in summer weather, the hinges should be lift-off butts, and then the entire door could be taken off the hinges and removed. The handyman is strongly advised to contrive, somewhere inside the building, racks where the window sashes and door could stand out of harm's way when thus taken down.

Flooring.—A wooden floor composed of inch board nailed down on to joists 3in. × 2in. is prepared on the site, after the ground has been levelled. The joists run from front to back of the building, so that the boards run the long way. First dig out any loose soil, clear away any vegetable matter, and lay down about four inches of hardcore, clinker, or similar hard material all over the site, rolling it firm. Level this with a long straight-edge and a spirit-level. Nine joists will be needed; the boards should project all round about four inches beyond the outside of the shelter; this means that the joists should be about 8ft. 9in. long, and the boarding about 12ft. 8in. long.

Frameworks.—Sound deal, 3in. × 2in. in section, is used for most of the framing, but the outside posts of the front and back units may well be of 3in. × 3in. section. If it is desired to lessen the cost, the outside posts of the end units may be of 3in. × 2in. timber, and the bottom and middle horizontal pieces also, but the rest in these two units may be of 2in. × 2in. quartering.

Use mortise-and-tenon joints for the principal members, making the tenons a tight fit and driving the frame together with blows of a mallet, or by hammer with a piece of waste wood interposed between hammer and framework. The arrangement of posts and rails is clearly shown in Fig. 4: the posts rest on the sills (the horizontal lower members), tenons going into mortises in the sills. The top horizontal members are mortised to fit on to stub tenons formed on the top of the posts. When a framed unit is completed, raise it and allow it to lean against a wall in its natural position ("top" at the top, etc.) until ready for erection. Meanwhile apply two good coats of creosote or gas-tar, as a preservative.

Cladding.—Figs. 1 to 3 show matchboarding nailed vertically to the frames; it should not be thinner than $\frac{5}{8}$in. actual (which means $\frac{3}{4}$in. nominal) thickness. The cladding for the front unit can be left until the shelter frame has been erected in position. As for the three remaining units, let us take the left-hand end unit as an example of procedure. First note that the roofing sheets are fastened to purlins cut from 2in. × 2in. deal; these purlins run lengthwise of the roof, and rest upon the top members of the unit frames. It follows that the boarding, if it is to cover the depth of the purlins, must be approximately 2in. longer than the height of the end unit, and be cut away at certain places to allow the ends of the purlins to come through. Examine Fig. 1; begin nailing on matching at the left-hand side, allowing for the width of the post of the back frame, which has also to be covered by the first width of matching. Cut a length of board to the proper slant at the top (this can be marked with an adjustable bevel, setting the latter by the top and side of the end frame). Push the board up until it projects 2in. above the sloping top members of the end frame, and mark where it comes to the foot of this unit at the bottom; cut it off $\frac{1}{2}$in. shorter.

Tack on this first piece with nails that do not go far into the studding, so that it can be taken off later. Fit and tack the next piece in the same way, also the third length, which has to be cut around the window opening at the top. These three lengths are not to be permanently fixed at present. Proceed now with the remaining boards, which come below the window opening; but do not attach the short pieces on top of this opening for the time being.

The number of boards will depend on the width of matching available and chosen; if a narrower board has to be used to make up the width, fit it in somewhere at the middle of the unit. The groove or tongue of the commencing board would have to be planed off, of course, and similarly the edge of the final (right-hand) board. Proceeding along this unit, we come to the last three boards, which should be fitted and tacked only. The remaining end unit is to be dealt with precisely in the same manner. The back unit also should have the first three and last three boards loosely attached for the present.

Assembling and Erecting.—The three boards temporarily tacked are to be taken down before moving the units on to the platform, but first clearly mark these boards for their proper place. Three temporary struts made of quartering (2in. × 2in. will do) will be needed here; a helper should be ready to give a hand. Lift the back unit on to the floor and stand it in the proper position. In order to keep this position during the rest of the assembly, nail down two pieces of stout board at the back of the back unit, on the floor, close against the side of the woodwork. While the helper steadies the unit, nail one piece of strut to the top rail, the strut coming down slantwise in front and resting on the floor; drive a couple of spikes into the foot of the strut and through into the floor. Put another strut at the back of the unit, if there is room for it. With the aid of the assistant, lift the left-hand unit on to the floor and edge it into proper position. Secure it with a strut from top to the floor.

Get three hexagon head bolts ready, size $\frac{3}{8}$in. × 6in., with nuts and washers. Also have at hand a strong G-cramp big enough to span the two adjacent posts of the end unit and back unit. Put on the cramp at about the middle of the height. Test the end unit for level, and use thin wedges under the sill if needed to bring it horizontal. The first hole is to be bored a few inches below the middle horizontal rail. Fix a 1in. centre-bit in a brace and standing at the back of the back unit, bore into the post about $\frac{3}{4}$in. with this bit; replace the bit now with a $\frac{3}{8}$in. twist-bit. Complete the hole, right through both posts, with the smaller bit; withdraw it gently so as not to displace the units.

Next, insert the bolt from the back, and tap it gently through so that its tail projects from the left-hand post of the end unit. In order to get the nut screwed up tight, it may be necessary to interpose a thin plate of wood, about $\frac{1}{2}$in. thick, between the nut and the face of the post. (For we actually need bolts only about 5$\frac{1}{2}$in. long, but this is not a stock size). Have such a piece of wood, about 2in. square, all ready. Put on the wood plate, which forms a sort of washer; then slip on the steel washer, and screw on the nut. Finally, put an ordinary spanner on the nut and twist it up tightly. Here the bolt itself may turn round, so the handyman will now need a tubular spanner to put in the recess made by the large centre-bit and grip the spanner head. Let the helper see to this end, while the handyman now uses the long spanner on the nut.

Next, use a stool or an old chair to reach the topmost bolt-hole, and repeat the operation here. The third bolt, near the floor, must now go in in the same way. Final tightening may wait until later, but the bolts must be firm enough to hold the units steady. Nail a piece of board at the outside of the end unit, as was done with the back one, to keep these units from shifting along the floor. Let the struts stay in place while the right-hand unit is erected, bored and bolted. Then lay a piece of quartering, or a length of 1in. board, across the roof-space about 9in. from the front, and temporarily spike it down so that the distance between the two side units at the front is exactly the same as at the back, where the back unit settles this dimension.

Now the front unit is to be offered up to the rest of the building, and discrepancy corrected, by gentle taps with a hammer to one or other end frame, and a pair of G-cramps put on for the time. Bore for bolts at the left-hand end, taking the middle hole first and putting in that bolt. Move over to the right-hand side next, and insert a similar bolt (middle one) here. The rest of the assembly is easy. The strut to the back may have to be taken off before the front unit can be got in place.

Securing the Units of the Floor.—By taking off three first and last boards of the back and end units we incidentally exposed part of the sill of those frames. This space will probably be wide enough to allow a brace and bit to be used to bore a hole through sill and floor, to take a bolt which will fix the sill to the flooring. Two such bolts in each sill are needed. Another method is to bore a hole through the sill, and take it a little way into the flooring (where one of the joists comes in a suitable place) with a bit of smaller diameter. Then we can use a coach-screw instead of a bolt, and take it down into the joist as well as into the floor. Unless the building is fixed in some such way, it may move on the floor in high winds. Bolts are more satisfactory where they are able to be used.

Roof.—Four purlins will be needed—one over the front top rail, one over the back top rail, and two more equi-distant between these outer ones. Fix and mark the positions on the sloping top rails, for the two middle purlins. Plane off the top edges of the two outer purlins (which rest on the front and back frames) until the slope is in line with that of the tops of the two middle purlins. All the purlins can be spiked down on to the tops of the units, or, where the top frame-member is accessible, a bolt can be put through instead.

Corrugated asbestos-cement sheeting is recommended for the roofing, though corrugated steel can be used instead. Directions are given on another page for cutting and fixing these materials, but we may point out here that asbestos-cement can be sawn with a hack-saw, or a wood saw with not too coarse a tooth. Holes must be drilled with a twist drill, and screws should be used to fix the sheets to the purlins. No hammering must be done. Holes are made in the tops of the corrugations, not in the hollows, and a sufficient overlap must be given to the side seams. Sheets 9ft. long will be suitable for the job, and as they are 2ft. 6in. wide, we shall need six in all, allowing for overlap and side projections. There are specially designed screws and washers for corrugated roofing. Do not buy the "drive-screws" also sold for such work, since they have to be knocked in with a hammer. Ordinary galvanized screws are available for the job.

Trimming.—At the eaves a piece of inch board can be screwed on lengthwise to make a neat finish to the end units. A similar length of board, about 2½in. to 3in. deep, should be fixed to the top of the front unit, close under the roof, as a fascia. Window sills, cut from 1in. or 1¼in. board, can be fitted to all window openings; a bevelled-off piece of 3in. × 2in. deal or oak will make a threshold for the door opening, nailed down at the front and level with the top of the bottom frame member here. The spaces for the purlins can be cut away in the matchboard, and this board finally fixed; the first three and last three are already "off," so we can deal with them at the bench. Fix these boards with galvanized screws; they cover the bolts, and if we ever take down the shelter we shall need to remove the boards to give access to the bolts. The short boards on top of the window opening in the end units have not yet been fixed, so we can easily cut them where needed for the purlin ends. They can be nailed on permanently.

Suggestions for Windows.—Probably enough ventilation can be afforded by making one sash in the back window to open, with the usual stay and latch. If this plan is adopted, divide the back window space into three vertically, and make two of the divisions "fixed" sashes. The windows in the end units will normally be fixed glazing also. There is a simple way of glazing these, by adopting vertical glazing bars such as are used in greenhouse work. A glance at any glasshouse will give the handyman the details needed. Simple sashes on a similar plan can be made for the front of the sun parlour. A door (half-glass) is better bought than made, and probably a suitable one can occasionally be picked up second-hand.

The framing of the front unit would then have to be settled after obtaining the door. A transom can be inserted at the top of the doorway to suit, or the top panelled in with matchboard to fit the height of the door. There is much to be said, having gone to the trouble of building a substantial shelter, for making it an all-weather resort by these little extra details.

The entire inside of the building may be lined with sheets of building board screwed to the framework, which will give a better appearance and added comfort. The roof also can be finished off inside in this way.

When erecting the sun parlour, choose a day that is not windy. Go through the operations with your assistant beforehand, and make sure all the tools and appliances are conveniently near.

Cloches

A USEFUL size for the glass sides is 18in. × 12in. If the frames are sloped at an angle of 30 degrees, the height at the centre is approximately 10¼in. See Fig. 1, which shows how to set out a board as a jig for bending the wire end-frames. The board can be formed out of pieces of odd 6in. flooring battened together to give the necessary width and length. The board itself should be securely cramped to the bench or to a table while the bending is done. It will be seen that we need a baseline, on which are marked off points at 1in., 6in. and 12in. Then from the 6in. mark we must erect a perpendicular; the mark for the apex point comes between 10¼in. and 10⅓in. up from the baseline.

Pegs are needed around which to bend the wire; bore holes at the marked points and insert Gauge 12 wood screws, letting the shanks stand up about ¾in. above the base board. Then saw off the screw-heads with a hacksaw, so that they will not prevent lifting off the wires when completed. Galvanized or tinned iron wire, in Gauge 10, is suitable for the job, and no thinner gauge should be used, or the wires will not be stiff enough. Slip a piece of string around the pegs and allow 3in. for surplus; then cut off a piece of wire to the length measured by the string. The frame has an eye at the apex, through which the top wire shown in Fig. 3 is passed to assemble the cloche; note also, as seen in Fig. 2, that the external ends of the frame are bent up somewhat in the form of a hook to support the glass.

Start the hook on one end by bending gently in a vice; hook this end tightly on the left-hand peg, (Figs. 1 and 2 show the baseboard as it would be fixed on the bench) and take the wire up to and around the apex peg at the top. Here it should make a complete turn to form the eye, and should continue down to the right-hand peg, around which it is bent from the inside. Start the second hook or upturn, which can be finished off in the vice. A gentle tap with a light hammer, or a pull with a strong pair of pliers, will aid in forming the bends. Now take off the frame; the apex eye will probably need closing down with a hammer blow.

Cut off the surplus wire with a hacksaw; failing this tool, make a deep nick with a three-square file on two opposite sides of the wire at the point needed, when the pliers will finish the severence. (But if the file nicks are not taken deep enough the wire may be bent and damaged in trying to break it).

Bending the Top Wire.—After as many pairs of the end-frames have been formed up we must deal with the top member of the assembly, as shown in Fig. 3. This is turned up at the ends, and formed into a loop or handle at the middle of its length. A simple jig should be formed, screwing in pegs where needed, and screwing down a disk of hardwood as the "former" for the circular hoop, which is shown as having a circle of ¾in. radius. Pegs are needed wherever the wire changes direction except when the wood disk takes care of the lifting hoop. Although it would be more difficult to bend, a wire of even stouter gauge would be an advantage for this member. The handyman who is dextrous with the soldering bit could omit the central loop, which is the hardest piece of bending, and solder on a separately made loop formed from the 10-gauge wire.

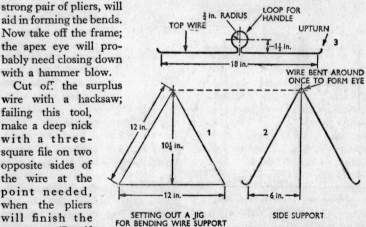

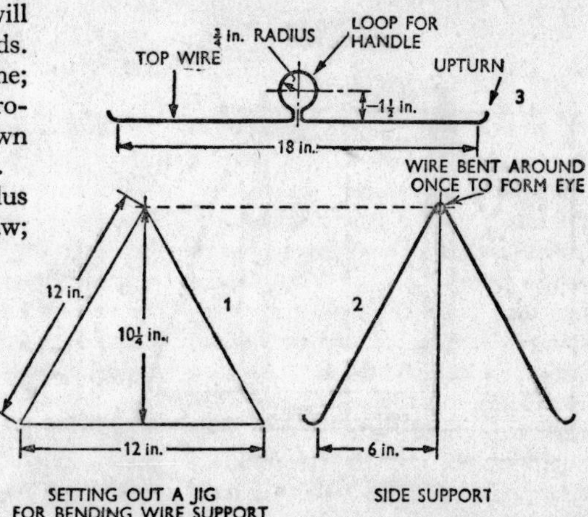

Figs. 1, 2 and 3. Show a wooden jig, a side frame and top wire respectively. The jig is used to form the side frame shown in Fig. 2. Loops at base of side frame support glass.

Again, the eyes at the apexes of the end frames could likewise be omitted, and a separate eye soldered into the top of the bend there.

Glass.—It may be possible to get glass in a size near 18in. × 12in., but not in these actual dimensions. In such case the size of the wire frames should be modified to suit. In any case, the top and lower edges on the long sides should be protected from harm by a strip of tinplate, or, much better, sheet zinc, about an inch wide and 18in. long, bent over to enclose the edge and stand up about ⅜in. on each side. If it is desired to save cost, the edge clips may be only about 6in. long, and be placed one at each outer side of the sheet, where it will lie against the hooks of the end-frames.

Assembly.—Take one top wire and a pair of end-frames; pass the ends of the top wire through the eyes of the end-frames, and stand the assembly approximately in place on the ground. Then lay a sheet of glass with the lower edge in the hooks and leaning against the side wires; follow by inserting the opposite sheet. Adjust finally, and secure the frames to the ground with simple wooden pegs. The end-frames may be kept at the proper distance apart, at the apex, by a few turns of tinned iron binding wire, or copper wire.

Longer Pattern with Wooden Frames.—Fig. 4 shows a method of protecting a row of plants. Wood frames are made up to support the glass, the one illustrated representing the end-frames. Intermediate frames of similar construction should be made up as required, the footboard (A) in this case being centralized on the frame, and the uprights being furnished with a *pair* each of cross-pieces (B and D), one at either side of the uprights C. An intermediate is needed wherever two 18in. lengths of glass abut. The end-frames and the intermediate ones are connected by passing a length of dowel rod, or a piece of ⅛in. (nominal) gas-barrel, through holes bored in the top member (D) of all the frames to suit. These holes register, and coincide in all the frames.

Begin by sawing sufficient foot-boards (A) from a piece of sound deal or hardwood not less than full ⅜in. in thickness. Following the dimensions given in Fig. 4, the total length would

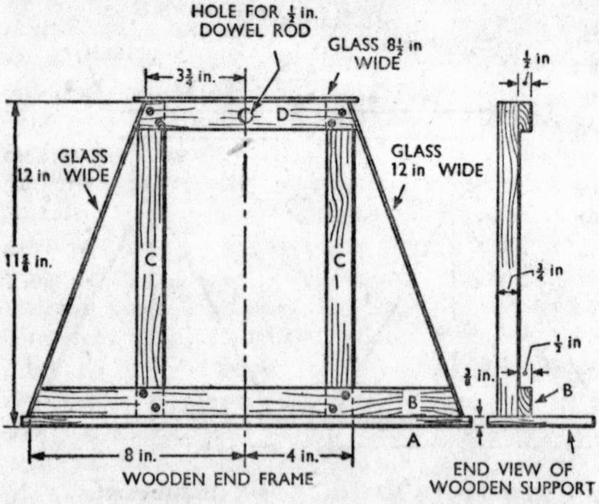

Fig. 4. A wooden frame cloche, showing dimensions and arrangement of A, foot board; B, bottom cross-piece; C, uprights; D, top cross-piece drilled to take a dowel rod.

be about 18¾in., the projection at each end being just enough to support the lower edge of the glass sheets. To the footboard is screwed a cross-piece (B) though this, with the two uprights (C) and the top cross-piece (D), had better be assembled first. For a stronger job the pieces (C) may be of 1in. × 1in. hardwood, and be halved to the cross-pieces as well as screwed. Non-rusting screws should be used throughout, which means that they must be of brass. The basic dimensions are given in Fig. 4, but a test should be made after constructing the first frame, by trying two sheets of glass in place and resting the top flat piece on the uprights. The glass for the sides is given as 18in. × 12in. and that for the top piece as 18in. × 8½in.

A length of ⅜in. barrel can be bought from a gasfitter or a builder's merchant. It should be painted with two coats of lead or aluminium paint before use. The holes in the cross-pieces (D) must be an easy fit. If the assembly is not more than 3ft. in length a piece of wood dowel rod will serve as the central support, but gas-barrel is better. Apply two coatings of creosote to all woodwork before use. The glass can be kept in place by simple clips made of small pieces cut from zinc sheet, screwed to the woodwork with brass screws, round-head pattern. The frames can be kept steady by inserting pieces of half-inch dowel rod at each end, putting them through holes bored in the footboards so that these pegs enter the ground a few inches. Of course, all the frames must be levelled up approximately if assembly is to be stable.

Strengthening the Glass.—The glasses can be framed with a strip of zinc in the passe-partout manner. Sheet zinc in Gauge 13 (approx. Gauge 22 in B.W.G.) is suitable. Cut a strip as long as the four sides of the glass, plus a little extra; the strip should be about 1¼ in. wide. Lay it flat on the bench and rule parallel lines to show where the flanges stand up; leave ample room for the thickness of the glass. At each point where the strip is to change direction, a vee-notch must be cut, as in passe-partout work, to allow a clean junction on the flanges. The point in the strip will come in the middle of the *lower edge* of the glass. Therefore measure from one end of the strip inwards, half the length of the long side; cut a notch at each flange; next measure for one short side (notch); the top long side (notch), the remaining short side (notch), and for the remaining half-length of the bottom side.

Start the bend for one flange by slipping the strip down a crack between two boards of the bench top, and gently bending over; complete the flanges by bending the zinc up over a thin lath, or a strip of brass, of the same thickness as the glass. Lay the strip on the bench and stand a sheet of glass over the points for the top long side. Bend upwards at the angles; take out glass and bend further inwards a little; replace glass and now bend partly over for the bottom half-lengths, just enough to get the accurate positions. Take out glass, and bend down *one* more half-length with glass finally in position, close-in both half-lengths. Solder on a piece of zinc, bent to the same form, over the join.

SECTION TEN

IN THE GARAGE

Garage Layout and Equipment

In contemplating the building of a garage a householder should take several matters into account. He must, in the first place, make quite sure that there is nothing forbidding its erection in the tenancy agreement. If the consent of the landlord has been obtained, and a garage is erected, this will automatically become the landlord's property at the end of the tenancy unless the structure is of a portable nature. Even if the builder of the garage owns the property there may be provisions in the deeds forbidding its erection altogether or permitting only a building of a certain type. Apart from these difficulties the local building regulations must be complied with. These may prohibit the erection within a specific distance of the road, or may demand the use of special materials and suitable drainage. Furthermore, Home Office regulations govern the location of places in which petrol may be kept, and the tank of a motor comes within this category. When the garage is attached to the house, further restrictions are usually imposed with the idea of safe-guarding the communicating door against fire. In this respect it might also affect the validity of the insurance policy covering the house.

These difficulties account for the popularity of the portable type of garage, such being exempt from the greater part of the restrictions outlined. The addition of a garage, portable or permanent, will, however, immediately raise your assessment for rates by £4 per annum.

Even so, it is as well to remember that any old shed will not make a garage, and if the owner is anxious to treat his car well and relieve himself of as much trouble as possible, he will set about building in the right way. Primarily, the garage should be dry, and if possible, built adjacent to the house. It will thus receive a certain amount of heat from the house and be warm in comparison with an isolated shed. If this is not possible, and the garage is to be isolated, see that provision is made to keep it dry and warm in frosty weather. More cars give starting trouble due to moisture and condensation than from any other cause. Also, although the use of anti-freeze solutions eliminates the bogey of frost fractures to a large extent, too much faith should not be placed in them during very hard weather, and in any case they can do nothing to make starting easier.

If the owner is really enthusiastic he will want to do most of his own maintenance work, and he should make sure there is sufficient room to pass round the car easily when it is in the garage. A garage into which the car just fits soon becomes a strain on the temper, and further, room for a work bench will certainly be required. If anything beyond pure maintenance work is aspired to, one of the first additions to the bench will be a vice. Also, with a view to keeping the floor space clear of miscellaneous articles, there should be ample provision of shelves and storage room.

If it is not too much of a luxury it is advisable to get electricity laid on, and water supply for a hose. These two amenities cannot be too highly recommended.

Equipment.—Having acquired a satisfactory garage, the car owner will now require to equip it for the efficient care of his car.

Care of the coachwork will no doubt take pride of place, and this is where an abundant supply of water will be appreciated. If a hose is available, it is a simple matter just to hose the worst of the mud off when coming in from a spell of wet weather. If this is done the draining process is robbed of a lot of hard work. A large sponge, a spoke type brush, a good quality chamois leather and a bucket should be obtained. A tin of reputable body polish, several soft polishing cloths, and a stiff hand-brush for brushing down the upholstery, mats, etc., are other necessities which are possibly already in the house.

It is a good plan to obtain a lubrication chart of your car, and to fix it to the garage wall for reference. You can obtain one free of charge by applying to the makers or to any reputable oil company. Next obtain a supply of lubricants as recommended by the manufacturer; by buying a 5-gallon drum of oil and a small quantity of other greases, etc., you will get the benefit of bulk supply prices and assure yourself of a constant stock of the correct, that is to say, approved lubricants.

Fig. 1 shows the *essential* tools one should possess in order to carry out most maintenance jobs. Should you decide to attend to the valves yourself you will require in addition to the above a valve clearance gauge, a set of tappet spanners, and a valve spring compressor.

In some cases the following special items are also included, and will no doubt be required at some time or another:

1 hub extractor.
1 carburettor jet key.
1 "C" spanner for water pump gland.
1 "C" spanner for differential adjustment.
1 hub cap spanner.
1 pinion nut spanner.
1 steering wheel nut spanner.
1 Lockheed brake bleeder tube.
1 Lockheed brake bleeder spanner.

Special spanners may also be needed for use if unorthodox drain plugs are fitted to the engine sump, gearbox and rear axle units. In addition, it is recommended that a reliable tyre pressure gauge, a wire brush for cleaning the sparking plugs, and a contact breaker points dressing-slip are obtained at the first opportunity. Other useful equipment would include a water can, oil funnel, and some distilled water for topping-up the battery. At a later date an oil-drain tray can be added, and a pair of axle stands will be found invaluable when carrying out a brake job.

In the course of time the amateur mechanic will be certain to require the following additional tools that will enable him to carry

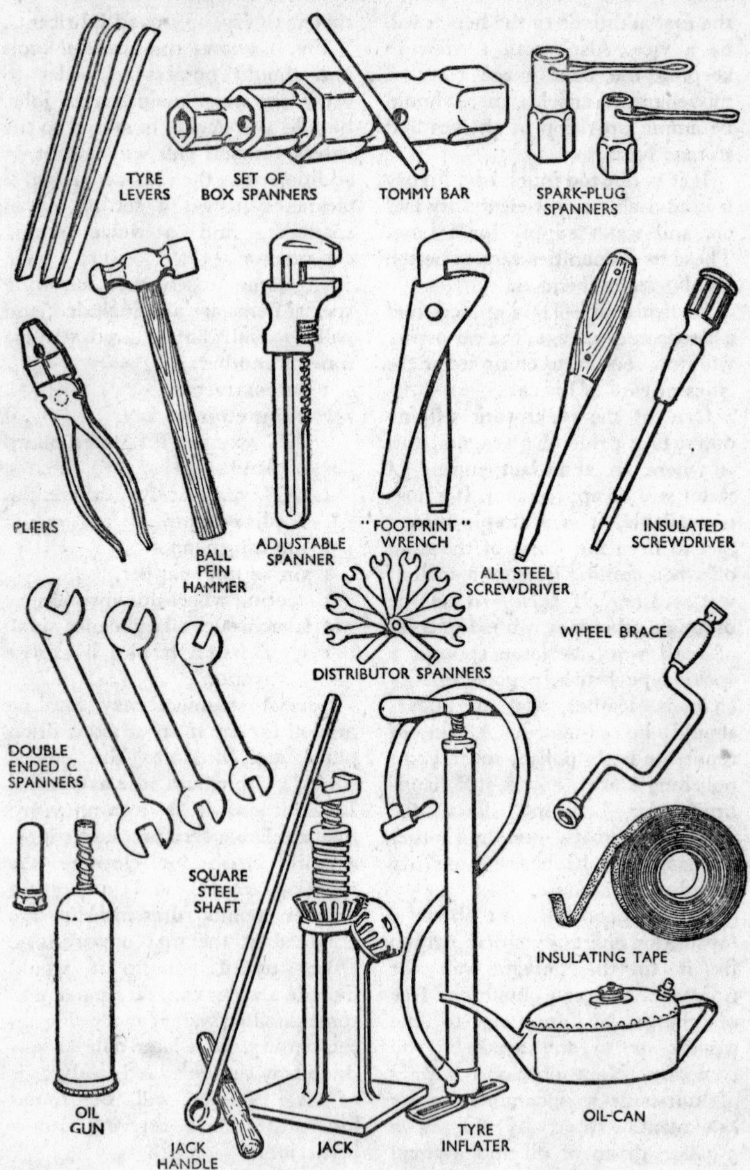

Fig. 1. A useful tool kit for the car owner. These tools should be stored in the tool kit box of the car. If a tool roll is not used wrap the tools in cleaning rags before storing them so as to prevent rattle. If the pump and jack cannot be stored in tool kit box keep them in luggage container or similar convenient space.

out small repairs on the car:

1 hack saw and blades.
1 12in. second cut file.
1 12in. smooth file.
1 hand brace.
1 set drills for above.
1 pair footprints or pipe grips.
1 solder iron (electric if power available).

A quantity of clean rags, paraffin, and a cleaning brush should always be on hand for cleaning down the engine, and its various auxiliaries.

Later on the collection of tools may be usefully augmented with additional spanners, screwing tackle and possibly a small stock of nuts and bolts. If this is contemplated first make sure what standard the car employs. For instance, most American cars adopt S.A.E. nuts and bolts and consequently require S.A.E. spanners, etc. Continental manufacturers employ the Metric Standard, and British makers Whitworth or B.S.F.

Motor Car Maintenance

MAKERS invariably issue instructions for the maintenance of the vehicles they manufacture. These instructions may or may not be fully comprehensive, but will, of necessity, apply only to a particular model. They will, however, be correct in the information given and consequently should be strictly adhered to. Also, the owner will realize that although the manufacturer can produce the finest piece of mechanism in creation, it will not give satisfaction if it is incorrectly serviced. The onus of taking proper care of a vehicle is therefore on the owner or driver, and not on the manufacturers.

Bodywork.—Whether the bodywork is finished with varnish, or with the cellulose enamel finish of most modern cars, the process of washing is much the same. Dirt and mud which cannot be dusted off must be removed with a jet of water, and a soft brush or sponge. Let the water soften the dirt to avoid scratching the paint. A strong jet of water is best for removing encrusted mud from under the mudguards and chassis, and from the axles. When the worst has been removed, the bodywork may be finally washed down with plenty of clean water, which may be slightly warm and contain a little soap free from alkali. Grease or oil on the body should be removed by the application of paraffin or petrol, but in this case a second rinse with clean water should be given. Dry off with a leather which should be rinsed and wrung out from time to time.

Wait until the body is thoroughly dry before applying a good body polish. Such polish should be thinly applied and well rubbed until bright. Finally, finish off the polishing with a special polishing cloth kept solely for the purpose.

Tar spots can be removed with turpentine applied with a soft cloth or brush, but a little petrol should afterwards be used to wash off the affected part prior to polishing.

Car hoods should be washed with soap and water and never folded until quite dry.

Chromium plated fittings, if dirty, should be cleaned with a damp leather and finished off with a soft rag. Do not use any abrasive polish.

The interior of the car should be regularly brushed out and the upholstery sponged over and leathered occasionally. Dirty mats can be rejuvenated with carpet soap. Door hinges, locks, window-winders, adjustable seat-runners, and roof-slides (if any) require periodical lubrication. The webbing on which the bonnet rests should also be greased. This will eliminate many elusive squeaks, but most motorists know by experience that after a sustained dry spell of weather numerous squeaks do occur. This is due to lack of moisture between the various wing and running board valances, for water acts as a lubricant before rusting sets in. The cure is to spray all round these parts with penetrating oil prior to washing down. Dirty cord upholstery can be renovated with a cloth and a good brushing, stains having previously been removed with petrol or liquid cleanser.

Rattling doors can usually be cured by slackening the screws securing the lock striking plate, moving the plate slightly until the door has to be closed sharply before the lock registers. The plate may have to be shifted several times until the position is satisfactory. Do not forget finally to tighten the fixing screws.

Fig. 1. Testing the sparking plug gap by feeler gauge. When adjusting the gap do not alter the position of the central electrode. Adjust on outer electrode.

Chassis.—A lubrication chart of a stripped chassis applying to a particular make of car, to fix on the garage wall for reference, may be obtained free of charge from any of the reputable oil companies. A study of the chart will show that there are many points which require regular attention, some more often than others. Apart from this, it is essential that the right kind and grade of lubricant is given to each specific part. Therefore, it cannot be too strongly advised that lubricants as recommended by the manufacturers of the vehicle should be used.

Pay attention to all the points shown. Clean greasers before applying the gun, and make sure they are not clogged. If they are, clear or replace them, otherwise the part served will suffer. Some greasers may be awkward to get at, others may be overlooked because they are not visible. Make it your business to become conversant with every lubrication point on your vehicle, and see that it gets regular attention. So much for general chassis lubrication, but other maintenance work consists of such adjustments as may be necessary to keep the vehicle up to as high a standard of efficiency as is consistent with normal service. We will therefore proceed to deal with each unit separately.

Power Unit.—The owner should always store the oil container in the cleanest part of the garage and keep it tightly covered so that no foreign matter can get into it. Funnels and any tins for transference or storage of oil must also be kept clean. He should for safety's sake make a daily check of the engine oil level. Inspect by means of a dip stick or gauge with the vehicle on level ground, and top up to correct level with the oil recommended by the manufacturers. Drain off after first 500 miles and every subsequent 1,000 to 2,000 miles, and flush out with light flushing oil (*not paraffin*) before refilling with fresh oil. Also take the opportunity of cleaning the filters in the oil system; you should locate these as soon as you acquire the car, by referring to the instruction manual. Those of the renewable cartridge type are usually changed about every 10,000 miles. Do not forget the air cleaner, generally fitted to the carburettor intake. This should be washed out with petrol, dried and re-oiled with engine oil, the surplus being allowed to drain off before refitting. Try and arrange the draining off and refilling of the engine at the period of change over from summer to winter grade oil, or vice versa. It is best to drain off oil when the engine is warm, as the oil is then thinned by the heat, and much of the sediment will be suspended in the oil. This sediment cannot be entirely removed, of course, without dropping the sump and cleaning out the system.

At the time the engine oil is renewed, the fuel system should be cleansed. Remove the carburettor float chamber, blow through the jets with the tyre pump, wipe clean the float chamber before replacing, and clean the petrol filter. Drain off any sediment in the fuel pump by using the drain plug provided. Otherwise, clean out the pump when removing the gauge filter for cleaning. When replacing, make sure the cover washer is in good condition and that the cap makes an air-tight joint when tightened down. With electric pumps it should be necessary only to clean the filter. If there are any other filters in the supply system, and reference to your instruction book should inform you on this point, they should also be cleaned at the same time.

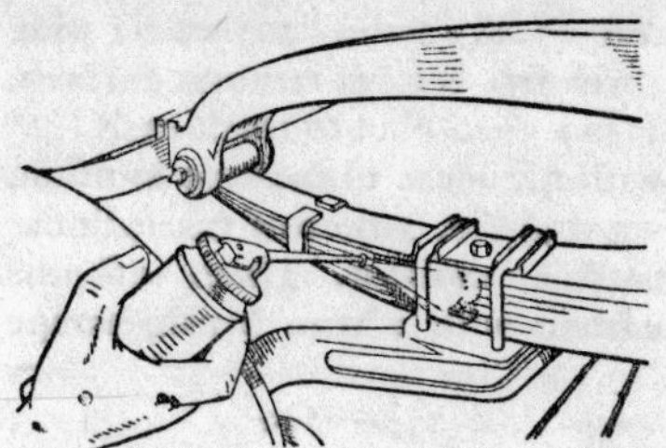

Fig. 2. Using oil-spray can to lubricate springs. Use an approved penetrating oil. Clean the surface before spraying.

About every 1,000 miles the valve clearances should be tested. It is impossible to give any hard and fast rule regarding correct tappet clearance, as designs vary from ·004in. to ·045in., so definite data must be obtained either from reference to the instruction book or from the makers. It is also particularly important that the clearances are set when the valve concerned is on the lowest position of the cam. In the absence of definite details of procedure the safest method is to adjust the clearance on both valves of one cylinder when the piston is at the top of its *firing* stroke.

The sparking plugs should also be cleaned and the electrodes reset about every 10,000 miles, see Fig. 1. Make sure you can replace the H.T. wires to each plug correctly before removing them. It is a good plan to mark each lead with file nicks to indicate location, starting No. 1 nearest the cylinder to the radiator. Clean off the carbon with a wire brush, scrape

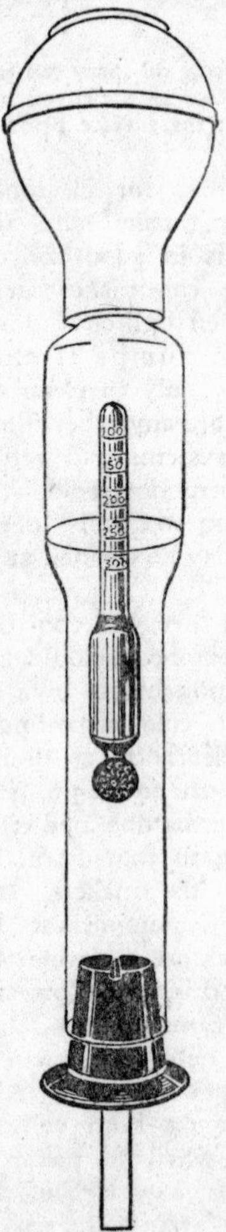

Fig. 3. Hydrometer for testing specific gravity of acid. Specific gravity of acid from battery shown on floating scale.

as clean as possible, and reset the points as recommended. Never try to bend the central electrode; always set the side one.

It is as well to check over the contact breaker at the same time as the plugs are cleaned. Clean the points with a special file or carborundum slip made for this purpose. Make sure that the rocker arm moves freely on its pivot and set the points to the particular gap recommended. A spot of lubricant on the operating cam will reduce wear on the fibre heel of the rocker arm and eliminate any tendency to squeak. Clean and wipe away any moisture that may be present in the distributor cap. After standing idle for a time, condensation occurs here at the sparking plug points, causing difficulty in starting up.

Clutch.—Clutches on modern cars are generally of the single plate type and require no lubrication. The few that operate in oil are generally fed from the engine system. Where ball thrust races are employed in the withdrawal mechanism they must *never* be neglected, but lubricated strictly in accordance with maker's instructions. Special thrust washers are now extensively employed with the object of eliminating the necessity for lubrication. About an inch of lost movement should be maintained at the pedal. When this becomes appreciably more, or the pedal fouls the toe board without fully disengaging the clutch, it is time for adjustment. Actual details vary with the design, and reference should therefore be made to the instruction book. Provision for this adjustment is always embodied in the clutch assembly. Closely observe the makers' instructions.

Gearbox.—The gearboxes of new cars should be drained, flushed out with thin oil, and replenished after the first 500 miles. This is necessary as metallic dust created during the running-in period would be harmful if left in. The level should be regularly checked every 1,000 miles and replenished to correct level. Drain and refill every subsequent 5,000 miles. Always drain off when the lubricant is warm and agitated, as in this condition impurities are more easily carried off and the oil flows more easily.

Rear Axle.—The rear axle should be given attention on similar lines to the gearbox, the only difference being that the grade of lubricant used will be different. Use only that recommended by the manufacturers.

Spring and Front Axle.—All points on the front axle and spring should be lubricated every 500 miles. Check and replenish lubricant in the steering box every 1,000 miles. Tighten up the steering knuckle joints every 10,000 miles if of the adjustable type, and check the front wheel track. Adjustable steering joints are now being favoured by manufacturers, and if play becomes excessive in these joints they must be renewed.

Many car manufacturers employ adjustable type bearings in the hubs of the road wheels. Excessive play in these bearings should be taken up by removing the split pin securing the spindle nut and tightening up same. They should be checked about every 10,000 miles, or at the same time as the brakes are adjusted. The opportunity should be taken to repack the hubs with the right lubricant.

General Chassis.—The road springs, if they are of the laminated or leaf type, require lubricating about every 10,000 miles. If there is no provision for this it is best done by jacking up the chassis so that the axle hangs on the spring thereby tending to open up the leaves. Graphite grease may then be introduced between the leaves, or the operation can be facilitated by spraying penetrating oil between them, see Fig. 2.

It is necessary to do the spraying rather more often, and while you have the spraying can in action give all the brake connections a spray. Lubricate them with a liberal dose of oil from the oil can after spraying. Also check the bolts or U-clips anchoring the springs to the axles, and tighten them up if they are loose. At the same time, the shock absorbers should be checked and topped up with the correct fluid. Make sure you use the correct fluid for your particular make as there are several different grades only one of which will be suitable. Also clean off the dirt before removing the filter plugs. Take the opportunity of making sure that the shock absorbers themselves are absolutely tight, and that the connecting linkage, etc., is secure.

Electrical Equipment.—With regard to the electrical equipment, first and foremost comes the battery. The electrolyte should be checked every month. Remove the vent plugs and see that the level of the acid is just above the tops of the plates. If necessary, top up with *distilled* water only; it is advisable to complete the check over by measuring the specific gravity of the acid, as this gives a good indication of the state of the battery. A hydrometer (Fig. 3) is used for this purpose and the acid should give a reading of 1·285 to 1·300. The terminal connections should be kept clean and tight; smear them with vaseline to prevent corrosion. Finally wipe all dirt and moisture from the tops leaving the batteries quite clean and dry.

Lubrication.—Correct lubrication in accordance with the engine manufacturers' specifications is of great importance. The viscosity and characteristics of lubricants vary considerably. One type of engine oil may be ideal for a certain engine but will be quite unsuitable for others. It is the special interest of the engine manufacturer to select, scientifically, from a very wide range of lubricants those which are particularly suitable for the engine concerned. The lubricants recommended generally consist of four classes, an engine oil possessing the correct viscosity at normal engine working temperatures, a lubricant with high pressure characteristics for the gearbox and rear axle, a special heavy grade grease suited to the working load imposed on wheel hub bearings,

Drain and Refill.

Engine.—After first 500 miles and every subsequent 1,000 to 2,000 miles, flush out with light flushing oil, not paraffin, before refilling with fresh oil.

Gearbox and Rear Axle.—After first 500 miles and every subsequent 5,000 miles.

Miles.	*Parts requiring attention.*	*How to lubricate.*
250	Engine.	Check oil level by dipstick and replenish.
500	Fan bearing, spring eye bolts and shackles, king pins, brake shafts, spring box and connections.	Use oil gun at nipples provided.
500	Brake linkage joints and clutch withdrawal bearing.	Apply oil generously with oil can.
1,000	Gearbox and rear axle.	Check oil and replenish to correct level.
1,000	Universal joints.	Attach oil gun and fill three-quarters full.
1,000	Distributor and water pump.	Give greaser one turn.
2,000	Wheel hubs.	Remove hub cap and replace hub.

etc. and a high speed non-separating lubricant for the universal joints.

The periodicity of inspection, replenishing or priming is detailed in the table below. The figures in the table indicate (as a general practical guide) the mileages at which attention is required.

Distributor, Magneto and Dynamo.—Every 1,000 miles place two or three drops of machine oil in oilers provided.

Occasionally remove the distributor cap and wipe out dry with a clean rag. Clean the electrodes with a rag moistened with petrol. See that the carbon pick-up brush is clean and moves freely in the cap. Clean and examine the contact breaker points, and reset to correct gap. Give the lubricator two turns every 500 miles, and a spot of oil on the rocker arm pivot every 5,000 miles. Lift off the rotor arm from the spindle and add a few drops of machine oil for lubricating the automatic mechanism, every 5,000 miles. See also Fig. 4.

The dynamo commutator and brushes should be kept clean. Dirty brushes should be cleaned with a cloth moistened in petrol; see that they move freely in their holders. Badly worn brushes can easily be replaced with new ones obtained from any service depot. At the same time see that the commutator is clean and free from oil and brush dust. If burned black it can be redressed with No. 00 sandpaper—never use emery cloth. Similar treatment should be given to the starter motor. As a rule these machines do not need lubrication as the bearings are primarily packed with special grease when assembled. Where greasers are provided, however, give them attention as per lubrication chart. On occasion, the starter pinion may fail to engage on the flywheel. When this happens, if it is not due to a run-down battery make sure that the screwed end on the armature spindle is not contaminated with oil and dirt. If it is, clean off with paraffin. Should the starter jam into mesh at any time, it can be disengaged by turning the squared end of the armature shaft with a spanner.

About every three months raise the arms of the direction indicators and apply a little vaseline with a small camel hair brush between the brass knob or profile and the small copper tongue spring and copper spindle.

Miscellaneous Work.—In conjunction with the foregoing notes the reader should refer, for further details, to the other entries dealing with the motor car.

Other items requiring attention from time to time include:

The fan belt, this should be kept tight.

When the dynamo or other auxiliaries are driven by chain in the timing case, provision will be made for tightening the chain when it becomes slack. Flush out the cooling system twice a year. The best time to do this is when safeguarding against frost with anti-freeze solution, and at the end of the winter where such protection is no longer necessary.

Regularly check over the wheel nuts for tightness. If wheels have not been removed for some considerable time, it is as well to detach them and to grease the registers and oil the nuts before replacing. Take the opportunity

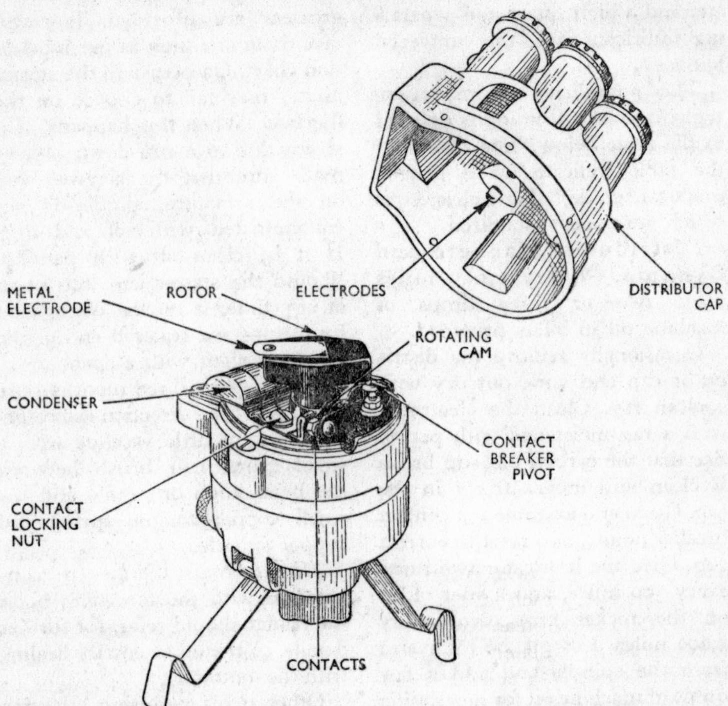

Fig. 4. Typical distributor head and cap. The internal components of this unit must be kept free from moisture and dirt. Test contact breaker points for clearance.

to change the wheels round as recommended in Wheels and Tyres, page 398.

All engine control joints and brake linkage pins should be lubricated occasionally with the oil can. Brake cables (if used), and the footbrake pedal shafts, should be lubricated regularly.

The engine oil sump should be removed once a season, to enable the filter tray to be cleaned and all sediment, etc. to be washed out before replacing.

Occasionally tighten down the cylinder head nuts, commencing with those at the centre.

Tighten the exhaust and inlet manifold nuts from time to time.

Disconnect the speedometer cable and lubricate the inner driving cable once every season.

If attention is given on the lines suggested above, trouble on the road is not likely to be experienced, and the wear and tear of all parts will be reduced to a minimum. There will, however, come a time when wear between working parts in the engine reaches a stage which requires more than adjustment to bring the engine back to something like its original efficiency. This condition, apart from mechanical defects, usually manifests itself in high petrol and oil consumption, lack of compression and excessive oil fumes. When any of these symptoms become apparent, repairs should be put in hand before a final breakdown occurs. Excessive wear of the engine internal components, such as may occur in big end bearings, gudgeon pins and bushes, cylinder walls, pistons, etc., is a job for professional car repair service, particularly if the wear is general.

Power Unit

The internal combustion engine, power unit of modern road vehicles, depends on petrol or oil fuel for the development of motive power. The combustion of fuel, which constitutes the energy converted into a driving force, occurs inside the combustion chamber of the cylinders. It is to this principle that the internal combustion engine owes its name, as distinct from the earlier type of power plant, the steam engine, which it has supplanted; for in the steam engine the conversion of the latent energy of fuel is effected at a point external to the engine body.

Although internal combustion engines vary considerably in design all embody the same fundamental components. All make use of a cylinder in which a piston, moving up and down, transfers movement, by a connecting rod, to a crankshaft mounted in bearings. The cylinder, which is sealed at the head, incorporates two valves. One valve, the Inlet, controls the entry of fuel and air mixture into the cylinder; the other valve, the Exhaust, controls the exit of gases after the fuel has been burned. See Fig. 1. A camshaft, driven from the crankshaft, operates the two valves at intervals directly co-ordinated with the movement and position of the piston. The fuel and air mixture in the cylinder combustion chamber, which is immediately above the piston head, is ignited at a predetermined point in the cycle of piston movement. The movement of the piston is converted into a reciprocating action by means of a connecting rod, attached at its lower end to the crankshaft crankpin, by which piston movement is translated into a rotary motion of the crankshaft. A flywheel, secured to the crankshaft, is embodied to absorb surplus energy, to damp out any irregular rotation of the crankshaft and, by its momentum, to carry the piston over the top dead centre position. Before dealing further with the detailed principles of operation the reader should familiarize himself with the following nomenclature. See also Figs. 1 and 2.

Cylinder Casting.—The bores of 1, 2, 4, 6 or 8 cylinder castings are invariably contained in one specially moulded block of cast iron. The cylinder block also generally includes the top half of the crankcase and the upper sections of the bearing housings for the crankshaft.

Cylinder Head.—This is a separate casting, often in similar material, and designed to seal off the tops of the cylinder bores. The joint made by head and block is made gas-tight by means of a

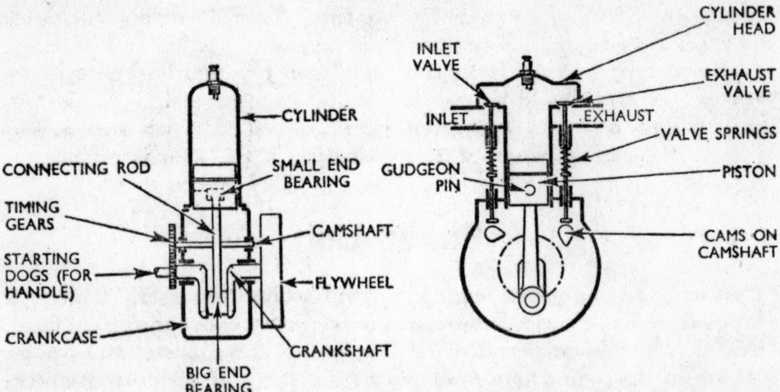

Fig. 1. Two diagrammatic views of a typical four stroke internal combustion engine. The right hand view shows the valve operating cams which are driven off the crankshaft by the timing gears as shown in the left hand view.

special washer called a gasket. Provision is made in the design of both cylinder head and cylinder block to permit the flow of cooling liquid round the walls and heads of the cylinders. This detail of design is described in the COOLING and LUBRICATION paragraphs.

Valves.—The valves are located either in the cylinder head or the cylinder block according to the design of the engine manufacturer. The valves when closed are designed to make an efficient gas-tight seal.

Camshaft.—This operates the valves through "tappets" or "rockers", and is carried either in bearings in the cylinder block, or at the cylinder head, depending on the location of the valves. It is driven from the crankshaft by suitable timing gears or chain drive.

Valve Operating Mechanism.—This is interposed between the cams on the camshaft and the valves, and may be in the form of tappets or, if of overhead valve design, in the form of rockers.

Crankshaft.—The crankshaft rotates freely in bearings secured in the crankcase and is operated by the reciprocating movement of the connecting rod.

Pistons.—These are contained within the bores of the cylinders and are provided with piston rings to prevent fuel or gas leaking past them as they move up and down the cylinders.

Connecting Rods.—These are attached, at the upper ends, to the pistons by gudgeon pins and small-end bearings, and the lower ends are mounted on the crankshaft, to operate on the specially machined journals of the shaft, in anti-friction big-end bearings.

Flywheel.—The flywheel is a heavy circular mass of metal, and is usually secured to the rear end of the crankshaft. By its rotation this heavy disk absorbs energy, and its momentum tends to keep the mechanism running smoothly between successive power strokes. It is invariably utilized as a component part of the clutch. See also the paragraphs dealing with

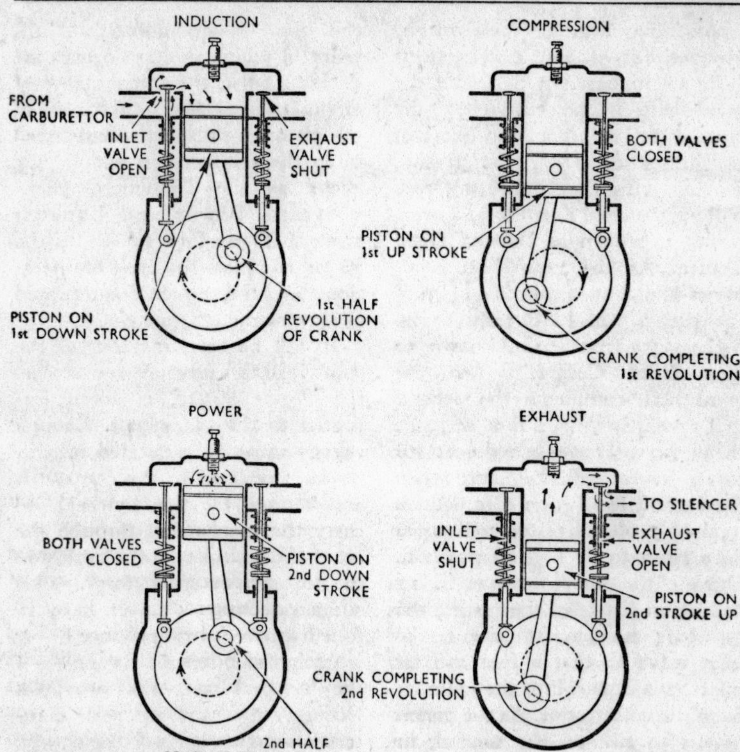

Fig. 2. Shows the four phases or strokes which make up the cycle of a four-stroke engine. Induction, inlet valve open, exhaust valve closed. Compression, both valves closed. Power, compressed mixture ignited. Exhaust, exhaust valve open to expel burnt gases. Four strokes are completed in two complete revolutions of crankshaft.

TRANSMISSION in this section.

Oil Sump.—The sump consists of a suitable receptacle bolted to the bottom of the cylinder block. It encases all the lower mechanism of the engine, and at the same time acts as a reservoir for the lubricating oil.

Oil Pump.—The oil pump is generally placed inside the sump, from which it draws oil. It may be driven by the camshaft or crankshaft, and delivers oil to all the working parts by suitable pipes, oil passages, ducts or galleries. It is essential that an oil film is maintained between all working parts, to eliminate friction and reduce wear. This requirement is an essential consideration in the initial design of the engine.

How the Engine Works.—Internal combustion engines operate on a four-stroke or two-stroke cycle of operations, brief outlines of which are as follows:

Four-Stroke Cycle.—The cycle or complete sequence of operations consists of *two* revolutions of the crankshaft and *four* strokes of the piston. See Fig. 2. This will be obvious for if the piston starts from its highest position, and the crankshaft is turned, when the crankshaft has completed one-half revolution or 180°, the piston, moving with the connecting rod, will have moved down to its lowest position, known as Bottom Dead Centre. As the crankshaft completes the first revolution of 360° the piston will have risen to its highest position again, known as Top Dead Centre. When the crankshaft completes the second half revolution, i.e. a total of 540°, the piston will have again descended to its lowest position, and when the second revolution completes a total of 720° the piston will again have risen to its highest position. During the first downward, or Induction stroke of the piston, the camshaft mechanism opens the inlet valve so that a fuel and air mixture is drawn into the cylinder from the carburettor. As the piston begins to rise on the second, or Compression stroke, the inlet valve closes and the mixture is compressed in the cylinder by the rising piston. As the piston reaches T.D.C., and the fuel is fully compressed, an electric spark at the sparking plug, provided by either a magneto or coil and distributor, ignites the mixture of air and fuel. The sudden expansion of the burning fuel constitutes the explosion which forces the piston down on its third, or Power stroke. When the piston rises on its fourth or Exhaust stroke, the exhaust valve is opened and the expended gases are expelled from the cylinder combustion chamber. The exact phases at which the inlet and exhaust valves open and close in the cycle of operations and the point at which ignition occurs are determined in the initial stages of engine design. The four strokes of the piston are respectively referred to in the sequence in which they occur as the Induction, Compression, Power and Exhaust strokes. These four strokes of the piston complete the cycle of operations, and the sequence is repeated as long as the engine runs.

It will be seen that out of the four strokes, only on one stroke, the Power stroke, is force imparted to the crankshaft. Enough energy must be generated on this stroke, imparted to the crankshaft and stored by the flywheel, to carry the mechanism through the other three strokes of the cycle and to do any external work. This sudden delivery of power on every fourth stroke would produce heavy vibration and irregular running if the flywheel were not provided. Often, when an internal combustion engine is revolving slowly, or a load is applied too suddenly, the engine will then stop abruptly. Most motorists have experienced this occurrence when letting in the clutch without first speeding up the engine sufficiently. This is a characteristic inherent in internal combustion engines and occurs when the load imposed on the engine exceeds the energy developed by the power stroke. But it is less noticeable as the number of cylinders is increased. This will be readily understood, for with the single cylinder only one power stroke occurs in a crankshaft rotation of 720°, but in an eight cylinder engine a power stroke occurs every 90°; consequently a more continuous impulse is given

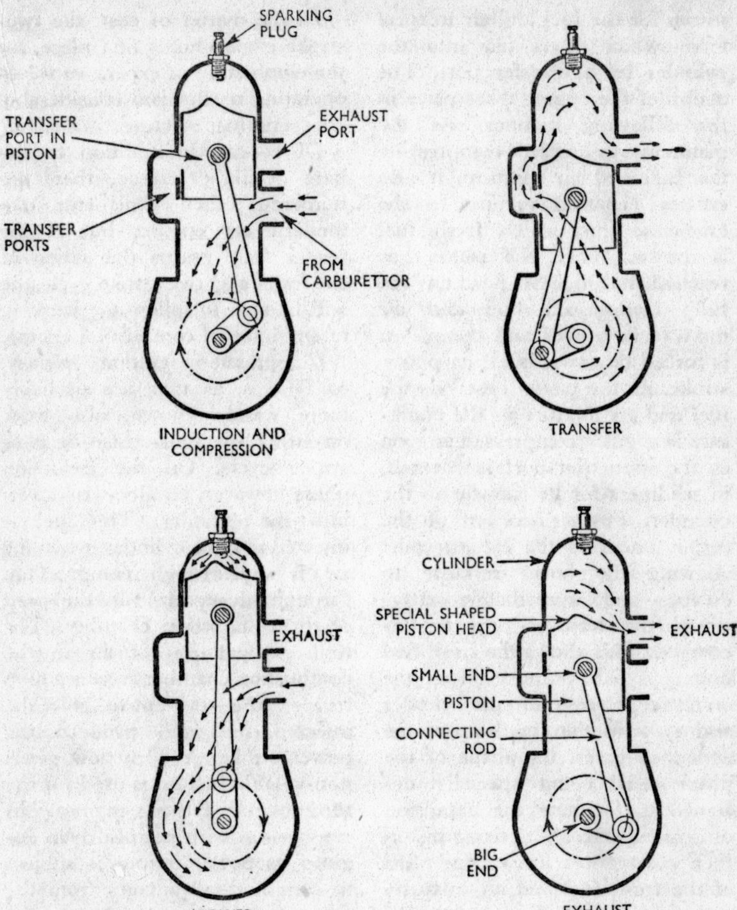

Fig. 3. Diagrammatic arrangement of two-stroke engine. Cycle of rotation, induction, compression transfer, power and exhaust is completed in one revolution of crankshaft; the piston being utilized to open and seal inlet and exhaust ports.

to the crankshaft even at low engine speeds.

Two-Stroke Cycle.—Some power units, chiefly those installed in motor cycles or other small machines, operate on the two-stroke cycle. See Fig. 3. This cycle of operations is completed in one revolution of the crankshaft and two strokes of the piston, every down stroke of the piston being a power stroke. This is made possible by placing the induction and exhaust ports in such a way that the piston, during its travel up and down the cylinder, is itself employed to open and close them without the assistance of independent valves. The crankcase, which is gas-tight, is utilized as a pump for the fuel and air mixture from which it is fed into the cylinder by a transfer port. The action of the engine takes place in the following manner. As the piston moves upwards compressing the fuel and air mixture, it also creates a partial vacuum in the crankcase into which fresh fuel is drawn. When the piston has reached its highest position the fully compressed fuel and air mixture is ignited and the piston is forced downwards on its power stroke. As the piston descends the fuel and air mixture in the crank-case is slightly compressed as soon as the induction port is covered, in readiness for its transfer to the cylinder. Further descent of the piston uncovers the exhaust port allowing the burnt mixture to escape, and immediately afterwards the transfer port is uncovered. This allows the fresh fuel under partial compression in the crankcase, to pass into the cylinder and assist in the expulsion of the expended gases, the shape of the piston head being specially designed to facilitate the expulsion of exhaust gases. The rising piston then commences the compression of the fresh fuel and air mixture, and a new cycle of operations.

With two engines of equal capacity, one working on the four-stroke cycle and the other on the two-stroke cycle, one might be led to expect double power from the two-stroke considering that it has one power stroke in every two compared with the four-stroke engine's one power stroke in every four. This, however, is not the case as the two-stroke cycle is wasteful of fuel and its efficiency is lower for reasons inherent in the design.

In the matter of cost, the two-stroke engine holds first place, for the elimination of expensive valve-operating mechanism considerably cheapens manufacture.

Of course, in addition to the bare details described, there are numerous other refinements in a modern car engine, but if the reader fully grasps the action of the four- and two-stroke cycles he will be able to follow the working of any internal combustion engine.

Compression ignition engines, or Diesels, as they are probably more widely known, also work on either the four-stroke or two-stroke cycle. On the induction phase however, air alone is drawn into the cylinder. The fuel is injected into the cylinder, when the air is under high compression, through an atomizer in the head of the combustion chamber. The high compression of air in the combustion chamber creates a high temperature sufficient to ignite the injected fuel and produce the power stroke. A fairly low grade non-volatile fuel oil is used for the running of Diesel engines. In comparison with petrol-driven engines its power output is subject to certain disadvantages from the aspect of engine weight to the horse power developed.

Power developed by an engine increases as its speed of rotation increases, but the speed range varies according to the design within which it operates most satisfactorily and economically.

The following charts which give engine data and typical causes of engine running defects are appended for quick reference in addition to the general information contained in this section.

Engine Data

MAKE AND MODEL	No. of cyls.	Batt. vol. tage	Dist. gaps in thous. in.	Plug gaps in thous. in.	Tappet Clearances min.	Tappet Clearances max.
AUSTIN						
8 H.P.	4	6	12	18	·004	·004 (hot)
10 H.P.	4	12	12	18/25	·004	·004 (hot)
12 H.P.	6	12	12	18	·004	·004 (hot)
14 H.P.	6	12	12	18	·004	·004 (hot)
FORD					Non. adj.	
8 H.P.	4	6	12	22	·011 to ·013	
10 H.P.	4	6	12	22	·011 to ·013	
V8 30 H.P.	8	6	15	25	·011 to ·013	
HILLMAN						
Minx	4	6	10	32	·010	·015 (cold)
14 H.P.	4	12	10	32	·010	·010 (cold)
20 H.P.	6	12	10	22	·006	·010 (cold)
HUMBER						
12 H.P.	4	12	10	22	·010	·015 (cold)
18 H.P.	6	12	10	22	·006	·010 (cold)
Snipe and Pullman	6	12	10	22	·006	·010 (cold)
LANCHESTER						
11 H.P.	4	12	12	20	·058	·058 (hot)
14 H.P.	6	12	12	20	·052	·052 (hot)
18 H.P.	6	12	12	20	·056	·056 (hot)
M.G.						
Midget T	4	12	12	18	·015	·015 (hot)
1½ Litre	4	12	12	18	·010	·015 (hot)
2 Litre	6	12	12	18	·015	·015 (hot)
MORGAN						
4/4	4	12	12/15	22/25	·006	·010 (cold)
MORRIS						
8 H.P.	4	6	12	20	·019	·019 (hot)
1939, 10 H.P.	4	12	12	20	·019	·019 (hot)
1939, 12 H.P.	4	12	12	20	·015	·015 (hot)
1939, 14 H.P.	6	12	12	20	·015	·015 (hot)
1939, 25 H.P.	6	12	12	20	·015	·015 (hot)

Engine Data

MAKE AND MODEL	No. of cyls.	Batt. vol. tage	Dist. gaps in thous. in.	Plug gaps in thous. in.	Tappet Clearances min.	Tappet Clearances max.
RILEY						
9 H.P.	4	12	Coil 18	20	·002	·003 (hot)
1½ Litre Sprite	4	12	Mag.	20	·004	·004 (hot)
1½ Standard	4	12	14	20	·004	·004 (hot)
ROVER						
10 H.P.	4	12	12	18	·010	·010 (hot)
14 H.P.	6	12	12	18	·010	·010 (hot)
SINGER						
Bantam	4					
10 H.P.	4	12	12	20	·005	·005 (hot)
12 H.P.	4					
STANDARD						
All models	—	12	12	X20	·012	·012 (hot)
V-8	8	12	12	20	·012	·012 (hot)
TALBOT						
BE, 10 H.P.	4					
BP, 3 Litre	6	12	18	22	·010	·015 (cold)
BG 110 3½ Litre	6					
TRIUMPH						
1½ Litre	4	12	15	20		
14/40 Special	4	12	15	20	·004	·004 (hot)
VAUXHALL						
10 H.P. H	4	6	12	37/40	·006	·013
12 H.P. DY	6	12	12	37/40	·008	·010
14 H.P. DX	6	12	12	37/40	·008	·010
WOLSELEY						
12 H.P.	4				·019	·019 (hot)
14/60 111	6				·015	·015 (hot)
18/85 111	6	12	12	19	·015	·015 (hot)
21 H.P. 111	6				·015	·015 (hot)
25 H.P. 111	6				·015	·015 (hot)

Petrol Engine Fault Tracing Chart

Symptom	Type	No.	Fault
Starter will not turn engine but engine will start by hand	E	1	Battery discharged or corroded terminals
	E	2	Starter switch contacts faulty or loose connections
	E	3	Starter motor brush or commutator trouble
Starter turns engine slowly, but engine will start by hand			Any of faults 1, 2, or 3
	M	4	Engine partially seized or too thick oil being used for cold weather
			MAGNETO
	E	5	Not switched on or faulty switch wire
	E	6	Contact breaker points incorrectly set or dirty
	E	7	Seized contact breaker arm
	E	8	Plugs damp or points need cleaning or resetting
	E	9	H.T. cables leaking badly
	E	10	Magneto damp or weak
	E	11	Drive partially sheared or stripped
			COIL
			Any of faults 1, 5, 6, 7, 8, 9, or 11
	E	12	Loose or faulty L.T. wires to coil
	E	13	Damp or faulty condenser
Starter turns engine briskly but engine does not start	E	14	Faulty coil
	E	15	Damaged distributor rotor or H.T. pick-up contact
	C	16	Lack of petrol or turned off
	C	17	Filters or pipes choked
	C	18	Petrol supply pump defective
	C	19	Autovac out of order
	C	20	Starting device controls not operating correctly
	C	21	Air leaks in induction system
			Either faults 11 or 18
	M	22	Sticking or leaking valve
	M	23	Valve timing incorrect
	M	24	Ignition timing incorrect
	M	25	Leakage past pistons and cylinders
			All faults 4, 27, 45
	–	—	Engine still tight (not run in)
Engine overheats	–	—	Fan defective—blades bent or belt slipping
	–	—	Cooling system faulty—radiator choked, pump not working
	–	—	Slipping clutch or binding brakes

Electrical (E), Carburation (C), Mechanical (M).

Petrol Engine Fault Tracing Chart

Symptom	Type	No.	Cause
			Any of faults 6, 9, 11, 12, 13, 14
	E	26	Plug insulation defective, sooted up or gaps too wide
	E	27	Ignition too retarded
	E	28	H.T. leads wrongly connected
			Fuel supply inadequate, due to 17, 18 or 19
Engine fires but dies out	C	29	Saturated plugs due to overstrangling
	C	30	Sticking carburettor dashpot (S.U.)
	C	31	Mixture controls incorrectly set
	C	32	Water in carburettor
	C	33	Vent hole in petrol tank cap blocked
	M	34	Timing chain jumped when engine last stopped
	M	35	Valve sticking, maladjustment, bent or broken spring
			Fault 21
	C	36	Slow running adjustment incorrectly set
	C	37	Slow running jet blocked
Engine will not slow run	C	38	Throttle spindle badly worn
	M	39	Worn valves, guides or piston rings
	M	40	Valve clearances wrongly adjusted
			Any of faults 13, 14, 26, 27
Engine will not open up and lacks power	C	41	Main jet blocked
	C	42	Petrol shortage
	M	43	Choked exhaust system
			All ignition faults 6, 13, 14, 27
	E	44	Unsuitable sparking plugs
Engine misfiring and spitting back	–	—	All carburation troubles, 18, 41, 42
	C	45	Weak mixture
	–	—	All mechanical faults, 22, 23, 24, 40
	M	46	Weak valve springs
	M	47	Throttle not opening fully
Engine cuts out suddenly	E	—	Electrical trouble usually
Engine dies out slowly	C	—	Carburation trouble usually
Medium low pitch knock	–	—	Big end bearing slack or run
High pitch tap	–	—	Worn gudgeon pins
Low pitch thud	–	—	Main bearing slack or run
Intermittent thuds	–	—	Loose flywheel or end play on crankshaft
Shrill squeaking	–	—	Dynamo brushes or distribution cam
Whistling or hissing	–	—	Air leaks in induction system
Continual tapping	–	—	Excessive valve clearances

Electrical (E), Carburation (C), Mechanical (M).

Frame

THE frame of a vehicle is generally rectangular in shape, comprising two main side members braced together by suitable cross members. Attached to this framework are the power unit, gearbox, rear axle, front axle and steering gear, the whole assembly being referred to as the chassis. Mounted on the frame, and attached thereto by suitable fittings, is the body.

The side members are usually of channel section steel, which has been found most suitable to withstand the stresses and strains peculiar to road transport vehicles. Where necessary, the side members are strengthened by deepening the dimensions of the section. It is now becoming common practice to use a box section for the side members, as this imparts a much greater degree of rigidity to the frame.

The cross members do not conform to any standard, and are placed wherever it is most convenient in the general design for positioning the various units. They are of steel and of a cross-section that will lend itself to the mounting of the units. To resist any tendency to "lozenging," i.e. one side member being set back relative to the other side member by impact, the "crucification" frame, in which two large diagonal cross members brace the two side members together, was at one time very popular. Today, however, there is a tendency to utilize the structure of the body for this purpose, the principle being referred to as "frameless construction" or "monoshell."

To obtain a reasonable turning circle on the steering, the distance between the side members at the front is smaller than at the rear so that the front wheels will not foul the frame when on the turn. It is also usual to upsweep the side members at the rear so as to clear the rear axle and make a low body line possible.

It is important that the frame should retain its true shape, otherwise the front axle will probably get out of alignment with the rear axle, and the steering stability and efficiency of transmission will be impaired. If the vehicle has been involved in an accident, or the truth of the frame is suspected for any other reason, tests should be made on the lines depicted in Fig. 1, page 366

The orthodox frame for the motor cycle is a diamond shape constructed of tubular steel, and was originally a development of the pedal cycle frame. But so many improvements and modifications have taken place that the modern product bears little resemblance to a bicycle. In most designs, the top tube runs roughly parallel with the ground from the steering head to the saddle pillar. The front down tube running from the steering head to the bottom tube is inclined rearwards to miss the front wheel. The bottom tube, roughly parallel with the top tube, runs from the front down tube to the rear hub, where the rear down tube meets it, the bottom and rear down tubes being split into forks to accommodate the rear wheel. Another down tube from the saddle pillar runs roughly diagonally across the diamond shape to the junction where the front down and bottom tube join. This braces the whole diamond shape. Some manufacturers favour a "duplex" frame, in which all the main tubes are doubled, hence the name. Pressed steel shapes have also been tried, but in all cases they conform roughly to the triangular diamond shape.

Here again the truth of the frame is essential to stability on the road, for a twisted frame will

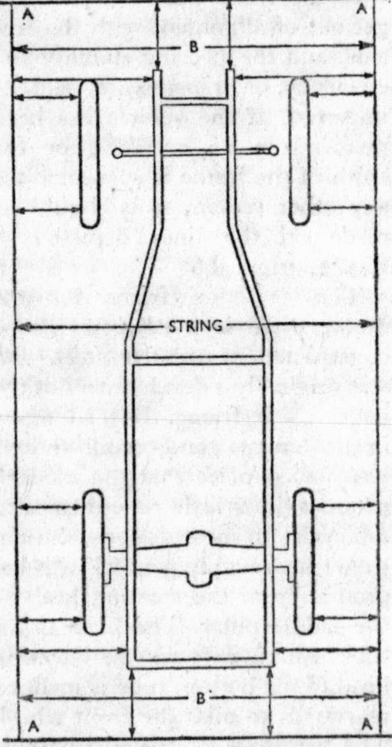

Fig. 1. Plan view and diagrammatic arrangement of car chassis showing the comparative dimensions for checking the chassis, road wheels and axle for any evidence of malalignment.

throw the axes of the two wheels and the steering head out of alinement. When a sidecar is attached, the wheels should all be in truly vertical and parallel planes. This should be regularly checked as shown in Fig. 2 and rectified, if necessary.

Furthermore, when the driving chains have to be adjusted, usually by sliding the gearbox to adjust the primary chain, and by sliding the rear wheel for the drive chain, the alignment of the sprockets must be maintained. This is best done be removing the chain and lining up the faces of the sprockets with a straightedge.

Springing.—Apart from contributing to the comfort of the passengers, the springing of a vehicle protects frame and body from shocks due to road irregularities. All springs have a distinct vibration rate defined by the term frequency, according to their structure, and this frequency (or periodicity) varies between 90 and 145 vibrations per minute. A vibration frequency of about 90 would give a much more smooth and comfortable ride than a short harsh spring with a frequency of 140. Unfortunately, the sensitive spring, while being very satisfactory at moderate speeds, allows too much freedom of movement at high speeds, when the car would bounce and roll and possess poor road-holding qualities. Also, with many vehicles there is a very great difference between the unladen and laden weights, and if the springs were made strong enough to carry the full load satisfactorily they would be too stiff when riding light, and would then transmit even the smallest shocks. It is therefore usual to effect a compromise between these two extremes, and to introduce further control by fitting additional devices in the form of dampers or shock absorbers. Some designers favour the use of "helpers", springs which only come into effect when the main springs have deflected a certain degree under load. With

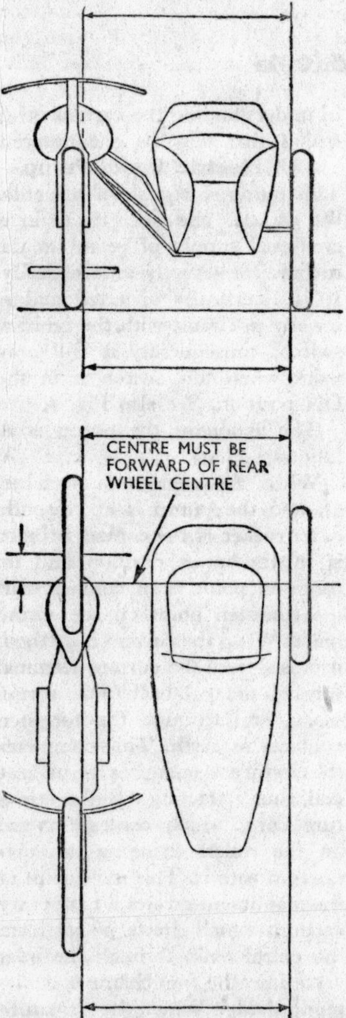

Fig. 2. Front elevation and plan view of motor cycle and side car showing points at which dimensions should be taken to test alignment of wheels.

this arrangement it is possible to have a sensitive light spring giving maximum riding comfort when the vehicle is running light, but when the load is applied the helper comes into play, and the required result of a strong spring is effected.

The most common type of spring fitted to both cars and lorries is the curved, laminated or leaf spring. This is built up of a number of leaves of gradually decreasing length piled on top of each other and secured to the largest or master leaf by a centre bolt. When the spring flexes—i.e. tends to straighten out—the leaves slide over each other at their outer ends; consequently, if they are not regularly lubricated, the sliding action of the springs will become progressively harsh and heavy wear will occur. There are many forms of the leaf spring under various designs from full elliptical to quarter elliptical and cantilever types, but it is unnecessary here to go into details as they all function similarly and all require lubrication. The shackle pins or spring eye bolts, which attach the springs to the frame, also require lubrication. The full weight comes on these components and there is continual movement at these points as the springs flex.

Today, with the advent of independent suspension, each wheel is allowed independence of movement, free from any influence of the other three road wheels. Coil springs, helical springs, and torque bars are becoming more popular. These forms of spring are not subject to friction and do not therefore require lubrication.

The springing of motor cycles is usually confined to the front forks and the rider's saddle. Coil springs, with suitable linkage, are invariably employed to spring the front wheel, and the pins in the linkage must be regularly lubricated. The rate of flexing is regulated by shock absorbers and these may be adjusted very efficiently to riding conditions to suit the rider, by a hand adjuster.

Fuel Systems

In nearly all modern motor vehicles the petrol tank is situated well below the level of the carburettor. Consequently, as the petrol will not flow to the float chamber some means must be provided to deliver fuel to the carburettor. In the past, it was sometimes the practice to locate the tank under the scuttle and feed the carburettor by gravity, and this was especially popular with commercial vehicles. But now it has become the practice to position the tank at the rear of private cars, and at the side of commercial vehicles. This very often involves lifting the petrol a matter of 2ft. to the carburettor float chamber. Suction pumps which utilized engine induction pressure for the operation of a vacuum for the delivery of fuel from tank to carburettor were once very popular, but these are now obsolescent; having been replaced by pumps with positive drives, electrically or mechanically operated.

These pumps (of the diaphragm type) have now become the standardized fitting on all vehicles. To see how these pumps work we will describe the action of a typical electrically operated pump of popular design, and also that of another pump operated mechanically by the engine. If the working of these two typical pumps is understood, no difficulty should be experienced in understanding the various other makes that may be encountered.

S.U. Electric Petrol Pump.—This pump is capable of a suction lift of 4ft. and will maintain a continual supply of petrol to the carburettor entirely automatically. It is electrically operated and is usually in circuit with the ignition switch, consequently it will only work when this switch is in the ON position. See also Fig. 1.

The action of the pump is as follows:

When the current is switched off and the pump is at rest, the outer rocker of the contact breaker is in the outer position and its tungsten point is in contact with the tungsten point on the spring blade. When the current is earthed, it passes from the current terminal through the coil, back to the spring blade, and through the tungsten contacts to earth. This completes the circuit and energizes the magnet coil, thus attracting the iron armature core, which comes forward on the rollers bringing the diaphragm with it. This movement of the diaphragm creates a temporary vacuum which draws petrol from the petrol tank, through the inlet valve into the fuel chamber of the pump body. When the armature has advanced nearly to the end of its stroke, the contact breaker rod, which moves with it, operates a "throw over" mechanism on the

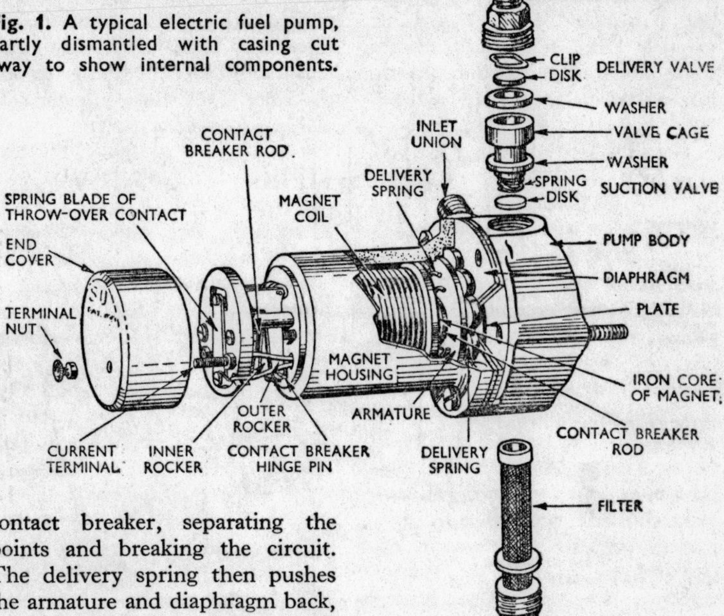

Fig. 1. A typical electric fuel pump, partly dismantled with casing cut away to show internal components.

contact breaker, separating the points and breaking the circuit. The delivery spring then pushes the armature and diaphragm back, forcing petrol through the outlet or delivery valve to the carburettor. As soon as the armature gets near the end of this stroke the "throw over" mechanism again operates, the breaker points again make contact, and the cycle of operations is repeated. The quantity of fuel delivered to the carburettor float chambers is governed by the float chamber needle valve, which, when closed, sets up a back pressure exceeding the strength of the fuel pump diaphragm return spring.

If trouble is experienced, and the pump ceases to function, first make sure that current is available at the pump terminal by shorting the wire to earth and seeing if it sparks. If there is no current the trouble is obviously not the pump but in the electrical system. But if current is available and the pump still ceases to operate it is probably due to dirty contact points. These should be cleaned by dressing with a breaker-point dressing slip, after which the pump will probably begin to operate again. If this does not cure the trouble, make sure that the breaker points are making contact. If they are not, it means that the contact breaker rod wants adjusting. As this is a somewhat complicated job necessitating the dismantling of the pump, it is advisable to obtain the assistance of a competent mechanic before effecting re-adjustment.

On the other hand, if the pump works noisily an air leak on the suction side may be suspected. Obviously, if the petrol tank is empty the pump will be working without delivering petrol, so do not overlook this point. Also do not

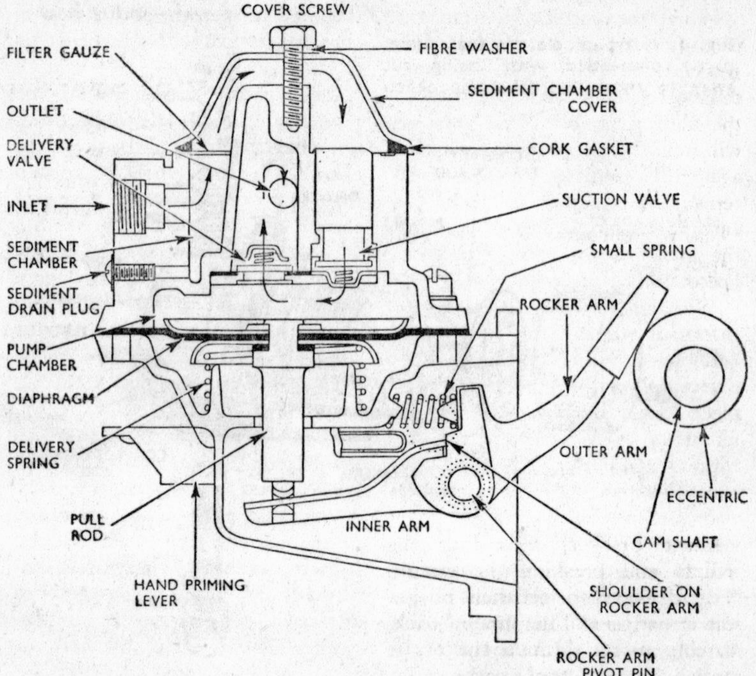

Fig. 2. A popular type of mechanically operated fuel pump. Eccentric on camshaft, driven off engine, operates the rocker arm causing diaphragm to draw in fuel from delivery tank and pump it to carburettor. Fuel delivery to carburettor varies in direct proportion to the speed at which engine crankshaft rotates.

neglect cleaning the filter regularly. Dirt underneath the suction or delivery valves will cause the pump to continue noisily working with little or no delivery of petrol. Each valve can be cleaned easily by unscrewing the top union from the body and lifting out the valve cage.

A.C. Mechanical Petrol Pump.—This fully mechanical pump is particularly popular, and its manufacturers maintain a very fine service organization. See Fig. 2.

The pump is usually bolted to the crankcase of the engine and operated directly by an eccentric on the camshaft, or by push rod.

As the camshaft rotates, the eccentric lifts the rocker-arm which pulls the connecting rod, together with the diaphragm, downward against the pressure of the return spring, thus creating a vacuum in the pump chamber. Fuel from the tank is then sucked through the inlet connection, into the sediment chamber, through the gauze filter and inlet valve into the pump chamber. On the return stroke the pressure of the return spring pushes the diaphragm upward forcing fuel from the pump chamber through the outlet or delivery valve and outlet connection to the carburettor.

When the correct level in the carburettor float chamber is reached, the needle valve will close, thus creating a back pressure in the pump chamber. This pressure will hold the diaphragm downward against the return spring and it will remain in this position until the carburettor requires more fuel and the float chamber needle valve opens.

When the fuel pump is subjected to a back pressure the diaphragm connecting rod forces the interior, pivoted portion or lever of the two-piece rocker arm to the bottom of its stroke. As the outer part of the rocker arm, which is in direct contact with the eccentric cam, is also secured to the same pivot centre as the lever, the rocker arm will cease to operate the lever until the diaphragm is returned to its initial position. The small spring at the rocker arm shoulder is intended to keep the rocker arm in constant contact with the eccentric, to eliminate noise.

The gauze filter should be regularly cleaned. It can be taken out when the cover of the sediment chamber is removed. Make certain that the cork gasket is properly seated and that the fibre washer is under the head of the screw when re-assembling, so that there is no air leak into the sediment chamber. Any deposit in the sediment chamber can usually be drained off by removing the drain plug. See Fig. 2.

Seepage of fuel at the edge of the diaphragm can generally be cured by tightening up the body screws. A continual fuel leakage from the drain hole in the body casting usually indicates a punctured diaphragm. Should this happen it is advisable to get the pump exchanged for a serviceable unit.

Carburettors

A GOOD example of the simple principles of carburation may be found in an examination of the Zenith Ordinary carburettor; a prototype, by the way, of more advanced Zenith type carburettors.

Petrol enters the float chamber through the tubular filter and needle valve (Fig. 1). When the correct level is reached, and this is just below the orifice of the main jet, the float closes the needle valve by means of the balance weights, and cuts off any further entry of petrol. When the engine is running fuel is drawn from the float chamber and the fuel level falls. The float also drops, and reopens the needle valve, thus ensuring that the correct level is maintained.

To start the engine the air strangler is closed and the throttle opened very slightly. The ignition is switched on and the starter engaged. The engine will suck petrol and air mixture through the slow running tube only, since the main air intake is closed. After several revolutions the engine will start up, and the air strangler should be opened slightly. When the engine has been warmed up, the air strangler can be opened fully and the throttle closed down to its stop. The engine will now be ticking over entirely on the slow running tube until the accelerator pedal is depressed and the throttle

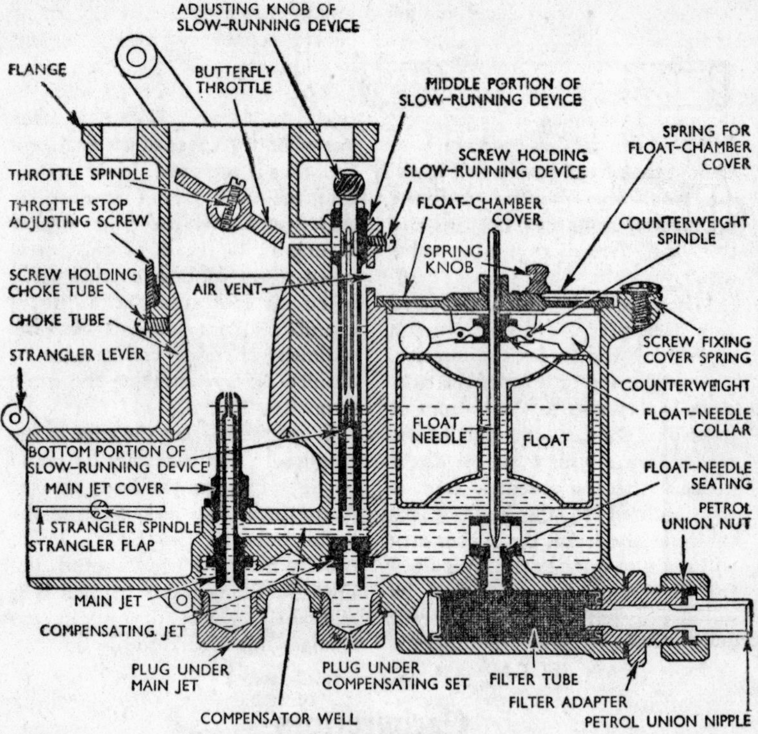

Fig. 1. Cross section of Zenith type carburettor showing arrangement of components and the fuel delivery from the float chamber to the main and slow-running jets. Note slow-running jet outlet passage at butterfly throttle.

opened. Then there will be an immediate rush of air past the main jet, drawing a petrol spray from the main jet itself. As the engine speed increases, a tendency to over richness is neutralized in the following manner by the balancing effect of the compensating jet. The size of the compensating jet is such that it does not allow petrol to pass into the well of the jet in any quantity at high engine speeds, when air, instead, is sucked in. At the same time, however, it provides an additional supply of fuel to the main jet at slow running speeds, such as when climbing hills or picking up speed. Actually the main jet exerts most influence at high speed, while the compensator jet corrects the fuel supply deficiencies of the main jet at low speed.

The carburettor is supplied with the correct size choke tube, and main and compensator jets, for a particular engine. As however, individual engines vary slightly, the general adjustment of the carburettor is carried out in the following manner. Start up the engine and, when it is warm, set the throttle at the required position to give the best slow running

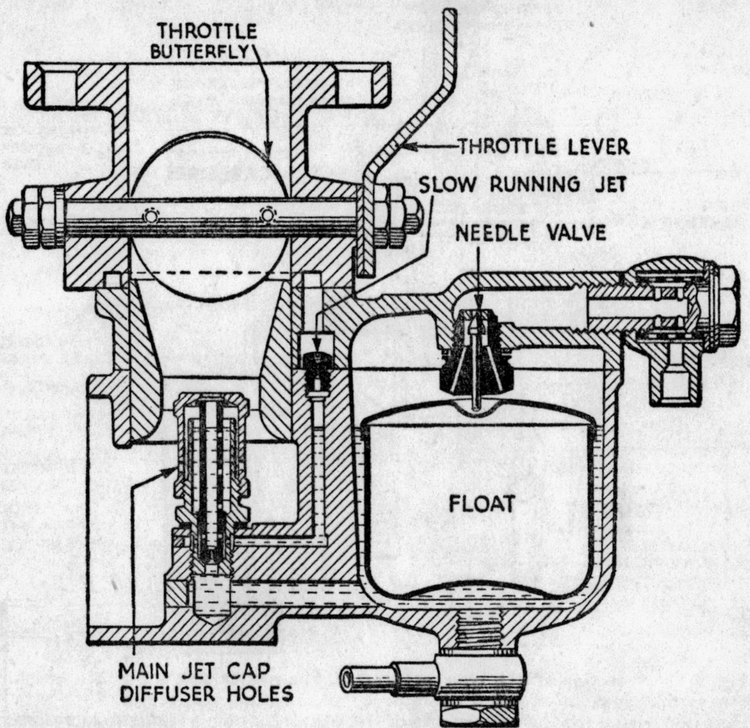

Fig. 2. Cross-section of a Solex type carburettor showing fuel passages from float chamber to main and slow running jets. Note that main jet is submerged at calibrated orifice at the base of the main jet immediately above the jet well.

speed, by screwing in or out the throttle stop adjusting screw. This will control the speed at which the engine will run. It may be found, however, that the engine is not running evenly. After the slow running tube has been adjusted it may be necessary to make another small adjustment to the stop screw on the throttle lever.

Solex Carburettor.—This popular carburettor consists of a float chamber, throttle butterfly valve, choke tube, and main and slow running jets. The petrol level is maintained by the direct operation of the float on the needle valve; the latter being situated in the head of the float chamber. The vent to the slow running jet is on the engine side of the throttle, so that when the throttle is closed the engine draws on the slow running jet. As soon as the throttle is opened air flows up past the main jet drawing a petrol spray from the jet. The main jet consists of the actual jet submerged at its lower level by a well of petrol, which is delivered to the air intake through a restricted orifice at the base of the jet. Consequently the initial rich mixture required for getting away or slow slogging hard work, is

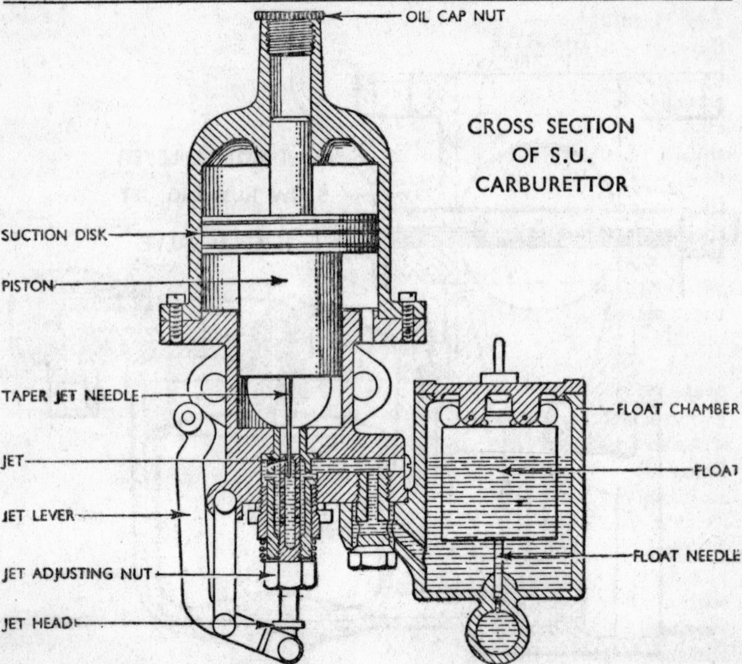

Fig. 3. Cross-section of S.U. type carburettor. The suction disk and piston which carries the taper jet needle is operated by suction from the engine. Thus with increased engine speed a greater rate of fuel delivery is obtained due to increased suction on disk and its withdrawal together with taper jet needle at main jet.

supplied by the petrol in the well of the jet. If the rate of consumption is in excess of the supply through the restricted orifice in the base of the jet, the mixture ratio is weakened by air which is drawn in through diffuser holes. Consequently, at high engine speeds the small orifice limits the supply of fuel and the tendency to enrichment is compensated. See Fig. 2.

When the engine is normally warm, set the throttle at the position where the engine runs best by screwing the throttle stop screw in or out. This will regulate the slow running of the engine but will not alter the ratio of the mixture. This may be incorrect, causing the engine to "hunt" or stall. To rectify this state of affairs the slow running mixture control screw should be first screwed fully home, and the throttle stop screw set to the lowest possible idling position. The engine should now have a tendency to "hunt", but by gradually screwing out the slow running mixture control screw this will be gradually rectified until the position is found where the engine runs regularly and evenly.

S.U. Carburettor.—The flow of petrol to the carburettor (Fig. 3), is maintained in the usual way with an orthodox float chamber. Petrol from the float chamber is fed to a jet which is always of standard size. Petrol delivery to the engine is regulated by a tapered needle attached to the lower end of a piston controlled by the suction from the engine. As the suction increases the needle is gradually withdrawn from the jet, enlarging its effective opening and permitting it to pass more petrol. The lower end of the suction operated piston also functions as a variable choke, regulating the area of the air passage around the jet as it rises and falls. It thus maintains a practically constant suction on the jet under varying engine loads and speeds. It is in this particular feature that it differs from the other carburettors already described where the choke size remains unaltered. The jet is so mounted that it can be moved up or down in relation to the needle, in order to enrich or weaken the mixture by a lever operated by the mixture control knob at the hand of the driver. Thus a rich mixture can be provided for starting and warming up a cold engine, and the correct mixture ratio available as soon as normal running conditions prevail. See also Fig. 4.

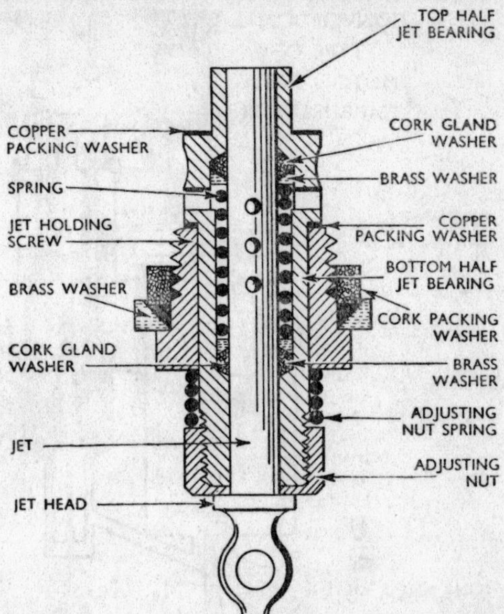

Fig. 4. The main jet can be raised or lowered by manual operation of the jet lever control, as required.

Obviously the correct size of carburettor and needle will have to be supplied for a particular engine. Tuning the carburettor is simplicity itself as all jets are of standard size, and with the right size of needle the only adjustment possible is to set the jet in the correct position for slow running. This adjustment not only sets the carburettor for idling but for the whole range of speeds. It is carried out in the following way:

Run the engine until it attains its normal running temperature. Adjust the jet to such a position that the engine idles on the correct mixture. An easy way to do this is to screw the jet adjusting nut up higher than its normal position and then adjust the jet correctly; as the jet adjusting nut only acts as a stop to prevent the jet from coming beyond its correct position; it can then be screwed down until it butts up against the jet head. This will be the normal running position, with the mixture control set at weak.

This is the only adjustment provided, and if the road per-

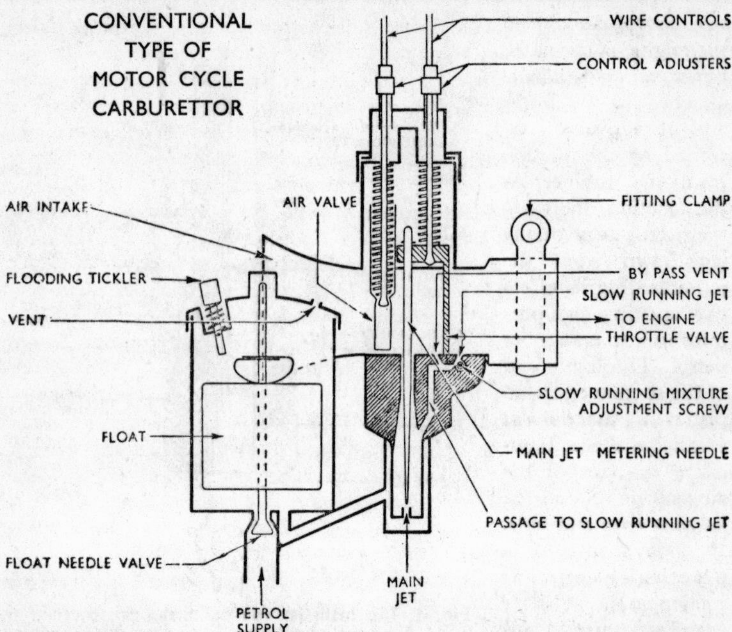

Fig. 5. Diagrammatic arrangement of typical motor cycle carburettor. Throttle valve and main jet metering needle are operated together by a single control. Air valve separately operated by similar control cable. Note by-pass for slow-running jet which operates when the throttle is in the normal closed position.

formance is not satisfactory, a larger or smaller needle will be necessary. But if the car has been running satisfactorily on previous journeys it is not likely that another needle is required; in the majority of cases correct adjustment is all that is necessary.

General Information.—It is obviously not possible to give detailed instructions but the following summary applies to all ordinary carburettors:

Slow Running.—There is usually some adjustable stop provided for regulating the closed position of the throttle. In conjunction with this, there is usually another adjustment for correcting the slow running mixture.

General Performance.—If the carburettor has been supplied with the engine it should not be necessary to make a change, but the choke tube and jets can be removed and new ones fitted to suit individual tastes. Obviously the combination fitted by the makers gives the best compromise for an all round performance with reasonable economy. The following factors should be grasped before any alterations are undertaken.

Choke Tubes.—Although too large a choke gives good consumption figures, it results in bad acceleration under all conditions. On the other hand, with too small a choke tube acceleration will generally be good but maximum possible speed will be cut down. This is due to the fact that the volume of air passing through the choke is being restricted.

Main Jets.—Too large a main jet generally causes high petrol consumption, and woolly or irregular running at medium and high speeds. Too small a main jet will cause loss of power and popping back when accelerating, and the engine will be inclined to over-heat.

Carburettor Troubles.—For general maintenance refer to section on CARE AND MAINTENANCE. The following notes on carburettor trouble assume that the engine is mechanically sound and that the ignition and fuel systems are in order, and also that the carburettor itself has previously been tuned. See also Fault Chart, p. 363.

Flooding.—This is usually due to dirt under the needle valve. It may, if persistent, be caused by a leaking float, in which case fit a new float. Another, less frequent, cause of flooding may be traced to wear on the face of the needle seating. If this is the cause a new needle must be fitted.

Bad Starting Cold.—The throttle may be opened too much or the float chamber dry. This latter condition is very often experienced when the car has been idle for a day or two, the petrol in the float chamber having evaporated. The float chamber should be primed before attempting to start up.

Bad Starting Hot.—This is often due to excessive richness resulting from the misuse of the strangler or mixture control. Accelerate the engine with the throttle fully open to clear, and then shut to usual closed position.

Bad Slow Running.—If the engine has been running satisfactorily, and no alteration of adjustment has been made, the cause is almost invariably dirt in the slow running jet.

Will not Accelerate.—This is most likely due to dirt in the main and compensator jets.

Lacks Full Power.—This is possibly due to shortage of fuel, caused by partially choked filters, or choked main jet.

Motor Cycle Carburettors.—These instruments retain the usual float chamber mechanism for maintaining the petrol level, as that used in car models. Otherwise they are much simpler and have fewer adjustments than their car prototypes. In most cases a separate air control besides the throttle control is also provided. Also the throttle generally incorporates a variable jet and choke, so that the size of the choke increases as the size of the jet increases. In fact, the action is similar to that of the S.U. Carburettor, but it is effected manually by hand control instead of by air suction. As an example, it will be convenient to take the working of the Amal carburettor, which is both typical and popular.

The petrol level is maintained in the usual manner by float and tapered needle valve. A tickler is provided which, when depressed, floods the float chamber. Slow running is provided for by an independent running jet with mixture adjustment by the slow running mixture control screw. It is augmented at small throttle openings by the by-pass vent. The air-valve is independently operated and serves the purpose of obstructing the air intake passage for starting and mixture regulation. The throttle control operates both the main jet metering needle and the throttle valve; uniform mixture strength is thus maintained throughout the full range. The size of the main jet is the limiting factor to the maximum amount of fuel passed at full throttle. An adjustable stop is also provided to determine the position at which the throttle valve may be shut down, by which the position of the throttle is regulated independently of the cable control adjustment.

The attachment of the carburettor controls at both the hand levers or twist grips must be efficient otherwise wear at the points may be excessive, for the cable controls are subject to a fair degree of manual operation. If the points of attachment are not secure fraying of the cable may ensue.

The run of the control cables from handlebars to carburettor should be free of sharp bends or kinks which would tend to cause the cable to bind in the outer casing and result in unnecessary wear and fraying of the cable

Cooling and Lubrication

MOST readers are aware that much heat is generated by an internal combustion engine while it is working and no known materials would stand continuous high working temperatures unless means were taken to dissipate the heat within practical limits. The usual running temperatures lie between 180 and 200 degrees Fahrenheit, or 80 and 90 degrees Centigrade. Sometimes control is achieved by *direct cooling*, and the heat is dissipated directly from the cylinders into the atmosphere. An engine cooled in this way is said to be air cooled. Or, alternatively, temperature control may be effected by *indirect cooling*, as when fluid is circulated through appropriate jackets surrounding the cylinders, and conveys the heat to a radiator which, in its turn, is cooled by the atmosphere. Water is usually employed for this purpose on motor vehicles and will be the only fluid to concern us, but glycol, having a basis of glycerine, is extensively employed on aircraft engines.

Air-cooled cylinders are furnished with a large number of fins to increase the surface area for the radiation of heat. Such engines are confined chiefly to motor cycles, but when used on larger vehicles, a fan is sometimes employed to deliver a forced draught through the system. Air-cooled engines installed in aircraft are fitted with special cowlings and baffles designed to concentrate the flow of cooling air over the cylinder cooling fins. Generally speaking, with air-cooled engines it is difficult to regulate the temperature, and consequently nearly all motor car engines use a water-cooling system in which either the water circulates by natural means, called thermo-siphon (see Fig. 1), or is forced round by a pump.

Thermo-Siphon System.—In this system the heated water circulates, by convection current, to the highest point in the system. For successful operation the bores.

of all pipes and jackets should be free of obstruction and as large as possible. The cylinders themselves are placed as low as possible, relative to the radiator, so as to accelerate the natural upward flow of heated water from the jackets to the radiator. The hot water cools as it passes into the hollow cellular structure of the radiator. It then flows down through the radiator into the cylinder jackets to take the place of the hot water flowing out. This circulation is maintained so long as the water level in the radiator is kept above the delivery pipe from the cylinders to the radiator. Otherwise the circulation will cease and the water in the jackets will boil away. So it is most important with this system to keep the water level well up in the radiator. It should be checked every day. This is particularly important where an aluminium cylinder head is embodied, for overheating will tend to produce cracks during the cooling of the

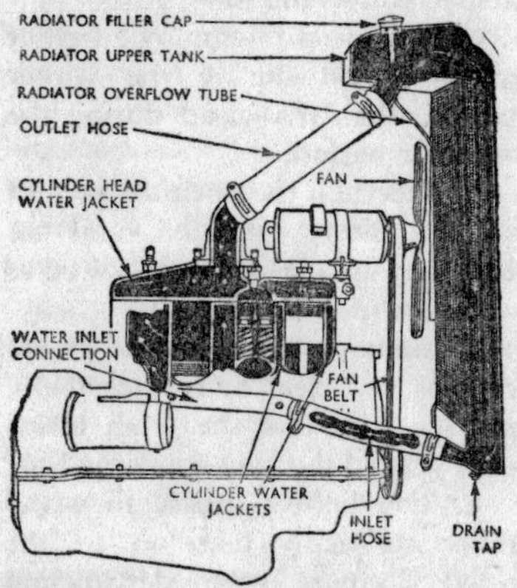

Fig. 1. Diagrammatic arrangement of engine cooling system. Water in cylinder jackets absorbs heat from cylinder and rises, by natural convection, and down through the radiator.

metal. Another advantage of this system is that it prevents the engine from being run too cold, for the circulation will not commence until a certain heat is reached.

Pump Circulation.—In this system the water is circulated under pressure by a pump or impeller, usually located between the radiator and the inlet into the cylinder jackets. The pump is driven by the engine and commences to circulate the water immediately the engine is started. A normal consequence would be for the engine to run too cold for some considerable time, to its detriment, and it is therefore the modern practice to instal a thermostatic valve in the outlet pipe from the cylinders to the radiator. This valve remains closed, preventing the water from circulating, but it automatically opens when a predetermined temperature is reached. In fact, the temperature of the engine is automatically regulated under all conditions. There is, however, a further consideration which must not be overlooked. Suppose the vehicle is held up in a traffic jam, with the engine running. It is true that the pump will circulate the water and the thermostatic valve will allow it to pass into the radiator, but, since the vehicle is not in motion, air-draught through the radiator will be absent and the engine will tend to over-heat. To counteract this disadvantage it has become a general practice to provide a fan to create a suitable flow of air through the radiator when the engine is running.

Caution.—Always refill the cooling system with soft water—ordinary tap water usually deposits substances detrimental to the system. If anti-freeze solutions are not used, or the garage is not heated, do not forget to drain the cooling system in frosty weather.

Lubrication.—All the moving parts of a vehicle, whether they are components of the engine, gearbox, transmission or chassis, are subject to friction and wear. It is the all-important job of a lubricant to reduce this wear to a minimum. No doubt the reader is aware that many different systems of lubrication are used in different designs for this purpose, but though he may not be particularly interested in the system itself, he must acquaint himself with the makers' instructions. It is, for instance, most important to use a suitable lubricant for a specific job. There are many different oils and greases whose properties and useful characteristics vary considerably. Nobody knows better what is suitable in the way of lubricants for a particular vehicle than the manufacturers, and one cannot do better than take their advice. For example, an oil which might be very suitable, and give good results in an engine employing a full force feed lubrication system would probably be entirely unsuitable for another engine employing splash lubrication. Also, the grade of grease specially suited to the lubrication of wheel hub bearings would be quite unsuitable for lubricating the water pump spindle. While not embarking on a detailed analysis of the various lubricants and their uses, we must point out that whereas the designer has equipped the vehicle with suitable means of lubrication at all places where it is required, it is the responsibility of the driver to see that regular maintenance is carried out with the lubricants as recommended. A lubrication chart is generally issued with the vehicle, or is available on application to any of the reputable oil companies.

For those who do their own maintenance, the points to watch in collaboration with the instruction book are:

1. Use the right lubricant for the right part.

2. Never mix oils or greases of different makes.

3. When checking engine oil level, always see that the vehicle is standing on level ground. The check should be made a few minutes after the engine is shut off.

4. When changing the lubricant in engine, gearbox or rear axle units, drain off the old lubricant immediately after a run—the lubricant, being hot, will then run most freely.

5. It is not good practice to use paraffin as a flushing medium. Use a special flushing oil.

6. It is usual to employ a lighter grade of oil during the winter period, than that used during the summer period.

7. Ascertain the position, etc., of *all* the filters provided, and see that they are cleaned or renewed as occasion requires.

8. Remove any blocked grease nipples and clear or replace them, making sure that the fresh lubricant gets to the part concerned.

9. Too light a grease in wheel hubs invariably gets on to the brake linings, with detrimental effect.

10. Never over-do the use of the carburettor strangler. Excessive use causes dilution of the engine oil.

Transmission

TRANSMISSION may be said to mean, the efficient conversion of engine crankshaft rotation into a motive force, to be transferred to the road wheels, by means of those mechanical components which link the engine crankshaft to the road wheels. Briefly, the transmission system includes the clutch, gearbox, propeller shaft and rear axles, which latter are driven through a set of differential gears by the main propeller shaft. The location of each of these components, in relation to the engine and car chassis, is illustrated in Fig. 1 and the functions of each are described in the following paragraphs.

Before proceeding further with a description of these components the reader's attention is drawn to the fact that the type of transmission herein described relates only to the more general principles of transmission. There are, for instance, car transmission designs which incorporate front wheel drive; others are so designed as to locate the engine power unit at the rear of the car with a transmission materially affected in design by this measure. There may also be minor variations in design at any point throughout the whole of the transmission system for cars of different makes, which incorporate transmission of the more orthodox type and, occasionally, extensive differences in clutch design. These are the main characteristics which distinguish one make of car from another. Since these variations are numerous they cannot be dealt with in detail and it is proposed to describe only the fundamental requirements and functions of car transmission.

The problem of the suitable conversion of engine power into a motive force by means of the transmission system is not confined to the simple transference of a mere rotation of the driving road wheels. Several requirements in design must be satisfied before effective transmission is possible.

The first of these is the necessity of isolating the engine, at will, from the transmission. This requirement is fulfilled by the embodiment of a foot operated clutch and a neutral position of the gears in the gearbox.

The clutch, situated between the rear of the engine and the forward face of the gearbox remains in effective operation until it is operated by the foot lever, or, as it is generally known, the clutch pedal.

The gearbox, incorporating a selection of gears, remains inoperative to the transmission of crankshaft rotation, via the clutch, when the gear selector lever is in neutral position, i.e. out of gear. Thus it will be understood that until the gear selector is moved to a different position the propeller shaft (directly connected to the gearbox main driven shaft by a universal coupling joint) will not rotate although the engine is running. The clutch, therefore, is necessary for the temporary isolation of the transmission system for the changing of gears either from the stationary position or during actual motion of the car. A second requirement influences the design of the propeller shaft and its connec-

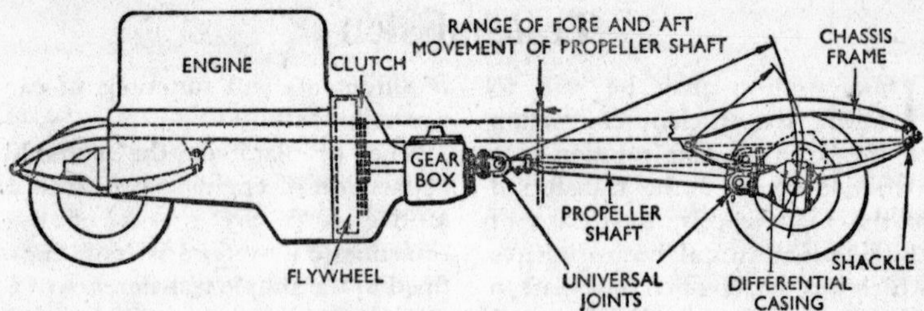

Fig. 1. Representative diagram of car frame and transmission arrangement. Note that the propeller shaft is secured to gearbox and differential gears by two universal joints to offset deflection caused by upward and downward movement of rear axle such as will occur when the vehicle is being driven.

tion to the gearbox. This is raised by the necessity of mounting the rear axle cover (or housing) on springs to absorb the shock normal to the movement of the car over uneven road surfaces. In consequence some point along the propeller shaft must be flexible to up and down movement of the rear axle without impairing the efficiency of transmission. This need is met by the introduction of a universal coupling at the point of attachment between the forward end of the propeller shaft and the rear end of the gearbox main driven shaft.

A further requirement, essential to the safe driving of a car, quite apart from the excessive wear which would be incurred by the tyres of the driving road wheels, is the necessity of ensuring that each of the rear driving road wheels shall turn at the correct speed required when negotiating a bend or corner on the road. Obviously the inner wheel should rotate more slowly than the outer wheel in relation to the bend in the road. This problem in design is solved by the incorporation of a differential gearbox located in the rear axle cover and it is at this point that the pinion wheel of the propeller shaft imparts its rotation, via the differential gears, to the axles of the driving road wheels. These three main requirements are, however, complicated by other considerations, the specialized reasons for which are described separately under the headings of the transmission components, the clutch, gearbox, propeller shaft, differential gears and rear axles.

Clutch.—This component is generally enclosed within the gearbox casing but is, in effect, a separate unit from the gearbox assembly. The clutch comprises three main members; the clutch pressure plate, flywheel and the clutch disk or centre plate, which covered with a material possessing a high coefficient of friction is interposed between clutch pressure plate, and the rear face of the flywheel, the clutch pressure plate only being operated by a foot lever located on the toe board of the interior of the car. A popular type of clutch known as the Single Plate Clutch is shown, together with a general arrangement of components, in Fig. 2. In simple terms of operation, when the clutch pedal is fully depressed the clutch pressure plate is drawn away from the clutch disk, thus isolating the engine from the gearbox. The clutch pressure plate is heavily spring loaded and if the foot pressure is relaxed on the clutch lever the pressure plate will return to its initial position, firmly contacting the clutch disk and forcing the disk against the flywheel face. The flywheel, which is driven direct from the engine, then transmits its rotation without slip, to the clutch disk. As the clutch disk or centre plate is keyed to the gearbox shaft this shaft will be turned as soon as the pressure on the clutch pedal is relaxed. If a gear has been engaged by movement of the gear selector lever, rotation will be transferred to the propeller shaft and thence to the road wheels.

The leverage of the clutch pedal is so arranged as to permit a sensitive application of the clutch pressure plate to the clutch disk. This feature is an essential, otherwise the sudden load imposed on the engine by the inert weight of the whole car would cause excessive strain on the transmission system. Thus it will be seen that slow application of the clutch provides for a gradual transference of loading to the engine when the car is stationary, eliminating jerky starting from the stationary position and smoothing out any sharp differences in engine loading when the gears are changed during car motion.

Gearbox.—The gearbox is closely inter-related, in function with the clutch, as it would be impracticable to change gears without the intermediate aid of the clutch assembly. But before describing the function of the gearbox it would be advisable to consider certain innate characteristics of the internal combustion engine.

It is obvious that an engine turning slowly will not develop so much power as when it is turning over at great speed. Thus at low engine speeds the power unit will, as previously mentioned, cut out if a sudden load, in excess of the power developed, is applied to the crankshaft. If, however, in the absence of a clutch, the engine is suddenly geared to the transmission the whole car will be jerked forward at a speed directly proportional to the power developed and transferred to the road wheels, before the engine cuts out. The effects of such a sudden loading on the various components can be imagined. Hence another reason for embodiment of the clutch.

Another significant factor in the employment of a gearbox is the variation in the load applied to the engine, such as would occur when the car negotiates hills, down slopes and level road surfaces. This will explain the range of gear ratios available in the gearbox. Since it is occasionally necessary to reverse the car a separate gear for this purpose is embodied in the gearbox. Each of the gear ratios is calculated to suit the power developed by the engine as against the range of loads likely to be encountered and speeds required during the normal running of the car. Thus the gearbox is there to ensure an appropriate transmission of adequate driving power to the road wheels in all conditions. To understand the operation of a gearbox it is necessary to realize that the average

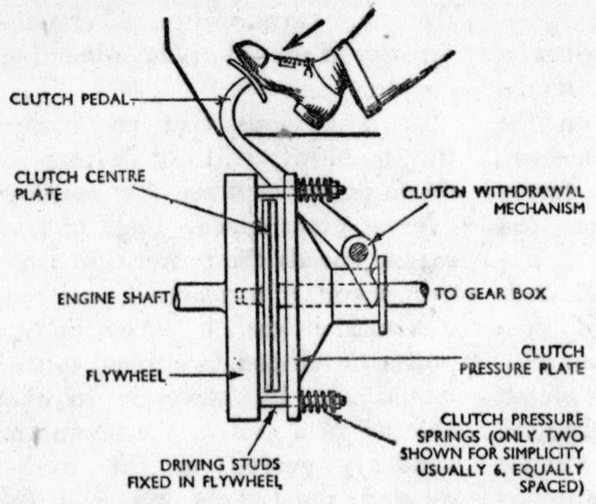

Fig. 2. Diagrammatic arrangement of single plate clutch. Foot pressure on pedal releases clutch pressure plate, isolating engine shaft from gearbox.

individual can, with the aid of a crane, lift a heavy weight which could not normally be lifted by hand. It is this principle which is applied in the design and incorporation of different gears in the gearbox. Briefly, if a large gear, attached to the drum of the crane, is turned by a small gear fixed to the spindle of the crane handle, a heavy weight may be easily lifted from the floor. The rate or speed at which the load is lifted will, however, be slower than would be the case if a somewhat larger gear was used with the crane handle (turned at a uniform speed) to operate the drum, but in the latter instance the speed and exertion of lifting the load would be proportionately greater.

For example, if the large gear in the drum has 40 teeth and the small gear has 20 teeth the gear ratio will be 2 to 1. If the large gear has 80 teeth and the small gear has 20 teeth the gear ratio will be 4 to 1, and less exertion will be necessary to lift the load; but, if in both instances, the handle is turned the same number of revolutions per minute the speed of lifting will be faster in the former instance where the gear ratio is 2 to 1.

That in its most simple form is what happens in the gearbox.

Low ratio gearing being utilized for heavy loads, such as those imposed when the car is stationary and about to be put in motion, hill climbing, etc. The intermediate gear ratios are utilized for those transitional phases of car motion to ensure smooth engagement in top gear, one of high ratio, when the car has negotiated an incline or has gathered speed on a level road surface.

Another mechanical feature in gear running must be noted. If a gear having 60 teeth is driven direct by the engine crankshaft, rotating at 1,000 r.p.m., and a gear having 120 teeth is meshed with the former, the speed of the larger gear will be 500 r.p.m. If a lower gear ratio for the driven gear was used, say with a gear having 240 teeth, the speed of this gear would be 250 r.p.m. Thus by drawing a comparison it will be seen that speed of car motion is sacrificed in low gear ratios but the ability to apply higher engine r.p.m. ensures that the engine will be capable of overcoming the load imposed without any danger of cutting out. The following table, which gives approximate figures and average

1st Gear Ratio 8 to 1		2nd Gear Ratio 10 to 1		3rd Gear Ratio 5 to 1	
Engine speed. r.p.m.	Road speed. m.p.h.	Engine speed. r.p.m.	Road speed. m.p.h.	Engine speed. r.p.m.	Road speed. m.p.h.
1170	5	1300	10	1300	20
2340	10	2600	20	2000	30
—	—	3750	30	2650	40
—	—	—	—	3300	50
—	—	—	—	3900	60

ratios with resulting road speeds for an 8 h.p. car will serve to correlate the foregoing information, bearing in mind the fact that the higher the r.p.m. the higher is the engine power output.

Fig. 3 shows two quite simple diagrammatic arrangements of a set of gears in a gearbox. The first and top gear trains only are shown in operation in the diagrams; the other gears are operated by the selector mechanism on similar lines. The names of the various components comprising the gearbox are also shown.

It will be noted that the small gear on the main driven shaft is always in mesh with the larger gear secured on the layshaft (sometimes called the countershaft). These are known as the Constant Mesh Gears. Thus the layshaft will rotate when the engine is running, but, as has been previously mentioned, no transmission of rotation will be imparted to the propeller shaft when the gear change or selector lever is in the neutral position. Furthermore, the layshaft will rotate at a lower speed than the engine crankshaft which drives it. It will be noted that the layshaft will also carry other fixed gears which may in turn be meshed with one or other of the sliding gears each of which, being of different gear ratios, will transmit a different speed of rotation to the propeller shaft, assuming that the engine is turning at a uniform rate. First, second, top and third speed sliding gears are all free to move *along* the splined main or driven shaft but all must rotate with the driven shaft when one or other of the sliding gears has been meshed with its appropriate gear on the layshaft.

When the driver disengages the clutch and moves the gear selector lever to first gear speed, the sliding first gear is moved along the splined driven shaft and into mesh with its fixed mating gear on the layshaft, the other sliding gears remaining free.

When the pressure on the clutch pedal is released the clutch will transmit the crankshaft rotation to the constant mesh gears and the layshaft will transmit its turning moment, via the first gears, to the main driven gear shaft which will cause the propeller shaft to rotate.

The same operation will apply

to the selection of any of the different gears and the conditions of use will be governed by the duties imposed on the engine during car running. In top gear, however, the main driven shaft in the gearbox is driven direct from the engine at crankshaft speed.

Propeller Shaft.—The propeller shaft is coupled direct to the rear end of the gearbox main driven shaft by a special fitting known as a universal joint. This fitting, necessary to the efficient operation of the propeller shaft, ensures that the up and down movement of the axle cover or housing, to which the shaft housing is secured, will not interfere with the rotation of the shaft; for the axle cover is secured to the rear springs of the car and a certain degree of flexing movement at the springs, due to uneven road surface, will be encountered. The propeller shaft is contained in roller and thrust bearings situated in the shaft housing and at its rear end is secured a driving pinion which meshes with a large driven gear in the interior of the axle cover or differential gear box. The rotation of the propeller shaft driving pinion is transferred to the axles which operate in the following manner.

Rear Axles.—The rear axle cover or housing, it should be noted, is braced by two torque tubes which are firmly secured, in horizontal positions, to the propeller shaft and the outer extremities of the axle housing. Furthermore the weight of the rear of the car is imposed on the axle cover only, the axles being free to

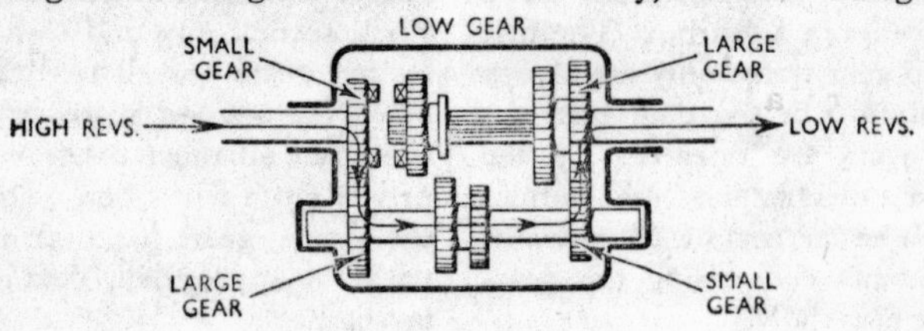

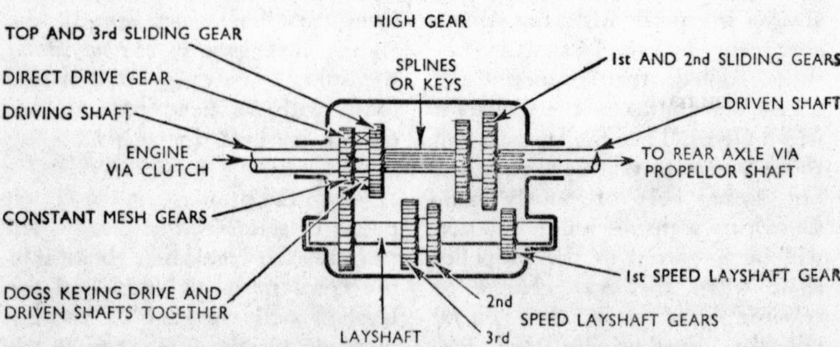

Fig. 3. Representative diagrams of a gearbox. Lower diagram shows driving shaft from engine in direct mesh with drive to rear axle. Layshaft not in mesh with sliding gears. Upper diagram shows 1st sliding gear in mesh with small gear on layshaft thus permitting high engine power output at slow car speed

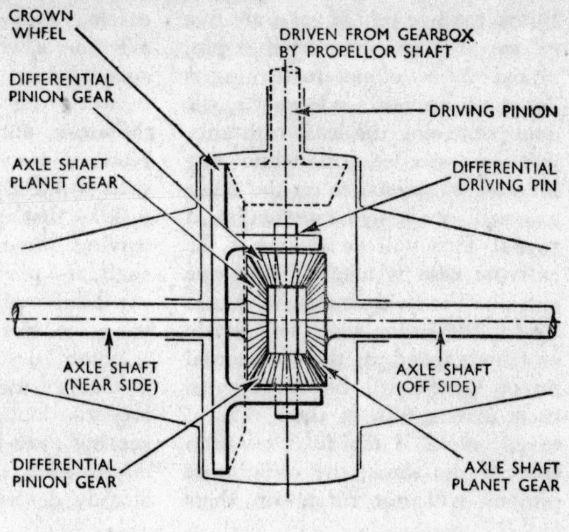

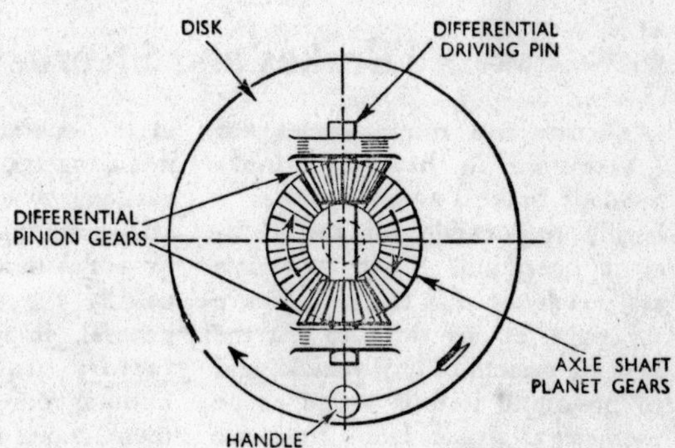

Fig. 4. Differential gears. Two diagrams illustrating the function of differential gearing at the axle shafts.

rotate within special type roller bearings located in the axle cover.

The large driven gear, previously mentioned as being in mesh with the propeller shaft driving pinion, carries the differential gear cage which is secured to its face.

It is at this point that a further reduction in the ratio of engine speed to road wheels is made, about 4 to 1 for private cars and approximately 10 to 1 for commercial vehicles.

Differential Gears.—To show how the differential gears are operated by the propeller shaft driving pinion, reference should be made to Fig. 4 when reading the following description of working principles.

First you have to imagine that the disk depicted in the lower sketch, is fitted with a handle so that it can be turned in the direction indicated by the arrow. On the face of the disk are two bosses in which the differential driving pin is fixed so that when the disk is turned by the handle the pin turns with it. Mounted on the differential driving pin are the two differential pinion gears so that they must run round with the pin and disk, but they are also free to revolve on the pin. In mesh with these two differential pinion gears are the two planet gears fixed to the axle shafts. Consequently if the disk is turned by the handle, the differential driving pin and the two differential pinion gears will turn with it as one. As the differential pinion gears are in mesh with the two planet gears, they and the axle shafts will also have to revolve.

But as the two pinion gears are free to revolve on the driving pin, unless the resistance to turning is the same on both axle shafts, the axle possessing the least resistance will be speeded up while any increase of resistance on the other axle will result in its reduction in speed. This will be clearer if the extreme case is taken, i.e. if one axle shaft is held so that it cannot rotate, the other shaft will rotate at a high speed, as the differential pinion gears will be turning on their driving pin at their highest speed. Next if the load on each shaft is the same, the differential pinions will not rotate on their driving pin, and therefore both axle shafts will rotate at the same speed. Any variation in speed between the two rear wheels is, therefore, automatically balanced. Now, if the handle is dispensed with and teeth are provided on the disk so that it can be turned by a driving pinion on the propeller shaft, the principle of operation in the differential gears will be exactly the same. See Fig. 4.

Some designs employ worm instead of bevel gear teeth, and recently double helical and hypoid gearing have become popular, but all function broadly on the lines already described in this section.

Brakes and Steering

All cars and motor cycles are required to have two independent brakes, and the driver is legally responsible for their efficient operation. Some motorists are not aware that the police have the right, at any time, to test the braking system of any vehicle, and to prosecute if it is found to be inefficient. Apart from this, the driver has a big responsibility to the rest of the community to keep them in good order for any emergency.

Types of Brakes.—It is not possible here to describe more than a few representative designs of brake, but there are general principles which are common to most makes. The most popular systems are the Lockheed Hydraulic, Bendix or Bendix-Cowdrey, and Girling, or some combination of these. In all these systems provision for adjustment against wear is made at the shoe assemblies, not in the operating mechanism, and it is dangerous to jump to the conclusion, when the brakes need attention, that the operating rods or cables need adjustment, as was usually the case in the past. In general, it is true that unsatisfactory brake operation needs nothing more drastic than adjustment, since modern systems give efficient results throughout the life of the brake linings, but they need the right kind of adjustment. Another point to be borne in mind is the difference between what is termed a *compensating* system and a *non-compensating* system of road wheel braking.

In a non-compensating system it is possible, by adjustment, to vary the braking effort of each individual wheel, but with a fully compensating system it is impossible to vary the braking of individual wheels. Thus, in a compensating system, should three

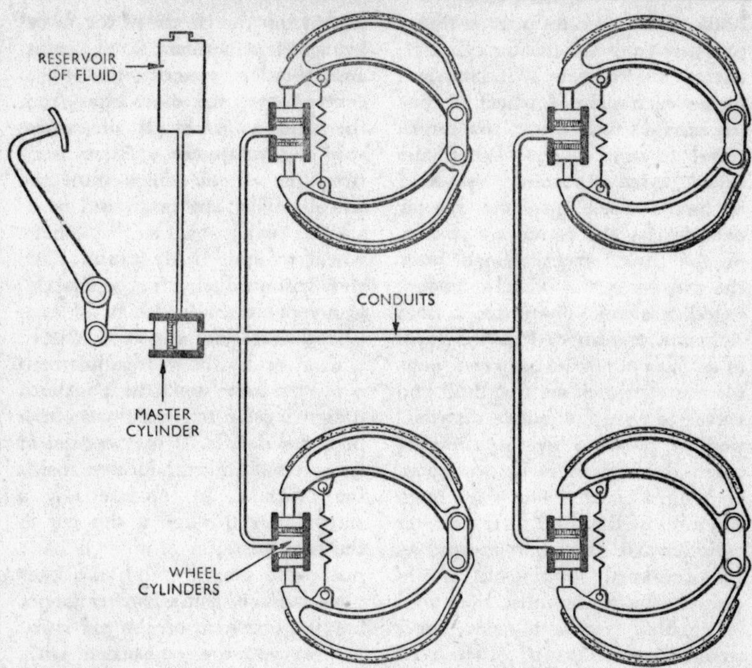

Fig. 1. Diagrammatic layout of a hydraulic brake system. Depression of brake pedal causes piston in master cylinder to force brake fluid along pipe lines and into the wheel brake cylinders thereby forcing brake shoes against brake drums.

wheels lock and the fourth fail to do so, it is not possible to rectify matters by adjustment. The trouble must be due to such causes as oil getting through on to the linings of the faulty brake, shoes seized on their pivots, or some other mechanical trouble at the shoes themselves.

Lockheed System.—We will review the Lockheed system first, as it will be evident that no adjustment can be carried out on the fluid conduits (there are no rods or cables); also the system is fully compensated, it being impossible to alter the braking at any one wheel in relation to any of the others. The only adjustment to correct lining wear is provided at the brake back plates on the brake shoes themselves, but this will affect the position of the shoes only, in relation to the drums, and not the braking effort. See Fig. 1.

Briefly the system works in the following manner: When the driver depresses the brake pedal, the hydraulic piston is forced into the master cylinder which contains the brake fluid. The fluid in the master cylinder is delivered under pressure, along the pipes leading to the four wheel cylinders, situated one in each wheel drum, between each pair of brake shoes. These wheel cylinders embody double pistons, and each piston moves one brake shoe. The fluid, now under pressure from the master cylinder, enters the wheel cylinders and forces each pair of wheel pistons to extend and apply the brake shoes to the drums. When the brake pedal is released the fluid is forced back into the master cylinder by the retracting springs of the brake shoes, which force the pistons in the wheel cylinders together again. There are certain refinements provided in the form of seals to eliminate seepage, plugs for the replenishment of fluid and valves to ensure effective distribution of pressure in the conduits when the system is in operation. Care must be exercised to maintain the level of the fluid in the master cylinder at all times. If more than an occasional topping-up is required, the cause must be traced and rectified without delay, for a progressive loss of fluid will seriously affect the efficiency of the brakes. At all times there should be about ½in. free movement of the brake pedal before resistance is felt. This is to ensure that the piston in the master cylinder is fully retarded to its stop and uncovers the compensator vent.

If the stroke of the pedal is excessive, so that it nearly fouls the toe board before the brakes are fully applied, worn brake linings are indicated; a condition that can be rectified by re-adjustment of the brake shoes. The shoe adjusters in most common use consist of two snail cams on the brake back plate which when turned bring the shoes into contact with, or away from the drum. Jack up each wheel in turn, and with a suitable spanner rotate the hexagon heads of the snail cams; rotation away from the centre of the wheel brings the shoes nearer the drums, and rotation towards the wheel centre moves the shoes away from the drums. So, with the wheel spinning, rotate the adjusters away from the wheel centre until the wheel stops spinning and then slacken back just sufficiently for the wheel to spin freely again. Each shoe will need adjusting separately. Carry out the adjustment of each pair of shoes similarly at all wheels.

Caution: as the shoe adjustment is not the same in all the Lockheed designs, refer to your instruction book for details. It may consist of an internal adjuster located inside the brake drum, operated by a screwdriver through a slot cut in the back plate, or of a single hand nut protruding through the back plate surface. But whatever device may be provided on the particular vehicle you are concerned with, that will be the only adjustment in the system.

Should a feeling of springiness develop when the brake pedal is depressed, or should a conduit pipe have been disconnected or the fluid reservoir been allowed to run dry, air will have entered the system. In normal conditions this should not happen, but before the system will function properly the air will have to be expelled. This is called bleeding the system, and should be carried out as follows. Keep the supply reservoir full of fluid during the whole operation. Commence with one wheel and attach a drain tube (usually supplied with a suitable connection in the tool kit) to the bleeder valve at the top of the wheel cylinder on the brake back plate. Submerge the other end of the drain tube in some

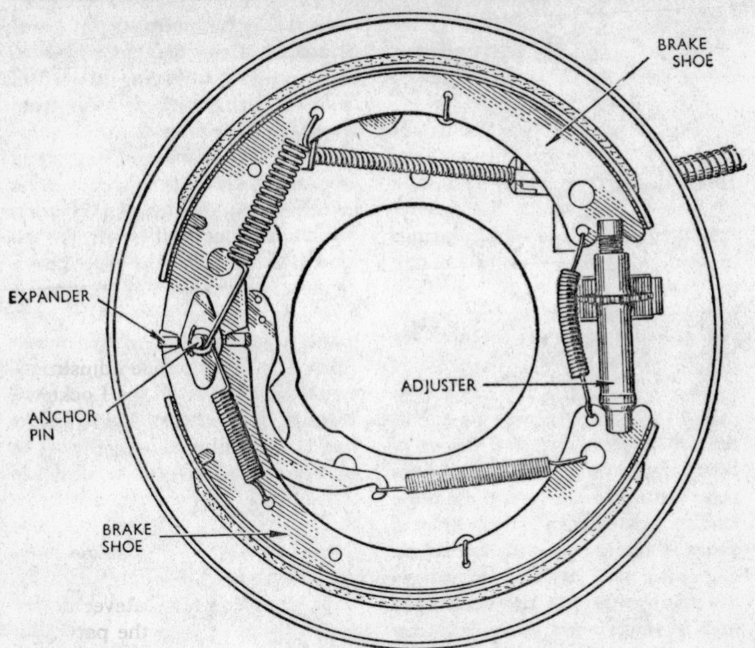

Fig. 2. Shows the interior arrangement of brake shoe assembly. Adjuster is utilized to take up wear on brake lining. Expander on left is connected to the brake controls which when operated cause shoes to bear against brake drum.

brake fluid in a clean glass jar. Slacken the bleeder screw one turn, and get an assistant to depress the brake pedal quickly, allowing it to return slowly and then a slight pause to refill master cylinder before again depressing. The pedal should be pumped in this way until all air bubbles cease to rise through the fluid in the jar. Ensure that the tube is kept submerged all the time, and until the bleeder valve is again screwed down on the cessation of the air bubbles. The operation should be carried out similarly at all wheels, and the brake fluid reservoir should be replenished from time to time, as necessary, and be *left full* (i.e. at the proper level).

Only genuine Lockheed brake fluid should be used. Spurious fluid or oil will wreck all the composition cups and seals to the detriment of the whole system.

Bendix Brakes.—In this system cables are generally used to operate the brakes, but sometimes rods or hydraulic operation is utilized. When cables are used the system is definitely non-compensating, and when adjusting the system care must be taken to balance the braking effort at all four wheels. The shoe assembly, as shown in Fig. 2, consists of two shoes forced open by an expander which is free to move circumferentially. The adjuster, provided to take up excessive movement of the shoes

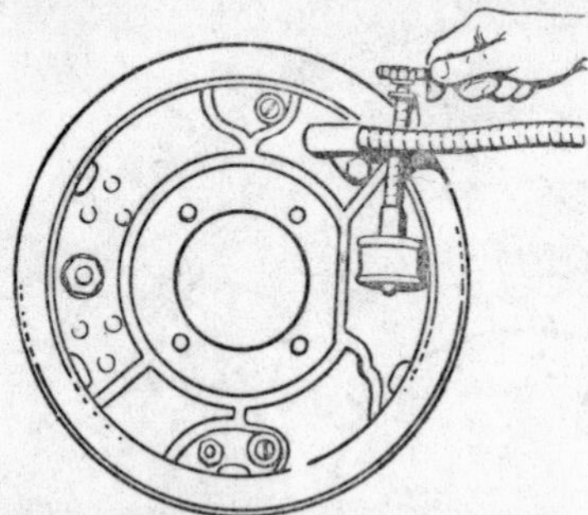
Fig. 3. Adjusting the brake shoes. Illustration shows spindle with hexagon head which operates a spur gear adjuster.

due to lining wear, is also free to float circumferentially. The only rigid fixture to the back plate is the anchor pin which prevents the shoes from turning with the drum. Consequently, as the shoes are not rigidly fixed to the back plate in any way, when expanded they move out until contact is made with the drum over practically the whole surface of the linings. Furthermore the rotation of the drum tends to carry the shoes round with it, until the shoes pile up on the fixed anchor pin. This creates a self-wrapping or self-energizing action, the result of

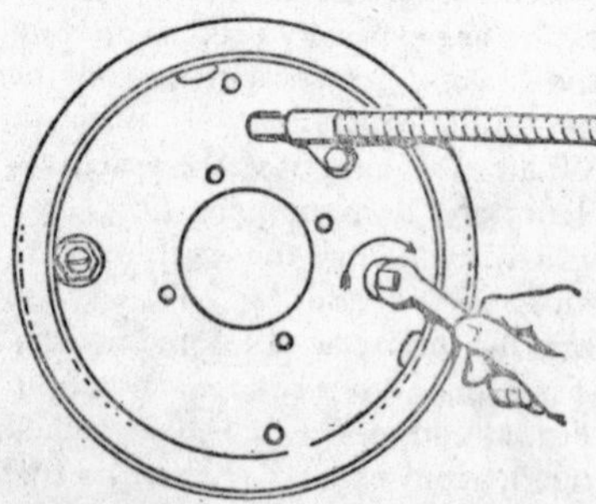
Fig. 4. Another type of brake shoe adjuster. Brake adjustment is obtained by turning square head on short spindle.

which may be increased, by gentle pressure of the foot on the pedal, into a powerful braking effort. This self-energizing effect, sometimes erroneously referred to as servo, should not be confused with systems employing separate servo assistance units. So much for a brief survey of the system. We will now proceed with the vital matter of keeping the system in efficient working order.

As wear occurs on the brake linings, it will be noticed that the stroke of the pedal increases until it nearly fouls the toe board before the brakes become effective. The brakes will also show a tendency

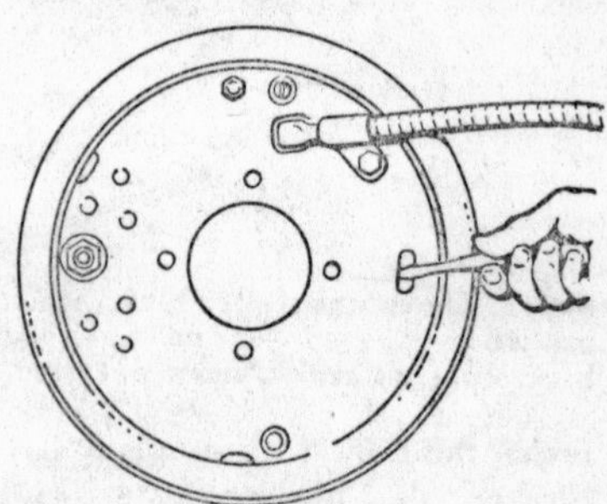
Fig. 5. Third type of brake shoe adjuster. Design similar to adjuster in Fig. 2.

to grab due to excessive movement of the shoes. Before this stage is reached, the brakes should be adjusted, and to do this it will be necessary to jack up the vehicle and have all four wheels clear of the ground. Normal wear can be taken up by means of the eccentric adjuster, this is only fitted to cars with brake drums over 8in. diameter, or, on later models, by a spring centralizer, and a shoe adjuster. There are several different types of shoe adjusters according to make of vehicle, and three are shown in the illustrations (Figs. 3 to 5). Expand the shoes until a brake drag is felt when turning the wheel by hand. Then slacken off until the wheel spins freely. Proceed similarly, with all the wheels, and it is advisable to give the brake pedal several sharp jabs to settle the shoes, after which closer adjustment can often be made. As the system is non-compensating it will be necessary to equalize the braking effect at all wheels. Apply the handbrake; when cable operation is used the handbrake applies all four brakes, otherwise an assistant will have to apply the footbrake, until the wheels will only just turn by hand. Go round all the brakes and slacken off the adjusters on the brakes that are hardest until all are approximately equal. Generally speaking, if the operating cables have been regularly lubricated during maintenance, nothing more will be required to put the brakes in efficient working order again. The cables should never be altered to accomplish lining wear adjustment.

After continual use, and if for some reason the result of the foregoing adjustments is not satisfactory, it may be necessary to check over the whole system. Jack up all four wheels, and detach the four cables at the centre cross shaft by removing the fork end pins. While the cables are disconnected, make sure that they are free in the outer conduits, that the cross shaft works freely in its bearings, and that when the brakes are off the brake pedal and operating levers return against their stops. Now proceed to centralize the brake shoes in the drums, by slackening off the lock nut and turning the eccentric adjuster in the direction the wheel revolves when car is moving forward, until a slight brake drag is felt. Then slacken off the eccentric slightly until the wheel is just free, and then tighten the lock nut. Next, expand the shoes fully in the drums by screwing out the shoe adjusters. Do not strain the adjusters by over screwing. Now adjust the length of the cables, so that they are just long enough to pull tight, and insert the pins into their fork ends, and cross shaft levers. There should be no slack left in the cables. Split pin the fork pins and tighten the lock nut of the screwed end. Then slacken off all the shoe adjusters until the wheels spin freely. Finally balance the braking effort at all wheels in the manner already described.

Bendix-Cowdrey.—In this system the shoe assembly is very similar to the Bendix, making use of the same advantage of self-wrapping effect of the floating shoes. But the cables are superseded by a fully compensated operating linkage whereby an all-square pull up is ensured even if shoe lining wear or adjustment is uneven. See also Figs. 6 and 7.

The only adjustment provided is to take up lining wear at the shoes themselves. The operating linkage should on no account be altered. When the pedal stroke becomes excessive, intimating that adjustment is called for, it is only necessary to use these adjusters on the brake back plate. There is no need to jack up the vehicle for this operation; just screw up the adjusters in a clockwise direction until tight, and then slacken back

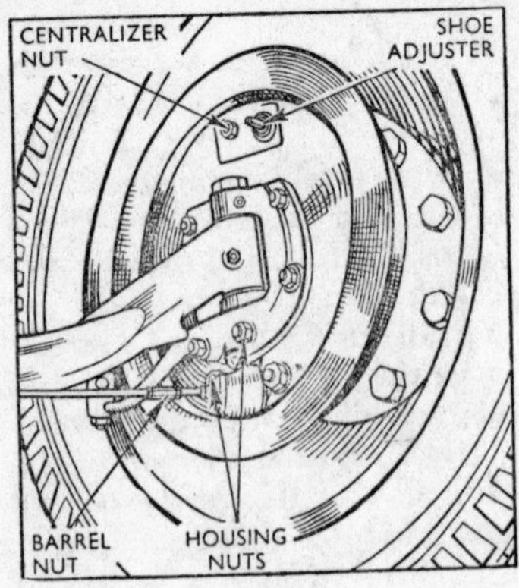

Fig. 6. To adjust this type of brake, turn shoe adjuster until shoes bear in drum then turn back adjuster six "clicks."

approximately six notches or three-quarters of a turn. Provided the operating linkage is moving freely and has not been damaged (this is easily done by careless jacking, binding or jamming the linkage) this should be all that is required.

If the brakes do not pull up squarely, remember that as it is a fully compensated system it is no use trying to improve matters by using the shoe adjusters. Oil on the brake linings, or some such cause, is the probable trouble and must be rectified before looking farther afield. Check over the nuts securing the axles to the springs and tighten them up if slack; see that the linkage pivots at front and rear axles are moving freely, and lubricate if required. *But do not alter the adjustment of the linkage rods.*

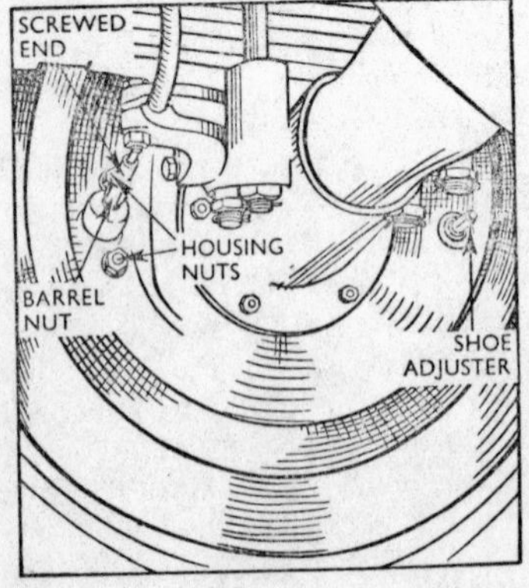

Fig. 7. This brake is similar to that shown in Fig 6 but mounted on rear axle casing.

Girling Brakes.—This system is simplicity itself, in that it is foolproof against neglect or maladjustment. The operating mechanism is fully compensating and does not require maintenance in the form of lubrication. The design is such that a large increase in braking effort is effected at the shoe expanders themselves by means of which the operating linkage is relieved of strain.

The shoes are free to make contact with the drum over practically the whole of the lining surface. Lining wear is provided for by the adjuster on the brake back plate. This is the only adjustment in the system and the operating linkage must never be altered in this respect. When the pedal stroke intimates that adjustment is required, it is only necessary to rotate the adjuster clockwise until resistance of the shoes contacting the drums is felt. The adjusters are then slackened back one notch. This is the only adjustment provided or required, and recourse to jacking up of the vehicle is unnecessary. The handbrake must, of course, be in the OFF position when the adjustments are carried out. If the resultant braking effect is unsatisfactory check over the linkage for damage, oil on brake linings, slack bolts securing springs, etc.,

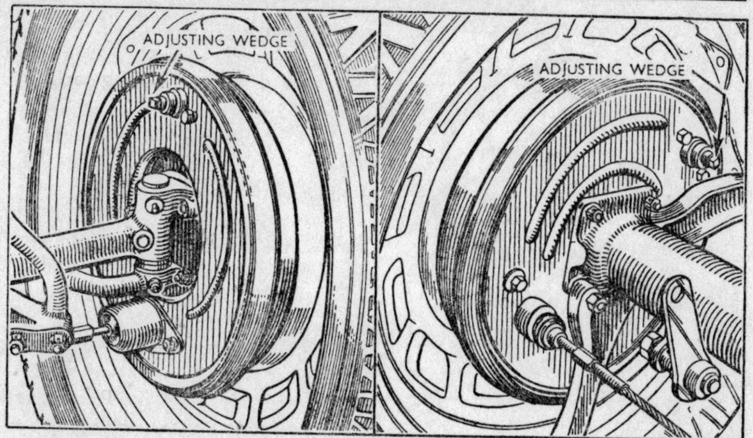

Figs. 8 and 9. Front and rear wheel brakes. Adjustment on this type of brake is obtained by turning the adjusting wedge in a clockwise direction until the brake shoes are just contacting the drums. Adjusting wedge is then turned back one notch.

for it is of no use altering the shoe adjusters further, or the linkage, in an endeavour to correct uneven braking as the system is fully compensating. See also Figs. 8 and 9.

Two entirely independent brakes, kept in efficient working order, are the rule for motor cycles. Generally, the practice is for a handbrake working on the front wheel operated by Bowden cables, and a footbrake operated by rod and lever on the rear wheel. The single expanding shoe with self-wrapping action, working in hub drums, is usually favoured. Adjustment is either by wing nuts or the usual Bowden adjuster, a simple and straightforward design that should present no difficulty.

Steering.—Any excessive lost motion due to wear or lack of stability should be rectified without delay. Usually, all that is needed is adjustment, but here again it is correct adjustment that counts. Therefore a brief outline of the principles involved will not be amiss, as all designs incorporate the same basic principles. These are as follows: Ackermann angle, castor, camber, and toe-in or toe-out, brief descriptions of which are given below.

Ackermann Angle.—When a car is moving along a circular path it will be obvious that the outer wheel will describe a circle of larger radius than the inner wheel. Therefore the front wheels will not be parallel with each other except in the straight ahead position, otherwise the tyres will have to accommodate slip, and excessive wear will inevitably result. To obviate this difficulty recourse is made to linkage based on the Ackermann principle. Referring to Fig. 10, it will be seen that the front wheels are coupled together by the track rod connected to their respective steering arms. An imaginary line drawn through the king pin and steering knuckle centres, will intersect on the centre-line of the car and rear axle. This linkage thus

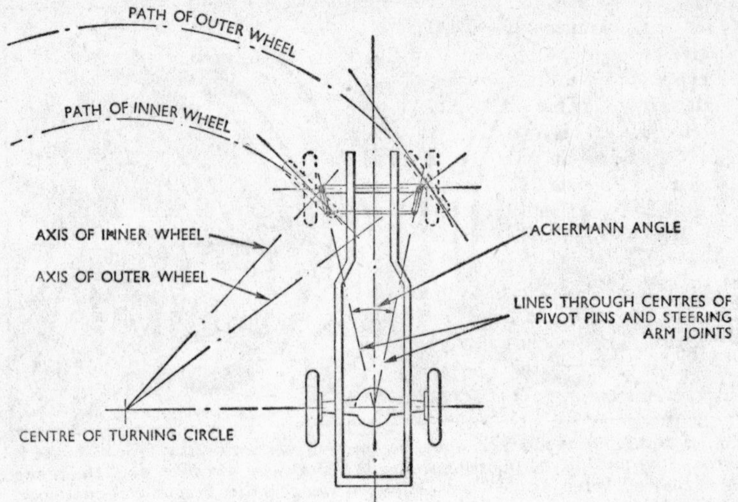

Fig. 10. Illustrates the principle of the Ackermann angle which ensures that the axes of the front wheels intersect at centre of turning circle described by car.

ensures that the axes of the front wheels intersect at the centre of the turning circle which the car is describing.

Castor Action.—All drivers are aware of the tendency for a car automatically to travel in a straight-ahead path. This self-centring is brought about by incorporating the action of a castor wheel. Take a trolley wagon fitted with castor wheels and push it along; all the wheels will swivel round until they trail in line and the wagon will tend to travel in a straight line. This is accomplished on both motor cycles

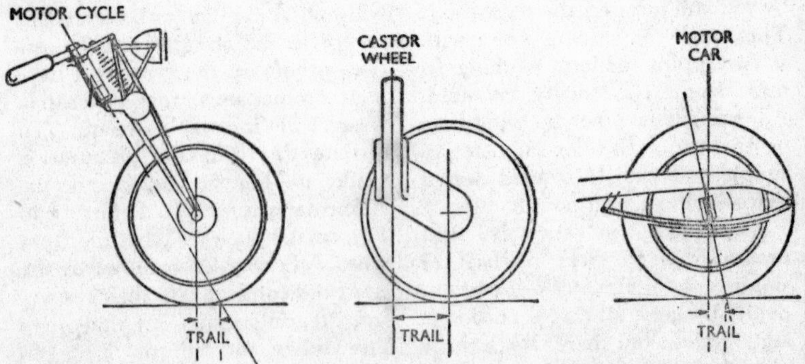

Fig. 11. Illustrates the principle of castor action on front wheel of motor cycle, castor wheel, and motor car front wheel. Note that the trail on the motor cycle and the car wheels is ahead of the centre line of the wheels: i.e. axle **hub.**

and cars by making the centre-line of the steering pin strike the ground at a point ahead of the point of contact of the wheel with the ground. This will be clear on reference to Fig. 11.

Camber.—It will be noticed that on most cars the front wheels are not vertical but that they cant outwards, being wider apart at the top than at the bottom. This is done in an endeavour to get as near as possible to what is termed centre-point steering, and the resultant light steering. Again, reference to Fig. 12 will make this point clear.

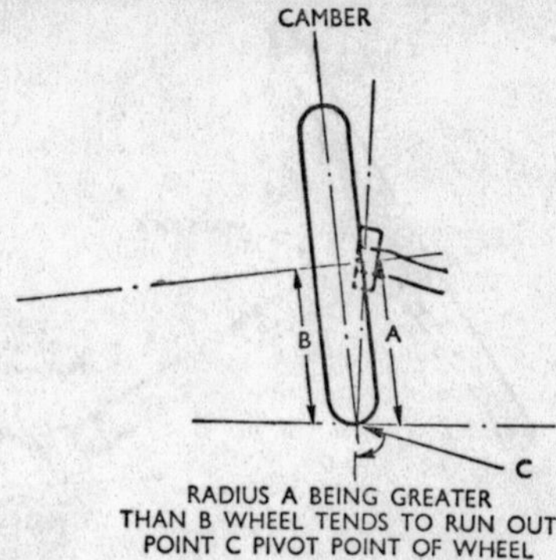

Fig. 12. Shows the camber angle of a front road wheel. Camber is used in this manner to obtain centre-point steering and small effort on steering wheel.

Toe-In or Toe-Out.—There is always a tendency for the front wheels to splay outwards. This is increased as the camber angle is increased due to the inclined axis of the wheel. Reference to Fig. 13 will make this clear also. To counteract this tendency and eliminate scruffing and wear on the tyres, the front wheels are given toe-in. Even if the wheels are vertical without camber, as in some commercial vehicles, a certain amount of toe-in is necessary.

Where, however, the front wheels are used as driving wheels as in front-wheel-drive vehicles, this splaying tendency is largely counteracted and no toe-in may be required. With some independent suspension systems the designers recommend toe-out.

From the foregoing it will be clearly understood that the Ackermann angle will alter with the wheelbase, castor, camber and toe-in or toe-out, according to design; and that they are all inter-related. Therefore it is impossible to give any general rules. Their correct maintenance and adjustment must be made according to the maker's instruc-

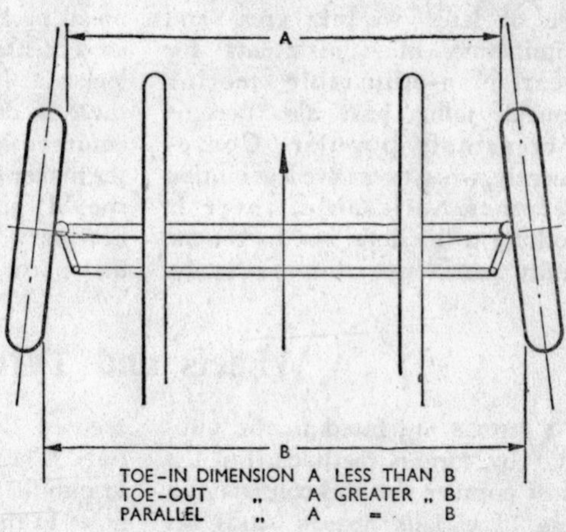

Fig. 13. Plan view of front steering wheels showing the wheels turned inwards, i.e. toed-in, thus counteracting tendency of front wheels to splay outwards.

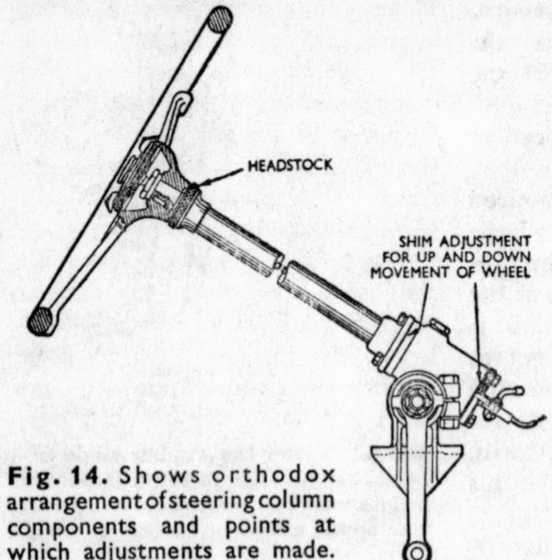

Fig. 14. Shows orthodox arrangement of steering column components and points at which adjustments are made.

Alternatively, where the spring knuckles are adjustable, these should be adjusted to eliminate wear whenever it develops. This is usually done by removing a split pin and tightening up a screwed cup end. In this type of adjustment, screw in the cup as tightly as possible and then just slacken back sufficiently to prevent binding. Do not forget to replace the split pin, and to check all the joints similarly.

Wear can develop at

tions, so consult your instruction manual. Also, refrain from driving the car over obstacles at speed, hitting the curb with the front wheels, and other practices likely to derange the steering mechanism.

Regarding the steering box itself, there is a general tendency in design which seems to favour the use of large wearing areas and elimination of adjustments for wear. Non-adjustable steering knuckle joints have also become increasingly popular. Consequently, when excessive lost motion becomes noticeable, there is nothing to be done but to get the faulty part renewed immediately.

the bearings and between the operating mechanism in the box. Provision may be provided at the headstock, or at the box, to eliminate excessive end-float of the column. Wear between the screw element and drop arm may occur in the box itself, and this may be counteracted by the use of thin metal packing washers (Fig. 14), or an eccentric bush or screw and lock nut. It is impossible to specify these in detail as the designs vary enormously. However, reference to the maker's official instruction book should give the reader all the necessary details which will apply to his particular make of vehicle.

Wheels and Tyres

Wheels are fitted to the hubs by various methods, but the most popular method consists of a ring of equally spaced studs set in the flange of the hub. These studs correspond with holes in the wheel plate and the wheel is secured to the studs by special nuts. The bevel edges of the nuts fit into the countersunk faces of the holes in the wheel thus preventing any movement of the wheel on the studs or slackening of the nuts. It is usual to bevel both end faces of the nuts as a safety measure against incorrect fitting, but as wheel nuts bevelled on one end face only are still in use, care should be taken to see that they are fitted correctly.

As an extra precaution against the wheel nuts slackening off, some manufacturers favour using left-hand threads on the studs fitted to the near side hubs, and right-hand threads on the off side hubs. The nuts are usually marked L for left-hand and R for right-hand, and this should always be borne in mind when struggling to remove a tight nut at any time.

The Rudge Whitworth single centre nut fitting is very popular with the sports type of car. The driving and braking strains are taken on serrations on both hub and wheel centre, and the wheel is pulled firmly on to a cone section of the hub by a large single nut. These nuts always undo in the same direction as the rotation of the wheel to which they are fitted, and will be left-hand threaded on the near-side wheels, and right-hand threaded on the off-side wheels. If the hubs are removed at any time care must be taken to see that they are not refitted to the wrong side, the wheels would tend to work loose and in all probability come off. These centre locking nuts are often fitted with ears so that they can be tightened or loosened with a hide or copper hammer.

With motor cycles it is usually the practice to mount the wheels on a non-rotating spindle mounted on bearings in the hub of the wheel and rigidly held in the fork ends of the frame. When the nuts securing this spindle in the forks are undone the wheel can be removed. The chain sprocket of the rear wheel is generally integral with the hub, the driving or braking strains are transmitted from hub to wheel through suitable dowels or dogs.

Whenever wheels are removed, the wheel registers and studs should be greased before replacing, to prevent rust. The correct procedure to be observed when removing or remounting wheels is as follows:

Initially slacken each nut before jacking up; if the nuts are extra tight it is easier to start them with the weight on the wheel to prevent it turning. Then jack up and remove all nuts and finally the wheel. As already suggested, take the opportunity of greasing studs and registers, etc., before replacing. When remounting, each nut should be given a few turns only at a time. This should be done with the wheel clear of the ground, and nuts, diametrically opposite, should be tightened in turn. The object is to enable the wheels gradually to seat themselves evenly on the faces of the studs and nuts. It is very bad practice to finish tightening one nut before moving to the others. Finally, jack down the car, and with the weight of the vehicle on

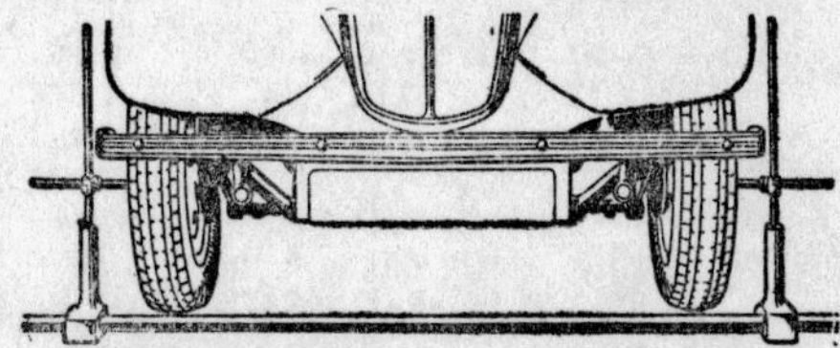

Fig. 1. Checking the track of the front road wheels. The dimensions at front and rear points of the front road wheels should conform to maker's requirements, the steering being centralized.

the wheel, tighten nuts right home.

Tyres.—It is very important that the tyres should not be kept at less than their minimum recommended pressures for the type of vehicle on which they are being used. Slack tyres, besides being conducive to wheel wobble and skidding, will show early disintegration of the cord foundation due to abnormal flexing. Tyres are liable to lose pressure through diffusion, even though there is no abnormal porosity or leakage due to a puncture or faulty valve. This loss may vary between 1 and 3 lb. per sq. in. per tyre per week, so one can judge how important it is to check over the pressures weekly with a reliable pressure gauge and to rectify any discrepancies. But a cursory glance should be given daily to see that none of the tyres is unduly slack. The instruction book issued by the car manufacturer will specify the correct pressures, but a short list of tyre pressures advocated by the Dunlop Rubber Co. Ltd. is given below for general reference. It will be appreciated, of course, that this list is not comprehensive and where high pressure, low pressure and extra low pressure tyres are concerned the undermentioned pressure specifications are not applicable.

It will be noted that the air pressure for any given size of tyre will vary in accordance with the load imposed. The necessary inflation pressure may be determined by weighing the vehicle (full normal load) and dividing the results by four.

The tyres should be examined occasionally for flints or other similar foreign matter which may have become embedded in the tread. If these are left in, they may eventually work through the cover and puncture the tube. Fill up any large cuts or gashes with a suitable filler, or if serious return for repair by specialists. Care should be taken to avoid getting oil on the covers, it should be cleaned off with petrol sparingly used. Should the front tyres at any time show signs of rapid wear, suspect misalinement of the front wheels. Provision is provided by the manufacturers for the adjustment of the track of the front wheels, which are given toe-in or toe-out according to design. Toe-in is most usual, but front wheel driven cars invariably have toe-out, and in many independent suspension models the wheels are parallel.

PRESSURE (lbs. per sq. in.)	TYRE SIZE IN INCHES 4.50	4.75	5.00	5.25	5.50
	Load per Tyre.			(Cwt.)	
24	5	5½	6	7	8
26	5½	6	6½	7½	8½
28	6	6½	7	8	9
32	7	7½	8	9	10
36	8	8½	9	10	11

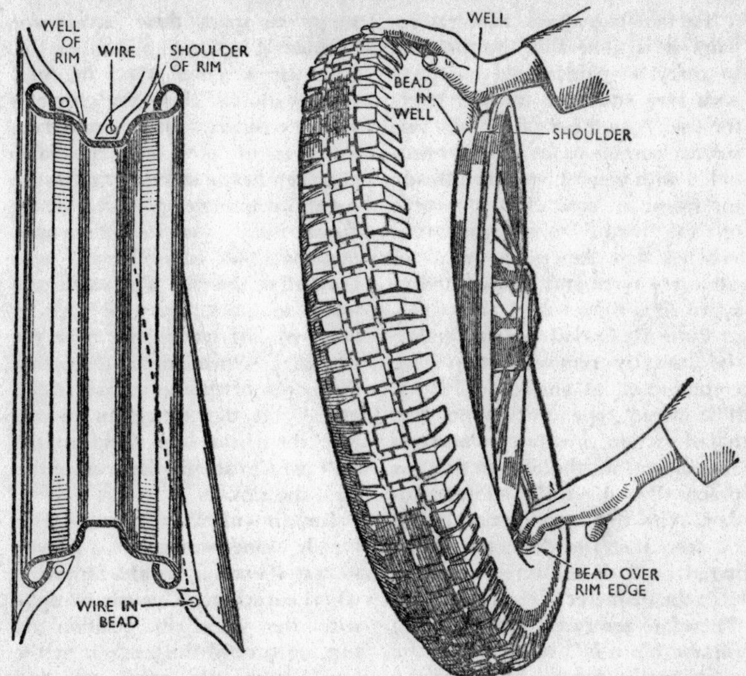

Fig. 2. Shows two views of wheel and tyre. When removing the tyre from the wheel inner tube valve should be free and the bead of the tyre pressed right into well of wheel. Ease off tyre by lever or hand at opposite point as indicated. Take care that the inner tube is not pinched between tyre and wheel during removal of tyre and avoid, as far as possible, the use of improvised sharp edged tyre levers.

Refer to the instruction book before making any adjustment. The operation of adjustment, illustrated in Fig. 1, is performed in the following manner. The steering is set in the straight ahead position and the distance between the two front rims is measured at a height approximately equal to the centre of the wheels. By means of a suitable gauge compare this measurement as taken in front of the axle with it taken behind the axle. The variation (if any) should conform to maker's specification. Periodically change the wheels round from front O/S to rear N/S and vice versa. Use the spare wheel in turn with the others, and so equalize wear of all 5 wheels. Big discrepancies in tyre mileages may be apparent when comparing drivers, and these can invariably be traced to the driving methods employed. In an endeavour to get improved mileage the driver should avoid wheel spin due to rapid acceleration, and allow the engine to slow down the car in preference to driving on the brakes. The wear at 50 m.p.h. is double that at 30 m.p.h. Avoid driving with the wheels in tram lines. Do not bump against curbs as this is liable to fracture the casing and to upset the wheel alignment.

To facilitate quick running repairs it is generally the practice to carry a spare wheel complete with tyre and tube inflated ready for use. A number of motor cycle sidecar combinations are also provided with a complete wheel ready for fitting in case of tyre trouble on the road. Some commercial vehicles and American makes of car carry tyres and tubes fitted to spare rims only.

Tyre Removal.—First deflate the tyre by removing the valve components, as shown in Fig. 2. The wired type of tyre on well based section rims (a tyre and rim are shown in the illustration) is practically universally adopted today. With this combination it will be seen that the diameter of the wired bead of the tyre is smaller than the diameter of the rim flange. Therefore the tyre (when inflated) cannot blow off, neither can the edges be lifted over the rim as the wire is inextensible. So do not attempt to stretch the wire edges of the tyre over the rim. Force is entirely unnecessary, for if the beads of the tyre at a *part diametrically opposite the valve* are pushed down into the well of the rim, the *cover edge near the valve* can easily be levered over the rim edge.

To fit the tyre, push one edge of the cover over the edge of the rim. It will go quite easily if the part first put on is pushed right down into the well of the rim. Very slightly inflate the tube, not sufficiently to disturb it, but only so that it takes shape, and place it in the cover with the valve through the hole in the rim. Take care that the valve (which is *off-set*) is on the correct side of the rim. Also, it is the practice for some manufacturers to mark their covers for balance. The Dunlop Rubber Co. Ltd. use a red spot on the wall which should coincide with the valve position. Make sure the cover is in its correct position, and then fit the second edge of the cover, commencing at a point *diametrically opposite the valve*, pushing the edge down into the well of the rim. The small tyre levers in the kit may be used to ease the last few inches over the rim edge. Whilst inflating see that the edges of the cover are seated evenly on the shoulders of the rim; there is a line circle on the wall which should be concentric with the rim.

Repair of Punctures.—If a tyre is losing pressure it is as well to test the valve before removing wheel cover, etc. This can be done with the wheel in position by turning it until the valve is at the top. Remove the valve cap, and immerse valve in a glass of water. If bubbles are visible fit a new valve core, reinflate and test again.

When cover and tube are removed for the repair of a puncture, inspect the inside of the cover for, and remove, any sharp object which may have penetrated the cover and caused the puncture. Take the opportunity of extracting any other matter embedded in the bead of the cover. Wherever possible it is advisable to have punctures repaired by vulcanized patches in preference to stick-on patches, which are liable to lift and leak in warm weather.

The reader is reminded that it is a legal offence for the motorist to run a vehicle on tyres with bald treads. It has sometimes been the practice in the past to have smooth tyres re-cut, provided there is sufficient rubber left.

The tread on a tyre is not only a means of improving the drive of the rear road wheels by increasing the grip between road surface and tyre; it also reduces the risk of skidding on wet roads, etc.

Care of Pedal Cycles

Loose nuts and slack bearings are the cause of most mechanical defects, not to mention defects arising from lack of lubrication. Neglect to make a minor adjustment may result in considerable labour and inconvenience in replacing a broken or worn part. The golden rule for the cyclist is to keep all nuts tight, all bearings free but not slack, and all moving parts well lubricated and free from dirt.

When tightening nuts always use a well fitting spanner and never exert brute force. To attempt to lock a nut once and for all is to expect it to serve the purpose of a rivet, and the attempt often results in damage to the bolt, the nut, or the knuckles. Nuts and bolts are used for securing components to one another, because they may be removed easily when required. Nevertheless, nuts may work loose by vibration and should, therefore, be tightened periodically, going over the machine with suitable spanners.

The aim of oiling and greasing should be to maintain a thin film of lubricant between the bearing surfaces of all moving parts. Surplus oil on external parts only collects dirt, to the detriment of any clothing that may come into contact with it. Therefore oil sparingly and often, using the oil can in one hand and a rag in the other to wipe off surplus oil.

Checking the nuts and oiling is a ten-minute job and should be made a weekly routine. The amount of time spent on cleaning and polishing is a matter of individual temperament. Dullness of plating and enamel will not impair efficiency, but regular cleaning and polishing of the frame and fittings will prevent the formation of rust on exposed metallic surfaces, will preserve the enamel from flaking and retain something of the pleasant neatness in appearance which characterized the bicycle when new. See Rust Prevention, p. 411.

Regular attention to the details outlined above will reduce running repairs and adjustments to the minimum, but wear is inevitable in long service and certain adjustments are necessary to keep the machine in first class condition.

Adjustment of Bearings.—There are six main bearings in the structure of a pedal cycle (see Fig. 1), all of the ball and cone type. These are: the hub bearings in the two wheels, the two pedals, the crankshaft or bottom bracket bearings, and the steering head bearings.

In all cases the adjustment should be tight enough to eliminate all play, without preventing free rotation.

Hub Bearings.—If the wheel rim shows any lateral movement between the forks the hub bearings need adjusting. Place the machine

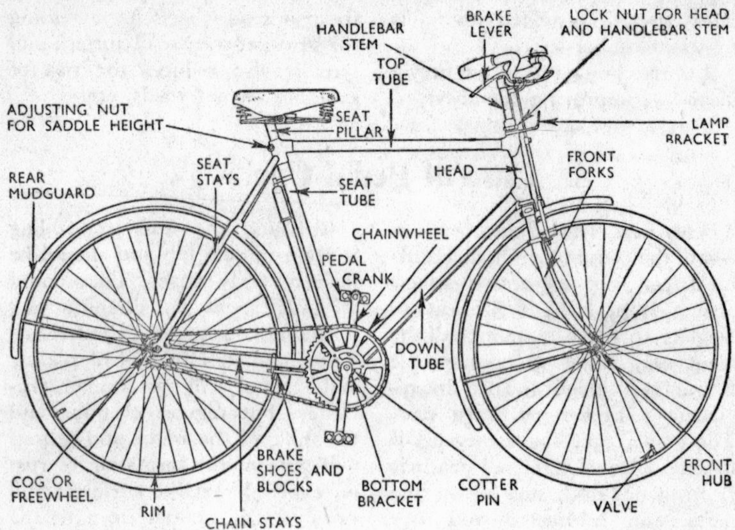

Fig. 1. View of bicycle. Note that the height of the handle bars is slightly greater than that of the seat. The distance between the seat and bottom dead centre of the pedal should suit the individual leg length of the rider.

inverted on a level floor and protect the handlebars from abrasion with a cloth pad. Loosen the spindle nut on one side and screw in the cone sufficiently to take up excess play, using a cone spanner. If the cone is taken in too much the wheel will not spin freely and will emit a slight grinding noise when rotated. Use a light touch and go by the feel of the adjustment. Finally tighten the spindle nut. Then spin the wheel by hand to ensure that it rotates freely. See also Fig. 2.

Crankshaft Bearing.—This bearing is housed in the bottom bracket and has an adjustable cup on the opposite side from the chain-wheel. The cup is held by a locking ring which must be loosened, and re-locked after adjusting the cup. Both cup and locking ring are turned by the use of the reverse end of the cone spanner which has two spigots that engage in special holes drilled in the face of the ring and similarly in the cup. See also Fig. 3.

Steering Head Bearing.—Slackness in this bearing, though it may not noticeably affect the steering, gives rise to an unpleasant "juddering" when the front brake is applied, and if neglected, sets up uneven wear in the bearing races. At the top of the steering head there is a collar that is locked by means of a nut and bolt passing through a split lug. The adjustment is made by loosening the nut and tapping the collar down to take up the slack, after which the nut is re-tightened. An alternative to the collar is a knurled ring locked by means of a hexagon lock nut. In this case the nut is first slackened anti-clockwise and the ring screwed down sufficiently to take up the slack without restricting free rotation. It is then locked tight with the lock nut. In either case it is well to take the weight off the bearing while making the adjustment, by supporting the front wheel clear of the ground.

Pedals.—The pedal bearings are adjusted by means of an adjustable cone and lock nut. After removing the dust cap the lock nut is loosened and cone adjusted by screwing clockwise with a cone spanner, the same care being exercised to feel the right setting.

If it is necessary to remove a damaged pedal, use the cone spanner which fits the flats on the shoulder of the spindle which screws into the crank arm. Note that the pedal on the right-hand, or chain wheel side, is screwed with a right-hand thread and the one on the left-hand side with a left-hand thread, the object being to prevent the left-hand pedal from coming unscrewed by the action of pedalling. See also Fig. 4.

Adjustments and Repairs.—The chain. This item being exposed to the effects of road grit and mud, requires a little extra attention. Accumulations of dirt should be wiped off with a rag and each link should be given a spot of oil that is thin enough to penetrate between the rollers. This may be followed with a smear of grease on the rollers or the teeth of the chain wheel. The chain is joined by a link that has a detachable side plate held in place by a spring clip. When the spring clip is prized off and the plate removed, the link can be extracted to allow the chain to be removed for cleaning. It should be thoroughly flushed in a bowl of paraffin and then placed on a hot stove to dry out all trace of residual paraffin. It is then immersed in a bath of fairly thick oil (containing graphite) heated to ensure complete penetration.

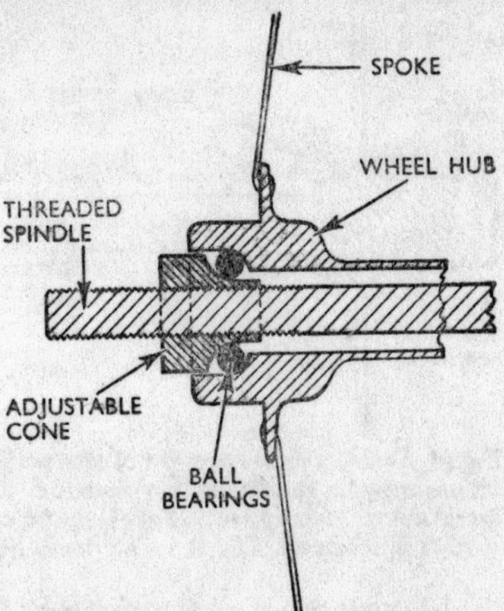

Fig. 2. A part cross-section of wheel hub, threaded spindle, spindle bearing, adjustable cone and ball bearings. Cone must not bear tightly on the bearings.

The chain adjustments should be such as to give ¾in. of sag when depressed at a point half way between the two sprocket wheels. The adjustment is made by loosening the nuts on the rear wheel spindle and sliding the spindle in

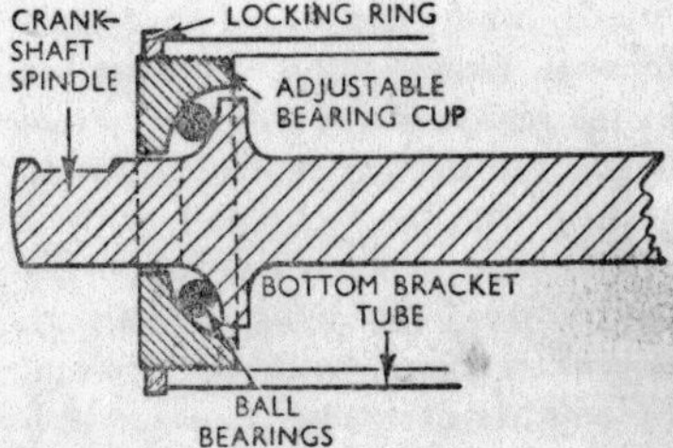

Fig. 3. A part cross-section of bottom bracket crankshaft bearing, adjustable bearing cup, ball bearings and the locking ring to secure bearing cup.

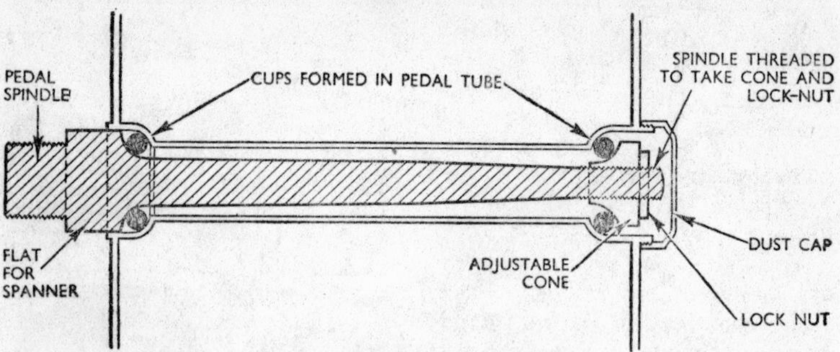

Fig. 4. Shows a cross-section of the pedal spindle. Bearing adjustment is obtained by unscrewing the adjustable cone lock nut and by turning the cone in a clockwise direction to take up wear. Pedal should spin freely after end float has been reduced to a minimum. Tighten the lock nut without altering position of cone.

the slotted forks to the required position. In re-tightening the nuts make sure that the wheel is in true alinement, i.e. that the spindle is set at right angles to the longitudinal axis of the machine.

Road Wheels.—To check for a twisted or buckled wheel the cycle is placed inverted on the ground, and, with the wheel spinning, a stick of chalk is held against the forks with its point lightly touching the rim. If this produces a continuous chalk line all round the rim, all is well. Any gap in the line denotes that the wheel is out of true. If the amount of error is not great it should be possible to bring the rim back into line by manipulation of the spoke tension. Examination of the spokes in the region of the gap may reveal loose or broken spokes. Loose spokes can be tightened with a nipple key after their opposing spokes have been slightly slackened. A broken spoke should be replaced by another of exactly equal length and gauge. It should be threaded through the appropriate hole in the flange of the hub with the head facing either inwards or outwards after the manner of the old spoke. The screwed end is then inserted in its hole in the rim of the wheel when the nipple may be engaged on the spoke thread and correctly tensioned with the nipple key. A wheel that is seriously out of truth or buckled should be placed in the hands of a capable cycle repairer as the job requires specialized skill.

Handlebars.—At the top of the handlebar stem is the hexagon head of a long bolt which passes right down inside the stem to a conical nut at the bottom. When the screw is tight, the nut is drawn upwards into the stem, which is split at the lower end, and is thus expanded to grip the fork tube. To alter the height of the handlebars, the screw is undone several turns and tapped down to free the cone from the bottom of the handlebar stem. The handlebars can then be raised or lowered with an alternate twisting motion while the front wheel is gripped between the knees. The screw is re-tightened when the handlebars are at the desired height and at right angles to the front wheel. The height of the handlebars should be slightly above the saddle level.

Saddle.—The position of the saddle must be adjusted to suit the individual needs of the rider. As a general guide the tip of the saddle should be 2in. back from an imaginary line perpendicular to the bottom bracket, and the height should be such that it is possible to reach the pedals with the heels at the fully extended position.

A nut underneath the saddle provides for adjusting the position forwards or backwards and setting the tilt, which should be slightly upwards. The height can be altered after loosening the nut at the top rear of the seat tube.

Brakes.—Wear in the brake blocks should be taken up by means of the adjusting nut on either the Bowden cable or rods. There should be equal clearances between the brake blocks and the rim on either side of the wheel. Unequal clearances may indicate that the wheel is buckled or not in true alinement between the forks. Hub brakes are fitted with internal expanding shoes and are adjusted at the arm on the outside.

Variable Gears.—The two chief types of gear changing devices are: (a) the hub gear, in which the mechanism consists of a set of gear trains enclosed within the rear hub, and (b) the Derailleur system in which the rear wheel is equipped with two or more related cogs with a cable-operated device for transposing the chain to any selected cog.

The hub gear, being totally enclosed, runs in oil and is protected from dirt and grit. In normal use it needs no attention other than oiling. It is controlled by a cable connected to a selector lever mounted on the top tube or the handlebars. The setting of the selector is a sensitive one. Any stretch or play in the cable that develops in use must be taken up by means of the adjusting nut provided on the cable so as to retain the correct setting. Lubrication of the moving parts of the control should not be overlooked in the general oiling routine.

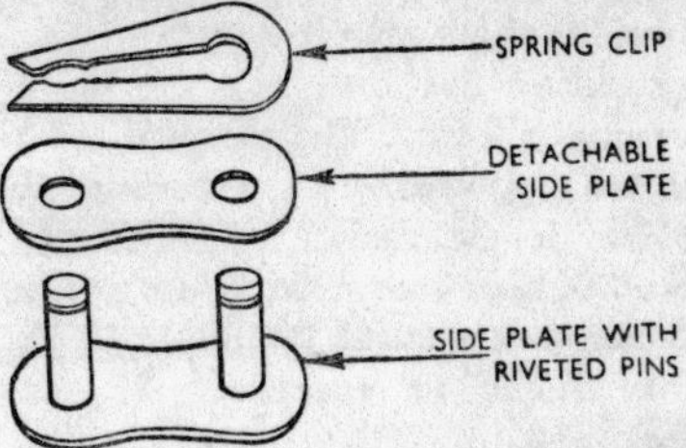

Fig. 5. Dismantled front link of a bicycle chain. The two pins on bottom plate are recessed at the heads to accommodate spring clip side plate retainer.

The same applies to the control of the Derailleur gear. This system, having a direct drive to the selected cog, is more robust than the hub type gear where the drive is transmitted through an intermediate train of gears. It is therefore particularly favoured for use on tandems where the transmission is subjected to the extra strain imposed by two riders. It has a further advantage to the enthusiast in that with little extra expense an alternative set of gear ratios can be obtained by substituting cogs of different sizes.

Lamps.—If a lamp fails and the bulb and battery are in good order, the fault will probably be found in the switch. Where a dynamo supplies front and rear lamps the wiring and connections should be examined for breaks, faulty insulation, or short circuit due to a loose strand of flex touching the lamp casing or frame. The circuit can be tested by connecting a battery in place of the dynamo, and if the fault is thus narrowed down to the dynamo it should be returned to the dealer or manufacturer for servicing.

Tyres.—Tyres should be kept hard to ensure long life, and embedded flints should be picked out with an old pen-knife. Any open gash left after the removal of a large flint should be filled with tyre filler, obtainable from any cycle dealer.

Instructions for patching a punctured tube are given with the puncture repair outfit; but first it is necessary to find the puncture. A fast puncture, one that lets the tyre down in say half an hour or less, is in most cases easily traced. Examine the tread for such things as a nail or flint. If one is found extract it, and having pumped air into the tyre, place a wetted finger over the hole and look for bubbles. If you are able to locate the puncture in this manner mark the location of the puncture with chalk. Next let down the tyre by removing the valve, and lever the cover off the rim in the locality of the leak. Pull out the tube and find the hole by visual inspection.

Clean the area around the puncture with a rag moistened with petrol. In the absence of petrol the head of a match makes an effective cleansing agent. First apply a small quantity of water on the spot to be cleaned, then rub the match over the area until a paste of sulphur is formed and wipe dry with a clean cloth. Apply a thin coat of rubber solution worked in with the finger tip. Select a suitable patch and peel off the linen backing. Leave both tyre and patch exposed to the air for as long as possible to dry out the volatile solvents. This is important; many cyclists experience trouble with patches lifting in the heat of the summer, causing a slow leakage of air that is sometimes difficult to trace. This trouble is the result of using too much solution and not letting it dry out. To repair a puncture and adjourn for tea while the solution dries, is a practical insurance against future trouble.

Place the patch in position and press firmly, dust the patch generously with French chalk, re-fit the tube to the wheel and replace the cover. Take care when using tyre levers, not to pinch the tube and create a new puncture. A little air pumped into the tube reduces the risk of pinching.

To trace a slow puncture the tube must be taken wholly out of the cover; in the case of the rear wheel it should be taken out on the side away from the chain. The tube is then pumped to stretching point and it may be possible, in quiet surroundings, to hear the escaping air by passing the tube slowly round close to the ear. Having thus located the approximate position, examine it closely for a minute pinhole and test by a wet finger for bubbles to prove the existence of the puncture. Failing this, the last resort is to pass the tube slowly through a bowl of water and look for bubbles.

Last, but not the least of the precautions for locating a puncture is the testing of the valve with a globule of water on the inlet stem before attempting to remove the tube. If this is overlooked, a leak due to faulty valve seating may be temporarily rectified in the course of deflating and re-inflating the tube, causing some perplexity when all subsequent efforts fail to reveal a leak.

In any case valve rubbers need to be changed from time to time. In doing so, see that the valve seating is free from adhering fragments of perished rubber, and that the new valve rubber fits well over the tapered shoulder of the inlet stem and extends a little beyond the bottom of the stem.

Cyclists' Tool Kit.—Puncture repair outfit containing patches, rubber solution, and French chalk.

Pump and connector.

Oil can, cycle oil, graphite grease, and rags.

Screwdriver.

Combined cone spanner and cup key.

Selection of set spanners to fit $\frac{1}{8}$in., $\frac{3}{16}$in., $\frac{1}{4}$in. and $\frac{5}{16}$in. nuts.

Spoke nipple key.

Spare chain joint link.

Spare bulb.

The manufacture of a cycle stand is described under that heading in SIMPLE CARPENTRY.

Re-enamelling.—Secondhand bicycles when purchased are fairly frequently in need of a coat of enamel and even the well cared for machine may eventually require re-enamelling. The first consideration is the selection of a room or shed from which the dust on the floor has been thoroughly removed. The room air should from this point of view be as free from dust particles as possible.

There is a large variety of cycle enamels on the market, many of which give excellent results but it is advisable to purchase a well known and generally approved enamel as the constituents do vary fairly considerably in the inferior brands.

Having purchased the enamel and found a suitable room for the enamelling, carefully dismantle the bicycle and clean all the enamelled components such as the frame and front forks, etc. with hot water and soap. Dry them off and using a metal scraping tool remove all the defective enamel, then with a medium grain emery paper thoroughly clean the metal. Wipe the surfaces with a rag soaked in petrol or turpentine. There are proprietary liquids on the market for the removal of enamel but the former method if thorough gives very good results.

Before attempting to enamel the components remove all the flakes of enamel from the floor and the bench if the latter is used. This is an important point as the enamel flakes have an insidious tendency to reappear as spots in the freshly enamelled surfaces.

A good brush with fine soft bristles is also an important accessory to efficient enamelling. Do not purchase a cheap and obviously inferior brush. One about $\frac{1}{2}$-in. wide rather like "a flat fitch" with softer bristles, is large enough.

Now apply the enamel to the surfaces. The first coat should be very thin. It does not matter if the metal shows opaquely through the film of enamel. Having treated the appropriate components suspend them by wire or some similar means so that they hang free of each other (i.e. not touching) and allow the enamel to dry and harden thoroughly.

They should then be lightly glass-papered with a fine grain glass-paper and wiped with a clean napless rag. Apply the second coat of enamel which will adhere quite readily. The second coat may be somewhat thicker than the first but only just thick enough to hide the metal. Allow the second coat to dry and harden. Repeat the glass-papering if necessary and wipe down with a clean rag. The second coat may be satisfactory, however, in which event glass-papering and the application of another coat may not be required, although a series of thin coats does produce excellent results. Never overload the brush with enamel, and do not allow excess of enamel to accumulate at joint angles, etc. as this will cause the enamel to run or collect in unsightly blobs.

General Information.—When removing the inner tube from the rim of the rear wheel, (i.e. with the wheel still in the frame) to repair a puncture do not take it out on the chain side of the wheel. This measure will avoid the risk of contaminating the tube and the hands with oil from the chain.

If the bicycle carries electric battery or dynamo lamps always take extra bulbs either in the pockets or stored in the saddlebag when travelling at night.

Repairing Mudguards.—Steel mudguards are the usual standard as fitted to new machines. Some are very satisfactory but others tend to crack or fracture as a result of unavoidable vibration at the points of attachment. If the mudguard is of thin gauge material of the inferior type it may be well worth while replacing it altogether by a new mudguard which can, if required, be of celluloid or aluminium alloy. Temporary repairs at the strut attachment may be made by soldering the crack, riveting on a patch of sheet-metal, or if practicable fitting two large washers at the bolthole from which the fracture radiates. Cracks in celluloid mudguards can be repaired by the application of a transparent celluloid patch after treating the affected area with a suitable solvent. Amyl acetate solutions, available under proprietory names, should be used for this purpose. Fractures in aluminium mudguards may be repaired by riveted patches of similar material if replacement by a new mudguard is not contemplated.

Mudguards sometimes tend to twist or warp. This defect can often be remedied, if the attachments are secure, by bending the supporting struts as required. Ensure that the mudguard is not in contact with the wheel.

Tyre Sizes.—Wheels are identified by their diameters. Thus a 26in. wheel is 26in. in diameter and only 26in. tyres can be fitted. On the side face of the tyre will be seen a specification such as this:—$26 \times 1\frac{3}{8}$. The latter measurement indicates the depth and width of the tyre when it has been fully inflated by the inner tube. This measurement must conform to the fitting width of the wheel rim. Wheels may be 28in. diameter for large frames and the width of rim for both 26 and 28in. wheels may be $1\frac{1}{4}$in. or $1\frac{3}{8}$in.; but in any event the outer cover and inner tube to be fitted must agree with diameter and rim width of the wheel.

Spokes.—After considerable use the top ends of the spokes (i.e. in the rim of the wheel) tend to rust and the canvas protective band, which protects the inner tube from contact with any possible sharp edges at the ends of the spokes, deteriorates, allowing the inner tube to bear against the metal. If this is the case remove the canvas band and fit a new band after cleaning the groove of the rim. Smear a very small quantity of petroleum jelly on the inner ends of the spokes, not enough to cause it to soak into the canvas band, as otherwise this will affect the rubber of the inner tube.

Verifying the gear number.—To determine the fixed gear ratio of the pedal or front sprocket to the hub sprocket is quite an easy matter. It is assumed for the sake of example that the wheels are 26in. type. Count the number of teeth in the front sprocket and multiply by 26—e.g. 52 teeth × 26 =1352. Now count the number of teeth on the rear or hub sprocket which we will assume is 14. Divide 1352 by 14. The ratio then is 96.5. The number of teeth on the front sprocket may be anything from 40 to 60 and the number of teeth on the hub or rear wheel sprocket from 12 to 22, thus it will be seen that a wide range of ratios will be obtainable by changing the front and/or rear sprockets For general purposes a gearing of about 65 will be suitable for men and about 59-60 for women.

It should be noted that the numbers 96.5 or 65, 59 or 60 are meant to represent the diameters of circles in inches, and the distance travelled in feet by the bicycle can be expressed by multiplying the diameter by following a simple formula. $(96\frac{1}{2} \times 3\frac{1}{7}) \div 12 = 25$ ft. approximately.

It will be seen then that the cycle owner may alter the ratios of the front and rear sprockets to suit individual requirements or, alternately, variable speed gear hubs may be fitted.

Rust Prevention.—The enamel on the frame can best be preserved by observing two simple rules. When not in use keep the bicycle under a dry shelter and never allow rain water or mud to remain overlong on the surfaces. Obviously it will not always be possible to store the machine under shelter during inclement weather and also the cycle may often be in use during rainy conditions. But at the earliest opportunity moisture and mud should be removed. Particular attention should be paid to the crevices and joint angles of the frame both on enamel and chromium parts. Do not neglect the under sides of the mudguards, the spokes, hubs and rims of the wheels. Other points that repay inspection are the pedals, brake levers and control rods or cables, etc. Water will readily seep into the small gaps, threads, bushes, shackles, etc. and it is a good practice to prevent ingress of moisture by applying a small quantity of petroleum jelly to these parts so as to seal them off. This procedure should be carried out at intervals especially during the more rainy months of the year. Nuts and threads should be smeared with oil or petroleum jelly as otherwise they tend to rust after a fairly long period. This will obviate any difficulty in replacement of small parts due to a nut having seized on its thread.

Replacing Brake Blocks.—Do not allow the brake blocks to wear right down to the shoes. Renew them when they are worn to approximately one-half their original depth. Note also that the ordinary pull-up brake block shoes have a stop at one end so that the block will not slide out of position when it is fitted in place and applied to the rim of the wheel. If new brake blocks and shoes are purchased together this is a point to remember when fitting them to the cycle. The shoes should be just clear of the wheel rim.

Brake Cables.—If brake cables are used all sharp kinks or bends in the run of the cable should be avoided. Lubricate the cable by allowing oil to filter in at highest point. Do not over-lubricate.

Guarding the Bike.—The maker's number will be found on some part of the framework of the cycle, usually on the frame just beneath the saddle. Make a note of this number. It will be useful in tracing the machine should it ever be stolen. The expense of a small padlock and chain is well worth while as a preventive against theft. Both the lock and chain should be of good strong construction. The lock, particularly, should be of the type that is not easily broken.

Speedometers.—Speedometers and cyclometers are generally regarded as luxuries, except for pace-making, racing, etc. But if there is any extensive touring to be done, a speedometer will be extremely useful. A speedometer, of course, enables the cyclist to check and maintain the speed at which he desires to travel. A cyclometer, which measures the distance covered, will afford the additional pleasure of keeping a record book of the distances travelled, and also a reminder on day trips how far the cyclist has travelled and, therefore, how far he will need to go on the return journey.

Tandems.—Tandems require more or less the same treatment as ordinary cycles, but there are one or two points to be remembered. When buying a tandem, do not forget that two people have got to ride it, and the measurements of the machine should suit both persons. The measurements for the front rider are the more important of the two. Special attention should be paid to the brakes, owing to the additional weight; and three speed hubs are recommended.

Preparing a Tour.—Remember these hints when preparing a tour. Travel as light as possible, but be prepared for bad weather and carry a cape. Do not wear clothes that hold perspiration: badly ventilated clothes will spoil your enjoyment. Remember the tool kit and puncture outfit. See that the cycle is well oiled before starting out. Do not be over-ambitious in the distance to be covered. Mark out the route on a map beforehand.

Safety First.—Cyclists are bound by law to have proper brakes and to give proper signals. It is illegal to be towed or to hang on to the back of any vehicle. Remember the safety first rules. Keep well to the left. Never pass on the inside of any vehicles. Keep a sharp look-out on the traffic. Do not ride more than two abreast.

INDEX

Made and Printed in Great Britain by C. Tinling & Co., Ltd. Liverpool, London and Prescot.